P9-DNX-569

MAPPING THE SOCIAL LANDSCAPE

Readings in Sociology

Mapping the Social Landscape

Readings in Sociology

Third Edition

SUSAN J. FERGUSON
Grinnell College

Boston   Burr Ridge, IL   Dubuque, IA   Madison, WI   New York
San Francisco   St. Louis   Bangkok   Bogotá   Caracas   Kuala Lumpur
Lisbon   London   Madrid   Mexico City   Milan   Montreal   New Delhi
Santiago   Seoul   Singapore   Sydney   Taipei   Toronto

McGraw-Hill Higher Education

*A Division of The **McGraw-Hill** Companies*

Copyright © 2002, 1999, 1996 by The McGraw-Hill Companies, Inc. All rights reserved. Printed in the United States of America. Except as permitted under the United States Copyright Act of 1976, no part of this publication may be reproduced or distributed in any form or by any means, or stored in a data base or retrieval system, without the prior written permission of the publisher.

1 2 3 4 5 6 7 8 9 0 MAL/MAL 0 9 8 7 6 5 4 3 2 1

Library of Congress Cataloging-in-Publication Data
Mapping the social landscape : readings in sociology / [compiled by]
   Susan J. Ferguson.—3rd ed.
      p.   cm.
   Includes bibliographical references.
   ISBN 0-7674-2093-4
   1. Social institutions.   2. Socialization.   3. Equality.
4. Social change.   5. Sociology.   I. Ferguson, Susan J.
HM826 .M36   2001
301—dc21   2001030391

Sponsoring editor, Serina Beauparlant; production, Publishing Support Services; manuscript editor, Margaret Moore; design manager, Susan Breitbard; text designer, Linda M. Robertson; cover designer, Laurie Anderson; manufacturing manager, Randy Hurst. The text was set in 10/12 Book Antiqua by G&S Typesetters, Inc., and printed on 45# Scholarly Matte by Malloy Lithographing.

Cover photos: (large, top to bottom) © David Bradford/Nonstock; © Giuseppe Ceschi/ Nonstock. *(small, top to bottom)* © Giuseppe Ceschi/Nonstock; © Ligia Boterno/ Nonstock; © David Bradford/Nonstock.

www.mhhe.com

With love to my grandmother, Edna Catherine Clark, who always believed that an education would open the doors of the world to me. She was right.

Preface

As the title suggests, *Mapping the Social Landscape* is about exploration and discovery. It means taking a closer look at a complex, ever-changing social world in which locations, pathways, and boundaries are not fixed. Because sociology describes and explains our social surroundings, it enables us to understand this shifting landscape. Thus, sociology is about discovering society and discovering ourselves. The purpose of this anthology is to introduce the discipline of sociology and to convey the excitement and the challenge of the sociological enterprise.

Although a number of readers in introductory sociology are already available for students, I have yet to find one that exposes students to the broad diversity of scholarship, perspectives, and authorship that exists within the field of sociology. This diversity goes beyond recognizing gender, racial-ethnic, and social class differences to acknowledging a plurality of voices and views within the discipline. Like other anthologies, this one includes classic works by authors such as Karl Marx, Max Weber, W. E. B. Du Bois, and C. Wright Mills; in addition, however, I have also drawn from a wide range of contemporary scholarship, some of which provides newer treatments of traditional concepts. This diversity of viewpoints and approaches should encourage students to evaluate and analyze the ideas and research findings presented.

In addition, because I find it invaluable in my own teaching to use examples from personal experiences to enable students to see the connection between "private troubles and public issues," as Mills phrased it, I have included in this collection a few personal narratives to help students comprehend how social forces affect individual lives. Thus, this anthology includes classic as well as contemporary writings, and the voices of other social scientists who render provocative sociological insights. The readings also exemplify functionalist, conflict, and symbolic interactionist perspectives and different types of research methodology. Each article is preceded by a brief headnote that sets the context within which the reader can seek to understand the sociological work. Thus, the selections communicate an enthusiasm for sociology while illustrating sociological concepts, theories, and methods.

During the last 25 years, sociology has benefited from a rich abundance of creative scholarship, but many of these original works have not been adequately presented in textbooks or readers. I believe an introductory anthology needs to reflect the new questions concerning research and theory within the discipline. Moreover, I find that students enjoy reading the actual research and words of sociologists. This anthology, therefore, includes many cutting-edge pieces of sociological scholarship and some very recent publications by recognized social analysts. Current issues are examined, including the tattoo subculture, the mythopoetic men's movement, the effects of globalization, the political influence of corporate PACs, teen suicide, the rise of paramilitary subcultures, and eating disorders. In essence, I have attempted, not to break new ground, but to compile a collection that provides a fresh, innovative look at the discipline of sociology.

Changes to the Third Edition

With this third edition, I maintain a balance of classical and contemporary readings. In addition to many of the classic pieces that appeared in the second edition, I have included Zimbardo's classic study of social interaction in a simulated prison. I also have added fourteen selections of cutting-edge contemporary sociological research that illustrate analyses of timely social issues and the intersection between race, social class, and gender. These new selections examine school cliques, TV talk shows, teen pregnancy, cosmetic surgery, the Internet, white privilege, the mass media, the U.S. health care system, the soft money in political campaigns, and other current social issues. Among these readings are some selections that I consider to be contemporary classics in that they provide an overview of the discipline of sociology or a specific content area. These readings include an essay by Earl Babbie on the science of sociology; Barbara Risman's reading on "Gender as Structure," which provides an overview of theories on sex and gender; Roger Finke and Rodney Stark's important work on social change within the institution of religion; Vicente Navarro's reading on why the U.S. health care system does not respond to people's needs; and an excerpt from Allan G. Johnson's recent book, *Privilege, Power, and Difference* (2001). Based on reviewers' comments I also have completely revised the sections on social research, religion, and health and medicine. I think students will find the newer pieces in these sections more accessible and interesting. Of course, for all of the readings, I have tried to choose selections that are compelling to students and demonstrate well the diversity within the discipline of sociology. Please note that I welcome feedback from professors and students on this edition of *Mapping the Social Landscape: Readings in Sociology*.

Printed Test Bank

I also have written an accompanying test manual that contains numerous examination and discussion questions for each reading. As the editor of this anthology, I developed these items with the goal of helping instructors test students' understanding of key sociological concepts and themes.

Acknowledgments

The completion of this book involved the labor and support of many people. I would like to begin by acknowledging the support of my colleagues in the sociology department at Grinnell College. I also am indebted to the Carnegie secretaries, Faun Black, Vicki Bunnell, Karen Groves, and Linda Price, for their time typing and copying portions of the manuscript. My student research assistants, Michelle Brunner, Margaret Hainline, and Emily Larson, also need to be commended for copying material and carrying innumerable pounds of books between my office and the library. I also am indebted to Grinnell College for its generous research support.

Many sociologists reviewed earlier drafts of the manuscript and provided me with valuable observations. First and foremost, I want to acknowledge the early insights of Agnes Riedmann, who suggested several key pieces in the first draft. I also appreciate the suggestions for selections made by Joan Ferrante, Annette Lareau, and Michael Messner.

My special thanks go to Arnold Arluke, Northeastern University; Joanne M. Badagliacco, University of Kentucky; Gary L. Brock, Southwest Missouri State University; Tom Gerschick, Illinois State University; Thomas B. Gold, University of California at Berkeley; Jack Harkins, College of DuPage; Paul Kamolnick, East Tennessee State University; Peter Kivisto, Augustana College; Fred Kniss, Loyola University; Diane E. Levy, University of North Carolina at Wilmington; Peter Meiksins, Cleveland State University; Roslyn Arlin Mickelson, University of North Carolina at Charlotte; and Carol Ray, San Jose State University, for their feedback on the first edition of the manuscript. As a team of reviewers, your detailed comments were enormously helpful in the tightening and refining of the manuscript. And more important, your voices reflect the rich and varied experiences with teaching introductory sociology.

For the second edition, I would like to thank the following team of reviewers: Angela Danzi, State University of New York at Farmingdale; Diane Diamond, State University of New York at Stony Brook; Yvonne Downs, State University of New York at Fredonia; Kay Forest, Northern Illinois University; Bob Granfield, University of Denver; Susan Greenwood, University of Maine; Kate Hausbeck, University of Nevada at Las Vegas; Arthur J. Jipson, Miami University; James Jones, Mississippi State University; Carolyn A. Kapinus, Penn State University; J. Richard Kendrick, Jr., State University of New York at Cortland; M. Kris McIlwaine, University of Arizona; Kristy McNamara, Furman University; Tracy Ore, University of Illinois at Urbana; Denise Scott, State University of New York at Geneseo; Maynard Seider, Massachusetts College of Liberal Arts; Tom Soltis, Westmoreland Community

College; Martha Thompson, Northeastern Illinois University; Huiying Wei-Arthus, Weber State University; Adam S. Weinberg, Colgate University; Amy S. Wharton, Washington State University; and John Zipp, University of Wisconsin at Milwaukee.

For the third edition, I thank the following reviewers: Stephen Adair, Central Connecticut State University; Javier Auyero, State University of New York, Stony Brook; David K. Brown, University of Illinois at Urbana-Champaign; Kay B. Forest, Northern Illinois University; Angela J. Hattery, Wake Forest University; Karen Honeycutt, University of Michigan; Neal King, Belmont University; Judith N. Lasker, Lehigh University; Rosemary F. Powers, Eastern Oregon University; Melissa Riba, Michigan State University; Deirdre Royster, University of Massachusetts, Amherst; James T. Salt, Lane Community College; H. Lovell Smith, Loyola College in Maryland; and Thomas Soltis, Westmoreland County Community College.

At Mayfield Publishing Company, I would like to recognize the creative and patient efforts of several individuals, including Mary Johnson, Jeanne M. Schreiber, Susan Breitbard, Marty Granahan, Brian Pecko, and Lynn Rabin Bauer. I also want to acknowledge the detailed work of the copyeditor, Margaret Moore, and the production management skills of Vicki Moran. My highest appreciation goes to Serina Beauparlant, the acquisitions editor. Serina, if I am a clutch hitter, then you are the phenomenal batting coach. I could not have asked for a more thoughtful and attentive sociology editor. Thank you.

Contents

GENDER

RACE AND ETHNICITY

Part VII   SOCIAL INSTITUTIONS

POWER AND POLITICS

THE ECONOMY AND WORK

THE FAMILY

Part VIII   SOCIAL CHANGE   625

Tell me the landscape in which you live, and I will tell you who you are.

José Ortega y Gasset

1

THE PROMISE

C. WRIGHT MILLS

The initial three selections examine the sociological perspective. The first of these is written by C. Wright Mills (1916–1962), a former professor of sociology at Columbia University. During his brief academic career, Mills became one of the best known and most controversial sociologists. He was critical of the U.S. government and other social institutions where power was unfairly concentrated. He also believed that academics should be socially responsible and speak out against social injustice. The excerpt that follows is from Mills' acclaimed book, *The Sociological Imagination*. Since its original publication in 1959, this text has been a required reading for most introductory sociology students around the world. Mills' sociological imagination perspective not only compels the best sociological analyses but also enables the sociologist and the individual to distinguish between "personal troubles" and "public issues." By separating these phenomena, we can better comprehend the sources of and solutions to social problems.

Nowadays men often feel that their private lives are a series of traps. They sense that within their everyday worlds, they cannot overcome their troubles, and in this feeling, they are often quite correct: What ordinary men are directly aware of and what they try to do are bounded by the private orbits in which they live; their visions and their powers are limited to the close-up scenes of job, family, neighborhood; in other milieux, they move vicariously and remain spectators. And the more aware they become,

---

This article was written in 1959 before scholars were sensitive to gender inclusivity in language. The references to masculine pronouns and men are, therefore, generic to both males and females and should be read as such. Please note that I have left the author's original language in this selection and other readings. —*Editor*

From *The Sociological Imagination*, pp. 3–13. Copyright © 2000 by Oxford University Press, Inc. Reprinted with the permission of Oxford University Press.

however vaguely, of ambitions and of threats which transcend their immediate locales, the more trapped they seem to feel.

Underlying this sense of being trapped are seemingly impersonal changes in the very structure of continent-wide societies. The facts of contemporary history are also facts about the success and the failure of individual men and women. When a society is industrialized, a peasant becomes a worker; a feudal lord is liquidated or becomes a businessman. When classes rise or fall, a man is employed or unemployed; when the rate of investment goes up or down, a man takes new heart or goes broke. When wars happen, an insurance salesman becomes a rocket launcher; a store clerk, a radar man; a wife lives alone; a child grows up without a father. Neither the life of an individual nor the history of a society can be understood without understanding both.

Yet men do not usually define the troubles they endure in terms of historical change and institutional contradiction. The well-being they enjoy, they do not usually impute to the big ups and downs of the societies in which they live. Seldom aware of the intricate connection between the patterns of their own lives and the course of world history, ordinary men do not usually know what this connection means for the kinds of men they are becoming and for the kinds of history making in which they might take part. They do not possess the quality of mind essential to grasp the interplay of man and society, of biography and history, of self and world. They cannot cope with their personal troubles in such ways as to control the structural transformations that usually lie behind them.

Surely it is no wonder. In what period have so many men been so totally exposed at so fast a pace to such earthquakes of change? That Americans have not known such catastrophic changes as have the men and women of other societies is due to historical facts that are now quickly becoming "merely history." The history that now affects every man is world history. Within this scene and this period, in the course of a single generation, one-sixth of mankind is transformed from all that is feudal and backward into all that is modern, advanced, and fearful. Political colonies are freed; new and less visible forms of imperialism installed. Revolutions occur; men feel the intimate grip of new kinds of authority. Totalitarian societies rise and are smashed to bits—or succeed fabulously. After two centuries of ascendancy, capitalism is shown up as only one way to make society into an industrial apparatus. After two centuries of hope, even formal democracy is restricted to a quite small portion of mankind. Everywhere in the underdeveloped world, ancient ways of life are broken up and vague expectations become urgent demands. Everywhere in the overdeveloped world, the means of authority and of violence become total in scope and bureaucratic in form. Humanity itself now lies before us, the super-nation at either pole concentrating its most co-ordinated and massive efforts upon the preparation of World War Three.

The very shaping of history now outpaces the ability of men to orient themselves in accordance with cherished values. And which values? Even when they do not panic, men often sense that older ways of feeling and thinking have collapsed and that newer beginnings are ambiguous to the point of moral stasis. Is it any wonder that ordinary men feel they cannot cope with the larger worlds with which they are so suddenly confronted? That they cannot understand the meaning of their epoch for their own lives? That—in defense of selfhood—they become morally insensible, trying to remain altogether private men? Is it any wonder that they come to be possessed by a sense of the trap?

It is not only information that they need—in this Age of Fact, information often dominates their attention and overwhelms their capacities to assimilate it. It is not only the skills of reason that they need—although their struggles to acquire these often exhaust their limited moral energy.

What they need, and what they feel they need, is a quality of mind that will help them to use information and to develop reason in order to achieve lucid summations of what is going on in the world and of what may be happening within themselves. It is this quality, I am going to contend, that journalists and scholars, artists and publics, scientists and editors are coming to expect of what may be called the sociological imagination.

The sociological imagination enables its possessor to understand the larger historical scene in terms of its meaning for the inner life and the external career of a variety of individuals. It enables him to take into account how individuals, in the welter of their daily experience, often become falsely conscious of their social positions. Within that welter, the framework of modern society is sought, and within that framework the psychologies of a variety of men and women are formulated. By such means the personal uneasiness of individuals is focused upon explicit troubles and the indifference of publics is transformed into involvement with public issues.

The first fruit of this imagination—and the first lesson of the social science that embodies it—is the idea that the individual can understand his own experience and gauge his own fate only by locating himself within his period, that he can know his own chances in life only by becoming aware of those of all individuals in his circumstances. In many ways it is a terrible lesson; in many ways a magnificent one. We do not know the limits of man's capacities for supreme effort or willing degradation, for agony or glee, for pleasurable brutality or the sweetness of reason. But in our time we have come to know that the limits of "human nature" are frighteningly broad. We have come to know that every individual lives, from one generation to the next, in some society; that he lives out a biography, and that he lives it out within some historical sequence. By the fact of his living he contributes, however minutely, to the shaping of this society and to the course of its history, even as he is made by society and by its historical push and shove.

The sociological imagination enables us to grasp history and biography and the relations between the two within society. That is its task and its promise. To recognize this task and this promise is the mark of the classic social analyst. It is characteristic of Herbert Spencer—turgid, polysyllabic, comprehensive; of E. A. Ross—graceful, muckraking, upright; of Auguste Comte and Emile Durkheim; of the intricate and subtle Karl Mannheim. It is the quality of all that is intellectually excellent in Karl Marx; it is the clue to Thorstein Veblen's brilliant and ironic insight, to Joseph Schumpeter's many-sided constructions of reality; it is the basis of the psychological sweep of W. E. H. Lecky no less than of the profundity and clarity of Max Weber. And it is the signal of what is best in contemporary studies of man and society.

No social study that does not come back to the problems of biography, of history and of their intersections within a society, has completed its intellectual journey. Whatever the specific problems of the classic social analysts, however limited or however broad the features of social reality they have examined, those who have been imaginatively aware of the promise of their work have consistently asked three sorts of questions:

1. What is the structure of this particular society as a whole? What are its essential components, and how are they related to one another? How does it differ from other varieties of social order? Within it, what is the meaning of any particular feature for its continuance and for its change?
2. Where does this society stand in human history? What are the mechanics by which it is changing? What is its place within and its meaning for the development of humanity as a whole? How does any particular feature we are examining affect, and how is it affected by, the historical period in which it moves? And this period—what are its essential features? How does it differ from other periods? What are its characteristic ways of history making?
3. What varieties of men and women now prevail in this society and in this period? And what varieties are coming to prevail? In what ways are they selected and formed, liberated and repressed, made sensitive and blunted? What kinds of "human nature" are revealed in the conduct and character we observe in this society in this period? And what is the meaning for "human nature" of each and every feature of the society we are examining?

Whether the point of interest is a great power state or a minor literary mood, a family, a prison, a creed—these are the kinds of questions the best social analysts have asked. They are the intellectual pivots of classic studies of man in society—and they are the questions inevitably raised by any mind possessing the sociological imagination. For that imagination is the capacity to shift from one perspective to another—from the political to the psychological; from examination of a single family to comparative assessment of the national budgets of the world; from the theological school to the military establishment; from considerations of an oil industry to studies of contemporary poetry. It is the capacity to range from the most impersonal and remote transformations to the most intimate features of the human self—and to see the relations between the two. Back of its use there is always the urge to know the social and historical meaning of the individual in the society and in the period in which he has his quality and his being.

That, in brief, is why it is by means of the sociological imagination that men now hope to grasp what is going on in the world, and to understand what is happening in themselves as minute points of the intersections of biography and history within society. In large part, contemporary man's self-conscious view of himself as at least an outsider, if not a permanent stranger, rests upon an absorbed realization of social relativity and of the transformative power of history. The sociological imagination is the most fruitful form of this self-consciousness. By its use men whose mentalities have swept only a series of limited orbits often come to feel as if suddenly awakened in a house with which they had only supposed themselves to be familiar. Correctly or incorrectly, they often come to feel that they can now provide themselves with adequate summations, cohesive assessments, comprehensive orientations. Older decisions that once appeared sound now seem to them products of a mind unaccountably dense. Their capacity for astonishment is made lively again. They acquire a new way of thinking, they experience a transvaluation of values: in a word, by their reflection and by their sensibility, they realize the cultural meaning of the social sciences.

———————

Perhaps the most fruitful distinction with which the sociological imagination works is between "the personal troubles of milieu" and "the public issues of social structure." This distinction is an essential tool of the sociological imagination and a feature of all classic work in social science.

Troubles occur within the character of the individual and within the range of his immediate relations with others; they have to do with his self and with those limited areas of social life of which he is directly and personally aware. Accordingly, the statement and the resolution of troubles properly lie within the individual as a biographical entity and within the scope of his immediate milieu—the social setting that is directly open to his personal experience and to some extent his willful activity. A trouble is a private matter: Values cherished by an individual are felt by him to be threatened.

Issues have to do with matters that transcend these local environments of the individual and the range of his inner life. They have to do with the organization of many such milieux into the institutions of a historical society as a whole, with the ways in which various milieux overlap and interpenetrate to form the larger structure of social and historical life. An issue is a public matter: Some value cherished by publics is felt to be threatened. Often there is a debate about what that value really is and about what it is that really threatens it. This debate is often without focus if only because it is the very nature of an issue, unlike even widespread trouble, that it cannot very well be defined in terms of the immediate and everyday environments of ordinary men.

An issue, in fact, often involves a crisis in institutional arrangements, and often too it involves what Marxists call "contradictions" or "antagonisms."

———

In these terms, consider unemployment. When, in a city of 100,000, only one man is unemployed, that is his personal trouble, and for its relief we properly look to the character of the man, his skills, and his immediate opportunities. But when in a nation of 50 million employees, 15 million men are unemployed, that is an issue, and we may not hope to find its solution within the range of opportunities open to any one individual. The very structure of opportunities has collapsed. Both the correct statement of the problem and the range of possible solutions require us to consider the economic and political institutions of the society, and not merely the personal situation and character of a scatter of individuals.

Consider war. The personal problem of war, when it occurs, may be how to survive it or how to die in it with honor; how to make money out of it; how to climb into the higher safety of the military apparatus; or how to contribute to the war's termination. In short, according to one's values, to find a set of milieux and within it to survive the war or make one's death in it meaningful. But the structural issues of war have to do with its causes; with what types of men it throws up into command; with its effects upon economic and political, family and religious institutions, with the unorganized irresponsibility of a world of nation-states.

Consider marriage. Inside a marriage a man and a woman may experience personal troubles, but when the divorce rate during the first four years of marriage is 250 out of every 1,000 attempts, this is an indication of a structural issue having to do with the institutions of marriage and the family and other institutions that bear upon them.

Or consider the metropolis—the horrible, beautiful, ugly, magnificent sprawl of the great city. For many upper-class people, the personal solution to "the problem of the city" is to have an apartment with private garage under it in the heart of the city, and forty miles out, a house by Henry Hill, garden by Garrett Eckbo, on a hundred acres of private land. In these two controlled environments—with a small staff at each end and a private helicopter connection—most people could solve many of the problems of personal milieux caused by the facts of the city. But all this, however splendid, does not solve the public issues that the structural fact of the city poses. What should be done with this wonderful monstrosity? Break it all up into scattered units, combining residence and work? Refurbish it as it stands? Or, after evacuation, dynamite it and build new cities according to new plans in new places? What should those plans be? And who is to decide and to accomplish whatever choice is made? These are structural issues; to confront them and to solve them requires us to consider political and economic issues that affect innumerable milieux.

Insofar as an economy is so arranged that slumps occur, the problem of unemployment becomes incapable of personal solution. Insofar as war is inherent in the nation-state system and in the uneven industrialization of the world, the ordinary individual in his restricted milieu will be powerless— with or without psychiatric aid—to solve the troubles this system or lack of system imposes upon him. Insofar as the family as an institution turns women into darling little slaves and men into their chief providers and un-weaned dependents, the problem of a satisfactory marriage remains inca-pable of purely private solution. Insofar as the overdeveloped megalopolis and the overdeveloped automobile are built-in features of the overdeveloped society, the issues of urban living will not be solved by personal ingenuity and private wealth.

What we experience in various and specific milieux, I have noted, is often caused by structural changes. Accordingly, to understand the changes of many personal milieux we are required to look beyond them. And the num-ber and variety of such structural changes increase as the institutions within which we live become more embracing and more intricately connected with one another. To be aware of the idea of social structure and to use it with sen-sibility is to be capable of tracing such linkages among a great variety of mi-lieux. To be able to do that is to possess the sociological imagination.

2

TEENAGE WASTELAND
Suburbia's Dead-End Kids

DONNA GAINES

This reading by Donna Gaines is excerpted from her internationally ac-claimed book, *Teenage Wasteland: Suburbia's Dead-End Kids* (1990). *Rolling Stone* declared *Teenage Wasteland* "the best book on youth culture," and it is a required reading for university course lists in several disciplines. Gaines is a journalist, cultural sociologist, and New York State certified social worker. She is currently a senior fellow at the Institute for Cultural Studies in New York City and is a features writer for several magazines.

This excerpt is an example of sociological research that employs C. Wright Mills' sociological imagination and, specifically, his distinction

From *Teenage Wasteland: Suburbia's Dead-Ends Kids,* pp. 3, 5, 6–10, 12, 68–69, 86–87, 93, 102–103, 150–51, 152–55, 250–52, Pantheon Books. Copyright © 1990, 1991 by Donna Gaines. Reprinted with the permission of the author.

between personal troubles and public issues. As Gaines illustrates, when one teenager commits suicide it is a personal tragedy, but when groups of teenagers form a suicide pact and successfully carry it out, suicide becomes a matter of public concern. In order to explain adequately why this incident occurred, Gaines examines both the history and the biography of suburban teens.

In Bergenfield, New Jersey, on the morning of March 11, 1987, the bodies of four teenagers were discovered inside a 1977 rust-colored Chevrolet Camaro. The car, which belonged to Thomas Olton, was parked in an unused garage in the Foster Village garden apartment complex, behind the Foster Village Shopping Center. Two sisters, Lisa and Cheryl Burress, and their friends, Thomas Rizzo and Thomas Olton, had died of carbon monoxide poisoning.

Lisa was 16, Cheryl was 17, and the boys were 19—they were suburban teens, turnpike kids like the ones in the town I live in. And thinking about them made me remember how it felt being a teenager too. I was horrified that it had come to this. I believed I understood why they did it, although it wasn't a feeling I could have put into words.

You could tell from the newspapers that they were rock and roll kids. The police had found a cassette tape cover of AC/DC's *If You Want Blood, You've Got It* near the bodies. Their friends were described as kids who listened to thrash metal, had shaggy haircuts, wore lots of black and leather. "Dropouts," "druggies," the papers called them. Teenage suburban rockers whose lives revolved around their favorite bands and their friends. Youths who barely got by in school and at home and who did not impress authority figures in any remarkable way. Except as fuck-ups.

My friends, most of whom were born in the 1950s, felt the same way about the kids everyone called "burnouts." On the weekend following the suicides, a friend's band, the Grinders, were playing at My Father's Place, a Long Island club. That night the guys dedicated a song, "The Kids in the Basement," to the four teens from Bergenfield—"This is for the suicide kids." In the weeks following the suicide pact, a number of bands in the tri-state area also dedicated songs to them. Their deaths had hit close to home. . . .

A week or two after the suicide pact, *The Village Voice* assigned me to go to Bergenfield. Now this was not a story I would've volunteered for. . . . But one day my editor at the *Voice* called to ask if I wanted to go to Bergenfield. She knew my background—that I knew suburbia, that I could talk to kids. By now I fully embraced the sociologist's ethical commitment to the "rights of the researched," and the social worker's vow of client confidentiality. As far as suicidal teenagers were concerned, I felt that if I couldn't help them, I didn't want to bother them.

But I was really pissed off at what I kept reading. How people in Bergenfield openly referred to the four kids as "troubled losers." Even after they were dead, nobody cut them any slack. "Burnouts," "druggies," "dropouts." Something was wrong. So I took the opportunity.

From the beginning, I believed that the Bergenfield suicides symbolized a tragic defeat for young people. Something was happening in the larger society that was not yet comprehended. Scholars spoke ominously of "the postmodern condition," "societal upheaval," "decay," "anomie." Meanwhile, American kids kept losing ground, showing all the symptoms of societal neglect. Many were left to fend for themselves, often with little success. The news got worse. Teenage suicides continued, and still nobody seemed to be getting the point.

Now, in trying to understand this event, I might have continued working within the established discourse on teenage suicide. I might have carried on the tradition of obscuring the bigger picture, psychologizing the Bergenfield suicide pact, interviewing the parents of the four youths, hounding their friends for the gory details. I might have spent my time probing school records, tracking down their teachers and shrinks for insights, focusing on their personal histories and intimate relationships. I might have searched out the individual motivations behind the words left in the note written and signed by each youth on the brown paper bag found with their bodies on March 11. But I did not.

Because the world has changed for today's kids. We also engaged in activities that adults called self-destructive. But for my generation, "doing it" meant having sex; for them, it means committing suicide.

"Teenage suicide" was a virtually nonexistent category prior to 1960. But between 1950 and 1980 it nearly tripled, and at the time of the Bergenfield suicide pact it was described as the second leading cause of death among America's young people; "accidents" were the first. The actual suicide rate among people aged 15 to 24—the statistical category for teenage suicide—is estimated to be even higher, underreported because of social stigma. Then there are the murky numbers derived from drug overdoses and car crashes, recorded as accidents. To date, there are more than 5,000 teen suicides annually, accounting for 12 percent of youth mortalities. An estimated 400,000 adolescents attempt suicide each year. While youth suicide rates leveled off by 1980, by mid-decade they began to increase again. Although they remained lower than adult suicide rates, the acceleration at which youth suicide rates increased was alarming. By 1987, we had books and articles detailing "copycat" and "cluster" suicides. Teenage suicide was now described as an epidemic.

Authors, experts, and scholars compiled the lists of kids' names, ages, dates, and possible motives. They generated predictive models: Rural and suburban white kids do it more often. Black kids in America's urban teenage wastelands are more likely to kill each other. Increasingly, alcohol and drugs are involved. In some cases, adults have tried to identify the instigating factor as a lyric or a song—Judas Priest, Ozzy Osbourne. Or else a popular film about the subject—the suicide of a celebrity; too much media attention or not enough.

Some kids do it violently: drowning, hanging, slashing, jumping, or crashing. Firearms are still the most popular. Others prefer to go out more peacefully, by gas or drug overdose. Boys do it more than girls, though girls try it more often than boys. And it does not seem to matter if kids are rich or poor.

Throughout the 1980s, teenage suicide clusters appeared across the country—six or seven deaths, sometimes more, in a short period of time in a single community. In the boomtown of Plano, Texas. The fading factory town of Leominster, Massachusetts. At Bryan High School in a white, working-class suburb of Omaha, Nebraska. A series of domino suicides among Arapaho Indian youths at the Wind River Reservation in Wyoming. Six youth suicides in the county of Westchester, New York, in 1984; five in 1985 and seven in 1986.

Sometimes they were close friends who died together in pacts of two. In other cases, one followed shortly after the other, unable to survive apart. Then there were strangers who died alone, in separate incidents timed closely together.

The Bergenfield suicide pact of March 11 was alternately termed a "multiple-death pact," a "quadruple suicide," or simply a "pact," depending on where you read about it. Some people actually called it a *mass* suicide because the Bergenfield case reminded them of Jonestown, Guyana, in 1978, where over 900 followers of Jim Jones poisoned themselves, fearing their community would be destroyed.

As experts speculated over the deaths in Bergenfield, none could recall a teenage suicide pact involving four people dying together; *it was historically unique.*

I wondered, did the "burnouts" see themselves as a community under siege? Like Jim Jones' people, or the 960 Jews at Masada who jumped to their deaths rather than face defeat at the hands of the Romans? Were the "burnouts" of Bergenfield choosing death over surrender? Surrender to what? Were they martyrs? If so, what was their common cause?

Because the suicide pact was a *collective act,* it warrants a social explanation—a portrait of the "burnouts" in Bergenfield as actors within a particular social landscape.

For a long time now, the discourse of teenage suicide has been dominated by atomizing psychological and medical models. And so the larger picture of American youth as members of a distinctive generation with a unique collective biography, emerging at a particular moment in history, has been lost.

The starting-off point for this research, then, is a teenage suicide pact in an "upper-poor" white ethnic suburb in northern New Jersey. But, of course, the story did not begin and will not end in Bergenfield.

Yes, there were specific sociocultural patterns operating in Bergenfield through which a teenage suicide pact became objectively possible. Yes, there were particular conditions which influenced how the town reacted to the event. Yes, there were reasons—that unique constellation of circumstances congealed in the lives of the four youths in the years, weeks, and days prior to March 11—that made suicide seem like their best alternative.

Given the four youths' personal histories, their losses, their failures, their shattered dreams, the motivation to die in this way seems transparent. Yet, after the suicide pact, in towns across the country, on television and in the press, people asked, "Why did they do it?" But I went to Bergenfield with other questions.

This was a suicide pact that involved close friends who were by no accounts obsessed, star-crossed lovers. What would make four people want to die together? Why would they ask, in their collective suicide note, to be waked and buried together? Were they part of a suicide cult?

If not, what was the nature of the *social* bond that tied them so closely? What could be so intimately binding that in the early morning hours of March 11 not one of them could stop, step back from the pact they had made to say, "Wait, I can't do this"? Who were these kids that everybody called "burnouts"?

"Greasers," "hoods," "beats," "freaks," "hippies," "punks." From the 1950s onward, these groups have signified young people's refusal to cooperate. In the social order of the American high school, teens are expected to do what they are told—make the grade, win the prize, play the game. Kids who refuse have always found something else to do. Sometimes it kills them; sometimes it sets them free.

In the 1980s, as before, high school kids at the top were the "preps," "jocks," or "brains," depending on the region. In white suburban high schools in towns like Bergenfield, the "burnouts" are often the kids near the bottom—academically, economically, and socially.

To outsiders, they look tough, scruffy, poor, wild. Uninvolved in and unimpressed by convention, they create an alternative world, a retreat, a refuge. Some burnouts are proud; they "wave their freak flags high." They call themselves burnouts to flaunt their break with the existing order, as a form of resistance, a statement of refusal.

But the meaning changes when "burnout" is hurled by an outsider. Then it hurts. It's an insult. Everyone knows you don't call somebody a burnout to their face unless you are looking for a fight. At that point, the word becomes synonymous with "troubled loser," "druggie"—all the things the press and some residents of the town called the four kids who died together in Tommy Olton's Camaro.

How did kids in Bergenfield *become* "burnouts," I wondered. At what point were they identified as outcasts? Was this a labeling process or one of self-selection? What kinds of lives did they have? What resources were available for them? What choices did they have? What ties did these kids have to the world outside Bergenfield? Where did their particular subculture come from? Why in the 1980s, the Reagan years, in white, suburban America?

What were their hopes and fears? What did heavy metal, Satan, suicide, and long hair mean to them? Who were their heroes, their gods? What saved them and what betrayed them in the long, cold night?

And what was this "something evil in the air" that people spoke about? Were the kids in Bergenfield "possessed"? Was the suicide pact an act of cowardice by four "losers," or the final refuge of kids helplessly and hopelessly trapped? How different was Bergenfield from other towns?

Could kids be labeled to death? How much power did these labels have? I wanted to meet other kids in Bergenfield who were identified as "burnouts" to find out what it felt like to carry these labels. I wanted to understand the existential situation they operated in—not simply as hapless losers, helpless victims, or tragic martyrs, but also as *historical actors* determined in their choices, resistant, defiant.

Because the suicide pact in Bergenfield seemed to be a symptom of something larger, a metaphor for something more universal, I moved on from there to other towns. For almost two years I spent my time reading thrash magazines, seeing shows, and hanging out with "burnouts" and "dirtbags" as well as kids who slip through such labels. . . .

From the beginning, I decided I didn't want to dwell too much on the negatives. I wanted to understand how alienated kids survived, as well as how they were defeated. How did they maintain their humanity against what I now felt were impossible odds? I wondered. What keeps young people together when the world they are told to trust no longer seems to work? What motivates them to be decent human beings when nobody seems to respect them or take them seriously? . . .

Joe's[1] been up for more than a day already. He's fried, his clothes are getting crusty, and he points to his armpits and says he smells (he doesn't). He's broke, he misses his girlfriend. He says he can't make it without someone. His girlfriend dumped him last year. He's gone out with other girls, but it's not the same. And he knows he can't win in this town. He's got a bad name. What's the use. He's tried it at least six times. Once he gashed at his vein with an Army knife he picked up in Times Square. He strokes the scars.

Tonight, he says, he's going to a Bible study class. Some girl he met invited him. Shows me a God pamphlet, inspirational literature. He doesn't want anyone to know about this, though. He thought the Jesus girl was nice. He's meeting her at seven. Bobby comes back in the room with Nicky, looking for cigarettes.

Later in the living room Joe teases Doreen. Poking at her, he gets rough. Bobby monitors him. "Calm down, Joe." We are just sitting around playing music, smoking cigarettes. Fooling around. "Did you see those Jesus freaks down at Cooper's Pond the other day?" Randy laughs. Nicky tells Joe to forget it. Jesus chicks won't just go with you; you have to date them for a long time, pretend you're serious about them. They don't fuck you right away. "It's not worth the bother."

Suicide comes up again. Joan and Susie have razor scars. The guys make Susie show me her freshly bandaged wrists. I look at her. She's such a beautiful girl. She's sitting there with her boyfriend, Randy, just fooling around. I ask her quietly, "Why are you doing this?" She smiles at me seductively. She doesn't say anything. What the fuck is this, erotic? Kicks? Romantic? I feel cold panic.

Nicky slashed his wrists when his old girlfriend moved out of state. His scars are much older. I motion to him about Susie. Discreetly he says, "It's best just to ignore it, don't pay too much attention." Throughout the afternoon I try every trick I know to get Susie to talk to me. She won't. She's shy, quiet; she's all inside herself.

And I really don't want to push too hard. The kids say they're already going nuts from all the suicide-prevention stuff. You can't panic. But I have to figure out if this is a cult, a fad, a hobby, or something I'm supposed to report to the police. I'm afraid to leave.

I wonder, do they know the difference between vertical and horizontal cuts? Don't their parents, their teachers, the cops, and neighbors see this shit going on? Maybe they feel as confused as I do. Maybe this is why they didn't see it coming here, and in the other towns. You can't exactly go around strip-searching teenagers to see if they have slash wounds. . . .

After the suicide pact, parents complained that the kids really did need somewhere to go when school let out. The after-school activities were limited to academics, sports, or organized school clubs. Even with part-time after-school jobs, a number of the town's young people did not find the conventional activities offered by the town particularly intriguing.

But according to established adult reasoning, if you didn't get absorbed into the legitimate, established routine of social activity, you'd be left to burn out on street corners, killing time, getting wasted. It was impossible for anyone to imagine any autonomous activity that nonconforming youth en masse might enjoy that would not be self-destructive, potentially criminal, or meaningless.

Parents understood that the lack of "anything to do" often led to drug and alcohol abuse. Such concerns were aired at the volatile meeting in the auditorium of Bergenfield High School. It was agreed that the kids' complaint of "no place to go" had to be taken seriously. Ten years ago, in any suburban town, teenagers' complaints of "nothing to do" would have been met with adult annoyance. But not anymore.

In Bergenfield, teenage boredom could no longer be dismissed as the whining of spoiled suburban kids. Experts now claimed that national rates of teenage suicide were higher in suburbs and rural areas because of teen isolation and boredom. In Bergenfield, adults articulated the fact that many local kids did hang out on street corners and in parks looking for drugs because things at home weren't too good.

Youngsters have always been cautioned by adults that the devil would make good use of their idle hands. But now they understood something else: boredom led to drugs, and boredom could kill. Yet it was taken for granted that if you refused to be colonized, if you ventured beyond the boundaries circumscribed by adults, you were "looking for trouble." But in reality, it was adult organization of young people's social reality over the last few hundred years that had *created* this miserable situation: one's youth as wasted years. Being wasted and getting wasted. Adults often wasted kids' time with meaningless activities, warehousing them in school; kids in turn wasted their own time on drugs. Just to have something to do.

So by now whenever kids hang out, congregating in some unstructured setting, adults read *dangerousness.* Even if young people are talking about serious things, working out plans for the future, discussing life, jobs, adults just assume they are getting wasted. They are. . . .

For the duration of my stay, in almost every encounter, the outcast members of Bergenfield's youth population would tell me these things: The cops are dicks, the school blows, the jocks suck, Billy Milano (lead singer of now defunct S.O.D.—Stormtroopers of Death) was from a nearby town, and Iron Maiden had dedicated "Wasted Years" to the Burress sisters the last time the band played Jersey. These were their cultural badges of honor, unknown to the adults.

Like many suburban towns, Bergenfield is occupationally mixed. Blue-collar aristocrats may make more money than college professors, and so one's local class identity is unclear. Schools claim to track kids in terms of "ability," and cliques are determined by subculture, style, participation, and refusal.

Because the myth of a democratized mass makes class lines in the suburbs of the United States so ambiguous to begin with, differences in status become the critical lines of demarcation. And in the mostly white, mainly Christian town of Bergenfield, where there are neither very rich nor very poor people, this sports thing became an important criterion for determining "who's who" among the young people.

The girls played this out, too, as they always have, deriving their status by involvement in school (as cheerleaders, in clubs, in the classroom). And just as important, by the boys they hung around with. They were defined by who they were, by what they wore, by where they were seen, and with whom.

Like any other "Other," the kids at the bottom, who everybody here simply called burnouts, were actually a conglomerate of several cliques—serious druggies, Deadheads, dirtbags, skinheads, metalheads, thrashers, and punks. Some were good students, from "good" families with money and prestige. In any other setting all of these people might have been bitter rivals, or at least very separate cliques. But here, thanks to the adults and the primacy of sports, they were all lumped together—united by virtue of a common enemy, the jocks. . . .

For a bored, ignored, lonely kid, drug oblivion may offer immediate comfort; purpose and adventure in the place of everyday ennui. But soon it has a life of its own—at a psychic and a social level, the focus of your life becomes *getting high* (or *well* as some people describe it). Ironically, the whole miserable process often begins as a positive act of self-preservation.

Both the dirts and the burnt may understand how they are being fucked over and by whom. And while partying rituals may actually celebrate the refusal to play the game, neither group has a clue where to take it beyond the parking lot of 7-Eleven.

So they end up stranded in teenage wasteland. They devote their lives to their bands, to their friends, to partying; they live in the moment. They're going down in flames, taking literally the notion that "rust never sleeps," that it is "better to burn out than fade away." While left-leaning adults have valorized the politically minded punks and right-wing groups have engaged some fascistic skins, nobody really thinks too much about organizing dirts or burnouts. Law enforcement officials, special education teachers, and drug treatment facilities are the adults who are concerned with these kids.

Such wasted suburban kids are typically not politically "correct," nor do they constitute an identifiable segment of the industrial working class. They are not members of a specific racial or ethnic minority, and they have few political advocates. Only on the political issues of abortion and the death penalty for minors will wasted teenage girls and boys be likely to find adults in their corner.

Small in numbers, isolated in decaying suburbs, they aren't visible on any national scale until they are involved in something that really horrifies us, like a suicide pact, or parricide, or incest, or "satanic" sacrifice. For the most part, burnouts and dirtbags are anomic small town white boys and girls, just trying to get through the day. Their way of fighting back is to have enough fun to kill themselves before everything else does. . . .

In the scheme of things, average American kids who don't have rich or well-connected parents have had these choices: Play the game and try to get ahead. Do what your parents did—work yourself to death at a menial job and find solace in beer, God, or family. Or take risks, cut deals, or break the law. The Reagan years made it hard for kids to "put their noses to the grindstone" as their parents had. Like everyone, these people hoped for better lives. But they lived in an age of inflated expectations and diminishing returns. Big and fast money was everywhere, and ever out of reach. America now had an economy that worked sort of like a cocaine high—propped up by hot air and big debt. The substance was absent. People's lives were like that too, and at times they were crashing hard.

In the meantime, wherever you were, you could still dream of becoming spectacular. A special talent could be your ticket out. Long Island kids had role models in bands like the Crumbsuckers, Ludichrist, Twisted Sister, Steve Vai, and Pat Benatar. North Jersey was full of sports celebrities and rock millionaires—you grew up hoping you'd end up like Mike Tyson or Jon Bon Jovi. Or like Keith Richards, whose father worked in a factory; or Ozzy, who also came from a grim English factory town, a hero who escaped the drudge because he was spectacular. This was the hip version of the American dream.

Kids who go for the prize now understand there are only two choices— rise to the top or crash to the bottom. Many openly admit that they would rather end it all now than end up losers. The nine-to-five world, corporate grunt life, working at the same job for 30 years, that's not for them. They'd prefer to hold out until the last possibility and then just piss on it all. The big easy or the bottomless pit, but never the everyday drone. And as long as there are local heroes and stories, you can still believe you have a chance to emerge from the mass as something larger than life. You can still play the great lottery and dream.

Schools urge kids to make these choices as early as possible, in a variety of ways. In the terse words of the San Francisco hardcore band MDC, "There's no such thing as cheating in a loser's game." Many kids who start out as nobody from nowhere with nothing will end up that way. Nevertheless, everyone pretends that everything is possible if you give it your best shot. We actually believe it. While educators hope to be as efficient as possible in figuring out where unspectacular students can plug into the workforce, kids try to play at being one in a million, some way of shining, even if it's just for a while. . . .

Girls get slightly different choices. They may hope to become spectacular by virtue of their talents and their beauty. Being the girlfriend of a guy in a band means you might get to live in his mansion someday if you stick it out with him during the lean years. You might just end up like Bon Jovi's high school sweetheart, or married to someone like Cinderella's lead singer—he married his hometown girlfriend and helped set her up in her own business. These are suburban fairy tales.

Around here, some girls who are beautiful and talented hope to become stars, too, like Long Island's local products Debbie Gibson and Taylor Dayne. Some hope to be like actress Heather Locklear and marry someone really hot like Motley Crüe's drummer, Tommy Lee. If you could just get to the right place at the right time.

But most people from New Jersey and Long Island or anywhere else in America don't end up rich and famous. They have some fun trying, though, and for a while life isn't bad at all.

Yet, if you are unspectacular—not too book-smart, of average looks and moderate creative ability—there have always been places for you. Much of your teachers' efforts will be devoted to your more promising peers, and so will your nation's resources. But your parents will explain to you that this is the way it is, and early on, you will know to expect very little from school.

There are still a few enclaves, reservations. The shop and crafting culture of your parents' class of origin is one pocket of refuge. In the vocational high school, your interests are rewarded, once you have allowed yourself to be dumped there. And if the skills you gather there don't really lead to anything much, there's always the military.

Even though half the kids in America today will never go to college, the country still acts as if they will. At least, most schools seem to be set up to prepare you for college. And if it's not what you can or want to do, their attitude is tough shit, it's your problem.

And your most devoted teachers at vocational high school will never tell you that the training you will get from them is barely enough to get your foot in the door. You picture yourself getting into something with a future only to find that your skills are obsolete, superficial, and the boss prefers people with more training, more experience, more promise. So you are stuck in dead-end "youth employment jobs," and now what?

According to the William T. Grant Commission on Work, Family and Citizenship, 20 million people between the ages of 16 and 24 are not likely to go to college. The "forgotten half," as youth advocates call them, will find jobs in service and retail. But the money is bad, only half that of typical manufacturing jobs. The good, stable jobs that don't require advanced training have been disappearing rapidly. From 1979 to 1985 the U.S.A. suffered a net loss of 1.7 million manufacturing jobs. What's left?

In my neighborhood, the shipping and warehousing jobs that guys like the Grinders took, hedging their bets against rock stardom, are now seen as "good jobs" by the younger guys at Metal 24. I am regularly asked to . . . "find out if they're hiring" down at [the] shipping company. Dead-end kids around here who aren't working with family are working "shit jobs."

The skills used in a typical "shit job" . . . involve slapping rancid butter on stale hard rolls, mopping the floor, selling Lotto tickets, making sure shelves and refrigerators are clean, sorting and stacking magazines, taking delivery on newspapers, and signing out videos. They are also advised to look out for shoplifters, to protect the register, and to be sure that the surveillance camera is running. Like most kids in shit jobs, they are most skilled at getting over on the boss and in developing strategies to ward off boredom. It is not unusual to see kids at the supermarket cash register or the mall clothing shop standing around with a glazed look in their eyes. And you will often hear them complain of boredom, tiredness, or whine, "I can't wait to get out of here." Usually, in shit jobs this is where it begins and ends. There aren't many alternatives.

Everywhere, such kids find getting into a union or having access to supervisory or managerial tracks hard to come by. Some forms of disinvestment are more obvious than others. In a company town, you will be somewhat clear about what is going on. At the end of the 1980s, the defense industry of Long Island seemed threatened; people feared that their lives would soon be devastated.

But the effect of a changing economic order on most kids only translates into scrambling for a new safety zone. It is mostly expressed as resentment against entrepreneurial foreigners (nonwhites) and as anomie—a vague sense of loss, then confusion about where they might fit in. . . .

So where are we going? Some people fear we are polarizing into a two-class nation, rich and poor. More precisely, a privileged knowledge-producing class and a low-paid, low-status service class. It is in the public high school that this division of labor for an emergent postindustrial local economy is first articulated. At the top are the kids who will hold jobs in a highly competitive technological economic order, who will advance and be respected if they cooperate and excel.

At the bottom are kids with poor basic skills, short attention spans, limited emotional investment in the future. Also poor housing, poor nutrition, bad schooling, bad lives. And in their bad jobs they will face careers of unsatisfying part-time work, low pay, no benefits, and no opportunity for advancement.

There are the few possibilities offered by a relative—a coveted place in a union, a chance to join a small family business in a service trade, a spot in a small shop. In my neighborhood, kids dream of making a good score on the cop tests, working up from hostess to waitress. Most hang out in limbo hoping to get called for a job in the sheriff's department, or the parks, or sanitation. They're on all the lists, although they know the odds for getting called are slim. The lists are frozen, the screening process is endless.

Meantime they hold jobs for a few months here and there, or they work off the books, or at two bad jobs at once. . . .

When he gave the eulogy at his godson's funeral, Tommy Olton's uncle Richard was quoted as saying, "When I held you in my arms at your baptism, I wanted it to be a fresh start, for you to be more complete than we had ever been ourselves, but I wonder if we expected too much. In thinking only of ourselves, maybe we passed down too great a burden."

Trans-historically, cross-culturally, humans have placed enormous burdens on their young. Sometimes these burdens have been primarily economic: The child contributes to the economy of the family or tribe. Sometimes the burden has been social—the child is a contribution to the immortality of our creed. Be fruitful and multiply.

But the spiritual burden we pass on to the child may be the most difficult to bear. We do expect them to fulfill an incompleteness in ourselves, in our world. Our children are our vehicle for the realization of unfulfilled human dreams: our class aspirations, our visions of social justice and world peace, of a better life on earth.

Faith in the child, in the next generation, helps get us through this life. Without this hope in the future *through the child* we could not endure slavery, torture, war, genocide, or even the ordinary, everyday grind of a "bad life." The child-as-myth is an empty slate upon which we carve our highest ideals. For human beings, the child is God, utopia, and the future incarnate. The Bergenfield suicide pact ruptured the sacred trust between the generations. It was a negation.

After I had been to Bergenfield, people asked me, "Why did they do it?" People want to know in 25 words or less. But it's more complicated than that. I usually just say, "They had bad lives," and try to explain why these lives ended where, when, and how they did. But I still wonder, at what point are people pushed over the line?

On the surface the ending of the four kids' bad lives can be explained away by the "case history" approach. Three of the four had suicidal or self-destructive adult role models: the suicide of Tommy Olton's father, the drug-related death of the Burress sisters' father. Tommy Rizzo, along with his three friends, had experienced the recent loss of a beloved friend, Joe Major. Before Joe, the death of three other local "burnouts." Then there was the chronic drug and alcohol abuse, an acknowledged contributing factor in suicide. Families ruptured by divorce, death, estrangement. Failure at school.

But these explanations alone would not add up to a suicide pact among four kids. If they did, the teenage suicide rate would be much, much higher. The personal problems experienced by the four kids were severe, painful, but by the 1980s, they were no longer remarkable.

For a while I wondered if the excessive labeling process in Bergenfield was killing off the "burnouts." Essentially, their role, their collective identity in their town was that of the "nigger" or "Jew." Us and Them, the One and the Other. And once they were constituted as "burnouts" by the town's hege-monic order, the kids played out their assigned role as self-styled outcasts with irony, style, and verve.

Yes, Bergenfield was guilty of blaming the victim. But only slightly more guilty than any other town. Labeling, blaming the victim, and conferring rewards on more cooperative kids was cruel, but also not remarkable in the eighties.

As I felt from the beginning, the unusually cloying geography of Ber-genfield seemed somehow implicated in the suicide pact. The landscape appeared even more circumscribed because of the "burnouts'" lack of legiti-mate space in the town: they were too old for the [roller skating] Rink, and the Building [an abandoned warehouse taken over by the teens] was avail-able for criminal trespass only. Outcast, socially and spatially, for years the "burnouts" had been chased from corner to parking lot, and finally, to the garage bays of Foster Village. They were nomads, refugees in the town of their birth. *There was no place for them.* They felt unloved, unwanted, deval-ued, disregarded, and discarded.

But this little town, not even two miles long from north to south, was just a dot on a much larger map. It wasn't the whole world. Hip adults I know, friends who grew up feeling like outcasts in their hometown, were very sym-pathetic to the plight of the "burnouts." Yet even they often held out one last question, sometimes contemptuously: "Why didn't they *just leave*?" As if the four kids had failed even as outcasts. My friends found this confusing. "No matter how worthless the people who make the rules say you are, you don't have to play their game. You can always walk and not look back," they would argue. People who feel abject and weird in their hometown simply move away.

But that has always been a class privilege. The townies are the poor kids, the wounded street warriors who stay behind. And besides, escape was eas-ier for everyone 20 years ago. American society had safety nets then that don't exist now—it's just not the same anymore.

During the eighties, dead-end kids—kids with personal problems and unspectacular talents living in punitive or indifferent towns with a sense of futility about life—became more common. There were lots of kids with bad lives. They didn't all commit suicide. But I believe that in another decade, Tommy Rizzo, Cheryl Burress, Tommy Olton, and Lisa Burress would not have "done it." They might have had more choices, or choices that really meant something to them. Teenage suicide won't go away until kids' bad lives do. Until there are other ways of moving out of bad lives, suicide will remain attractive.

ENDNOTE

[1] As I promised the kids I met hanging out on the streets of Bergen County and on Long Island, "No names, no pictures." Names such as "Joe," "Eddie," and "Doreen" are fictitious, changed to protect their privacy.

3

INTERSECTION OF BIOGRAPHY AND HISTORY
My Intellectual Journey

MARY ROMERO

This selection by Mary Romero is another example of C. Wright Mills' sociological imagination. Romero is a professor in the School of Justice Studies at Arizona State University, where she teaches sociology and Chicano studies. In this excerpt, Romero explains how biography and history influenced her investigation of domestic service work done by Chicanas. In particular, she describes her research process, which involved reinterpreting her own and others' domestic service experiences within the larger work history of Mexican Americans and the devaluation of housework. Thus, this selection is from the introduction to Romero's 1992 book, *Maid in the U.S.A.*, a study of domestic work and the social interactions between domestics and their employers.

From *Maid in the U.S.A.*, pp. 1–15. Copyright © 1992 by Routledge, Chapman and Hall, Inc. Reprinted with permission of the publisher.

When I was growing up many of the women whom I knew worked cleaning other people's houses. Domestic service was part of my taken-for-granted reality. Later, when I had my own place, I considered housework something you did before company came over. My first thought that domestic service and housework might be a serious research interest came as a result of a chance encounter with live-in domestics along the U.S.–Mexican border. Before beginning a teaching position at the University of Texas at El Paso, I stayed with a colleague while apartment hunting. My colleague had a live-in domestic to assist with housecleaning and cooking. Asking around, I learned that live-in maids were common in El Paso, even among apartment and condominium dwellers. The hiring of maids from Mexico was so common that locals referred to Monday as the border patrol's day off because the agents ignored the women crossing the border to return to their employers' homes after their weekend off. The practice of hiring undocumented Mexican women as domestics, many of whom were no older than fifteen, seemed strange to me. It was this strangeness that raised the topic of domestic service as a question and made problematic what had previously been taken for granted.

I must admit that I was shocked at my colleague's treatment of the 16-year-old domestic whom I will call Juanita. Only recently hired, Juanita was still adjusting to her new environment. She was extremely shy, and her timidity was made even worse by constant flirting from her employer. As far as I could see, every attempt Juanita made to converse was met with teasing so that the conversation could never evolve into a serious discussion. Her employer's sexist, paternalistic banter effectively silenced the domestic, kept her constantly on guard, and made it impossible for her to feel comfortable at work. For instance, when she informed the employer of a leaky faucet, he shot her a look of disdain, making it clear that she was overstepping her boundaries. I observed other encounters that clearly served to remind Juanita of her subservient place in her employer's home.

Although Juanita was of the same age as my colleague's oldest daughter and but a few years older than his two sons, she was treated differently from the other teenagers in the house. She was expected to share her bedroom with the ironing board, sewing machine, and other spare-room types of objects.[1] More importantly, she was assumed to have different wants and needs. I witnessed the following revealing exchange. Juanita was poor. She had not brought toiletries with her from Mexico. Since she had not yet been paid, she had to depend on her employer for necessities. Yet instead of offering her a small advance in her pay so she could purchase the items herself and giving her a ride to the nearby supermarket to select her own toiletries, the employer handled Juanita's request for toothbrush, toothpaste, shampoo, soap, and the like in the following manner. In the presence of all the family and the houseguest, he made a list of the things she needed. Much teasing and joking accompanied the encounter. The employer shopped for her and purchased only generic brand items, which were a far cry from the brand-name products that filled the bathroom of his 16-year-old daughter. Juanita looked at the toothpaste, shampoo, and soap with confusion; she may never have seen generic products before, but she obviously knew that a distinction had been made.

One evening I walked into the kitchen as the employer's young sons were shouting orders at Juanita. They pointed to the dirty dishes on the table and pans in the sink and yelled "WASH!" "CLEAN!" Juanita stood frozen next to the kitchen door, angry and humiliated. Aware of possible repercussions for Juanita if I reprimanded my colleague's sons, I responded awkwardly by reallocating chores to everyone present. I announced that I would wash the dishes and the boys would clear the table. Juanita washed and dried dishes alongside me, and together we finished cleaning the kitchen. My colleague returned from his meeting to find us in the kitchen washing the last pan. The look on his face was more than enough to tell me that he was shocked to find his houseguest—and future colleague—washing dishes with the maid. His embarrassment at my behavior confirmed my suspicion that I had violated the normative expectations of class behavior within the home. He attempted to break the tension with a flirtatious and sexist remark to Juanita which served to excuse her from the kitchen and from any further discussion.

The conversation that followed revealed how my colleague chose to interpret my behavior. Immediately after Juanita's departure from the kitchen, he initiated a discussion about "Chicano radicals" and the Chicano movement. Although he was a foreign-born Latino, he expressed sympathy for *la causa*. Recalling the one Chicano graduate student he had known to obtain a Ph.D. in sociology, he gave several accounts of how the student's political behavior had disrupted the normal flow of university activity. Lowering his voice to a confidential whisper, he confessed to understanding why Marxist theory has become so popular among Chicano students. The tone of his comments and the examples that he chose made me realize that my "outrageous" behavior was explained, and thus excused, on the basis of my being one of those "Chicano radicals." He interpreted my washing dishes with his maid as a symbolic act; that is, I was affiliated with *los de abajo*.

My behavior had been comfortably defined without addressing the specific issue of maids. My colleague then further subsumed the topic under the rubric of "the servant problem" along the border. (His reaction was not unlike the attitude employers have displayed toward domestic service in the United States for the last hundred years.)[2] He began by providing me with chapter and verse about how he had aided Mexican women from Juarez by helping them cross the border and employing them in his home. He took further credit for introducing them to the appliances found in an American middle-class home. He shared several funny accounts about teaching country women from Mexico to use the vacuum cleaner, electric mixer, and microwave (remember the maid scene in the movie *El Norte*?) and implicitly blamed them for their inability to work comfortably around modern conveniences. For this "on-the-job training" and introduction to American culture, he complained, his generosity and goodwill had been rewarded by a high turnover rate. As his account continued, he assured me that most maids were simply working until they found a husband. In his experience they worked for a few months or less and then did not return to work on Monday morning after their first weekend off. Of course it never dawned on him that they may simply have found a job with better working conditions.

The following day, Juanita and I were alone in the house. As I mustered up my best Spanish, we shared information about our homes and families. After a few minutes of laughter about my simple sentence structure, Juanita lowered her head and in a sad, quiet voice told me how isolated and lonely she felt in this middle-class suburb literally within sight of Juarez. Her feelings were not the consequence of the work or of frustrations with modern appliances, nor did she complain about the absence of Mexican people in the neighborhood; her isolation and loneliness were in response to the norms and values surrounding domestic service. She described the situation quite clearly in expressing puzzlement over the social interactions she had with her employer's family: Why didn't her employer's children talk to her or include her in any of their activities when she wasn't working? Her reaction was not unlike that of Lillian Pettengill, who wrote about her two-year experience as a domestic in Philadelphia households at the turn of the century: "I feel my isolation alone in a big house full of people." [3]

Earlier in the day, Juanita had unsuccessfully tried to initiate a conversation with the 16-year-old daughter while she cleaned her room. She was of the same age as the daughter (who at that moment was in bed reading and watching TV because of menstrual cramps—a luxury the maid was not able to claim). She was rebuffed and ignored and felt that she became visible only when an order was given. Unable to live with this social isolation, she had already made up her mind not to return after her day off in Juarez. I observed the total impossibility of communication. The employer would never know why she left, and Juanita would not know that she would be considered simply another ungrateful Mexican whom he had tried to help.

After I returned to Denver, I thought a lot about the situations of Juanita and the other young undocumented Mexican women living in country club areas along the border. They worked long days in the intimacy of American middle-class homes but were starved for respect and positive social interaction. Curiously, the employers did not treat the domestics as "one of the family," nor did they consider themselves employers. Hiring a domestic was likely to be presented within the context of charity and good works; it was considered a matter of helping "these Mexican women" rather than recognized as a work issue.

I was bothered by my encounter along the border, not simply for the obvious humanitarian reasons, but because I too had once worked as a domestic, just as my mother, sister, relatives, and neighbors had. As a teenager, I cleaned houses with my mother on weekends and vacations. My own working experience as a domestic was limited because I had always been accompanied by my mother or sister instead of working alone. Since I was a day worker, my time in the employer's home was limited and I was able to return to my family and community each day. In Juanita's situation as a live-in domestic, there was no distinction between the time on and off work. I wondered whether domestic service had similarly affected my mother, sister, and neighbors. Had they too worked beyond the agreed-upon time? Did they have difficulty managing relationships with employers? I never worked alone and was spared the direct negotiations with employers. Instead, I cooperated with my mother or sister in completing the housecleaning as efficiently and quickly as possible.

I could not recall being yelled at by employers or their children, but I did remember anger, resentment, and the humiliation I had felt at kneeling to scrub other people's toilets while they gave step-by-step cleaning instructions. I remember feeling uncomfortable around employers' children who never acknowledged my presence except to question where I had placed their belongings after I had picked them up off the floor to vacuum. After all, my experience was foreign to them; at the age of 14 I worked as a domestic while they ran off to swimming, tennis, and piano lessons. Unlike Juanita, I preferred to remain invisible as I moved around the employer's house cleaning. Much later, I learned that the invisibility of workers in domestic service is a common characteristic of the occupation. Ruth Schwartz Cowan has commented on the historical aspect of invisibility:

> The history of domestic service in the United States is a vast, unresolved puzzle, because the social role "servant" so frequently carries with it the unspoken adjective *invisible*. In diaries and letters, the "invisible" servant becomes visible only when she departs employment ("Mary left today"). In statistical series, she appears only when she is employed full-time, on a live-in basis; or when she is willing to confess the nature of her employment to a census taker, and (especially since the Second World War) there have frequently been good reasons for such confessions to go unmade.[4]

Although I remained invisible to most of the employers' family members, the mothers, curiously enough, seldom let me move around the house invisibly, dusting the woodwork and vacuuming carpets. Instead, I was subjected to constant supervision and condescending observations about "what a good little girl I was, helping my mother clean house." After I had moved and cleaned behind a hide-a-bed and Lazy-boy chair, vacuumed three floors including two sets of stairs, and carried the vacuum cleaner up and downstairs twice because "little Johnny" was napping when I was cleaning the bedrooms—I certainly didn't feel like a "little girl helping mother." I felt like a domestic worker!

There were employers who attempted to draw parallels between my adolescent experience and their teenagers' behavior: they'd point to the messy bedrooms and claim, "Well, you're a teenager, you understand clothes, books, papers, and records on the floor." Even at 14, I knew that being sloppy and not picking up after yourself was a privilege. I had two brothers and three sisters. I didn't have my own bedroom but shared a room with my sisters. Not one of us would think of leaving our panties on the floor for the others to pick up. I didn't bother to set such employers straight but continued to clean in silence, knowing that at the end of the day I would get cash and confident that I would soon be old enough to work elsewhere.

Many years later, while attending graduate school, I returned to domestic service as an "off-the-record" means to supplement my income. Graduate fellowships and teaching assistantships locked me into a fixed income that frequently was not enough to cover my expenses.[5] So once again I worked alongside my mother for seven hours as we cleaned two houses. I earned about 50 dollars for the day. Housecleaning is strenuous work, and I returned home exhausted from climbing up and down stairs, bending over, rubbing, and scrubbing.

Returning to domestic service as a graduate student was awkward. I tried to reduce the status inconsistency in my life by electing to work only in houses from which families were absent during the day. If someone appeared while I worked, I ignored their presence as they did mine. Since working arrangements had been previously negotiated by my mother, I had limited face-to-face interactions with employers. Most of the employers knew I was a graduate student, and fortunately, most seemed reluctant to ask me too many questions. Our mutual silence served as a way to deal with the status inconsistency of a housewife with a B.A. hiring an ABD to clean her house.

I came to El Paso with all of these experiences unquestioned in my memory. My presuppositions about domestic service were called into question only after observing the more obviously exploitative situation in the border town. I saw how vulnerable undocumented women employed as live-in domestics are and what little recourse they have to improve their situation, short of finding another job. Experiencing Juanita's shame and disgust at my colleague's sons' behavior brought back a flood of memories that eventually influenced me to study the paid housework that I had once taken for granted. I began to wonder professionally about the Chicanas employed as domestics that I had known throughout my own life: how vulnerable were they to exploitation, racism, and sexism? Did their day work status and U.S. citizenship provide protection against degradation and humiliation? How did Chicanas go about establishing a labor arrangement within a society that marked them as racial and cultural inferiors? How did they deal with racial slurs and sexist remarks within their employers' homes? How did Chicanas attempt to negotiate social interactions and informal labor arrangements with employers and their families?

An Exploratory Study

The Research Process

Intending to compare my findings with the research on U.S. minority women employed as domestics, I chose to limit my study to Chicanas, that is, women of Mexican descent born and raised in the United States. Although many women born in Mexico and living in the United States consider themselves Chicanas, my sample did not include women born outside the United States. My major concern in making this distinction was to avoid bringing into the analysis immigration issues that increase the vulnerability of the women employed as domestics. I wanted to keep conditions as constant as possible to make comparisons with the experiences Judith Rollins, Bonnie Thornton Dill, and Soraya Moore Coley report among African American women and with Evelyn Nakano Glenn's study of Japanese American women.[6] In order to duplicate similar residential and citizenship characteristics of these studies, I restricted my sample to Chicanas living in Denver whose families had migrated from rural areas of New Mexico and Colorado. All of the women interviewed were U.S. citizens and lived in Denver most of their adult lives.

I began the project by soliciting the cooperation of current and former domestics from my own family. I relied on domestics to provide entree into informal networks. These networks turned out to be particularly crucial in gaining access to an occupation that is so much a part of the underground economy. My mother, sister, and sister-in-law agreed to be interviewed and to provide names of relatives, friends, and neighbors. I also identified Chicana domestics in the community with the assistance of outreach workers employed by local churches and social service agencies. The snowball sampling was achieved by asking each interviewee to recommend other Chicana domestics as potential interviewees.

The women were extremely cautious about offering the names of friends and relatives. In most cases, they contacted the person first and only then gave me the name and telephone number. This actually turned out to be quite helpful. Potential interviewees had already heard about my study from someone who had been interviewed. They had a general idea of the questions I was going to ask and in some cases a little background information about who I was. However, on three occasions, I called women to ask for an interview and was confronted with resistance and shame. The women expressed embarrassment at being identified by their work—as a "housekeeper" or "cleaning lady." I responded by sharing my research interests in the occupation and in the relationship between work and family. I also shared my previous experience as a domestic.[7] One woman argued with me for 20 minutes about conducting research on an occupation that was low status, suggesting instead that I study Chicana lawyers or doctors, that is, "another occupation that presents our people in a more positive light." Another woman denied ever having worked as a domestic even though several

women, including her sister-in-law, had given me her name as someone currently employed as a domestic.

The stigma of domestic service was a problem during the interviews as
well. From the outset, it was very important for each woman to establish
herself as someone more than a private household worker. Conducting non-
structured, free-flowing, and open-ended interviews allowed the women
to establish multiple identities, particularly diffuse family and community
roles.

The interviews were conducted in the women's homes, usually while sitting in the living room or at the dining room table with the radio or television
on in the background. Although family members peeked in, for the most part
there were few interruptions other than an occasional telephone call. From
time to time, the women called to their husbands in the other room to ask the
name of a street where they had once lived or the year the oldest son had
been born in order to figure out when they had left and returned to work. The
average interview lasted two hours, but I often stayed to visit and chat long
after the interview was over. They told me about their church activities and
plans to remodel the house and asked me for my opinion on current Chicano
politics. Some spread out blankets, tablecloths, and pillow covers to exhibit
their needlework. They showed me pictures of their children and grandchildren, giving me a walking tour of living rooms and bedrooms where
wedding and high school portraits hung. As each one was identified, I
learned more about their lives.

I conducted 25 open-ended interviews with Chicanas living and working
in the greater Denver metropolitan area. The most visible Chicano communities in Denver are in the low-income neighborhood located in the downtown area or in one of two working-class neighborhoods in the northern and
western areas of the city. I interviewed women from each of these communities. I asked them to discuss their overall work histories, with particular emphasis on their experiences as domestics. I probed for detailed information
on domestic work, including strategies for finding employers, definitions of
appropriate and inappropriate tasks, the negotiation of working conditions,
ways of doing housework efficiently, and the pros and cons of domestic service. The accounts included descriptions of the domestics' relationships with
white middle-class mistresses and revealed Chicanas' attitudes toward their
employers' lifestyles.

All of the interviewees' families of orientation were from northern New
Mexico or southern Colorado, where many of them had lived and worked on
small farms. Some of the women had arrived in Denver as children with their
parents, others as young brides, and still others as single women to join siblings and cousins in Denver's barrios. Several women recalled annual migra-
tions to northern Colorado to pick sugar beets, prior to their permanent
relocation to Denver. In some cases, the women's entire families of orientation had migrated to Denver; in others, parents and siblings had either remained behind or migrated to other cities. Many older women had migrated

with their husbands after World War II, and several younger women interviewed had arrived at the same time, as children. Women who had migrated as single adults typically had done so in the last 10 or 15 years. Now they were married and permanently living in Denver. . . .

Historical Background

After the Mexican American War, Mexicans were given the option to maintain their Mexican citizenship and leave the country or become U.S. citizens. Many reluctantly chose the latter in order to keep their homes. Although the Treaty of Guadalupe Hidalgo was supposed to guarantee land grant provisions to those who chose to remain in occupied territory, legal and illegal maneuvers were used to eliminate communal usage of land and natural resources. Between 1854 and 1930, an estimated 2,000,000 acres of private land and 1,700,000 acres of communal land were lost.[8] In the arid Southwest, small plots were insufficient to continue a subsistence-based farming economy, thus the members of the Hispano community were transformed from landowners to wage laborers. Enclosure of the common lands forced Mexicans from their former economic roles, "freed" Mexicans for wage labor, and established a racially stratified labor force in the Southwest.

As early as 1900, the Hispano farming and ranching communities of northern New Mexico and southern Colorado began to lose their population. A combination of push-pull factors conspired to force rural Hispanos off the land and attracted them to urban areas like Denver. Rural northern New Mexico and southern Colorado experienced drastic depopulation as adults left to find jobs. During the Depression, studies conducted in cooperation with the Works Progress Administration (WPA) noted the desperate situation:

> The Tewa Basin Study by the U.S. Department of Agriculture showed that in eleven Spanish-American villages containing 1,202 families, an average of 1,110 men went out of the villages to work for some part of each year prior to 1930. In 1934, only 157 men out of 1,202 families had found outside work.[9]

Migration in search of jobs became a way of life for many families. New Mexicans and southern Coloradans joined the migratory farm labor stream from Texas, California, and Mexico. World War II further depopulated the rural villages as people flocked to the cities in response to job openings in defense plants and related industries. Postwar migration from New Mexico was estimated to be one-fifth of the 1940 rural Chicano population.[10] This pattern continued in the following decades. For instance, Thomas Malone found that during the decade of the 1950s, only one of seven northern counties in New Mexico had not experienced a decrease in its former predominantly Spanish-speaking population.[11] By 1960, 61 percent of the population had been urbanized,[12] and between 1950 and 1960, an additional 24 percent left their rural communities.[13]

Perhaps because research on population movement among Chicanos has been so overwhelmingly concerned with emigration from Mexico, this type of internal population movement among Chicanos has not been well studied. What research is available has focused primarily on male workers and the relationship between urbanization and acculturation.[14] Chicanas have been either ignored or treated simply as family members—mothers, daughters, or wives, accompanying male relatives in search of work—rather than as wage earners in their own right. Nevertheless, for many women migration to an urban area made it necessary that they enter the labor market. Domestic service became a significant occupation in the experience.

Profile of Chicana Household Workers

Only the vaguest statistical data on Chicana private household workers are available; for the most part these workers remain a doubly hidden population. The reasons are themselves instructive. Domestic workers tend to be invisible because paid domestic work has not been one of the occupations recorded in social science surveys, and the U.S. Census Bureau uses a single code lumping together all private household workers, including launderers, cooks, housekeepers, child-care workers, cleaners, and servants. Even when statistics on domestics can be teased out of the census and labor data bases, they are marred by the common practice of underreporting work in the informal sector. Unlike some of the private household workers in the East, Chicana domestics are not unionized and remain outside the "counted" labor force. Many private household workers are not included in the statistics collected by the Department of Labor. The "job" involves an informal labor arrangement made between two people, and in many cases payment is simply a cash transaction that is never recorded with the Internal Revenue Service (IRS).

Governmental undercounting of Chicanos and Mexican immigrants in the United States further adds to the problem of determining the number of Chicanas and Mexicanas employed as private household workers. For many, domestic service is part of the underground economy, and employing undocumented workers is reported neither to the IRS nor to the Immigration and Naturalization Service (INS), thus making another source of statistical information unreliable. Chicanos continue to be an undercounted and obscure population. Problems with the categorization of domestics have been still further complicated by changing identifiers for the Mexican American population: Mexican, Spanish-speaking, Hispanic, Spanish-surnamed, and the like make it impossible to segment out the Chicano population.

The 25 Chicanas whom I interviewed included welfare recipients as well as working-class women, ranging in age from 29 to 68. Thirteen of the 25 women were between 29 and 45 years old. The remaining 12 were over 52 years old. All the women had children, and the older women also had grandchildren. The smallest family consisted of one child, and the largest family had seven children. The average was three children. All but one of the women had been married. Five of the women were single heads of house-holds, two of them were divorced, and the other three were single, separated, or widowed. The married women were currently living with husbands employed in blue-collar positions, such as construction and factory work. At the time of the interview, the women who were single heads of households were financially supporting no more than two children.

Educational backgrounds ranged from no schooling to completion of high school. Six women had completed high school, and seven had no high school experience, including one who had never attended school at all. The remaining 12 had at least a sixth-grade education. Although the least educated were the older women, eight of the women under 42 had not completed high school. The youngest woman with less than an eighth-grade education was 53 years old. The 12 women over 50 averaged eight years of schooling. Three of the high school graduates were in their early thirties, two were in their early forties, and one was 57 years old. Although one woman preferred to be interviewed in Spanish, all the women spoke English.

Work experience as a private household worker ranged from five months to 30 years. Women 50 years and older had worked in the occupation from eight to 30 years, while four of the women between the ages of 33 and 39 had worked as domestics for 12 years. Half of the women had worked for more than 10 years as private household workers. Only three women had worked as domestics prior to marriage; each of these women had worked in live-in situations in rural areas in Colorado. Several years later, after marriage and children, they returned as day workers. All the other women, however, had turned to nonresidential day work in response to a financial crisis; in the majority of cases, it was their first job after marriage and having children. Some of the women remained domestics throughout their lives, but others moved in and out of domestic work. Women who returned to domestic service after having other types of jobs usually did so following a period of unemployment.

The work histories revealed that domestic service was only one of several low-paying, low-status jobs the women had held during their lives. They had been hired as waitresses, laundresses, janitors, farmworkers, nurses aides, fast-food servers, cooks, dishwashers, receptionists, school aides, cashiers, baby-sitters, salesclerks, factory workers, and various types of line workers in poultry farms and car washes. Almost half of the women had worked as janitors in hospitals and office buildings or as hotel maids. About one-fourth of the women had held semiskilled and skilled positions such as beauticians, typists, and medical-record clerks. Six of the women had worked only as domestics.

Paid and Unpaid Domestic Work

In describing their daily routine activities, these Chicanas drew my attention to the interrelationship between paid and unpaid housework. As working women, Chicana private household workers face the "double day" or "second shift," but in their case both days consisted of the same types of tasks. Paid housework done for an employer was qualitatively different from housework done for their own families.

In the interviews, Chicanas described many complexities of domestic service. They explained how they used informal networks to find new employers for themselves and for relatives and friends. As they elaborated on the advantages and disadvantages of particular work arrangements and their reasons for refusing certain household tasks, I soon realized that these women not only knew a great deal about cleaning and maintaining homes, but they understood the influence of social relationships on household tasks. Analysis of the extensive planning and negotiation involved in the informal and underground arrangements of domestic service highlighted the significance of the social relationships surrounding housework.

Their work histories included detailed explanations of beginning, returning to, and continuing in domestic service. In the discussions, I began to understand the paradox of domestic service: On the one hand, cleaning houses is degrading and embarrassing; on the other, domestic service can be higher paying, more autonomous, and less dehumanizing than other low-status, low-skilled occupations. Previous jobs in the beet fields, fast-food restaurants, car washes, and turkey farms did not offer annual raises, vacations, or sick leave. Furthermore, these jobs forced employees to work long hours and to keep rigid time schedules, and they frequently occurred outside or in an unsafe work environment. Unlike the other options available, domestic service did have the potential for offering flexible work schedules and autonomy. In most cases, domestic service also paid much more. Although annual raises, vacation, and social security were not the norm for most Chicanas in domestic service, there remained the possibility that such benefits could be negotiated with employers. Furthermore, as former farmworkers, laundresses, and line workers, the women found freedom in domestic work from exposure to dangerous pesticides, poor ventilation, and other health risks. This paradox foreshadowed a critical theoretical issue, the importance of understanding the social process that constructs domestic service as a low-status occupation.

Stigma as a perceived occupational hazard of domestic service emerged during the initial contact and throughout most of the interviews. The stigma attached to domestic service punctuated the interviews. I knew that many women hid their paid household labor from the government, but I did not realize that this secrecy encompassed neighbors, friends, and even extended family members. Several women gave accounts that revealed their families' efforts to conceal their employment as domestics. Children frequently stated that their mothers "just did housework," which was ambiguous enough to define them as full-time homemakers and not necessarily as domestics.

Faced with limited job opportunities, Chicanas selected domestic service and actively sought to make the most of the situation. In comparison with other jobs they had held, domestic service usually paid more and offered greater flexibility in arranging the length of the workday and workweek. Although other jobs did not carry the stigma of servitude, workers were under constant supervision, and the work was similarly low status. Therefore, the women who chose domestic service over other low-paying, low-status jobs based their selection on the occupation that offered some possibility of control. Their challenge was to structure the work so as to reap the most benefits: pay, work hours, labor, and autonomy. Throughout the interviews, the women emphasized job flexibility as the major advantage of domestic service over previous jobs. Nonrigid work schedules allowed time to do their own housework and fulfill family obligations, such as caring for sick children or attending school functions. By stressing the benefits gained by doing day work, Chicanas diffused the low status in their work identities and emphasized their family and community identities. The ways in which they arranged both work and family revealed coping strategies used to deal with the stigma, and this drew me to analyze housework as a form of labor having both paid and unpaid manifestations.

The conventional social science separation of work and family is an analytical construct and is not found in the lived reality of Chicana domestics. Invariably the interviewees mixed and intertwined discussions of work and family. Moreover, the actual and practical relationships between work and family were explicit in their descriptions of daily activities: The reasons for seeking employment included the family's financial situation and the desire to raise its standard of living; earning extra money for the household was viewed as an extension of these women's roles as mothers and wives; arranging day work involved planning work hours around the children's school attendance, dentist and doctor appointments, and community and church activities; in some cases, young mothers even took their preschool-age children with them to work. The worlds of paid and unpaid housework were not disconnected in the lives of these women.

Attending to the importance of the relationship between paid and unpaid domestic work led me to ponder new questions about the dynamics of buying and selling household labor. How does housework differ when it is paid work? How does the housewife role change when part of her work is allocated to another woman? What is the range of employer–employee relationship in domestic service today? And is there a difference in the type of relationships developed by employed and unemployed women buying household labor?

The importance of attending to both paid and unpaid housework in researching domestic service became more apparent as I began presenting my research to academic audiences. When I read papers on the informal labor market or on family and community networks used to find work, some of my colleagues responded as women who employed domestics. Frequently question-and-answer sessions turned into a defense of such practices as hiring undocumented workers, not filing income taxes, or gift giving in lieu of raises and benefits. Although I was aware that as working women, many academics employed someone to clean their houses, I was not prepared for scholars and feminists to respond to my scholarly work as housewives or employers. I was also surprised to discover that many of the maternalistic practices traditionally found in domestic service were common practices in their homes. The recurring responses made me realize that my feminist colleagues had never considered their relationships with the "cleaning woman" on the same plane as those with secretaries, waitresses, or janitors; that is, they thought of the former more or less in terms of the mistress–maid relationship. When, through my research, I pointed out the contradiction, many still had difficulty thinking of their homes—the haven from the cruel academic world—as someone's workplace. Their overwhelming feelings of discomfort, guilt, and resentment, which sometimes came out as hostility, alerted me to the fact that something more was going on.

Although written over a decade ago, Margaret Mead's depiction of the middle-class woman's dilemma still seems to capture the contradictory feelings and attitudes that I hear among feminists today.

> Traveling around the country, I meet a great many young wives and mothers who are struggling with the problem that seems to have no solution—how to hold down two full-time jobs at once. . . . As I listen I realize how many of them—guiltily but wistfully—yearn for the bygone days of servants. . . . They are guilty because they don't quite approve of anyone's working as a servant in someone else's home.[15]

In a society that espouses egalitarian values, we can expect yearnings "for the bygone days of servants" to be experienced as a contradiction. A century ago, Jane Addams discussed the awkward feelings and apprehensiveness academic women feel:

> I should consider myself an unpardonable snob if, because a woman did my cooking, I should not hold myself ready to have her for my best friend, to drive, to read, to attend receptions with her, but that friendship might or might not come about, according to her nature and mine, just as it might or might not come about between me and my college colleague. On the other hand, I would consider myself very stupid if merely because a woman cooked my food and lived in my house I should insist upon having a friendship with her, whether her nature and mine responded to it or not. It would be folly to force the companionship of myself or my family upon her when doubtless she would vastly prefer the companionship of her own friends and her own family.[16]

In her book on black domestics and white employers in the South, Susan Tucker addresses the deeper psychological and class factors involved in hiring servants.

Most studies of domestic work maintain that the prime motivation for hiring a servant is the enhancement of the employer's image as a superior being. Yet, many women certainly must feel some discomfort, even when paying a decent wage, about the possibility of such a motivation. . . . There are many conflicting principles and traditions surrounding the employment of a socially and economically disadvantaged woman who goes daily into a wealthy home. One might feel discomfort if one were aware of any number of different types of ideas—feminist, egalitarian, religious.[17]

Domestic service must be studied because it raises a challenge to any feminist notion of "sisterhood." A growing number of employed middle- and upper-middle-class women escape the double-day syndrome by hiring poor women of color to do housework and child care. David Katzman underscored the class contradiction:

Middle-class women, the employers, gained freedom from family roles and household chores and assumed or confirmed social status by the employment of a servant. . . . The greater liberty of these middle-class women, however, was achieved at the expense of working-class women, who, forced to work, assumed the tasks beneath, distasteful to, or too demanding for the family members.[18]

Housework is ascribed on the basis of gender, and it is further divided along class lines and, in most cases, by race and ethnicity. Domestic service accentuates the contradiction of race and class in feminism, with privileged women of one class using the labor of another woman to escape aspects of sexism.

ENDNOTES

[1] The conditions I observed in El Paso were not much different from those described by D. Thompson in her 1960 article, "Are Women Bad Employers of Other Women?" *Ladies Home Journal:* "Quarters for domestic help are usually ill placed for quiet. Almost invariably they open from pantry or kitchen, so that if a member of the family goes to get a snack at night he wakes up the occupant. And the live-in maid has nowhere to receive a caller except in the kitchen or one [of] those tiny rooms." "As a general rule anything was good enough for a maid's room. It became a catchall for furniture discarded from other parts of the house. One room was a cubicle too small for a regular-sized bed." Cited in Linda Martin and Kerry Segrave, *The Servant Problem: Domestic Workers in North America* (Jefferson, NC: McFarland, 1985), p. 25.

[2] David Katzman addresses the "servant problem" in his historical study of domestic service, *Seven Days a Week: Women and Domestic Service in Industrializing America* (Chicago: University of Illinois Press, 1981). Defined by middle-class housewives, the problem includes both the shortage of servants available and the competency of women willing to enter domestic service. Employers' attitudes about domestics have been well documented in women's magazines. Katzman described the topic as "the bread and butter of women's magazines between the Civil War and World War I"; moreover, Martin and Segrave, *The Servant Problem,* illustrate the continuing presence of articles on the servant problem in women's magazines today.

[3] Lillian Pettengill's account *Toilers of the Home: The Record of a College Woman's Experience As a Domestic Servant* (New York: Doubleday, 1903) is based on two years of employment in Philadelphia households.

[4] Ruth Schwartz Cowan, *More Work for Mother: The Ironies of Household Technology from the Open Hearth to the Microwave* (New York: Basic Books, 1983), p. 228.

[5] Earning money as domestic workers to pay college expenses not covered by scholarships is not that uncommon among other women of color in the United States. Trudier Harris interviewed several African American women public school and university college teachers about their college day experiences in domestic service. See *From Mammies to Militants: Domestics in Black American Literature* (Philadelphia: Temple University Press, 1982), pp. 5–6.

[6] Judith Rollins, *Between Women: Domestics and Their Employers* (Philadelphia: Temple University Press, 1985); Bonnie Thornton Dill, "Across the Boundaries of Race and Class: An Exploration of the Relationship between Work and Family among Black Female Domestic Servants" (Ph.D. dissertation, New York University, 1979): Judith Rollins, "'Making Your Job Good Yourself': Domestic Service and the Construction of Personal Dignity," in *Women and the Politics of Empowerment,* ed. Ann Bookman and Sandra Morgen (Philadelphia: Temple University Press, 1988), pp. 33–52; Soraya Moore Coley, "'And Still I Rise': An Exploratory Study of Contemporary Black Private Household Workers" (Ph.D. dissertation, Bryn Mawr College, 1981); Evelyn Nakano Glenn, *Issei, Nisei, War Brides: Three Generations of Japanese American Women in Domestic Service* (Philadelphia: Temple University Press, 1986).

[7] In some cases, it was important to let women know that my own background had involved paid housework and that my mother and sister were currently employed full-time as private household workers. Sharing this information conveyed that my life had similarities to theirs and that I respected them. This sharing of information is similar to the concept of "reciprocity" (R. Wax, "Reciprocity in Field Work," in *Human Organization Research: Field Relationships and Techniques,* ed. R. N. Adams and J. J. Preiss [New York: Dorsey, 1960], pp. 90–98).

[8] Clark Knowlton, "Changing Spanish-American Villages of Northern New Mexico," *Sociology and Social Research* 53 (1969): 455–75.

[9] Nancie Gonzalez, *The Spanish-Americans of New Mexico* (Albuquerque: University of New Mexico Press, 1967), p. 123.

[10] William W. Winnie, "The Hispanic People of New Mexico" (Master's thesis, University of Florida, 1955).

[11] Thomas J. Malone, "Recent Demographic and Economic Changes in Northern New Mexico," *New Mexico Business* 17 (1964): 4–14.

[12] Donald N. Barrett and Julian Samora, *The Movement of Spanish Youth from Rural to Urban Settings* (Washington, DC: National Committee for Children and Youth, 1963).

[13] Clark Knowlton, "The Spanish Americans in New Mexico," *Sociology and Social Research* 45 (1961): 448–54.

[14] See Paul A. Walter, "The Spanish-Speaking Community in New Mexico," *Sociology and Social Research* 24 (1939): 150–57; Thomas Weaver, "Social Structure, Change and Conflict in a New Mexico Village" (Ph.D. dissertation, University of California, 1965); Florence R. Kluckhohn and Fred L. Stodtbeck, *Variations in Value Orientations* (Evanston, IL: Row, Peterson, 1961); Frank Moore, "San Jose, 1946: A Study in Urbanization" (Master's thesis, University of New Mexico, 1947); Donald N. Barrett and Julian Samora, *The Movement of Spanish Youth* (Washington, DC: National Committee for Children and Youth, 1963).

[15] Margaret Mead, "Household Help," *Redbook Magazine,* October 1976, pp. 42, 45, 47.

[16] See page 545 of Jane Addams, "A Belated Industry," *American Journal of Sociology* 1 (1896): 536–50.

[17] Susan Tucker, *Telling Memories among Southern Women: Domestic Workers and Their Employers in the Segregated South* (Baton Rouge: Louisiana State University Press, 1988), p. 231.

[18] David Katzman, *Seven Days a Week* (Chicago: University of Illinois Press, 1981), pp. 269–70.

<hr>

SOCIAL RESEARCH

4

AN IDEA WHOSE TIME HAS COME

EARL BABBIE

Most sociologists agree that the best way to learn about research is through the hands-on experience gained by conducting a study. The research process, examined in the next three readings, often turns up new questions and challenges for the researcher. The first reading is by Earl Babbie, a professor of sociology at Chapman University, and is excerpted from his 1994 book, *The Sociological Spirit: Critical Essays in a Critical Science.* In this selection, Babbie explains what the domain of sociology is and how sociology is a science. Specifically, he provides an overview of both the theories and research methods used in sociology, and explains the critical connection between the two.

There is a more pressing need for sociological insights today than at any time in history. In 1822, the French philosopher Auguste Comte first proclaimed the possibility of studying society scientifically. A century and a half later, sociology is an idea whose time has come, and not a minute too soon.

<hr>

From Sociological Spirit: Critical Essays in a Critical Science, Second Edition by E. R. Babbie. Copyright © 1994 Wadsworth. Reprinted with permission of Wadsworth, an imprint of the Wadsworth Group, a division of Thomson Learning. Fax 800 730-2215.

It is no secret that this generation faces several unprecedented dangers. No sooner has the Cold War seemingly ended than we have come to recognize the danger of localized wars among ethnic groups spilling over into wider, global conflict. This danger is made worse by the possibility that relatively small, impoverished nations could gain access to nuclear weapons, giving terrorists the opportunity to spark an international conflagration. The more we learn about the prospects of a "nuclear winter"—the likely result of the first truly nuclear war—the more evident it is that there would be no real survivors of such a large-scale nuclear exchange.

If, on the other hand, we escape the threat of nuclear extinction, there is a real possibility that we will overpopulate and pollute the planet beyond its carrying capacity. As a single indicator of this problem, some 13 to 18 million people die of starvation around the world every year, three-fourths of them children. Approximately one-fifth of all humans on the planet go to bed hungry every night.

Add to this such persistent problems as crime, inflation, unemployment, prejudice, totalitarianism, and national debts, and you have sufficient grounds for understanding the ancient Chinese curse: "May you live in interesting times."

These are unquestionably interesting times. But the picture is not completely gloomy. These are also the times of great achievements in space: humans landing on the moon, a remote-controlled craft landing on Mars, and others photographing the more distant planets. These are the times when human beings, working cooperatively around the globe, eradicated smallpox—a scourge throughout history. These are the times of an awakening of awareness and commitment to ending world hunger. And the breakup of the former USSR, along with its domination of Eastern Europe, is regarded by most as a positive development.

If it were possible to make comparable lists of the positive and negative aspects of life today, my hunch is that they might be about equal in length. At any rate, both lists would be long ones, indicating that you and I and our fellow human beings face both trying challenges and promising opportunities ahead of us.

Assuming that we'd agree in favoring peace over war, prosperity over hunger and poverty, and so forth, the question you should be asking yourself is: what determines how things turn out? Specifically, what would it take for peace to triumph over the continuing specter of wars large and small? We'd all like the answer to that question. . . .

The point of this discussion on war and peace is to suggest that what we need to know to establish peace around the world is not likely to arise from military technology. If such an answer is to be found at all, we must look elsewhere: in the study of why people relate to one another as they do—sometimes peacefully, sometimes hostilely. This, as we'll see, lies in the domain of sociology.

The Domain of Sociology

Sociology involves the study of human beings. More specifically, it is the study of interactions and relations *among* human beings. Whereas psychology is the study of what goes on inside individuals, sociology addresses what goes on between them. Sociology addresses simple, face-to-face interactions such as conversations, dating behavior, and students asking a professor to delay the term paper deadline. Equally, sociology is the study of formal organizations, the functioning of whole societies, and even relations among societies.

Sociology is the study of how human beings live together—in both the good times and the bad. It is no more a matter of how we cooperate and get along than of how we compete and conflict. Both are fundamental aspects of our living together and, hence, of sociology.

You might find it useful to view sociology as the study of our *rules for living together.* Let's take a minute to look at that.

To begin, let's consider some of the things that individuals need or want out of life: food, shelter, companionship, security, satisfaction—the list could go on and on. My purpose in considering such a list is to have us see that the things you and I need or want out of life create endless possibilities for conflict and struggle. When food is scarce, for example, I can only satisfy my need at your expense. Even in the case of companionship—where both people get what they want—you and I may fight over a particular companion.

The upshot of all this is that human beings do not seem to be constructed in a way that ensures cooperation. Bees and ants, by contrast, just seem to be wired that way. As a consequence, human beings *create rules* to establish order in the face of chaos. Sometimes we agree on the rules voluntarily, and other times some people impose the rules on everyone else. In part, sociology is the study of how rules come into existence.

Sociology is also the study of how rules are *organized* and *perpetuated.* It would be worth taking a minute to reflect on the extent and complexity of the rules by which you and I live. There is a rule, for example, that Americans must pay taxes to the government. But it doesn't end there. The rule for paying taxes has been elaborated on by a great many more specific rules indicating how much, when, and to whom taxes are to be paid. In recent years, the index to the IRS tax code has run more than 1,000 pages long, which should give you some idea of the complexity of that set of rules. The much-touted tax simplification of 1986 was 1,855 pages long.

The rules governing our lives are not all legal ones. There are rules about shaking hands when you meet someone, rules about knives and forks at dinner, rules about how long to wear your hair, and rules about what to wear to class, to the symphony, and to mud-wrestling. There are rules of grammar, rules of good grooming, and rules of efficient computer programming.

Many of the rules we've been considering were here long before you and I showed up, and many will still be here after we've left. Moreover, I doubt that you have the experience of having taken part in creating any of the rules I've listed. Nobody asked you to vote on the rules of grammar, for example. But in a critical way, you *did* vote on those rules: you voted by obeying them.

Consider the rule about not going naked in public. Even though you don't recall being asked what you thought about that one, there was a public referendum on that issue this morning—and you voted in favor of clothes. So did I. If this seems silly, by the way, realize that there are other societies in which people voted to accept a different rule this morning.

Sometime today you are likely to be asked to vote on a set of rules about eating. Some of the possibilities are eating spaghetti with a knife, pouring soup on your dessert, and throwing your food against the wall. Let's see how you vote.

The persistence of our rules is largely a function of one generation teaching them to the next generation. We speak of **socialization** as the process of learning the rules, and it becomes apparent that we are all socializing each other all the time through the use of positive and negative **sanctions**—rewards and punishments.

All the rules we've been discussing are fundamentally *arbitrary*—that is, different rules would work just as well. Although Americans have a rule that cars must be driven on the right side of the road, other societies (e.g., England, Japan) manage equally well with people driving on the left side.

Once we've established a rule, however, we tend to add weight to it. We act as though it were better than the other possibilities, that it somehow represents an eternal and universal *truth*. Sociologists often use the term **reification** in reference to the pretense that things are real when they are not, and we often *reify* the rules of society. We make the right side of the road the *right* side for cars to drive on, and we think the British and Japanese strange for not knowing that.

The rules of society take their strongest hold when they are **internalized** by individuals—taken inside ourselves and made our own. Imagine this situation, which you may have actually experienced. It is three o'clock in the morning, and you are driving along a street leading out of a small town. There is no traffic on the street in any direction as you come to a red light at an intersection. You can see there are no cars coming for a mile in every direction. There is no one around. What do you do? There's a good chance that you will sit and wait for the light to change. If someone questioned you about it, you might say, "It just wouldn't feel right."

In the event you would drive through the light and generally regard yourself as above reification and internalization, think again. You have reified and internalized countless rules. How would you feel about having live ants and cockroaches for dinner tonight, for example? Are you willing to give them a try? How do you feel about murder, rape, and child abuse? Are you pretty casual about them, or do you feel they are *really wrong*? If you think about it, you'll find you feel pretty strongly about a lot of our rules.

All of this notwithstanding, sociology is also the study of how we *break* the rules. Some people use bad grammar and pour their soup on the floor, not to mention drive too fast, steal, fix prices, commit murder, and everything in between. Although this may seem like the study of "bad people," beware.

First, the rules of society are so extensive and complex that no one can possibly keep them all. For example, there is probably a street near you that is posted with a twenty-five-mile-per-hour speed limit; that's certainly a rule. And yet if you drive twenty-five miles an hour on that street during rush hour, you may discover you're breaking another rule. Your clue will be the honking horns and shaking fists.

Beyond the impossibility of obeying all the rules, you and I might agree that some of them ought to be broken. Consider the rule, in force a few years ago, that black people had to sit in the back of the bus in some parts of America. The people who finally broke that rule are considered heroes today. By the same token, you might disagree with rules that women can't fix carburetors, that men shouldn't cry, or that professors always know better than students.

The study of how people break the rules is closely related to the study of how the rules *change* over time. Although we are always living in a sea of rules, and many seem to last forever, it is also true that the rules of society are always in a process of change. Rules pertaining to hemlines, hair length, and political views operate a little like yo-yos. Others seem to change in only one direction.

Sociology, then, is an examination of the rules that govern our living together: what they are, how they arise, and how they change. Sociology, however, is a special approach to the rules of social life. As we'll see, there are other approaches.

A Science of Society

Sociology shouldn't be confused with social philosophy. It is not a point of view about the way things ought to be. Rather, sociology deals with the way things *are*. Moreover, sociology is more than just an *opinion* about the way things are.

Sociology is a science of social life. Like other sciences, sociology has a **logical/empirical** basis. This means that, to be accepted, assertions must (1) make sense and (2) correspond to the facts. In this sense, sociology can be characterized by a current buzzword: *critical thinking*. The simple fact is that most of us, most of the time, are uncritical in our thinking. Much of the time we simply believe what we read or hear. Or, when we disagree, we do so on the basis of ideological points of view and prejudices that are not very well thought out.

Suppose you were talking with a friend about the value of going to col-

TABLE 4.1 Median Income by Educational Level

Educational Level	Median Income
Less than 8 years	$ 9,221
8 years	11,811
1–3 years high school	13,705
4 years high school	20,800
1–3 years college	24,606
4 years college or more	34,709

Source: U.S. Bureau of the Census, *Statistical Abstract of the United States,* Washington, DC: U.S. Government Printing Office, 1985, p. 443.

lege. Your friend disagrees: "College is a waste of time. You should get a head start in the job market instead. Most of today's millionaires never went to college, and there are plenty of college graduates pumping gas or out of work altogether." That's the kind of thing people sometimes say, and it can be convincing—especially if it's said with conviction. But does it stand up to logical and empirical testing?

Logically, it doesn't seem to make much sense, since a college education would seem to give a person access to high-paying occupations not open to people with less education.

How does the assertion stack up empirically? Table 4.1 lists the median incomes of families headed by individuals of different educational levels as reported by the Census Bureau.

There isn't any scientific support for the assertion that education is a worthless financial investment—even though there are some individual exceptions to the rule.

It's important to recognize that human beings generally have opinions about everything. . . . It needs saying here that the people you deal with every day have a tendency to express opinions about the way things are—and what they say isn't always so. Consequently, you need to protect yourself from false information. That's what critical thinking is all about, and sociology provides some powerful critical-thinking tools.

I hope these few examples will indicate that sociology is not just something you might study in college and never think about again. Sociology deals with powerful issues that determine the quality of your life. Understanding sociology can empower you to be a more effective participant in the social affairs around you whether you are a conscious player or not. Marriage, employment, prejudice, crime, and politics are only a few of the areas of social life that can be importantly affected by your ability to engage in sociological reasoning.

Let's look at the twin foundations of critical thinking and of science in more detail—seeing how they apply to sociology in particular. Let's start with the determination of *facts*.

The Search for Facts: Research

At his August 5, 1985, news conference, then-President Ronald Reagan noted the fortieth anniversary of the Hiroshima bombing in the context of an unabated nuclear arms race and increasing popular demands for a freeze on the manufacture and deployment of nuclear weapons. In defense of his administration's military policies, the president suggested that our store of nuclear weapons, coupled with the horrible example of Hiroshima, "is a deterrent that kept us at peace for the longest stretch we've ever known, 40 years of peace."

Regardless of how you feel about the nuclear arms race—whether we should be in it and who's winning—the argument that our nuclear arsenal had at least kept us at peace was a compelling one. In my review of the media and public comments following the news conference, people disagreed on whether the nuclear deterrent was the reason for the forty years of peace. Yet to my amazement, no one questioned the empirical accuracy of the assertion. A simple historical review of the period from 1945 to 1985 turned up the Korean War from 1950 to 1953 and the extensive and expensive war in Vietnam, which claimed 47,318 American lives between 1959 and 1973. This has to have been the bloodiest forty years of peace in our national history.

Much of what you read and hear simply doesn't correspond to the empirical facts, but the inaccuracy gets overlooked in the heat of rhetoric. For example, when the newspaper *USA Today* focused its attention on the national budget deficit, reporters interviewed seven men and women "in the street" to get their opinions. One of those interviewed, Glen Cemer, a retired photographer from Battle Creek, Michigan, responded as follows: "One way to lower the deficit would be to reduce the amount of foreign aid we provide to other countries—it's not winning any friends for us. Let's use that money to lower the deficit." [1]

This comment is often heard when people discuss ways to reduce the federal budget deficit. On the one side, some people, like Mr. Cemer, can point to instances of foreign aid being wasted in various ways and cases where countries we have aided have subsequently turned against us. On the other side, people who support foreign aid point to positive accomplishments against a general backdrop of our moral urge to help others less fortunate than ourselves.

Regardless of how you happen to feel about foreign aid in general, it is possible to determine, empirically, whether reducing foreign aid would be an effective way of reducing the federal budget deficit. In 1990, the United States gave a total of $10.8 billion in economic (nonmilitary) aid to other countries. Our budget deficit that year was $238 billion. Canceling our foreign aid program altogether, therefore, would have reduced the deficit by only 4.5 percent. Whereas the budget deficit is sometimes expressed on a per capita basis, canceling foreign aid in 1990 would have reduced the 1990 deficit of each American from $956.98 to $913.55—not much of a reduction.[2]

One of the things I hope you'll gain from this introduction to critical thinking is an ability to balance what you read and hear in your day-to-day life against empirical evidence. That's one of the keystones of sociology.

Over the past 150 years, sociologists have developed a number of research methods to assist in determining the facts of social life. **Survey research,** for example, involves the use of questionnaires to collect information. Sometimes it's appropriate to have people fill out the questionnaires themselves; other times interviewers read the questions and take down the answers. In recent years, telephone interviewing has become increasingly popular and effective. In particular, computers have been adapted to support the interviewing process: selecting telephone numbers at random, showing interviewers what questions to ask, and recording the answers given for immediate analysis.

Usually, surveys are conducted among samples of people, selected in such a way that a few hundred or thousand respondents can provide an accurate assessment of much larger populations. For example, a political poll among a properly selected sample of 1,600 voters can provide an accurate estimate of how all 100 million American voters feel: accurate within 2.5 percentage points. I know that may be hard to believe, but sociologists are putting the logic and techniques of survey sampling to effective use every day.

Sometimes, laboratory **experiments** are a more effective method of getting at the facts of social life. This technique is commonly used in the study of small group dynamics, for example. As a practical example, some sociologists have used this technique to study the dynamics of jury deliberations. Hiring subjects to serve as pseudo-jurors, the researchers can then observe their subjects argue their way to a verdict.

A ready resource for sociological analysis exists in the great masses of data regularly compiled by government agencies and various groups in the private sector. As in the example of education and income that we examined earlier, it's often possible to find appropriate answers without the time and expense of conducting a survey, experiment, or comparable research project. Even in this situation, however, you need to exercise critical thinking, since the facts never really "speak for themselves.". . .

The Role of Reason: Theory

In the midst of national concern over the persistence of hunger in America, then-President Reagan appointed a thirteen-member Task Force on Food Assistance to determine the nature and extent of the problem and to recommend government action. One of the panel's members, Dr. George Graham, attracted considerable attention by indicating his belief that the problem of malnutrition among children had been exaggerated—especially with regard to black children. He was quoted as stating:

> National data show that black children are now taller than white children—obviously, they must be getting more to eat. . . . If you think that blacks as a group are undernourished, look around at the black athletes on television—they're a pretty hefty bunch.[3]

As you can see, Dr. Graham cited two pieces of evidence—one statistical and one impressionistic—to support his thesis that black Americans are no more likely to suffer malnutrition than other Americans. But take a minute to consider these assertions logically.

First, Graham said black children are taller, on the average, than white children. But, even if this is true, does it mean that black children "must be getting more to eat"? What other factors might affect height? If you said "genetics," go to the head of the class. Racial and ethnic groups differ in average height. Consider the African Tutsi tribe, for example. These poor cattle-herders of Burundi and Rwanda, noted for their spectacular height, are commonly over seven feet tall. It would be absurd to conclude that they must eat more than Americans just because they are taller.

Second, what about the black athletes on television? Does their heftiness mean that black Americans as a whole must be getting a lot to eat? In this instance, you might have asked whether the black athletes are typical of all black Americans. Of course not. They are no more typical of blacks in general than white athletes are typical of all whites. Otherwise, we would need to look at Japanese sumo wrestlers and conclude that the Japanese people in general must be bigger and better fed than Americans.

As another example of the function of logical reasoning in everyday discourse, let's consider the broad public concern over acquired immune deficiency syndrome (AIDS). This extremely deadly disease has been disproportionately concentrated among homosexuals in America, especially during the early years of the epidemic, thereby coloring the public and political response to the disease. American gays and those sympathetic to the gay community have frequently charged that research on the disease has been slow in coming, due to prejudice against homosexuality.

Regardless of whether the charge of prejudice is true in general, there is no question that some people feel AIDS is a fitting punishment for gays. Some have even argued that AIDS is God's way of expressing divine displeasure with homosexuality. The discovery that AIDS is also commonly spread by contaminated needles of drug users and that it is also spread by prostitutes only confirms the theory of divine retribution.

Evangelist Don Boys, writing a guest editorial for *USA Today*, expressed his feelings this way: "The AIDS epidemic indicates that national morality has broken its mooring and drifted into a miasmic swamp, producing disease, degeneracy, and death. . . . God's plan is for each man to have one woman—his wife—for a lifetime, and be faithful to her. God's plan still works."[4]

Although sociology has no direct pipeline to divine will, critical thinking can shed some light on this assertion. To begin, AIDS has also been disproportionately common among Haitians in America. The divine retribution theory would need to include God's displeasure with them. The susceptibility of hemophiliacs and others needing blood transfusions further complicates the matter. The fact that AIDS is primarily transmitted through heterosexual sex in Africa muddies the water still further.

But let's put the divine retribution theory to its acid test. If AIDS is a sign of God's preference for lifestyles, then lesbians must be the most favored of all, for AIDS is least common among lesbian women! In short, the divine retribution theory, as generally conceived, simply doesn't hold up under logical scrutiny.

Logical reasoning, then, is another key component in critical thinking. As a science, sociology is consciously and deliberately committed to logical reasoning, and, as the above examples indicate, such a concern has real, practical implications. In part, this involves the development of **theories.** To understand the function of theory, we need to consider a few of its elements.

First, **concepts** are the mental images we use to bring order to the mass of specific experiences we have. Basically, we form concepts in order to group similar things together and to distinguish dissimilar ones. For example, the concept "human being" groups nearly 6 billion creatures into a single category and distinguishes them from billions and billions of other creatures. "Male" and "female" divide the 6 billion human beings into two categories.

Other concepts that distinguish different kinds of human beings include "infants," "Ethiopians," "mail-carriers," "college students," and so forth. All of us use concepts like these every day. We also commonly use concepts that do not necessarily distinguish different kinds of people. We may speak of "anxiety" and "alienation," for example. "Crime" is a concept; so is "unemployment."

Sociologists work with many of the same concepts that people commonly use in everyday life, but, as scientists, sociologists are more deliberate in their use of concepts. For example, sociologists are particularly concerned with the precise definitions of concepts such as those we've been considering. How do we decide, for example, if a person is unemployed? We probably wouldn't say a newborn baby was unemployed, but what about a wealthy playboy who never had a job and doesn't plan on ever having one? Specifying exactly what we will mean by the concepts we use is a fundamental part of sociology.

Equally important, sociologists seek to discover order among concepts. The concepts "male" and "female" are often referred to as **attributes** of individuals. The **variable** "gender" is a concept that brings together those two attributes. The variable "religion" brings order to such attributes as "Protestant," "Catholic," "Jew," and "Hindu."

It could be said that sociology is devoted to discovering relationships among the variables that distinguish different kinds of people. The earlier example of education and income illustrates that. The relationships to be explored are limitless. Are married people happier than single people? Are conservatives more prejudiced than liberals? Do broken homes produce juvenile delinquency?

Sociological theory goes a step beyond the questions of relationships between pairs of variables, however. Ultimately, we seek to develop a more or less comprehensive picture of the interrelations among a great many variables—ideally to understand the functioning of social life in general.

As a basis for such comprehensive understanding, sociologists begin with overarching models or **paradigms** of social life. . . .

There are three major paradigms commonly used in modern sociology. Some sociologists find it most useful to regard social life as a multitude of **interactions** among people. Consider a conversation, for example. Let's assume that you and I have met for the first time, waiting in the dentist's office. There are no magazines, not even old ones. All we have is each other.

After staring at the ceiling a while, I break the ice by saying, "Waiting for the dentist?" You confirm my brilliant insight. "Been here before?" you ask. I reply that I come for a check-up every six months, that I floss every day, and that I have three gold crowns. Pretty soon we are engaged in an adventure of mutual discovery. Before long, we've discovered that we both grew up in Vermont, that we tend to vote for different political parties, and that we both own malamute dogs. When I say I'm a sociology professor, you say you took a course in sociology once. Now, I may begin trying to shape the conversation into a pattern appropriate to a professor–student exchange, and you try to get back to the topic of malamutes.

The **interactionist paradigm** in sociology focuses on social life as the process of give and take in which individuals come to grips with each other, forming common definitions of the situation they find themselves in. This paradigm is particularly useful in understanding the ways in which we create the rules of social life.

A very different paradigm, the **social systems paradigm,** or **functionalist paradigm,** tends to focus on the structure of social life. A group of people, as large as a whole society, can usefully be seen as constituting an integrated system in which each individual has a part to play.

Consider a symphony orchestra, for example. The violins have a particular job to do (or function to perform), the horns have a different job, and the conductor's job is different from any of the players. Taken together, all the members of the orchestra constitute a whole system that is greater than the sum of its parts.

A football team offers another illustration of how we might use the social systems paradigm. The quarterback has one set of functions, and the running backs, linemen, and receivers have different functions.

Shifting to a whole society, we might examine the functions played by groups and organizations such as factory workers, police, teachers, children, ministers, and so forth. This paradigm is particularly useful in understanding the organization of the rules of life we've created.

Finally, the **conflict paradigm** focuses on the competitive struggle among individuals and groups in society. Criminals conflict with police, workers with owners, students with teachers, Protestants with Catholics, blacks with whites, and so forth. Typically, these struggles grow out of the unequal distribution of quantities perceived as desirable and limited, such as money, property, prestige, and power. This paradigm is particularly useful in understanding how and why people break the rules and how the rules themselves change.

Be clear that none of these paradigms is intended as a complete statement of how social life operates. Rather, each offers a different point of view that reveals certain aspects of social life and conceals others. The obvious implication of this is the value of using more than one paradigm for the purpose of achieving an integrated, well-rounded view. . . .

Sociological Questions and Answers

The common image of science is of scientists finding the answers to questions. I will conclude with a somewhat different view of science and of sociology in particular. Science is sometimes better at raising questions than at finding answers to them. It would be useful for you to regard science as an ongoing inquiry, recognizing that questions initiate new avenues of inquiry, while answers close them down.

Science makes an especially powerful contribution when it calls into question those things that "everyone knows." Everyone used to "know," for example, that blacks were inferior to whites and that women were inferior to men. As you'll see, sociological points of view very often raise questions about things everyone else thought had already been answered. Even when we discover new and seemingly better answers about something, it's important to hold them as tentative.

There is a particular **recursive** quality in human life that makes anything we know tentative. Whenever we learn something about ourselves, what we've learned may bring about changes—even to the extent of making what we learned no longer accurate.

Suppose we studied employment opportunities across the country, for example. When our study was complete, we listed the ten cities with the most jobs available. As soon as our findings became widely known, of course, a lot of unemployed people would move to those cities, and soon those cities would not have as many jobs available as before. This is the same thing that happens when a newspaper columnist identifies a local restaurant that has great food, low prices, and no waiting. The "no waiting" part probably won't last another twenty-four hours, and the other two characteristics may disappear, too. In sociology, anything we learn can change things, so no knowledge can be counted on to remain true. Thus, we need to keep asking questions.

Even more fundamentally, sociology deals with a number of questions that will never be answered fully. Who am I? What is a human being? Are we more the result of our genes or of our environment? Is order possible without restricting freedom? These are a few of the questions [sociologists ask in their research], and it is unlikely that they will ever be completely answered. As we'll see, however, it can be very useful to keep asking them anyway.

I point all this out to give you an appropriate context for your own inquiry into sociology. Although there are some facts about sociology that are worth learning, it is more important for you to learn to use sociology for your own ongoing critical thinking. If you were studying brain surgery or medieval history, you might not have an opportunity to use what you learned in your day-to-day life. Sociology is very different. Every day you will wake up into a sociological laboratory with a massive experiment underway. We're all subjects in the experiment, and you now have the opportunity to join the researchers.

ENDNOTES

[1] *USA Today*, September 25, 1985, p. 10A.

[2] U.S. Bureau of the Census, *Statistical Abstract of the United States*, 1992, Washington, DC: Government Printing Office, 1992, pp. 8, 279, 794.

[3] "Big Changes Made in Hunger Report," *San Francisco Chronicle*, December 30, 1983, p. 10.

[4] Don Boys, "Don't Spend Money; Stop Sinners Instead," *USA Today*, October 7, 1985, p. 6A.

5

INTERPERSONAL DYNAMICS
IN A SIMULATED PRISON

CRAIG HANEY • W. CURTIS BANKS
PHILIP G. ZIMBARDO

Ethical questions concerning social research are a rather recent discussion in the history of social science. It was not until the 1960s and early 1970s that we began to question research protocols and the effects of social experiments on humans. This second reading in the social research section, by Craig Haney, W. Curtis Banks, and Philip G. Zimbardo, reviews the research methodology used in Zimbardo's famous prison study conducted in 1971. Zimbardo, a professor of psychology at Stanford University, was fascinated with the social dynamics of prisons, especially the social interaction that takes place between guards and prisoners. The selection below takes us inside the research world of the prison environment and reveals many ethical and logistical concerns about using social experiments to study human behavior.

A lthough we have passed through many periods of so-called prison "reform," in which physical conditions within prisons have improved and in which the rhetoric of rehabilitation has replaced the language of punitive incarceration, the social institution of prison has continued to fail. On purely pragmatic grounds, there is substantial evidence that prisons really neither "rehabilitate" nor act as a deterrent to future crime—in America, recidivism rates upwards of 75 percent speak quite decisively to these criteria. And, to perpetuate what is additionally an economic failure, American taxpayers alone must provide an expenditure for "corrections" of 1.5 billion dollars annually. On humanitarian grounds as well, prisons have failed: our mass media are increasingly filled with accounts of atrocities committed daily, man against man, in reaction to the penal system or in the name of it.

Attempts at explaining the deplorable condition of our penal system, and its dehumanizing effects upon prisoners and guards, characteristically focus upon what can be called the *dispositional hypothesis*. Rarely expressed

Source: Abridged from Craig Haney, W. Curtis Banks, and Philip G. Zimbardo, "Interpersonal Dynamics in a Simulated Prison," *International Journal of Criminology and Penology*, 1973, 1. 69–97. Reprinted with permission.

explicitly, it is central to a prevalent nonconscious ideology: The state of the social institution of prison is due to the "nature" of the people who administrate it, or the "nature" of the people who populate it, or both. The dispositional hypothesis has been embraced by the proponents of the prison status quo (blaming violence on the criminal dispositions of prisoners), as well as by its critics (attributing brutality of guards and staff to their sadistic personality structures). The appealing simplicity of this proposition localizes the source of prison riots, recidivism, and corruption in these "bad seeds" and not in the conditions of the "prison soil." The system itself goes on essentially unchanged, its basic structure unexamined and unchallenged.

A critical evaluation of the dispositional hypothesis, however, cannot be made directly through observation in existing prison settings, since such naturalistic observation necessarily confounds the acute effects of the environment with the chronic characteristics of the inmate and guard populations. To partial out the situational effects of the prison environment per se from those attributable to a priori dispositions of its inhabitants requires a research strategy in which a "new" prison is constructed, comparable in its fundamental social-psychological milieu to existing prison systems but entirely populated by individuals who are undifferentiated in all essential dimensions from the rest of society.

Such was the approach taken in the present empirical study, namely, to create a prisonlike situation in which the guards and inmates were initially comparable and characterized as being "psychologically healthy," and then to observe the patterns of behavior which resulted and to record the cognitive, emotional, and attitudinal reactions that emerged.

No specific hypotheses were advanced other than the general one that assignment to the treatment of "guard" or "prisoner" would result in significantly different reactions on behavioral measures of interaction, emotional measures of mood state and pathology, and attitudes toward self, as well as other indices of coping and adaptation to this extreme situation.

Method

The effects of playing the role of "guard" or "prisoner" were studied in the context of an experimental simulation of a prison environment. The research design was a relatively simple one, involving as it did only a single treatment variable, the random assignment to either a "guard" or "prisoner" condition. These roles were enacted over an extended period of time (nearly one week) within an environment which had been physically constructed to closely resemble a prison. Central to the methodology of creating and maintaining the psychological state of imprisonment was the functional simulation of significant properties of "real prison life" (established through information from former inmates, correctional personnel, and texts).

Subjects

The 22 subjects who participated in the experiment were selected from an initial pool of 75 respondents who answered a newspaper ad asking for male volunteers to participate in a psychological study of "prison life," in return for payment of $15 per day. Those who responded to the notice completed an extensive questionnaire concerning their family background, physical and mental health history, prior experience, and attitudinal propensities with respect to any possible sources of psychopathology (including their involvements in crime). Each respondent who completed the background questionnaire was interviewed by one of two experimenters. Finally, the 24 subjects who were judged to be *most stable* (physically and mentally) were selected to participate in the study. On a random basis, half of the subjects were assigned the role of "guard," half were assigned to the role of "prisoner."

The subjects were normal, healthy males attending colleges throughout the United States who were in the Stanford [University] area during the summer. They were largely of middle-class background and Caucasians (with the exception of one Asian subject). Initially they were strangers to each other, a selection precaution taken to avoid the disruption of any preexisting friendship patterns and to mitigate against any transfer of previously established relationships or patterns of behavior into the experimental situation.

Procedure

Role Instructions   All subjects had been told that they would be randomly assigned either the guard or the prisoner role, and all had voluntarily agreed to play either role for $15 per day for up to two weeks. They signed a contract guaranteeing a minimally adequate diet, clothing, housing, and medical care, as well as the financial remuneration, in return for their stated "intention" of serving in the assigned role for the duration of the study.

It was made explicit in the contract that those assigned to be prisoners should expect to be under surveillance (have little or no privacy) and to have some of their basic civil rights suspended during their imprisonment. They were aware that physical abuse was explicitly prohibited. Subjects were given no other information about what to expect and no instructions about behavior "appropriate" for the prisoner role. Those actually assigned to this treatment were informed by phone to be available at their place of residence on a given Sunday, when we would start the experiment.

The subjects assigned to be guards attended an orientation meeting on the day prior to the induction of the prisoners. At this time they were introduced to the principal investigators, the "superintendent" of the prison (P.G.Z.) and an undergraduate research assistant who assumed the administrative role of "warden." They were told that we were attempting to simulate a prison environment within the limits imposed by pragmatic and ethical considerations. Their assigned task was to "maintain the reasonable degree of order within the prison necessary for its effective functioning," although the specifics of how this duty might be implemented were not explicitly detailed. To involve the subjects in their roles even before the first prisoner was incarcerated, the guards assisted in the final phases of completing the prison complex—putting the cots in the cells, posting signs on the walls, setting up the guards' quarters, and moving furniture, water coolers, and refrigerators.

The guards generally believed that we were interested primarily in studying the behavior of prisoners. Of course, we were also concerned with effects which enacting the role of guard in this environment would have on their behavior and subjective states. For this reason, they were given few explicit instructions on what it meant to be a guard and were left to "fill in" their own definitions of the role. A notable exception was the explicit and categorical prohibition against the use of physical punishment or aggression, which we emphasized from the outset of the study.

The prisoner subjects remained in the mock prison 24 hours a day for the duration of the study. Three were arbitrarily assigned to each of the three cells, and two others were on standby call at their homes. The guard subjects worked on three-man, eight-hour shifts, remaining in the prison environment only during their work shifts and going about their usual routines at other times. The one subject assigned to be a standby guard withdrew just before the simulation phase began. Final data analysis, then, is based on 11 prisoners and 10 guards.

Physical Aspects of the Prison   The prison was built in a 35-foot section of a basement corridor in the psychology building at Stanford University. It was partitioned by two fabricated walls, one of which was fitted with the only entrance door to the cell block; the other contained a small observation screen. Three small cells (6 × 9 feet) were made from converted laboratory rooms by replacing the usual doors with steel-barred doors painted black and removing all furniture. A cot (with mattress, sheet, and pillow) for each prisoner was the only furniture in the cells. A small closet across from the cells served as a solitary confinement facility; its dimensions were extremely small (2 × 2 × 7 feet), and it was unlit.

In addition, several rooms in an adjacent wing of the building were used as guards' quarters (to change in and out of uniform or for rest and relaxation), a bedroom for the "warden" and "superintendent," and an interview-testing room. Concealed video recording equipment was located in the testing room and behind the observation screen at one end of the "yard," where there was also sufficient space for several observers.

Uniforms   In order to promote feelings of anonymity in the subjects, each group was issued uniforms. For the guards, this consisted of plain khaki shirts and trousers, a whistle, a police nightstick (wooden baton), and reflecting sunglasses which made eye contact impossible. The prisoners' uniforms were loosely fitting muslin smocks with an identification number on front and back. A light chain and lock were placed around one ankle. On their feet they wore rubber sandals, and their hair was covered with a nylon stocking made into a cap. Each prisoner was also issued a toothbrush, soap, soapdish, towel, and bed linen. No personal belongings were allowed in the cells. The outfitting of both prisoners and guards in this manner served to enhance group identity and reduce individual uniqueness within the two groups.

Induction Process   With the cooperation of the Palo Alto City Police Department, all of the subjects assigned to the prisoner treatment were unexpectedly "arrested" at their residences. A police officer charged them either with suspicion of burglary or armed robbery, advised them of their legal rights, handcuffed them, thoroughly searched them (often as curious neighbors looked on), and carried them off to the police station in the rear of the police car. At the station they went through the standard booking routines of being fingerprinted, having an identification file prepared, and then being placed in a detention cell. Subsequently, each prisoner was blindfolded and driven by one of the experimenters and a subject-guard to our mock prison. Throughout the entire arrest procedure, the police officers involved maintained a formal, serious attitude, avoiding answering any questions of clarification as to the relation of this "arrest" to the mock prison study.

Upon arrival at our experimental prison, each prisoner was stripped, sprayed with a delousing preparation (deodorant spray), and made to stand alone, naked, in the cell yard before being outfitted. After being given their uniforms and having an I.D. picture ("mug shot") taken, each prisoner was put in his cell.

Administrative Routine   When all the cells were occupied, the warden greeted the prisoners and read them the rules of the institution (developed the previous day by the guards and the warden). They were to be memorized and to be followed. Prisoners were to be referred to only by the number of their uniforms, in a further effort to depersonalize them.

The prisoners were served three bland meals per day, were allowed three supervised toilet visits, and were given two hours daily for the privilege of reading or letter writing. Work assignments were issued for which the prisoners were to receive an hourly wage to constitute their $15 daily payment. Two visiting periods per week were scheduled, as were movie rights and exercise periods. Three times a day all prisoners were lined up for a "count" (one on each guard work-shift). The initial purpose of the count was to ascertain that all prisoners were present and to test them on their knowledge of the rules and of their I.D. numbers. The first perfunctory counts lasted only about ten minutes, but on each successive day (or night) they were spontaneously increased in duration by the guards until some lasted several hours. Many of the preestablished features of administrative routine were modified or abandoned by the guards, and some privileges were forgotten by the staff over the course of study.

Data Collection: Dependent Measures

The exploratory nature of this investigation and the absence of specific hypotheses led us to adopt the strategy of surveying as many behavioral and psychological manifestations of the prison experience on the guards and the prisoners as was possible. The dependent measures were of two general types: (1) transactions between and within each group of subjects, recorded on video- and audiotape as well as directly observed, and (2) individual reactions on questionnaires, mood inventories, personality tests, daily guard shift reports, and postexperimental interviews.

Data collection was organized around the following sources:

1. *Videotaping*   Using the concealed video equipment, about 12 hours of recordings were made of daily, regularly occurring events such as the counts and meals, as well as unusual interactions such as a prisoner rebellion; visits from a priest, a lawyer, and parents; parole board meetings; and others.

2. *Audio recording*   Concealed microphones recorded over 30 hours of verbal interactions between guards and prisoners in the prison yard, as well as some within the cells and in the testing-interview room.

3. *Rating scales*   Mood adjective checklists and sociometric measures were administered on several occasions to assess emotional changes in affective state and interpersonal dynamics among the guard and prisoner groups.

4. *Individual difference scales*   Prior to the start of the simulation, all subjects had completed a series of paper-and-pencil personality tests selected to provide dispositional indicators of interpersonal behavior styles—the F scale of Authoritarian Personality (Adorno, Frenkel-Brunswik, Levinson, and Sanford 1950) and the Machiavellianism Scale (Christie and Geis 1970)—and to isolate areas of possible personality pathology through the newly developed Comrey Personality Scale (Comrey 1970).

5. *Personal observations*   The guards made daily reports of their observations after each shift, the experimenters kept informal diaries, and all subjects completed postexperimental questionnaires of their reactions to the experience about a month after the study was over.

Data Analysis: Video Recordings

Special analyses were required only of the video and audio material. The other data sources were analyzed following established scoring procedures. Since the present discussion is based primarily on the videotaped material, details of this analysis are outlined here.

There were 25 relatively discrete incidents identifiable on the tapes of prisoner-guard interactions. Each incident or scene was scored for the presence of nine behavioral (and verbal) categories by two judges who had not been involved with the simulation study. These categories were defined as follows:

▼ *Question*   All questions asked, requests for information or assistance (excluding rhetorical questions).

▼ *Command*   An order to commence or abstain from a specific behavior, directed to either individuals or groups. Also generalized orders; e.g., "Settle down."

▼ *Information*   A specific piece of information proffered by anyone, whether requested or not, dealing with any contingency of the simulation.

▼ *Individuating reference*   Positive: use of a person's real name, nickname, or allusion to special positive physical characteristics. Negative: use of prison number, title, generalized "you," or reference to derogatory characteristic.

▼ *Threat*   Verbal statement of contingent negative consequences of a wide variety; e.g., no meal, long count, pushups, lock-up in hole, no visitors.

▼ *Deprecation/insult*   Use of obscenity, slander, malicious statement directed toward individuals or groups, e.g., "You lead a life of mendacity," "You guys are really stupid."

▼ *Resistance*   Any physical resistance, usually prisoners to guards, such as holding onto beds, blocking doors, shoving guard or prisoner, taking off stocking caps, refusing to carry out orders.

▼ *Help*   Person physically assisting another (excludes verbal statements of support); e.g., guard helping another to open door, prisoner helping another prisoner in cleanup duties.

▼ *Use of instruments*   Use of any physical instrument to either intimidate, threaten, or achieve specific end; e.g., fire extinguisher, batons, whistles.

Results

The results of the present experiment support many commonly held conceptions of prison life and validate anecdotal evidence supplied by articulate ex-convicts. The environment of arbitrary custody had great impact upon *the affective states* of both guards and prisoners as well as upon *the interpersonal processes* between and within those role-groups.

In general, guards and prisoners showed a marked decrease in positive affect or emotion, and their overall outlook became increasingly negative. As the experiment progressed, prisoners expressed intentions to do harm to others more frequently. For both prisoners and guards, self-evaluations were more deprecating as the experience of the prison environment became internalized.

Overt behavior was generally consistent with the subjective self-reports and affective expressions of the subjects. While guards and prisoners were essentially free to engage in any form of interaction (positive or negative, supportive or affrontive, etc.), the characteristic nature of their encounters tended to be negative, hostile, affrontive, and dehumanizing. Prisoners immediately adopted a generally passive style of responding, while guards assumed a very active initiative role in all interactions. Throughout the experiment, commands were the most frequent form of verbal behavior and, generally, verbal exchanges were strikingly impersonal, with few references to individual identity. Although it was clear to all subjects that the experimenters would not permit physical violence to take place, varieties of less direct aggressive behavior were observed frequently (especially on the part of guards). In fact, varieties of verbal affronts became the most frequent form of interpersonal contact between guards and prisoners.

The most dramatic evidence of the impact of the mock prison upon the participants was seen in the gross reactions of five prisoners who had to be released from the study because of extreme emotional depression, crying, rage, or acute anxiety. The pattern of symptoms was quite similar in four of the subjects and began as early as the second day of imprisonment. The fifth subject was released after being treated for a psychosomatic rash which covered portions of his body. Of the remaining prisoners, only two said they were unwilling to forfeit all the money they had earned in return for being "paroled" from the study. When the experiment was terminated prematurely after only six days, all the remaining prisoners were delighted by their unexpected good fortune; in contrast, most of the guards seemed to be distressed by the decision to stop the experiment. It appeared to us that the guards had become sufficiently involved in their roles so that they now enjoyed the extreme control and power they exercised and were reluctant to give it up. One guard, who did report being personally upset at the suffering of the prisoners, claimed to have considered asking to change his role to become one of them—but never did so. None of the guards ever failed to come to work on time for their shift, and indeed, on several occasions guards remained on duty voluntarily and uncomplainingly for extra hours—without additional pay.

The extreme reactions which emerged in both groups of subjects provide clear evidence of the power of the social forces operating in this pathological setting. There were, however, individual differences observed in *styles* of coping with this stressful experience, as well as varying degrees of success in adaptation to it. While all were somewhat adversely affected by it, half the prisoners did "endure" the oppressive atmosphere—at least in the sense that they remained until the study was completed. Not all of the guards resorted to the overt and inventive forms of hostility employed by others. Some guards were tough but fair ("played by the rules"), some went far beyond their roles to engage in cruelty and harassment, while a few were passive and rarely instigated any coercive control over the prisoners. It is important to emphasize, however, that at some time during the six days *all* guards participated in what could be characterized as sadistic treatment of prisoners. . . .

Representative Personal Statements

Much of the flavor and impact of this prison experience has been unavoidably lost in the relatively formal, objective analyses outlined in [other papers]. The following quotations taken from interviews, conversations, and questionnaires provide a more personal view of what it was like to be a prisoner or guard in the "Stanford County Prison" experiment.

GUARDS' COMMENTS

They [the prisoners] seemed to lose touch with the reality of the experiment—they took me so seriously.

I didn't interfere with any of the guards' actions. Usually if what they were doing bothered me, I would walk out and take another duty.

. . . looking back, I am impressed by how little I felt for them.

They [the prisoners] didn't see it as an experiment. It was real and they were fighting to keep their identity. But we were always there to show them just who was boss.

I was tired of seeing the prisoners in their rags and smelling the strong odors of their bodies that filled the cells. I watched them tear at each other, on orders given by us.

Acting authoritatively can be fun. Power can be a great pleasure.

During the inspection, I went to cell 2 to mess up a bed which the prisoner had made and he grabbed me, screaming that he had just made it, and he wasn't going to let me mess it up. He grabbed my throat, and although he was laughing I was pretty scared. I lashed out with my stick and hit him in the chin (although not very hard) and when I freed myself I became angry.

PRISONERS' COMMENTS

The way we were made to degrade ourselves really brought us down, and that's why we all sat docile toward the end of the experiment.

I realize now (after it's over) that no matter how together I thought I was inside my head, my prison behavior was often less under my control than I realized. No matter how open, friendly, and helpful I was with other prisoners I was still operating as an isolated, self-centered person, being rational rather than compassionate.

I began to feel I was losing my identity, that the person I call _____ , the person who volunteered to get me into this prison (because it was a prison to me, it still is a prison to me, I don't regard it as an experiment or a simulation . . .) was distant from me, was remote until finally I wasn't that person, I was 416. I was really my number and 416 was really going to have to decide what to do.

I learned that people can easily forget that others are human.

Debriefing Encounter Sessions

Because of the unexpectedly intense reactions (such as the above) generated by this mock prison experience, we decided to terminate the study at the end of six days rather than continue for the second week. Three separate encounter sessions were held, first for the prisoners, then for the guards, and finally for all participants together. Subjects and staff openly discussed their reactions, and strong feelings were expressed and shared. We analyzed the moral conflicts posed by this experience and used the debriefing sessions to make explicit alternative courses of action that would lead to more moral behavior in future comparable situations.

Follow-ups on each subject over the year following termination of the study revealed that the negative effects of participation had been temporary, while the personal gain to the subjects endured.

Conclusions and Discussion

It should be apparent that the elaborate procedures (and staging) employed by the experimenters to ensure a high degree of "mundane realism" in this mock prison contributed to its effective functional simulation of the psychological dynamics operating in "real" prisons. We observed empirical relationships in the simulated prison environment which were strikingly isomorphic to the internal relations of real prisons, corroborating many of the documented reports of what occurs behind prison walls. Most dramatic and distressing to us were the ease with which sadistic behavior could be elicited from individuals who were not "sadistic types" and the frequency with which acute emotional breakdowns could occur in persons selected precisely for their emotional stability.

Authors' Note: This research was funded by an ONR grant: N00014-67-A-0112-0041 to Professor Philip G. Zimbardo.

The ideas expressed in this paper are those of the authors and do not imply endorsement of ONR or any sponsoring agency. We wish to extend our thanks and appreciation for the contributions to this research by David Jaffe who served as "warden" and pretested some of the variables in the mock prison situation. In addition, Greg White provided invaluable assistance during the data reduction phase of this study. Many others (most notably Carolyn Burkhart, Susie Phillips, and Kathy Rosenfeld) helped at various stages of the experiment, with the construction of the prison, prisoner arrest, interviewing, testing, and data analysis—we extend our sincere thanks to each of these collaborators. Finally, we especially wish to thank Carlo Prescott, our prison consultant, whose personal experience gave us invaluable insights into the nature of imprisonment.

REFERENCES

Adorno, T. W., E. Frenkel-Brunswik, D. J. Levinson, and R. N. Sanford. 1950. *The Authoritarian Personality.* New York: Harper.

Charrière, H. 1969. *Papillon.* Robert Lafont.

Christie, R., and F. L. Geis, eds. 1970. *Studies in Machiavellianism.* New York: Academic Press.

Comrey, A. L. 1970. *Comrey Personality Scales.* San Diego, CA: Educational and Industrial Testing Service.

6

NOT OUR KIND OF GIRL

ELAINE BELL KAPLAN

Social research is concerned with the definition and assessment of social phenomena. Many social concepts such as teen pregnancy are difficult to study because of stereotyping and ideological pronouncements that blame the victim for the social problem. For example, this selection by Elaine Bell Kaplan is taken from her dissertation research in which she challenges the myths of black teenage motherhood and reveals the complex interaction of social factors such as racism, social class, and gender relations that influence black teenagers to become mothers. Kaplan, an assistant professor of sociology at the University of Southern California, revised her dissertation into the 1995 book *Not Our Kind of Girl: Unraveling the Myths of Black Teenage Pregnancy.* The excerpt below summarizes the ethnographic research methods Kaplan used to find and interview African American teen mothers.

"If we want to solve the problems of the Black community, we have to do something about illegitimate babies born to teenage mothers." The caller, who identified himself as Black, was responding to a radio talk show discussion about the social and economic problems of the Black community. According to this caller's view, Black teen mothers' children grow up in fatherless households with mothers who have few moral values and little control over their offspring. The boys join gangs; the girls stand a good chance of becoming teen mothers themselves. The caller's perspective captures the popular view of many Americans: that marital status and age-

From: Elaine Bell Kaplan. 1995. *Not Our Kind of Girl: Unraveling the Myths of Black Teenage Motherhood.* Berkeley: University of California Press, pp. xviii–xxiii, 10–26. Copyright © 1997 Regents of the University of California. Used with permission from the publisher.

appropriate sexual behavior ensure the well-being of the family and the community. . . .

According to mainstream ideology, men who through hard work have moved up the career ladder and provide their families with decent food on the dinner table, clothes on their backs, and an occasional family vacation have achieved the American Dream. Women's achievements are measured by their marriage and child rearing, done in proper order and at an appropriate age. Teenage girls are expected to replicate these values by refraining from sexual relations before adulthood and marriage.

Certainly, such traditional ideas held sway over the Black community I knew. Two decades ago unmarried teenagers with babies were a rare and unwelcome presence in my Harlem community. These few girls would be subjected to gossip about their lack of morals and stigmatized if they were on welfare. But by the 1980s so many young Black girls were pushing strollers around inner-city neighborhoods that they became an integral part of both the reality and the myth concerning the sexuality of Black underclass culture and Black family values. These Black teenage mothers did not fit in with the American ethic of hard work and strong moral character. . . .

If this conservative ideology is extended to teen mothers, their situation can be explained only as a result of aberrant moral character. If Black adolescent girls fail to achieve, something in their nature prevents them from doing so. As president, Ronald Reagan often urged teenage mothers to "just say no" so that taxpayers would no longer be forced to pay for their sexual behavior. The "Just Say No" slogan invoked by the Reagan and Bush administrations in the 1980s was utilized in the 1990s by both Black and White conservatives in the attempt "to change welfare as we know it." If these politicians have their way, teenage mothers will be shunned, hidden, and ignored.

As I made my way through East Oakland and downtown Richmond [California] to interview teen mothers,* I witnessed a different scenario from the one devised by politicians. Teenage mothers are housed in threatening, drug-infested environments, schooled in jail-like institutions, and obstructed from achieving the American Dream. In our ostensibly open society, teenage mothers are disqualified from full participation and are marked as deviant. Black teenage girls aged fourteen, fifteen, and sixteen—many of them just beginning to show an adolescent interest in wearing makeup, dressing in the latest fashions, and reading teen magazines—are stigmatized. These teen mothers attempt to cope as best they can by redefining their situation in terms that involve the least damage to their self-respect.

---

*Except when necessary for clarification, all teenage mothers and older women who were previously teenage mothers will for the sake of brevity be referred to as teen mothers—a term they use. When appropriate the teen mothers' own mothers will be referred to as adult mothers. All names and places have been changed to protect confidentiality.

Are Black teenage mothers responsible for the socioeconomic problems besetting the Black community, as the radio show caller would have us believe? Do Black teenage mothers have different moral values than most Americans? Do they have babies in order to collect welfare, as politicians suggest? Do the families of Black teenage mothers condone their deviant behavior, as the popular view contends? Or, as William J. Wilson's economic theory suggests, is Black teenage motherhood simply a response to the economic problems of the Black community? Black teenage girls confront a world in which gender norms, poverty, and racism are intertwined. Accordingly, to answer questions about these young mothers, we must sort out a host of complex economic and social problems that pervade their lives. I hope the questions I have asked and the answers given will provide portraits of real teenage mothers involved in real experiences.

The reality of these teenage mothers is that they have had to adopt strategies for survival that seem to them to make sense within their social environment but are as inadequate for them as they were for teenage mothers in the past.

These ethnographic pictures illuminate the way structural contradictions act on psychological well-being and the way people construct and reconstruct their lives in order to cope on a daily basis. One issue that comes through quite clearly in this study, and one that is often overlooked by politicians and various studies on Black teenage mothers, is that these teenagers know what constitutes a successful life. Black teenage mothers . . . struggle against being considered morally deviant, underclass, and unworthy.

If we are to understand the stories of these teenage mothers and generalize from their experiences in any significant way, we must place them within the current theoretical and political discussions concerning Black teenage mothers. As T. S. Eliot noted long ago, reality is often more troubling than myth.

What is begging for our attention is the fact that adolescence is a time when Black girls, striving for maturity, lose the support of others in three significant ways. First, they are abandoned by the educational system; second, they become mere sexual accompanists for boys and men; third, these problems create a split between the girls and their families and significant others. What is needed to understand the losses, the stresses, and the large and small violences that render such teenage girls incapable of successfully completing their adolescent tasks, is a gender, race, and class analysis. When early motherhood is added to these challenges, they become insurmountable. The adolescent mothers I saw were deprived of every resource needed for any human being to function well in our society: education, jobs, food, medical care, a secure place to live, love and respect, the ability to securely connect with others. In addition, these girls were silenced by the insidious and insistent stereotyping of them as promiscuous and aberrant teenage girls. . . .

Talking to Teen Mothers

I began my search to understand the rise in Black motherhood by interviewing two teen mothers referred to me by friends. They came to my house early one Saturday morning and stayed for three hours. Although I had prepared a series of general questions, the young women had so much more to say that I was compelled to create a more extensive set. Next, the director of a local family planning center let me attend a teen parent meeting, where I left a letter of introduction inviting those who were interested in my project to contact me. These teen mothers referred me to others. Eventually, I created a list of fifteen teen mothers.

The director of the family planning center also introduced me to Mary Higgins, the director of the Alternative Center in East Oakland. The Center operated with a grant from a large charity organization that allowed it to develop outreach programs geared to the needs of the local teenage population. These programs included an alternative school, day care, self-esteem development, parenting skills training, and personal counseling. Mary in turn introduced me to Ann Getty, a counselor at the center. Through Ann I met Claudia Wilson, a counselor for the Richmond Youth Counseling program. A short time after that meeting, I began to work as a volunteer consultant for the Alternative Center and to attend meetings with counselors and others who visited the center.

Through my contacts at the center, in the autumn of 1985 I met DeVonya Smalls and twenty of the sample of thirty-two teen mothers who participated in this study. The rest of my sample was drawn from other contacts I made in a network of community workers at the Richmond Youth Service Agency and through my work as a volunteer consultant there. The youth agency's counselors introduced me to teenage mothers who lived in the downtown Richmond area. As a consultant, I was able to talk extensively with the adolescents who took part in teen mother programs.

After several months of making contacts, losing some, and making new ones, I was able to pull together the sample of thirty-two teenage mothers. Of this sample, I "hung out" with a core group of seven teen mothers for a period of seven months, including sixteen-year-old DeVonya Smalls. The other six teen mothers who participated were sixteen-year-old Susan Carter, a mother of a two-month-old baby, who was living with her mother and sister in East Oakland; seventeen-year-old Shana Leeds, a mother with a nine-month-old baby, who was living with a family friend in downtown Richmond; and eighteen-year-old Terry Parks, a mother of a two-year-old, who was sharing her East Oakland apartment with twenty-year-old Dana Little and her five-year-old son. The group also included twenty-year-old Diane Harris, who had become pregnant at seventeen and within months had exchanged a middle-class lifestyle for that of a welfare mother and was now living in a run-down apartment in East Oakland; Lois Patterson, a twenty-seven-year-old mother of two and long-term welfare recipient, who was living with her extended family in a small, crowded house in East Oakland; and Evie Jenkins, a forty-three-year-old mother of two, who was living on monthly disability insurance in a housing project near downtown Richmond. Like Diane Harris, Evie lost her middle-class status when she became a teenage welfare mother at age seventeen.

I accompanied these women to the Alternative Center, to the welfare office, and to visits with their mothers. Some of the teen mothers could not find private places to talk, so we talked in the back seat of my car, over lunch or dinner in coffee shops, in a shopping mall, at teenage program meetings, or while moving boxes to a new apartment—in other words, anywhere they would let me join them.

Interviewing the teen mothers on a regular basis was difficult: they frequently moved, appointments were missed, telephones were disconnected. One day I tried to call five mothers about planned participant observation sessions only to find all their telephones disconnected. A few mothers were willing to be interviewed because they thought they would benefit in some way. One mother let me interview her because she thought I had access to housing and could get her an apartment. Another thought I would be able to get her into a teen parent program. A few mothers did not bother returning my telephone calls once they discovered I could not pay them.

I did not pay the teen mothers or the others for taking part in these interviews. In exchange for their information, I told the teen mothers about my own family, gave out information about welfare assistance and teen parent programs, and drove them to various stores. I helped De Vonya Smalls move into her first apartment. I went out with the teen mothers to eat Chinese food, shared takeout dinners, and bought potato chips and sodas for, so it seemed, everyone's sisters, brothers, and cousins. I was in some homes so often that the families began to treat me like a friend.

I found myself caught up in the teen mothers' lives more than I had planned. I was able to capture changes in their lives. I watched a teen mother break up with her baby's father. I witnessed DeVonya Smalls and Shana Leeds move in and out of three different homes. I saw Shana Leeds go through the process of applying for AFDC. I sat through long afternoons with Diane Harris discussing her baby's "womanizing" father, only to attend their wedding a few months later.

I also talked to everyone else I could, including the teen mothers' mothers, Black and White teenage girls who were not mothers, teachers, counselors, directors of teen programs, social workers, and Planned Parenthood counselors. Many have definite views about teenage mothers, some representing a more conservative voice than we usually hear in the Black community

Sadly, most of the teen mothers' fathers and their babies' fathers were not involved in their lives in any significant way. The teen mothers' lack of knowledge about the babies' fathers' whereabouts made it impossible for me to interview the men. The few men who were still involved with the teen mothers refused to be interviewed. The best I could do was to observe some of the dynamics between two teen fathers and mothers.

Personal Histories

The teen mothers' ages ranged from fourteen to forty-three. Seventeen of them were currently teen mothers (aged fourteen to nineteen), and fifteen were older women who had previously been teen mothers (aged twenty to forty-three). The presence of the two age groups enabled me to appreciate the dynamic quality and long-term effects of teenage pregnancy on the mothers. The current teen mothers brought to the study a "here and now" aspect: I witnessed some of the family drama as it unfolded. The older women brought a sense of history and their reflective skills; the problems of being a teenage mother did not disappear when the teenage mothers became adults. The older women's stories served two goals for this [study]: to show that the black community has a history of not condoning teenage motherhood, and to locate emerging problems within the structural changes of our society that have affected everyone in recent years. . . .

As a group, the teen mothers' personal histories reveal both common and not so common patterns among teenage mothers. The youngest teen mother was fourteen and the oldest was eighteen at the time of their first pregnancies. Seventeen teen mothers were currently receiving welfare aid. But contrary to the commonly held assumption that welfare mothers beget welfare mothers, only five teen mothers reported that their families had been on welfare for longer than five years. Twenty-four of the teen mothers had grown up in families headed by a single mother—a common pattern among teenage mothers. Thirteen reported that their mothers had been teenage mothers. Unlike other studies that focus on poor teenage mothers, this study also included five middle-class and three working-class teenage mothers whose parents were teachers, civil service managers, or nursing assistants. Nine of the teen mothers were attending high school (of whom six were attending alternative high school). Several had taken college courses, and two had managed to obtain a college degree.

Along with capturing an ethnographic snapshot of the seven teen mothers, I conducted semistructured interviews in which I asked all the teen mothers specific questions about their experiences before, during, and after their pregnancies. I asked questions about various common perceptions: the idea of passive and promiscuous teenage girls, the role of men in their lives, the notion of strong cultural support for their pregnancies, the concept of extended family support networks, and the idea that teenage mothers have babies in order to receive welfare aid. Each teenage mother was interviewed for two to two and one-half hours. I audiotaped and transcribed all of the interviews.

I transcribed the material verbatim except for names and other identifying markers, which were changed during the transcription. I coded each teen mother on background variables and patterns. I read and reread my fieldnotes, supporting documents, and relevant literature. For [my research] I chose those quotations that would best represent typical responses, overall categories, and major themes. I used quotations from the core sample of seven as well as from the larger sample of thirty-two to include a wide range of responses.

Whenever possible I have tried to capture the teen mothers' emotional responses to the questions or issues. Often a teen mother would express through a sigh or a laugh feelings about some issue that contradicted her verbal response. For instance, when Terry Parks laughed as she described her feelings about being on welfare, I added a note about her laughter because it indicated to me that she was embarrassed about the subject. Without that notation, I would not have been able to communicate the emotional intensity with which she said the word "welfare" as she talked about her welfare experiences.

Through the Ethnographic Lens

I use an ethnographic approach to provide an intricate picture of how gender and poverty dictate the lives of these young teenage mothers and how societal gender, race, and class struggles are played out at the personal level. An ethnographic approach can bridge the gap between the sociological discussion of field research and the actual field experience. Studying these women through the lens of ethnography helped me move the teen mothers' personal stories to an objective level of analysis. The ethnographic method allowed the teen mothers to express to me personal information that was close to the heart. The method also allowed me to bring these Black teenage mothers into sociology's purview, to better understand them as persons, to make their voices heard, and to make their lives important to the larger society. The interviews and observations show that Black teenage girls' experiences are structural and troublesome. At all times I have attempted to make these teen mothers' stories real and visible by presenting the teen mothers' own words with as little editing as possible and by revealing their own insights into the interlocking structures of gender, race, and class.

The Insider Interviewer

I could not walk easily into some teen mothers' lives. Being close to the people being interviewed made me both pleased and tense. Being an insider—someone sharing the culture, community, ethnicity, or gender background of the study participants—has its advantages and disadvantages. When the interviewer can identify with the class and ethnic background of the person being interviewed, there is a greater chance of establishing rapport. The person will express a greater range of attitudes and opinions, especially when the opinions to be expressed are somewhat opposed to general public opinion. The situation is more complex when interviewees are asked to reveal information that may serve the researcher's interest but not that of the group involved. "Don't wash dirty linen in public," they remind the researcher.

The most difficult questions I faced, as do most insider interviewers, had to do with the politics of doing interviews in my own community. As an insider I had to decide whether making certain issues public would benefit the group at the same time that it served my research goals. I imagine that these interviews will raise questions. How will the White community perceive Black families if I discuss the conflicts between teen mothers and their mothers, or fathers who refuse to support their children, or the heavy negative sanctioning of these teen mothers by some in the Black community? My work would be taken out of context, several people warned me.

Every Black researcher who works on issues pertaining to her or his community grapples with these questions. We think about the possibility that our findings may contradict what the Black community wants outsiders to know. Some researchers select nonthreatening topics. Others romanticize Black life despite the evidence that life is hard for those on the bottom. And others simply adopt a code of silence, taking a position similar to that of the Black college teacher who in another context made the point to me, "I'm socialized to bear my pain in silence and not go blabbing about my problems to White folks, let alone strangers."

Being an insider did not help me gain the confidence of the teen mothers and others immediately. Most were suspicious of researchers. I lost a chance to interview one group of teen mothers involved in a special school project because the counselors who worked with them did not like the way a White male researcher had treated the teen mothers previously. Indeed, these teen mothers had the right to be suspicious. What these girls and women say about their lives can be used against them by public policy makers, since the Black community is often blamed for its own social and economic situations.

But overall, being a Black woman was helpful, because eventually the teen mothers, realizing we had much in common, stopped being suspicious of me and began to talk candidly of their lives. Occasionally I could not find a babysitter and had to bring my little boy along. I found my son's presence helped reduce the aloofness of my role as researcher and the powerlessness of the teens' position as interview subjects. I was surprised at how helpful my son was in breaking through the first awkward moments. We made him the topic of discussion—mothers can always compare child-care problems. His presence also helped me counter some of the teenagers' tendencies to deny problems. When I talked to DeVonya Smalls about my son's effects on my own schedule, like having to get up at five in the morning instead of at seven, she relaxed and told me about her efforts to study for a test while her baby cried for attention. She also admitted to doing poorly in school.

I decided to study these teenage mothers because Black teenage mothers are not going away, no matter how much we ignore, romanticize, or remain silent about their lives. I strongly disagree with approaches that let the group's code of silence supersede the need to understand the problems and issues of Black teenage mothers. That kind of false ideology only perpetuates the myths about Black teenage motherhood and causes researchers to neglect larger sociological issues or fail to ask pertinent questions about the lives of these mothers. In the name of racial pride, then, we essentially overlook how the larger society shares a great deal of responsibility for these problems. The only way to reduce the number of teenage pregnancies or to improve the lives of teenage mothers is to understand the societal causes by examining the realities of these girls' lives. The time had arrived, as Nate Hare put it, for an end to the unrealistic view of Black lives.

PART II
Culture

7

THE NEW TATTOO SUBCULTURE

ANNE M. VELLIQUETTE • JEFF B. MURRAY

Culture is defined as the shared ways of a human social group. This definition includes the ways of thinking, understanding, and feeling that have
been gained through common experience in social groups and are passed on
from one generation to another. Thus, culture reflects the social patterns of
thought, emotions, and practices that arise from social interaction within a
given society. In this reading, the first of four to explore culture, Anne Velliquette and Jeff Murray explore the social and symbolic meanings of body
adornment in the new tattoo subculture. A *subculture* is defined as a system
of values, attitudes, modes of behavior, and lifestyles of a social group that
is distinct from, but related to, the dominant culture of a society. In particular, this ethnographic study investigates what tattoos, as cultural objects, signify for both the tattooist (the service provider) and the tattooee (the client).

*In the past, what you were determined what you looked like. Today, what you
choose to look like expresses who—or indeed what—you would like to be. The
choice is yours.*

—TED POLHEMUS

Humans are the only known species that deliberately alters its appearance through the customization of our bodies (Randall and Polhemus 1996). At the most basic level, we get up every morning and
make decisions about what to wear. The customization of our bodies, however, goes far beyond the clothing we choose to wear as a "second skin" (Randall and Polhemus 1996:79). At the surface level, our skin can be tattooed,
pierced, branded, scarred, and adorned with jewelry, cosmetics, and various
articles of clothing. Our hair can also be creatively modified and adorned. Beyond redefining our surface appearance, we can also alter the body's actual

---

Reprinted by permission from Anne M. Velliquette and Jeff B. Murray.

shape through techniques such as body building and plastic surgery. In all cultures, human beings spend time and effort customizing the body strictly for the sake of appearance (Randall and Polhemus 1996). This customization often involves not only time and energy, but pain and discomfort (Myers 1992; Randall and Polhemus 1996). This leads to an engaging question: Why do human beings of all cultures alter their natural inherited appearance?

In most societies, the likely reason for altering the body is that such alteration provides a vehicle for self-expression (Finkelstein 1991; Randall and Polhemus 1996; Velliquette, Murray, and Creyer 1997). Permanent as well as temporary forms of body adornment may signify a wide array of symbolic meanings. For example, permanent forms of body decoration (e.g., tattoos, piercings, and scarification) have been known to represent emblems of accomplishment, group membership, social status, personal identity, or a willingness to endure pain in order to please a lover (Bohannan 1988; Drewal 1988; Gathercole 1988; Gritton 1988; Sanders 1988; Velliquette et al. 1997). Temporary forms of body adornment also provide an invaluable means of self-expression. Our personal choice in clothing, hairstyle, body shape, and use of objects may display various identity features such as gender, status, values, interests, and a particular approach to life. Clearly, body adornment has become a way for human beings to present their desired self-image to others (Blumer 1969; Finkelstein 1991; Goffman 1959). Thus, understanding the way that individuals use nonverbal signs and symbols to construct, revise, and maintain symbolic meaning is important for the construction of self-identity.

Focusing on one type of body adornment, this article presents an ethnographic account of symbolic meaning as expressed by two segments of the *New Tattoo Subculture*,[1] the tattooist (the service provider) and the tattooee (the client). Although it is difficult to assess the number of people participating in the new tattoo subculture, it has been estimated that 12 to 20 million Americans have joined the ranks of the tattooed (Blouin 1996; Velliquette et al. 1997). This is not surprising given that in 1996, tattoo studios were among the top six growth businesses in the United States (American Business Information, Inc. 1996; Velliquette et al. 1997). During the 1990s, observers have also witnessed sharp increases in the sale of tattoo ink, books, magazines, videos, special clothing designed to show off the decorated body, and other tattoo-related odds and ends, as well as the expansion of tattoo associations and conventions, the growth of state regulations, and an increase in the number of advertisements featuring tattooed models and celebrities (Ball 1996; Blouin 1996; Krakow 1994; Peterson 1996).

Tattooing's recent popularity, as well as the increased interest in the tattoo as popular culture (e.g., Gap and Polo Ads featuring tattoos, and a tattooed Barbie doll by Mattel), leads to some interesting research questions. What is it about the tattoo as a cultural object that draws people to participate in this subculture? In what ways is the tattoo used as a form of expression?

What is involved in the experience of acquiring a tattoo? What transpires during the service interaction between the tattooist and tattooee? To address these questions, we begin with a brief discussion of the literature on tattooing as an art form, its rich history, and its cultural and subcultural roots. Next, we summarize the ethnographic method used for data collection. Following this summary, we offer an ethnographic account of the tattoo subculture in order to demonstrate the symbolic nature of the act of tattooing. We draw from our own experiences and observations (including fieldwork at two tattoo studios, a tattoo museum/archive, and a tattoo convention) to illustrate ways in which the tattoo is used as a form of expression. We also consider the process itself via interactions between tattooists and their clients. Finally, we consider emergent aspects of this research that may further illustrate what has been described as the New Tattoo Subculture.

Tattooing: Yesterday and Today

Tattoo is a word loaded with rich visual associations summoning images that range from circus sideshow freaks or tribal warriors to WWII sailors, the Holocaust, street gangs, criminals, or the more recent association of media stars and athletes (Velliquette et al. 1997). With such vivid associations spanning across decades, it becomes clear that tattoos have a long and fascinating history. . . . The practice of tattooing is one of the oldest art forms discovered by archaeologists (Ball 1996; Randall and Polhemus 1996). The word *tattoo* is derived from the Tahitian word *ta-tu* meaning "to strike." A *ta* was a sharp, jagged piece of antler or bone. Different types of bones, or *tas*, were used to create different designs by tapping or pushing ink, usually made from vegetable or fruit dyes, into the flesh (Ball 1996; Randall and Polhemus 1996). Because it is usually only the bones and not the skin of our distant ancestors that remain intact, it is impossible to determine just how old the tattoo really is. The oldest irrefutable evidence of tattooing entered the archaeological record only a few years ago, when the complete body of an Iceman was found frozen in a glacier in the Alps. Some 5,000 years old, this ancient hunter's body was adorned with 15 tattoos (Randall and Polhemus 1996). In order to appreciate the history of tattooing, one must appreciate its social logic and functions.

The social-symbolic role that tattoos have played in society varies a great deal, depending on factors such as historical period, geography, economic development, innovation, and cultural diffusion. In ancient societies, tattoos, as well as other forms of permanent body modification, were most commonly associated with permanency in one's life (e.g., gender and maturity), lifelong social connections (e.g., tribe membership), or a celebrated appearance style that showed considerable continuity through dozens of generations (Randall and Polhemus 1996; Sanders 1988). The permanency of the tattoo symbolized premodern society's need for social integration, order, and stability (Randall and Polhemus 1996). . . . The current trend in tattooing has been explained as serving a number of social-symbolic roles: as a mark of affiliation to express group commitment and belonging (e.g., the logo worn by Harley Davidson riders), as a mark of personal identity (e.g., a symbol that represents a unique personal experience), as a mark of resistance (e.g., a symbol that violates consumption codes), or as a mark of identity change (e.g., a symbol that emulates a media image) (Randall and Polhemus 1996; Sanders 1988; Velliquette et al. 1997).

The recent popular interest in tattoos, along with remarkable changes in the practices and styles of tattooing, has attracted a number of new artists, some of them classically trained at prestigious art institutes (e.g., the tattoo artist Jamie Summers; see Rubin 1988:256). The role the artist/tattooist plays becomes an important part of this "Tattoo Renaissance" (Rubin 1988:233). The tattooist engages in *impression management*[2] to set the stage for an artistic service encounter. For example, the tattooist sets an artistic tone by impressing upon the client that her shop is a studio, that her work is art, and that her identity is an artist (Sanders 1989). Thus tattooists who view themselves as artists are continually engaged in legitimation talk in order to neutralize the stigma that has been historically associated with tattooing (Sanders 1989). As tattoo artists legitimize their work as art, it seems that they in turn decrease the stigma for the consumer. This increased recognition of tattooing as an art form has not only led to its development as a creative medium for some artists, it has also led to a new creative form of expression for the consumer (Rubin 1988; Velliquette et al. 1997). The consumer engages in experiential consumption, and through negotiated order with the artist, the consumer embarks upon a symbolic journey where the choice in artist, design, colors, and body location are all linked to the consumer's personal experiences and sense of identity (Sanders 1988).

In summary, a review of literature suggests two central a priori themes: *collective legitimization* and *self-identity*. These themes are not mutually exclusive, but rather are intertwined analytical categories that are useful for the framework of discovery. Further, to allow for a discussion of several aspects of interaction, several "sensitizing concepts" are introduced within each theme (Blumer 1969:147–48). . . .

Ethnographic Method and Setting

Tattooing is one topic that "demands a plunge into the waters, not a comfortable observer's beach chair at the side of the ocean" (Steward 1990:198). According to Blumer (1969) and Hebdige (1979), immersion in the field (or hovering close) produces some of the most compelling and evocative accounts of subculture and human interaction. Given the symbolic complexity associated with the artist-client interaction, the choice of design, and the act of becoming tattooed, we decided to use ethnographic interviews and participant observation as our primary data-gathering techniques.

We collected the majority of the text for this study over a six-month period in 1996. We returned to the field in 1997 for approximately two to three
months in order to follow up on questions regarding support for both a
priori and emerging themes grounded in the data. The text consists of over
400 pages of typed fieldnotes composed immediately after each participant
observation in the everyday activities of two tattoo studios. Generally, we
spent two to four hours at a time, at least once a week, in one of the studios,
helping to maintain files of tattoo designs, working behind the front desk,
sitting with customers as they were tattooed, assisting with some technical
procedures, interviewing customers, and interviewing artists when they
were not tattooing. . . . In addition to participating in the studios, we collected
fieldnotes and took photographs at a 1996 national tattoo convention and
two tattoo artwork museum gallery exhibitions. Further, in order to gain
more historical appreciation, we traveled to the Tattoo Archive in Berkeley,
California. The Tattoo Archive is a national museum of tattoo history and col-
lectibles. We spent four days collecting relevant information and interviewing the curator.

Although the primary goal of ethnography is immersion in the life-
worlds and everyday experiences of a group of people, the researcher inevitably remains an outsider (Emerson, Fretz, and Shaw 1995). Since both
"outsider" and "insider" perspectives are important in this type of research
(Rubin 1988:11, n. 2), we decided to reinforce an insider's perspective by becoming tattooed. I (first author) chose a *cat* (ankle) for my first tattoo and
a *butterfly* (lower front hip) for my second. . . . I carefully recorded the details of this experience in a private journal. These notes also became part of
the text. . . .

Findings from the Field

As expected, we found support for many of the *collective legitimization* issues
that had been discussed in previous literature on tattooing. For example, we
found that tattooists often tried to convince their clients that tattooing is an
art form and that "tattoos aren't just for bikers anymore" (fieldnotes January
31, 1996). The tattooists worked hard to legitimize their field of work by becoming certified, referring to themselves as artists, attending national tattoo
conventions, showing their work at local art galleries, and studying other
artists in the field. The artists often conversed about different tattoo artists'
reputations in the field, often ranking them in terms of their favorites. . . .
The artists also discussed how bored they get with customer-requested designs that do not allow them to use their creative, artistic talent. One artist referred to these simplistic, uncreative designs as "cartoon characters." This
artist hated these simple designs because she felt "like a kid coloring in a
coloring book. . . . Something you do when you're five years old" (fieldnotes
April 15, 1997).

The artist says to me, "The owner is tired of doing the small cartoon characters like the tazmanian devil. . . . She hates doing that shit. She is into the big pieces that she can really get creative with. . . . You know, custom work." (fieldnotes April 9, 1997)

We also found that the artists worked hard to impress upon their clients that their studios were clean and met all of the health department's regulations. Several neutralization tactics were employed by the artists to change the perceptions of those individuals who viewed tattooing as deviant and tattoo shops as dirty, underground holes where deviants hung out. The following passage represents an attempt to neutralize the tattooing experience:

The male artist calls the Irish man back to the room and I stay to watch. The artist sits him down in the chair and shows him the needles that will be used. The artist tells him they are clean, new needles and that they are sealed in the bags. I ask the artist to repeat what he said and he says, "I like to let the customers see that the needles are new and sterile. I would want to see that if I were the customer." The artist then cuts open the sealed bags to get the needles out. (fieldnotes March 1, 1997)

The owners of the tattoo studios worked hard to legitimize their businesses further by creating a clinical atmosphere. For example, in the client rooms where tattooing took place, there were several glass jars on the counter filled with supplies (e.g., cotton, disposable razors, gauze), paper towels, antiseptic cleaning sprays, lotions, ointments, and tattooing equipment (e.g., guns, disposable ink trays, and ink). Some of the equipment was displayed on the wall (e.g., pliers and parts to the gun). There were also boxes of surgical gloves on the counter, a washing sink, and a hazardous waste container for disposal of needles and other infectious material. The room had an appearance similar to that of a doctor's office.

Although the tattoo artists employed these neutralization tactics, a certain amount of stigma remained, as viewed and expressed by a few informants. One informant described how he thought others would react to his tattoos in his profession: "I know it is not totally acceptable. I would catch crap if I ever showed up here in the future to teach with my tattoos hanging out. . . . They would lay down and die!" (fieldnotes April 17, 1997). Several customers stated that there are levels of social acceptance for various kinds of tattoos. One informant explained how the sun design she wanted on her hip was more socially acceptable than a skull and crossbones on a person's chest. To further illustrate the stigma associated with tattoos, we provide the following quoted passage:

I want to get it where I can cover it up. You know, so my mom won't see it. My mom hates tattoos. She lives in a place where she associates all tattoos with gang members. (fieldnotes March 1, 1997)

As discussed in the literature, collective legitimization is a process of *impression management* (Goffman 1959). Early in the ethnography, it became apparent that, in many respects, tattooists are performers. We often observed tattooists putting on a public display of professionalism. For example, tattooists often impressed upon their clients that they were artistic, friendly, and most of all technically competent and sterile. The following passage is representative of this theme:

> The artist and I continue to talk and she tells me, "I was so nervous when I had to do my first tongue piercing." She then tells me she was shaking when she did it, which made the guy nervous. Then the artist said, "You really have to pretend like you know what the hell you are doing." (fieldnotes February 15, 1997)

Within the studio setting, we observed the tattooists spending their time in two different regions: the front stage and the back stage areas of the shop. In the front stage, "permanent cosmetic/tattoo artist" certificates were hung on the wall in the lobby. The walls in the lobby area were covered with photographs of tattoos given to previous clients: the best and most unique work made the "wall." The wall attracted customers who were entering the shop and added to the credibility of the artists. Also included in the front stage region were the rooms where clients became tattooed. In the front stage region, including both the lobby and the tattoo rooms, we often observed tattooists engaging in what Goffman (1959:80) refers to as "team performance."

> The artist is finishing a large, colorful, elaborate design with a horse, clouds, and moon on a woman's arm. The artist calls the other artist in to come and look at the work. The female artist says, "This design is a dual effort between me and _____." The male artist had done the outline the week before and now the female artist was adding color. They were both happy with the results of their work. They complimented one another's artistic work (telling each other how good they were) in front of the client. (fieldnotes March 1, 1997)

Another important concept related to impression management is emotion management. The artists often managed their emotions when in the presence of clients. The artists typically refrained from displaying disappointment, anger, disgust, or impatience when interacting with their customers.

> A guy came in looking for someone to quote him a price on some touch-up work. The owner asked him where he got the tattoo done and he replied, "By a friend of mine in Oklahoma City. He is a paraplegic and he does real good work. I just don't want to have to drive to OK City to have it touched up." After he left the owner said, "He thought that was a good tattoo?" She then said, "It was hard not to laugh!! You really have to control yourself from laughing in situations like that." (fieldnotes March 28, 1997)

The tattooists usually segregated their audiences by keeping conversations like this one within the circle of the other artists. However, a few instances were observed where this segregation did not take place and customers were allowed to hear backstage talk:

> The male artist assists this time on a tongue piercing. The owner talks to the male artist about piercing and tells him the first time she did a navel, she was extremely nervous. She says this in front of the customer as if he is not there. She then says, "The only way to really practice is to just get in there and do one." The customer then asks with a nervous tone of voice, "Is this your first one?" He says this with surprise and anxiety. She said, "Oh no, I have done many, I am just saying that this is really the only way to get used to it." The male artist then tells the guy (as if to calm him down), "Everything we are using on you is sterile." The guy sits still as the two artists pierce his tongue and the client's friend and I watch. (fieldnotes March 19, 1997)

In the tattoo studio, the artists attempted to gain and maintain control during the service encounter by *negotiating order* (Strauss 1990). The artists claimed that the average client's lack of experience and knowledge necessitated the need for the artist to be in control at all times to ensure a successful interaction. . . .

As we observed, most negotiations appeared to go smoothly during artist–client interactions. A working consensus was usually achieved, because most clients seemed to realize the artist's role as the expert in the situation.

> The female customer then said, "It is not the pain I am worried about. . . . I just want to know where it will look best." The owner replies, "Well, ankles are a nice place because the skin is so smooth and tight there, so it is easier to tattoo a nice design on the ankle. The skin is stretched tight on the ankle unlike the spongy skin of the breast, stomach, back or hip area." The owner then also tells her that the "shoulders [back] make a nice canvas as well." The artist refers to the skin as canvas for the ink. . . . The girl continues to ask the owner for advice on colors, size, and location. (fieldnotes February 15, 1997)

It appeared to us that most interactions were controlled by the artists. It was discovered rather quickly that the customer is literally in the tattooist's hands.

> The artist didn't like the way she had drawn the leaf. She said she had kind of made a mistake when tattooing it. I asked her about making mistakes. She said, "It happens. . . . When you make a mistake, you just cover it up. The customer won't ever know." I thought about this and realized that the customer usually can't see what is going on up-close during the process and that they probably wouldn't know if a mistake had been made. (fieldnotes February 22, 1997)

Although most interactions and negotiations went smoothly, there were instances where this was not the case. The artists labeled the clients involved in the unsuccessful interactions as "bad clients" and the customers involved in the successful interactions as "good clients." The following passages provide examples of "bad clients" as defined by the artists:

> The owner explains, "This chick came in the other day for a navel piercing and she had the dirtiest belly button I had ever seen! It took me five minutes to pick all of the shit out of it! I thought about charging her extra just for that!" (fieldnotes April 9, 1997)

> The artist defines bad customers: "The ones where price is the most important thing. . . . The customers that will let you run with it and do whatever you want to, those are the great ones. . . . Unfortunately there aren't many of those. . . . Most people say, "I can only afford 50 dollars' worth." I sometimes give them a few free colors just to make it look better. . . . The whiny ones are bad too, when you step on your pedal and you're not even touching them and they are like, 'Ow! Quit!' you know. . . . You just feel like slapping them." (fieldnotes April 15, 1997) . . .

It was very common for customers to bring friends with them for support during the tattooing procedure. The social support often helped the potential client with such decisions as choice of design, size, colors, and body location. Friends offered further support by engaging in conversation to keep the client's mind off the painful procedure. We also observed this type of conversational support between the artists and their clients. One artist described how she felt this conversational support was part of the job:

> *You get to talk to a lot of people. Sitting there with them for an hour or an hour and a half, you get to talking and make new friends. We're actually like bartenders you know, people cry on our shoulder. . . . You usually know their life story by the time they leave.* (fieldnotes April 15, 1997)

The second a priori theme identified in the literature reveals how tattoos are used to reinforce one's *self-identity*. We discovered that the use of tattoos to express one's inner self was probably the most commonly stated motivation for acquiring a tattoo. In this context, the tattoo becomes an extension of the person, symbolizing the person's narrative story. One informant described how becoming tattooed "is more of a reflection of who you think you are" (fieldnotes April 17, 1997). As one artist explained, "The tattoo is already there inside those who really want it, it is already a part of them, the tattoo artist just brings it out" (fieldnotes July 12, 1996). . . . One of the informants, who had acquired tattoos from 35 different artists, described his tattoos as a "scrapbook" symbolizing his life story:

> I asked him if there was one he favored or if any particular one had great meaning. He said, "They all do." He told me that he considers his tattoo

art work "his personal scrapbook." Each and every tattoo reminds the informant of a person, place, time or period in his life. A personal scrapbook of one's life or self. (fieldnotes July 12, 1996)

During the ethnography, we discovered that customers choose tattoos to represent who they are in different ways. Some choose symbols for personal distinction, whereas others choose symbols for integration purposes. Both cases contributed to an expression of identity: the former case seemed to represent one's personal identity whereas the latter case represented one's social identity. One informant described how tattoos distinguish him from others in a crowd (and help create a sense of personal identity):

> *When you make the decision, 'I'm going to be a person with a tattoo,' you know you are different from most people. . . . Just the bottom line, standing in the line at Wal-Mart, I know I'm different. . . . It is fun being different, it is even more fun being more different.* (fieldnotes April 17, 1997)

Other examples from interviews in which the tattoo symbolized the owner's personal identity include a Mickey Mouse tattooed to the informant's arm because his grandfather called him "Mickey"; a butterfly tattooed to the client's hip symbolizing her given name; a rattlesnake design chosen in memory of being bitten and almost dying; a rose tattooed on the wrist for every child born and a butterfly tattooed on the ankle for every family member who had died; and a cat design that reflected a woman's long history of living with and loving cats. There were other instances where the design seemed to represent the client's social identity (integration):

> Back at the counter, a young man (30s) with an Irish accent comes in and asks to see the hog file. The owner asks him to clarify what kind of hog and he says, "You know, a razorback." Shortly after that remark he says, "I am not getting a hog because of THE Razorbacks basketball team, the hog is part of my family crest. It looks just like the razorback, only it's not running. . . . It is just standing there." I ask him where he is from and he says, "Dublin." He then tells me that every family name has a crest and that his has the hog in the design. (fieldnotes March 1, 1997)

Often the process of becoming tattooed could be explained as experiential consumption (Holbrook and Hirschman 1982), where the event was tied to a meaningful experience. The following passages are representative of this concept:

> The two girls who were best friends got matching tattoos on vacation in Mexico to bond their friendship. I ask her why the tribal piece and she says, "I don't know, we didn't really care what the design was. . . . We just wanted something simple . . . to represent our friendship." (fieldnotes April 15, 1997)

A young woman comes in (WF 20) with her mother to get a tattoo of a moon and fairy. She tells me that she had drawn the design herself. This will be her fourth tattoo as she has gotten one every year for her birthday since she was 16 years old. (fieldnotes March 19, 1997)

As discovered in this ethnography, tattoos are consumed for many different reasons. Most informants agreed, however, that tattoos are a form of self-expression, a way to communicate to others some aspect of the wearer's self-identity. . . .

Discussion and Conclusions

The preceding review of literature and ethnographic account suggests some feasible answers to the research questions stated in the introduction: What is it about the tattoo as a cultural object that draws people to participate in the tattoo subculture? In what ways is the tattoo used as a form of expression? What is involved in the experience of acquiring a tattoo? What transpires during the service interaction between the tattooist and tattooee? The a priori and emergent themes suggest that there are many reasons why individuals are drawn to participate in the new tattoo subculture. A subculture "signifies a way of life of a group of people" and is "characterized by interaction, continuity, and outsider and insider definitions of distinctiveness" (Prus 1996: 85). The tattoo subculture is no different in that the tattoo as a cultural object attracts people who want to express difference as well as integration. In this realm, the tattoo indicates the separate domains to which its wearers belong, while it expresses unity and connects otherwise diverse domains. For example, as we discovered in this ethnography, the tattoo was a common bond among all informants regardless of social class or background. Further, the tattoo was a form of distinction, separating the informants from the rest of society, or the non-tattooed.

Another reason that members are drawn to this subculture can be attributed to the phenomenon of certain objects becoming so firmly associated with an individual that they are understood as literal extensions of that individual's being. The tattoo as a cultural object is a "document that describes our past, an image that reflects our present, and a sign that calls us into the future" (Richardson 1989). Informants used tattoos to express symbolically the meanings they attached to themselves from past, present, and future perspectives. In other words, tattoos were used both to reflect one's past or current identity and to construct and revise one's future identity. Two of the most important themes used to represent this idea are *self-identity* and *simulated self*. Following the ideas presented under the self-identity theme, most informants used the tattoo to express the inner self; "to bring a little bit or a lot of their inner self out for others to see" (fieldnotes March 31, 1996). In this sense, tattoos were extensions of self-conceptions. In contrast, with the simulated self, informants believed that by adopting a symbol, they were changing their images and becoming someone different.

We conclude by stating that it is important and most "useful to examine subcultures by understanding the identities people achieve as participants, the activities deemed consequential in that context, the bonds participants develop with one another, and the sorts of commitments the people involved make with respect to the setting at hand" (Prus 1996:85). This study has achieved such a thorough examination of the new tattoo subculture. If the implications of the examples surveyed in this research can be summarized into a single idea, that idea would be the importance of cultural objects in constituting culture and human relations. Cultural artifacts, such as the tattoo, have properties and tendencies that in an era where material culture is rapidly increasing, deserve to be investigated in their own right.

ENDNOTES

[1] The modifier *New* signifies the recent expansion of popular interest in tattooing as a form of marking identity (Krakow 1994; Lautman 1994; Randall and Polhemus 1996; Velliquette et al. 1997).

[2] Erving Goffman (1959) argues that in everyday life, there is a clear understanding that first impressions are important and seldom overlooked. Those in service occupations have many motives for trying to control the impression they present during the service encounter. This process is called *impression management*.

REFERENCES

American Business Information, Inc. 1996. "1996 Business Changes Report." Omaha, NE: Marketing Research Division. Jeff Ferris, Project Manager.

Ball, Keith, ed. 1996. "Skin and Bones: Tools of the Trade." *Tattoo* 82 (June): 76–79.

Blouin, Melissa, ed. 1996. "Tattoo You: Health Experts Worried about Artful Trend." *Northwest Arkansas Times,* July 14, p. C4.

Blumer, Herbert. 1969. *Symbolic Interactionism: Perspective and Method.* Englewood Cliffs, NJ: Prentice-Hall.

Bohannan, Paul. 1988. "Beauty and Scarification amongst the Tiv." Pp. 77–82 in *Marks of Civilization,* edited by Arnold Rubin. Los Angeles: Museum of Cultural History.

Drewal, Henry John. 1988. "Beauty and Being: Aesthetics and Ontology in Yoruba Body Art." Pp. 83–96 in *Marks of Civilization,* edited by Arnold Rubin. Los Angeles: Museum of Cultural History.

Emerson, Robert M., Rachael I. Fretz, and Linda L. Shaw. 1995. *Writing Ethnographic Fieldnotes.* Chicago: University of Chicago Press.

Finkelstein, Joanne. 1991. *The Fashioned Self.* Philadelphia: Temple University Press.

Gathercole, Peter. 1988. "Contexts of Maori Moko." Pp. 171–78 in *Marks of Civilization,* edited by Arnold Rubin. Los Angeles: Museum of Cultural History.

Goffman, Erving. 1959. *The Presentation of Self in Everyday Life.* New York: Doubleday.

Gritton, Joy. 1988. "Labrets and Tattooing in Native Alaska." Pp. 181–90 in *Marks of Civilization,* edited by Arnold Rubin. Los Angeles: Museum of Cultural History.

Hebdige, Dick. 1979. *Subculture: The Meaning of Style.* New York: Routledge.

Holbrook, Morris B. and Elizabeth C. Hirschman. 1982. "The Experiential Aspects of Consumption: Consumer Fantasies, Feelings, and Fun." *Journal of Consumer Research* 9 (September): 132–40.

Krakow, Amy. 1994. *Total Tattoo Book.* New York: Warner Books.

Lautman, Victoria. 1994. *The New Tattoo.* New York, London, and Paris: Abbeville Press.

Myers, James. 1992. "Nonmainstream Body Modification: Genital Piercing, Branding, Burning, and Cutting." *Journal of Contemporary Ethnography* 21(3): 267–306.

Peterson, Andrea. 1996. "Parents Spur Laws against Tattoos for Kids." *Wall Street Journal,* September, pp. B1–B2.

Prus, Robert. 1996. *Symbolic Interaction and Ethnographic Research: Intersubjectivity and the Study of Human Lived Experience.* Albany: State University of New York Press.

Randall, Housk and Ted Polhemus. 1996. *The Customized Body.* London and New York: Serpent's Tail.

Rubin, Arnold. 1988. "The Tattoo Renaissance." Pp. 233–62 in *Marks of Civilization,* edited by Arnold Rubin. Los Angeles: Museum of Cultural History.

Sanders, Clinton R. 1988. "Drill and Frill: Client Choice, Client Typologies, and Interactional Control in Commercial Tattoo Settings." Pp. 219–33 in *Marks of Civilization,* edited by Arnold Rubin. Los Angeles: Museum of Cultural History.

———. 1989. "Organizational Constraints on Tattoo Images: A Sociological Analysis of Artistic Style." Pp. 232–41 in *The Meaning of Things,* edited by Ian Hodder. London: Unwin Hyman.

Steward, Samuel M. 1990. *Bad Boys and Tough Tattoos: A Social History of the Tattoo with Gangs, Sailors, and Street Corner Punks, 1950–1965.* New York: Harrington Park Press.

Velliquette, Anne M., Jeff B. Murray, and Elizabeth H. Creyer. 1997. "The Tattoo Renaissance: An Ethnographic Account of Symbolic Consumer Behavior." *Advances in Consumer Research.*

8

THE CODE OF THE STREETS

ELIJAH ANDERSON

In this selection, adapted from *Streetwise: Race, Class, and Change in an Urban Community* (1990), Elijah Anderson demonstrates how cultural values create new standards for behavior. Anderson, a professor of sociology and director of the Philadelphia Ethnography Project at the University of Pennsylvania, is an expert on the sociology of black America. The ethnographic study below analyzes the social norms governing street behavior and violence in the inner city. The resulting "code" is a complex system of norms, dress, rituals, and expected behavior. In order to survive within the subculture of the inner city, children and adults must learn the code and adapt their lives accordingly.

O f all the problems besetting the poor inner-city black community, none is more pressing than that of interpersonal violence and aggression. It wreaks havoc daily with the lives of community residents and increasingly spills over into downtown and residential middle-class areas. Muggings, burglaries, carjackings, and drug-related shootings, all of which may leave their victims or innocent bystanders dead, are now common enough to concern all urban and many suburban residents. The inclination to violence springs from the circumstances of life among the ghetto poor—the lack of jobs that pay a living wage, the stigma of race, the fallout from rampant drug use and drug trafficking, and the resulting alienation and lack of hope for the future.

Simply living in such an environment places young people at special risk of falling victim to aggressive behavior. Although there are often forces in the community which can counteract the negative influences, by far the most powerful being a strong, loving, "decent" (as inner-city residents put it) family committed to middle-class values, the despair is pervasive enough to have spawned an oppositional culture, that of "the streets," whose norms are often consciously opposed to those of mainstream society. These two orientations—decent and street—socially organize the community, and their coexistence has important consequences for residents, particularly children

From *The Code of the Streets*. Originally in *The Atlantic Monthly* 273, no. 5 (May 1994): 81–94. Copyright © 1994 by Elijah Anderson. Reprinted with the permission of W. W. Norton & Company, Inc.

growing up in the inner city. Above all, this environment means that even youngsters whose home lives reflect mainstream values—and the majority of homes in the community do—must be able to handle themselves in a street-oriented environment.

This is because the street culture has evolved what may be called a code of the streets, which amounts to a set of informal rules governing interpersonal public behavior, including violence. The rules prescribe both a proper comportment and a proper way to respond if challenged. They regulate the use of violence and so allow those who are inclined to aggression to precipitate violent encounters in an approved way. The rules have been established and are enforced mainly by the street-oriented, but on the streets the distinction between street and decent is often irrelevant; everybody knows that if the rules are violated, there are penalties. Knowledge of the code is thus largely defensive; it is literally necessary for operating in public. Therefore, even though families with a decency orientation are usually opposed to the values of the code, they often reluctantly encourage their children's familiarity with it to enable them to negotiate the inner-city environment.

At the heart of the code is the issue of respect—loosely defined as being treated "right," or granted the deference one deserves. However, in the troublesome public environment of the inner city, as people increasingly feel buffeted by forces beyond their control, what one deserves in the way of respect becomes more and more problematic and uncertain. This in turn further opens the issue of respect to sometimes intense interpersonal negotiation. In the street culture, especially among young people, respect is viewed as almost an external entity that is hard-won but easily lost, and so must constantly be guarded. The rules of the code in fact provide a framework for negotiating respect. The person whose very appearance—including his clothing, demeanor, and way of moving—deters transgressions feels that he possesses, and may be considered by others to possess, a measure of respect. With the right amount of respect, for instance, he can avoid "being bothered" in public. If he is bothered, not only may he be in physical danger but he has been disgraced or "dissed" (disrespected). Many of the forms that dissing can take might seem petty to middle-class people (maintaining eye contact for too long, for example), but to those invested in the street code, these actions become serious indications of the other person's intentions. Consequently, such people become very sensitive to advances and slights, which could well serve as warnings of imminent physical confrontation.

This hard reality can be traced to the profound sense of alienation from mainstream society and its institutions felt by many poor inner-city black people, particularly the young. The code of the streets is actually a cultural adaptation to a profound lack of faith in the police and the judicial system. The police are most often seen as representing the dominant white society and not caring to protect inner-city residents. When called, they may not respond, which is one reason many residents feel they must be prepared to take extraordinary measures to defend themselves and their loved ones against those who are inclined to aggression. Lack of police accountability has in fact been incorporated into the status system: The person who is believed capable of "taking care of himself" is accorded a certain deference, which translates into a sense of physical and psychological control. Thus the street code emerges where the influence of the police ends and personal responsibility for one's safety is felt to begin. Exacerbated by the proliferation of drugs and easy access to guns, this volatile situation results in the ability of the street-oriented minority (or those who effectively "go for bad") to dominate the public spaces.

Decent and Street Families

Although almost everyone in poor inner-city neighborhoods is struggling financially and therefore feels a certain distance from the rest of America, the decent and the street family in a real sense represent two poles of value orientation, two contrasting conceptual categories. The labels "decent" and "street," which the residents themselves use, amount to evaluative judgments that confer status on local residents. The labeling is often the result of a social contest among individuals and families of the neighborhood. Individuals of the two orientations often coexist in the same extended family. Decent residents judge themselves to be so while judging others to be of the street, and street individuals often present themselves as decent, drawing distinctions between themselves and other people. In addition, there is quite a bit of circumstantial behavior—that is, one person may at different times exhibit both decent and street orientations, depending on the circumstances. Although these designations result from so much social jockeying, there do exist concrete features that define each conceptual category.

Generally, so-called decent families tend to accept mainstream values more fully and attempt to instill them in their children. Whether married couples with children or single-parent (usually female) households, they are generally "working poor" and so tend to be better off financially than their street-oriented neighbors. They value hard work and self-reliance and are willing to sacrifice for their children. Because they have a certain amount of faith in mainstream society, they harbor hopes for a better future for their children, if not for themselves. Many of them go to church and take a strong interest in their children's schooling. Rather than dwelling on the real hardships and inequities facing them, many such decent people, particularly the increasing number of grandmothers raising grandchildren, see their difficult situation as a test from God and derive great support from their faith and from the church community.

Extremely aware of the problematic and often dangerous environment in which they reside, decent parents tend to be strict in their child-rearing practices, encouraging children to respect authority and walk a straight moral line. They have an almost obsessive concern about trouble of any kind and remind their children to be on the lookout for people and situations that might lead to it. At the same time, they are themselves polite and considerate of others, and teach their children to be the same way. At home, at work, and in church, they strive hard to maintain a positive mental attitude and a spirit of cooperation.

So-called street parents, in contrast, often show a lack of consideration for other people and have a rather superficial sense of family and community. Though they may love their children, many of them are unable to cope with the physical and emotional demands of parenthood and find it difficult to reconcile their needs with those of their children. These families, who are more fully invested in the code of the streets than the decent people are, may aggressively socialize their children into it in a normative way. They believe in the code and judge themselves and others according to its values. . . .

Campaigning for Respect

[The] realities of inner-city life are largely absorbed on the streets. At an early age, often even before they start school, children from street-oriented homes gravitate to the streets, where they "hang"—socialize with their peers. Children from these generally permissive homes have a great deal of latitude and are allowed to "rip and run" up and down the street. They often come home from school, put their books down, and go right back out the door. On school nights, eight- and nine-year-olds remain out until nine or ten o'clock (and teenagers typically come in whenever they want to). On the streets they play in groups that often become the source of their primary social bonds. Children from decent homes tend to be more carefully supervised and are thus likely to have curfews and to be taught how to stay out of trouble.

When decent and street kids come together, a kind of social shuffle occurs in which children have a chance to go either way. Tension builds as a child comes to realize that he must choose an orientation. The kind of home he comes from influences but does not determine the way he will ultimately turn out—although it is unlikely that a child from a thoroughly street-oriented family will easily absorb decent values on the streets. Youths who emerge from street-oriented families but develop a decency orientation almost always learn those values in another setting—in school, in a youth group, in church. Often it is the result of their involvement with a caring "old head" (adult role model).

In the street, through their play, children pour their individual life experiences into a common knowledge pool, affirming, confirming, and elaborating on what they have observed in the home and matching their skills against those of others. And they learn to fight. Even small children test one another, pushing and shoving, and are ready to hit other children over circumstances not to their liking. In turn, they are readily hit by other children, and the child who is toughest prevails. Thus the violent resolution of disputes, the hitting and cursing, gains social reinforcement. The child in effect is initiated into a system that is really a way of campaigning for respect.

In addition, younger children witness the disputes of older children, which are often resolved through cursing and abusive talk, if not aggression or outright violence. They see that one child succumbs to the greater physical and mental abilities of the other. They are also alert and attentive witnesses to the verbal and physical fights of adults, after which they compare notes and share their interpretations of the event. In almost every case the victor is the person who physically won the altercation, and this person often enjoys the esteem and respect of onlookers. These experiences reinforce the lessons the children have learned at home: Might makes right, and toughness is a virtue, while humility is not. In effect they learn the social meaning of fighting. When it is left virtually unchallenged, this understanding becomes an ever more important part of the child's working conception of the world. Over time the code of the streets becomes refined.

Those street-oriented adults with whom children come in contact—including mothers, fathers, brothers, sisters, boyfriends, cousins, neighbors, and friends—help them along in forming this understanding by verbalizing the messages they are getting through experience: "Watch your back." "Protect yourself." "Don't punk out." "If somebody messes with you, you got to pay them back." "If someone disses you, you got to straighten them out." Many parents actually impose sanctions if a child is not sufficiently aggressive. For example, if a child loses a fight and comes home upset, the parent might respond, "Don't you come in here crying that somebody beat you up; you better get back out there and whup his ass. I didn't raise no punks! Get back out there and whup his ass. If you don't whup his ass, I'll whup your ass when you come home." Thus the child obtains reinforcement for being tough and showing nerve.

While fighting, some children cry as though they are doing something they are ambivalent about. The fight may be against their wishes, yet they may feel constrained to fight or face the consequences—not just from peers but also from caretakers or parents, who may administer another beating if they back down. Some adults recall receiving such lessons from their own parents and justify repeating them to their children as a way to toughen them up. Looking capable of taking care of oneself as a form of self-defense is a dominant theme among both street-oriented and decent adults who worry about the safety of their children. There is thus at times a convergence in their child-rearing practices, although the rationales behind them may differ.

Self-Image Based on "Juice"

By the time they are teenagers, most youths have either internalized the code of the streets or at least learned the need to comport themselves in accordance with its rules, which chiefly have to do with interpersonal communication.

The code revolves around the presentation of self. Its basic requirement is the display of a certain predisposition to violence. Accordingly, one's bearing must send the unmistakable if sometimes subtle message to "the next person" in public that one is capable of violence and mayhem when the situation requires it, that one can take care of oneself. The nature of this communication is largely determined by the demands of the circumstances but can include facial expressions, gait, and verbal expressions—all of which are geared mainly to deterring aggression. Physical appearance, including clothes, jewelry, and grooming, also plays an important part in how a person is viewed; to be respected, it is important to have the right look.

Even so, there are no guarantees against challenges because there are always people around looking for a fight to increase their share of respect— or "juice," as it is sometimes called on the street. Moreover, if a person is assaulted, it is important, not only in the eyes of his opponent but also in the eyes of his "running buddies," for him to avenge himself. Otherwise, he risks being "tried" (challenged) or "moved on" by any number of others. To maintain his honor he must show he is not someone to be "messed with" or "dissed." In general, the person must "keep himself straight" by managing his position of respect among others; this involves in part his self-image, which is shaped by what he thinks others are thinking of him in relation to his peers.

Objects play an important and complicated role in establishing self-image. Jackets, sneakers, gold jewelry, reflect not just a person's taste, which tends to be tightly regulated among adolescents of all social classes, but also a willingness to possess things that may require defending. A boy wearing a fashionable, expensive jacket, for example, is vulnerable to attack by another who covets the jacket and either cannot afford to buy one or wants the added satisfaction of depriving someone else of his. However, if the boy forgoes the desirable jacket and wears one that isn't "hip," he runs the risk of being teased and possibly even assaulted as an unworthy person. To be allowed to hang with certain prestigious crowds, a boy must wear a different set of expensive clothes—sneakers and athletic suit—every day. Not to be able to do so might make him appear socially deficient. The youth comes to covet such items— especially when he sees easy prey wearing them.

In acquiring valued things, therefore, a person shores up his identity— but since it is an identity based on having things, it is highly precarious. This very precariousness gives a heightened sense of urgency to staying even with peers, with whom the person is actually competing. Young men and women who are able to command respect through their presentation of self—by allowing their possessions and their body language to speak for them—may not have to campaign for regard but may, rather, gain it by the force of their manner. Those who are unable to command respect in this way must actively campaign for it—and are thus particularly alive to slights.

One way of campaigning for status is by taking the possessions of others. In this context, seemingly ordinary objects can become trophies imbued with symbolic value that far exceeds their monetary worth. Possession of the trophy can symbolize the ability to violate somebody—to "get in his face," to take something of value from him, to "dis" him, and thus to enhance one's own worth by stealing someone else's. The trophy does not have to be something material. It can be another person's sense of honor, snatched away with a derogatory remark. It can be the outcome of a fight. It can be the imposition of a certain standard, such as a girl's getting herself recognized as the most beautiful. Material things, however, fit easily into the pattern. Sneakers, a pistol, even somebody else's girlfriend, can become a trophy. When a person can take something from another and then flaunt it, he gains a certain regard by being the owner, or the controller, of that thing. But this display of ownership can then provoke other people to challenge him. This game of who controls what is thus constantly being played out on inner-city streets, and the trophy—extrinsic or intrinsic, tangible or intangible—identifies the current winner.

An important aspect of this often violent give-and-take is its zero-sum quality. That is, the extent to which one person can raise himself up depends on his ability to put another person down. This underscores the alienation that permeates the inner-city ghetto community. There is a generalized sense that very little respect is to be had, and therefore everyone competes to get what affirmation he can of the little that is available. The craving for respect that results gives people thin skins. Shows of deference by others can be highly soothing, contributing to a sense of security, comfort, self-confidence, and self-respect. Transgressions by others which go unanswered diminish these feelings and are believed to encourage further transgressions. Hence one must be ever vigilant against the transgressions of others or even *appearing* as if transgressions will be tolerated. Among young people, whose sense of self-esteem is particularly vulnerable, there is an especially heightened concern with being disrespected. Many inner-city young men in particular crave respect to such a degree that they will risk their lives to attain and maintain it.

The issue of respect is thus closely tied to whether a person has an inclination to be violent, even as a victim. In the wider society, people may not feel required to retaliate physically after an attack, even though they are aware that they have been degraded or taken advantage of. They may feel a great need to defend themselves *during* an attack, or to behave in such a way as to deter aggression (middle-class people certainly can and do become victims of street-oriented youths), but they are much more likely than street-oriented people to feel that they can walk away from a possible altercation with their self-esteem intact. Some people may even have the strength of character to flee, without any thought that their self-respect or esteem will be diminished.

In impoverished inner-city black communities, however, particularly among young males and perhaps increasingly among females, such flight would be extremely difficult. To run away would likely leave one's self-esteem in tatters. Hence people often feel constrained not only to stand up and at least attempt to resist during an assault but also to "pay back"—to seek revenge—after a successful assault on their person. This may include going to get a weapon or even getting relatives involved. Their very identity and self-respect, their honor, is often intricately tied up with the way they perform on the streets during and after such encounters. This outlook reflects the circumscribed opportunities of the inner-city poor. Generally, people outside the ghetto have other ways of gaining status and regard, and thus do not feel so dependent on such physical displays.

By Trial of Manhood

On the street, among males these concerns about things and identity have come to be expressed in the concept of "manhood." Manhood in the inner city means taking the prerogatives of men with respect to strangers, other men, and women—being distinguished as a man. It implies physicality and a certain ruthlessness. Regard and respect are associated with this concept in large part because of its practical application: If others have little or no regard for a person's manhood, his very life and those of his loved ones could be in jeopardy. But there is a chicken-and-egg aspect to this situation: One's physical safety is more likely to be jeopardized in public *because* manhood is associated with respect. In other words, an existential link has been created between the idea of manhood and one's self-esteem, so that it has become hard to say which is primary. For many inner-city youths, manhood and respect are flip sides of the same coin; physical and psychological well-being are inseparable, and both require a sense of control, of being in charge.

The operating assumption is that a man, especially a real man, knows what other men know—the code of the streets. And if one is not a real man, one is somehow diminished as a person, and there are certain valued things one simply does not deserve. There is thus believed to be a certain justice to the code, since it is considered that everyone has the opportunity to know it. Implicit in this is that everybody is held responsible for being familiar with the code. If the victim of a mugging, for example, does not know the code and so responds "wrong," the perpetrator may feel justified even in killing him and may feel no remorse. He may think, "Too bad, but it's his fault. He should have known better."

So when a person ventures outside, he must adopt the code—a kind of shield, really—to prevent others from "messing with" him. In these circumstances it is easy for people to think they are being tried or tested by others even when this is not the case. For it is sensed that something extremely valuable is at stake in every interaction, and people are encouraged to rise to the occasion, particularly with strangers. For people who are unfamiliar with the code—generally, people who live outside the inner city—the concern with respect in the most ordinary interactions can be frightening and incomprehensible. But for those who are invested in the code, the clear object of their demeanor is to discourage strangers from even thinking about testing their manhood. And the sense of power that attends the ability to deter others can be alluring even to those who know the code without being heavily invested in it—the decent inner-city youths. Thus a boy who has been leading a basically decent life can, in trying circumstances, suddenly resort to deadly force.

Central to the issue of manhood is the widespread belief that one of the most effective ways of gaining respect is to manifest "nerve." Nerve is shown when one takes another person's possessions (the more valuable the better), "messes with" someone's woman, throws the first punch, "gets in someone's face," or pulls a trigger. Its proper display helps on the spot to check others who would violate one's person and also helps to build a reputation that works to prevent future challenges. But since such a show of nerve is a forceful expression of disrespect toward the person on the receiving end, the victim may be greatly offended and seek to retaliate with equal or greater force. A display of nerve, therefore, can easily provoke a life-threatening response, and the background knowledge of that possibility has often been incorporated into the concept of nerve.

True nerve exposes a lack of fear of dying. Many feel that it is acceptable to risk dying over the principle of respect. In fact, among the hard-core street-oriented, the clear risk of violent death may be preferable to being "dissed" by another. The youths who have internalized this attitude and convincingly display it in their public bearing are among the most threatening people of all, for it is commonly assumed that they fear no man. As the people of the community say, "They are the baddest dudes on the street." They often lead an existential life that may acquire meaning only when they are faced with the possibility of imminent death. Not to be afraid to die is by implication to have few compunctions about taking another's life. Not to be afraid to die is the quid pro quo of being able to take somebody else's life— for the right reasons, if the situation demands it. When others believe this is one's position, it gives one a real sense of power on the streets. Such credibility is what many inner-city youths strive to achieve, whether they are decent or street-oriented, both because of its practical defensive value and because of the positive way it makes them feel about themselves. The difference between the decent and the street-oriented youth is often that the decent youth makes a conscious decision to appear tough and manly; in another setting—with teachers, say, or at his part-time job—he can be polite and deferential. The street-oriented youth, on the other hand, has made the concept of manhood a part of his very identity; he has difficulty manipulating it—it often controls him.

Girls and Boys

Increasingly, teenage girls are mimicking the boys and trying to have their own version of "manhood." Their goal is the same—to get respect, to be recognized as capable of setting or maintaining a certain standard. They try to achieve this end in the ways that have been established by the boys, including posturing, abusive language, and the use of violence to resolve disputes, but the issues for the girls are different. Although conflicts over turf and status exist among the girls, the majority of disputes seem rooted in assessments of beauty (which girl in a group is "the cutest"), competition over boyfriends, and attempts to regulate other people's knowledge of and opinions about a girl's behavior or that of someone close to her, especially her mother.

A major cause of conflicts among girls is "he say, she say." This practice begins in the early school years and continues through high school. It occurs when "people," particularly girls, talk about others, thus putting their "business in the streets." Usually one girl will say something negative about another in the group, most often behind the person's back. The remark will then get back to the person talked about. She may retaliate or her friends may feel required to "take up for" her. In essence this is a form of group gossiping in which individuals are negatively assessed and evaluated. As with much gossip, the things said may or may not be true, but the point is that such imputations can cast aspersions on a person's good name. The accused is required to defend herself against the slander, which can result in arguments and fights, often over little of real substance. Here again is the problem of low self-esteem, which encourages youngsters to be highly sensitive to slights and to be vulnerable to feeling easily "dissed." To avenge the dissing, a fight is usually necessary.

Because boys are believed to control violence, girls tend to defer to them in situations of conflict. Often if a girl is attacked or feels slighted, she will get a brother, uncle, or cousin to do her fighting for her. Increasingly, however, girls are doing their own fighting and are even asking their male relatives to teach them how to fight. Some girls form groups that attack other girls or take things from them. A hard-core segment of inner-city girls inclined toward violence seems to be developing. As one 13-year-old girl in a detention center for youths who have committed violent acts told me, "To get people to leave you alone, you gotta fight. Talking don't always get you out of stuff." One major difference between girls and boys: Girls rarely use guns. Their fights are therefore not life-or-death struggles. Girls are not often willing to put their lives on the line for "manhood." The ultimate form of respect on the male-dominated inner-city street is thus reserved for men.

"Going for Bad"

In the most fearsome youths such a cavalier attitude toward death grows out of a very limited view of life. Many are uncertain about how long they are going to live and believe they could die violently at any time. They accept this fate; they live on the edge. Their manner conveys the message that nothing intimidates them; whatever turn the encounter takes, they maintain their attack—rather like a pit bull, whose spirit many such boys admire. The demonstration of such tenacity "shows heart" and earns their respect.

This fearlessness has implications for law enforcement. Many street-oriented boys are much more concerned about the threat of "justice" at the hands of a peer than at the hands of the police. Moreover, many feel not only that they have little to lose by going to prison but that they have something to gain. The toughening-up one experiences in prison can actually enhance one's reputation on the streets. Hence the system loses influence over the hard core who are without jobs, with little perceptible stake in the system. If mainstream society has done nothing *for* them, they counter by making sure it can do nothing *to* them.

At the same time, however, a competing view maintains that the true nerve consists in backing down, walking away from a fight, and going on with one's business. One fights only in self-defense. This view emerges from the decent philosophy that life is precious, and it is an important part of the socialization process common in decent homes. It discourages violence as the primary means of resolving disputes and encourages youngsters to accept nonviolence and talk as confrontational strategies. But "if the deal goes down," self-defense is greatly encouraged. When there is enough positive support for this orientation, either in the home or among one's peers, then nonviolence has a chance to prevail. But it prevails at the cost of relinquishing a claim to being bad and tough, and therefore sets a young person up as at the very least alienated from street-oriented peers and quite possibly a target of derision or even violence.

Although the nonviolent orientation rarely overcomes the impulse to strike back in an encounter, it does introduce a certain confusion and so can prompt a measure of soul-searching, or even profound ambivalence. Did the person back down with his respect intact or did he back down only to be judged a "punk"—a person lacking manhood? Should he or she have acted? Should he or she have hit the other person in the mouth? These questions beset many young men and women during public confrontations. What is the "right" thing to do? In the quest for honor, respect, and local status—which few young people are uninterested in—common sense most often prevails, which leads many to opt for the tough approach, enacting their own particular versions of the display of nerve. The presentation of oneself as rough and tough is very often quite acceptable until one is tested. And then that presentation may help the person pass the test, because it will cause fewer questions to be asked about what he did and why. It is hard for a person to explain why he lost the fight or why he backed down. Hence many will strive to appear to "go for bad," while hoping they will never be tested. But when they are tested, the outcome of the situation may quickly be out of their hands, as they become wrapped up in the circumstances of the moment.

An Oppositional Culture

The attitudes of the wider society are deeply implicated in the code of the streets. Most people in inner-city communities are not totally invested in the code, but the significant minority of hard-core street youths who are have to maintain the code in order to establish reputations, because they have—or feel they have—few other ways to assert themselves. For these young people the standards of the street code are the only game in town. The extent to which some children—particularly those who through upbringing have become most alienated and those lacking in strong and conventional social support—experience, feel, and internalize racist rejection and contempt from mainstream society may strongly encourage them to express contempt for the more conventional society in turn. In dealing with this contempt and rejection, some youngsters will consciously invest themselves and their considerable mental resources in what amounts to an oppositional culture to preserve themselves and their self-respect. Once they do, any respect they might be able to garner in the wider system pales in comparison with the respect available in the local system; thus they often lose interest in even attempting to negotiate the mainstream system.

At the same time, many less alienated young blacks have assumed a street-oriented demeanor as a way of expressing their blackness while really embracing a much more moderate way of life; they, too want a nonviolent setting in which to live and raise a family. These decent people are trying hard to be part of the mainstream culture, but the racism, real and perceived, that they encounter helps to legitimate the oppositional culture. And so on occasion they adopt street behavior. In fact, depending on the demands of the situation, many people in the community slip back and forth between decent and street behavior.

A vicious cycle has thus been formed. The hopelessness and alienation many young inner-city black men and women feel, largely as a result of endemic joblessness and persistent racism, fuels the violence they engage in. This violence serves to confirm the negative feelings many whites and some middle-class blacks harbor toward the ghetto poor, further legitimating the oppositional culture and the code of the streets in the eyes of many poor young blacks. Unless this cycle is broken, attitudes on both sides will become increasingly entrenched, and the violence, which claims victims black and white, poor and affluent, will only escalate.

9

WARRIOR DREAMS
Violence and Manhood in Post-Vietnam America

J. WILLIAM GIBSON

Sociologists are interested in how culture limits our free choice and shapes social interaction. Because each of us is born into a particular culture that has certain norms and values, our personal values and life expectations are profoundly influenced by our culture. For example, what are the values of American culture? Many scholars agree that dominant U.S. values are achievement, Judeo-Christian morals, material comfort, patriotism, and individualism. Contrast these dominant culture values with those expressed by men who are active in the paramilitary culture. What are the values and expected behaviors of men involved in paramilitary groups? J. William Gibson, a professor of sociology at California State University, Long Beach, has spent years studying the Vietnam War and the rise of paramilitary groups in its aftermath. The selection below takes us inside this subculture to reveal the beliefs, practices, and rituals of men who join paramilitary groups.

We couldn't see them, but we could hear their bugles sound the call. The Communist battalions were organizing for a predawn assault. Captain Kokalis smiled wickedly; he'd been through this before. A "human wave" assault composed of thousands of enemy soldiers was headed our way. The captain ordered the remaining soldiers in his command to check their .30- and .50-caliber machine guns. Earlier in the night, the demolitions squad attached to our unit had planted mines and explosive charges for hundreds of meters in front of our position.

And then it began. At a thousand meters, the soldiers emerged screaming from the gray-blue fog. "Fire!" yelled Captain Kokalis. The gun crews opened up with short bursts of three to seven rounds; their bullets struck meat. Everywhere I could see, clusters of Communist troops were falling by the second. But the wave still surged forward. At 500 meters, Kokalis passed the word to his gunners to increase their rate of fire to longer strings of 10 to

From *Warrior Dreams: Violence and Manhood in Post-Vietnam America*, pp. 3–13. Copyright © 1994 by James William Gibson. Reprinted with the permission of Hill and Wang, a division of Farrar, Straus & Giroux, Inc.

20 rounds. Sergeant Donovan, the demolitions squad leader, began to reap the harvest from the night's planting. Massive explosions ripped through the Communist troops. Fire and smoke blasted into the dawn sky. It was as if the human wave had hit a submerged reef; as the dying fell, wide gaps appeared in the line where casualties could no longer be replaced.

But still they kept coming, hundreds of men, each and every one bent on taking the American position and wiping us out. As the Communists reached 100 meters, Kokalis gave one more command. Every machine gun in our platoon went to its maximum rate of sustained full-automatic frenzy, sounding like chain saws that just keep cutting and cutting.

And then it was over. The attack subsided into a flat sea of Communist dead. No Americans had been killed or wounded. We were happy to be alive, proud of our victory. We only wondered if our ears would ever stop ringing and if we would ever again smell anything other than the bittersweet aroma of burning gunpowder. . . .

Although an astonishing triumph was achieved that day, no historian will ever find a record of this battle in the hundreds of volumes and thousands of official reports written about the Korean or Vietnam war. Nor was the blood spilt part of a covert operation in Afghanistan or some unnamed country in Africa, Asia, or Latin America.

No, this battle was fought inside the United States, a few miles north of Las Vegas, in September 1986. It was a purely *imaginary* battle, a dream of victory staged as part of the *Soldier of Fortune* [*SOF*] magazine's annual convention. The audience of several hundred men, women, and children, together with reporters and a camera crew from CBS News, sat in bleachers behind half a dozen medium and heavy machine guns owned by civilians. Peter G. Kokalis, *SOF*'s firearms editor, set the scene for the audience and asked them to imagine that the sandy brushland of the Desert Sportsman Rifle and Pistol Club was really a killing zone for incoming Communist troops. Kokalis was a seasoned storyteller; he'd given this performance before. When the fantasy battle was over, the fans went wild with applause. Kokalis picked up a microphone, praised Donovan (another *SOF* staff member)—"He was responsible for that whole damn Communist bunker that went up"—and told the parents in the audience to buy "claymores [anti-personnel land mines] and other good shit for the kids." A marvelous actor who knew what his audience wanted, Kokalis sneered, "Did you get that, CBS, on your videocam? Screw you knee-jerk liberals."[1]

The shoot-out and victory over Communist forces conducted at the Desert Sportsman Rifle and Pistol Club was but one battle in a cultural or imaginary "New War" that had been going on since the late 1960s and early 1970s. The bitter controversies surrounding the Vietnam War had discredited the old American ideal of the masculine warrior hero for much of the public. But in 1971, when Clint Eastwood made the transition from playing cowboys in old *Rawhide* reruns and spaghetti westerns to portraying San Francisco police detective Harry Callahan in *Dirty Harry*, the warrior hero returned in full force.

His backup arrived in 1974 when Charles Bronson appeared in *Death Wish,* the story of a mild-mannered, middle-aged architect in New York City who, after his wife is murdered and his daughter is raped and driven insane, finds new meaning in life through an endless war of revenge against street punks.

In the 1980s, Rambo and his friends made their assault. The experience of John Rambo, a former Green Beret, was the paradigmatic story of the decade. In *First Blood* (1982), he burns down a small Oregon town while suffering hallucinatory flashbacks to his service in Vietnam. Three years later, in *Rambo: First Blood, Part 2,* he is taken off a prison chain gang by his former commanding officer in Vietnam and asked to perform a special reconnaissance mission to find suspected American POWs in Laos, in exchange for a presidential pardon. His only question: "Do we get to win this time?" And indeed, Rambo does win. Betrayed by the CIA bureaucrat in charge of the mission, Rambo fights the Russians and Vietnamese by himself and brings the POWs back home.

Hundreds of similar films celebrating the victory of good men over bad through armed combat were made during the late 1970s and 1980s. Many were directed by major Hollywood directors and starred well-known actors. Elaborate special effects and exotic film locations added tens of millions to production costs. And for every large-budget film, there were scores of cheaper formula films employing lesser-known actors and production crews. Often these "action-adventure" films had only brief theatrical releases in major markets. Instead, they made their money in smaller cities and towns, in sales to Europe and the Third World, and most of all, in the sale of video-cassettes to rental stores. Movie producers could even turn a profit on "video-only" releases; action-adventure films were the largest category of video rentals in the 1980s.

At the same time, Tom Clancy became a star in the publishing world. His book *The Hunt for Red October* (1984) told the story of the Soviet Navy's most erudite submarine commander, Captain Markus Ramius, and his effort to defect to the United States with the Soviets' premier missile-firing submarine. *Red Storm Rising* (1986) followed, an epic of World War III framed as a high-tech conventional war against the Soviet Union. Clancy's novels all featured Jack Ryan, Ph.D., a former Marine captain in Vietnam turned academic naval historian who returns to duty as a CIA analyst and repeatedly stumbles into life-and-death struggles in which the fate of the world rests on his prowess. All were best-sellers.

President Reagan, Secretary of the Navy John Lehman, and many other high officials applauded Clancy and his hero. Soon the author had a multi-million-dollar contract for a whole series of novels, movie deals with Paramount, and a new part-time job as a foreign-policy expert writing op-ed pieces for the *Washington Post,* the *Los Angeles Times,* and other influential newspapers around the country. His success motivated dozens of authors, mostly active-duty or retired military men, to take up the genre. The "techno-thriller" was born.

At a slightly lower level in the literary establishment, the same publishing houses that marketed women's romance novels on grocery and drugstore paperback racks rapidly expanded their collections of pulp fiction for men. Most were written like hard-core pornography, except that inch-by-inch descriptions of penises entering vaginas were replaced by equally graphic portrayals of bullets, grenade fragments, and knives shredding flesh: "He tried to grab the handle of the commando knife, but the terrorist pushed down on the butt, raised the point and yanked the knife upward through the muscle tissue and guts. It ripped intestines, spilling blood and gore."[2] A minimum of 20 but sometimes as many as 120 such graphically described killings occurred in each 200-to-250-page paperback. Most series came out four times a year with domestic print runs of 60,000 to 250,000 copies. More than a dozen different comic books with titles like *Punisher*, *Vigilante*, and *Scout* followed suit with clones of the novels.

Along with the novels and comics came a new kind of periodical which replaced the older adventure magazines for men, such as *True* and *Argosy*, that had folded in the 1960s. Robert K. Brown, a former captain in the U.S. Army Special Forces during the Vietnam War, founded *Soldier of Fortune: The Journal of Professional Adventurers* in the spring of 1975, just before the fall of Saigon. *SOF*'s position was explicit from the start: The independent warrior must step in to fill the dangerous void created by the American failure in Vietnam. By the mid-1980s *SOF* was reaching 35,000 subscribers, had newsstand sales of another 150,000, and was being passed around to at least twice as many readers.[3]

Half a dozen new warrior magazines soon entered the market. Some, like *Eagle*, *New Breed*, and *Gung-Ho*, tried to copy the *SOF* editorial package—a strategy that ultimately failed. But most developed their own particular pitch. *Combat Handguns* focused on pistols for would-be gunfighters. *American Survival Guide* advertised and reviewed everything needed for "the good life" after the end of civilization (except birth control devices—too many Mormon subscribers, the editor said), while *S.W.A.T.* found its way to men who idealized these elite police teams and who were worried about home defense against "multiple intruders."

During the same period, sales of military weapons took off. Colt offered two semiautomatic versions of the M16 used by U.S. soldiers in Vietnam (a full-size rifle and a shorter-barreled carbine with collapsible stock). European armories exported their latest products, accompanied by sophisticated advertising campaigns in *SOF* and the more mainstream gun magazines. Israeli Defense Industries put a longer, 16-inch barrel on the Uzi submachine gun (to make it legal) and sold it as a semiautomatic carbine. And the Communist countries of Eastern Europe, together with the People's Republic of China, jumped into the market with the devil's own favorite hardware, the infamous AK47. The AK sold in the United States was the semiautomatic version of the assault rifle used by the victorious Communists in Vietnam and by all kinds of radical movements and terrorist organizations around the world. It retailed for $300 to $400, half the price of an Uzi or an AR-15; complete with three 30-round magazines, cleaning kit, and bayonet, it was truly a bargain.

To feed these hungry guns, munitions manufacturing packaged new "generic" brands of military ammo at discount prices, often selling them in cases of 500 or 1,000 rounds. New lines of aftermarket accessories offered parts for full-automatic conversions, improved flash-hiders, scopes, folding stocks, and scores of other goodies. In 1989, the U.S. Bureau of Alcohol, Tobacco and Firearms (ATF) estimated that two to three million military-style rifles had been sold in this country since the Vietnam War. The Bureau released these figures in response to the public outcry over a series of mass murders committed by psychotics armed with assault rifles.

But the Bureau's statistics tell only part of the story. In less than two decades, millions of American men had purchased combat rifles, pistols, and shotguns and began training to fight their own personal wars. Elite combat shooting schools teaching the most modern techniques and often costing $500 to over $1,000 in tuition alone were attended not only by soldiers and police but by increasing numbers of civilians as well. Hundreds of new indoor pistol-shooting ranges opened for business in old warehouses and shopping malls around the country, locations ideal for city dwellers and suburbanites.

A new game of "tag" blurred the line between play and actual violence: men got the opportunity to hunt and shoot other men without killing them or risking death themselves. The National Survival Game was invented in 1981 by two old friends, one a screenwriter for the weight-lifting sagas that gave Arnold Schwarzenegger his first starring roles, and the other a former member of the Army's Long Range Reconnaissance Patrol (LRRP) in Vietnam.[4] Later called paintball because it utilized guns firing balls of watercolor paint, by 1987 the game was being played by at least fifty thousand people (mostly men) each weekend on both outdoor and indoor battlefields scattered across the nation. Players wore hard-plastic face masks intended to resemble those of ancient tribal warriors and dressed from head to toe in camouflage clothes imported by specialty stores from military outfitters around the world. The object of the game was to capture the opposing team's flag, inflicting the highest possible body count along the way.

One major park out in the Mojave Desert 70 miles southeast of Los Angeles was named Sat Cong Village. *Sat Cong* is a slang Vietnamese phrase meaning "Kill Communists" that had been popularized by the CIA as part of its psychological-warfare program. Sat Cong Village employed an attractive Asian woman to rent the guns, sell the paintballs, and collect the $20 entrance fee. Players had their choice of playing fields: Vietnam, Cambodia, or Nicaragua. On the Nicaragua field, the owner built a full-size facsimile of the crashed C-47 cargo plane contracted by Lieutenant Colonel Oliver North to supply the contras. The scene even had three parachutes hanging from trees; the only thing missing was the sole survivor of the crash, Eugene Hasenfus.

The 1980s, then, saw the emergence of a highly energized culture of war and the warrior. For all its varied manifestations, a few common features stood out. The New War culture was not so much military as paramilitary. The new warrior hero was only occasionally portrayed as a member of a conventional military or law enforcement unit; typically, he fought alone or with a small, elite group of fellow warriors. Moreover, by separating the warrior from his traditional state-sanctioned occupations—policeman or soldier—the New War culture presented the warrior role as the ideal identity for *all* men. Bankers, professors, factory workers, and postal clerks could all transcend their regular stations in life and prepare for heroic battle against the enemies of society.

To many people, this new fascination with warriors and weapons seemed a terribly bad joke. The major newspapers and magazines that arbitrate what is to be taken seriously in American society scoffed at the attempts to resurrect the warrior hero. Movie critics were particularly disdainful of Stallone's Rambo films. *Rambo: First Blood, Part 2* was called "narcissistic jingoism" by *The New Yorker* and "hare-brained" by the *Wall Street Journal.* The *Washington Post* even intoned that "Sly's body looks fine. Now can't you come up with a workout for his soul?"

But in dismissing Rambo so quickly and contemptuously, commentators failed to notice the true significance of the emerging paramilitary culture. They missed the fact that quite a few people were not writing Rambo off as a complete joke; behind the Indian bandanna, necklace, and bulging muscles, a new culture hero affirmed such traditional American values as self-reliance, honesty, courage, and concern for fellow citizens. Rambo was a worker and a former enlisted man, not a smooth-talking professional. That so many seemingly well-to-do, sophisticated liberals hated him for both his politics and his uncouthness only added to his glory. Further, in their emphasis on Stallone's clownishness the commentators failed to see not only how widespread paramilitary culture had become but also its relation to the historical moment in which it arose.

Indeed, paramilitary culture can be understood only when it is placed in relation to the Vietnam War. America's failure to win that war was a truly profound blow. The nation's long, proud tradition of military victories, from the Revolutionary War through the century-long battles against the Indians to World Wars I and II, had finally come to an end. Politically, the defeat in Vietnam meant that the post–World War II era of overwhelming American political and military power in international affairs, the era that in 1945 *Time* magazine publisher Henry Luce had prophesied would be the "American Century," was over after only 30 years. No longer could U.S. diplomacy wield the big stick of military intervention as a ready threat—a significant part of the American public would no longer support such interventions, and the rest of the world knew it.

Moreover, besides eroding U.S. influence internationally, the defeat had subtle but serious effects on the American psyche. America has always celebrated war and the warrior. Our long, unbroken record of military victories has been crucially important both to the national identity and to the personal identity of many Americans—particularly men. The historian Richard Slotkin locates a primary "cultural archetype" of the nation in the story of a heroic warrior whose victories over the enemy symbolically affirm the country's fundamental goodness and power; we win our wars because, morally, we deserve to win. Clearly, the archetypical pattern Slotkin calls "regeneration through violence" was broken with the defeat in Vietnam.[5] The result was a massive disjunction in American culture, a crisis of self-image: If Americans were no longer winners, then who were they?

This disruption of cultural identity was amplified by other social transformations. During the 1960s, the civil rights and ethnic pride movements won many victories in their challenges to racial oppression. Also, during the 1970s and 1980s, the United States experienced massive waves of immigration from Mexico, Central America, Vietnam, Cambodia, Korea, and Taiwan. Whites, no longer secure in their power abroad, also lost their unquestionable dominance at home; for the first time, many began to feel that they too were just another hyphenated ethnic group, the Anglo-Americans.

Extraordinary economic changes also marked the 1970s and 1980s. U.S. manufacturing strength declined substantially; staggering trade deficits with other countries and the chronic federal budget deficits shifted the United States from creditor to debtor nation. The post–World War II American Dream—which promised a combination of technological progress and social reforms, together with high employment rates, rising wages, widespread home ownership, and ever increasing consumer options—no longer seemed a likely prospect for the great majority. At the same time, the rise in crime rates, particularly because of drug abuse and its accompanying violence, made people feel more powerless than ever.

While the public world dominated by men seemed to come apart, the private world of family life also felt the shocks. The feminist movement challenged formerly exclusive male domains, not only in the labor market and in many areas of political and social life but in the home as well. Customary male behavior was no longer acceptable in either private relationships or public policy. Feminism was widely experienced by men as a profound threat to their identity. Men had to change, but to what? No one knew for sure what a "good man" was anymore.

It is hardly surprising, then, that American men—lacking confidence in the government and the economy, troubled by the changing relations between the sexes, uncertain of their identity or their future—began to *dream,* to fantasize about the powers and features of another kind of man who could retake and reorder the world. And the hero of all these dreams was the paramilitary warrior. In the New War he fights the battles of Vietnam a thousand times, each time winning decisively. Terrorists and drug dealers are blasted into oblivion. Illegal aliens inside the United States and the hordes of non-whites in the Third World are returned by force to their proper place. Women are revealed as dangerous temptresses who have to be mastered, avoided, or terminated.

Obviously these dreams represented a flight from the present and a rejection and denial of events of the preceding 20 years. But they also indicated a more profound and severe distress. The whole modern world was damned as unacceptable. Unable to find a rational way to face the tasks of rebuilding society and reinventing themselves, men instead sought refuge in myths from both America's frontier past and ancient times. Indeed, the fundamental narratives that shape paramilitary culture and its New War fantasies are often nothing but reinterpretations or reworkings of archaic warrior myths.

In ancient societies, the most important stories a people told about themselves concerned how the physical universe came into existence, how their ancestors first came to live in this universe, and how the gods, the universe, and society were related to one another. These cosmogonic, or creation, myths frequently posit a violent conflict between the good forces of order and the evil forces dedicated to the perpetuation of primordial chaos.[6] After the war in which the gods defeat the evil ones, they establish the "sacred order," in which all of the society's most important values are fully embodied. Some creation myths focus primarily on the sacred order and on the deeds of the gods and goddesses in paradise. Other myths, however, focus on the battles between the heroes and villains that lead up to the founding.[7] In these myths it is war and the warrior that are most sacred. American paramilitary culture borrows from both kinds of stories, but mostly from this second, more violent, type.

In either case, the presence, if not the outright predominance, of archaic male myths at the moment of crisis indicates just how far American men jumped psychically when faced with the declining power of their identities and organizations. The always-precarious balance in modern society between secular institutions and ways of thinking on the one hand and older patterns of belief informed by myth and ritual on the other tilted decisively in the direction of myth. The crisis revealed that at some deep, unconscious level these ancient male creation myths live on in the psyche of many men and that the images and tales from this mythic world of warriors and war still shape men's fantasies about who they are as men, their commitments to each other and to women, and their relationships to society and the state.

———

The imaginary New War that men created is a coherent mythical universe, formed by the repetition of key features in thousands of novels, magazines, films, and advertisements. As the sociologist Will Wright points out, the component elements of myth work to create a common "theoretical idea of a social order."[8] These New War stories about heroic warriors and their evil adversaries are ways of arguing about what is wrong with the modern world and what needs to be done to make society well again. . . .

War games took these fantasies one step further and allowed men to act on their desires in paramilitary games and theme parks that one would-be warrior described as "better than Disneyland." Here, away from the ordinary routines of world and family life, men could meet, mingle, and share their warrior dreams. Three major types of imaginary war zones developed: the National Survival Game, or paintball; the annual *Soldier of Fortune* convention in Las Vegas; and combat shooting schools and firing ranges. In these special environments, the gods of war could be summoned for games played along the edges of violence.

Finally, the imaginary New War turned into the real nightmares of "War Zone America." Since the 1970s, a number of racist groups, religious sects, mercenaries, and madmen have literally lived their own versions of the New War. At the same time, as hundreds of thousands of military-style rifles have entered the domestic gun market and become the weapon of choice for some killers, the gun-control debate has escalated to a new level. And not surprisingly, the myths of the New War have profoundly influenced several presidential administrations, affecting both those leaders who make military policy decisions and the lower-ranking personnel who carry out covert and overt operations.

Only at the surface level, then, has paramilitary culture been merely a matter of the "stupid" movies and novels consumed by the great unwashed lower-middle and working classes, or of the murderous actions of a few demented, "deviant" men. In truth, there is nothing superficial or marginal about the New War that has been fought in American popular culture since the 1970s. It is a war about basics: power, sex, race, and alienation. Contrary to the *Washington Post* review, Rambo was no shallow muscle man but the emblem of a movement that at the very least wanted to reverse the previous 20 years of American history and take back all the symbolic territory that had been lost. The vast proliferation of warrior fantasies represented an attempt to reaffirm the national identity. But it was also a larger volcanic upheaval of archaic myths, an outcropping whose entire structural formation plunges into deep historical, cultural, and psychological territories. These territories have kept us chained to war as a way of life; they have infused individual men, national political and military leaders, and society with a deep attraction to both imaginary and real violence. This terrain must be explored, mapped, and understood if it is ever to be transformed.

ENDNOTES

[1] Peter G. Kokalis, speaking at the *Soldier of Fortune* firepower demonstration at the Desert Sportsman Rifle and Pistol Club, Las Vegas, Nevada, September 20, 1986.

[2] Gar Wilson, *The Fury Bombs,* vol. 5 of *Phoenix Force* (Toronto: Worldwide Library, 1983), p. 30.

[3] *SOF* regularly hired the firm of Starch, Inra, Hopper to study their readership. A condensed version of their 1986 report, from which these figures were taken, was made available to the press at the September 1986 *SOF* convention in Las Vegas.

[4]Lionel Atwill, *Survival Game: Airgun National Manual* (New London, NH: The National Survival Game, Inc., 1987), pp. 22–30.

[5]Richard Slotkin, *Regeneration through Violence: The Mythology of the American Frontier, 1660–1860* (Middletown, CT: Wesleyan University Press, 1973).

[6]Mircea Eliade, *Myth and Reality*, trans. Willard R. Trask (New York: Harper & Row, 1963).

[7]Richard Stivers, *Evil in Modern Myth and Ritual* (Athens: University of Georgia Press, 1982).

[8]Will Wright, *Sixguns and Society: A Structural Study of the Western* (Berkeley: University of California Press, 1975), p. 20.

10

LOVELY HULA HANDS
Corporate Tourism and the Prostitution of Hawaiian Culture

HAUNANI-KAY TRASK

Many U.S. racial-ethnic groups, including Native Americans, Latinos, and African Americans, have experienced cultural exploitation. Exploitation occurs when aspects of a subculture, such as its beliefs, rituals, and social customs, are commodified and marketed without the cultural group's permission. This selection by Haunani-Kay Trask explores the cultural commodification and exploitation of Hawaiian culture. Trask, a descendant from the Pi'ilani line of Maui and the Kahakumakaliua line of Kaua'i, is a professor of Hawaiian studies at the University of Hawai'i at Manoa. In this excerpt, taken from her 1993 book, *From a Native Daughter: Colonialism and Sovereignty in Hawai'i*, Trask argues that several aspects of Polynesian and Hawaiian cultures, including their language, dress, and dance forms, have been marketed as products for the mass consumption of tourists.

I am certain that most, if not all, Americans have heard of Hawai'i and have wished, at some time in their lives, to visit my native land. But I doubt that the history of how Hawai'i came to be territorially incorporated, and economically, politically, and culturally subordinated to the United States is

From *From a Native Daughter: Colonialism and Sovereignty in Hawai'i*, pp. 179–81, 183–84, 184–87. Reprinted with the permission of Common Courage Press.

known to most Americans. Nor is it common knowledge that Hawaiians have been struggling for over 20 years to achieve a land base and some form of political sovereignty on the same level as American Indians. Finally, I would imagine that most Americans could not place Hawai'i or any other Pacific island on a map of the Pacific. But despite all this appalling ignorance, five million Americans will vacation in my homeland this year *and* the next, and so on into the foreseeable capitalist future. Such are the intended privileges of the so-called American standard of living: ignorance of, and yet power over, one's relations to native peoples.

Thanks to postwar American imperialism, the ideology that the United States has no overseas colonies and is, in fact, the champion of self-determination the world over holds no greater sway than in the United States itself. To most Americans, then, Hawai'i is *theirs:* to use, to take, and, above all, to fantasize about long after the experience.

Just five hours away by plane from California, Hawai'i is a thousand light years away in fantasy. Mostly a state of mind, Hawai'i is the image of escape from the rawness and violence of daily American life. Hawai'i—the word, the vision, the sound in the mind—is the fragrance and feel of soft kindness. Above all, Hawai'i is "she," the Western image of the native "female" in her magical allure. And if luck prevails, some of "her" will rub off on you, the visitor.

This fictional Hawai'i comes out of the depths of Western sexual sickness which demands a dark, sin-free native for instant gratification between imperialist wars. The attraction of Hawai'i is stimulated by slick Hollywood movies, saccharine Andy Williams music, and the constant psychological deprivations of maniacal American life. Tourists flock to my native land for escape, but they are escaping into a state of mind while participating in the destruction of a host people in a native place.

To Hawaiians, daily life is neither soft nor kind. In fact, the political, economic, and cultural reality for most Hawaiians is hard, ugly, and cruel.

In Hawai'i, the destruction of our land and the prostitution of our culture are planned and executed by multinational corporations (both foreign-based and Hawai'i-based), by huge landowners (like the missionary-descended Castle and Cook—of Dole Pineapple fame—and others) and by collaborationist state and county governments. The ideological gloss that claims tourism to be our economic savior and the "natural" result of Hawaiian culture is manufactured by ad agencies (like the state supported Hawai'i Visitors' Bureau) and tour companies (many of which are owned by the airlines), and spewed out to the public through complicitous cultural engines like film, television and radio, and the daily newspapers. As for the local labor unions, both rank and file and management clamor for more tourists while the construction industry lobbies incessantly for larger resorts. . . .

My use of the word *tourism* in the Hawai'i context refers to a mass-based, corporately controlled industry that is both vertically and horizontally integrated such that one multinational corporation owns an airline, the tour buses that transport tourists to the corporation-owned hotel where they eat in a corporation-owned restaurant, play golf and "experience" Hawai'i on corporation-owned recreation areas, and eventually consider buying a second home built on corporation land. Profits, in this case, are mostly repatriated back to the home country. In Hawai'i, these "home" countries are Japan, Taiwan, Hong Kong, Canada, Australia, and the United States. . . .

With this as a background on tourism, I want to move now into the area of cultural prostitution. "Prostitution" in this context refers to the entire institution which defines a woman (and by extension the "female") as an object of degraded and victimized sexual value for use and exchange through the medium of money. The "prostitute" is then a woman who sells her sexual capacities and is seen, thereby, to possess and reproduce them at will, that is, by her very "nature." The prostitute and the institution which creates and maintains her are, of course, of patriarchal origin. The pimp is the conduit of exchange, managing the commodity that is the prostitute while acting as the guard at the entry and exit gates, making sure the prostitute behaves as a prostitute by fulfilling her sexual–economic functions. The victims participate in their victimization with enormous ranges of feeling, including resistance and complicity, but the force and continuity of the institution are shaped by men.

There is much more to prostitution than my sketch reveals but this must suffice for I am interested in using the largest sense of this term as a metaphor in understanding what has happened to Hawaiian culture. My purpose is not to exact detail or fashion a model but to convey the utter degradation of our culture and our people under corporate tourism by employing "prostitution" as an analytic category.

Finally, I have chosen four areas of Hawaiian culture to examine: our homeland, or *one hānau* that is Hawai'i, our lands and fisheries, the outlying seas and the heavens; our language and dance; our familial relationships; and our women.

Nā Mea Hawai'i—Things Hawaiian

The *mo'ōlelo*, or history of Hawaiians, is to be found in our genealogies. From our great cosmogonic genealogy, the *Kumulipo*, derives the Hawaiian identity. The "essential lesson" of this genealogy is "the interrelatedness of the Hawaiian world, and the inseparability of its constituent parts." Thus, "the genealogy of the land, the gods, chiefs, and people intertwine one with the other, and with all aspects of the universe."[1]

In the *mo'ōlelo* of Papa and Wākea, earth-mother and sky-father, our islands are born: Hawai'i, Maui, O'ahu, Kaua'i, and Ni'ihau. From their human offspring came the *taro* plant and from the taro came the Hawaiian people.

The lessons of our genealogy are that human beings have a familial relationship to land and to the *taro,* our elder siblings or *kua'ana.*

In Hawai'i, as in all of Polynesia, younger siblings must serve and honor elder siblings who, in turn, must feed and care for their younger siblings. Therefore, Hawaiians must cultivate and husband the land which will feed and provide for the Hawaiian people. This relationship of people to land is called *mālama 'āina* or *aloha 'āina,* care and love of the land.

When people and land work together harmoniously, the balance that results is called *pono.* In Hawaiian society, the *ali'i* or chiefs were required to maintain order, abundance of food, and good government. The *maka'āinana* or common people worked the land and fed the chiefs; the *ali'i* organized production and appeased the gods.

Today, *mālama 'āina* is called stewardship by some, although that word does not convey spiritual and genealogical connections. Nevertheless, to love and make the land flourish is a Hawaiian value. *'Āina,* one of the words for land, means *that which feeds. Kama'āina,* a term for native-born people, means *child of the land.* Thus is the Hawaiian relationship to land both familial and reciprocal.

Our deities are also of the land: Pele is our volcano, Kāne and Lono our fertile valleys and plains, Kanaloa our ocean and all that lives within it, and so on with the 40,000 and 400,000 gods of Hawai'i. Our whole universe, physical and metaphysical, is divine.

Within this world, the older people or *kūpuna* are to cherish those who are younger, the *mo'opuna.* Unstinting generosity is a value and of high status. Social connections between our people are through *aloha,* simply translated as love but carrying with it a profoundly Hawaiian sense that is, again, familial and genealogical. Hawaiians feel *aloha* for Hawai'i whence they come and for their Hawaiian kin upon whom they depend. It is nearly impossible to feel or practice *aloha* for something that is not familial. This is why we extend familial relations to those few non-natives whom we feel understand and can reciprocate our *aloha.* But *aloha* is freely given and freely returned, it is not and cannot be demanded, or commanded. Above all, *aloha* is a cultural feeling and practice that works among the people and between the people and their land.

The significance and meaning of *aloha* underscores the centrality of the Hawaiian language or *'ōlelo* to the culture. *'Ōlelo* means both language and tongue; *mo'ōlelo,* or history, is that which comes from the tongue, that is, a story. *Haole* or white people say we have oral history, but what we have are stories passed on through the generations. These are different from the *haole* sense of history. To Hawaiians in traditional society, language had tremendous power, thus the phrase, *i ka 'ōlelo ke ola; i ka 'ōlelo ka make*—in language is life, in language is death.

After nearly 2,000 years of speaking Hawaiian, our people suffered the near extinction of our language through its banning by the American-imposed government in 1896. In 1900, Hawai'i became a territory of the

United States. All schools, government operations, and official transactions were thereafter conducted in English, despite the fact that most people, including non-natives, still spoke Hawaiian at the turn of the century.

Since 1970, *'ōlelo Hawai'i,* or the Hawaiian language, has undergone a tremendous revival, including the rise of language immersion schools. The state of Hawai'i now has two official languages, Hawaiian and English, and the call for Hawaiian language speakers and teachers grows louder by the day.[2]

Along with the flowering of Hawaiian language has come a flowering of Hawaiian dance, especially in its ancient form, called *hula kahiko.* Dance academies, known as *hālau,* have proliferated throughout Hawai'i as have *kumu hula,* or dance masters, and formal competitions where all-night presentations continue for three or four days to throngs of appreciative listeners. Indeed, among Pacific Islanders, Hawaiian dance is considered one of the finest Polynesian art forms today.

Of course, the cultural revitalization that Hawaiians are now experiencing and transmitting to their children is as much a *repudiation* of colonization by so-called Western civilization in its American form as it is a *reclamation* of our past and our own ways of life. This is why cultural revitalization is often resisted and disparaged by anthropologists and others: they see very clearly that its political effect is de-colonization of the mind. Thus our rejection of the nuclear family as the basic unit of society and of individualism as the best form of human expression infuriates social workers, the churches, the legal system, and educators. Hawaiians continue to have allegedly "illegitimate" children, to *hānai* or adopt both children and adults outside of sanctioned Western legal concepts, to hold and use land and water in a collective form rather than a private property form, and to proscribe the notion and the value that one person should strive to surpass and therefore outshine all others.

All these Hawaiian values can be grouped under the idea of *'ohana,* loosely translated as family, but more accurately imagined as a group of both closely and distantly related people who share nearly everything, from land and food to children and status. Sharing is central to this value since it prevents individual decline. Of course, poverty is not thereby avoided, it is only shared with everyone in the unit. The *'ohana* works effectively when the *kua'ana* relationship (elder sibling/younger sibling reciprocity) is practiced.

Finally, within the *'ohana,* our women are considered the lifegivers of the nation, and are accorded the respect and honor this status conveys. Our young women, like our young people in general, are the *pua,* or flower of our *lāhui,* or our nation. The renowned beauty of our women, especially their sexual beauty, is not considered a commodity to be hoarded by fathers and brothers but an attribute of our people. Culturally, Hawaiians are very open and free about sexual relationships, although Christianity and organized religion have done much to damage these traditional sexual values.

With this understanding of what it means to be Hawaiian, I want to move now to the prostitution of our culture by tourism.

Hawai'i itself is the female object of degraded and victimized sexual value. Our *'āina,* or lands, are not any longer the source of food and shelter, but the source of money. Land is now called real estate, rather than our mother, *Papa.* The American relationship of people to land is that of exploiter to exploited. Beautiful areas, once sacred to my people, are now expensive resorts; shorelines where net fishing, seaweed gathering, and crabbing occurred are more and more the exclusive domain of recreational activities: sunbathing, windsurfing, jet skiing. Now, even access to beaches near hotels is strictly regulated or denied to the local public altogether.

The phrase *mālama 'āina*—to care for the land—is used by government officials to sell new projects and to convince the locals that hotels can be built with a concern for "ecology." Hotel historians, like hotel doctors, are stationed in-house to soothe the visitors' stay with the pablum of invented myths and tales of the "primitive."

High schools and hotels adopt each other and funnel teenagers through major resorts for guided tours from kitchens to gardens to honeymoon suites in preparation for postsecondary jobs in the lowest-paid industry in the state. In the meantime, tourist appreciation kits and movies are distributed through the state department of education to all elementary schools. One film, unashamedly titled "What's in It for Me?," was devised to convince locals that tourism is, as the newspapers never tire of saying, "the only game in town."

Of course, all this hype is necessary to hide the truth about tourism, the awful exploitative truth that the industry is the major cause of environmental degradation, low wages, land dispossession, and the highest cost of living in the United States.

While this propaganda is churned out to local residents, the commercialization of Hawaiian culture proceeds with calls for more sensitive marketing of our native values and practices. After all, a prostitute is only as good as her income-producing talents. These talents, in Hawaiian terms, are the *hula;* the generosity, or *aloha,* of our people; the *u'i* or youthful beauty of our women and men; and the continuing allure of our lands and waters, that is, of our place, Hawai'i.

The selling of these talents must produce income. And the function of tourism and the state of Hawai'i is to convert these attributes into profits.

The first requirement is the transformation of the product, or the cultural attribute, much as a woman must be transformed to look like a prostitute, that is, someone who is complicitous in her own commodification. Thus *hula* dancers wear clownlike make-up, don costumes from a mix of Polynesian cultures, and behave in a manner that is smutty and salacious rather than powerfully erotic. The distance between the smutty and the erotic is precisely the distance between Western culture and Hawaiian culture. In the hotel version of the *hula,* the sacredness of the dance has completely evaporated while the athleticism and sexual expression have been packaged like ornaments. The purpose is entertainment for profit rather than a joyful and truly Hawaiian celebration of human and divine nature.

But let us look at an example that is representative of literally hundreds of images that litter the pages of scores of tourist publications. From an Aloha Airlines booklet—shamelessly called the "Spirit of Aloha"—there is a characteristic portrayal of commodified *hula* dancers, one male and one female. The costuming of the female is more South Pacific—the Cook Islands and Tahiti—while that of the male is more Hawaiian. (He wears a Hawaiian loincloth called a *malo*.) The ad smugly asserts the hotel dinner service as a *lū'au*, a Hawaiian feast (which is misspelled) with a continuously open bar, lavish "island" buffet, and "thrilling" Polynesian revue. Needless to say, Hawaiians did not drink alcohol, eat "island" buffets, or participate in "thrilling" revues before the advent of white people in our islands.

But back to the advertisement. Lahaina, the location of the resort and once the capital of Hawai'i, is called "royal" because of its past association with our *ali'i*, or chiefs. Far from being royal today, Lahaina is sadly inundated by California yuppies, drug addicts, and valley girls.

The male figure in the background is muscular, partially clothed, and unsmiling. Apparently, he is supposed to convey an image of Polynesian sexuality that is both enticing and threatening. The white women in the audience can marvel at this physique and still remain safely distant. Like the black American male, this Polynesian man is a fantasy animal. He casts a slightly malevolent glance at our costumed maiden whose body posture and barely covered breasts contradict the innocent smile on her face.

Finally, the "wondrous allure" referred to in the ad applies to more than just the dancers in their performances; the physical beauty of Hawai'i "alive under the stars" is the larger reference.

In this little grotesquerie, the falseness and commercialism fairly scream out from the page. Our language, our dance, our young people, even our customs of eating are used to ensnare tourists. And the price is only a paltry $39.95, not much for two thousand years of culture. Of course, the hotel will rake in tens of thousands of dollars on just the *lū'au* alone. And our young couple will make a pittance.

The rest of the magazine, like most tourist propaganda, commodifies virtually every part of Hawai'i: mountains, beaches, coastlines, rivers, flowers, our volcano goddess, Pele, reefs and fish, rural Hawaiian communities, even Hawaiian activists.

The point, of course, is that everything in Hawai'i can be yours, that is, you the tourist, the non-native, the visitor. The place, the people, the culture, even our identity as a "native" people is for sale. Thus, the magazine, like the airline that prints it, is called *Aloha*. The use of this word in a capitalist context is so far removed from any Hawaiian cultural sense that it is, literally, meaningless.

Thus, Hawai'i, like a lovely woman, is there for the taking. Those with only a little money get a brief encounter; those with a lot of money, like the Japanese, get more. The state and counties will give tax breaks, build infrastructure, and have the governor personally welcome tourists to ensure they keep coming. Just as the pimp regulates prices and guards the commodity of the prostitute, so the state bargains with developers for access to Hawaiian land and culture. Who builds the biggest resorts to attract the most affluent tourists gets the best deal: more hotel rooms, golf courses, and restaurants approved. Permits are fast-tracked, height and density limits are suspended, new groundwater sources are miraculously found.

Hawaiians, meanwhile, have little choice in all this. We can fill up the unemployment lines, enter the military, work in the tourist industry, or leave Hawai'i. Increasingly, Hawaiians are leaving, not by choice but out of economic necessity.

Our people who work in the industry—dancers, waiters, singers, valets, gardeners, housekeepers, bartenders, and even a few managers—make between $10,000 and $25,000 a year, an impossible salary for a family in Hawai'i. Psychologically, our young people have begun to think of tourism as the only employment opportunity, trapped as they are by the lack of alternatives. For our young women, modeling is a "cleaner" job when compared to waiting on tables, or dancing in a weekly revue, but modeling feeds on tourism and the commodification of Hawaiian women. In the end, the entire employment scene is shaped by tourism.

Despite their exploitation, Hawaiians' participation in tourism raises the problem of complicity. Because wages are so low and advancement so rare, whatever complicity exists is secondary to the economic hopelessness that drives Hawaiians into the industry. Refusing to contribute to the commercialization of one's culture becomes a peripheral concern when unemployment looms.

Of course, many Hawaiians do not see tourism as part of their colonization. Thus tourism is viewed as providing jobs, not as a form of cultural prostitution. Even those who have some glimmer of critical consciousness don't generally agree that the tourist industry prostitutes Hawaiian culture. To me, this is a measure of the depth of our mental oppression: We can't understand our own cultural degradation because we are living it. As colonized people, we are colonized to the extent that we are unaware of our oppression. When awareness begins, then so too does de-colonization. Judging by the growing resistance to new hotels, to geothermal energy and manganese nodule mining which would supplement the tourist industry, and to increases in the sheer number of tourists, I would say that de-colonization has begun, but we have many more stages to negotiate on our path to sovereignty.

My brief excursion into the prostitution of Hawaiian culture has done no more than give an overview. Now that you have heard a native view, let me just leave this thought behind. If you are thinking of visiting my homeland, please don't. We don't want or need any more tourists, and we certainly don't like them. If you want to help our cause, pass this message on to your friends.

ENDNOTES

Author's Note: "Lovely Hula Hands" is the title of a famous and very saccharine song written by a *haole* who fell in love with Hawai'i in the pre-statehood era. It embodies the worst romanticized views of *hula* dancers and Hawaiian culture in general.

[1] Lilikalā Kame'eleihiwa, *Native Land and Foreign Desires* (Honolulu: Bishop Museum Press, 1992), p. 2.

[2] See Larry Kimura, 1983. "Native Hawaiian Culture," in *Native Hawaiians Study Commission Report,* Vol. 1 (Washington, DC: U.S. Department of the Interior), pp. 173–97.

11

"NIGHT TO HIS DAY"
The Social Construction of Gender

JUDITH LORBER

In this and the following three selections, we examine socialization, the process of learning cultural values and norms. *Socialization* refers to those so-cial processes through which an individual becomes integrated into a social group by learning the group's culture and his or her roles in that group. It is largely through this process that an individual's concept of self is formed. Thus, socialization teaches us the cultural norms, values, and skills neces-sary to survive in society. Socialization also enables us to form social identi-ties and an awareness about ourselves as individuals. The following reading by Judith Lorber, a professor of sociology at the Graduate Center of the City University of New York, is taken from her comprehensive study *Paradoxes of Gender* (1993). Here, Lorber examines socialization and how we learn our gender identities following birth.

[Gethenians] do not see each other as men or women. This is almost impossible for our imagination to accept. What is the first question we ask about a new-born baby?

—URSULA LE GUIN

Talking about gender for most people is the equivalent of fish talking about water. Gender is so much the routine ground of everyday activi-ties that questioning its taken-for-granted assumptions and presuppo-sitions is like thinking about whether the sun will come up.[1] Gender is so pervasive that in our society we assume it is bred into our genes. Most people find it hard to believe that gender is constantly created and re-created out of

From *Paradoxes of Gender*, pp. 3–15 and 17–27. Copyright © 1993 by Yale University. Reprinted with the permission of Yale University Press.

human interaction, out of social life, and is the texture and order of that social life. Yet gender, like culture, is a human production that depends on everyone constantly "doing gender" (West and Zimmerman 1987).

And everyone "does gender" without thinking about it. Today, on the subway, I saw a well-dressed man with a year-old child in a stroller. Yesterday, on a bus, I saw a man with a tiny baby in a carrier on his chest. Seeing men taking care of small children in public is increasingly common—at least in New York City. But both men were quite obviously stared at—and smiled at, approvingly. Everyone was doing gender—the men who were changing the role of fathers and the other passengers, who were applauding them silently. But there was more gendering going on that probably fewer people noticed. The baby was wearing a white crocheted cap and white clothes. You couldn't tell if it was a boy or a girl. The child in the stroller was wearing a dark blue T-shirt and dark print pants. As they started to leave the train, the father put a Yankee baseball cap on the child's head. Ah, a boy, I thought. Then I noticed the gleam of tiny earrings in the child's ears, and as they got off, I saw the little flowered sneakers and lace-trimmed socks. Not a boy after all. Gender done.

Gender is such a familiar part of daily life that it usually takes a deliberate disruption of our expectations of how women and men are supposed to act to pay attention to how it is produced. Gender signs and signals are so ubiquitous that we usually fail to note them—unless they are missing or ambiguous. Then we are uncomfortable until we have successfully placed the other person in a gender status; otherwise, we feel socially dislocated. In our society, in addition to man and woman, the status can be *transvestite* (a person who dresses in opposite-gender clothes) and *transsexual* (a person who has had sex-change surgery). Transvestites and transsexuals carefully construct their gender status by dressing, speaking, walking, gesturing in the ways prescribed for women or men—whichever they want to be taken for—and so does any "normal" person.

For the individual, gender construction starts with assignment to a sex category on the basis of what the genitalia look like at birth.[2] Then babies are dressed or adorned in a way that displays the category because parents don't want to be constantly asked whether their baby is a girl or a boy. A sex category becomes a gender status through naming, dress, and the use of other gender markers. Once a child's gender is evident, others treat those in one gender differently from those in the other, and the children respond to the different treatment by feeling different and behaving differently. As soon as they can talk, they start to refer to themselves as members of their gender. Sex doesn't come into play again until puberty, but by that time, sexual feelings and desires and practices have been shaped by gendered norms and expectations. Adolescent boys and girls approach and avoid each other in an elaborately scripted and gendered mating dance. Parenting is gendered, with different expectations for mothers and for fathers, and people of different genders work at different kinds of jobs. The work adults do as mothers and fathers and as low-level workers and high-level bosses, shapes women's and men's life experiences, and these experiences produce different feelings, consciousness, relationships, skills—ways of being that we call feminine or masculine.[3] All of these processes constitute the social construction of gender.

Gendered roles change—today fathers are taking care of little children, girls and boys are wearing unisex clothing and getting the same education, women and men are working at the same jobs. Although many traditional social groups are quite strict about maintaining gender differences, in other social groups they seem to be blurring. Then why the one-year-old's earrings? Why is it still so important to mark a child as a girl or a boy, to make sure she is not taken for a boy or he for a girl? What would happen if they were? They would, quite literally, have changed places in their social world.

To explain why gendering is done from birth, constantly and by everyone, we have to look not only at the way individuals experience gender but at gender as a social institution. As a social institution, gender is one of the major ways that human beings organize their lives. Human society depends on a predictable division of labor, a designated allocation of scarce goods, assigned responsibility for children and others who cannot care for themselves, common values and their systematic transmission to new members, legitimate leadership, music, art, stories, games, and other symbolic productions. One way of choosing people for the different tasks of society is on the basis of their talents, motivations, and competence—their demonstrated achievements. The other way is on the basis of gender, race, ethnicity—ascribed membership in a category of people. Although societies vary in the extent to which they use one or the other of these ways of allocating people to work and to carry out other responsibilities, every society uses gender and age grades. Every society classifies people as "girl and boy children," "girls and boys ready to be married," and "fully adult women and men," constructs similarities among them and differences between them, and assigns them to different roles and responsibilities. Personality characteristics, feelings, motivations, and ambitions flow from these different life experiences so that the members of these different groups become different kinds of people. The process of gendering and its outcome are legitimated by religion, law, science, and the society's entire set of values. . . .

Western society's values legitimate gendering by claiming that it all comes from physiology—female and male procreative differences. But gender and sex are not equivalent, and gender as a social construction does not flow automatically from genitalia and reproductive organs, the main physiological differences of females and males. In the construction of ascribed social statuses, physiological differences such as sex, stage of development, color of skin, and size are crude markers. They are not the source of the social statuses of gender, age grade, and race. Social statuses are carefully constructed through prescribed processes of teaching, learning, emulation, and enforcement. Whatever genes, hormones, and biological evolution contribute to human social institutions is materially as well as qualitatively transformed by social practices. Every social institution has a material base, but culture and social practices transform that base into something with qualitatively different patterns and constraints. The economy is much more than producing food and goods and distributing them to eaters and users; family and kinship are not the equivalent of having sex and procreating; morals and religions cannot be equated with the fears and ecstasies of the brain; language goes far beyond the sounds produced by tongue and larynx. No one eats "money" or "credit"; the concepts of "god" and "angels" are the subjects of theological disquisitions; not only words but objects, such as their flag, "speak" to the citizens of a country.

Similarly, gender cannot be equated with biological and physiological differences between human females and males. The building blocks of gender are *socially constructed statuses*. Western societies have only two genders, "man" and "woman." Some societies have three genders—men, women, and *berdaches* or *hijras* or *xaniths*. Berdaches, hijras, and xaniths are biological males who behave, dress, work, and are treated in most respects as social women; they are therefore not men, nor are they female women; they are, in our language, "male women."[4] There are African and American Indian societies that have a gender status called *manly hearted women*—biological females who work, marry, and parent as men; their social status is "female men" (Amadiume 1987; Blackwood 1984). They do not have to behave or dress as men to have the social responsibilities and prerogatives of husbands and fathers; what makes them men is enough wealth to buy a wife.

Modern Western societies' *transsexuals* and *transvestites* are the nearest equivalent of these crossover genders, but they are not institutionalized as third genders (Bolin 1987). Transsexuals are biological males and females who have sex-change operations to alter their genitalia. They do so in order to bring their physical anatomy in congruence with the way they want to live and with their own sense of gender identity. They do not become a third gender; they change genders. Transvestites are males who live as women and females who live as men but do not intend to have sex-change surgery. Their dress, appearance, and mannerisms fall within the range of what is expected from members of the opposite gender, so that they "pass." They also change genders, sometimes temporarily, some for most of their lives. Transvestite women have fought in wars as men soldiers as recently as the nineteenth century; some married women, and others went back to being women and married men once the war was over.[5] Some were discovered when their wounds were treated; others not until they died. In order to work as a jazz musician, a man's occupation, Billy Tipton, a woman, lived most of her life as a man. She died at 74, leaving a wife and three adopted sons for whom she was husband and father, and musicians with whom she had played and traveled, for whom she was "one of the boys" (*New York Times* 1989).[6] There have been many other such occurrences of women passing as men to do more prestigious or lucrative men's work (Matthaei 1982:192–93).[7]

Genders, therefore, are not attached to a biological substratum. Gender boundaries are breachable, and individual and socially organized shifts from one gender to another call attention to "cultural, social, or aesthetic dissonances" (Garber 1992:16). These odd or deviant or third genders show us what we ordinarily take for granted—that people have to learn to be women and men. Men who cross-dress for performances or for pleasure often learn from women's magazines how to "do femininity" convincingly (Garber 1992: 41–51). Because transvestism is direct evidence of how gender is constructed, Marjorie Garber (1992) claims it has "extraordinary power . . . to disrupt, expose, and challenge, putting in question the very notion of the 'original' and of stable identity" (p. 16).

Gender Bending

It is difficult to see how gender is constructed because we take it for granted that it's all biology, or hormones, or human nature. The differences between women and men seem to be self-evident, and we think they would occur no matter what society did. But in actuality, human females and males are physiologically more similar in appearance than are the two sexes of many species of animals and are more alike than different in traits and behavior (Epstein 1988). Without the deliberate use of gendered clothing, hairstyles, jewelry, and cosmetics, women and men would look far more alike.[8] Even societies that do not cover women's breasts have gender-identifying clothing, scarification, jewelry, and hairstyles.

The ease with which many transvestite women pass as men and transvestite men as women is corroborated by the common gender misidentification in Westernized societies of people in jeans, T-shirts, and sneakers. Men with long hair may be addressed as "miss," and women with short hair are often taken for men unless they offset the potential ambiguity with deliberate gender markers (Devor 1987, 1989). Jan Morris, in *Conundrum*, an autobiographical account of events just before and just after a sex-change operation, described how easy it was to shift back and forth from being a man to being a woman when testing how it would feel to change gender status. During this time, Morris (1975) still had a penis and wore more or less unisex clothing; the context alone made the man and the woman:

> Sometimes the arena of my ambivalence was uncomfortably small. At the Travellers' Club, for example, I was obviously known as a man of sorts— women were only allowed on the premises at all during a few hours of the day, and even then were hidden away as far as possible in lesser rooms or alcoves. But I had another club, only a few hundred yards away, where I was known only as a woman, and often I went directly from one to the other, imperceptibly changing roles on the way—"Cheerio, sir,"

the porter would say at one club, and "Hello, madam," the porter would greet me at the other. (P. 132)

Gender shifts are actually a common phenomenon in public roles as well. Queen Elizabeth II of England bore children, but when she went to Saudi Arabia on a state visit, she was considered an honorary man so that she could confer and dine with the men who were heads of a state that forbids unrelated men and women to have face-to-unveiled face contact. In contemporary Egypt, lower-class women who run restaurants or shops dress in men's clothing and engage in unfeminine aggressive behavior, and middle-class educated women of professional or managerial status can take positions of authority (Rugh 1986:131). In these situations, there is an important status change: These women are treated by the others in the situation as if they are men. From their own point of view, they are still women. From the social perspective, however, they are men.[9]

In many cultures, gender bending is prevalent in theater or dance—the Japanese kabuki are men actors who play both women and men; in Shakespeare's theater company, there were no actresses—Juliet and Lady Macbeth were played by boys. Shakespeare's comedies are full of witty comments on gender shifts. Women characters frequently masquerade as young men, and other women characters fall in love with them; the boys playing these masquerading women, meanwhile, are acting out pining for the love of men characters.[10] . . .

But despite the ease with which gender boundaries can be traversed in work, in social relationships, and in cultural productions, gender statuses remain. Transvestites and transsexuals do not challenge the social construction of gender. Their goal is to be feminine women and masculine men (Kando 1973). Those who do not want to change their anatomy but do want to change their gender behavior fare less well in establishing their social identity. . . .

Paradoxically, then, bending gender rules and passing between genders does not erode but rather preserves gender boundaries. In societies with only two genders, the gender dichotomy is not disturbed by transvestites, because others feel that a transvestite is only transitorily ambiguous—is "really a man or woman underneath." After sex-change surgery, transsexuals end up in a conventional gender status—a "man" or a "woman" with the appropriate genitals (Eichler 1989). When women dress as men for business reasons, they are indicating that in that situation, they want to be treated the way men are treated; when they dress as women, they want to be treated as women:

By their male dress, female entrepreneurs signal their desire to suspend the expectations of accepted feminine conduct without losing respect and reputation. By wearing what is "unattractive" they signify that they are not intending to display their physical charms while engaging in public activity. Their loud, aggressive banter contrasts with the modest demeanor that attracts men. . . . Overt signalling of a suspension of the rules preserves normal conduct from eroding expectations. (Rugh 1986:131)

For Individuals, Gender Means Sameness

Although the possible combinations of genitalia, body shapes, clothing, mannerisms, sexuality, and roles could produce infinite varieties in human beings, the social institution of gender depends on the production and maintenance of a limited number of gender statuses and of making the members of these statuses similar to each other. Individuals are born sexed but not gendered, and they have to be taught to be masculine or feminine.[11] As Simone de Beauvoir said: "One is not born, but rather becomes, a woman . . . ; it is civilization as a whole that produces this creature . . . which is described as feminine" ([1949] 1953:267).

Children learn to walk, talk, and gesture the way their social group says girls and boys should. Ray Birdwhistell (1970: 39–46), in his analysis of body motion as human communication, calls these learned gender displays *tertiary* sex characteristics and argues that they are needed to distinguish genders because humans are a weakly dimorphic species—their only sex markers are genitalia. Clothing, paradoxically, often hides the sex but displays the gender.

In early childhood, humans develop gendered personality structures and sexual orientations through their interactions with parents of the same and opposite gender. As adolescents, they conduct their sexual behavior according to gendered scripts. Schools, parents, peers, and the mass media guide young people into gendered work and family roles. As adults, they take on a gendered social status in their society's stratification system. Gender is thus both ascribed and achieved (West and Zimmerman 1987).

The achievement of gender was most dramatically revealed in a case of an accidental transsexual—a baby boy whose penis was destroyed in the course of a botched circumcision when he was seven months old (Money and Ehrhardt 1972:118–23). The child's sex category was changed to "female," and a vagina was surgically constructed when the child was 17 months old. The parents were advised that they could successfully raise the child, one of identical twins, as a girl. Physicians assured them that the child was too young to have formed a gender identity. Children's sense of which gender they belong to usually develops around the age of three, at the time that they start to group objects and recognize that the people around them also fit into categories—big, little; pink-skinned, brown-skinned; boys, girls. Three has also been the age when children's appearance is ritually gendered, usually by cutting a boy's hair or dressing him in distinctively masculine clothing. In Victorian times, English boys wore dresses up to the age of three, when they were put into short pants (Garber 1992:1–2).

The parents of the accidental transsexual bent over backward to feminize the child—and succeeded. Frilly dresses, hair ribbons, and jewelry created a pride in looks, neatness, and "daintiness." More significant, the child's dominance was also feminized:

> The girl had many tomboyish traits, such as abundant physical energy, a high level of activity, stubbornness, and being often the dominant one in a girls' group. Her mother tried to modify her tomboyishness: ". . . I teach her to be more polite and quiet. I always wanted those virtues. I never did manage, but I'm going to try to manage them to—my daughter—to be more quiet and ladylike." From the beginning the girl had been the dominant twin. By age of three, her dominance over her brother was, as her mother described it, that of a mother hen. The boy in turn took up for his sister, if anyone threatened her. (Money and Ehrhardt 1972:122)

This child was not a tomboy because of male genes or hormones; according to her mother, she herself had also been a tomboy. What the mother had learned poorly while growing up as a "natural" female she insisted that her physically reconstructed son-daughter learn well. For both mother and child, the social construction of gender overrode any possibly inborn traits.

People go along with the imposition of gender norms because the weight of morality as well as immediate social pressure enforces them. Consider how many instructions for properly gendered behavior are packed into this mother's admonition to her daughter: "This is how to hem a dress when you see the hem coming down and so to prevent yourself from looking like the slut I know you are so bent on becoming" (Kincaid 1978).

Gender norms are inscribed in the way people move, gesture, and even eat. In one African society, men were supposed to eat with their "whole mouth, wholeheartedly, and not, like women, just with the lips, that is half-heartedly, with reservation and restraint" (Bourdieu [1980] 1990:70). Men and women in this society learned to walk in ways that proclaimed their different positions in the society:

> The manly man . . . stands up straight into the face of the person he approaches, or wishes to welcome. Ever on the alert, because ever threatened, he misses nothing of what happens around him. . . . Conversely, a well brought-up woman . . . is expected to walk with a slight stoop, avoiding every misplaced movement of her body, her head or her arms, looking down, keeping her eyes on the spot where she will next put her foot, especially if she happens to have to walk past the men's assembly. (P. 70)

Many cultures go beyond clothing, gestures, and demeanor in gendering children. They inscribe gender directly into bodies. In traditional Chinese society, mothers bound their daughters' feet into three-inch stumps to enhance their sexual attractiveness. Jewish fathers circumcise their infant sons to show their covenant with God. Women in African societies remove the clitoris of prepubescent girls, scrape their labia, and make the lips grow together to preserve their chastity and ensure their marriageability. In Western societies, women augment their breast size with silicone and reconstruct their faces with cosmetic surgery to conform to cultural ideals of feminine beauty. . . .

Most parents create a gendered world for their newborn by naming, birth announcements, and dress. Children's relationships with same-gendered and different-gendered caretakers structure their self-identifications and personalities. Through cognitive development, children extract and apply to their own actions the appropriate behavior for those who belong in their own gender, as well as race, religion, ethnic group, and social class, rejecting what is not appropriate. If their social categories are highly valued, they value themselves highly; if their social categories are low status, they lose self-esteem (Chodorow 1974). Many feminist parents who want to raise androgynous children soon lose their children to the pull of gendered norms (Gordon 1990: 87–90). My son attended a carefully nonsexist elementary school, which didn't even have girls' and boys' bathrooms. When he was seven or eight years old, I attended a class play about "squares" and "circles" and their need for each other and noticed that all the girl squares and circles wore makeup, but none of the boy squares and circles did. I asked the teacher about it after the play, and she said, "Bobby said he was not going to wear makeup, and he is a powerful child, so none of the boys would either." In a long discussion about conformity, my son confronted me with the question of who the conformists were, the boys who followed their leader or the girls who listened to the woman teacher. In actuality, they both were, because they both followed same-gender leaders and acted in gender-appropriate ways. (Actors may wear makeup, but real boys don't.)

For human beings there is no essential femaleness and maleness, femininity or masculinity, womanhood or manhood, but once gender is ascribed, the social order constructs and holds individuals to strongly gendered norms and expectations. Individuals may vary on many of the components of gender and may shift genders temporarily or permanently, but they must fit into the limited number of gender statuses their society recognizes. In the process, they re-create their society's version of women and men: "If we do gender appropriately, we simultaneously sustain, reproduce, and render legitimate the institutional arrangements. . . . If we fail to do gender appropriately, we as individuals—not the institutional arrangements—may be called to account (for our character, motives, and predispositions)" (West and Zimmerman 1987:146).

The gendered practices of everyday life reproduce a society's view of how women and men should act (Bourdieu [1980] 1990). Gendered social arrangements are justified by religion and cultural productions and backed by law, but the most powerful means of sustaining the moral hegemony of the dominant gender ideology is that the process is made invisible; any possible alternatives are virtually unthinkable (Foucault 1972; Gramsci 1971).[12]

For Society, Gender Means Difference

The pervasiveness of gender as a way of structuring social life demands that gender statuses be clearly differentiated. Varied talents, sexual preferences, identities, personalities, interests, and ways of interacting fragment the individual's bodily and social experiences. Nonetheless, these are organized in Western cultures into two and only two socially and legally recognized gender statuses, "man" and "woman."[13] In the social construction of gender, it does not matter what men and women actually do; it does not even matter if they do exactly the same thing. The social institution of gender insists only that what they do is *perceived* as different.

If men and women are doing the same tasks, they are usually spatially segregated to maintain gender separation, and often the tasks are given different job titles as well, such as executive secretary and administrative assistant (Reskin 1988). If the differences between women and men begin to blur, society's "sameness taboo" goes into action (Rubin 1975:178). At a rock and roll dance at West Point in 1976, the year women were admitted to the prestigious military academy for the first time, the school's administrators "were reportedly perturbed by the sight of mirror-image couples dancing in short hair and dress gray trousers," and a rule was established that women cadets could dance at these events only if they wore skirts (Barkalow and Raab 1990:53).[14] Women recruits in the U.S. Marine Corps are required to wear makeup—at a minimum, lipstick and eye shadow—and they have to take classes in makeup, hair care, poise, and etiquette. This feminization is part of a deliberate policy of making them clearly distinguishable from men Marines. Christine Williams (1989) quotes a 25-year-old woman drill instructor as saying: "A lot of the recruits who come here don't wear makeup; they're tomboyish or athletic. A lot of them have the preconceived idea that going into the military means they can still be a tomboy. They don't realize that you are a *Woman* Marine" (pp. 76–77).[15]

If gender differences were genetic, physiological, or hormonal, gender bending and gender ambiguity would occur only in hermaphrodites, who are born with chromosomes and genitalia that are not clearly female or male. Since gender differences are socially constructed, all men and all women can enact the behavior of the other, because they know the other's social script: "'Man' and 'woman' are at once empty and overflowing categories. Empty because they have no ultimate, transcendental meaning. Overflowing because even when they appear to be fixed, they still contain within them alternative, denied, or suppressed definitions" (Scott 1988:49). Nonetheless, though individuals may be able to shift gender statuses, the gender boundaries have to hold, or the whole gendered social order will come crashing down.

Paradoxically, it is the social importance of gender statuses and their external markers—clothing, mannerisms, and spatial segregation—that makes gender bending or gender crossing possible—or even necessary. The social viability of differentiated gender statuses produces the need or desire to shift statuses. Without gender differentiation, transvestism and transsexuality would be meaningless. You couldn't dress in the opposite gender's clothing if all clothing were unisex. There would be no need to reconstruct genitalia to match identity if interests and lifestyles were not gendered. There would be no need for women to pass as men to do certain kinds of work if jobs were not typed as "women's work" and "men's work." Women would not have to dress as men in public life in order to give orders or aggressively bargain with customers.

Gender boundaries are preserved when transsexuals create congruous autobiographies of always having felt like what they are now. The transvestite's story also "recuperates social and sexual norms" (Garber 1992:69). In the transvestite's normalized narrative, he or she "is 'compelled' by social and economic forces to disguise himself or herself in order to get a job, escape repression, or gain artistic or political 'freedom'" (Garber 1992:70). The "true identity," when revealed, causes amazement over how easily and successfully the person passed as a member of the opposite gender, not a suspicion that gender itself is something of a put-on.

ENDNOTES

[1] Gender is, in Erving Goffman's (1983) words, an aspect of *Felicity's Condition:* "any arrangement which leads us to judge an individual's . . . acts not to be a manifestation of strangeness. Behind Felicity's Condition is our sense of what it is to be sane" (p. 27). Also see Bem 1993; Frye 1983, pp. 17–40; Goffman 1977.

[2] In cases of ambiguity in countries with modern medicine, surgery is usually performed to make the genitalia more clearly male or female.

[3] See J. Butler 1990 for an analysis of how doing gender *is* gender identity.

[4] On the hijras of India, see Nanda 1990; on the xaniths of Oman, Wikan 1982, pp. 168–86; on the American Indian berdaches, W. L. Williams 1986. Other societies that have similar institutionalized third-gender men are the Koniag of Alaska, the Tanala of Madagascar, the Mesakin of Nuba, and the Chukchee of Siberia (Wikan 1982, p. 170).

[5] Durova 1989; Freeman and Bond 1992; Wheelwright 1989.

[6] Gender segregation of work in popular music still has not changed very much, according to Groce and Cooper 1990, despite considerable androgyny in some very popular figures. See Garber 1992 on the androgyny. She discusses Tipton on pp. 67–70.

[7] In the nineteenth century, not only did these women get men's wages, but they also "had male privileges and could do all manner of things other women could not: open a bank account, write checks, own property, go anywhere unaccompanied, vote in elections" (Faderman 1991, p. 44).

[8] When unisex clothing and men wearing long hair came into vogue in the United States in the mid-1960s, beards and mustaches for men also came into style again as gender identifications.

[9] For other accounts of women being treated as men in Islamic countries, as well as accounts of women and men cross-dressing in these countries, see Garber 1992, pp. 304–52.

[10] Dollimore 1986; Garber 1992, pp. 32–40; Greenblatt 1987, pp. 66–93; Howard 1988. For Renaissance accounts of sexual relations with women and men of ambiguous sex, see Lacqueur 1990, pp. 134–39. For modern accounts of women passing as men that other women find sexually attractive, see Devor 1989, pp. 136–37; Wheelwright 1989, pp. 53–59.

[11] For an account of how a potential man-to-woman transsexual learned to be feminine, see Garfinkel 1967, pp. 116–85, 285–88. For a gloss on this account that points out how, throughout his encounters with Agnes, Garfinkel failed to see how he himself was constructing his own masculinity, see Rogers 1992.

[12] The concepts of moral hegemony, the effects of everyday activities (praxis) on thought and personality, and the necessity of consciousness of these processes before political change can occur are all based on Marx's analysis of class relations.

[13] Other societies recognize more than two categories, but usually no more than three or four (Jacobs and Roberts 1989).

[14] Carol Barkalow's book has a photograph of 11 first-year West Pointers in a math class, who are dressed in regulation pants, shirts, and sweaters, with short haircuts. The caption challenges the reader to locate the only woman in the room.

[15] The taboo on males and females looking alike reflects the U.S. military's homophobia (Bérubé 1989). If you can't tell those with a penis from those with a vagina, how are you going to determine whether their sexual interest is heterosexual or homosexual unless you watch them having sexual relations?

REFERENCES

Amadiume, Ifi. 1987. *Male Daughters, Female Husbands: Gender and Sex in an African Society*. London: Zed Books.

Barkalow, Carol, with Andrea Raab. 1990. *In the Men's House*. New York: Poseidon Press.

Beauvoir, Simone de. [1949] 1953. *The Second Sex*, translated by H. M. Parshley. New York: Knopf.

Bem, Sandra Lipsitz. 1993. *The Lenses of Gender: Transforming the Debate on Sexual Inequality*. New Haven, CT: Yale University Press.

Bérubé, Allan. 1989. "Marching to a Different Drummer: Gay and Lesbian GIs in World War II." In *Hidden from History: Reclaiming the Gay and Lesbian Past*, edited by Martin Bauml Duberman, Martha Vicinus, and George Chauncey Jr. New York: New American Library.

Birdwhistell, Ray L. 1970. *Kinesics and Context: Essays on Body Motion Communication*. Philadelphia: University of Pennsylvania Press.

Blackwood, Evelyn. 1984. "Sexuality and Gender in Certain Native American Tribes: The Case of Cross-Gender Females." *Signs* 10:27–42.

Bolin, Anne. 1987. "Transsexualism and the Limits of Traditional Analysis." *American Behavior Scientist* 31:41–65.

Bourdieu, Pierre. [1980] 1990. *The Logic of Practice*. Stanford, CA: Stanford University Press.

Butler, Judith. 1990. *Gender Trouble: Feminism and the Subversion of Identity.* New York: Routledge.

Chodorow, Nancy. 1974. "Family Structure and Feminine Personality." In *Woman, Culture and Society,* edited by Michelle Zimbalist Rosaldo and Louise Lamphere. Stanford, CA: Stanford University Press.

Devor, Holly. 1987. "Gender Blending Females: Women and Sometimes Men." *American Behavior Scientist* 31:12–40.

———. 1989. *Gender Blending: Confronting the Limits of Duality.* Bloomington: University of Indiana Press.

Dollimore, Jonathan. 1986. "Subjectivity, Sexuality, and Transgression: The Jacobean Connection." *Renaissance Drama,* n.s. 17:53–81.

Durova, Nadezhda. 1989. *The Cavalry Maiden: Journals of a Russian Officer in the Napoleonic Wars,* translated by Mary Fleming Zirin. Bloomington: Indiana University Press.

Eichler, Margrit. 1989. "Sex Change Operations: The Last Bulwark of the Double Standard." In *Feminist Frontiers II,* edited by Laurel Richardson and Verta Taylor. New York: Random House.

Epstein, C. F. 1988. *Deceptive Distinctions: Sex, Gender and the Social Order.* New Haven, CT: Yale University Press.

Faderman, Lillian. 1991. *Odd Girls and Twilight Lovers: A History of Lesbian Life in Twentieth-Century America.* New York: Columbia University Press.

Foucault, Michel. 1972. *The Archeology of Knowledge and the Discourse on Language,* translated by A. M. Sheridan Smith. New York: Pantheon.

Freeman, Lucy and Alma Halbert Bond. 1992. *America's First Woman Warrior: The Courage of Deborah Sampson.* New York: Paragon.

Frye, Marilyn. 1983. *The Politics of Reality: Essays in Feminist Theory.* Trumansburg, NY: Crossing Press.

Garber, Marjorie. 1992. *Vested Interests: Cross-Dressing and Cultural Anxiety.* New York: Routledge.

Garfinkel, Harold. 1967. *Studies in Ethnomethodology.* Englewood Cliffs, NJ: Prentice-Hall.

Goffman, Erving. 1977. "The Arrangement between the Sexes." *Theory and Society* 4:301–33.

———. 1983. "Felicity's Condition." *American Journal of Sociology* 89:1–53.

Gordon, Tuula. 1990. *Feminist Mothers.* New York: New York University Press.

Gramsci, Antonio. 1971. *Selections from the Prison Notebooks,* translated and edited by Quintin Hoare and Geoffrey Nowell Smith. New York: International Publishers.

Greenblatt, Stephen. 1987. *Shakespearean Negotiations: The Circulation of Social Energy in Renaissance England.* Berkeley: University of California Press.

Groce, Stephen B. and Margaret Cooper. 1990. "Just Me and the Boys? Women in Local-Level Rock and Roll." *Gender & Society* 4:220–29.

Howard, Jean E. 1988. "Crossdressing, the Theater, and Gender Struggle in Early Modern England." *Shakespeare Quarterly* 39:418–41.

Jacobs, Sue-Ellen and Christine Roberts. 1989. "Sex, Sexuality, Gender, and Gender Variance." In *Gender and Anthropology,* edited by Sandra Morgen. Washington, DC: American Anthropological Association.

Kando, Thomas. 1973. *Sex Change: The Achievement of Gender Identity among Feminized Transsexuals.* Springfield, IL: Charles C. Thomas.

Kincaid, Jamaica. 1978. "Girl." *The New Yorker,* June 26.

Lacqueur, Thomas. 1990. *Making Sex: Body and Gender from the Greeks to Freud.* Cambridge, MA: Harvard University Press.

Matthaei, Julie A. 1982. *An Economic History of Woman's Work in America.* New York: Schocken.

Money, John and Anke A. Ehrhardt. 1972. *Man and Woman, Boy and Girl.* Baltimore, MD: Johns Hopkins University Press.

Morris, Jan. 1975. *Conundrum.* New York: Signet.

Nanda, Serena. 1990. *Neither Man nor Woman: The Hijras of India.* Belmont, CA: Wadsworth.

New York Times. 1989. "Musician's Death at 74 Reveals He Was a Woman." February 2.

Reskin, Barbara F. 1988. "Bringing the Men Back In: Sex Differentiation and the Devaluation of Women's Work." *Gender & Society* 2:58–81.

Rogers, Mary R. 1992. "They Were All Passing: Agnes, Garfinkel, and Company." *Gender & Society* 6:169–91.

Rubin, Gayle. 1975. "The Traffic in Women: Notes on the Political Economy of Sex." In *Toward an Anthropology of Women,* edited by Rayna Rapp Reiter. New York: Monthly Review Press.

Rugh, Andrea B. 1986. *Reveal and Conceal: Dress in Contemporary Egypt.* Syracuse, NY: Syracuse University Press.

Scott, Joan Wallach. 1988. *Gender and the Politics of History.* New York: Columbia University Press.

West, Candace and Don Zimmerman. 1987. "Doing Gender." *Gender & Society* 1:125–51.

Wheelwright, Julie. 1989. *Amazons and Military Maids: Women Who Cross-Dressed in Pursuit of Life, Liberty and Happiness.* London: Pandora Press.

Wikan, Unni. 1982. *Behind the Veil in Arabia: Women in Oman.* Baltimore, MD: Johns Hopkins University Press.

Williams, Christine L. 1989. *Gender Differences at Work: Women and Men in Nontraditional Occupations.* Berkeley: University of California Press.

Williams, Walter L. 1986. *The Spirit and the Flesh: Sexual Diversity in American Indian Culture.* Boston: Beacon Press.

12

BOYHOOD, ORGANIZED SPORTS, AND THE CONSTRUCTION OF MASCULINITIES

MICHAEL MESSNER

An important point about socialization is that societal values, identities, and social roles are learned and *not* instinctual. We have to learn the social norms and behaviors our society expects from us. In this reading, published in 1990, Michael Messner challenges the notion that gender identity formation is biological or natural. Instead, Messner examines how masculinity is learned

From *Journal of Contemporary Ethnography* 18, no. 4 (January 1990): 416–44. Copyright © 1990 by Sage Publications, Inc. Reprinted with the permission of the publishers.

through socialization, especially through the participation of boys and men in organized sports. Messner, an associate professor and graduate director of sociology at the University of Southern California, has studied men, masculinity, and sports for over 10 years.

I view gender identity not as a "thing" that people "have," but rather as a *process of construction* that develops, comes into crisis, and changes as a person interacts with the social world. Through this perspective, it becomes possible to speak of "gendering" identities rather than "masculinity" or "femininity" as relatively fixed identities or statuses.

There is an agency in this construction: People are not passively shaped by their social environment. As recent feminist analyses of the construction of feminine gender identity have pointed out, girls and women are implicated in the construction of their own identities and personalities, both in terms of the ways that they participate in their own subordination and the ways that they resist subordination (Benjamin 1988; Haug 1987). Yet this self-construction is not a fully conscious process. There are also deeply woven, unconscious motivations, fears, and anxieties at work here. So, too, in the construction of masculinity. Levinson et al. (1978) have argued that masculine identity is neither fully "formed" by the social context, nor is it "caused" by some internal dynamic put into place during infancy. Instead, it is shaped and constructed through the interaction between the internal and the social. The internal gendering identity may set developmental "tasks," may create thresholds of anxiety and ambivalence, yet it is only through a concrete examination of people's interactions with others within social institutions that we can begin to understand both the similarities and differences in the construction of gender identities.

In this study I explore and interpret the meanings that males themselves attribute to their boyhood participation in organized sport. In what ways do males construct masculine identities within the institution of organized sports? In what ways do class and racial differences mediate this relationship and perhaps lead to the construction of different meanings, and perhaps different masculinities? And what are some of the problems and contradictions within these constructions of masculinity?

Description of Research

Between 1983 and 1985, I conducted interviews with 30 male former athletes. Most of the men I interviewed had played the (U.S.) "major sports"— football, basketball, baseball, track. At the time of the interview, each had been retired from playing organized sports for at least five years. Their ages ranged from 21 to 48, with the median, 33; 14 were black, 14 were white, and 2 were Hispanic; 15 of the 16 black and Hispanic men had come from poor or working-class families, while the majority (9 of 14) of the white men had come from middle-class or professional families. All had at some time in their lives based their identities largely on their roles as athletes and could therefore be said to have had "athletic careers." Twelve had played organized sports through high school, 11 through college, and 7 had been professional athletes. Though the sample was not randomly selected, an effort was made to see that the sample had a range of difference in terms of race and social class backgrounds, and that there was some variety in terms of age, types of sports played, and levels of success in athletic careers. Without exception, each man contacted agreed to be interviewed.

The tape-recorded interviews were semistructured and took from one and one-half to six hours, with most taking about three hours. I asked each man to talk about four broad eras in his life: (1) his earliest experiences with sports in boyhood, (2) his athletic career, (3) retirement or disengagement from the athletic career, and (4) life after the athletic career. In each era, I focused the interview on the meanings of "success and failure," and on the boy's/man's relationships with family, with other males, with women, and with his own body.

In collecting what amounted to life histories of these men, my overarching purpose was to use feminist theories of masculine gender identity to explore how masculinity develops and changes as boys and men interact within the socially constructed world of organized sports. In addition to using the data to move toward some generalizations about the relationship between "masculinity and sport," I was also concerned with sorting out some of the variations among boys, based on class and racial inequalities, that led them to relate differently to athletic careers. I divided my sample into two comparison groups. The first group was made up of 10 men from higher-status backgrounds, primarily white, middle-class, and professional families. The second group was made up of 20 men from lower-status backgrounds, primarily minority, poor, and working-class families.

Boyhood and the Promise of Sports

Zane Grey once said, "All boys love baseball. If they don't they're not real boys" (as cited in Kimmel 1990). This is, of course, an ideological statement: In fact, some boys do *not* love baseball, or any other sports, for that matter. There are millions of males who at an early age are rejected by, become alienated from, or lose interest in organized sports. Yet all boys are, to a greater or lesser extent, judged according to their ability, or lack of ability, in competitive sports (Eitzen 1975; Sabo 1985). In this study I focus on those males who did become athletes—males who eventually poured thousands of hours into the development of specific physical skills. It is in boyhood that we can discover the roots of their commitment to athletic careers.

How did organized sports come to play such a central role in these boys' lives? When asked to recall how and why they initially got into playing sports, many of the men interviewed for this study seemed a bit puzzled: After all, playing sports was "just the thing to do." A 42-year-old black man who had played college basketball put it this way:

> *It was just what you did. It's kind of like, you went to school, you played athletics, and if you didn't, there was something wrong with you. It was just like brushing your teeth: It's just what you did. It's part of your existence.*

Spending one's time playing sports with other boys seemed as natural as the cycle of the seasons: baseball in the spring and summer, football in the fall, basketball in the winter—and then it was time to get out the old baseball glove and begin again. As a black 35-year-old former professional football star said:

> *I'd say when I wasn't in school, 95 percent of the time was spent in the park playing. It was the only thing to do. It just came as natural.*

And a black 34-year-old professional basketball player explained his early experiences in sports:

> *My principal and teacher said, "Now if you work at this you might be pretty damned good." So it was more or less a community thing—everybody in the community said, "Boy, if you work hard and keep your nose clean, you gonna be good." Cause it was natural instinct.*

"It was natural instinct." "I was a natural." Several athletes used words such as these to explain their early attraction to sports. But certainly there is nothing "natural" about throwing a ball through a hoop, hitting a ball with a bat, or jumping over hurdles. A boy, for instance, may have amazingly dexterous inborn hand-eye coordination, but this does not predispose him to a career of hitting baseballs any more than it predisposes him to a life as a brain surgeon. When one listens closely to what these men said about their early experiences in sports, it becomes clear that their adoption of the self-definition of "natural athlete" was the result of what Connell (1990) has called "a collective practice" that constructs masculinities. The boyhood development of masculine identity and status—truly problematic in a society that offers no official rite of passage into adulthood—results from a process of interaction with people and social institutions. Thus, in discussing early motivations in sports, men commonly talk of the importance of relationships with family members, peers, and the broader community.

Family Influences

Though most of the men in this study spoke of their mothers with love, respect, even reverence, their descriptions of their earliest experiences in sports are stories of an exclusively male world. The existence of older brothers or uncles who served as teachers and athletic role models—as well as sources of competition for attention and status within the family—was very common. An older brother, uncle, or even close friend of the family who was a successful athlete appears to have acted as a sort of standard of achievement against whom to measure oneself. A 34-year-old black man who had been a three-sport star in high school said:

> *My uncles—my Uncle Harold went to the Detroit Tigers, played pro ball—all of 'em, everybody played sports, so I wanted to be better than anybody else. I knew that everybody in this town knew them—their names were something. I wanted my name to be just like theirs.*

Similarly, a black 41-year-old former professional football player recalled:

> *I was the younger of three brothers and everybody played sports, so consequently I was more or less forced into it. 'Cause one brother was always better than the next brother and then I came along and had to show them that I was just as good as them. My oldest brother was an all-city ballplayer, then my other brother comes along—he's all-city and all-state—and then I have to come along.*

For some, attempting to emulate or surpass the athletic accomplishments of older male family members created pressures that were difficult to deal with. A 33-year-old white man explained that he was a good athlete during boyhood, but the constant awareness that his two older brothers had been better made it difficult for him to feel good about himself, or to have fun in sports:

> *I had this sort of reputation that I followed from the playgrounds through grade school, and through high school. I followed these guys who were all-conference and all-state.*

Most of these men, however, saw their relationship with their athletic older brothers and uncles in a positive light; it was within these relationships that they gained experience and developed motivations that gave them a competitive "edge" within their same-aged peer group. As a 33-year-old black man describes his earliest athletic experiences:

> *My brothers were role models. I wanted to prove—especially to my brothers— that I had heart, you know, that I was a man.*

When asked, "What did it mean to you to be 'a man' at that age?" he replied:

> *Well, it meant that I didn't want to be a so-called scaredy-cat. You want to hit a guy even though he's bigger than you to show that, you know, you've got this macho image. I remember that at that young an age, that feeling was exciting to me. And that carried over, and as I got older, I got better and I began to look around me and see, well hey! I'm competitive with these guys, even though I'm younger, you know? And then of course all the compliments come—and I began to notice a change, even in my parents—especially in my father—he was proud*

of that, and that was very important to me. He was extremely important. . . .
He showed me more affection, now that I think of it.

As this man's words suggest, if men talk of their older brothers and uncles mostly as role models, teachers, and "names" to emulate, their talk of their relationships with their fathers is more deeply layered and complex. Athletic skills and competition for status may often be learned from older brothers, but it is in boys' relationships with fathers that we find many of the keys to the emotional salience of sports in the development of masculine identity.

Relationships with Fathers

The fact that boys' introductions to organized sports are often made by fathers who might otherwise be absent or emotionally distant adds a powerful emotional charge to these early experiences (Osherson 1986). Although playing organized sports eventually came to feel "natural" for all of the men interviewed in this study, many needed to be "exposed" to sports, or even gently "pushed" by their fathers to become involved in activities like Little League baseball. A white 33-year-old man explained:

> *I still remember it like it was yesterday—Dad and I driving up in his truck, and I had my glove and my hat and all that—and I said, "Dad, I don't want to do it." He says, "What?" I says, "I don't want to do it." I was nervous. That I might fail. And he says, "Don't be silly. Lookit: There's Joey and Petey and all your friends out there." And so Dad says, "You're gonna do it, come on." And in my memory he's never said that about anything else; he just knew I needed a little kick in the pants and I'd do it. And once you're out there and you see all the other kids making errors and stuff, and you know you're better than those guys, you know: Maybe I do belong here. As it turned out, Little League was a good experience.*

Some who were similarly "pushed" by their fathers were not so successful as the aforementioned man had been in Little League baseball, and thus the experience was not altogether a joyous affair. One 34-year-old white man, for instance, said he "inherited" his interest in sports from his father, who started playing catch with him at the age of four. Once he got into Little League, he felt pressured by his father, one of the coaches, who expected him to be the star of the team:

> *I'd go 0-for-four sometimes, strike out three times in a Little League game, and I'd dread the ride home. I'd come home and he'd say, "Go in the bathroom and swing the bat in the mirror for an hour," to get my swing level. . . . It didn't help much, though, I'd go out and strike out three or four times again the next game too [laughs ironically].*

When asked if he had been concerned with having his father's approval, he responded:

Failure in his eyes? Yeah, I always thought that he wanted me to get some kind of [athletic] scholarship. I guess I was afraid of him when I was a kid. He didn't hit that much, but he had a rage about him—he'd rage, and that voice would just rattle you.

Similarly, a 24-year-old black man described his awe of his father's physical power and presence, and his sense of inadequacy in attempting to emulate him:

My father had a voice that sounded like rolling thunder. Whether it was intentional on his part or not, I don't know, but my father gave me a sense, an image of him being the most powerful being on earth, and that no matter what I ever did I would never come close to him. . . . There were definite feelings of physical inadequacy that I couldn't work around.

It is interesting to note how these feelings of physical inadequacy relative to the father lived on as part of this young man's permanent internalized image. He eventually became a "feared" high school football player and broke school records in weight-lifting. . . .

Using sports activities as a means of identifying with and "living up to" the power and status of one's father was not always such a painful and difficult task for the men I interviewed. Most did not describe fathers who "pushed" them to become sports stars. The relationship between their athletic strivings and their identification with their fathers was more subtle. A 48-year-old black man, for instance, explained that he was not pushed into sports by his father, but was aware from an early age of the community status his father had gained through sports. He saw his own athletic accomplishments as a way to connect with and emulate his father:

I wanted to play baseball because my father had been quite a good baseball player in the Negro leagues before baseball was integrated, and so he was kind of a model for me. I remember, quite young, going to a baseball game he was in—this was before the war and all—I remember being in the stands with my mother and seeing him on first base, and being aware of the crowd. . . . I was aware of people's confidence in him as a serious baseball player. I don't think my father ever said anything to me like "play sports." . . . [But] I knew he would like it if I did well. . . . His admiration was important. . . . He mattered. . . .

First experiences in sports might often come through relationships with brothers or other male relatives, and the early emotional salience of sports was often directly related to a boy's relationship with his father. The sense of commitment that these young boys eventually made to the development of athletic careers is best explained as a process of development of masculine gender identity and status in relation to same-sex peers.

Masculine Identity and Early Commitment to Sports

When many of the men in this study said that during childhood they played sports because "it's just what everybody did," they of course meant that it was just what *boys* did. They were introduced to organized sports by older brothers and fathers, and once involved, found themselves playing within an exclusively male world. Though the separate (and unequal) gendered worlds of boys and girls came to appear as "natural," they were in fact socially constructed. Thorne's observations of children's activities in schools indicated that rather than "naturally" constituting "separate gendered cultures," there is considerable interaction between boys and girls in classrooms and on playgrounds. When adults set up legitimate contact between boys and girls, Thorne observed, this usually results in "relaxed interactions." But when activities in the classroom or on the playground are presented to children as sex-segregated activities and gender is marked by teachers and other adults ("boys line up here, girls over there"), "gender boundaries are heightened, and mixed-sex interaction becomes an explicit arena of risk" (Thorne 1986: 70). Thus sex-segregated activities such as organized sports as structured by adults, provide the context in which gendered identities and separate "gendered cultures" develop and come to appear natural. For the boys in this study, it became "natural" to equate masculinity with competition, physical strength, and skills. Girls simply did not (could not, it was believed) participate in these activities.

Yet it is not simply the separation of children, by adults, into separate activities that explains why many boys came to feel such a strong connection with sports activities, while so few girls did. As I listened to men recall their earliest experiences in organized sports, I heard them talk of insecurity, loneliness, and especially a need to connect with other people as a primary motivation in their early sports strivings. As a 42-year-old white man stated, "The most important thing was just being out there with the rest of the guys— being friends." Another 32-year-old interviewee was born in Mexico and moved to the United States at a fairly young age. He never knew his father, and his mother died when he was only nine years old. Suddenly he felt rootless, and threw himself into sports. His initial motivations, however, do not appear to be based on a need to compete and win:

> *Actually, what I think sports did for me is it brought me into kind of an instant family. By being on a Little League team, or even just playing with all kinds of different kids in the neighborhood, it brought what I really wanted, which was some kind of closeness. It was just being there, and being friends.*

Clearly, what these boys needed and craved was that which was most problematic for them: connection and unity with other people. But why do these young males find *organized sports* such an attractive context in which to establish "a kind of closeness" with others? . . . For the boy who both seeks and fears attachment with others, the rule-bound structure of organized sports can promise to be a safe place in which to seek nonintimate attachment with others within a context that maintains clear boundaries, distance, and separation.

Competitive Structures and Conditional Self-Worth

Young boys may initially find that sports gives them the opportunity to experience "some kind of closeness" with others, but the structure of sports and athletic careers often undermines the possibility of boys learning to transcend their fears of intimacy, thus becoming able to develop truly close and intimate relationships with others (Kidd 1990; Messner 1987). The sports world is extremely hierarchical, and an incredible amount of importance is placed on winning, on "being number one." For instance, a few years ago I observed a basketball camp put on for boys by a professional basketball coach and his staff. The youngest boys, about eight years old (who could barely reach the basket with their shots), played a brief scrimmage. Afterward, the coaches lined them up in a row in front of the older boys who were sitting in the grandstands. One by one, the coach would stand behind each boy, put his hand on the boy's head (much in the manner of a priestly benediction), and the older boys in the stands would applaud and cheer, louder or softer, depending on how well or poorly the young boy was judged to have performed. The two or three boys who were clearly the exceptional players looked confident that they would receive the praise they were due. Most of the boys, though, had expressions ranging from puzzlement to thinly disguised terror on their faces as they awaited the judgments of the older boys.

This kind of experience teaches boys that it is not "just being out there with the guys—being friends," that ensures the kind of attention and connection that they crave; it is being *better* than the other guys—*beating* them—that is the key to acceptance. Most of the boys in this study did have some early successes in sports, and thus their ambivalent need for connection with others was met, at least for a time. But the institution of sport tends to encourage the development of what Schafer (1975) has called "conditional self-worth" in boys. As boys become aware that acceptance by others is contingent upon being good—a "winner"—narrow definitions of success, based upon performance and winning, become increasingly important to them. A 33-year-old black man said that by the time he was in his early teens

> it was expected of me to do well in all my contests—I mean by my coaches, my peers, and my family. So I in turn expected to do well, and if I didn't do well, then I'd be very disappointed.

The man from Mexico, discussed above, who said that he had sought "some kind of closeness" in his early sports experiences began to notice in his

early teens that if he played well, was a *winner*, he would get attention from others:

> It got to the point where I started realizing, noticing that people were always there for me, backing me all the time—sports got to be really fun because I always had some people there backing me. Finally my oldest brother started going to all my games, even though I had never really seen who he was [laughs]—after the game, you know, we never really saw each other, but he was at all my baseball games, and it seemed like we shared a kind of closeness there, but only in those situations. Off the field, when I wasn't in uniform, he was never around.

By high school, he said, he felt "up against the wall." Sports hadn't delivered what he had hoped it would, but he thought if he just tried harder, won one more championship trophy, he would get the attention he truly craved. Despite his efforts, this attention was not forthcoming. And, sadly, the pressures he had put on himself to excel in sports had taken most of the fun out of playing.

For many of the men in this study, throughout boyhood and into adolescence, this conscious striving for successful achievement became the primary means through which they sought connection with other people (Messner 1987). But it is important to recognize that young males' internalized ambivalences about intimacy do not fully determine the contours and directions of their lives. Masculinity continues to develop through interaction with the social world—and because boys from different backgrounds are interacting with substantially different familial, educational, and other institutions, these differences will lead them to make different choices and define situations in different ways. Next, I examine the differences in the ways that boys from higher- and lower-status families and communities related to organized sports.

Status Differences and Commitments to Sports

In discussing early attractions to sports, the experiences of boys from higher- and lower-status backgrounds are quite similar. Both groups indicate the importance of fathers and older brothers in introducing them to sports. Both groups speak of the joys of receiving attention and acceptance among family and peers for early successes in sports. Note the similarities, for instance, in the following descriptions of boyhood athletic experiences of two men. First, a man born in a white, middle-class family:

> I loved playing sports so much from a very early age because of early exposure. A lot of the sports came easy at an early age, and because they did, and because you were successful at something, I think that you're inclined to strive for that gratification. It's like, if you're good, you like it, because it's instant gratification. I'm doing something that I'm good at and I'm gonna keep doing it.

Second, a black man from a poor family:

> *Fortunately I had some athletic ability, and, quite naturally, once you start doing good in whatever it is—I don't care if it's jacks—you show off what you do. That's your ability, that's your blessing, so you show it off as much as you can.*

For boys from both groups, early exposure to sports, the discovery that they had some "ability," shortly followed by some sort of family, peer, and community recognition, all eventually led to the commitment of hundreds and thousands of hours playing, practicing, and dreaming of future stardom. Despite these similarities, there are also some identifiable differences that begin to explain the tendency of males from lower-status backgrounds to develop higher levels of commitment to sports careers. The most clear-cut difference was that while men from higher-status backgrounds are likely to describe their earliest athletic experiences and motivations almost exclusively in terms of immediate family, men from lower-status backgrounds more commonly describe the importance of a broader community context. For instance, a 46-year-old man who grew up in a "poor working class" black family in a small town in Arkansas explained:

> *In that community, at the age of third or fourth grade, if you're a male, they expect you to show some kind of inclination, some kind of skill in football or basketball. It was an expected thing, you know? My mom and my dad, they didn't push at all. It was the general environment.*

A 48-year-old man describes sports activities as a survival strategy in his poor black community:

> *Sports protected me from having to compete in gang stuff, or having to be good with my fists. If you were an athlete and got into the fist world, that was your business, and that was okay—but you didn't have to if you didn't want to. People would generally defer to you, give you your space away from trouble.*

A 35-year-old man who grew up in "a poor black ghetto" described his boyhood relationship to sports similarly:

> *Where I came from, either you were one of two things: You were in sports or you were out on the streets being a drug addict, or breaking into places. The guys who were in sports, we had it a little easier, because we were accepted by both groups. . . . So it worked out to my advantage, 'cause I didn't get into a lot of trouble—some trouble, but not a lot.*

The fact that boys in lower-status communities faced these kinds of realities gave salience to their developing athletic identities. In contrast, sports were important to boys from higher-status backgrounds, yet the middle-class environment seemed more secure, less threatening, and offered far more options. By the time most of these boys got into junior high or high school, many had made conscious decisions to shift their attentions away from athletic careers to educational and (nonathletic) career goals. A 32-year-

old white college athletic director told me that he had seen his chance to pursue a pro baseball career as "pissing in the wind" and, instead, focused on education. Similarly, a 33-year-old white dentist who was a three-sport star in high school decided not to play sports in college so he could focus on getting into dental school. As he put it,

> *I think I kind of downgraded the stardom thing. I thought it was small potatoes. And sure, that's nice in high school and all that, but on a broad scale, I didn't think it amounted to all that much.*

This statement offers an important key to understanding the construction of masculine identity within a middle-class context. The status that this boy got through sports had been *very* important to him, yet he could see that "on a broad scale," this sort of status was "small potatoes." This sort of early recognition is more than a result of the oft-noted middle-class tendency to raise "future-oriented" children (Rubin 1976; Sennett and Cobb 1973). Perhaps more important, it is that the *kinds* of future orientations developed by boys from higher-status backgrounds are consistent with the middle-class context. These men's descriptions of their boyhoods reveal that they grew up immersed in a wide range of institutional frameworks, of which organized sports was just one. And—importantly—they could see that the status of adult males around them was clearly linked to their positions within various professions, public institutions, and bureaucratic organizations. It was clear that access to this sort of institutional status came through educational achievement, not athletic prowess. A 32-year-old black man who grew up in a professional-class family recalled that he had idolized Wilt Chamberlain and dreamed of being a pro basketball player, yet his father discouraged his athletic strivings:

> *He knew I liked the game. I loved the game. But basketball was not recommended; my dad would say, "That's a stereotyped image for black youth. . . . When your basketball is gone and finished, what are you gonna do? One day, you might get injured. What are you gonna look forward to?" He stressed education.*

Similarly, a 32-year-old man who was raised in a white, middle-class family, had found in sports a key means of gaining acceptance and connection in his peer group. Yet he was simultaneously developing an image of himself as a "smart student," and becoming aware of a wide range of nonsports life options:

> *My mother was constantly telling me how smart I was, how good I was, what a nice person I was, and giving me all sorts of positive strokes, and those positive strokes became a self-motivating kind of thing. I had this image of myself as smart, and I lived up to that image.*

It is not that parents of boys in lower-status families did not also encourage their boys to work hard in school. Several reported that their parents "stressed books first, sports second." It's just that the broader social context—education, economy, and community—was more likely to *narrow* lower-status boys' perceptions of real-life options, while boys from higher-status backgrounds faced an expanding world of options. For instance, with a different socioeconomic background, one 35-year-old black man might have become a great musician instead of a star professional football running back. But he did not. When he was a child, he said, he was most interested in music:

> *I wanted to be a drummer. But we couldn't afford drums. My dad couldn't go out and buy me a drum set or a guitar even—it was just one of those things; he was just trying to make ends meet.*

But he *could* afford, as could so many in his socioeconomic condition, to spend countless hours at the local park, where he was told by the park supervisor

> *that I was a natural—not only in gymnastics or baseball—whatever I did, I was a natural. He told me I shouldn't waste this talent, and so I immediately started watching the big guys then.*

In retrospect, this man had potential to be a musician or any number of things, but his environment limited his options to sports, and he made the best of it. Even within sports, he, like most boys in the ghetto, was limited:

> *We didn't have any tennis courts in the ghetto—we used to have a lot of tennis balls, but no racquets. I wonder today how good I might be in tennis if I had gotten a racquet in my hands at an early age.*

It is within this limited structure of opportunity that many lower-status young boys found sports to be *the* place, rather than *a* place, within which to construct masculine identity, status, the relationships. A 36-year-old white man explained that his father left the family when he was very young and his mother faced a very difficult struggle to make ends meet. As his words suggest, the more limited a boy's options, and the more insecure his family situation, the more likely he is to make an early commitment to an athletic career:

> *I used to ride my bicycle to Little League practice—if I'd waited for someone to pick me up and take me to the ball park I'd have never played. I'd get to the ball park and all the other kids would have their dad bring them to practice or games. But I'd park my bike to the side and when it was over I'd get on it and go home. Sports was the way for me to move everything to the side—family problems, just all the embarrassments—and think about one thing, and that was sports. . . . In the third grade, when the teacher went around the classroom and asked everybody, "What do you want to be when you grow up?," I said, "I want to be a major league baseball player," and everybody laughed their heads off.*

This man eventually did enjoy a major league baseball career. Most boys from lower-status backgrounds who make similar early commitments to athletic careers are not so successful. As stated earlier, the career structure of organized sports is highly competitive and hierarchical. In fact, the chances of attaining professional status in sports are approximately 4:100,000 for a white man, 2:100,000 for a black man, and 3:1 million for a Hispanic man in the United States (Leonard and Reyman 1988). Nevertheless, the immediate rewards (fun, status, attention), along with the constricted (nonsports) structure of opportunity, attract disproportionately large numbers of boys from lower-status backgrounds to athletic careers as their major means of constructing a masculine identity. These are the boys who later, as young men, had to struggle with "conditional self-worth," and, more often than not, occupational dead ends. Boys from higher-status backgrounds, on the other hand, bolstered their boyhood, adolescent, and early adult status through their athletic accomplishments. Their wider range of experiences and life chances led to an early shift away from sports careers as the major basis of identity (Messner 1989).

Conclusion

The conception of the masculinity-sports relationship developed here begins to illustrate the idea of an "elective affinity" between social structure and personality. Organized sports is a "gendered institution"—an institution constructed by gender relations. As such, its structure and values (rules, formal organization, sex composition, etc.) reflect dominant conceptions of masculinity and femininity. Organized sports is also a "gendering institution"—an institution that helps to construct the current gender order. Part of this construction of gender is accomplished through the "masculinizing" of male bodies and minds.

Yet boys do not come to their first experiences in organized sports as "blank slates," but arrive with already "gendering" identities due to early developmental experiences and previous socialization. I have suggested here that an important thread running through the development of masculine identity is males' ambivalence toward intimate unity with others. Those boys who experience early athletic successes find in the structure of organized sport an affinity with this masculine ambivalence toward intimacy: The rule-bound, competitive, hierarchical world of sport offers boys an attractive means of establishing an emotionally distant (and thus "safe") connection with others. Yet as boys begin to define themselves as "athletes," they must learn that in order to be accepted (to have connection) through sports, they must be winners. And in order to be winners, they must construct relationships with others (and with themselves) that are consistent with the competitive and hierarchical values and structure of the sports world. As a result, they often develop a "conditional self-worth" that leads them to construct more instrumental relationships with themselves and others. This ultimately exacerbates their difficulties in constructing intimate relationships with others. In effect, the interaction between the young male's preexisting internalized ambivalence toward intimacy with the competitive, hierarchical institution of sport has resulted in the construction of a masculine personality that is characterized by instrumental rationality, goal-orientation, and difficulties with intimate connection and expression (Messner 1987).

This theoretical line of inquiry invites us not simply to examine how social institutions "socialize" boys, but also to explore the ways that boys' already-gendering identities interact with social institutions (which, like organized sport, are themselves the product of gender relations). This study has also suggested that it is not some singular "masculinity" that is being constructed through athletic careers. It may be correct, from a psychoanalytic perspective, to suggest that all males bring ambivalences toward intimacy to their interactions with the world, but "the world" is a very different place for males from different racial and socioeconomic backgrounds. Because males have substantially different interactions with the world, based on class, race, and other differences and inequalities, we might expect the construction of masculinity to take on different meanings for boys and men from differing backgrounds (Messner 1989). Indeed, this study has suggested that boys from higher-status backgrounds face a much broader range of options than do their lower-status counterparts. As a result, athletic careers take on different meanings for these boys. Lower-status boys are likely to see athletic careers as *the* institutional context for the construction of their masculine status and identities, while higher-status males make an early shift away from athletic careers toward other institutions (usually education and nonsports careers). A key line of inquiry for future studies might begin by exploring this irony of sports careers: Despite the fact that "the athlete" is currently an example of an exemplary form of masculinity in public ideology, the vast majority of boys who become most committed to athletic careers are never well rewarded for their efforts. The fact that class and racial dynamics lead boys from higher-status backgrounds, unlike their lower-status counterparts, to move into nonsports careers illustrates how the construction of different kinds of masculinities is a key component of the overall construction of the gender order.

REFERENCES

Benjamin, J. 1988. *The Bonds of Love: Psychoanalysis, Feminism and the Problem of Domination.* New York: Pantheon.

Connell, R. W. 1990. "An Iron Man: The Body and Some Contradictions of Hegemonic Masculinity." In *Sport, Men and the Gender Order: Critical Feminist Perspectives,* edited by M. A. Messner and D. F. Sabo. Champaign, IL: Human Kinetics.

Eitzen, D. S. 1975. "Athletics in the Status System of Male Adolescents: A Replication of Coleman's *The Adolescent Society.*" *Adolescence* 10:268–76.

Haug, F. 1987. *Female Sexualization.* London: Verso.

Kidd, B. 1990. "The Men's Cultural Centre: Sports and the Dynamic of Women's Oppression / Men's Repression." In *Sport, Men and the Gender Order: Critical Feminist*

Perspectives, edited by M. A. Messner and D. F. Sabo. Champaign, IL: Human Kinetics.

Kimmel, M. S. 1990. "Baseball and the Reconstitution of American Masculinity: 1880– 1920." In *Sport, Men and the Gender Order: Critical Feminist Perspectives,* edited by M. A. Messner and D. F. Sabo. Champaign, IL: Human Kinetics.

Leonard, W. M., II, and J. M. Reyman. 1988. "The Odds of Attaining Professional Athlete Status: Refining the Computations." *Sociology of Sport Journal* 5:162–69.

Levinson, D. J. et al. 1978. *The Seasons of a Man's Life.* New York: Ballantine.

Messner, M. 1987. "The Meaning of Success: The Athletic Experience and the Development of Male Identity." Pp. 193–210 in *The Making of Masculinities: The New Men's Studies,* edited by H. Brod. Boston: Allyn & Unwin.

———. 1989. "Masculinities and Athletic Careers." *Gender and Society* 3:71–88.

Osherson, S. 1986. *Finding Our Fathers: How a Man's Life Is Shaped by His Relationship with His Father.* New York: Fawcett Columbine.

Rubin, L. B. 1976. *Worlds of Pain: Life in the Working Class Family.* New York: Basic Books.

Sabo, D. 1985. "Sport, Patriarchy and Male Identity: New Questions about Men and Sport." *Arena Review* 9:2.

Schafer, W. E. 1975. "Sport and Male Sex Role Socialization." *Sport Sociology Bulletin* 4:47–54.

Sennett, R., and J. Cobb. 1973. *The Hidden Injuries of Class.* New York: Random House.

Thorne, B. 1986. "Girls and Boys Together . . . but Mostly Apart: Gender Arrangements in Elementary Schools." Pp. 167–84 in *Relationships and Development,* edited by W. W. Hartup and Z. Rubin. Hillsdale, NJ: Erlbaum.

13

MAKING IT BY FAKING IT
Working-Class Students in an Elite Academic Environment

ROBERT GRANFIELD

Learning an occupation is a common form of adult socialization. Occupational socialization occurs during formal education, during job training, and during time spent on the job. Every profession has a set of values that it wants its colleagues to embrace. For example, to become a doctor one needs to learn the skills and knowledge of practicing medicine as well as the attitudes and values of the medical profession. Medical students experience

From *Journal of Contemporary Ethnography* 20, no. 3 (October 1991): 331–51. Copyright © 1991 by Sage Publications, Inc. Reprinted with the permission of the publishers.

an intense period of professional socialization during the years, almost a decade, they spend in medical school and residency. Law students are socialized as well, and the following reading by Robert Granfield (1991), an assistant professor of sociology at the University of Denver, discusses how working-class students are socialized into elite law schools and into the legal profession.

R esearch on stigma has generated significant insights into the complex relationship between self and society. The legacy of Goffman's (1963) seminal work on the subject can be found in studies on alcoholism, mental illness, homosexuality, physical deformities, and juvenile delinquency. Even the literature on gender and racial inequality has benefited from an emphasis on stigma. Goffman's attention to the social processes of devaluation and the emerging self-concepts of discredited individuals not only created research opportunities for generations of sociologists but contributed to a humanistic ideology that viewed stigma assignment and its effects as unjust.

One of the most vibrant research programs that emerged from Goffman's classic work has been in the area of stigma management. A host of conceptual terms have been employed to describe the process through which discreditable individuals control information about themselves so as to manage their social identity. Concepts such as passing, deviance disavowal, accounts, disclaimers, and covering have often been used in analyzing accommodations and adjustments to deviance, as Pfuhl's (1986) review shows. These tactics, while offering rewards associated with being seen as normal, frequently contribute to psychological stress. Possessing what Goffman (1963:5) referred to as "undesired differentness" often has significant consequences for one's personal identity as well as for available life chances. . . .

In this article, I focus on class stigma by examining a group of highly successful, upwardly mobile, working-class students who gained admission to a prestigious Ivy League law school in the East. While upward mobility from the working class occurs far less often within elite branches of the legal profession (Heinz and Laumann 1982; Smigel 1969) or corporate management (Useem and Karabel 1986), a certain amount of this type of mobility does take place. Working-class aspirants to the social elite, however, must accumulate cultural capital (Bourdieu and Passeron 1990; Cookson and Persell 1985) before they are able to transcend their status boundaries.

First, this article examines the ways in which working-class students experience a sense of differentness and marginality within the law school's elite environment. Next, I explore how these students react to their emerging class stigma by managing information about their backgrounds. I then demonstrate that the management strategies contribute to identity ambivalence and consider the secondary forms of adjustment students use to resolve this tension. Finally, I discuss why an analysis of social class can benefit from the insights forged by Goffman's work on stigma.

Setting and Methodology

The data analyzed for this article were collected as part of a much larger project associated with law school socialization (Granfield 1989). The subjects consist of students attending a prestigious, national law school in the eastern part of the United States. The school has had a long reputation of training lawyers who have become partners in major Wall Street law firms, Supreme Court judges, United States presidents and other politicians, heads of foundations, and . . . [have assumed many] other eminent leadership positions. Throughout the school's history, it has drawn mostly on the talents of high-status males. It was not until the second half of the twentieth century that women, minorities, and members of the lower classes were allowed admission into this esteemed institution (Abel 1989).

Most of the students attending the university at the time the study was being conducted were white and middle class.[1] The overwhelming majority are the sons and daughters of the professional-managerial class. Over 70 percent of those returning questionnaires had Ivy League or other highly prestigious educational credentials. As one would expect, fewer working-class students possessed such credentials.

A triangulated research design (Fielding and Fielding 1986) was used to collect the data. The first phase consisted of extensive fieldwork at the law school from 1985 to 1988, during which time I became a "peripheral member" (Adler and Adler 1987) in selected student groups. My activities while in the field consisted of attending classes with students, participating in their Moot Court[2] preparations, studying with students on campus, and at times, in their apartments, lunching with them, becoming involved in student demonstrations over job recruiting and faculty hiring, attending extracurricular lectures presented on campus, and participating in orientation exercises for first-year students. Throughout the entire fieldwork phase, I assumed both overt and covert roles. During the observation periods in classrooms, I recorded teacher-student interactions that occurred.

To supplement these observations, I conducted in-depth interviews with 103 law students at various stages in their training. Both personal interviews and small-group interviews with three or four students were recorded. The interviews lasted approximately two hours each and sought to identify the lived process through which law students experience legal training.

Finally, I administered a survey to 50 percent of the 1,540 students attending the law school. The survey examined their backgrounds, motives for attending law school, subjective perceptions of personal change, expectations about future practice, and evaluations of various substantive areas of practice. Over half (391) of the questionnaires were returned—a high rate of response for a survey of six pages requiring approximately 30 minutes of the respondent's time.

For this article, a subset of working-class students was selected for extensive analysis. Of the 103 students interviewed for the larger study, 23 came from working-class backgrounds, none of these from either the labor aristocracy or the unstable sectors of the working class. Typical parental occupations include postal worker, house painter, factory worker, fireman, dock worker, and carpenter. Many of these students were interviewed several times during their law school career. Many of the students selected for interviews were identified through questionnaires, while others were selected through the process of snowball sampling (Chadwick, Bahr, and Albrecht 1984).

Feeling Out of Place

Working-class students entered this elite educational institution with a great deal of class pride. This sense of class pride is reflected in the fact that a significantly larger proportion of working-class students reported entering law school for the purposes of contributing to social change than their non-working-class counterparts (see Granfield and Koenig 1990). That these students entered law school with the desire to help the downtrodden suggests that they identified with their working-class kin. In fact, students often credited their class background as being a motivating factor in their decision to pursue a career in social justice. One third-year student, whose father worked as a postal worker, recalled her parental influence:

> I wanted a career in social justice. It seemed to me to be a good value for someone who wanted to leave this world a little better than they found it. My parents raised me with a sense that there are right things and wrong things and that maybe you ought to try to do some right things with your life.

A second-year student said that he was influenced by the oppressive experiences that his father endured as a factory laborer. Coming to law school to pursue a career in a labor union, this student explained, "I was affected by my father, who had a job as a machinist. My father believes that corporations have no decency. I would term it differently but we're talking about the same thing." Identifying with their working-class heritage produced not only a sense of pride but a system of values and ideals that greatly influenced their initial career objectives.

However, identification with the working class began to diminish soon after these students entered law school. Not long after arriving, most working-class students encountered an entirely new moral career. Although initially proud of their accomplishments, they soon came to define themselves as different and their backgrounds a burden. Lacking the appropriate cultural capital (Bourdieu 1984) associated with their more privileged counterparts, working-class students began to experience a crisis in competency. Phrases such as "the first semester makes you feel extremely incompetent," "the first year is like eating humble pie," and "I felt very small, powerless, and dumb" were almost universal among these working-class students. Some students felt embarrassed by their difficulty in using the elaborated speech codes (Bernstein 1977) associated with the middle class. One working-class woman said that she was very aware of using "proper" English, adding that "it makes me self-conscious when I use the wrong word or tense. I feel that if I had grown up in the middle class, I wouldn't have lapses. I have difficulty expressing thoughts while most other people here don't."

The recognition of their apparent differentness is perhaps best noted by examining the students' perception of stress associated with the first year of studies. Incoming working-class students reported significantly higher levels of personal stress than did their counterparts with more elite backgrounds. Much of this anxiety came from fears of academic inadequacy. Despite generally excellent college grades and their success in gaining admission to a nationally ranked law school, these students often worried that they did not measure up to the school's high standards. Nearly 62 percent of the first-year working-class students reported experiencing excessive grade pressure, compared to only 35 percent of those students from higher social class backgrounds.

In the words of Sennett and Cobb (1973), this lack of confidence is a "hidden injury of class," a psychological burden that working-class students experienced as they came to acquire the "identity beliefs" associated with middle-class society. While most students experience some degree of uncertainty and competency crisis during their first year, working-class students face the additional pressure of being cultural outsiders. Lacking manners of speech, attire, values, and experiences associated with their more privileged counterparts, even the most capable working-class student felt out of place:

> I had a real problem my first year because law and legal education are based on upper-middle-class values. The class debates had to do with profit maximization, law and economics, atomistic individualism. I remember in class we were talking about landlords' responsibility to maintain decent housing in rental apartments. Some people were saying that there were good reasons not to do this. Well, I think that's bullshit because I grew up with people who lived in apartments with rats, leaks, and roaches. I feel really different because I didn't grow up in suburbia.

Another student, a third-year working-class woman, felt marginalized because even her teachers assumed class homogeneity:

> I get sensitive about what professors have to say in class. I remember in a business class the professor seemed to assume that we all had fathers that worked in business and that we all understood about family investments. He said, "You're all pretty much familiar with this because of your family background."

> *I remember thinking, doesn't he think there's any people in this law school who come from a working-class background?*

Such experiences contributed to a student's sense of living in an alien world. The social distance these students experienced early in their law school career produced considerable discomfort.

This discomfort grew more intense as they became increasingly immersed into this new elite world. Within a short span of time, these students began to experience a credential gap vis-à-vis other students who possessed more prestigious academic credentials. A first-year male student who attended a state school in the Midwest explained:

> *I'm not like most people here. I didn't go to prestigious schools. I'm a bit of a minority here because of that. When I got here I was really intimidated by the fact of how many Yale and Harvard people there were here.*

At times, working-class law students were even embarrassed by their spouse's lower status. One first-year student described how her husband's credential gap caused her some anxiety:

> *People would ask me what my husband did and I would say he works for Radio Shack. People would be surprised. That was hard. Lately, we haven't done as much with [law school] people.*

Thus students sometimes pruned contacts that would potentially result in stigma disclosure. In general, then, as working-class students progressed through law school, they began to adopt a view of themselves as different. The recognition of this difference subsequently led them to develop techniques of adjusting to their perceived secondary status.

Faking It

The management of identity has critical strategic importance not only for group affiliation and acceptance but for life chances. Stigma limits one's opportunities to participate in social life as a complete citizen, particularly so for those possessing gender or racial stigmas. However, because of the visibility of these stigmas, a person's adjustment to second-class citizenship is accomplished typically through either role engulfment in which a person accepts a spoiled identity (Schur 1971) or through direct confrontation where assignment of secondary status is itself challenged (Schur 1980). Rarely are these groups able to employ the concealment tactics typical among those groups whose stigma is not overtly visible.

Unlike gender or racial stigma, however, individuals often adjust to class stigma by learning to conceal their uniqueness. The practice of concealing one's class background, for instance, is not unusual. Certainly, members of the elite frequently learn that it is in "bad taste" to flaunt their privileged background and that it is more gracious to conceal their eminent social status (Baltzell 1958). Similarly, individuals who experience downward mobility often attempt to maintain their predecline image by concealing loss of status. Camouflaging unemployment in the world of management by using such terms as "consultant" and by doctoring résumés are ways that downwardly mobile executives "cover" their spoiled status (Newman 1988). Concealing one's social class circumstances and the stigma that may be associated with it assist individuals in dealing with any rejection and ostracism that may be forthcoming were the person's actual status known.

Initially, students who took pride in having accomplished upward mobility openly displayed a working-class presentation of self. Many went out of their way to maintain this presentation. One first-year student who grew up in a labor union family in New York explained that "I have consciously maintained my working-class image. I wear work shirts or old flannel shirts and blue jeans every day." During his first year, this student flaunted his working-class background, frequently also donning an old army jacket, hiking boots, and a wool hat. Identifying himself as part of the "proletarian left," he tried to remain isolated from what he referred to as the "elitist" law school community.

This attempt to remain situated in the working class, however, not only separated these students from the entire law school community but alienated them from groups that shared their ideological convictions. While much of the clothing worn by non-working-class students suggests resistance to being identified as a member of the elite, working-class students become increasingly aware of their differentness. Although these students identify with the working class, others, despite their appearance, possess traits and lifestyles that are often associated with more privileged groups (see Lurie 1983; Stone 1970). One first-year woman who described herself as "radical" complained that the other law school radicals were really "a bunch of upper-class white men." Subsequently, working-class students must disengage from their backgrounds if they desire to escape feeling discredited.

Working-class students disengaged from their previous identity by concealing their class backgrounds. Just as deviants seek to manage their identity by "passing" as nondeviants (Goffman 1963), these working-class law students often adopted identities that were associated with the more elite social classes.[3] Concealment allowed students to better participate in the culture of eminence that exists within the law school and reap available rewards.

This concealment meant, for instance, that students needed to acquire new dress codes. As Stone (1970) illustrated, appearance signifies identity and exercises a regulatory function over the responses of others. Such cultural codes pertaining to appearance often are used to exclude individuals from elite social positions (Bourdieu 1984; Jackell 1988; Lamont and Lareau 1988). Although working-class students lacked the cultural capital of higher social classes, they began to realize that they could successfully mimic their more privileged counterparts. Like undistinguished prep school students (Cookson and Persell 1985), working-class law students learned how to behave in an upper-class world, including how to dress for a new audience whose favorable appraisal they must cultivate. One second-year male discussed this process:

> *I remember going to buy suits here. I went to Brooks Brothers for two reasons. One, I don't own a suit. My father owns one suit, and it's not that good. Second, I think it's important to look good. A lot of my friends went to Brooks Brothers, and I feel it's worth it to do it right and not to have another hurdle to walk in and have the wrong thing on. It's all a big play act. . . . During my first year, I had no luck with interviews. I was in my own little world when I came here. I wished I had paid more attention to the dressing habits of second- and third-year students.*

Being in their own "working-class world" forced these students to begin recognizing the importance of different interpersonal skills. A second-year woman commented that

> *I have really begun to see the value of having good social skills. I think that is one of the ways that law firms weed out people. In order to get jobs you have to have those social skills. I'm real conscious of that when I go out on interviews now.*

The recognition among working-class students that they were able to imitate upper-class students increasingly encouraged them to conceal their backgrounds. One second-year student, whose father worked as a house painter, boasted of his mastery of "passing":

> *I generally don't tell people what my father does or what my mother does. I notice that I'm different, but it's not something other people here notice because I can fake it. They don't notice that I come from a blue-collar background.*

Paying attention to the impression that one presents becomes extremely important for the upwardly mobile working-class student.

These students were sometimes assisted in their performances by professional career counselors employed by the law school. These professionals gave students instructions on how to present themselves as full-fledged members of this elite community. Students were taught that unless they downplayed their social class background, the most lucrative opportunities would be denied them. A third-year woman from a working-class area in Boston recalled learning this new norm of presentation:

> *I'm sort of proud that I'm from South Boston and come from a working-class background. During my second year, however, I wasn't having much luck with my first interviews. I went to talk with my adviser about how to change my résumé a bit or how to present myself better. I told my adviser that on the interviews I was presenting myself as a slightly unusual person with a different*

background. We talked about that, and he told me that it probably wasn't a good idea to present myself as being a little unusual. I decided that he was right and began to play up that I was just like them. After that, the interviews and offers began rolling in. I began to realize that they [interviewers] really like people who are like themselves.

Recognizing that job recruiters seek homogeneity is an important lesson that upwardly mobile working-class students must learn if they are to gain admission into high status and financially rewarding occupations.[4] Kanter (1977) demonstrated, for instance, that managers come to reward those who resemble themselves. More recently, Jackell (1988) documented how the failure of managers to "fit in" resulted in suspicion and subsequent exclusion from advancement. Fitting in is particularly important in prestigious law firms which tend to resemble the high-status clients they represent (Abel 1989). During interviews, however, working-class law students faced a distinct disadvantage, as the interviewers who actively pursued new recruits rarely posed questions about the student's knowledge of law.[5] Most seemed intent on finding students who fit into the law firm's corporate structure. The entire recruitment process itself, from the initial interview to "fly out," represents ceremonial affirmation of these students' elite status in which they need only demonstrate their "social" competence. Working-class students typically found such interactions stressful. One third-year student explained her experiences:

They [the recruiters] didn't test my knowledge of law. They were interested in finding out what kind of person I was and what my background was. I tried to avoid talking about that and instead stressed the kind of work I was interested in. I think that most firms want a person who they can mold, that fits into their firm.

Some of the most successful working-class students enjoyed the accolades bestowed on them because of their hard work and natural abilities. In speaking of her success, a third-year student on law review said that when she entered law school, it never occurred to her that she would clerk for the Supreme Court and then work for a major Wall Street law firm, adding that "once you begin doing well and move up the ladder and gain a whole new set of peers, then you begin to think about the possibilities." However, such success comes at a price, particularly for working-class students of color. Although having achieved success, many of these students continued to feel like outsiders. One such student, a third-year black male, reflected on what he considered the unfortunate aspects of affirmative action programs:

I have mixed feelings about the law review because of its affirmative action policies. On the one hand, I think it's good that minorities are represented on the law review. On the other hand, there's a real stigma attached to it. Before law school, I achieved by my own abilities. On law review, I don't feel I get respect. I find myself working very hard and getting no respect. Other students don't work as hard. I spend a lot of time at the review because I don't want to turn in a bad assignment. I don't want them [other law review members] to think that I don't have what it takes.

Students who perceived themselves as outsiders frequently overcompensated for their failings because they felt judged by the "master status" associated with their social identity. This reaction to class stigma is typical among working-class students in educational institutions. In addition to developing their educational skills, working-class students are confronted with learning social skills as well. This makes succeeding particularly difficult for these students and is a task fraught with the fear of being discovered as incompetent (Sennett and Cobb 1973).

Ambivalence

Despite their maneuvers, these working-class students had difficulty transcending their previous identity. The attempt by these students to manage their stigma resulted in what Goffman (1963:107) termed "identity ambivalence." Working-class students who sought to exit their class background could neither embrace their group nor let it go. This ambivalence is often felt by working-class individuals who attain upward mobility into the professional-managerial class (Steinitz and Solomon 1986). Many experience the "stranger in paradise" syndrome, in which working-class individuals feel like virtual outsiders in middle-class occupations (Ryan and Sackrey 1984). Such experiences frequently lead to considerable identity conflict among working-class individuals who attempt to align themselves with the middle class.

The working-class law students in my sample typically experienced identity conflicts on their upward climb. Not only did they feel deceptive in their adjustment strategies, but many felt the additional burden of believing they had "sold out" their own class and were letting their group down. Like other stigmatized individuals who gain acceptance among dominant groups (Goffman 1963), these students often felt they were letting down their own group by representing elite interests. One third-year female student ruefully explained:

My brother keeps asking me whether I'm a Republican yet. He thought that after I finished law school I would go to work to help people, not work for one of those firms that do business. In a way, he's my conscience. Maybe he's right. I've got a conflict with what I'm doing. I came from the working class and wanted to do public interest law. I have decided not to do that. It's been a difficult decision for me. I'm not completely comfortable about working at a large firm.

Another student, who grew up on welfare, expressed similar reservations about his impending career in law:

I'm not real happy about going to a large firm. I make lots of apologies. I'm still upset about the fact that my clients are real wealthy people, and it's not clear as to what the social utility of that will be.

Like the previous example, this student experienced a form of self-alienation as a result of his identity ambivalence. Students often experience a sense of guilt as they transcend their working-class backgrounds. Such guilt, however, needs to be abated if these students are to successfully adjust to their new reference group and reduce the status conflict they experience. For these working-class students, making the primary adjustment to upward mobility required strategies of accommodation in personal attitudes regarding their relationship to members of less privileged social classes. Secondary identity adjustments were therefore critical in helping students mitigate the ambivalence they experienced over their own success and subsequent separation from the working class.

Resolving Ambivalence

Although accommodation strategies were typical throughout the entire student body,[6] working-class students at this law school were more likely to employ particular types of strategies to help manage their identity. Students sought to manage their ambivalence by remaining "ideologically" distanced from the very social class their elite law school credential had facilitated alignment with. Many of these students became deliberate role models, unreservedly immersing themselves in higher social classes for that specific purpose. Such adjustments might be thought of as political since they were intended to directly challenge the domination of social elites. A black working-class student described how his actions would benefit the less fortunate:

I get slammed for being a corporate tool. People feel that I have sold out. I'm irritated by that. For years, blacks have been treated as slaves, sharecroppers, or porters. So I think that whether I want to be a partner at Cravath or to be an NAACP defense attorney, either of these positions are politically correct. We need black people with money and power. I think that I can make significant contributions to black causes.

For many students who experienced ambivalence, working in elite law firms was seen as the best way to help those they left behind. Other students redefined the value of large corporate law firms for the opportunities that such positions offered in contributing to social change. One third-year student suggested:

I used to think that social change would come about by being an activist. That's why I originally wanted to do public interest law. But you really can't accomplish much by doing this. The hiring partner at [a major New York law firm] convinced me that this is the only way to get things done. He served as the under secretary of state in the [former president's] administration. He made sense when he told me that if I wanted to contribute to social change I had to become an important person.

Students became less convinced that directly serving the less-privileged social classes would effectively resolve the problems that concerned them. A third-year student explained how disenchanted she had become with public interest law:

I used to think that you could do good things for people. . . . I don't think that anymore. I'm no longer troubled by the idea of being a corporate lawyer as opposed to a public interest one. I'm still concerned about social problems like poverty or poor housing, but I'm not sure that being a public interest attorney is the way to resolve those things. The needs of the people that public interest lawyers serve are just beyond what I can do as an attorney. I think I can do more good for people if I commit myself to working with community groups or activities in the bar during my spare time.

The offering of such accounts helps students resolve the contradiction they experience by choosing a large law firm practice, as does the practical planning to use one's spare time (e.g., to do community activities). Unfortunately, given the structure of contemporary large law firms, spare time is a rarity (Nelson 1988; Spangler 1986). Adopting these new definitions regarding the pursuit of effective social change means that working-class students need not feel penitent over their upward mobility. Such strategies, of course, are attractive, as they suggest that the student is becoming elite not solely because he or she is striving for personal reward and success but as a means to best pursue the noble ideals of public service and social activism.

A more drastic accommodation involved avoidance of those who reminded working-class students of their social obligations toward helping the less fortunate. Just associating with individuals whose career path was geared toward helping the downtrodden caused considerable uneasiness in working-class students who had decided to enter large law firms. One third-year student said that he had begun to avoid law students who had retained their commitment to work with the poor:

It's taken for granted here that you can work for a large firm and still be a good person. The people who don't reinforce that message make me uncomfortable now. Frankly, that's why I'm not hanging out with the public interest people. They remind me of my own guilt.

In some cases, avoidance turned into open hostility. Another third-year student described how she now saw other students who remained committed to their ideals of helping the less fortunate: "They're so single-minded at times and I think a little naive. They've really pushed me away from wanting to do public interest work as a full-time occupation." Condemning her condemn-ers helped this student neutralize the guilt she felt over working for a corporate law firm.

Conclusion

Upwardly mobile working-class students in this study, as well as in others, interpret and experience their social class from the perspective of stigma. However, since the stigma of being a member of the lower classes is thought to be just, upwardly mobile working-class students frequently construct identities in which they seek to escape the taint associated with their affiliation. Overcoming this stigma is therefore considered an individual rather than a collective effort. As was demonstrated in this study, such efforts often involve managing one's identity in the ways that Goffman outlined. Research that explores identity struggles as they relate to class could offer further extensions of Goffman's comments on stigma. Such research also has potential value in contributing to our understanding of working-class movements in the United States. Indeed, exploring the experience of class from the perspective of stigma and its management could offer great insight into the social psychology of working-class disempowerment.

ENDNOTES

Author's Note: Partial funding for this research was provided by the Woodrow Wilson Foundation.

[1] The following are the percentage distributions of social class background on the random sample of questionnaire returnees I collected for the larger project: upper class (2.8), upper-middle (44.6), middle (30.0), lower-middle (8.0), working (13.1), and lower (0.5).

[2] This is a first-year exercise in which students select a case to argue in front of a three-person panel consisting of a law professor, a third-year student, and an invited guest from the legal community. First-year students prepare their cases for several months in advance before formally presenting their oral argument.

[3] Similar findings were reported by Domhoff and Zweigenhaft (1991) in which they described the experiences of black students who were enrolled in elite prep schools as a result of affirmative action.

[4] Students are actively pursued. During the 1987 recruitment seasons at the law school, an average of 44 recruiters from commercial law firms conducted interviews with students each day. This represents nearly one law firm for each law student eligible to interview. In most cases, law firms are looking to hire more than one student.

[5] A study of hiring policies among large law firms found that "personal characteristics" ranked second among the criteria for selecting new lawyers (see Buller and Beck-Dudley 1990).

[6] Many students are confronted with identity conflicts that stem from the separation of personal values from professional roles. This is felt most among those students

who entered law school with social activist ideals (for further discussion of this, see Granfield 1986, 1989, forthcoming).

REFERENCES

Abel, R. 1989. *American Lawyers.* New York: Oxford University Press.
Adler, P. and P. Adler. 1987. *Membership Roles in Field Research.* Newbury Park, CA: Sage.
Baltzell, E. D. 1958. *Philadelphia Gentlemen.* New York: Free Press.
Bernstein, B. 1977. *Class Codes and Control.* Vol. 3, *Towards a Theory of Educational Transmission.* London: Routledge & Kegan Paul.
Bourdieu, P. 1984. *Distinction: A Social Critique of the Judgment of Taste.* Cambridge, MA: Harvard University Press.
Bourdieu, P. and J. C. Passeron. 1990. *Reproduction in Education, Society and Culture.* London: Routledge & Kegan Paul.
Buller, P. and C. Beck-Dudley. 1990. "Performance, Policies and Personnel." *American Bar Association Journal* 76:94.
Chadwick, B., H. Bahr, and S. Albrecht. 1984. *Social Science Research Methods.* Englewood Cliffs, NJ: Prentice-Hall.
Cookson, P. and C. Persell. 1985. *Preparing for Power: America's Elite Boarding Schools.* New York: Basic Books.
Domhoff, G. W. and R. Zweigenhaft. 1991. *Blacks in the White Establishment: A Study of Race and Class in America.* New Haven, CT: Yale University Press.
Fielding, N. and J. Fielding. 1986. *Linking Data.* Beverly Hills, CA: Sage.
Goffman, E. 1963. *Stigma: Notes on the Management of Spoiled Identity.* Englewood Cliffs, NJ: Prentice-Hall.
Granfield, R. 1986. "Legal Education As Corporate Ideology: Student Adjustment to the Law School Experience." *Sociological Forum* 1:514–23.
———. 1989. "Making the Elite Lawyer: Culture and Ideology in Legal Education." Ph.D. dissertation, Northeastern University, Boston.
———. Forthcoming. *Making Elite Lawyers.* New York: Routledge, Chapman & Hall.
Granfield, R. and T. Koenig. 1990. "From Activism to Pro Bono: The Redirection of Working Class Altruism at Harvard Law School." *Critical Sociology* 17:57–80.
Heinz, J. and E. Laumann. 1982. *Chicago Lawyers: The Social Structure of the Bar.* New York: Russell Sage.
Jackell, R. 1988. *Moral Mazes: The World of the Corporate Manager.* New York: Oxford University Press.
Kanter, R. 1977. *Men and Women of the Corporation.* New York: Basic Books.
Lamont, M. and A. Lareau. 1988. "Cultural Capital: Allusions, Gaps and Glissandos in Recent Theoretical Development." *Sociological Theory* 6:153–68.
Lurie, A. 1983. *The Language of Clothes.* New York: Vintage.
Nelson, R. 1988. *Partners with Power: The Social Transformation of the Large Law Firm.* Berkeley: University of California Press.
Newman, K. 1988. *Falling from Grace: The Experience of Downward Mobility in the American Middle Class.* New York: Free Press.
Pfuhl, E. 1986. *The Deviance Process.* Belmont, CA: Wadsworth.
Ryan, J. and C. Sackrey. 1984. *Strangers in Paradise: Academics from the Working Class.* Boston: South End Press.
Schur, E. 1971. *Labeling Deviant Behavior.* New York: Harper & Row.
———. 1980. *The Politics of Deviance.* Englewood Cliffs, NJ: Prentice-Hall.
Sennett, R. and R. Cobb. 1973. *The Hidden Injuries of Class.* New York: Random House.
Smigel, E. 1969. *The Wall Street Lawyer.* Bloomington: Indiana University Press.

Spangler, E. 1986. *Lawyers for Hire: Salaried Professionals at Work.* New Haven, CT: Yale University Press.

Steinitz, V. and E. Solomon. 1986. *Starting Out: Class and Community in the Lives of Working Class Youth.* Philadelphia: Temple University Press.

Stone, G. 1970. "Appearance and the Self." Pp. 394–414 in *Social Psychology through Symbolic Interaction,* edited by G. Stone and H. Farberman. New York: Wiley.

Useem, M. and J. Karabel. 1986. "Paths to Corporate Management." *American Sociological Review* 51:184–200.

14

ANYBODY'S SON WILL DO

GWYNNE DYER

An important point about socialization is that if culture is learned, it also can be unlearned. Sociologists call this process *resocialization*. This situation occurs when an individual gives up one way of life and one set of values for another. Examples of resocialization include the experience of new immigrants, of a person changing careers, of someone joining a feminist consciousness-raising group, or of an individual undergoing a religious conversion, such as a woman entering a convent to become a nun or a person being initiated into a cult. The following reading by journalist Gwynne Dyer is from his 1985 book, *War: Past, Present, and Future.* Here, Dyer focuses on the intense resocialization civilians experience during military basic training.

You think about it and you know you're going to have to kill but you don't understand the implications of that, because in the society in which you've lived murder is the most heinous of crimes . . . and you are in a situation in which it's turned the other way round. . . . When you do actually kill someone the experience, my experience, was one of revulsion and disgust. . . .

I was utterly terrified—petrified—but I knew there had to be a Japanese sniper in a small fishing shack near the shore. He was firing in the other direction at Marines in another battalion, but I knew as soon as he picked off the people there—there was a window on our side—that he would start picking

From *War: Past, Present, and Future,* pp. 101–105, 108–16, and 125. Copyright © 1985 by Media Resources. Reprinted with the permission of Crown Publishers, a division of Random House, Inc.

us off. And there was nobody else to go . . . and so I ran towards the shack and broke in and found myself in an empty room. . . .

There was a door which meant there was another room and the sniper was in that—and I just broke that down. I was just absolutely gripped by the fear that this man would expect me and would shoot me. But as it turned out he was in a sniper harness and he couldn't turn around fast enough. He was entangled in the harness so I shot him with a .45, and I felt remorse and shame. I can remember whispering foolishly, "I'm sorry" and then just throwing up. . . . I threw up all over myself. It was a betrayal of what I'd been taught since a child.

—Wɪʟʟɪᴀᴍ Mᴀɴᴄʜᴇsᴛᴇʀ

Yet he did kill the Japanese soldier, just as he had been trained to—the revulsion only came afterward. And even after Manchester knew what it was like to kill another human being, a young man like himself, he went on trying to kill his "enemies" until the war was over. Like all the other tens of millions of soldiers who had been taught from infancy that killing was wrong, and had then been sent off to kill for their countries, he was almost helpless to disobey, for he had fallen into the hands of an institution so powerful and so subtle that it could quickly reverse the moral training of a lifetime.

The whole vast edifice of the military institution rests on its ability to obtain obedience from its members even unto death—and the killing of others. It has enormous powers of compulsion at its command, of course, but all authority must be based ultimately on consent. The task of extracting that consent from its members has probably grown harder in recent times, for the gulf between the military and the civilian worlds has undoubtedly widened: Civilians no longer perceive the threat of violent death as an everyday hazard of existence, and the categories of people whom it is not morally permissible to kill have broadened to include (in peacetime) the entire human race. Yet the armed forces of every country can still take almost any young male civilian and turn him into a soldier with all the right reflexes and attitudes in only a few weeks. Their recruits usually have no more than twenty years' experience of the world, most of it as children, while the armies have had all of history to practice and perfect their techniques.

Just think of how the soldier is treated. While still a child he is shut up in the barracks. During his training he is always being knocked about. If he makes the least mistake he is beaten, a burning blow on his body, another on his eye, perhaps his head is laid open with a wound. He is battered and bruised with flogging. On the march . . . they hang heavy loads round his neck like that of an ass.

—Egyptian, ca. 1500 B.C.[1]

The moment I talk to the new conscripts about the homeland I strike a land mine. So I kept quiet. Instead, I try to make soldiers of them. I give them hell from morning to sunset. They begin to curse me, curse the army, curse the state. Then they begin to curse together, and become a truly cohesive group, a unit, a fighting unit.

—Israeli, ca. A.D. 1970[2]

All soldiers belong to the same profession, no matter what country they serve, and it makes them different from everybody else. They have to be different, for their job is ultimately about killing and dying, and those things are not a natural vocation for any human being. Yet all soldiers are born civilians. The method for turning young men into soldiers—people who kill other people and expose themselves to death—is basic training. It's essentially the same all over the world, and it always has been, because young men everywhere are pretty much alike.

Human beings are fairly malleable, especially when they are young, and in every young man there are attitudes for any army to work with: the inherited values and postures, more or less dimly recalled, of the tribal warriors who were once the model for every young boy to emulate. Civilization did not involve a sudden clean break in the way people behave, but merely the progressive distortion and redirection of all the ways in which people in the old tribal societies used to behave, and modern definitions of maleness still contain a great deal of the old warrior ethic. The anarchic machismo of the primitive warrior is not what modern armies really need in their soldiers, but it does provide them with promising raw material for the transformation they must work in their recruits.

Just how this transformation is wrought varies from time to time and from country to country. In totally militarized societies—ancient Sparta, the samurai class of medieval Japan, the areas controlled by organizations like the Eritrean People's Liberation Front today—it begins at puberty or before, when the young boy is immersed in a disciplined society in which only the military values are allowed to penetrate. In more sophisticated modern societies, the process is briefer and more concentrated, and the way it works is much more visible. It is, essentially, a conversion process in an almost religious sense—and as in all conversion phenomena, the emotions are far more important than the specific ideas. . . .

Armies know this. It is their business to get men to fight, and they have had a long time to work out the best way of doing it. All of them pay lip service to the symbols and slogans of their political masters, though the amount of time they must devote to this activity varies from country to country. . . . Nor should it be thought that the armies are hypocritical—most of their members really do believe in their particular national symbols and slogans. But their secret is that they know these are not the things that sustain men in combat.

What really enables men to fight is their own self-respect, and a special kind of love that has nothing to do with sex or idealism. Very few men have died in battle, when the moment actually arrived, for the United States of

America or for the sacred cause of Communism, or even for their homes and families; if they had any choice in the matter at all, they chose to die for each other and for their own vision of themselves. . . .

The way armies produce this sense of brotherhood in a peacetime environment is basic training: a feat of psychological manipulation on the grand scale which has been so consistently successful and so universal that we fail to notice it as remarkable. In countries where the army must extract its recruits in their late teens, whether voluntarily or by conscription, from a civilian environment that does not share the military values, basic training involves a brief but intense period of indoctrination whose purpose is not really to teach the recruits basic military skills, but rather to change their values and their loyalties. "I guess you could say we brainwash them a little bit," admitted a U.S. Marine drill instructor, "but you know they're good people."

The duration and intensity of basic training, and even its major emphases, depend on what kind of society the recruits are coming from, and on what sort of military organization they are going to. It is obviously quicker to train men from a martial culture than from one in which the dominant values are civilian and commercial, and easier to deal with volunteers than with reluctant conscripts. Conscripts are not always unwilling, however; there are many instances in which the army is popular for economic reasons. . . .

It's easier if you catch them young. You can train older men to be soldiers; it's done in every major war. But you can never get them to believe that they like it, which is the major reason armies try to get their recruits before they are 20. There are other reasons too, of course, like the physical fitness, lack of dependents, and economic dispensability of teenagers, that make armies prefer them, but the most important qualities teenagers bring to basic training are enthusiasm and naiveté. Many of them actively want the discipline and the closely structured environment that the armed forces will provide, so there is no need for the recruiters to deceive the kids about what will happen to them after they join.

> *There is discipline. There is drill. . . . When you are relying on your mates and they are relying on you, there's no room for slackness or sloppiness. If you're not prepared to accept the rules, you're better off where you are.*
> —British army recruiting advertisement, 1976

> *People are not born soldiers, they become soldiers. . . . And it should not begin at the moment a new recruit is enlisted into the ranks, but rather much earlier, at the time of the first signs of maturity, during the time of adolescent dreams.*
> —*Red Star* (Soviet army newspaper), 1973

Young civilians who have volunteered and have been accepted by the Marine Corps arrive at Parris Island, the Corps's East Coast facility for basic training, in a state of considerable excitement and apprehension: Most are aware that they are about to undergo an extraordinary and very difficult experience. But they do not make their own way to the base; rather, they trickle in to Charleston airport on various flights throughout the day on which their training platoon is due to form, and are held there, in a state of suppressed but mounting nervous tension, until late in the evening. When the buses finally come to carry them the 76 miles to Parris Island, it is often after midnight—and this is not an administrative oversight. The shock treatment they are about to receive will work most efficiently if they are worn out and somewhat disoriented when they arrive.

The basic training organization is a machine, processing several thousand young men every month, and every facet and gear of it has been designed with the sole purpose of turning civilians into Marines as efficiently as possible. Provided it can have total control over their bodies and their environment for approximately three months, it can practically guarantee converts. Parris Island provides that controlled environment, and the recruits do not set foot outside it again until they graduate as Marine privates 11 weeks later.

> *They're allowed to call home, so long as it doesn't get out of hand—every three weeks or so they can call home and make sure everything's all right, if they haven't gotten a letter or there's a particular set of circumstances. If it's a case of an emergency call coming in, then they're allowed to accept that call; if not, one of my staff will take the message. . . .*
>
> *In some cases I'll get calls from parents who haven't quite gotten adjusted to the idea that their son had cut the strings—and in a lot of cases that's what they're doing. The military provides them with an opportunity to leave home but they're still in a rather secure environment.*
>
> —Captain Brassington, USMC

For the young recruits, basic training is the closest thing their society can offer to a formal rite of passage, and the institution probably stands in an unbroken line of descent from the lengthy ordeals by which young males in precivilized groups were initiated into the adult community of warriors. But in civilized societies it is a highly functional institution whose product is not anarchic warriors, but trained soldiers.

Basic training is not really about teaching people skills; it's about changing them so that they can do things they wouldn't have dreamt of otherwise. It works by applying enormous physical and mental pressure to men who have been isolated from their normal civilian environment and placed in one where the only right way to think and behave is the way the Marine Corps wants them to. The key word the men who run the machine use to describe this process is *motivation*.

> *I can motivate a recruit and in third phase, if I tell him to jump off the third deck, he'll jump off the third deck. Like I said before, it's a captive audience and I can train that guy; I can get him to do anything I want him to do. . . . They're good kids and they're out to do the right thing. We get some bad kids, but you know,*

we weed those out. But as far as motivation—here, we can motivate them to do anything you want, in recruit training.

—USMC drill instructor, Parris Island

The first three days the raw recruits spend at Parris Island are actually relatively easy, though they are hustled and shouted at continuously. It is during this time that they are documented and inoculated, receive uniforms, and learn the basic orders of drill that will enable young Americans (who are not very accustomed to this aspect of life) to do everything simultaneously in large groups. But the most important thing that happens in "forming" is the surrender of the recruits' own clothes, their hair—all the physical evidence of their individual civilian identities.

During a period of only 72 hours, in which they are allowed little sleep, recruits lay aside their former lives in a series of hasty rituals (like being shaven to the scalp) whose symbolic significance is quite clear to them even though they are quite deliberately given absolutely no time for reflection, or any hint that they might have the option of turning back from their commitment. The men in charge of them know how delicate a tightrope they are walking, though, because at this stage the recruits are still newly caught civilians who have not yet made their ultimate inward submission to the discipline of the Corps.

Forming Day One makes me nervous. You've got a whole new mob of recruits, you know, 60 or 70 depending, and they don't know anything. You don't know what kind of a reaction you're going to get from the stress you're going to lay on them, and it just worries me the first day. . . .

Things could happen, I'm not going to lie to you. Something might happen. A recruit might decide he doesn't want any part of this stuff and maybe take a poke at you or something like that. In a situation like that it's going to be a spur-of-the-moment thing and that worries me.

—USMC drill instructor

But it rarely happens. The frantic bustle of forming is designed to give the recruit no time to think about resisting what is happening to him. And so the recruits emerge from their initiation into the system, stripped of their civilian clothes, shorn of their hair, and deprived of whatever confidence in their own identity they may previously have had as 18-year-olds, like so many blanks ready to have the Marine identity impressed upon them.

The first stage in any conversion process is the destruction of an individual's former beliefs and confidence, and his reduction to a position of helplessness and need. It isn't really as drastic as all that, of course, for three days cannot cancel out 18 years; the inner thoughts and the basic character are not erased. But the recruits have already learned that the only acceptable behavior is to repress any unorthodox thoughts and to mimic the character the Marine Corps wants. Nor are they, on the whole, reluctant to do so, for they *want* to be Marines. From the moment they arrive at Parris Island, the vague notion that has been passed down for a thousand generations that masculinity means being a warrior becomes an explicit article of faith, relentlessly preached: To be a man means to be a Marine.

There are very few 18-year-old boys who do not have highly romanticized ideas of what it means to be a man, so the Marine Corps has plenty of buttons to push. And it starts pushing them on the first day of real training: The officer in charge of the formation appears before them for the first time, in full dress uniform with medals, and tells them how to become men.

> *The United States Marine Corps has 205 years of illustrious history to speak for itself. You have made the most important decision in your life . . . by signing your name, your life, your pledge to the Government of the United States, and even more importantly, to the United States Marine Corps—a brotherhood, an elite unit. In 10.3 weeks you are going to become a member of that history, those traditions, this organization—if you have what it takes. . . .*
>
> *All of you want to do that by virtue of your signing your name as a man. The Marine Corps says that we build men. Well, I'll go a little bit further. We develop the tools that you have—and everybody has those tools to a certain extent right now. We're going to give you the blueprints, and we are going to show you how to build a Marine. You've got to build a Marine—you understand?*
>
> —Captain Pingree, USMC

The recruits, gazing at him in awe and adoration, shout in unison, "Yes, sir!" just as they have been taught. They do it willingly, because they are volunteers—but even conscripts tend to have the romantic fervor of volunteers if they are only 18 years old. Basic training, whatever its hardships, is a quick way to become a man among men, with an undeniable status, and beyond the initial consent to undergo it, it doesn't even require any decisions.

> *I had just dropped out of high school and I wasn't doing much on the street except hanging out, as most teenagers would be doing. So they gave me an opportunity—a recruiter picked me up, gave me a good line, and said that I could make it in the Marines, that I have a future ahead of me. And since I was living with my parents, I figured that I could start my own life here and grow up a little.*
>
> —USMC recruit, 1982

> *I like the hand-to-hand combat and . . . things like that. It's a little rough going on me, and since I have a small frame I would like to become deadly, as I would put it. I like to have them words, especially the way they've been teaching me here.*
>
> —USMC recruit (from Brooklyn), Parris Island, 1982

The training, when it starts, seems impossibly demanding physically for most of the recruits—and then it gets harder week by week. There is a constant barrage of abuse and insults aimed at the recruits, with the deliberate purpose of breaking down their pride and so destroying their ability to resist the transformation of values and attitudes that the Corps intends them to undergo. At the same time, the demands for constant alertness and for instant obedience are continuously stepped up, and the standards by which the dress and behavior of the recruits are judged become steadily more unforgiving. But it is all carefully calculated by the men who run the machine, who think and talk in terms of the stress they are placing on the recruits: "We take so many c.c.'s of stress and we administer it to each man—they should be a little bit scared and they should be unsure, but they're adjusting." The aim is to keep the training arduous but just within most of the recruits' capability to withstand. One of the most striking achievements of the drill instructors is to create and maintain the illusion that basic training is an extraordinary challenge, one that will set those who graduate apart from others, when in fact almost everyone can succeed.

There has been some preliminary weeding out of potential recruits even before they begin basic training, to eliminate the obviously unsuitable minority, and some people do "fail" basic training and get sent home, at least in peacetime. The standards of acceptable performance in the U.S. armed forces, for example, tend to rise and fall in inverse proportion to the number and quality of recruits available to fill the forces to the authorized manpower levels. (In 1980, about 15% of Marine recruits did not graduate from basic training.) But there are very few young men who cannot be turned into passable soldiers if the forces are willing to invest enough effort in it.

Not even physical violence is necessary to effect the transformation, though it has been used by most armies at most times.

> *It's not what it was 15 years ago down here. The Marine Corps still occupies the position of a tool which the society uses when it feels like that is a resort that they have to fall to. Our society changes as all societies do, and our society felt that through enlightened training methods we could still produce the same product—and when you examine it, they're right. . . . Our 100 c.c.'s of stress is really all we need, not two gallons of it, which is what used to be. . . . In some cases with some of the younger drill instructors it was more an initiation than it was an acute test, and so we introduced extra officers and we select our drill instructors to "fine-tune" it.*
>
> —Captain Brassington, USMC

There is, indeed, a good deal of fine-tuning in the roles that the men in charge of training any specific group of recruits assume. At the simplest level, there is a sort of "good cop–bad cop" manipulation of recruits' attitudes toward those applying the stress. The three younger drill instructors with a particular serial are quite close to them in age and unremittingly harsh in their demands for ever higher performance, but the senior drill instructor, a man almost old enough to be their father, plays a more benevolent and understanding part and is available for individual counseling. And generally off-stage, but always looming in the background, is the company commander, an impossibly austere and almost godlike personage.

At least these are the images conveyed to the recruits, although of course all these men cooperate closely with an identical goal in view. It works: In the end they become not just role models and authority figures, but the focus of the recruits' developing loyalty to the organization.

> *I imagine there's some fear, especially in the beginning, because they don't know what to expect. . . . I think they hate you at first, at least for a week or two, but it turns to respect. . . . They're seeking discipline, they're seeking someone to take charge, 'cause at home they never got it. . . . They're looking to be told what to do and then someone is standing there enforcing what they tell them to do, and it's kind of like the father-and-son game, all the way through. They form a fatherly image of the DI whether they want to or not.*
> —Sergeant Carrington, USMC

Just the sheer physical exercise, administered in massive doses, soon has recruits feeling stronger and more competent than ever before. Inspections, often several times daily, quickly build up their ability to wear the uniform and carry themselves like real Marines, which is a considerable source of pride. The inspections also help to set up the pattern in the recruits of unquestioning submission to military authority: Standing stock-still, staring straight ahead, while somebody else examines you closely for faults is about as extreme a ritual act of submission as you can make with your clothes on.

But they are not submitting themselves merely to the abusive sergeant making unpleasant remarks about the hair in their nostrils. All around them are deliberate reminders—the flags and insignia displayed on parade, the military music, the marching formations and drill instructors' cadenced calls—of the idealized organization, the "brotherhood" to which they will be admitted as full members if they submit and conform. Nowhere in the armed forces are the military courtesies so elaborately observed, the staffs' uniforms so immaculate (some DIs change several times a day), and the ritual aspects of military life so highly visible as on a basic training establishment.

Even the seeming inanity of close-order drill has a practical role in the conversion process. It has been over a century since mass formations of men were of any use on the battlefield, but every army in the world still drills its troops, especially during basic training, because marching in formation, with every man moving his body in the same way at the same moment, is a direct physical way of learning two things a soldier must believe: that orders have to be obeyed automatically and instantly, and that you are no longer an individual, but part of a group.

The recruits' total identification with the other members of their unit is the most important lesson of all, and everything possible is done to foster it. They spend almost every waking moment together—a recruit alone is an anomaly to be looked into at once—and during most of that time they are enduring shared hardships. They also undergo collective punishments, often for the misdeed or omission of a single individual (talking in the ranks, a bed not swept under during barracks inspection), which is a highly effective way of suppressing any tendencies toward individualism. And, of course, the DIs place relentless emphasis on competition with other "serials" in training: There may be something infinitely pathetic to outsiders about a marching group of anonymous recruits chanting, "Lift your heads and hold them high, 3313 is a-passin' by," but it doesn't seem like that to the men in the ranks.

Nothing is quite so effective in building up a group's morale and solidarity, though, as a steady diet of small triumphs. Quite early in basic training, the recruits begin to do things that seem, at first sight, quite dangerous: descend by ropes from 50-foot towers, cross yawning gaps hand-over-hand on high wires (known as the Slide for Life, of course), and the like. The common denominator is that these activities are daunting but not really dangerous: The ropes will prevent anyone from falling to his death off the rappelling tower, and there is a pond of just the right depth—deep enough to cushion a falling man, but not deep enough that he is likely to drown— under the Slide for Life. The goal is not to kill recruits, but to build up their confidence as individuals and as a group by allowing them to overcome apparently frightening obstacles.

> *You have an enemy here at Parris Island. The enemy that you're going to have at Parris Island is in every one of us. It's in the form of cowardice. The most rewarding experience you're going to have in recruit training is standing on line every evening, and you'll be able to look into each other's eyes, and you'll be able to say to each other with your eyes: "By God, we've made it one more day! We've defeated the coward."*
>
> —Captain Pingree, USMC

> *Number on deck, sir, 45 . . . highly motivated, truly dedicated, rompin', stompin', bloodthirsty, kill-crazy United States Marine Corps recruits, SIR!*
>
> —Marine chant, Parris Island, 1982

If somebody does fail a particular test, he tends to be alone, for the hurdles are deliberately set low enough that most recruits can clear them if they try. In any large group of people there is usually a goat: someone whose intelligence or manner or lack of physical stamina marks him for failure and contempt. The competent drill instructor, without deliberately setting up this unfortunate individual for disgrace, will use his failure to strengthen the solidarity and confidence of the rest. When one hapless young man fell off the Slide for Life into the pond, for example, his drill instructor shouted the usual invective—"Well, get out of the water. Don't contaminate it all day"—and then delivered the payoff line: "Go back and change your clothes. You're useless to your unit now."

"Useless to your unit" is the key phrase, and all the recruits know that what it means is "useless *in battle*." The Marine drill instructors at Parris Island know exactly what they are doing to the recruits, and why. They are not rear-echelon people filling comfortable jobs, but the most dedicated and intelligent NCOs the Marine Corps can find; even now, many of them have combat experience. The Corps has a clear-eyed understanding of precisely what it is training its recruits for—combat—and it ensures that those who do the training keep that objective constantly in sight.

The DIs "stress" the recruits, feed them their daily ration of synthetic triumphs over apparent obstacles, and bear in mind all the time that the goal is to instill the foundations for the instinctive, selfless reactions and the fierce group loyalty that is what the recruits will need if they ever see combat. They are arch-manipulators, fully conscious of it, and utterly unashamed. These kids have signed up as Marines, and they could well see combat; this is the way they have to think if they want to live.

> *I've seen guys come to Vietnam from all over. They were all sorts of people that had been scared—some of them had been scared all their life and still scared. Some of them had been a country boy, city boys—you know, all different kinds of people—but when they got in combat they all reacted the same—99 percent of them reacted the same. . . . A lot of it is training here at Parris Island, but the other part of it is survival. They know if they don't conform—conform I call it, but if they don't react in the same way other people are reacting, they won't survive. That's just it. You know, if you don't react together, then nobody survives.*
>
> —USMC drill instructor, Parris Island, 1982

> *When I went to boot camp and did individual combat training they said if you walk into an ambush what you want to do is just do a right face—you just turn right or left, whichever way the fire is coming from, and assault. I said, "Man, that's crazy. I'd never do anything like that. It's stupid." . . .*
>
> *The first time we came under fire, on Hill 1044 in Operation Beauty Canyon in Laos, we did it automatically. Just like you look at your watch to see what time it is. We done a right face, assaulted the hill—a fortified position with concrete bunkers emplaced, machine guns, automatic weapons—and we took it. And we killed—I'd estimate probably 35 North Vietnamese soldiers in the assault, and we only lost three killed. I think it was about two or three, and about eight or ten wounded. . . .*
>
> *But you know, what they teach you, it doesn't faze you until it comes down to the time to use it, but it's in the back of your head, like, What do you do when you come to a stop sign? It's in the back of your head, and you react automatically.*
>
> —USMC sergeant, 1982

Combat is the ultimate reality that Marines—or any other soldiers, under any flag—have to deal with. Physical fitness, weapons training, battle drills, are all indispensable elements of basic training, and it is absolutely essential that the recruits learn the attitudes of group loyalty and interdependency which will be their sole hope of survival and success in combat. The training inculcates or fosters all of those things, and even by the halfway point in the 11-week course, the recruits are generally responding with enthusiasm to their tasks. . . .

In basic training establishments, . . . the malleability is all one way: in the direction of submission to military authority and the internalization of military values. What a place like Parris Island produces when it is successful, as it usually is, is a soldier who will kill because that is his job.

ENDNOTES

[1] Leonard Cottrell, *The Warrior Pharaohs* (London: Evans Brothers, 1968).
[2] Samuel Rolbart, *The Israeli Soldier* (New York: A. S. Barnes, 1970), p. 206.

PART IV
Groups and Social Structure

15

PEER POWER
Clique Dynamics among School Children

PATRICIA A. ADLER • PETER ADLER

The following four selections explore groups and social structure. The basic components of social structure are the roles and social statuses of individuals. Over the course of a lifetime, people occupy numerous statuses and roles. A *status* is a social position an individual holds within a group or a social system. A *role* is a set of expectations about the behavior assigned to a particular social status. Each role helps to define the nature of interaction with others and contributes to social organization by creating patterns of interpersonal and group relationships. Because we modify social roles more than we do our social statuses, roles are the dynamic aspect of social status. In the first reading, Patricia and Peter Adler investigate the social roles and social statuses children hold in social cliques. Of particular interest to the Adlers is how social hierarchies are formed and how power is distributed among the friendship groups of third- to sixth-grade students.

A dominate feature of children's lives is the clique structure that organizes their social world. The fabric of their relationships with others, their levels and types of activity, their participation in friendships, and their feelings about themselves are tied to their involvement in, around, or outside the cliques organizing their social landscape. Cliques are, at their base, friendship circles, whose members tend to identify each other as mutually connected.[1] Yet they are more than that; cliques have a hierarchical structure, being dominated by leaders, and are exclusive in nature, so that not all individuals who desire membership are accepted. They function as bodies of power within grades, incorporating the most popular individuals, offering the most exciting social lives, and commanding the most interest and attention from classmates (Eder and Parker 1987). As such, they represent a vibrant component of the preadolescent experience, mobilizing powerful forces that produce important effects on individuals.[2] . . .

From *Peer Power* by Patricia A. Adler and Peter Adler. Copyright © 1998 by Patricia A. Adler and Peter Adler. Reprinted by permission of Rutgers University Press.

In this [reading] we look at these dynamics and their association, at the way clique leaders generate and maintain their power and authority (leadership, power/dominance), and at what it is that influences followers to comply so readily with clique leaders' demands (submission). These interactional dynamics are not intended to apply to all children's friendship groups, only those (populated by one-quarter to one-half of the children) that embody the exclusive and stratified character of cliques.

Techniques of Inclusion

The critical way that cliques maintained exclusivity was through careful membership screening. Not static entities, cliques irregularly shifted and evolved their membership, as individuals moved away or were ejected from the group and others took their place. In addition, cliques were characterized by frequent group activities designed to foster some individuals' inclusion (while excluding others). Cliques had embedded, although often unarticulated, modes for considering and accepting (or rejecting) potential new members. These modes were linked to the critical power of leaders in making vital group decisions. Leaders derived power through their popularity and then used it to influence membership and social stratification within the group. This stratification manifested itself in tiers and subgroups within cliques composed of people who were hierarchically ranked into levels of leaders, followers, and wannabes. Cliques embodied systems of dominance, whereby individuals with more status and power exerted control over others' lives.

Recruitment

... Potential members could be brought to the group by established members who had met and liked them. The leaders then decided whether these individuals would be granted a probationary period of acceptance during which they could be informally evaluated. If the members liked them, the newcomers would be allowed to remain in the friendship circle, but if they rejected them, they would be forced to leave.

Tiffany, a popular, dominant girl, reflected on the boundary maintenance she and her best friend Diane, two clique leaders, had exercised in fifth grade:

Q: Who defines the boundaries of who's in or who's out?

Tiffany: *Probably the leader. If one person might like them, they might introduce them, but if one or two people didn't like them, then they'd start to get everyone up. Like in fifth grade, there was Dawn Bolton and she was new. And the girls in her class that were in our clique liked her, but Diane and I didn't like her, so we kicked her out. So then she went to the other clique, the Emily clique.*

Timing was critical to recruitment. The beginning of the year, when classes were being reconstructed and people formed new social configurations, was the major time when cliques considered additions. Once these al-liances were set, cliques tended to close their boundaries once again and stick to socializing primarily within the group. Kara, a fifth-grade girl, offered her view: *"In the fall, right after school starts, when everyone's lining up and checking each other out, is when people move up, but not during the school year. You can move down during the school year, if people decide they don't like you, but not up."* . . .

Most individuals felt that invitation to membership in the popular clique represented an irresistible offer. They repeatedly asserted that the popular group could get anybody they wanted to join them. One of the strategies used was to try to select new desirables and go after them. This usually meant separating the people from their established friends. Melody, an un-popular fourth-grade girl, described her efforts to hold on to her best friend who was being targeted for recruitment by the popular clique:

> *She was saying that they were really nice and stuff. I was really worried. If she joined their group, she would have to leave me. She was over there, and she told me that they were making fun of me, and she kind of sat there and went along with it. So I kind of got mad at her for doing that. 'Why didn't you stick up for me?' She said, 'Because they wouldn't like me anymore.'*

Melody subsequently lost her friend to the clique.

When clique members wooed someone to join them, they usually showed only the better side of their behavior. It was not until they had the new person firmly committed to the group that the shifts in behavior associated with lead-ers' dominance and status stratification activities began. Diane recalled her inclusion into the popular clique and its aftermath:

> *In fifth grade I came into a new class and I knew nobody. None of my friends from the year before were in my class. So I get to school, a week late, and Tiffany comes up to me and she was like, 'Hi Diane, how are you? Where were you? You look so pretty.' And I was like, wow, she's so nice. And she was being so nice for like two weeks, kiss-ass major. And then she started pulling her bitch moves. Maybe it was for a month that she was nice. And so then she had clawed me into her clique and her group, and so she won me over that way, but then she was a bitch to me once I was inside it, and I couldn't get out because I had no other friends. 'Cause I'd gone in there and already been accepted into the popular clique, so everyone else in the class didn't like me, so I had nowhere else to go.*

Eder (1985) also notes that popular girls are often disliked by unpopular people because of their exclusive and elitist manner (as befits their status).

Application

A second way for individuals to gain initial membership into a clique oc-curred through their actively seeking entry (Blau 1964). . . . According to Rick, a fifth-grade boy who was in the popular clique but not a central member, application for clique entry was more easily accomplished by individuals than groups. He described the way individuals found routes into cliques:

> *It can happen any way. Just you get respected by someone, you do something nice, they start to like you, you start doing stuff with them. It's like you just kind of follow another person who is in the clique back to the clique, and he says, "Could this person play?" So you kind of go out with the clique for a while and you start doing stuff with them, and then they almost like invite you in. And then soon after, like a week or so, you're actually in. It all depends. . . . But you can't bring your whole group with you, if you have one. You have to leave them behind and just go in on your own.*

Successful membership applicants often experienced a flurry of immediate popularity. Because their entry required clique leaders' approval, they gained associational status.

Friendship Realignment

Status and power in a clique were related to stratification, and people who remained more closely tied to the leaders were more popular. Individuals who wanted to be included in the clique's inner echelons often had to work regularly to maintain or improve their position.

Like initial entry, this was sometimes accomplished by people striving on their own for upward mobility. In fourth grade, Danny was brought into the clique by Mark, a longtime member, who went out of his way to befriend him. After joining the clique, however, Danny soon abandoned Mark when Brad, the clique leader, took an interest in him. Mark discussed the feelings of hurt and abandonment this experience left him with:

> *I felt really bad, because I made friends with him when nobody knew him and nobody liked him, and I put all my friends to the side for him, and I brought him into the group, and then he dumped me. He was my friend first, but then Brad wanted him. . . . He moved up and left me behind, like I wasn't good enough anymore.*

The hierarchical structure of cliques, and the shifts in position and relationships within them, caused friendship loyalties within these groups to be less reliable than they might have been in other groups. People looked toward those above them and were more susceptible to being wooed into friendship with individuals more popular than they. When courted by a higher-up, they could easily drop their less popular friends.

Cliques' stratification hierarchies might motivate lower-echelon members to seek greater inclusion by propelling themselves toward the elite inner circles, but membership in these circles was dynamic, requiring active effort to sustain. More popular individuals had to put repeated effort into their friendship alignments as well, to maintain their central positions relative to people just below them, who might rise up and gain in group esteem. Efforts to protect themselves from the potential incursions of others took several forms, among them co-optation, position maintenance, follower realignment, and membership challenge, only some of which draw upon inclusionary dynamics.

Follower realignment involved the perception that other clique members were gaining in popularity and status and might challenge leaders' position. But instead of trying to hold them in place (position maintenance) or exclude them from the group (membership challenge), leaders shifted their base of support; they incorporated lesser but still loyal members into their activities, thereby replacing problematic supporters with new ones. . . .

Co-optation involved leaders diminishing others' threats to their position by drawing them into their orbit, increasing their loyalty, and diminishing their independence. Clique members gaining in popularity were sometimes given special attention. At the same time, leaders might try to cut out their rivals' independent base of support from other friends.

Darla, a fourth grader, had occupied a second-tier leadership position with Kristy, her best friend. She explained what happened when Denise, the clique leader, came in and tore their formerly long-standing friendship apart:

> *Me and Kristy used to be best friends, but she [Denise] hated that. 'Cause even though she was the leader, we were popular and we got all the boys. She didn't want us to be friends at all. But me and Kristy were, like, getting to be a threat to her, so Denise came in the picture and tore me and Kristy apart, so we weren't even friends. She made Kristy make totally fun of me and stuff. And they were so mean to me. . . .*

. . . Hence, friendship realignment involved clique members' abandoning previous friendships or plowing through existing ones in order to assert themselves into relationships with those in central positions. These actions were all geared toward improving instigators' positions and thus their inclusion. Their outcome, whether anticipated or not, was often the separation of people and the destruction of their relationships.

Ingratiation

Currying favor with people in the group, like previous inclusionary endeavors, can be directed either upward (supplication) or downward (manipulation). Addressing the former, Dodge et al. (1983) note that children often begin their attempts at entry into groups with low-risk tactics; they first try to become accepted by more peripheral members, and only later do they direct their gaze and inclusion attempts toward those with higher status. The children we observed did this as well, making friendly overtures toward clique followers and hoping to be drawn by them into the center.

The more predominant behavior among group members, however, involved currying favor with the leader to enhance their popularity and attain greater respect from other group members. One way they did this was by imitating the style and interests of the group leader. Marcus and Adam, two fifth-grade boys, described the way borderline people would fawn on their clique and its leader to try to gain inclusion:

> Marcus: *Some people would just follow us around and say, "Oh yeah, whatever he says, yeah, whatever his favorite kind of music is, is my favorite kind of music."*
>
> Adam: *They're probably in a position where they want to be more in because if they like what we like, then they think more people will probably respect them. Because if some people in the clique think this person likes their favorite group, say it's REM, or whatever, so it's say Bud's [the clique leader's], this person must know what we like in music and what's good and what's not, so let's tell him that he can come up and join us after school and do something.*

Fawning on more popular people not only was done by outsiders and peripherals but was common practice among regular clique members, even those with high standing. Darla, the second-tier fourth-grade girl mentioned earlier, described how, in fear, she used to follow the clique leader and parrot her opinions:

> *I was never mean to the people in my grade because I thought Denise might like them and then I'd be screwed. Because there were some people that I hated that she liked and I acted like I loved them, and so I would just be mean to the younger kids, and if she would even say, 'Oh she's nice,' I'd say, 'Oh yeah, she's really nice!'*

Clique members, then, had to stay abreast of the leader's shifting tastes and whims if they were to maintain status and position in the group. Part of their membership work involved a regular awareness of the leader's fads and fashions, so that they could accurately align their actions and opinions with the current trends in a timely manner. (See also Eder and Sanford 1986.)

Besides outsiders supplicating to insiders and insiders supplicating to those of higher standing, individuals at the top had to think about the effects of their actions on their standing with those below them. While leaders did not have to explicitly imitate the style and taste of their followers, they did have to act in a way that held their adulation and loyalty. This began with people at the top making sure that those directly below them remained firmly placed where they could count on them. Any defection, especially by the more popular people in a clique, could seriously threaten their standing.

Leaders often employed manipulation to hold the attention and loyalty of clique members.[3] Another manipulative technique involved acting different ways toward different people. Rick recalled how Brad, the clique leader in fifth grade, used this strategy to maintain his position of centrality: "*Brad would always say that Trevor is so annoying. 'He is such an idiot, a stupid baby,' and everyone would say, 'Yeah, he is so annoying. We don't like him.' So they would all be mean to him. And then later in the day, Brad would go over and play with Trevor and say that everyone else didn't like him, but that he did. That's how Brad maintained control over Trevor.*" Brad employed similar techniques of manipulation to ensure that all the members of his clique were similarly tied to him. Like many leaders, he would shift his primary attention among the different clique members, so that everyone experienced the power and status associated with his favor. Then, when they were out of favor, his followers felt relatively deprived and strove to regain their privileged status. This ensured their loyalty and compliance.

To a lesser degree, clique members curried friendship with outsiders. Although they did not accept them into the group, they sometimes included them in activities and tried to influence their opinions. While the leaders had their in-group followers, lower-status clique members, if they cultivated them well, could look to outsiders for respect, admiration, and imitation. This attitude and behavior were not universal, however; some popular cliques were so disdainful and mean to outsiders that nonmembers hated them. Diane, Tiffany, and Darla, three popular girls who had gone to two different elementary schools, reflected on how the grade school cliques to which they had belonged displayed opposing relationships with individuals of lesser status:

> Darla: *We hated it if the dorks didn't like us and want us to be with them. 'Cause then we weren't the popularest ones 'cause we always had to have them look up to us, and when they wouldn't look up to us we would be nice to them.*
>
> Diane: *The medium people always hated us.*
>
> Tiffany: *They hated us royally, and we hated them back whenever they started.*
>
> Darla: *Sometimes we acted like we didn't care, but it bothered me.*
>
> Tiffany: *We always won, so it didn't matter.*

Thus, while there were notable exceptions (see Eder 1985), many popular clique members strove to ingratiate themselves with people less popular than they, from time to time, to ensure that their dominance and adulation extended beyond their own boundaries, throughout the grade.

Techniques of Exclusion

Although inclusionary techniques reinforced individuals' popularity and prestige while maintaining the group's exclusivity and stratification, they failed to contribute to other, essential, clique features such as cohesion and integration, the management of in-group and out-group relationships, and submission to clique leadership. These features are rooted, along with further sources of domination and power, in cliques' exclusionary dynamics.

Out-Group Subjugation

When they were not being nice to try to keep outsiders from straying too far from their realm of influence, clique members predominantly subjected outsiders to exclusion and rejection.[4] They found sport in picking on these lower-status individuals. As one clique follower remarked, "*One of the main things is to keep picking on unpopular kids because it's just fun to do."* Eder (1991) notes that this kind of ridicule, where the targets are excluded and not enjoined to participate in the laughter, contrasts with teasing, where friends make fun of each other in a more lighthearted manner but permit the targets to remain included in the group by also jokingly making fun of themselves. Diane, a clique leader in fourth grade, described the way she acted toward outsiders: *"Me and my friends would be mean to the people outside of our clique. Like, Eleanor Dawson, she would always try to be friends with us, and we would be like, 'Get away, ugly.'"*

Interactionally sophisticated clique members not only treated outsiders badly but managed to turn others in the clique against them. Parker and Gottman (1989) observe that one of the ways people do this is through gossip. Diane recalled the way she turned all the members of her class, boys as well as girls, against an outsider:

> *I was always mean to people outside my group like Crystal, and Sally Jones; they both moved schools. . . . I had this gummy bear necklace, with pearls around it and gummy bears. She [Crystal] came up to me one day and pulled my necklace off. I'm like, 'It was my favorite necklace,' and I got all of my friends, and all the guys even in the class, to revolt against her. No one liked her. That's why she moved schools, because she tore my gummy bear necklace off and everyone hated her. They were like, 'That was mean. She didn't deserve that. We hate you.'*

Turning people against an outsider served to solidify the group and to assert the power of the strong over the vulnerability of the weak. Other classmates tended to side with the dominant people over the subordinates, not only because they admired their prestige but also because they respected and feared the power of the strong.

Insiders' ultimate manipulation in leading the group to pick on outsiders involved instigating the bullying and causing others to take the blame. Davey, the fifth-grade clique follower mentioned earlier, described, with some mystery and awe, the skilled maneuvering of Joe, his clique leader: *"He'd start a fight and then he would get everyone in it, cause everyone followed him, and then he would get out of it so he wouldn't get in trouble."*

Q: How'd he do that?

Davey: *One time he went up to this kid Morgan, who nobody liked, and said, "Come on Morgan, you want to talk about it?" and started kicking him, and then everyone else started doing it. Joe stopped and started watching, and then some parapro[fessional] came over and said, "What's going on here?" And then everyone got in trouble except for him.*

Q: Why did he pick on Morgan?

Davey: *'Cause he couldn't do anything about it, 'cause he was a nerd.*

Getting picked on instilled outsiders with fear, grinding them down to accept their inferior status and discouraging them from rallying together to challenge the power hierarchy.[5] In a confrontation between a clique member and an outsider, most people sided with the clique member. They knew that clique members banded together against outsiders, and that they could easily become the next target of attack if they challenged them. Clique members picked on outsiders with little worry about confrontation or repercussion. They also knew that their victims would never carry the tale to teachers or administrators (as they might against other targets; see Sluckin 1981) for fear of reprisal. As Mike, a fifth-grade clique follower, observed, *"They know if they tell on you, then you'll 'beat them up,' and so they won't tell on you, they just kind of take it in, walk away."*

In-Group Subjugation

Picking on people within the clique's confines was another way to exert dominance. More central clique members commonly harassed and were mean to those with weaker standing.[6] Many of the same factors prompting the ill treatment of outsiders motivated high-level insiders to pick on less powerful insiders. Rick, a fifth-grade clique follower, articulated the systematic organization of downward harassment:

> *Basically the people who are the most popular, their life outside in the playground is picking on other people who aren't as popular, but are in the group. But the people just want to be more popular so they stay in the group, they just kind of stick with it, get made fun of, take it. . . . They come back everyday, you do more ridicule, more ridicule, more ridicule, and they just keep taking it because they want to be more popular, and they actually like you but you don't like them. That goes on a lot, that's the main thing in the group. You make fun of someone, you get more popular, because insults is what they like, they like insults.*

The finger of ridicule could be pointed at any individual but the leader. It might be a person who did something worthy of insult, it might be someone who the clique leader felt had become an interpersonal threat, or it might be someone singled out for no apparent reason (see Eder 1991). Darla, the second-tier fourth grader discussed earlier, described the ridicule she encountered and her feelings of mortification when the clique leader derided her hair:

> *Like I remember, she embarrassed me so bad one day. Oh my God, I wanted to kill her! We were in music class and we were standing there and she goes, 'Ew! what's all that shit in your hair?' in front of the whole class. I was so embarrassed, 'cause, I guess I had dandruff or something.*[7]

Often, derision against insiders followed a pattern, where leaders started a trend and everyone followed it. This intensified the sting of the mockery by compounding it with multiple force. Rick analogized the way people in cliques behaved to the links on a chain: *"Like it's a chain reaction, you get in a fight with the main person, then the person right under him will not like you, and the person under him won't like you, and et cetera, and the whole group will take turns against you. A few people will still like you because they will do their own thing, but most people will do what the person in front of them says to do, so it would be like a chain reaction. It's like a chain; one chain turns, and the other chain has to turn with them or else it will tangle."*

Compliance

Going along with the derisive behavior of leaders or other high-status clique members could entail either active or passive participation. Active participation occurred when instigators enticed other clique members to pick on their friends. For example, leaders would often come up with the idea of placing phony phone calls to others and would persuade their followers to do the dirty work. They might start the phone call and then place followers on the line to finish it, or they might pressure others to make the entire call, thus keeping one step distant from becoming implicated, should the victim's parents complain.

Passive participation involved going along when leaders were mean and manipulative, as when Trevor submissively acquiesced in Brad's scheme to convince Larry that Rick had stolen his money. Trevor knew that Brad was hiding the money the whole time, but he watched while Brad whipped Larry into a frenzy, pressing him to deride Rick, destroy Rick's room and possessions, and threaten to expose Rick's alleged theft to others. It was only when Rick's mother came home, interrupting the bedlam, that she uncovered the money and stopped Larry's onslaught. The following day at school, Brad and Trevor could scarcely contain their glee. As noted earlier, Rick was demolished by the incident and cast out by the clique; Trevor was elevated to the status of Brad's best friend by his co-conspiracy in the scheme.

Many clique members relished the opportunity to go along with such exclusive activities, welcoming the feelings of privilege, power, and inclusion. Others were just thankful that they weren't the targets. This was especially true of new members, who, as Sanford and Eder (1984) describe, often feel unsure about their standing in a group. Marcus and Adam, two fifth-grade clique followers introduced earlier, expressed their different feelings about such participation:

Q: What was it like when someone in your group got picked on?
Marcus: *If it was someone I didn't like or who had picked on me before, then I liked it. It made me feel good.*
Adam: *I didn't really enjoy it. It made me feel better if they weren't picking on me. But you can't do too much about it, so you sort of get used to it.*

Like outsiders, clique members knew that complaining to persons in authority did them no good. Quite the reverse, such resistance tactics made their situation worse, as did showing their vulnerabilities to the aggressors.[8]

Kara, a popular fifth-grade girl, explained why such declarations had the opposite effect from that intended: *"Because we knew what bugged them, so we could use it against them. And we just did it to pester 'em, aggravate 'em, make us feel better about ourselves. Just to be shitty."*

When people saw their friends in tenuous situations, they often reacted in a passive manner. Popular people who got in fights with other popular people might be able to count on some of their followers for support, but most people could not command such loyalty. Jeff, a fifth-grade boy, explained why people went along with hurtful behavior:

> *It's a real risk if you want to try to stick up for someone because you could get rejected from the group or whatever. Some people do, and nothing happens because they're so high up that other people listen to them. But most people would just find themselves in the same boat. And we've all been there before, so we know what that's like.*

Clique members thus went along with picking on their friends, even though they knew it hurt, because they were afraid (see also Best 1983). They became accustomed to living within a social world where the power dynamics could be hurtful, and accepted it.

Stigmatization

Beyond individual incidents of derision, clique insiders were often made the focus of stigmatization for longer periods of time. Unlike outsiders who commanded less enduring interest, clique members were much more involved in picking on their friends, whose discomfort more readily held their attention. Rick noted that the duration of this negative attention was highly variable: *"Usually at certain times, it's just a certain person you will pick on all the time, if they do something wrong. I've been picked on for a month at a time, or a week, or a day, or just a couple of minutes, and then they will just come to respect you again."* When people became the focus of stigmatization, as happened to Rick, they were rejected by all their friends. The entire clique rejoiced in celebrating their disempowerment. They would be made to feel alone whenever possible. Their former friends might join hands and walk past them through the play yard at recess, physically demonstrating their union and the discarded individual's aloneness.

Worse than being ignored was being taunted. Taunts ranged from verbal insults to put-downs to singsong chants. Anyone who could create a taunt was favored with attention and imitated by everyone (see Fine 1981). Even outsiders, who would not normally be privileged to pick on a clique member, were able to elevate themselves by joining in on such taunting (see Sanford and Eder 1984).

The ultimate degradation was physical. Although girls generally held themselves to verbal humiliation of their members, the culture of masculinity gave credence to boys' injuring each other (Eder and Parker 1987; Oswald et al. 1987; Thorne 1993). Fights would occasionally break out in which boys were punched in the ribs or stomach, kicked, or given black eyes. When this happened at school, adults were quick to intervene. But after hours or on the school bus, boys could be hurt. Physical abuse was also heaped on people's homes or possessions. People spit on each other or others' books or toys, threw eggs at their family's cars, and smashed pumpkins in front of their house.

Expulsion

While most people returned to a state of acceptance following a period of severe derision (see Sluckin 1981 for strategies children use to help attain this end), this was not always the case. Some people became permanently excommunicated from the clique. Others could be cast out directly, without undergoing a transitional phase of relative exclusion. Clique members from any stratum of the group could suffer such a fate, although it was more common among people with lower status.

When Davey, mentioned earlier, was in sixth grade, he described how expulsion could occur as a natural result of the hierarchical ranking, where a person at the bottom rung of the system of popularity was pushed off. He described the ordinary dynamics of clique behavior:

Q: How do clique members decide who they are going to insult that day?

Davey: *It's just basically everyone making fun of everyone. The small people making fun of smaller people, the big people making fun of the small people. Nobody is really making fun of people bigger than them because they can get rejected, because then they can say, "Oh yes, he did this and that, this and that, and we shouldn't like him anymore." And everybody else says, "Yeah, yeah, yeah," 'cause all the lower people like him, but all the higher people don't. So the lowercase people just follow the highercase people. If one person is doing something wrong, then they will say, "Oh yeah, get out, good-bye."*

Being cast out could result either from a severely irritating infraction or from individuals standing up for their rights against the dominant leaders. Sometimes expulsion occurred as a result of breakups between friends or friendship realignments leading to membership challenges (mentioned earlier), where higher-status people carried the group with them and turned their former friends into outcasts. . . .

On much rarer occasions, high-status clique members or even leaders could be cast out of the group (see Best 1983). One sixth-grade clique leader, Tiffany, was deposed by her former lieutenants for a continued pattern of petulance and self-indulgent manipulations:

Q: Who kicked you out?

Tiffany: *Robin and Tanya. They accepted Heidi into their clique, and they got rid of me. They were friends with her. I remember it happened in one blowup in the cafeteria. I asked for pizza and I thought I wasn't getting enough attention anymore, so I was pissed and in a bitchy mood all the time and stuff, and so I asked them for some, so she [Robin] said like, "Wait, hold on, Heidi is taking a bite," or something, and I got so mad I said, "Give the whole fuckin' thing to Heidi," and something like that, and they got so sick of me right then, and they said like, "Fuck you."*

When clique members get kicked out of the group, they leave an established circle of friends and often seek to make new ones. Some people have relatively easy time making what Davies (1982) calls "contingency friends" (temporary replacements for their more popular friends), and, according to one fifth-grade teacher, they are "hot items" for the unpopular crowd. . . .

Many cast-outs found new friendships harder to establish, however. They went through a period where they kept to themselves, feeling rejected, stigmatized, and cut off from their former social circle and status. Because of their previous behavior and their relations with other classmates, they had trouble being accepted by unpopular kids. Others had developed minimum acceptability thresholds for friends when they were in the popular crowd, and had difficulty stooping to befriend unpopular kids. When Mark was ejected from his clique in fifth grade, he explained why he was unsuccessful in making friends with the unpopular people: *"Because there was nobody out there I liked. I just didn't like anybody. And I think they didn't like me because when I was in the popular group we'd make fun of everyone, I guess, so they didn't want to be around me, because I had been too mean to them in the past."*

Occasionally, rejects from the popular clique had trouble making friends among the remainder of the class due to the interference of their former friends. If clique members got angry at one of their friends and cast him or her out, they might want to make sure that nobody else befriended that individual. By soliciting friendship with people outside the clique, they could influence outsiders' behavior, causing their outcast to fall beyond the middle crowd to the status of pariah, or loner. Darla explained why and how people carried out such manipulations:

Q: Have you ever seen anyone cast out?

Darla: *Sure, like, you just make fun of them. If they don't get accepted to the medium group, if they see you like, "Fuck, she's such a dork," and like you really don't want them to have any friends, so you go to the medium group, and you're like, "Why are you hanging out with THAT loser, she's SUCH a dork, we HATE her," and then you be nice to them so they'll get rid of her so she'll be such a dork. I've done that just so she'll be such a nerd that no one will like her. You're just getting back at them. And then they will get rid of her just 'cause you said to, so then, you've done your way with them. If you want something, you'll get it.*

People who were cast out of their group often kept to themselves, staying in from the playground at recess and coming home after school alone. They took the bus to school, went to class, did what they had to do, but didn't have friends. Their feelings about themselves changed, and this was often reflected in the way they dressed and carried themselves. Being ejected from the clique thus represented the ultimate form of exclusion, carrying with it severe consequences for individuals' social lives, appearance, and identity.

The techniques of inclusion and exclusion represent the means by which the behavioral dynamics of cliques are forged. As such, they offer the basis for a generic model of clique functioning that interweaves these processes with the essential clique features of exclusivity, power and dominance, status stratification, cohesion and integration, popularity, submission, and in-group and out-group relations. . . .

These two dynamics work hand in hand. The inclusionary dynamic is central to cliques' foundation of attraction. Cliques' boundary maintenance makes them exclusive. They can recruit the individuals they want, wooing them from competing friendships, and reject the supplications of others they evaluate as unworthy. The popularity of their membership (with leaders to lend status and followers to lend power) strengthens their position at the center of activity. Upheavals and friendship realignments within cliques keep the hierarchical alignment of prestige and influence fluid, giving those successful at maneuvering toward and staying near the top the greatest esteem among their peers. The systematic upward ingratiation of individuals toward the leading members, and leading members' ability to easily ingratiate themselves downward with others, thereby securing the favors they desire, enhance the attractiveness of inclusion in the clique.

The exclusionary dynamic is central to cliques' bases of cohesion. Clique members solidify together in disparaging outsiders, learning that those in the in-group can freely demean out-group members, only to have their targets return for renewed chances at acceptance. They learn sensitivity toward changes in group boundaries, acting one way toward insiders and another way toward outsiders. This lesson manifests itself not only at the group's outer edges but within the clique, as individuals move in and out of relative favor and have to position themselves carefully to avoid the stigma of association with the disfavored. They learn the hierarchy of group positions and the perquisites of respect and influence that go with those roles, submitting to the dominance of clique leaders in order to earn a share of their reflected status and position. The periodic minicyclings of exclusion serve to manipulate followers into dependence and subservience, at the same time enhancing leaders' centrality and authority. The ultimate sanction of expulsion represents a dramatic example of the effects of exclusion, weakening or bringing down potential rivals from positions of power while herding other group members into cohesion. The dynamic of inclusion lures members into cliques, while the dynamic of exclusion keeps them there.[9]

ENDNOTES

[1] See Hallinan (1979), Hubbell (1965), Peay (1974), and Varenne (1982) for a discussion of cliques' sociometric characteristics.

[2] They are primary groups, offering individuals the opportunity to select close friendships of their own choosing (Elkin and Handel 1989), to learn about society, to practice their behavior, and to evolve their selves and identities. Autonomous from the world of adults (Fine 1981), they are often forged in opposition to adult values (Elkin and Handel 1989), with a culture of resistance to adult standards (Corsaro 1985). They thus encompass a robust form of children's peer culture that is both unique in its own right yet at the same time a staging ground for future adult behavior.

[3] Oswald, Krappmann, Chowdhuri, and von Salisch (1987) note that one way children assert superiority over others and indebt them with loyalty is to offer them "help," either materially or socially.

[4] Hogg and Abrams (1988) find that denigrating out-group members enhances a group's solidarity and improves the group status of people participating in such denigration. This tendency is particularly strong where two groups perceive themselves to be in conflict or competition.

[5] Eder and Sanford (1986) and Merten (1994) note the same tendency among adolescent peer groups in middle school.

[6] Eder (1991) also notes that when insiders pick on other members of their clique, this can have good-natured overtones, indicating that they like them.

[7] Eder and Sanford (1986) and Eder and Parker (1987) discuss the importance of physical appearance, particularly hair, in adhering to group norms and maintaining popularity.

[8] Merten (1994; 1996) discusses the dilemma faced by children who are picked on, who would like to report the problem to a teacher but cannot do so out of fear that the teacher's intervention would incur the wrath of others. He notes the consequences for one boy whose mother complained to other parents about the way their children treated her son: when these others came to school the next day, they ridiculed the boy even more, taunting and deriding him for being a tattletale.

[9] Bigelow, Tesson, and Lewko (1996) also note this "Lord of the Flies" phenomenon.

REFERENCES

Best, Raphaela. 1983. *We've All Got Scars.* Bloomington: Indiana University Press.

Bigelow, Brian J., Geoffrey Tesson, and John H. Lewko. 1996. *Learning the Rules.* New York: Guilford Press.

Blau, Peter M. 1964. *Exchange and Power in Social Life.* New York: Wiley.

Corsaro, William A. 1985. *Friendship and Peer Culture in the Early Years.* Norwood, NJ: Ablex.

Davies, Bronwyn. 1982. *Life in the Classroom and Playground: The Accounts of Primary School Children.* London: Routledge and Kegan Paul.

Dodge, Kenneth A., David C. Schlundt, Iris Schocken, and Judy D. Delugach. 1983. "Social Competence and Children's Sociometric Status: The Role of Peer Group Entry Strategies." *Merrill-Palmer Quarterly* 29:309–36.

Eder, Donna. 1985. "The Cycle of Popularity: Interpersonal Relations among Female Adolescents." *Sociology of Education* 58:154–65.

———. 1991. "The Role of Teasing in Adolescent Peer Group Culture." Pp. 181–97 in *Sociological Studies of Child Development,* vol. 1, edited by P. A. Adler and P. Adler. Greenwich, CT: JAI Press.

Eder, Donna and Stephen Parker. 1987. "The Cultural Production and Reproduction of Gender: The Effect of Extracurricular Activities on Peer-Group Culture." *Sociology of Education* 60:200–213.

Eder, Donna and Stephanie Sanford. 1986. "The Development and Maintenance of Interactional Norms among Early Adolescents." Pp. 283–300 in *Sociological Studies of Child Development,* vol. 1, edited by P. A. Adler and P. Adler. Greenwich, CT: JAI Press.

Elkin, Frederick and Gerald Handel. 1989. *The Child and Society.* 5th ed. New York: Random House.

Fine, Gary Alan. 1981. "Friends, Impression Management, and Preadolescent Behavior." Pp. 29–52 in *The Development of Children's Friendships,* edited by S. Asher and J. Gottman. New York: Cambridge University Press.

Hallinan, Maureen. 1979. "Structural Effects on Children's Friendships and Cliques." *Social Psychology Quarterly* 42:43–54.

Hogg, Michael A. and Dominic Abrams. 1988. *Social Identifications.* New York: Routledge.

Hubbell, Charles H. 1965. "An Input-Output Approach to Clique Identification." *Sociometry* 28:377–99.

Merten, Don E. 1994. "The Cultural Context of Aggression: The Transition to Junior High School." *Anthropology and Education Quarterly* 25:29–43.

———. 1996. "Visibility and Vulnerability: Responses to Rejection by Nonaggressive Junior High School Boys." *Journal of Early Adolescence* 16:5–26.

Oswald, Hans, Lothar Krappmann, Irene Chowdhuri, and Maria von Salisch. 1987. "Gaps and Bridges: Interactions between Girls and Boys in Elementary School." Pp. 205–23 in *Sociological Studies of Child Development,* vol. 1, edited by P. A. Adler and P. Adler. Greenwich, CT: JAI Press.

Parker, Jeffrey G. and John M. Gottman. 1989. "Social and Emotional Development in a Relational Context." Pp. 95–131 in *Peer Relationships in Child Development,* edited by T. J. Berndt and G. W. Ladd. New York: Wiley.

Peay, Edmund R. 1974. "Hierarchical Clique Structures." *Sociometry* 37:54–65.

Sanford, Stephanie and Donna Eder. 1984. "Adolescent Humor during Peer Interaction." *Social Psychology Quarterly* 47:235–43.

Sluckin, Andy. 1981. *Growing Up in the Playground.* London: Routledge and Kegan Paul.

Thorne, Barrie. 1993. *Gender Play.* New Brunswick, NJ: Rutgers University Press.

Varenne, Herve. 1982. "Jocks and Freaks: The Symbolic Structure of the Expression of Social Interaction among American Senior High School Students." Pp. 210–35 in *Doing the Ethnography of Schooling,* edited by G. Spindler. New York: Holt, Rinehart, and Winston.

16

GANG BUSINESS
Making Ends Meet

MARTÍN SÁNCHEZ JANKOWSKI

This selection by Martín Sánchez Jankowski is excerpted from his book, *Islands in the Street: Gangs and American Urban Society* (1991). Sánchez Jankowski, a professor of sociology at the University of California at Berkeley, studies the *primary group* of social gangs that exist in urban settings across the United States. Examples of other primary groups are families, friendship cliques, sororities and fraternities, neighborhood coffee klatches, and small work groups. Thus, primary groups emerge when people live or work closely together. As this reading by Sánchez Jankowski shows, gangs are similar to other primary groups in that they are small, intimate, and informal. Sánchez Jankowski also argues that, contrary to the stereotype of gang culture, gangs have some social values that are similar to those of other American groups, including a work ethic and an entrepreneurial spirit.

Cunning and deceit will serve a man better than force to rise from a base condition to great fortune.
            —NICCOLÒ MACHIAVELLI, THE DISCOURSES (1517?)

If there is one theme that dominates most studies of gangs, it is that gangs are collectives of individuals who are social parasites, and that they are parasitic not only because they lack the skills to be productive members of society but, more important, because they lack the values, particularly the work ethic, that would guide them to be productive members of society.[1] However, one of the most striking factors I observed was how much the entrepreneurial spirit, which most Americans believe is the core of their productive culture, was a driving force in the worldview and behavior of gang members.[2] If entrepreneurial spirit denotes the desire to organize and manage business interests toward some end that results in the accumulation of capital, broadly defined, nearly all the gang members that I studied possessed, in varying degrees, five attributes that are either entrepreneurial in character or that reinforce entrepreneurial behavior.

Martín Sánchez Jankowski: *Islands in the Street: Gangs and American Urban Society*, pp. 101–105, 119–126. Copyright © 1991 The Regents of the University of California. Reprinted by permission of the University of California Press.

The first of these entrepreneurial attitudes is competitiveness. Most gang members I spoke with expressed a strong sense of self-competence and a drive to compete with others. They believed in themselves as capable of achieving some level of economic success and saw competition as part of human nature and an opportunity to prove one's self-worth. This belief in oneself often took on a dogmatic character, especially for those individuals who had lost in some form of economic competition. The losers always had ready excuses that placed the blame on something other than their own personal inadequacy, thereby artificially reinforcing their feelings of competence in the face of defeat.[3]

Gang members' sense of competitiveness also reflected their general worldview that life operates under Social Darwinist principles. In the economic realm, they believed there is no ethical code that regulates business ventures, and this attitude exempted them from moral constraints on individual economic-oriented action.[4] The views of Danny provide a good example of this Social Darwinist outlook. Danny was a 20-year-old Irish gang member from Boston:

> *I don't worry about whether something is fair or not when I'm making a business deal. There is nothing fair or unfair, you just go about your business of trying to make a buck, and if someone feels you took advantage of him, he has only himself to blame. If someone took advantage of me, I wouldn't sit around belly-aching about it, I'd just go and try to get some of my money back. One just has to ask around here [the neighborhood] and you'd find that nobody expects that every time you're going to make a business deal, that it will be fair—you know, that the other guy is not going to be fair, hell, he is trying to make money, not trying to be fair. This is the way those big business assholes operate too! The whole thing [the system] operates this way. . . .*

The second entrepreneurial attribute I observed is the desire and drive to accumulate money and material possessions. Karl Marx, of course, described this desire as the "profit motive" and attributed it primarily to the bourgeoisie.[5] There is a profit-motive element to the entrepreneurial values of gang members, but it differs significantly from Marx's analysis of the desire to accumulate material and capital for their own sake, largely divorced from the desire to improve one's material condition. Nor is gang members' ambition to accumulate material possessions related to a need for achievement, which the psychologist David McClelland identifies as more central to entrepreneurial behavior in certain individuals than the profit motive per se.[6] Rather, the entrepreneurial activity of gang members is predicated on their more basic understanding of what money can buy.[7] The ambition to accumulate capital and material possessions is related, in its initial stages (which can last for a considerable number of years), to the desire to improve the comfort of everyday living and the quality of leisure time.

This desire, of course, is shared by most people who live in low-income neighborhoods. Some of them resign themselves to the belief that they will never be able to secure their desires. Others attempt to improve their life situation by using various "incremental approaches," such as working in those jobs that are made available to them and saving their money, or attempting to learn higher-level occupational skills. In contrast, the entrepreneurs of low-income neighborhoods, especially those in gangs, attempt to improve their lives by becoming involved in a business venture, or a series of ventures, that has the potential to create large changes in their own or their family's socioeconomic condition.

The third attribute of entrepreneurial behavior prevalent in gangs is status-seeking. Mirroring the dominant values of the larger society, most gang members attempt to achieve some form of status with the acquisition of possessions. However, most of them cannot attain a high degree of status by accumulation alone. To merit high status among peers and in the community, gang members must try, although most will be unsuccessful, to accumulate a large number of possessions and be willing to share them. Once gang members have accumulated sufficient material possessions to provide themselves with a relative level of comfort or leisure above the minimal, they begin to seek the increase in status that generosity affords. (For philanthropic purposes, accumulating cash is preferable to accumulating possessions, because the more money one has, the more flexibility one has in giving away possessions.)

The fourth entrepreneurial attribute one finds among gang members is the ability to plan. Gang members spend an impressive amount of time planning activities that will bring them fortune and fame, or, at least, plenty of spending money in the short term. At their grandest, these plans have the character of dreams, but as the accounts of renowned business tycoons show, having big dreams has always been a hallmark of entrepreneurial endeavors.[8] At the other end of the spectrum are short-range plans (also called small scams) that members try to pull on one another, usually to secure a loan. . . .

Gang members also engage in intermediary and long-range planning. A typical intermediary plan might concern modest efforts to steal some type of merchandise from warehouses, homes, or businesses. Because most of the sites they select are equipped with security systems, a more elaborate plan involving more time is needed than is the case for those internal gang scams just described. Long-range planning and organization, sometimes quite elaborate, are, as other studies have reported, at times executed with remarkable precision.[9]

Finally, the fifth entrepreneurial attribute common among gang members is the ability to undertake risks. Generally, young gang members (nine to fifteen years of age) do not understand risk as part of a risk-reward calculus, and for this age group, risk-taking is nearly always pursued for itself, as an element of what Thrasher calls the "sport motive,"[10] the desire to test oneself. As gang members get older, they gradually develop a more sophisticated understanding of risk-taking, realizing that a certain amount of risk is necessary to secure desired goals. Now they attempt to calculate the risk factors involved for nearly every venture, measuring the risk to their physical well-being, money, and freedom. Just like mainstream businessmen, they discover that risk tends to increase proportionally to the level of innovation undertaken to secure a particular financial objective. Most of these older gang members are willing to assume risks commensurate with the subjective "value" of their designated target, but they will not assume risks just for the sake of risk-taking. . . .

Economic Activity: Accumulating

With a few exceptions, nearly all the literature on gangs focuses on their economic delinquency.[11] This is a very misleading picture, however, for although gangs operate primarily in illegal markets, they also are involved in legal markets. Of the 37 gangs observed in the present study, 27 generated some percentage of their revenues through legitimate business activity. It is true that gangs do more of their business activity in the illegal markets, but none of them wants to be exclusively active in these markets.[12]

In the illegal market, gangs concentrate their economic activities primarily in goods, services, and recreation. In the area of goods, gangs have been heavily involved in accumulating and selling drugs, liquor, and various stolen products such as guns, auto parts, and assorted electronic equipment. These goods are sometimes bought and sold with the gang acting as the wholesaler and/or retailer. At other times, the gang actually produces the goods it sells. For example, while most gangs buy drugs or alcohol and retail them, a few gangs manufacture and market homemade drugs and moonshine liquor. Two gangs (one African American and one Irish) in this study had purchased stills and sold their moonshine to people on the street, most of whom were derelicts, and to high school kids too young to buy liquor legally.[13] Three other gangs (two Puerto Rican and one Dominican) made a moonshine liquor from fermented fruit and sold it almost exclusively to teenagers. Both types of moonshine were very high in alcohol, always above one hundred proof. While sales of this liquor were not of the magnitude to create fortunes, these projects were quite surprisingly capable of generating substantial amounts of revenue.

The biggest money-maker and the one product nearly every gang tries to market is illegal drugs.[14] The position of the gang within the illegal drug market varies among gangs and between cities. In New York, the size of the gang and how long it has been in existence have a great deal to do with whether it will have access to drug suppliers. The older and larger gangs are able to buy drugs from suppliers and act as wholesalers to pushers. They shun acting as pushers (the lowest level of drug sales) themselves because there are greater risks and little, if any, commensurate increase in profit. In addition, because heroin use is forbidden within most gangs, the gang leaders prefer to establish attitudes oriented to the sale rather than the consumption of drugs within the organization. In the past, when the supply was controlled by the Italian Mafia, it was difficult for gangs to gain access to the quantity of drug supplies necessary to make a profit marketing them. In the past ten years, though, the Mafia has given way (in terms of drug supply) to African American, Puerto Rican, and Mexican syndicates.[15] In addition, with the increased popularity of cocaine in New York, the African American, Puerto Rican, and Dominican syndicates' connections to Latin American sources of cocaine supply rival, and in many cases surpass, those of Mafia figures.[16] With better access to supplies, gangs in New York have been able to establish a business attitude toward drugs and to capitalize on the opportunities that drugs now afford them.

Some gangs have developed alternative sources of supply. They do so in two ways. Some, particularly the Chicano gangs, have sought out pharmacies where an employee can be paid off to steal pills for the gang to sell on the street.[17] Other gangs, particularly in New York, but also some in Los Angeles, have established "drug mills" to produce synthetic drugs such as LSD (or more recently crack cocaine) for sale on the street. The more sophisticated drug mills, which are controlled by various organized crime families, manufacture a whole line of drugs for sale, including cut heroin, but gangs are almost never involved in them. Those gangs that have established a production facility for generating drugs, no matter how crude it may be, generate sizable sums of money. Whether a gang is able to establish a sophisticated production and distribution system for drug sales depends on the sophistication of the gang organization and the amount of capital available for start-up purposes.

Stolen guns are another popular and profitable product. Gangs sometimes steal guns and then redistribute them, but most often they buy them from wholesale gun peddlers and then resell them. Sometimes the gangs will buy up a small number of shotguns and then cut the barrel and stock down to about 13 to 15 inches in length and then sell them as "easily concealable." A prospective buyer can get whatever gun he wants if he is willing to pay the going price. In the present study, the Irish gangs have been, commercially speaking, the most involved with guns, often moving relatively large shipments, ranging from sawed-off shotguns to fully automatic rifles and pistols of the most sophisticated types.[18] It was reported that these guns were being moved, with the help of the Irish social clubs, to the Catholics of Northern Ireland for their struggle with the Protestants there. No matter what the destination, rather large sums of money were paid to the Irish gangs for their efforts in acquiring the weapons or in helping move them. Although all the gangs studied were involved in the sale of illegal guns, illegal gun sales constituted a larger proportion of the economic activities of Irish gangs than they did for the others.

Gangs in all three cities were also involved in the selling of car parts. All the parts sold were stolen, some stolen to fill special orders from customers and others stolen and reworked in members' home garages into customized parts for resale. Business was briskest in Los Angeles, where there is a large market, especially among the low-rider clientele, for customized auto parts.[19] The amount of money made from stolen auto parts varies according to the area, whether or not the gang has an agent to whom to sell the parts, and the types of parts sold. On the whole, revenues from stolen auto parts are not nearly as high as those from selling illegal drugs, guns, or liquor, and so less time is devoted by gangs to this activity.

Gangs' business activities also include a number of services, the three most common being protection, demolition (usually arson), and indirect participation in prostitution. Protection is the most common service, both because there is a demand for it in the low-income areas in which gangs operate and because the gangs find it the easiest service to deliver, since it requires little in the way of resources or training. Gangs offer both personal and business protection. Nearly all the gangs had developed a fee schedule according to the type of protection desired. Most, but certainly not all, of the protection services offered by the gangs in this study involved extortion. Usually the gang would go into a store and ask the owner if he felt he needed protection from being robbed. Since it was clear what was being suggested, the owner usually said yes and asked how much it would cost him. When dealing with naive owners, those who did not speak English very well or did not know American ghetto customs, or with owners who flatly resisted their services, the gang would take time to educate or persuade them to retain its services. In the case of the immigrants (most of whom were Asian or Near Eastern), the gang members would begin by explaining the situation, but usually such owners did not understand, and so the gang would demonstrate its point by sending members into the store to steal. Another tactic was to pay a dope addict to go in and rob the store. After such an incident occurred, the gang would return and ask the owner if he now needed protection. If he refused, the tactics were repeated, and almost all the owners were finally convinced. However, for those owners who understood and resisted from the start, more aggressive tactics were used, such as destruction of their premises or harassment of patrons. More often than not, continued pressure brought the desired result. However, it should be noted that in the vast majority of cases, no coercion was needed, because store owners in high-crime areas were, more often than not, happy to receive protection. As one owner said to me: "I would need to hire a protection company anyway, and frankly the gang provides much more protection than they could ever do."

Gangs also offer their services as enforcers to clients who need punishment administered to a third party. Small-time hustlers or loan sharks, for example, hired some gangs to administer physical coercion to borrowers delinquent in their repayments. More recently one gang offered and apparently was hired by a foreign government to undertake terrorist attacks against the government and people of the United States.[20] Although that was an extreme case, nearly all gangs seek enforcement contracts because the fee is usually high, few resources have to be committed, and relatively little in the way of planning (compared to other projects) is needed.

The permanent elimination of or damage to property is another service gangs offer. This more often than not involves arson, and the buildings hit are commonly dilapidated. The gangs' clients are either landlords who want to torch the building to get the insurance money or residents who are so frustrated by the landlord's unwillingness to provide the most basic services that they ask the gang to retaliate. In both cases, there is usually much preliminary discussion of the project within the gang. These service jobs require a good deal of discussion and planning because there is the potential to hurt someone living in the building or to create enormous hardship if people have no alternative place to live, and the gang will do almost anything to avoid injuring people in its community. The gangs of New York have had the most business along these lines, particularly in the South Bronx, but arson is a service offered in Detroit, Chicago, and Philadelphia as well. As one gang leader from the Bronx said:

> *You just don't bomb or torch any building that someone wants down. You got to find out who lives there, if they got another place to go, if they would be for takin' out the building and if they'd be OK with the folks [law enforcement authorities]. Then you got to get organized to get everybody out and sometimes that ain't many people and sometimes it is. If there is lots of people in the building, we'd just pass [refuse] on the job. . . . Now if we can work all these things out, we take the job and we deliver either a skeleton [outer walls are standing, but nothing else] or a cremation [just ashes].*

Many potential clients know that a gang will refuse to burn down a building in its neighborhood if some type of harm will come to residents of its community, and so they contract with a gang from another area to do the job. Such incidents always ignite a war not only between the affected gangs but also between the communities. Take the example of the Hornets, a gang from one borough in New York that had contracted to set on fire a building in another borough. Although no one was killed in the fire, a few people were slightly burned, and of course everyone who lived in the building became homeless. At the request of a number of residents, the Vandals, a gang from the affected area, began to investigate and found out who had contracted to torch the building and which gang had been responsible. Then, at the request of an overwhelming majority of the community, the Vandals retaliated by burning down a building in the culprit gang's community. Hipper, a 20-year-old member of the Vandals, said:

> *We got to protect our community, they depend on us and they want us to do something so this [the burning of an apartment building in the neighborhood] don't happen again. . . . We be torchin' one of their buildings. I hope this don't*

*hurt anybody, but if we don't do this, they be back hurting the people in our com-
munity and we definitely don't be letting that happen!*

This is an excellent example of the bond that exists between the community
and the gang. There is the understanding, then, among the community that
the gang is a resource that can be counted on, particularly in situations where
some form of force is necessary. Likewise, the gang knows that its legitimacy
and existence are tied to being integrated in and responsible to community
needs.

Prostitution is one illegal service in which gangs do not, for the most
part, become directly involved. Gangs will accept the job of protecting pimps
and their women for a fee (fifteen, or 40 percent, of the gangs in this study
had), and in this way they become indirectly associated with the prostitution
business. Yet they generally avoid direct involvement because they feel protective of the females in their communities, and their organizations are wary
of being accused by neighborhood residents of exposing female members of
the community to the dangers associated with prostitution.

The last type of illegal ecomomic activity in which all of the gangs in the
present study were involved has to do with providing recreation. Some
gangs establish numbers games in their neighborhoods. One New York gang
had rented what had been a small Chinese food take-out place and was running numbers from the back where the kitchen had once been. (When I first
observed the place, I thought it was a Chinese take-out and even proposed
we get some quick food from it, which met with much laughter from the
members of the gang I was with.) This gang became so successful that it
opened up two other numbers establishments. One had been a pizza place
(and was made to look as though it still served pizza slices); the other was a
small variety store, which still functioned in that capacity, but also housed
the numbers game in the back rooms.

Setting up gambling rooms is another aspect of the recreation business.
Eleven of the gangs (or 30 percent) rented small storefronts, bought tables
and chairs, and ran poker and/or domino games. The gang would assume
the role of the "house," receiving a commission for each game played. Some
of the gangs bought slot machines and placed them in their gambling rooms.
Five (or 14 percent) of the gangs had as many as fifteen machines available
for use.

Finally, ten gangs (27 percent), primarily those with Latino members,
rented old buildings and converted them to accommodate cockfights. The
gang would charge each cock owner a fee for entering his bird and an entrance fee for each patron. All of these ventures could, at various times, generate significant amounts of capital. The exact amount would depend on how
often they were closed by the police and how well the gang managed the
competition in its marketplace.

Turning to the legal economic activities undertaken by gangs, I observed that two ran "mom and pop" stores that sold groceries, candy, and soft drinks. Three gangs had taken over abandoned apartment buildings, renovated them, and rented them very cheaply—not simply because the accommodations were rather stark, but also because the gang wanted to help the less fortunate members of its community. The gangs also used these buildings to house members who had nowhere else to live. Undertaken and governed by social as much as economic concerns, these apartment ventures did not generate much income.

Interestingly, the finances of these legal activities were quite tenuous. The gangs that operated small grocery stores experienced periodic failures during which the stores had to be closed until enough money could be acquired (from other sources) to either pay the increased rent, rebuild shelf stock, or make necessary repairs. For those gangs who operated apartment buildings, in every case observed, the absence of a deed to the building or the land forced the gang to relinquish its holdings to either the city or a new landlord who wanted to build some new structure. Though there was a plentiful supply of abandoned buildings, most gangs lost interest in the renovation-and-rental business because such projects always created a crisis in their capital flow, which in turn precipitated internal bickering and conflict.

Other legal economic activities undertaken by the gangs I studied were automobile and motorcycle repair shops, car parts (quasi junk yards), fruit stands, and hair shops (both barber and styling). However, most of these ventures contributed only very modest revenues to the gangs' treasuries. Furthermore, the gang leadership had difficulty keeping most of the legal economic activities functioning because the rank and file were, by and large, not terribly enthusiastic about such activities. Rank-and-file resistance to most of these activities was of three sorts: members did not want to commit regularly scheduled time to any specific ongoing operation; members felt that the legal activities involved considerable overhead costs that lowered the profit rate; and members calculated that the time required to realize a large profit was far too long when compared to illegal economic activity. Thus, when such projects were promoted by the gang leadership and undertaken by the rank and file, they were done under the rubric of community service aid projects. The comments of Pin, a 19-year-old African American gang member from New York, are representative of this general position on legal economic activity:

> No, I don't go for those deals where we [the gang] run some kind of hotel out of an old building or run some repair shop or something like that. When you do that you can't make no money, or if you do make something it so small and takes so long to get it that it's just a waste of our [the gang's] money. But when the leadership brings it up as a possibility, well, sometimes I vote for it because I figure you got to help the community, many of them [people in the community] say they sort of depend on our help in one way or another, so I always say this is

one way to help the community and me and the brothers go along with it. But everybody knows you can't make no money on shit like this.

ENDNOTES

[1] Nearly all studies of gangs incorporate this theme into their analysis. One of the exceptions is Cloward and Ohlin, *Delinquency and Opportunity,* which argues that many delinquents have the same values as other members of American society. However, even Cloward and Ohlin incorporate some of the conventional argument by accepting the premise that gang members' skills to compete in the larger society have been retarded by a lack of opportunity.

[2] See Charles Sabel, *Work and Politics* (Cambridge: Cambridge University Press, 1987), pp. 1–30, on the importance of worldviews in affecting the behavior of individuals in industrial organizations and politics.

[3] David Matza mentions a comparable tendency among delinquents to deny guilt associated with wrongdoing when he discusses the delinquent's belief that he is nearly always the victim of a "bum rap" (see Matza, *Delinquency and Drift* [New Brunswick, NJ: Transaction Books], pp. 108–10).

[4] I use the term *economic oriented action* the way Weber does: "Action will be said to be 'economical oriented' so far as, according to its subjective meaning, it is concerned with the satisfaction of a desire for 'utilities' *(Nutzleistung)"* (Weber, *Economy and Society* 1:63).

[5] See Karl Marx, *The Economic and Philosophical Manuscripts of 1844,* 4th rev. ed. (Moscow: Progress Publishers, 1974), p. 38.

[6] See David C. McClelland, *The Achieving Society* (New York: Free Press, 1961), pp. 233–37.

[7] See Lee Rainwater, *What Money Buys: Inequality and the Social Meanings of Income* (New York: Basic Books, 1974). Also see Richard P. Coleman and Lee Rainwater, *Social Standing in America: New Dimensions of Class* (New York: Basic Books, 1978), pp. 29–45.

[8] See the accounts of successful entrepreneurs from poor families who dreamed of grandeur and became America's most renowned business tycoons in Matthew Josephson, *The Robber Barons: The Great American Capitalists, 1861–1901* (New York: Harcourt, Brace & World, 1962), especially the chapter titled "What Young Men Dream," pp. 32–49.

[9] See Thrasher, *The Gang,* p. 86.

[10] Ibid., p. 86.

[11] Both the theoretical and empirical literature focus on the gang's criminal activity. For theoretical discussions, see Kornhauser, *Social Sources of Delinquency,* pp. 51–61. For empirical studies, see nearly all of the classic and contemporary work on gangs. A sample of this literature would include Thrasher, *The Gang;* Herman Schwendinger and Julia Schwendinger, *Adolescent Subcultures and Delinquency* (New York: Praeger, 1985); Cloward and Ohlin, *Delinquency and Opportunity;* Cohen, *Delinquent Boys.* Two exceptions are Horowitz, *Honor and the American Dream,* and Vigil, *Barrio Gangs.*

[12] There are two factors that have encouraged gangs to be more active in illegal markets. First, gangs, like organized crime syndicates, attempt to become active in many economic activities that are legal. However, because so much of the legal market is controlled by groups that have established themselves in strategic positions (because they entered that market a considerable time in the past), gangs have

found it difficult at best to successfully penetrate many legal markets. Further, there are financial incentives that have encouraged gangs to operate in the illegal market. These include the fact that costs are relatively low, and while personal risk (in terms of being incarcerated and/or physically hurt) is rather high, high demand along with high risk can produce greater profit margins. Despite the fact that these two factors have encouraged gangs to be more active in the illegal market, it is important to emphasize that nearly all the gangs studied attempted to, and many did, conduct business in the legal market as well.

[13] The Schwendingers indicate that "youthful tastes regulate the flow of goods and services in the [adolescent] market" and gangs do take advantage of these tastes. See Schwendinger and Schwendinger, *Adolescent Subcultures and Delinquency*, p. 286.

[14] See Fagan, "Social Organization of Drug Use and Drug Dealing among Urban Gangs," pp. 633–67; and Jerome H. Skolnick, *Forum: The Social Structure of Street Drug Dealing* (Sacramento: Bureau of Criminal Statistics/Office of the Attorney General, 1989).

[15] See Francis A. J. Ianni, *Black Mafia: Ethnic Succession in Organized Crime* (New York: Simon & Schuster, 1974). Also see Moore, *Homeboys*, pp. 86–92, 114–16.

[16] See Peter Lupsha and K. Schlegel, "The Political Economy of Drug Trafficking: The Herrera Organization (Mexico and the United States)" (Paper Presented at the Latin American Studies Association, Philadelphia, 1979).

[17] This paying off of employees for drug supplies began, according to Joan Moore, in Los Angeles in the 1940s and 1950s (see Moore, *Homeboys*, pp. 78–82).

[18] These gangs can procure fully automatic M-16s, Ingrams, and Uzzis.

[19] Low riders are people, nearly all of whom are of Mexican descent, who drive customized older automobiles (1950s and 1960s models are preferred), one of the characteristics being that the springs for each wheel are cut away so that the car rides very low to the ground. Some of these cars have hydraulic systems that can be inflated at the flip of a switch so that the car can ride low to the ground at one moment and at the normal level the next. For a discussion of the importance of customized automobiles in Los Angeles, especially among Chicano youth, see Schwendinger and Schwendinger, *Adolescent Subcultures and Delinquency*, pp. 234–45.

[20] The El Rukn gang in Chicago was recently indicted and convicted of contracting with the Libyan government to carry out terrorist acts within the United States. See *Chicago Tribune*, November 3, 4, 6, 7, 1987.

REFERENCES

Cloward, Richard A. and Lloyd B. Ohlin. 1960. *Delinquency and Opportunity: A Theory of Delinquent Gangs.* New York: Free Press.

Cohen, Albert K. 1955. *Delinquent Boys: The Culture of the Gang.* Glencoe, IL: Free Press.

Coleman, Richard P. and Lee Rainwater. 1978. *Social Standing in America: New Dimensions of Class.* New York: Basic Books.

Fagan, Jeffery. 1989. "The Social Organization of Drug Use and Drug Dealing among Urban Gangs." *Criminology* 27, no. 4 (November): 633–70.

Horowitz, Ruth. 1983. *Honor and the American Dream: Culture and Identity in a Chicano Community.* New Brunswick: Rutgers University Press.

Ianni, Francis, A. J. 1974. *Black Mafia: Ethnic Succession in Organized Crime.* New York: Simon & Schuster.

Josephson, Matthew. 1962. *The Robber Barons: The Great American Capitalists, 1861–1901.* New York: Harcourt, Brace & World.

Kornhauser, Ruth Rosner. 1978. *Social Sources of Delinquency: An Appraisal of Analytic Models.* Chicago: University of Chicago Press.

Lupsha, Peter and K. Schlegel. 1979. "The Political Economy of Drug Trafficking: The Herrera Organization (Mexico and the United States)." Paper presented at a meeting of the Latin American Studies Association, Philadelphia.

McClelland, David C. 1961. *The Achieving Society.* New York: Free Press.

Marx, Karl. 1974. *The Economic and Philosophical Manuscripts of 1844.* 4th rev. ed. Moscow: Progress Publishers.

Matza, David. 1990. *Delinquency and Drift.* New Brunswick, NJ: Transaction Books.

Moore, Joan W. 1978. *Homeboys: Gangs, Drugs, and Prisons in the Barrios of Los Angeles.* Philadelphia: Temple University Press.

———. 1985. "Isolation and Stigmatization in the Development of an Underclass: The Case of Chicano Gangs in East Los Angeles." *Social Problems* 33, no. 1 (October): 1–12.

Rainwater, Lee. 1970. *Behind Ghetto Walls: Black Family Life in a Federal Slum.* Chicago: Aldine Press.

———. 1974. *What Money Buys: Inequality and the Social Meanings of Income.* New York: Basic Books.

Thrasher, Frederic. 1928. *The Gang: A Study of 1303 Gangs in Chicago.* Chicago: University of Chicago Press.

Vigil, James Diego. 1988. *Barrio Gangs: Street Life and Identity in Southern California.* Austin: University of Texas Press.

Weber, Max. 1978. *Economy and Society: An Outline of Interpretive Sociology.* Edited by Guenther Roth and Claus Wittich. Berkeley: University of California Press.

17

WOMEN OF THE KLAN
Organizing 100 Percent American Women

KATHLEEN M. BLEE

This reading by Kathleen Blee, a professor of sociology at the University of Pittsburgh, is taken from Blee's 1991 book, *Women of the Klan: Racism and Gender in the 1920s.* Blee's study of the Women's Ku Klux Klan (WKKK) is an example of sociological research done on a secondary group. *Secondary groups* tend to be larger, less intimate, and more formal than primary groups. Moreover, most secondary groups are utilitarian in that they serve some function for society. Blee examines the history of the WKKK and the group char-

From *Women of the Klan: Racism and Gender in the 1920s*, pp. 27–41. Copyright © 1991 by Kathleen M. Blee. Reprinted with the permission of the University of California Press.

acteristics that distinguish this organization from the all-male KKK. She finds
that the WKKK had a particular social structure that enabled it to obtain a
large membership in a short period of time. Blee hopes that her research on
the politics of racial hatred and religious bigotry might help in the development of effective strategies to counteract the growth of organized racism in
the United States.

Judge R. M. Mann of the second division circuit court in Little Rock, Arkansas, officially chartered the Women of the Ku Klux Klan on June 10,
1923. Its national headquarters were set up in a three-room office in the
Ancient Order of United Workmen hall in Little Rock, Arkansas, at some distance from the male Klan's Atlanta headquarters to symbolize the purported
independence of the new women's order from its male counterpart.[1]

Membership in the WKKK was open to white Gentile female native-
born citizens over 18 years of age who owed no allegiance to any foreign
government or sect, that is, who were not Catholic, Socialist, Communist,
or so forth. Applicants were required to have been resident in a Klan jurisdiction for at least six months and to be endorsed by at least two Klanswomen or a WKKK kleagle or Imperial Commander. Klanswomen swore to
investigate "carefully and personally" the qualifications and background of
every candidate they proposed for office. Dues of $10 included one robe
and helmet but did not apply to wives of men who were members of the
original Klan or a similar organization during Reconstruction. The national
offices of the WKKK were supported (in lavish style) by a portion of all dues;
an Imperial Tax (a per capita assessment); profits from the sale of regalia,
uniforms, stationery, jewelry, and costumes; and by interest and profits from
investments.[2]

. . . The WKKK declared itself an organization "by women, for women,
and of women [that] no man is exploiting for his individual gain." The structure of the new women's Klan, worked out in a meeting of WKKK leaders in
Asheville, North Carolina, would focus on specific functions and each would
have a corresponding task department. The major areas of work for the
WKKK's initial efforts were Americanism, education, public amusements,
legislation, child welfare and delinquency, citizenship, civics, law enforcement, disarmament, peace, and politics.[3] . . .

The charter membership of the new WKKK numbered 125,000 women.
Most lived in the Midwest, Northwest, and Ozarks region, strongholds of the
KKK. Not satisfied with a membership drawn from among the wives, sisters,
sweethearts, and mothers of Klansmen, [WKKK leaders] immediately em-
barked on a recruiting trip throughout the West and Northwest, increasing
the WKKK's overall membership and giving the new organization visibility
in other regions. [Leaders] also hired female field agents and kleagles who
worked with KKK kleagles to bring the message of the women's Klan to all
areas of the country. WKKK kleagles, initially often the wives and sisters of

KKK officers, worked on a commission basis, retaining a percentage of the initiation dues collected from each new Klanswoman. Organizers used techniques proven effective in the men's Klan: they recruited through personal, family, and work contacts and held highly publicized open meetings to reach politically inactive women and women not from Klan families. In addition, WKKK kleagles worked to recruit women through existing organizations. Female nativist and patriotic societies, in particular, were courted by WKKK organizers who sought to persuade them to merge into the new national women's Klan organization.[4]

Organizers for the women's Klan were effective. Within four months, the WKKK claimed that its membership had doubled to 250,000. By November 1923, 36 states had chapters of the Women of the Ku Klux Klan. Throughout 1924 the WKKK continued to grow, accepting girls over 16 years old and chartering 50 locals a week in 1924. The following year an influential anti-Klan commentator declared that at least three million women had been initiated into the women's Klan. His estimate was no doubt inflated, perhaps by projecting from the recruitment successes of the strong Ohio and Indiana WKKK realms; indeed, modern scholars judge the entire 1920s Klan to have enrolled no more than three to five million members. It is clear, however, that the WKKK attracted a great many women within a short time.[5]

It is impossible to determine the exact number or location of WKKK chapters across the country in the absence of organizational records, but we can estimate the expansion of the women's Klan by examining the pages of Klan periodicals. During the mid-1920s the *Fellowship Forum* published news about WKKK chapters, women's rights organizations, and women's clubs—mingled with recipes and fashion tips. The September 1925 issue carried news from local WKKK chapters in 11 states: New York, Connecticut, Pennsylvania, Michigan, Ohio, Virginia, West Virginia, Kansas, Oklahoma, Texas, and Colorado. Most chapters were located in small towns; the exceptions were those of Oklahoma City and Norfolk. The following September, in 1926, the *Fellowship Forum* included news from WKKK chapters in 16 states: New York, Pennsylvania, Maryland, Virginia, Georgia, Florida, Illinois, Indiana, Ohio, Iowa, Minnesota, Wisconsin, Michigan, Nebraska, California, Washington, and in the District of Columbia as well. Again, most chapters were located outside major metropolitan areas although most members of the WKKK, as of the male Ku Klux Klan, probably resided in large or middle-sized cities. Other issues of the *Fellowship Forum* show a similar geographical dispersion of the women's Klan. Many chapters clustered in Pennsylvania, Ohio, Indiana, Michigan, and New York—states where the KKK was also strong—but chapters existed in the West, on the Atlantic Coast, and along the North-South border.[6] . . .

In chartering its new women's organization, the Klan emphasized the role of women as helpmates to Klansmen. Women's cooperation and assistance were needed, Klansmen insisted, to ensure that the political agenda of the men's Klan could be implemented. The KKK press talked often of the WKKK as its "women's auxiliary" and argued that the men's Klan had created the WKKK with the same ideals and principles as its father organization.[7]

Klansmen were unsure, however, about what Klan membership would mean for women. Women might be convenient symbols for mobilizing men into the Klan, but women's actual political participation was another matter. An early advertisement written by the KKK to solicit members for an organization of Klanswomen illustrates the men's ambivalence. Although it was a recruitment pitch for the WKKK, the advertisement also pointed to a fearful potential in political involvement to masculinize women. Many worry, the ad suggested, that "giving [women] the ballot would foster masculine boldness and restless independence, which might detract from the modesty and virtue of womanhood." To this dilemma, the KKK posed as a solution the creation of a separate organization for Klanswomen. The WKKK would allow women to be politically active without "sacrifice of that womanly dignity and modesty we all admire." The key to the delicate balancing act between a "masculine" and a "feminine" political involvement, according to the KKK, was acquiescence of Klanswomen in the political agenda of Klansmen. By adopting as a whole the Klan's agenda of support for white Protestantism, the English language, public schools, the Bible, and immigration restrictions, women could exercise their newly granted enfranchisement without relying on "masculine" traits of political judgment and strategizing.[8]

A related tactic of recruitment for the women's organization stressed women's political *potential*. Although ostensibly supporting women's involvement in politics, this approach emphasized women's ignorance and limited abilities in the political arena. Excluded from the world of political debate, white Protestant women had developed only a "moral influence" in politics. Their special roles in the family and home gave women good political instincts, the Klan argued, but not mature political judgment. Women now needed to be taught (by men) those principles and attitudes that the world of politics required: clear thinking, intelligence, and collective and individual responsibility for maintaining the principles of Anglo-Saxon Protestantism. Women might have gained the ballot by law, but the ability to use it intelligently required further education—an education the Klan was prepared to provide through its women's organization. . . .

The WKKK advertised its ability to champion the goals of white womanhood as a standard recruiting tool for new members. Its Washington chapter, for example, argued that white Protestant native-born women had common political interests and would be more effective in pursuing those interests if they were politically organized. Their recruitment advertisement posed a number of questions for women to consider:

> *Are you interested in the welfare of our Nation?*
> *As an enfranchised woman are you interested in Better Government?*
> *Do you not wish for the protection of Pure Womanhood?*
> *Shall we uphold the sanctity of the American Home?*

Should we not interest ourselves in Better Education for our children?
Do we not want American teachers in our American schools?

"Patriotic women," those who answered these questions in the affirmative,
were needed in the women's Klan. Protestant white women, the WKKK insisted, shared a concern for their children's education and the welfare of the
country. It is the "duty of the American Mother" to stamp out vice and immorality in the nation. Joining the Klan was an effective avenue for the political work that white Protestant women needed to do.[9]

The Women's Klan

To understand the nature of the new women's Klan, we need to examine
the beliefs, organizations, rituals, and activities of the WKKK in comparison
with those of the men's order. But we must use caution in our comparison.
When Klanswomen swore to uphold the "sanctity of the home and chastity
of womanhood" they echoed the words, but not necessarily the sentiments,
of their male Klan counterparts. Although a simple listing of WKKK and
KKK principles and rituals would suggest that there was little difference between the two organizations, we must understand how these were interpreted and justified by each organization.

Beliefs

On one level, many principles of the new women's Klan appear identical to
the racist and xenophobic politics of the first and second men's Klans. The
WKKK supported militant patriotism, national quotas for immigration, racial segregation, and antimiscegenation laws. Klanswomen cited the need to
safeguard the "eternal supremacy" of the white race against a "rising tide of
color" and decried Catholic and Jewish influence in politics, the schools, the
media, and the business world. [Lulu] Markwell [of Arkansas, the first Imperial Commander of the WKKK,] . . . saw the mission of the women's Klan as
"fighting for the same principles as the Knights of the Ku Klux Klan," although she reserved for the WKKK a special interest in "work peculiar to
women's organization, such as social welfare work [and] the prevention of
juvenile delinquency."[10]

Like the men's Klan, the WKKK often used politically palatable symbols
to present its agenda of nativism and racial hatred to the public. It called
for separation of church from state when crusading against Roman Catholic political influence, for free public schools when seeking to destroy parochial schools, and for the purity of race when seeking racial segregation
and restricted immigration. In private, the racial bigotry of the WKKK was

fully as vicious as that of the KKK, as in Klanswomen's condemnation of "mulatto leaders forced to remain members of the negro group [who] aspire to white association because of their white blood [thus] boldly preaching racial equality."[11]

But if many of the WKKK's basic principles followed existing doctrines of the men's Klan, women and men did not always have a common perception of the problems that required Klan action. Klansmen of the 1920s denounced interracial marriage for its destructive genetic outcomes; their Klan forefathers fought interracial sexuality to maintain white men's sexual access to white and black women. Klanswomen, however, saw a different danger in miscegenation: the destruction of white marriages by untrustworthy white men who "betray their own kind."

In many cases, women and men in the Klan took different messages from common symbols. Klansmen praised womanhood to underscore the correctness of male supremacy; Klanswomen used the symbol to point out the inequities that women faced in society and politics. Klansmen sought political inspiration in the "great achievements" of white American Protestantism, but Klanswomen read history differently. Rather than mimicking the men's empty gestures of praise for "true American women" in the past, the WKKK complained that women had been excluded from public politics throughout most of this glorious history, even though "our mothers have ever been Klanswomen at heart, sharing with our fathers the progress and development of our country." Klanswomen embraced the KKK's racist, anti-Catholic, and anti-Semitic agenda and symbols of American womanhood but they used these to argue as well for equality for white Protestant women.[12]

Organization

For the most part the WKKK adopted the militaristic hierarchical style of the KKK. An Excellent Commander served as president, with a four-year term of office and responsibility for issuing, suspending, and revoking the charters of locals and realms (state organizations). Next in the chain of command was the klaliff (vice-president), who acted as presiding officer of the Imperial Klonvokation; the klokard (lecturer), responsible for disseminating Klankraft; and the kludd (chaplain), who presided over Klan ritual. Other major officers included the kligrapp (secretary), bonded for $25,000 to handle minor Klan funds; the Klabee (treasurer), bonded for $50,000 to handle major Klan funds; and the officers of Klan ritual and ceremony, including the kladd (conductor), klagoro (inner guard), klexter (outer guard), night hawk (in charge of candidates), klokan (investigator and auditor), and kourier (messenger).

Each realm or group of realms of the WKKK was organized by a Major Kleagle with subjurisdictions organized by minor kleagles and supervised by a series of Realm Commanders and Imperial Commanders. Upon retirement from office, Excellent Commanders became Klan Regents, Realm Commanders became Grand Regents, and Imperial Commanders became Imperial Regents. In keeping with the military arrangement of the WKKK, nearly all offices were subdivided into further levels of authority. The rank of kourier, for example, was subdivided into that of kourier private, corporal, sergeant, lieutenant, captain, major, and colonel. Ranks carried more than symbolic authority, as failure to obey the command of an officer was defined as insubordination and could bring harsh punishment.[13]

The similarity between the organization of the male and female Klans is significant. Consistently, WKKK denied that it was like the auxiliary of a fraternal association, "merely a social order for social purposes." Instead, Klanswomen embraced the mixture of individualism and deference to authority that characterized the male Klan. Like Klansmen, Klanswomen had at least ostensible opportunities to rise within the organization through individual effort and talent; both organizations used a strict command hierarchy. In this, the WKKK claimed to stand apart from the outside world that discouraged women from individual efforts and achievements. By valuing both obedience and individual effort, the WKKK would "inculcate patriotism, upbuild character, and develop true clannishness among women."[14]

Other features of the WKKK show the contrasting aspects of obedience and commonality that characterized the KKK. Like their male counterparts, Klanswomen typically wore white robes with masks and helmets, although some chapters used red robes. Masks were clearly intended to disguise the identity of Klanswomen in public, but the WKKK insisted that masks had only a symbolic purpose. Through masking Klanswomen hid their individuality as well as identity, exemplifying the Klan motto "not for self, but for others." Similar claims were made about Klan robes. Although in fact officers' robes had more colors and accoutrements, Klanswomen asserted that their robes symbolized the equality of all women within Klankraft. Robes set Klanswomen apart from the invidious world of social class distinctions in fashion, leveling the divisions of wealth so pervasive in alien society. "As we look upon a body of women robed in white we realize that we are on a common level of sisterhood and fraternal union."[15]

The detailed laws and regulations of the WKKK ensured obedience to authority. Women, no less than men, were expected to conduct themselves according to klannish principles. The WKKK treated as major offenses those of treason to the Klan, violating the oath of allegiance, disrespect of virtuous womanhood, violation of the U.S. Constitution, the "pollution" of Caucasian blood through miscegenation, and other acts unworthy of a Klanswoman. Minor offenses included profane language or vulgarity during a klonklave, acts against the best interest of the Klan or a Klanswoman, and refusal or failure to obey the Excellent Commander. The Excellent Commander assessed penalties for minor offenses; a tribunal handled major offenses. Violators faced reprimand, suspension, banishment forever, or complete ostracism.

Ritual

At least as central as laws and hierarchy to both women's and men's Klans was an elaborate and intricate web of ceremonials, rites, and protocols designed to increase members' commitment to the order and to sharpen the distinctions between insiders and outsiders ("aliens"). Like the men's Klan, the WKKK used threatening, frightening, and challenging rituals to ensure loyalty and instill fear in its members. Both the WKKK and the KKK referred to themselves as "invisible empires," conveying the Klan's aspirations to universal jurisdiction. Secret klannish words gave members an immediate way to recognize sister and brother Klan members. In Klan ceremonies, days of the week were not Sunday, Monday, and so forth as in the alien world but were desperate, dreadful, desolate, doleful, dismal, deadly, and dark. Weeks of the month became weird, wonderful, wailing, weeping, and woeful. January through December were labeled appalling, frightful, sorrowful, mournful, horrible, terrible, alarming, furious, fearful, hideous, gloomy, and bloody.

The Klan changed historical time as well, setting it to the ascendancy of white Gentile Americans. The reign of Incarnation included all time up to the American Revolution. A first reign of Reincarnation lasted from the beginning of the revolutionary war until the organization of the first Ku Klux Klan in 1866. A second reign of Reincarnation extended from 1866 to 1872, the collapse of the first KKK. The third reign of Reincarnation began in 1915, the reorganization of the KKK, and extended from the present into the future.[16]

The naturalization klonklave was typical of women's Klan rituals. An altar was placed in the center of a room or in an open-air gathering place surrounded by stations with water, a Bible, a flag, and a sword. WKKK officers entered the klonklave, kissed the flag, proceeded to the altar, and saluted the Excellent Commander or other presiding officer, raising their masks to reveal their identities to this official. When all officers were assembled, the kladd certified that everyone present was a valid member of the WKKK. The entrance to the building or park was secured by the klexter and klagoro, and then all masks were removed.

Once assembled, officers were questioned about the seven sacred symbols of Klankraft in a ritualized catechism oddly patterned after the catechism ritual of the Roman Catholic church. Each officer repeated a litany of symbols: the Bible (God), fiery cross (sacrifice and service), flag (U.S. Constitution), sword (law enforcement and national defense), water (purity of life and unity of purpose), mask (secrecy, unselfishness, and banishment of individuality), and robe (purity and equality). Between each restatement of Klan doctrine, the audience and officers sang a Christian hymn.

During the naturalization ceremony, a klokard led the class of candidates through the oath of admission. Candidates swore that they were serious, qualified for admission, believers in klannishness, and willing to practice klannishness toward other Klanswomen and work for the eternal maintenance of white supremacy. Candidates then were greeted by officers and members and congratulated for their "womanly decision to forsake the world of selfishness and fraternal alienation and emigrate to the delectable bounds of the Invisible Empire and become its loyal citizens." At this point, the Excellent Commander conferred the obligation and oath of admission on the assembled candidates and baptized the new members by pouring water and saying:

> With this transparent, life-giving, powerful God-given fluid, more precious and far more significant than all the sacred oils of the ancients, I set you apart from the women of your daily association to the great and honorable task you have voluntarily allotted yourselves as citizens of the Invisible Empire, Women of the Ku Klux Klan. As Klanswomen, may your character be as transparent, your life purpose as powerful, your motive in all things as magnanimous and as pure, and your Klannishness as real and as faithful as the manifold drops herein.

As a quartet of Klanswomen sang and the assembly prayed, the klannish initiates responded with their own ritual. They dipped fingers in water and touched their shoulders, saying "In body," and their foreheads, saying "In mind," then waved their hands in the air, saying "In spirit," and made a circle above their heads saying "In life." The klokard then imparted the secret signs and words of the Klan. The ceremony closed with an opportunity to raise issues from the floor (probably an infrequent occurrence), followed by a restatement of the need for secrecy in the presence of aliens. The night hawk extinguished the fiery cross, the kludd performed a benediction, and the klonklave was declared closed.[17]

Ceremonies for higher levels in the WKKK followed a similar pattern, although more was required of the candidates. Acceptance into the second-degree obligation, the highest rank below officer level, required candidates to make pledges against slandering other Klanswomen or Klansmen, against materialism, and against selfishness and similar temptations. Candidates for advanced degrees also made greater pledges of duty, swearing that "when pleasure interferes with my duty as Klanswoman . . . I will set aside pleasure"; they affirmed their loyalty, vowing not to recommend "faithless, contemptuous, careless, or indifferent" women for advancement in the order.[18]

Activities

It is difficult to compare the political practices of the women's and men's Klans, as both varied considerably across the nation and over time but the national agendas of each organization give some indication of the differences.

The political agenda of the men's Klan ranged from infiltration into legislative and judicial politics on the state, municipal, and county level to acts of violence and terroristic intimidation against Jews, Catholics, and blacks. Many Klansmen, though, used the KKK as primarily a male fraternity, a social club of like-minded white Protestants.[19]

The women's Klan similarly showed a range of activities and purposes. On a national level, the women's Klan worked to legitimate the violence and terrorism of the men's order. It published and distributed a detailed guide to the proper display of the American flag and a pocket-sized version of the U.S. Constitution and circulated a card reminding Protestants to attend church faithfully; each item prominently displayed the WKKK logo. The WKKK involved itself in national legislative politics, although without much success. It actively supported the creation of a federal Department of Education to bolster public schools and undermine parochial education and opposed U.S. membership in the World Court. Although it claimed to be interested in safeguarding white Protestant children and the home, the WKKK opposed a 1924 bill outlawing child labor on the grounds that it was "a Communistic, Bolshevistic scheme." That same year Klanswomen were active in blocking an attempt by anti-Klan forces to introduce a plank in the national Democratic party platform condemning the Ku Klux Klan.[20]

At times the women's Klan sought to portray itself as an organization of social work and social welfare. One national WKKK speaker announced that she left social work for the "broader field of Klankraft" because of the Klan's effectiveness in promoting morality and public welfare. Many chapters claimed to collect food and money for the needy, although these donations typically went to Klan families, often to families of Klan members arrested for rioting and vigilante activities. A powerful Florida WKKK chapter operated a free day nursery, charging that Catholic teachers had ruined the local public schools.[21]

Some WKKK chapters ran homes for wayward girls. These homes served two purposes: to protect the virtue of Protestant women who were tempted by a life of vice and to underscore the danger faced by delinquent girls placed in Catholic-controlled reform schools. The Shreveport, Louisiana, WKKK chapter, for example, based its fund-raising for a Protestant girls' home on the story of a woman whose unhappy fate it was to be sent to a Catholic reform home after being convicted of selling whiskey and prostituting her teenaged daughters.[22]

Another activity of many WKKK locals was the crusade against liquor and vice. WKKK chapters worked to "clean up" a motion picture industry in which they claimed Jewish owners spewed a steady diet of immoral sex onto the screen. Other chapters fought against liquor, as evidenced by the case of Myrtle Cook, a Klanswoman and president of the Vinton, Iowa, WCTU, who was assassinated for documenting the names of suspected bootleggers. In death, Cook was eulogized by Klanswomen and WCTU members alike; all business in Vinton was suspended for the two hours of the funeral.[23]

WKKK chapters in many states were active also in campaigns to prohibit prenuptial religious agreements about future children, bar interracial marriage, outlaw the Knights of Columbus (a Catholic fraternal society), remove Catholic encyclopedias from public schools, bar the use of Catholic contractors by public agencies, and exclude urban (i.e., Jewish and Catholic) vacationers in majority-Protestant suburban resorts.[24]

Some WKKK locals, though, functioned largely for the personal and financial success of their members. F. C. Dunn of Lansing, Michigan, made a fortune after introducing her invention, a new antiseptic powder, at a local WKKK meeting.[25]

Klanswomen tended not to be involved in physical violence and rioting, but there were exceptions. In the aftermath of a 1924 Klan riot in Wilkinsburg, Pennsylvania, Mamie H. Bittner, a 39-year-old mother of three children and member of the Homestead, Pennsylvania, WKKK testified that she, along with thousands of other Klanswomen paraded through town, carrying heavy maple riot clubs. Moreover, Bittner claimed that the WKKK was teaching its members to murder and kill in the interest of the Klan.[26]

The activities of the women's Klan were shaped largely by the existing political agenda of the men's Klan. It is not accurate, however, to portray the WKKK as a dependent auxiliary of the men's order. Klanswomen created a distinctive ideology and political agenda that infused the Klan's racist and nativist goals with ideas of equality between white Protestant women and men. The ideology and politics of Klanswomen and Klansmen were not identical, though at many points they were compatible. But women and men of the Klan movement sometimes found themselves in contention as women changed from symbols to actors in the Klan.

The difference between the women's and men's Klan grew from an underlying message in the symbol of white womanhood. By using gender and female sexual virtue as prime political symbols, the Klan shaped its identity through intensely masculinist themes, as an organization of real men. Clearly, this was an effective recruitment strategy for the first Klan. But in the 1920s, as both financial and political expediency and significant changes in women's political roles prompted the Klan to accept female members, an identity based on symbols of masculine exclusivity and supremacy became problematic. In addition, if Klansmen understood that defending white womanhood meant safeguarding white Protestant supremacy and male supremacy, many women heard the message differently. The WKKK embraced ideas of racial and religious privilege but rejected the messages of white female vulnerability. In its place Klanswomen substituted support for women's rights and a challenge to white men's political and economic domination.

ENDNOTES

[1] *Arkansas Gazette,* June 10, 1923, 1.
[2] WKKK, *Constitution and Laws* (WKKK, 1927).

[3] *Fellowship Forum,* Feb. 23, 1924, p. 6; Nov. 17, 1923, p. 6; *Imperial Night-Hawk,* Oct. 31, 1923, p. 1; Aug. 1, 1923, p. 8.

[4] *The Truth;* also, *Fiery Cross,* July 13, 1923, p. 1; Sue Wilson Abbey ("The Ku Klux Klan in Arizona, 1921–25," *Journal of Arizona History* 14 [Spring 1973]: 10–30) discusses how Tom Akers was sent to organize the Phoenix, Arizona, chapter of the WKKK in 1923; Loucks, *The Ku Klux Klan in Pennsylvania,* pp. 150–56; *Arkansas Gazette,* June 10, 1925, p. 1.

[5] *Arkansas Gazette,* Oct. 7, 1923, p. 12; see also *Imperial Night-Hawk,* Oct. 31, 1923, p. 1; *New York Times,* Nov. 7, 1923, p. 15; Kenneth Jackson, *The Ku Klux Klan;* William M. Likins, *The Ku Klux Klan, Its Rise and Fall; Patriotism Capitalized or Religion Turned into Gold* (privately published, 1925).

[6] See Kenneth Jackson, *The Ku Klux Klan; Fellowship Forum,* 1924–1928.

[7] *Imperial Night-Hawk,* June 13, 1923, p. 5; Aug. 8, 1923, p. 6.

[8] *Fiery Cross,* Mar. 2, 1923, p. 4; *Fellowship Forum,* June 2, 1923, p. 8.

[9] *Watcher on the Tower,* Sept. 15, 1923, p. 12.

[10] *Imperial Night-Hawk,* June 20, 1923, p. 8.

[11] WKKK, *Ideals of the Women of the Ku Klux Klan* (WKKK, 1923), pp. 2–3, 4–5; WKKK, *Women of America!,* pp. 6–7, 9–10, 13–14 (WKKK, ca. 1923); WKKK, *Kreed* (WKKK, ca. 1924).

[12] WKKK, *Women of America!;* WKKK, *Constitution and Laws,* pp. 6–7; WKKK, *Kreed;* WKKK, *Ideals,* pp. 2–3, 4–5; *Imperial Night-Hawk,* June 20, 1923, p. 8; May 14, 1924, p. 7; advertisement in *Dawn,* Aug. 11, 1923, p. 2.

[13] WKKK, *Constitution and Laws.* From statement by Victoria Rogers, Major Kleagle for the Realm of Illinois, in *Dawn,* Feb. 2, 1924, p. 12.

[14] WKKK, *Women of America!*

[15] WKKK, *Catalogue of Official Robes and Banners* (WKKK, ca. 1923); WKKK, *Kloran or Ritual of the WKKK* (WKKK, 1923).

[16] WKKK, *Constitution and Laws.*

[17] WKKK, *Kloran or Ritual of the WKKK.* The *New York Times* (Aug. 19, 1923, p. 2) has detailed coverage of a naturalization ceremony involving 700 members of the women's Klan in Allenwood, New Jersey.

[18] WKKK, *Second Degree Obligation of the Women of the Ku Klux Klan* (WKKK, n.d.); see also WKKK, *Installation Ceremonies of the Women of the Ku Klux Klan* (WKKK, n.d.).

[19] Hiram Evans, *The Menace* and *The Attitude of the Knights of the Ku Klux Klan toward the Roman Catholic Hierarchy* (KKK, ca. 1923).

[20] WKKK, *Flag Book* (WKKK, 1923); Ku Klux Klan record collection (hereafter cited as KKK), Indiana State Library; WKKK, *U.S. Constitution* (WKKK, n.d.); *Fiery Cross,* Oct. 10, 1924, p. 5; *Fellowship Forum,* July 5, 1924, pp. 6–7.

[21] *Fellowship Forum,* Sept. 19, 1925, p. 6; July 5, 1924; Mar. 3, 1926, p. 6. The anonymous speaker is identified only as a "Klan female speaker." January 1925 issues of the *Fellowship Forum* have other examples of such self-promotion, as does that of May 1, 1926, p. 7; see also Chalmers, *Hooded Americanism.*

[22] *Imperial Night-Hawk,* May 9, 1923, p. 2; see also *New York Times,* July 11, 1926, p. 7.

[23] *Arkansas Gazette,* Sept. 8, 1925, p. 1; *Fiery Cross,* Mar. 30, 1923, p. 5; *Fellowship Forum,* Jan. 24, 1925, p. 6; *New York Times,* Sept. 9, 1925, p. 1; Sept. 19, 1925, p. 20; Sept. 11, 1925, p. 5.

[24] *New York Times,* June 3, 1923, sect. 1, pt. 2, p. 8; *Fellowship Forum,* Jan. 24, 1925, p. 6; *New York Times,* Mar. 21, 1922, p. 6; Dec. 8, 1922, p. 9; *Imperial Night-Hawk,* May 9, 1923, p. 3; *Fiery Cross,* Oct. 10, 1924, p. 5; *Fellowship Forum,* Jan. 17, 1925, p. 6; July 5, 1924, p. 6. For a detailed analysis of the conflict over the Klan during the 1924

election, especially during the Democratic party convention, see Lee Allen, "The McAdoo Campaign for the Presidential Nomination of 1924," *Journal of Southern History* 29 (1963): 211–18; "The Klan and the Democrats," *Literary Digest,* June 14, 1924, pp. 12–13; Rice, *Ku Klux Klan;* Chalmers, *Hooded Americanism,* pp. 282–90.

[25] *Fiery Cross,* July 18, 1924, p. 6. In an odd twist—"because of their affiliation with the KKK"—two women were excluded from the will of a third woman with whom they had lived for 16 years (will of Alice Reid, filed in surrogate's court in Brooklyn in 1928 and reported in the *New York Times,* Oct. 10, 1928, p. 16).

[26] Testimony of Mamie H. Bittner in U.S. District Court for the Western District of Pennsylvania, *Knights of the Ku Klux Klan, Plaintiff, v. Rev. John F. Strayer et al., Defendants,* 1928 (Equity 1897 in National Archives–Philadelphia Branch; William M. Likins, *The Trail of the Serpent* (n.p., 1928), pp. 64–67.

18

THE SEARCH FOR *COMMUNITAS* IN THE MEN'S MOVEMENT

MICHAEL SCHWALBE

Communities are another type of social structure often studied by sociologists. This selection by Michael Schwalbe, an associate professor of sociology at North Carolina State University, investigates the mythopoetic men's movement and a type of community, called *communitas,* that men in these groups try to create. Schwalbe spent three years investigating the mythopoetic men's movement, including doing participant observation, interviewing members, and studying the writings of current movement leaders. His work resulted in the book *Unlocking the Iron Cage: The Men's Movement, Gender Politics, and American Culture* (1996), which is excerpted here.

In the late 1980s and early 1990s, the commercial media discovered the mythopoetic men's movement. Newspapers, magazines, and television reported that thousands of middle-aged, middle-class white men were retreating to rustic settings to share their feelings, to cry, hug, drum, dance, tell poems and fairy tales, and enact primitive rituals. The men were supposedly trying to get in touch with the inner "wildman" and other masculine arche

Reprinted by permission of Michael Schwalbe.

types as urged by movement leader Robert Bly, a famous poet and author of the 1991 bestseller *Iron John*.[1] Mythopoetic activity was covered because it was offbeat, and so, not surprisingly, most stories played up its odd trappings. The serious side of the movement—its implicit critique of men's lives in American society—was not examined.

While most observers thought mythopoetic activity was harmless and silly, others saw it as dangerous. Feminist critics accused Bly and the mythopoetic men of nefarious doings at their all-male retreats: whining about men's relatively minor psychological troubles while ignoring the much greater oppression of other groups, especially women; "modernizing" rather than truly changing masculinity; retreating from tough political realities into boyish play; unfairly blaming mothers and wives for men's troubles; and reproducing sexism by using fairy tales and rituals from patriarchal cultures. Critics thus saw the mythopoetic movement as part of an antifeminist backlash, or as a New Age maneuver in the battle of the sexes.[2]

Much of the criticism of the movement was based on the same superficial stories fed to the public. More responsible critics at least read Bly's book, saw his 1990 PBS interview ("A Gathering of Men") with Bill Moyers, attended a retreat, or read other pieces of mythopoetic literature.[3] Even so, almost none of the criticism was based on firsthand knowledge of what the men involved in mythopoetic activity were thinking, feeling, and doing together. The men themselves either disappeared behind the inflated image of Bly, or critics presumed that there was no need to distinguish them from Bly. But while Bly was indeed the chief public figure of the movement and a main source of its philosophy, mythopoetic activity or, as the men themselves called it, "mythopoetic men's work," was much more than Robert Bly.

In the fall of 1990, before Bly's *Iron John* raised the visibility of the mythopoetic movement, I began a participant-observation study of a group of men, associated with a local men's center, who were engaged in mythopoetic activity. As a sociologist, I wanted to know how the men began doing "men's work" and how it was affecting them. I was especially interested in how it affected the meanings they gave to their identities as men. So from September 1990 to June 1993, I attended 128 meetings of various kinds; observed and participated in all manner of mythopoetic activities; attended events led by the movement's prominent teachers; read the movement's guiding literature; and interviewed 21 of the local men at length. The full account of my study appears elsewhere.[4]

Any sociologist who has studied a social movement from the inside will tell you that there is always more diversity within it than outsiders tend to see. This was true in the case of the mythopoetic men. As I was doing my research, people often asked me for a quick explanation of who the men were, what they were doing, and why—as if all the men were alike and one explanation would fit all. While there were commonalities of experience and outlook among the mythopoetic men, there were also significant differences.

The men did not all experience the same troubles, want the same things, or think similarly about gender politics. It's important to recognize this diversity, since in writing about any group of people there is a tendency to make internal diversity disappear.

Two other points may aid understanding of the mythopoetic men. One is that, while they held Robert Bly in high esteem, they did not see him as an infallible guru. Most of the men knew that Bly could be obnoxious, that he tended to exaggerate, and that he liked to be the center of attention. It would be fair to say that the men saw him as wise, entertaining, charismatic, and challenging—but hardly without fault. Many of the men had equally high regard for other teachers in the mythopoetic movement, especially the Jungian psychologist James Hillman and the drummer/storyteller Michael Meade. Even so, the mythopoetic men were wary of leaders and did not want to be dependent on them. They believed that men could and should learn to do men's work on their own.

The second point is that many of the men rejected the label "movement" for what they were doing, since to them this implied central organization, the imposition of a doctrine, and political goals. It's true that mythopoetic activity was not centrally coordinated, overtly oriented to political goals, or restricted to those who swore allegiance to a particular set of beliefs. There was, however, an underlying philosophy (derived in large part from Jungian psychology), a "circuit-riding" group of teachers, a body of inspirational literature, nationally circulated publications, and many similarities of practice among the mythopoetic men's groups that had sprung up around the country. So, to add all this up and call it a movement is a legitimate convenience.

Many of the men also shared certain goals, which they sought to achieve through mythopoetic work. As individuals they sought the therapeutic goals of self-acceptance, greater self-confidence, and better knowledge of themselves as emotional beings. As a group they sought to revalue "man" as a moral identity; that is, they collectively sought to define "man" as an identity that implied positive moral qualities. Identity work of this kind, which was partly a response to feminist criticism of men's behavior, was accomplished through talk at gatherings and through the movement's literature. Much of what the men sought to accomplish thus had to do with their feelings about themselves as men.

It's important to see, however, that mythopoetic men's work was not just about sharing feelings, as if the men knew what they were feeling and then met to talk about it. Things were not so simple. Often the work itself aroused feelings that surprised the men. And these feelings were not always pleasant. But even unpleasant feelings were resources for fashioning a special kind of collective experience. It was this experience, which the anthropologist Victor Turner calls *communitas*, that the men sought to create at their gatherings. This was a rare and seductive experience for men in a highly bureaucratized society such as ours.

Community and *Communitas*

Most of the mythopoetic men were between the ages of 35 and 60. Nearly all were white, self-identified as heterosexual, and college educated. Most had good jobs, owned homes, and helped maintain families. They were, by and large, successful in conventional, middle-class terms. Yet the men said that living out this conventional script had left them, at midlife, feeling empty and dissatisfied. They found that the external trappings of success were not spiritually fulfilling. What's more, many of the men felt isolated, cut off from other men, except for competitive contexts such as the workplace. Hence, many described mythopoetic activity as part of an effort to create a community where they could interact with other men in a supportive, noncompetitive way.

But it was not exactly community that these men created through mythopoetic work. Although they did sometimes establish serious friendships and networks of support, the men did not enter into relations of material dependence upon each other, live in close proximity to each other, work together, or interact on a daily basis. Usually, the men who met at gatherings and in support groups went home to their separate lives. Thus, strictly speaking, it was not a true community they created. What the mythopoetic men sought and tried to create at their gatherings was both more and less than community. It was *communitas*.

Victor Turner, an anthropologist who studied tribal rituals, describes *communitas* as both a shared feeling-state and a way of relating. To create *communitas*, people must relate to each other outside the constraints of formally defined roles and statuses. As Turner describes it:

> Essentially, *communitas* is a relationship between concrete, historical, idiosyncratic individuals. These individuals are not segmentalized into roles and statuses but confront one another rather in the manner of Martin Buber's "I and Thou." Along with this direct, immediate, and total confirmation of human identities, there tends to go a model of society as a homogeneous, unstructured *communitas*, whose boundaries are ideally coterminous with those of the human species.[5]

Communitas, as Turner says, can happen when the force of roles and statuses is suspended; that is, when individuals in a group feel themselves to be equals and there are no other significant differences to impede feelings of communality. Although the mythopoetic men did not use the term *communitas*, they sought to relate to each other in the way that Turner describes as characteristic of *communitas*. At gatherings they tried to engage each other in a way that was unmediated by the roles they played in their everyday work lives. The men tried to practice this kind of relating by talking about the feelings they had, which they believed arose out of their common experiences as men.

Turner distinguishes three types of *communitas:* normative, ideological, and spontaneous or existential. Of these, it is spontaneous or existential *communitas* that the mythopoetic men sought to create. Turner says that spontaneous *communitas* is "richly charged with affects, mainly pleasurable ones," that it "has something 'magical' about it," and that in it there is "the feeling of endless power."[6] He compares hippies and tribesmen in a passage that could also apply to the mythopoetic men:

> The kind of *communitas* desired by tribesmen in their rites and by hippies in their "happenings" is not the pleasurable and effortless comradeship that can arise between friends, coworkers, or professional colleagues any day. What they seek is a transformative experience that goes to the root of each person's being and finds in that root something profoundly communal and shared.[7]

There are several ways in which Turner's description of spontaneous *communitas* fits mythopoetic activity. First, the men sought personal growth through their experiences of "connection," as they called it, at mythopoetic gatherings. A connection was a feeling of emotional communion with another man or group of men. Such connections were made when a story, poem, dance, ritual, or psychodramatic enactment brought up strong feelings in one or more men, and this in turn induced emotional responses in others. In these moments the men learned about their own complexity as emotional beings. The changes they sought were greater awareness of their feelings, more clarity about them, and better ability to use those feelings constructively.

The mythopoetic men also presumed it was possible to establish deep emotional connections with each other because they were all, at root, men. This presumption grew out of the Jungian psychology that informed mythopoetic activity. The idea was that all men possessed the same set of masculine archetypes that predisposed them to think, feel, and act in similar ways.[8] In Jungian terms, these masculine archetypes are parts of the collective unconscious, to which we are all linked by our common humanity. Thus all men, simply by virtue of being male, were presumed to possess similar masculine energies and masculine ways of feeling. Mythopoetic activities were aimed at bringing out or tapping into these energies and feelings so that men could connect based on them and thereby mutually reinvigorate themselves.

Turner's references to pleasurable affects and mysterious feelings of power are echoed in how the mythopoetic men described their experiences. Mythopoetic activity was enjoyable, the men said, because "It's just being with men in a way that's very deep and powerful"; "There's a tremendous energy that grows out of men getting together and connecting emotionally"; and "It just feels great to be there connecting with other men in a noncompetitive way." And, indeed, the feelings were often intense. As one man said during a talking circle at the end of a weekend retreat, "I feel there's so much love in this room right now it hurts." Men also said that going back to their ordinary lives after a gathering meant "coming down from an emotional high." I, too, experienced this transition from the warm, open, supportive, emotionally charged atmosphere of a gathering to the relatively chilly atmosphere of a large research university.

The success of a gathering was measured by the intensity of the emotion it evoked and the connections thereby established. A less successful gathering was one where the emotional intensity was low and the men did not make strong connections. At a small two-day gathering, one man commented somewhat sadly, "We've had some good sharing, but only once did I feel much happening to me. That was when B. was talking. I felt tears welling up. So there's a deeper level we could get to." This was said at the beginning of the final talking circle, in hopes of prompting a more emotional discussion before the gathering was over. In addition to showing the desire for *communitas,* this statement also shows that it took effort to achieve. Spontaneous *communitas* did not happen spontaneously.

Creating Spontaneous *Communitas*

Mythopoetic men's work was in large part the conversation work required to create spontaneous *communitas.* I'll explain here how this work was done, through talk and other means. It should be understood that not all gatherings were aimed as intently at creating the same degree of spontaneous *communitas.* Some gatherings were more "heady," in that they were devoted to discussion of a topic, such as fathering or men's health or men's friendships. Often there were moments of *communitas* at these kinds of meetings; but it was at the retreats—those that had an explicit mythopoetic or "inner work" theme—where the greatest efforts were made to produce *communitas.* Talk, ritual, and drumming were the chief means for doing this.

Forms of Talk

At mythopoetic gatherings, men often made personal statements that revealed something shameful, tragic, or emotionally disturbing about their lives. Such statements might be made by each man in turn at the beginning of a retreat, as part of saying why he was there, what he was feeling, and what he hoped to accomplish at the retreat. Before any statements were made, the leader of the retreat or gathering would remind the men of the rules to follow in making statements: speak briefly, speak from the heart (i.e., focus on feelings), and speak to the other men—who were supposed to listen intently, make no judgments, and give no advice. The idea was that the statements should bring the unrehearsed truth up from a man's gut, since this would stir feelings in him and move other men to speak their "belly truth."

A great deal of feeling was stirred up as men talked about troubled relationships with fathers; being sexually abused as children; struggling to overcome addictions; repressed anger over past hurts and betrayals; grief and sadness over irreplaceable losses; efforts to be better fathers to their children. When men choked up, wept, shook with fear, or raged as they spoke, it induced strong feelings in other men in the group. The sequence in which personal statements were made amplified this effect. Men would often begin their remarks by saying, "What that [the previous statement] brings up for me is . . . ," or "I really identify with what ——— said, because . . ." The more disclosing, expressive, and moving a man's statement, the more likely it was to evoke from the other men heavy sighs, sympathetic "mmmms," or a loud chorus of "Ho!" (supposedly a Native American way of affirming that a man's statement has been heard and felt). If a statement seemed inauthentic or insufficiently revealing, it might evoke little or no reaction. In this way the men reinforced a norm of making risky, revealing, and evocative statements.

Thus, the men were not only sharing feelings but, by virtue of how they talked, knitting those feelings together into a group mood. In this way they were also creating *communitas*. It is important, too, that the settings in which these statements were made were defined as "safe," meaning that, by agreement, the men were not there to compete with or judge each other, but to listen and provide support. Even so, there was an element of risk and a degree of anxiety associated with making personal statements, since the mythopoetic men, like most men in American society, were unused to sharing feelings of hurt and vulnerability with other men. This anxiety aided the achievement of *communitas* because it created a higher-than-usual level of emotional arousal to begin with. It also allowed the men immediately to identify with one another over being anxious. As Turner likewise noted: "Danger is one of the chief ingredients in the production of spontaneous *communitas*."[9]

In making personal statements and in their general conversation at gatherings, the men could not help but refer to people, events, and circumstances outside themselves that evoked the feelings they had. In doing this, the men were careful to add to their statements the disclaimer "for me," as in "For *me*, the Gulf War was very depressing." This disclaimer signified that the man speaking was talking about *his* feelings based on *his* perceptions of things, and he was making no presumptions about how other men should feel. The use of this disclaimer helped the men maintain the fellow-feeling they sought by avoiding arguments about what was true of the external world. The mythopoetic men wanted their feelings validated, not challenged. As long as each man spoke the truth from his heart, no one could say he was wrong.

Talk about fathers was another way the men achieved *communitas*. It worked because almost every man had a father to talk about, and those few who didn't could talk about not having fathers. So every man could participate. Father talk also worked because it brought up feelings of sadness and anger for many of the men, and thus created the necessary emotional charge.

Because many of the men experienced their fathers as physically or emotionally absent, or in some way abusive, the men could identify with each other based on these common experiences. Father talk may have helped them to reach insights about their relationships to their fathers. But father talk went on to the extent it did because it was so useful for creating *communitas*.

Poems and fairy tales were also a staple part of mythopoetic activity.[10] Most of the time no commentary or discussion followed the reading or reciting of a poem. The men would just steep in the feelings the poem evoked. An especially stirring poem, like a moving personal statement, would elicit deep sighs, "mmmmm," "yeah," sometimes "Ho!", and, often, calls for the reader to "read it again!" And as with the personal statements, these responses, which were signs of shared feelings, served to turn the individual feelings into a collective mood, and thus helped to create *communitas*. When fairy tales were told, there usually was commentary and discussion in a form that also encouraged *communitas*.

When a story was told, the storyteller would usually instruct the men to look for an image that evoked strong feelings. That image, it was said, would be a man's "doorway into the story"—his way of discovering what the story could tell him about his life as a man. This is consistent with Turner's observation that the "concrete, personal imagist mode of thinking is highly characteristic of those in love with existential [or spontaneous] *communitas*, with the direct relation between man and man, and man and nature. Abstractions appear as hostile to live contact."[11] In the case of the mythopoetics, the emphasis on specific images grew out of Jungian psychology, according to which the psyche was best explored by working with emotionally evocative images.

After a story or part of a story was told, men would talk about the images that struck them and the feelings these images evoked. In a large group of men many different images might be mentioned. Sometimes men reacted strongly to the same image. Talking about the stories in this way created more chances for men to express feelings and to find that they shared feelings and experiences with other men. This was in part how feelings of isolation were overcome and connections were made. Again, the stories may have helped the men to better understand their lives. But it was *how* the stories were talked about that helped the men to experience the good feelings and mysterious power of spontaneous *communitas*.

Ritual

Ritual is different from routine. Routine is the repetition of a behavioral pattern, like brushing one's teeth every night before bed. Ritual involves the symbolic enactment of values, beliefs, or feelings. It is a way of making external, visible, and public things that are normally internal, invisible, and private. By doing this, members of a community create a shared reality, reaffirm their common embrace of certain beliefs and values, and thereby keep the community alive. Ritual can also be a way of acknowledging changes in community members or of actually inducing such changes. The mythopoetic men used ritual for the same purposes: to call up, express, and share their otherwise private feelings, and to make changes in themselves.

Not all gatherings were ritual gatherings, though most included some ritual elements. Those gatherings where an explicit attempt was made to create "ritual space" or "sacred space" usually began with a symbolic act of separation from the ordinary world. For example, sometimes men would dip their hands into a large bowl of water to symbolize a washing off of concerns and distractions linked to the outside world. Other times, at the outset of gatherings the "spirits of the four directions" (and sometimes of the earth and sky, too) would be invoked and asked to bring the men strength and wisdom. Still other times, the men would dance their way into the space where the meeting was to be held, while the men already inside drummed and chanted. The point was to perform some collective act to mark a boundary between outside life and the "ritual space."

The scene of a gathering also had to be properly set. Ritual gatherings were often held at rustic lodges, where various objects—candles, bird feathers, masks, antlers, strangely shaped driftwood, animal skulls—might be set up around the main meeting area. Sage was often burned (a practice called "smudging") to make the air pungent and to cleanse the ritual space for the action that was going to take place. Usually the leader or leaders of the gathering made sure these things were done. Again, the idea was to heighten the sense of separation from ordinary reality, to make the physical space where the gathering would take place seem special, and to draw the men together. This preparation was talked about in terms of "creating a container" that could safely hold the psychic energies about to be unleashed.

The separation from ordinary reality also helped the men let go of the concerns for status and power that influenced their interactions with other men in everyday life. In the ritual space, the men were supposed to be "present for each other" in a direct and immediate way, as equals, as "brothers," and not as inferiors and superiors. Defining the situation as one in which feelings and other psychic matters were the proper focus of attention and activity helped to create and sustain this sense of equality. Thus, the men seldom talked about their jobs, except to describe job-related troubles (and sometimes triumphs) in general terms. Too much talk about occupations would have introduced status concerns, which in turn would have corroded the sense of equality and brotherhood that fostered feelings of *communitas*.

Two examples can help show more concretely how the mythopoetic men used ritual to create *communitas*. One example is from a six-day gathering of about 120 men in a remote rural setting. At this gathering the men were divided into three clans: Trout, Ravens, and Lions. During the week each clan worked with a dance teacher to develop a dance of its own, a dance that would symbolize the spirit of the men in the clan. At the carnivale on the last night of the gathering, each clan was to share its dance with the rest of the men. One clan would drum while another danced and the third clan "witnessed."

The carnivale was held in a large, dimly lit lodge built of rough-cut logs. Many of the men wore the wildly decorated masks they had made earlier in the week. When their turn came, the 40 men in the Trout clan moved to the center of the room and formed a circle. The men stood for a few moments and then hunched down, extended their arms with their hands together in front of them, and began to dip and sway like fish swimming. Then half the men began moving to their right and half to their left, creating two flowing, interweaving circles. The Trout men also carried small stones, which they clicked together as they moved. About 30 men drummed as the Trout men danced. The rest of the men watched.

After a while the Trout men stopped and stood again, holding hands in a circle inside the larger circle of witnesses. They began a sweet and mournful African chant that they said was used to honor the passing away of loved ones. One by one, each of the Trout men moved to the center of their circle and put down the stones he was carrying. As he did so, he called out the name of a person or people whose passing he wished to honor. Another of the Trout men walked along the row of men standing in the outer ring and said, "We invite you to join us by putting a stone in the center of the circle to honor your dead." The drumming and chanting continued all the while.

At first a few, then more and more of the Raven and Lion men stepped outside to get stones. Each man as he returned went to the center of the circle, called the name of the dead he was honoring, put down a stone, and then stepped back. There was sadness in the men's voices as they spoke. This lent gravity to their acts and drew everyone into the ritual. By now all the men had picked up the chant and joined hands in one large circle. The sound filled the lodge. After about 20 minutes the chanting reached a lull—and then one man began to sing "Amazing Grace." Soon all the men joined in and again their voices rose in chorus and filled the lodge. When we finished singing we stood silent, looking at all the stones between us.

This example shows how a great deal of work went into creating spontaneous *communitas*. The dance was carefully choreographed and the stage was elaborately set (one could argue that the five days leading up to the carnivale were part of the stage setting). But later I talked to Trout men who said that they had planned the dance only up to the point of asking the other men to honor their dead. They were surprised by what happened after that, by how quickly and powerfully the other men were drawn in. No one had expected the surge of emotion and fellow-feeling that the ritual induced, especially when the men began to sing "Amazing Grace." Several men I talked to later cited this ritual as one of the most moving experiences they had had at a mythopoetic gathering.

Another example comes from a sweat-lodge ritual modeled on a traditional Native American practice.[12] In this case the lodge was tiny, consisting of a framework of saplings held together with twine upon which were draped several layers of old blankets and tarps. Before the frame was built, a fire pit was dug in the center of the spot on which the lodge stood. Although a lodge could be made bigger, here it was about ten feet in diameter and four feet high—big enough for a dozen men to squeeze in. From the outside it looked like a miniature domed stadium.

It was a drizzly 45-degree morning on the second day of a teacher-led weekend retreat. I was in the second group of 12 men who would go into the lodge together. This was the first "sweat" for all of us. The men in this group were almost giddy as we walked from the cabins to the shore of a small lake where the sweat lodge had been built. When we got there the men from the previous group had just finished.

The scene stopped us abruptly. Next to the lodge a large rock-rimmed fire was burning. A fierce, black-haired man with a beard stood by the fire, a five-foot staff in his hand. Some of the men who had just finished their sweat were standing waist-deep in the lake. Others were on shore hugging, their naked bodies still steaming in the cool air. Our moment of stunned silence ended when the leader of the retreat said to us, matter of factly, "Get undressed, stay quiet, keep your humility." We undressed and stashed our clothes under the nearby pine trees, out of the rain.

Before we entered the lodge, the teacher urged us to reflect on the specialness of the occasion and to approach it with seriousness. Upon entering the lodge through a small entry flap each man was to say, "all my relations," to remind himself of his connections to the earth, to his ancestors, and to the other men. Once we were inside, the teacher called for the fire tender to bring us fresh, red-hot rocks. As each rock was placed by shovel into the fire pit, we said in unison, "welcome Grandfather," again as symbolic acknowledgment of our connection to the earth. The teacher then burned sage on the rocks to scent the air. When he poured water on the rocks, the lodge became a sauna. The space was tightly packed, lit only by the glow of the rocks, and very hot. We were to do three sessions of ten to fifteen minutes each. Because of the intensity of the heat, a few men could not do all three sessions.

During one of the sessions, the teacher urged us to call upon the spirits of our ancestors from whom we wanted blessings. In the cacophony of voices it was hard to make out what was being said. Some men were calling the names of people not present. A few were doing what sounded like a Native American Indian chant learned from the movies. The man next to me was gobbling like a turkey. At first this all struck me as ridiculous. I looked around the lodge for signs of similar bemusement in other men's faces. Surely they couldn't be taking this seriously. But those whose faces I could see appeared absorbed in the experience. Some men seemed oddly distant, as if they were engaged in a conversation going on elsewhere.

Although I was still put off by the bogus chanting and baffled by the gobbling, I, too, began to feel drawn in. I found myself wanting to suspend disbelief and find some meaning in the ritual, no matter how culturally foreign it was. In large part this was because the teacher and the other men seemed to be taking it seriously. I certainly didn't want to ruin the experience for them by showing any sign of cynicism. These were men who had taken my feelings seriously during the retreat. I felt I owed them the same consideration in the sweat lodge.

In both examples, a carefully crafted set of appearances made *communitas* likely to happen. The physical props, the words and actions of the ritual leaders, and the sincere words and actions of some men evoked real feelings in others and drew them in.[13] Because it seemed that there were genuine emotions at stake, it would have taken a hard heart to show any sign of cynicism during the Trout dance or the sweat lodge. To do so would have risked hurting other men's feelings and dimming the glow of *communitas*. It would also have cut the cynic himself off from the good feelings and mysterious power being generated by these occasions. Whether or not everyone really "believed" in what was happening didn't matter. Appearances made it seem so, and to achieve the *communitas* they desired, all the men needed to do was to act on these appearances.

Another dynamic was at work in the case of the sweat lodge. On the face of it, the idea of late twentieth-century white men enacting a Native American sweat lodge ritual was absurd. And for most of these men, the idea of squatting naked, haunch to haunch, with other men would have been— within an everyday frame of reference—embarrassing and threatening to their identities as heterosexuals. Thus, to avoid feeling ridiculous, threatened, or embarrassed, the men had to stay focused on the form of the ritual and show no sign of doubting its content or propriety. Because there was such a gap between their everyday frame of reference and the ritual, the men had to exaggerate their absorption in the ritual reality just to keep a grip on it. In so doing the men truly did create a common focus and, again, the appearance that a serious collective spiritual activity was going on.

The sweat lodge example also illustrated how the creation of *communitas* was aided by literally stripping men of signs of their differences. In the sweat lodge, men were only men—as symbolized by their nakedness. As such they were also equals. When a small group of us spoke afterwards about the experience, one man said, "The closeness and physicality, and especially being naked, are what make it work. Everyone is just a man in there. You can't wear any merit badges."

Drumming

Next to Bly, the most widely recognized icon of the mythopoetic movement was the drum. Drumming was indeed an important part of mythopoetic activity. Some mythopoetic groups held gatherings just to drum, although the group I studied was more likely to mix drumming with other activities. Not all of the men drummed. A few didn't care for it; others preferred to use rattles or tambourines during drumming sessions. The most enthusiastic men had congas, African-styled djembes, or hand-held shaman's drums, though all manner of large and small folk drums appeared at gatherings. On one occasion a man used a five-gallon pail turned upside down.

Why did the mythopoetic men drum? Some of the men in the local group said that they began drumming after a visit by Michael Meade, a prominent teacher in the mythopoetic movement, who was skilled at using drumming to accompany his telling of folk tales. This is what inspired one man I interviewed:

> *Bly came and told his Iron John story and that was my first introduction to using stories as a way of illuminating dilemmas or emotional situations in your life. Michael Meade came the following year in the spring and introduced some drumming at that weekend. I just loved the energy of that right away. It just really opened me up. After drumming I felt wonderful. I liked the feeling of it and felt a connection with the mythopoetic [movement] ever since then, more to the drumming than to anything else.*

But on only a few occasions did any of the local men use drumming as accompaniment to story telling. Most of the drumming was done in groups, which varied in size from six to forty. And while the men who were better drummers might lead the group into a complex rhythm, often something samba-like, the drumming was usually free-form, leaderless, and simple.

The appeal of this activity had little to do with acquiring virtuosity at drumming. Rather, much of the appeal stemmed from the fact that the men could be bad drummers and still participate. It was, most importantly, another means to achieve *communitas.* Victor Turner notes that simple musical instruments are often used this way: "It is . . . fascinating to consider how expressions of *communitas* are culturally linked with simple wind instruments (flutes and harmonicas). Perhaps, in addition to their ready portability, it is their capacity to convey in music the quality of spontaneous human *communitas* that is responsible for this."[14] This was equally true of drums, which were also readily portable and required even less skill to play.

What the mythopoetic men say about their experiences drumming tells much about not only drumming, but about the *communitas* it helped create and about the mythopoetic experience in general. In another interview, a 48-year-old salesman spoke of drumming as both ordinary and special at the same time:

> *You can kind of lose yourself in it. It's like any hobby—fishing or playing ball or whatever. There is something that happens. You go into an altered state almost, hearing that music. At this national meeting in Minnesota a month ago the common thing was the drums. You could hear the beating of that drum. At break people would drum and we would dance. So it's this common bond.*

Put another way, drumming was an activity that gave men who were strangers a way to quickly feel comfortable and familiar with each other. Some of the mythopoetic men believed that men in general had a special facility for connecting with each other via nonverbal means. The way that men were able to quickly bond via drumming was seen as evidence of this.

Although the men were aware that drumming was not an activity limited to men, some clearly felt that it held a special appeal for them. Another man, a 33-year-old technical writer, said in an interview:

> *Drumming does something—connects me with men in ways that I can't under-stand, in the same way I've observed women who have babies connecting with each other. There's something in it that I don't participate in emotionally. In the same way, the drumming—society with other men—is emotionally important to men in ways that women don't understand. They can't.*

Some of the mythopoetic men's ideas about gender are exemplified by this statement. Many of them believed that women, no matter how empathic they might be, could not know what it was like to be a man, just as men could not know what it was like to be a woman. Hence, men needed the understanding and support that could come only from other men just as women needed the same things from other women.

For other men, drumming was both a communal and, sometimes, a personal, spiritual experience. A 42-year-old therapist told me:

> *There was one point where I was really deeply entranced just drumming and then all of a sudden I had this real powerful experience where I felt like I was on a hill, on some mountainside or some mountaintop, in some land far far away, in some time that was all time. And I was in the middle of my men, who were my brothers, who were all men. It was one of those powerful, mystical experiences where all of a sudden I felt planted in the community of men. And that changed my life, because I felt like I was a man among men in the community of men and we were drumming and the drum was in my bones and it was in my heartbeat and it was good.*

This statement captures in spirit, tone, and rhythm the experience that many of the men found in drumming. Even if they didn't report such flights of imagination, others said that drumming provided a similar sense of communality, of connection—*communitas.*

My own experience corroborates this. I found that when I would pick up a beat and help sustain it without thinking, the sense of being part of the group was strong. It was as if the sound testified to the reality of the group, and the rhythm testified to our connection. By drumming in synch each man attached himself to the group and to the other men in it. The men valued this also because the attachment was created by physical action rather than by talk, and because it seemed to happen at a nonrational level. Drumming thus helped the men to do two other things that mythopoetic philosophy called for: getting out of their heads and into feeling their bodies, and by-passing the rational ego that kept a lid on the archetypal masculine energies the men sought to tap.

Communitas and Politics

My point has been to show that much mythopoetic activity can be understood as a search for *communitas*. This experience was rare in these men's lives and precious on the occasions when it occurred. Sometimes the men talked about the activities at their gatherings as "inviting the sacred to happen." Particular forms of talk, the orchestration of ritual, and drumming were means to this end. Because *communitas* was so valuable to the men, there were also things they *avoided* doing to make *communitas* more likely to happen. One thing they avoided was serious talk about politics.

This is not to say that the men were apolitical. Most of the men I studied were well informed on social issues and supported progressive causes. They were also critical of the rapacious greed of big corporations, the duplicity and brutal militarism of Reagan and Bush, and the general oppressiveness of large bureaucracies. But there were two revealing ironies in the politics of the mythopoetic men. First, while they were critical of the behavior of corporations and government, they avoided saying that these institutions were run by men. Usually it was an unspecified, genderless "they" who were said to be responsible for destroying the environment or for turning all culture into mass marketable schlock. And second, while many of the men saw corporate power and greed as root problems in U.S. society, they were uninterested in collective action to address these problems. This is, as one might expect, because the white, middle-class mythopoetic men did not do so badly in reaping the material benefits of the economic system they occasionally criticized.

In other words, the men were selectively apolitical. They did not want to see that it was other *men* who were responsible for many of the social problems they witnessed and were sometimes affected by. To do so, and to talk about it, would have shattered the illusion of universal brotherhood among men that helped sustain feelings of *communitas*. Talk about power, politics, and inequality in the external world was incompatible with the search for *communitas*, because it would have led to arguments, or at least to intellectual discussions, rather than to warm emotional communion. When discussions at mythopoetic gatherings inadvertently turned political, disagreements surfaced and tensions arose; someone would usually say, "We're getting away from the important work here." Or, as one man said in trying to stop a conversation that was becoming an argument, "I think we're losing the power of the drums."

The mythopoetic men believed that engaging in political or sociological analysis would have led them away from their goals of self-acceptance, self-knowledge, emotional authenticity, and *communitas*. The men wanted to feel

better about themselves as men, to learn about the feelings and psychic energies that churned within them, to live fuller and more authentic emotional
lives, and to experience the pleasure and mysterious power of *communitas*.
They did not want to compete over whose interpretation of social reality was
correct. They wanted untroubled brotherhood in which their feelings were
validated by other men and in which their identities as men could be infused
with new value.

Here can be seen both the power and limits of mythopoetic men's work.
Through this work some men have begun to free themselves from the debilitating repression of emotion that was part of their socialization into traditional masculinity. Feminism provided the intellectual basis and political
impetus for this critique of traditional masculinity, although the mythopoetics have difficulty appreciating this. Yet they deserve credit for developing a
method that allows some men to explore and express more of the emotions
that make them human. Mythopoetic men's work has also helped men to see
how these emotions can be the basis for connections to men they might otherwise have feared, mistrusted, or felt compelled to compete with. And, to the
extent that men begin to see that they don't have to live out traditional masculinity and can even cooperate to heal the damage it causes, mythopoetic
men's work has progressive potential.

One problem is that the progressive potential of mythopoetic men's work
is limited, because it leads men to think about gender and gender inequality
in psychological or, at best, cultural terms. Mythopoetic men's work may
open men to seeing things in themselves and help them make connections
with each other, but it also blinds them to seeing important connections between themselves and society. For example, the mythopoetic men do not see
that, in a male-supremacist society, there can be no innocent celebration of
masculinity. In such a society the celebration of manhood and of masculinity—even if it is supposedly "deep" or "authentic" and thus a more fully human version of masculinity—reaffirms the lesser value of women, whether
this is intended or not. The therapeutic focus of mythopoetic men's work—
as done by a largely homogeneous group of middle-class white males—
also blinds them to matters of class inequality and to the exploitation of
working-class people and people of color by the elite white *men* who run the
economy.

Yet mythopoetic men's work is a form of resistance to domination. It's not
just an entertaining form of group therapy or collective whining over imagined wounds, or retrograde male bonding. These middle-class white men,
who are not the ruling elites, are responding to the alienation and isolation
that stem from living in a capitalist society that encourages people to be
greedy, selfish, and predatory. Their goal of trying to awaken the human sensibilities that have been benumbed by an exploitive economy is subversive.
But to get to the root of the problem men will have to do more than take
modest risks among themselves to try to heal their psyches. They will have
to take big risks in trying to abolish the race, class, and gender hierarchies

that damage us all. They will have to learn to create *communitas* in struggles for justice.

ENDNOTES

¹ Robert Bly, *Iron John: A Book about Men* (Reading, MA: Addison-Wesley, 1990).

² See Kay Leigh Hagan, editor, *Women Respond to the Men's Movement* (San Francisco: HarperCollins, 1992); Kenneth Clatterbaugh, *Contemporary Perspectives on Masculinity* (Boulder, CO: Westview, 1990), pp. 85–103; Susan Faludi, *Backlash: The Undeclared War against American Women* (New York: Crown, 1991), pp. 304–12; R. W. Connell, "Drumming Up the Wrong Tree," *Tikkun* 7, no. 1 (1992): 31–36; Sharon Doubiago, "Enemy of the Mother: A Feminist Response to the Men's Movement," *Ms.* March/April (1992): 82–85; Fred Pelka, "Robert Bly and Iron John," *On the Issues* Summer (1991): 17–19, 39; Diane Johnson, "Something for the Boys," *New York Review of Books* January 16 (1992): 13–17.

³ For a sampling of other writings in the mythopoetic genre, see Robert Moore and Douglas Gillette, *King, Warrior, Magician, Lover: Rediscovering the Archetypes of the Mature Masculine* (New York: HarperCollins, 1990); Wayne Liebman, *Tending the Fire: The Ritual Men's Group* (St. Paul, MN: Ally, 1991); Christopher Harding, editor, *Wingspan: Inside the Men's Movement* (New York: St. Martin's, 1992).

⁴ Michael Schwalbe, *Unlocking the Iron Cage: The Men's Movement, Gender Politics, and American Culture* (New York: Oxford University Press, 1996).

⁵ Victor Turner, *The Ritual Process* (Ithaca, NY: Cornell, 1969), pp. 94–165.

⁶ Ibid., pp. 131–32.

⁷ Ibid., p. 139.

⁸ For an introduction to the basic concepts of Jungian psychology, see Calvin Hall and Vernon Nordby, *A Primer of Jungian Psychology* (New York: Penguin, 1973); or Frieda Fordham, *An Introduction to Jung's Psychology* (New York: Penguin, 1966). For more detail, see Edward C. Whitmont, *The Symbolic Quest* (Princeton, NJ: Princeton, 1991).

⁹ Turner, p. 154.

¹⁰ Many of the poems frequently read at mythopoetic gatherings are collected in Robert Bly, James Hillman, and Michael Meade (eds.), *The Rag and Bone Shop of the Heart* (New York: HarperCollins, 1992). Many of the fairy tales told at gatherings, including Bly's "Iron John," originally known as "Iron Hans," are taken from the Grimm brothers' collection.

¹¹ Turner, p. 141.

¹² A description of the sweat-lodge ritual can be found in Joseph Epes Brown (recorder and editor), *The Sacred Pipe: Black Elk's Account of the Seven Rites of the Oglala Sioux* (Norman: University of Oklahoma, 1953), pp. 31–43. This account was a source of inspiration for some of the mythopoetic men. See also William K. Powers, *Oglala Religion* (Lincoln: University of Nebraska, 1977).

¹³ Catherine Bell writes about how ritual "catches people up in its own terms" and provides a "resistant surface to casual disagreement." See Bell, *Ritual Theory, Ritual Practice* (New York: Oxford University Press, 1992), pp. 214–15. Other observers have noted how the improvised rituals at mythopoetic gatherings had this power to draw the men in. See Richard Gilbert, "Revisiting the Psychology of Men: Robert Bly and the Mytho-Poetic Movement," *Journal of Humanistic Psychology* 32 (1992): 41–67.

¹⁴ Turner, p. 165.

PART V

Deviance, Crime, and Social Control

19

ON BEING SANE IN INSANE PLACES

DAVID L. ROSENHAN

Sociologists have a long-standing interest in the study of social deviance, which is explored in the next four readings. *Deviance* is the recognized violation of social norms. As norms cover a wide range of human behavior, deviant acts are plentiful in any given society. Moreover, whether a person is labeled deviant depends on how others perceive, define, and respond to that person's behavior. In this selection, originally published in 1973, David L. Rosenhan explores the social deviance of mental illness and the consequences of labeling people "sane" or "insane." Rosenhan is currently professor emeritus of psychology and law at Stanford University.

If sanity and insanity exist . . . how shall we know them? The question is neither capricious nor itself insane. However much we may be personally convinced that we can tell the normal from the abnormal, the evidence is simply not compelling. It is commonplace, for example, to read about murder trials wherein eminent psychiatrists for the defense are contradicted by equally eminent psychiatrists for the prosecution on the matter of the defendant's sanity. More generally, there is a great deal of conflicting data on the reliability, utility, and meaning of such terms as *sanity, insanity, mental illness,* and *schizophrenia.*[1] Finally, as early as 1934, Benedict suggested that normality and abnormality are not universal.[2] What is viewed as normal in one culture may be seen as quite aberrant in another. Thus, notions of normality and abnormality may not be quite as accurate as people believe they are.

To raise questions regarding normality and abnormality is in no way to question the fact that some behaviors are deviant or odd. Murder is deviant. So, too, are hallucinations. Nor does raising such questions deny the existence of the personal anguish that is often associated with "mental illness."

Reprinted with permission from *Science* 179 (January 19, 1973):250–58. Copyright © 1973 by American Association Academy for the Advancement of Science.

Anxiety and depression exist. Psychological suffering exists. But normality and abnormality, sanity and insanity, and the diagnoses that flow from them may be less substantive than many believe them to be.

At its heart, the question of whether the sane can be distinguished from the insane (and whether degrees of insanity can be distinguished from each other) is a simple matter: Do the salient characteristics that lead to diagnoses reside in the patients themselves or in the environments and contexts in which observers find them? From Bleuler, through Kretchmer, through the formulations of the recently revised [1968] *Diagnostic and Statistical Manual* of the American Psychiatric Association, the belief has been strong that patients present symptoms, that those symptoms can be categorized, and, implicitly, that the sane are distinguishable from the insane. More recently, however, this belief has been questioned. Based in part on theoretical and anthropological considerations, but also on philosophical, legal, and therapeutic ones, the view has grown that psychological categorization of mental illness is useless at best and downright harmful, misleading, and pejorative at worst. Psychiatric diagnoses, in this view, are in the minds of the observers and are not valid summaries of characteristics displayed by the observed.[3, 4, 5]

Gains can be made in deciding which of these is more nearly accurate by getting normal people (that is, people who do not have, and have never suffered, symptoms of serious psychiatric disorders) admitted to psychiatric hospitals and then determining whether they were discovered to be sane and, if so, how. If the sanity of such pseudopatients were always detected, there would be *prima facie* evidence that a sane individual can be distinguished from the insane context in which he is found. Normality (and presumably abnormality) is distinct enough that it can be recognized wherever it occurs, for it is carried within the person. If, on the other hand, the sanity of the pseudopatients were never discovered, serious difficulties would arise for those who support traditional modes of psychiatric diagnosis. Given that the hospital staff was not incompetent, that the pseudopatient had been behaving as sanely as he had been outside of the hospital, and that it had never been previously suggested that he belonged in a psychiatric hospital, such an unlikely outcome would support the view that psychiatric diagnosis betrays little about the patient but much about the environment in which an observer finds him.

This article describes such an experiment. Eight sane people gained secret admission to twelve different hospitals.[6] Their diagnostic experiences constitute the data of the first part of this article; the remainder is devoted to a description of their experiences in psychiatric institutions. Too few psychiatrists and psychologists, even those who have worked in such hospitals, know what the experience is like. They rarely talk about it with former patients, perhaps because they distrust information coming from the previously insane. Those who have worked in psychiatric hospitals are likely to have adapted so thoroughly to the settings that they are insensitive to the impact of that experience. And while there have been occasional reports of researchers who submitted themselves to psychiatric hospitalization,[7] these researchers have commonly remained in the hospitals for short periods of time, often with the knowledge of the hospital staff. It is difficult to know the extent to which they were treated like patients or like research colleagues. Nevertheless, their reports about the inside of the psychiatric hospital have been valuable. This article extends those efforts.

Pseudopatients and Their Settings

The eight pseudopatients were a varied group. One was a psychology graduate student in his 20s. The remaining seven were older and "established." Among them were three psychologists, a pediatrician, a psychiatrist, a painter, and a housewife. Three pseudopatients were women, five were men. All of them employed pseudonyms, lest their alleged diagnoses embarrass them later. Those who were in mental health professions alleged another occupation in order to avoid the special attentions that might be accorded by staff, as a matter of courtesy or caution, to ailing colleagues.[8] With the exception of myself (I was the first pseudopatient and my presence was known to the hospital administrator and chief psychologist and, so far as I can tell, to them alone), the presence of pseudopatients and the nature of the research program were not known to the hospital staffs.[9]

The settings were similarly varied. In order to generalize the findings, admission into a variety of hospitals was sought. The 12 hospitals in the sample were located in five different states on the East and West coasts. Some were old and shabby, some were quite new. Some were research-oriented, others not. Some had good staff-patient ratios, others were quite understaffed. Only one was a strictly private hospital. All of the others were supported by state or federal funds, or in one instance, by university funds.

After calling the hospital for an appointment, the pseudopatient arrived at the admissions office complaining that he had been hearing voices. Asked what the voices said, he replied that they were often unclear, but as far as he could tell they said "empty," "hollow," and "thud." The voices were unfamiliar and were of the same sex as the pseudopatient. The choice of these symptoms was occasioned by their apparent similarity to existential symptoms. Such symptoms are alleged to arise from painful concerns about the perceived meaninglessness of one's life. It is as if the hallucinating person were saying, "My life is empty and hollow." The choice of these symptoms was also determined by the *absence* of a single report of existential psychoses in the literature.

Beyond alleging the symptoms and falsifying name, vocation, and employment, no further alterations of person, history, or circumstances were made. The significant events of the pseudopatient's life history were presented as they had actually occurred. Relationships with parents and siblings, with spouse and children, with people at work and in school, consistent with the aforementioned exceptions, were described as they were or had been.

Frustrations and upsets were described along with joys and satisfactions. These facts are important to remember. If anything, they strongly biased the subsequent results in favor of detecting sanity, since none of their histories or current behaviors were seriously pathological in any way.

Immediately upon admission to the psychiatric ward, the pseudopatient ceased simulating *any* symptoms of abnormality. In some cases, there was a brief period of mild nervousness and anxiety, since none of the pseudo-patients really believed that they would be admitted so easily. Indeed, their shared fear was that they would be immediately exposed as frauds and greatly embarrassed. Moreover, many of them had never visited a psychiatric ward; even those who had, nevertheless had some genuine fears about what might happen to them. Their nervousness, then, was quite appropriate to the novelty of the hospital setting, and it abated rapidly.

Apart from that short-lived nervousness, the pseudopatient behaved on the ward as he "normally" behaved. The pseudopatient spoke to patients and staff as he might ordinarily. Because there is uncommonly little to do on a psychiatric ward, he attempted to engage others in conversation. When asked by the staff how he was feeling, he indicated that he was fine, that he no longer experienced symptoms. He responded to instructions from attendants, to calls for medication (which was not swallowed), and to dining-hall instructions. Beyond such activities as were available to him on the admissions ward, he spent his time writing down his observations about the ward, its patients, and the staff. Initially these notes were written "secretly," but as it soon became clear that no one much cared, they were subsequently written on standard tablets of paper in such public places as the dayroom. No secret was made of these activities.

The pseudopatient, very much as a true psychiatric patient, entered a hospital with no foreknowledge of when he would be discharged. Each was told that he would have to get out by his own devices, essentially by convincing the staff that he was sane. The psychological stresses associated with hospitalization were considerable, and all but one of the pseudopatients desired to be discharged almost immediately after being admitted. They were, therefore, motivated not only to behave sanely, but to be paragons of cooperation. That their behavior was in no way disruptive is confirmed by nursing reports, which have been obtained on most of the patients. These reports uniformly indicate that the patients were "friendly," "cooperative," and "exhibited no abnormal indications."

The Normal Are Not Detectably Sane

Despite their public "show" of sanity, the pseudopatients were never detected. Admitted, except in one case, with a diagnosis of schizophrenia,[10] each was discharged with a diagnosis of schizophrenia "in remission." The label "in remission" should in no way be dismissed as a formality, for at no time during any hospitalization had any question been raised about any pseudo-patient's simulation. Nor are there any indications in the hospital records that the pseudopatient's status was suspect. Rather, the evidence is strong that, once labeled schizophrenic, the pseudopatient was stuck with that label. If the pseudopatient was to be discharged, he must naturally be "in remission"; but he was not sane, nor, in the institution's view, had he ever been sane.

The uniform failure to recognize sanity cannot be attributed to the quality of the hospitals, for, although there were considerable variations among them, several are considered excellent. Nor can it be alleged that there was simply not enough time to observe the pseudopatients. Length of hospitalization ranged from 7 to 52 days, with an average of 19 days. The pseudopatients were not, in fact, carefully observed, but this failure clearly speaks more to the traditions within psychiatric hospitals than to lack of opportunity.

Finally, it cannot be said that the failure to recognize the pseudopatients' sanity was due to the fact that they were not behaving sanely. While there was clearly some tension present in all of them, their daily visitors could detect no serious behavioral consequences—nor, indeed, could other patients. It was quite common for the patients to "detect" the pseudopatients' sanity. During the first three hospitalizations, when accurate counts were kept, 35 of a total of 118 patients on the admissions ward voiced their suspicions, some vigorously. "You're not crazy. You're a journalist, or a professor [referring to the continual note-taking]. You're checking up on the hospital." While most of the patients were reassured by the pseudopatient's insistence that he had been sick before he came in but was fine now, some continued to believe that the pseudopatient was sane throughout his hospitalization.[11] The fact that the patients often recognized normality when staff did not raises important questions.

Failure to detect sanity during the course of hospitalization may be due to the fact that physicians operate with a strong bias toward what statisticians call the type 2 error.[12] This is to say that physicians are more inclined to call a healthy person sick (a false positive, type 2) than a sick person healthy (a false negative, type 1). The reasons for this are not hard to find: It is clearly more dangerous to misdiagnose illness than health. Better to err on the side of caution, to suspect illness even among the healthy.

But what holds for medicine does not hold equally well for psychiatry. Medical illnesses, while unfortunate, are not commonly pejorative. Psychiatric diagnoses, on the contrary, carry with them personal, legal, and social stigmas.[13] It was therefore important to see whether the tendency toward diagnosing the sane insane could be reversed. The following experiment was arranged at a research and teaching hospital whose staff had heard these findings but doubted that such an error could occur in their hospital. The staff was informed that at some time during the following three months, one or more pseudopatients would attempt to be admitted into the psychiatric hospital. Each staff member was asked to rate each patient who presented himself at admissions or on the ward according to the likelihood that the patient was a pseudopatient. A 10-point scale was used, with a 1 and 2 reflecting high confidence that the patient was a pseudopatient.

Judgments were obtained on 193 patients who were admitted for psychiatric treatment. All staff who had had sustained contact with or primary responsibility for the patient—attendants, nurses, psychiatrists, physicians, and psychologists—were asked to make judgments. Forty-one patients were alleged, with high confidence, to be pseudopatients by at least one member of the staff. Twenty-three were considered suspect by at least one psychiatrist. Nineteen were suspected by one psychiatrist and one other staff member. Actually, no genuine pseudopatient (at least from my group) presented himself during this period.

The experiment is instructive. It indicates that the tendency to designate sane people as insane can be reversed when the stakes (in this case, prestige and diagnostic acumen) are high. But what can be said of the 19 people who were suspected of being "sane" by one psychiatrist and another staff member? Were these people truly "sane," or was it rather the case that in the course of avoiding the type 2 error the staff tended to make more errors of the first sort—calling the crazy "sane"? There is no way of knowing. But one thing is certain: Any diagnostic process that lends itself so readily to massive errors of this sort cannot be a very reliable one.

The Stickiness of Psychodiagnostic Labels

Beyond the tendency to call the healthy sick—a tendency that accounts better for diagnostic behavior on admission than it does for such behavior after a lengthy period of exposure—the data speak to the massive role of labeling in psychiatric assessment. Having once been labeled schizophrenic, there is nothing the pseudopatient can do to overcome the tag. The tag profoundly colors others' perceptions of him and his behavior.

From one viewpoint, these data are hardly surprising, for it has long been known that elements are given meaning by the context in which they occur. Gestalt psychology made this point vigorously, and Asch[14] demonstrated that there are "central" personality traits (such as "warm" versus "cold") which are so powerful that they markedly color the meaning of other information in forming an impression of a given personality.[15] "Insane," "schizophrenic," "manic-depressive," and "crazy" are probably among the most powerful of such central traits. Once a person is designated abnormal, all of his other behaviors and characteristics are colored by that label. Indeed, that label is so powerful that many of the pseudopatients' normal behaviors were overlooked entirely or profoundly misinterpreted. Some examples may clarify this issue.

Earlier I indicated that there were no changes in the pseudopatient's personal history and current status beyond those of name, employment, and, where necessary, vocation. Otherwise, a veridical description of personal history and circumstances was offered. Those circumstances were not psychotic. How were they made consonant with the diagnosis of psychosis? Or were those diagnoses modified in such a way as to bring them into accord with the circumstances of the pseudopatient's life, as described by him?

As far as I can determine, diagnoses were in no way affected by the relative health of the circumstances of a pseudopatient's life. Rather, the reverse occurred: The perception of his circumstances was shaped entirely by the diagnosis. A clear example of such translation is found in the case of a pseudopatient who had had a close relationship with his mother but was rather remote from his father during his early childhood. During adolescence and beyond, however, his father became a close friend, while his relationship with his mother cooled. His present relationship with his wife was characteristically close and warm. Apart from occasional angry exchanges, friction was minimal. The children had rarely been spanked. Surely there is nothing especially pathological about such a history. Indeed, many readers may see a similar pattern in their own experiences, with no markedly deleterious consequences. Observe, however, how such a history was translated in the psychopathological context, this from the case summary prepared after the patient was discharged.

> This white 39-year-old male . . . manifests a long history of considerable ambivalence in close relationships, which begins in early childhood. A warm relationship with his mother cools during adolescence. A distant relationship to his father is described as becoming very intense. Affective stability is absent. His attempts to control emotionality with his wife and children are punctuated by angry outbursts and, in the case of the children, spankings. And while he says that he has several good friends, one senses considerable ambivalence embedded in those relationships also.

The facts of the case were unintentionally distorted by the staff to achieve consistency with a popular theory of the dynamics of schizophrenic reaction.[16] Nothing of an ambivalent nature had been described in relations with parents, spouse, or friends. To the extent that ambivalence could be inferred, it was probably not greater than is found in all human relationships. It is true the pseudopatient's relationships with his parents changed over time, but in the ordinary context that would hardly be remarkable—indeed, it might very well be expected. Clearly, the meaning ascribed to his verbalizations (that is, ambivalence, affective instability) was determined by the diagnosis: schizophrenia. An entirely different meaning would have been ascribed if it were known that the man was "normal."

All pseudopatients took extensive notes publicly. Under ordinary circumstances, such behavior would have raised questions in the minds of observers, as, in fact, it did among patients. Indeed, it seemed so certain that the notes would elicit suspicion that elaborate precautions were taken to remove them from the ward each day. But the precautions proved needless. The closest any staff member came to questioning these notes occurred when one pseudopatient asked his physician what kind of medication he was receiving and began to write down the response. "You needn't write it," he was told gently. "If you have trouble remembering, just ask me again."

If no questions were asked of the pseudopatients, how was their writing interpreted? Nursing records for three patients indicate that the writing was seen as an aspect of their pathological behavior. "Patient engages in writing behavior" was the daily nursing comment on one of the pseudopatients who was never questioned about his writing. Given that the patient is in the hospital, he must be psychologically disturbed. And given that he is disturbed, continuous writing must be a behavioral manifestation of that disturbance, perhaps a subset of the compulsive behaviors that are sometimes correlated with schizophrenia.

One tacit characteristic of psychiatric diagnosis is that it locates the sources of aberration within the individual and only rarely within the complex of stimuli that surrounds him. Consequently, behaviors that are stimulated by the environment are commonly misattributed to the patient's disorder. For example, one kindly nurse found a pseudopatient pacing the long hospital corridors. "Nervous, Mr. X?" she asked. "No, bored," he said.

The notes kept by pseudopatients are full of patient behaviors that were misinterpreted by well-intentioned staff. Often enough, a patient would go "berserk" because he had, wittingly or unwittingly, been mistreated by, say, an attendant. A nurse coming upon the scene would rarely inquire even cursorily into the environmental stimuli of the patient's behavior. Rather, she assumed that his upset derived from his pathology, not from his present interactions with other staff members. Occasionally, the staff might assume that the patient's family (especially when they had recently visited) or other patients had stimulated the outburst. But never were the staff found to assume that one of themselves or the structure of the hospital had anything to do with a patient's behavior. One psychiatrist pointed to a group of patients who were sitting outside the cafeteria entrance half an hour before lunchtime. To a group of young residents he indicated that such behavior was characteristic of the oral-acquisitive nature of the syndrome. It seemed not to occur to him that there were very few things to anticipate in the psychiatric hospital besides eating.

A psychiatric label has a life and an influence of its own. Once the impression has been formed that the patient is schizophrenic, the expectation is that he will continue to be schizophrenic. When a sufficient amount of time has passed, during which the patient has done nothing bizarre, he is considered to be in remission and available for discharge. But the label endures beyond discharge, with the unconfirmed expectation that he will behave as a schizophrenic again. Such labels, conferred by mental health professionals, are as influential on the patient as they are on his relatives and friends, and it should not surprise anyone that the diagnosis acts on all of them as a self-fulfilling prophecy. Eventually, the patient himself accepts the diagnosis, with all of its surplus meanings and expectations, and behaves accordingly.[17]

The inferences to be made from these matters are quite simple. Much as Zigler and Phillips have demonstrated that there is enormous overlap in the symptoms presented by patients who have been variously diagnosed,[18] so there is enormous overlap in the behaviors of the sane and the insane. The sane are not "sane" all of the time. We lose our tempers "for no good reason." We are occasionally depressed or anxious, again for no good reason. And we may find it difficult to get along with one or another person—again for no reason that we can specify. Similarly, the insane are not always insane. Indeed, it was the impression of the pseudopatients while living with them that they were sane for long periods of time—that the bizarre behaviors upon which their diagnoses were allegedly predicated constituted only a small fraction of their total behavior. If it makes no sense to label ourselves permanently depressed on the basis of an occasional depression, then it takes evidence that is presently available to label all patients insane or schizophrenic on the basis of bizarre behaviors or cognitions. It seems more useful, as Mischel[19] has pointed out, to limit our discussions to *behaviors*, the stimuli that provoke them, and their correlates.

It is not known why powerful impressions of personality traits, such as "crazy" or "insane," arise. Conceivably, when the origins of and stimuli that give rise to a behavior are remote or unknown, or when the behavior strikes us as immutable, trait labels regarding the *behavior* arise. When, on the other hand, the origins and stimuli are known and available, discourse is limited to the behavior itself. Thus, I may hallucinate because I am sleeping, or I may hallucinate because I have ingested a peculiar drug. These are termed sleep-induced hallucinations, or dreams, and drug-induced hallucinations, respectively. But when the stimuli to my hallucinations are unknown, that is called craziness, or schizophrenia—as if that inference were somehow as illuminating as the others.

The Consequences of Labeling and Depersonalization

Whenever the ratio of what is known to what needs to be known approaches zero, we tend to invent "knowledge" and assume that we understand more than we actually do. We seem unable to acknowledge that we simply don't know. The needs for diagnosis and remediation of behavioral and emotional problems are enormous. But rather than acknowledge that we are just embarking on understanding, we continue to label patients "schizophrenic," "manic-depressive," and "insane," as if in those words we had captured the essence of understanding. The facts of the matter are that we have known for a long time that diagnoses are often not useful or reliable, but we have nevertheless continued to use them. We now know that we cannot distinguish insanity from sanity. It is depressing to consider how that information will be used.

Not merely depressing, but frightening. How many people, one wonders, are sane but not recognized as such in our psychiatric institutions? How many have been needlessly stripped of their privileges of citizenship, from the right to vote and drive to that of handling their own accounts? How many have feigned insanity in order to avoid the criminal consequences of their behavior, and conversely, how many would rather stand trial than live interminably in a psychiatric hospital—but are wrongly thought to be mentally ill? How many have been stigmatized by well-intentioned, but nevertheless erroneous, diagnoses? On the last point, recall again that a "type 2 error" in psychiatric diagnosis does not have the same consequences it does in medical diagnosis. A diagnosis of cancer that has been found to be in error is cause for celebration. But psychiatric diagnoses are rarely found to be in error. The label sticks, a mark of inadequacy forever.

ENDNOTES

[1] P. Ash, *Journal of Abnormal and Social Psychology* 44 (1949): 272; A. T. Beck, *American Journal of Psychiatry* 119 (1962): 210; A. T. Boisen, *Psychiatry* 2 (1938): 233; J. Kreitman, *Journal of Mental Science* 107 (1961): 876; N. Kreitman, P. Sainsbury, J. Morrisey, J. Towers, and J. Scrivener, *Journal of Mental Science* 107 (1961): 887; H. O. Schmitt and C. P. Fonda, *Journal of Abnormal Social Psychology* 52 (1956): 262; W. Seeman, *Journal of Nervous Mental Disorders* 118 (1953): 541. For analysis of these artifacts and summaries of the disputes, see J. Zubin, *Annual Review of Psychology* 18 (1967): 373; L. Phillips and J. G. Draguns, *Annual Review of Psychology* 22 (1971): 447.

[2] R. Benedict, *Journal of General Psychology* 10 (1934): 59.

[3] See in this regard Howard Becker, *Outsiders: Studies in the Sociology of Deviance* (New York: Free Press, 1963); B. M. Braginsky, D. D. Braginsky, and K. Ring, *Methods of Madness: The Mental Hospital As a Last Resort* (New York: Holt, Rinehart and Winston, 1969); G. M. Crocetti and P. V. Lemkau, *American Sociological Review* 30 (1965): 577; Erving Goffman, *Behavior in Public Places* (New York: Free Press, 1964); R. D. Laing, *The Divided Self: A Study of Sanity and Madness* (Chicago: Quadrangle, 1960); D. L. Phillips, *American Sociological Review* 28 (1963): 963; T. R. Sarbin, *Psychology Today* 6 (1972): 18; E. Schur, *American Journal of Sociology* 75 (1969): 309; Thomas Szasz, *The Myth of Mental Illness: Foundations of a Theory of Mental Illness* (New York: Hoeber Harper, 1963). For a critique of some of these views, see W. R. Gave, *American Sociological Review* 35 (1970): 873.

[4] Erving Goffman, *Asylums* (Garden City, NY: Doubleday, 1961).

[5] T. J. Scheff, *Being Mentally Ill: A Sociological Theory* (Chicago: Aldine, 1966).

[6] Data from a ninth pseudopatient are not incorporated in this report because, although his sanity went undetected, he falsified aspects of his personal history, including his marital status and parental relationships. His experimental behaviors therefore were not identical to those of the other pseudopatients.

[7] A. Barry, *Bellevue Is a State of Mind* (New York: Harcourt Brace Jovanovich, 1971); I. Belknap, *Human Problems of a State Mental Hospital* (New York: McGraw-Hill, 1956); W. Caudill, F. C. Redlich, H. R. Gilmore, and E. B. Brody, *American Journal of Orthopsychiatry* 22 (1952): 314; A. R. Goldman, R. H. Bohr, and T. A. Steinberg, *Professional Psychology* 1 (1970): 427; *Roche Report* 1, no. 13 (1971): 8.

[8] Beyond the personal difficulties that the pseudopatient is likely to experience in the hospital, there are legal and social ones that, combined, require considerable attention before entry. For example, once admitted to a psychiatric institution, it is

difficult, if not impossible, to be discharged on short notice, state law to the contrary notwithstanding. I was not sensitive to these difficulties at the outset of the project, nor to the personal and situational emergencies that can arise, but later a writ of habeas corpus was prepared for each of the entering pseudopatients and an attorney was kept "on call" during every hospitalization. I am grateful to John Kaplan and Robert Bartels for legal advice and assistance in these matters.

[9] However distasteful such concealment is, it was a necessary first step to examining these questions. Without concealment, there would have been no way to know how valid these experiences were; nor was there any way of knowing whether whatever detections occurred were a tribute to the diagnostic acumen of the staff or to the hospital's rumor network. Obviously, since my concerns are general ones that cut across individual hospitals and staffs, I have respected their anonymity and have eliminated clues that might lead to their identification.

[10] Interestingly, of the 12 admissions, 11 were diagnosed as schizophrenic and one, with the identical symptomatology, as manic-depressive psychosis. This diagnosis has a more favorable prognosis, and it was given by the only private hospital in our sample. On the relations between social class and psychiatric diagnosis, see A. B. Hollinghead and F. C. Redlich, *Social Class and Mental Illness: A Community Study* (New York: Wiley, 1958).

[11] It is possible, of course, that patients have quite broad latitudes in diagnosis and therefore are inclined to call many people sane, even those whose behavior is patently aberrant. However, although we have no hard data on this matter, it was our distinct impression that this was not the case. In many instances, patients not only singled us out for attention, but came to imitate our behaviors and styles.

[12] Scheff, *Being Mentally Ill.*

[13] J. Cumming and E. Cumming, *Community Mental Health* 1 (1965): 135; A. Farina and K. Ring, *Journal of Abnormal Psychology* 40 (1965): 47; H. E. Freeman and O. G. Simmons, *The Mental Patient Comes Home* (New York: Wiley, 1963); W. J. Johannsen, *Mental Hygiene* 53 (1969): 218; A. S. Linsky, *Social Psychology* 5 (1970): 166.

[14] S. E. Asch, *Abnormal Social Psychology* 41 (1946): 258; S. E. Asch, *Social Psychology* (New York: Prentice-Hall, 1952).

[15] See also I. N. Mensch and J. Wishner, *Journal of Personality* 16 (1947): 188; J. Wishner, *Psychological Review* 67 (1960): 96; J. S. Bruner and K. R. Tagiuri in *Handbook of Social Psychology*, vol. 2, ed. G. Lindzey (Cambridge, MA: Addison-Wesley, 1954), pp. 634–54; J. S. Bruner, D. Shapiro, and R. Tagiuri in *Person Perception and Interpersonal Behavior*, ed. R. Tagiuri and L. Petrullo (Stanford, CA: Stanford University Press, 1958), pp. 277–88.

[16] For an example of a similar self-fulfilling prophecy, in this instance dealing with the "central" trait of intelligence, see R. Rosenthal and L. Jacobson, *Pygmalion in the Classroom* (New York: Holt, Rinehart and Winston, 1968).

[17] Scheff, *Being Mentally Ill.*

[18] E. Zigler and L. Phillips, *Journal of Abnormal and Social Psychology* 63 (1961): 69. See also R. K. Freudenberg and J. P. Robertson, *A.M.A. Archives of Neurological Psychiatry* 76 (1956): 14.

[19] W. Mischel, *Personality and Assessment* (New York: Wiley, 1968).

20

ANOREXIA NERVOSA AND BULIMIA
The Development of Deviant Identities

PENELOPE A. McLORG • DIANE E. TAUB

Symbolic interactionists claim that deviance is relative depending on the situation and who is perceiving the act of deviance. Thus, according to *labeling theory,* people label certain acts as deviant and others as normal. This reading by Penelope McLorg and Diane Taub, both professors at Southern Illinois University at Carbondale, further illustrates this subjective process of deviance identification. In the reading below, originally published in 1987, McLorg and Taub employ labeling theory to explain how eating disorders have become defined as deviant behaviors and how some young women acquire deviant identities by modifying their self-concepts to conform to the societal labels of a person with an eating disorder.

Introduction

Current appearance norms stipulate thinness for women and muscularity for men; these expectations, like any norms, entail rewards for compliance and negative sanctions for violations. Fear of being overweight—of being visually deviant—has led to a striving for thinness, especially among women. In the extreme, this avoidance of overweight engenders eating disorders, which themselves constitute deviance. Anorexia nervosa, or purposeful starvation, embodies visual as well as behavioral deviation; bulimia, binge-eating followed by vomiting and/or laxative abuse, is primarily behaviorally deviant.

Besides a fear of fatness, anorexics and bulimics exhibit distorted body images. In anorexia nervosa, a 20–25 percent loss of initial body weight occurs, resulting from self-starvation alone or in combination with excessive exercising, occasional binge-eating, vomiting and/or laxative abuse. Bulimia denotes cyclical (daily, weekly, for example) binge-eating followed by vomiting or laxative abuse; weight is normal or close to normal (Humphries,

From *Deviant Behavior* 8 (1987). Copyright © 1987 by Taylor and Francis, Inc. Reprinted with the permission of Taylor and Francis, Inc.

Wrobel, and Weigert 1982). Common physical manifestations of these eating disorders include menstrual cessation or irregularities and electrolyte imbalances; among behavioral traits are depression, obsessions/compulsions, and anxiety (Russell 1979; Thompson and Schwartz 1982).

Increasingly prevalent in the past two decades, anorexia nervosa and bulimia have emerged as major health and social problems. Termed an epidemic on college campuses (Brody, as quoted in Schur 1984:76), bulimia affects 13 percent of college students (Halmi, Falk, and Schwartz 1981). Less prevalent, anorexia nervosa was diagnosed in 0.6 percent of students utilizing a university health center (Stangler and Printz 1980). However, the overall mortality rate of anorexia nervosa is 6 percent (Schwartz and Thompson 1981) to 20 percent (Humphries et al. 1982); bulimia appears to be less life-threatening (Russell 1979).

Particularly affecting certain demographic groups, eating disorders are most prevalent among young, white, affluent (upper-middle to upper class) women in modern, industrialized countries (Crisp 1977; Willi and Grossman 1983). Combining all of these risk factors (female sex, youth, high socio-economic status, and residence in an industrialized country), prevalence of anorexia nervosa in upper-class English girls' schools is reported at 1 in 100 (Crisp, Palmer, and Kalucy 1976). The age of onset for anorexia nervosa is bimodal at 14.5 and 18 years (Humphries et al. 1982); the most frequent age of onset for bulimia is 18 (Russell 1979).

Eating disorders have primarily been studied from psychological and medical perspectives.[1] Theories of etiology have generally fallen into three categories: the ego psychological (involving an impaired child-maternal environment); the family systems (implicating enmeshed, rigid families); and the endocrinological (involving a precipitating hormonal defect). Although relatively ignored in previous studies, the sociocultural components of anorexia nervosa and bulimia (the slimness norm and its agents of reinforcement, such as role models) have been postulated as accounting for the recent, dramatic increases in these disorders (Boskind-White 1985; Schwartz, Thompson, and Johnson 1982).[2]

Medical and psychological approaches to anorexia nervosa and bulimia obscure the social facets of the disorders and neglect the individuals' own definitions of their situations. Among the social processes involved in the development of an eating disorder is the sequence of conforming behavior, primary deviance, and secondary deviance. Societal reaction is the critical mediator affecting the movement through the deviant career (Becker 1973). Within a framework of labeling theory, this study focuses on the emergence of anorexic and bulimic identities, as well as on the consequences of being career deviants.

Methodology

Sampling and Procedures

Most research on eating disorders has utilized clinical subjects or nonclinical respondents completing questionnaires. Such studies can be criticized for simply counting and describing behaviors and/or neglecting the social construction of the disorders. Moreover, the work of clinicians is often limited by therapeutic orientation. Previous research may also have included individuals who were not in therapy on their own volition and who resisted admitting that they had an eating disorder.

Past studies thus disregard the intersubjective meanings respondents attach to their behavior and emphasize researchers' criteria for definition as anorexic or bulimic. In order to supplement these sampling and procedural designs, the present study utilizes participant observation of a group of self-defined anorexics and bulimics.[3] As the individuals had acknowledged their eating disorders, frank discussion and disclosure were facilitated.

Data are derived from a self-help group, BANISH, Bulimics/Anorexics in Self-Help, which met at a university in an urban center of the mid-South. Founded by one of the researchers (D.E.T.), BANISH was advertised in local newspapers as offering a group experience for individuals who were anorexic or bulimic. Despite the local advertisements, the campus location of the meeting may have selectively encouraged university students to attend. Nonetheless, in view of the modal age of onset and socioeconomic status of individuals with eating disorders, college students have been considered target populations (Crisp et al. 1976; Halmi et al. 1981).

The group's weekly two-hour meetings were observed for two years. During the course of this study, 30 individuals attended at least one of the meetings. Attendance at meetings was varied: Ten individuals came nearly every Sunday; five attended approximately twice a month; and the remaining 15 participated once a month or less frequently, often when their eating problems were "more severe" or "bizarre." The modal number of members at meetings was 12. The diversity in attendance was to be expected in self-help groups of anorexics and bulimics:

> Most people's involvement will not be forever or even a long time. Most people get the support they need and drop out. Some take the time to help others after they themselves have been helped but even they may withdraw after a time. It is a natural and in many cases *necessary* process (emphasis in original). (American Anorexia and Bulimia Association 1983)

Modeled after Alcoholics Anonymous, BANISH allowed participants to discuss their backgrounds and experiences with others who empathized. For many members, the group constituted their only source of help; these respondents were reluctant to contact health professionals because of shame, embarrassment, or financial difficulties.

In addition to field notes from group meetings, records of other encounters with all members were maintained. Participants visited the office of one of the researchers (D.E.T.), called both researchers by phone, and invited them to their homes or out for a cup of coffee. Such interaction facilitated genuine communication and mutual trust. Even among the 15 individuals who did not attend the meetings regularly, contact was maintained with 10 members on a monthly basis.

Supplementing field notes were informal interviews with 15 group members, lasting from two to four hours. Because they appeared to represent more extensive experience with eating disorders, these interviewees were chosen to amplify their comments about the labeling process, made during group meetings. Conducted near the end of the two-year observation period, the interviews focused on what the respondents thought antedated and maintained their eating disorders. In addition, participants described others' reactions to their behaviors as well as their own interpretations of these reactions. To protect the confidentiality of individuals quoted in the study, pseudonyms are employed.

Description of Members

The demographic composite of the sample typifies what has been found in other studies (Crisp 1977; Fox and James 1976; Herzog 1982; Schlesier-Stropp 1984). Group members' ages ranged from 19 to 36, with the modal age being 21. The respondents were white, and all but one were female. The sole male and three of the females were anorexic; the remaining females were bulimic.[4]

Primarily composed of college students, the group included four nonstudents, three of whom had college degrees. Nearly all members derived from upper-middle- or lower-upper-class households. Eighteen students and two nonstudents were never married and uninvolved in serious relationships; two nonstudents were married (one with two children); two students were divorced (one with two children); and six students were involved in serious relationships. The duration of eating disorders ranged from 3 to 15 years.

Conforming Behavior

In the backgrounds of most anorexics and bulimics, dieting figures prominently, beginning in the teen years (Crisp 1977; Johnson et al. 1982; Lacey, Coker, and Birtchnell 1986). As dieters, these individuals are conformist in their adherence to the cultural norms emphasizing thinness (Garner et al. 1980; Schwartz et al. 1982). In our society, slim bodies are regarded as the most worthy and attractive; overweight is viewed as physically and morally unhealthy—"obscene," "lazy," "slothful," and "gluttonous" (DeJong 1980; Ritenbaugh 1982; Schwartz et al. 1982).

Among the agents of socialization promoting the slimness norm is advertising. Female models in newspaper, magazine, and television advertisements are uniformly slender. In addition, product names and slogans exploit the thin orientation; examples include "Ultra Slim Lipstick," "Miller Lite," and "Virginia Slims." While retaining pressures toward thinness, an Ayds commercial attempts a compromise for those wanting to savor food: "Ayds . . . so you can taste, chew, and enjoy, while you lose weight." Appealing particularly to women, a nationwide fast-food restaurant chain offers low-calorie selections, so individuals can have a "license to eat." In the latter two examples, the notion of enjoying food is combined with the message to be slim. Food and restaurant advertisements overall convey the pleasures of eating, whereas advertisements for other products, such as fashions and diet aids, reinforce the idea that fatness is undesirable.

Emphasis on being slim affects everyone in our culture, but it influences women especially because of society's traditional emphasis on women's appearance. The slimness norm and its concomitant narrow beauty standards exacerbate the objectification of women (Schur 1984). Women view themselves as visual entities and recognize that conforming to appearance expectations and "becoming attractive object[s] [are] role obligation[s]" (Laws, as quoted in Schur 1984:66). Demonstrating the beauty motivation behind dieting, a Nielson survey indicated that of the 56 percent of all women aged 24 to 54 who dieted during the previous year, 76 percent did so for cosmetic, rather than health, reasons (Schwartz et al. 1982). For most female group members, dieting was viewed as a means of gaining attractiveness and appeal to the opposite sex. The male respondent, as well, indicated that "when I was fat, girls didn't look at me, but when I got thinner, I was suddenly popular."

In addition to responding to the specter of obesity, individuals who develop anorexia nervosa and bulimia are conformist in their strong commitment to other conventional norms and goals. They consistently excel at school and work (Bruch 1981; Humphries et al. 1982; Russell 1979), maintaining high aspirations in both areas (Lacey et al. 1986; Theander 1970). Group members generally completed college-preparatory courses in high school, aware from an early age that they would strive for a college degree. Also, in college as well as high school, respondents joined honor societies and academic clubs.

Moreover, pre-anorexics and -bulimics display notable conventionality as "model children" (Humphries et al. 1982:199), "the pride and joy" of their parents (Bruch 1981:215), accommodating themselves to the wishes of others. Parents of these individuals emphasize conformity and value achievement (Bruch 1981). Respondents felt that perfect or near-perfect grades were expected of them; however, good grades were not rewarded by parents, because "A's" were common for these children. In addition, their parents suppressed conflicts, to preserve the image of the "all-American family" (Humphries et al. 1982). Group members reported that they seldom, if ever, heard their parents argue or raise their voices.

Also conformist in their affective ties, individuals who develop anorexia nervosa and bulimia are strongly, even excessively, attached to their parents. Respondents' families appeared close-knit, demonstrating palpable emotional ties. Several group members, for example, reported habitually calling home at prescribed times, whether or not they had any news. Such families have been termed "enmeshed" and "overprotective," displaying intense interaction and concern for members' welfare (Minuchin, Rosman, and Baker 1978; Selvini-Palazzoli 1978). These qualities could be viewed as marked conformity to the norm of familial closeness.[5]

Another element of notable conformity in the family milieu of pre-anorexics and -bulimics concerns eating, body weight and shape, and exercising (Humphries et al. 1982; Kalucy, Crisp, and Harding 1977). Respondents reported their fathers' preoccupation with exercising and their mothers' engrossment in food preparation. When group members dieted and lost weight, they received an extraordinary amount of approval. Among the family, body size became a matter of "friendly rivalry." One bulimic informant recalled that she, her mother, and her coed sister all strived to wear a size 5, regardless of their heights and body frames. Subsequent to this study, the researchers learned that both the mother and sister had become bulimic.

As pre-anorexics and -bulimics, group members thus exhibited marked conformity to cultural norms of thinness, achievement, compliance, and parental attachment. Their families reinforced their conformity by adherence to norms of family closeness and weight and body shape consciousness.

Primary Deviance

Even with familial encouragement, respondents, like nearly all dieters (Chernin 1981), failed to maintain their lowered weights. Many cited their lack of willpower to eat only restricted foods. For the emerging anorexics and bulimics, extremes such as purposeful starvation or binging accompanied by vomiting and/or laxative abuse appeared as "obvious solutions" to the problem of retaining weight loss. Associated with these behaviors was a regained feeling of control in lives that had been disrupted by a major crisis. Group members' extreme weight-loss efforts operated as coping mechanisms for entering college, leaving home, or feeling rejected by the opposite sex.

The primary inducement for both eating adaptations was the drive for slimness: With slimness came more self-respect and a feeling of superiority over "unsuccessful dieters." Brian, for example, experienced a "power trip" upon consistent weight loss through starvation. Binges allowed the purging respondents to cope with stress through eating while maintaining a slim appearance. As former strict dieters, Teresa and Jennifer used binging and purging as an alternative to the constant self-denial of starvation. Acknowledging their parents' desires for them to be slim, most respondents still felt it was a conscious choice on their part to continue extreme weight-loss efforts. Being thin became the "most important thing" in their lives—their "greatest ambition."

In explaining the development of an anorexic or bulimic identity, Lemert's (1951, 1967) concept of primary deviance is salient. Primary deviance refers to a transitory period of norm violations which do not affect an individual's self-concept or performance of social roles. Although respondents were exhibiting anorexic or bulimic behavior, they did not consider themselves to be anorexic or bulimic.

At first, anorexics' significant others complimented their weight loss, expounding on their new "sleekness" and "good looks." Branch and Eurman (1980) also found anorexics' families and friends describing them as "well groomed," "neat," "fashionable," and "victorious" (p. 631). Not until the respondents approached emaciation did some parents or friends become concerned and withdraw their praise. Significant others also became increasingly aware of the anorexics' compulsive exercising, preoccupation with food preparation (but not consumption), and ritualistic eating patterns (such as cutting food into minute pieces and eating only certain foods at prescribed times).

For bulimics, friends or family members began to question how the respondents could eat such large amounts of food (often in excess of 10,000 calories a day) and stay slim. Significant others also noticed calluses across the bulimics' hands, which were caused by repeated inducement of vomiting. Several bulimics were "caught in the act," bent over commodes. Generally, friends and family required substantial evidence before believing that the respondents' binging or purging was no longer sporadic.

Secondary Deviance

Heightened awareness of group members' eating behavior ultimately led others to label the respondents "anorexic" or "bulimic." Respondents differed in their histories of being labeled and accepting the labels. Generally first termed anorexic by friends, family, or medical personnel, the anorexics initially vigorously denied the label. They felt they were not "anorexic enough," not skinny enough; Robin did not regard herself as having the "skeletal" appearance she associated with anorexia nervosa. These group members found it difficult to differentiate between socially approved modes of weight loss— eating less and exercising more—and the extremes of those behaviors. In fact, many of their activities—cheerleading, modeling, gymnastics, aerobics— reinforced their pursuit of thinness. Like other anorexics, Chris felt she was being "ultra-healthy," with "total control" over her body.

For several respondents, admitting they were anorexic followed the realization that their lives were disrupted by their eating disorder. Anorexics' inflexible eating patterns unsettled family meals and holiday gatherings.

Their regimented lifestyle of compulsively scheduled activities—exercising, school, and meals—precluded any spontaneous social interactions. Realization of their adverse behaviors preceded the anorexics' acknowledgment of their subnormal body weight and size.

Contrasting with anorexics, the binge/purgers, when confronted, more readily admitted that they were bulimic and that their means of weight loss was "abnormal." Teresa, for example, knew "very well" that her bulimic behavior was "wrong and unhealthy," although "worth the physical risks." While the bulimics initially maintained that their purging was only a temporary weight-loss method, they eventually realized that their disorder represented a "loss of control." Although these respondents regretted the self-indulgence, "shame," and "wasted time," they acknowledged their growing dependence on binging and purging for weight management and stress regulation.

The application of anorexic or bulimic labels precipitated secondary deviance, wherein group members internalized these identities. Secondary deviance refers to norm violations which are a response to society's labeling: "Secondary deviation . . . becomes a means of social defense, attack or adaptation to the overt and covert problems created by the societal reaction to primary deviance" (Lemert 1967:17). In contrast to primary deviance, secondary deviance is generally prolonged, alters the individual's self-concept, and affects the performance of his/her social roles.

As secondary deviants, respondents felt that their disorders "gave a purpose" to their lives. Nicole resisted attaining a normal weight because it was not "her"—she accepted her anorexic weight as her "true" weight. For Teresa, bulimia became a "companion"; and Julie felt "every aspect of her life," including time management and social activities, was affected by her bulimia. Group members' eating disorders became the salient element of their self-concepts, so that they related to familiar people and new acquaintances as anorexics or bulimics. For example, respondents regularly compared their body shapes and sizes with those of others. They also became sensitized to comments about their appearance, whether or not the remarks were made by someone aware of their eating disorder.

With their behavior increasingly attuned to their eating disorders, group members exhibited role engulfment (Schur 1971). Through accepting anorexic or bulimic identities, individuals centered activities around their deviant role, downgrading other social roles. Their obligations as students, family members, and friends became subordinate to their eating and exercising rituals. Socializing, for example, was gradually curtailed because it interfered with compulsive exercising, binging, or purging.

Labeled anorexic or bulimic, respondents were ascribed a new status with a different set of role expectations. Regardless of other positions the individuals occupied, their deviant status, or master status (Becker 1973; Hughes 1958), was identified before all others. Among group members, Nicole, who was known as the "school's brain," became known as the "school's anorexic."

No longer viewed as conforming model individuals, some respondents were termed "starving waifs" or "pigs."

Because of their identities as deviants, anorexics' and bulimics' interactions with others were altered. Group members' eating habits were scrutinized by friends and family and used as a "catch-all" for everything negative that happened to them. Respondents felt self-conscious around individuals who knew of their disorders; for example, Robin imagined people "watching and whispering" behind her. In addition, group members believed others expected them to "act" anorexic or bulimic. Friends of some anorexic group members never offered them food or drink, assuming continued disinterest on the respondents' part. While being hospitalized, Denise felt she had to prove to others she was not still vomiting, by keeping her bathroom door open. Other bulimics, who lived in dormitories, were hesitant to use the restroom for normal purposes lest several friends be huddling at the door, listening for vomiting. In general, individuals interacted with the respondents largely on the basis of their eating disorder; in doing so, they reinforced anorexic and bulimic behaviors.

Bulimic respondents, whose weight-loss behavior was not generally detectable from their appearance, tried earnestly to hide their bulimia by binging and purging in secret. Their main purpose in concealment was to avoid the negative consequences of being known as a bulimic. For these individuals, bulimia connoted a "cop-out": Like "weak anorexics," bulimics pursued thinness but yielded to urges to eat. Respondents felt other people regarded bulimia as "gross" and had little sympathy for the sufferer. To avoid these stigmas or "spoiled identities," the bulimics shrouded their behaviors.

Distinguishing types of stigma, Goffman (1963) describes discredited (visible) stigmas and discreditable (invisible) stigmas. Bulimics, whose weight was approximately normal or even slightly elevated, harbored discreditable stigmas. Anorexics, on the other hand, suffered both discreditable and discredited stigmas—the latter due to their emaciated appearance. Certain anorexics were more reconciled than the bulimics to their stigmas: For Brian, the "stigma of anorexia was better than being fat." Common to the stigmatized individuals was an inability to interact spontaneously with others. Respondents were constantly on guard against topics of eating and body size.

Both anorexics and bulimics were held responsible by others for their behavior and presumed able to "get out of it if they tried." Many anorexics reported being told to "just eat more," while bulimics were enjoined to simply "stop eating so much." Such appeals were made without regard for the complexities of the problem. Ostracized by certain friends and family members, anorexics and bulimics felt increasingly isolated. For respondents, the self-help group presented a nonthreatening forum for discussing their disorders. Here, they found mutual understanding, empathy, and support. Many participants viewed BANISH as a haven from stigmatization by "others."

Group members, as secondary deviants, thus endured negative consequences, such as stigmatization, from being labeled. As they internalized the labels anorexic or bulimic, individuals' self-concepts were significantly influenced. When others interacted with the respondents on the basis of their eating disorders, anorexic or bulimic identities were encouraged. Moreover, group members' efforts to counteract the deviant labels were thwarted by their master status.

Discussion

Previous research on eating disorders has dwelt almost exclusively on medical and psychological facets. Although necessary for a comprehensive understanding of anorexia nervosa and bulimia, these approaches neglect the social processes involved. The phenomena of eating disorders transcend concrete disease entities and clinical diagnoses. Multifaceted and complex, anorexia nervosa and bulimia require a holistic research design, in which sociological insights must be included.

A limitation of medical and psychiatric studies, in particular, is researchers' use of a priori criteria in establishing salient variables. Rather than utilizing predetermined standards of inclusion, the present study allows respondents to construct their own reality. Concomitant to this innovative approach to eating disorders is the selection of a sample of self-admitted anorexics and bulimics. Individuals' perceptions of what it means to become anorexic or bulimic are explored. Although based on a small sample, findings can be used to guide researchers in other settings.

With only 5 to 10 percent of reported cases appearing in males (Crisp 1977; Stangler and Printz 1980), eating disorders are primarily a women's aberrance. The deviance of anorexia nervosa and bulimia is rooted in the visual objectification of women and attendant slimness norm. Indeed, purposeful starvation and binging and purging reinforce the notion that "a society gets the deviance it deserves" (Schur 1979:71). As noted (Schur 1984), the sociology of deviance has generally bypassed systematic studies of women's norm violations. Like male deviants, females endure label applications, internalizations, and fulfillments.

The social processes involved in developing anorexic or bulimic identities comprise the sequence of conforming behavior, primary deviance, and secondary deviance. With a background of exceptional adherence to conventional norms, especially the striving for thinness, respondents subsequently exhibit the primary deviance of starving or binging and purging. Societal reaction to these behaviors leads to secondary deviance, wherein respondents' self-concepts and master statuses become anorexic or bulimic. Within this framework of labeling theory, the persistence of eating disorders, as well as the effects of stigmatization, are elucidated.

Although during the course of this research some respondents alleviated their symptoms through psychiatric help or hospital treatment programs, no one was labeled "cured." An anorexic is considered recovered when weight is normal for two years; a bulimic is termed recovered after being symptom-free for one and one-half years (American Anorexia and Bulimia Association Newsletter 1985). Thus deviance disavowal (Schur 1971), or efforts after normalization to counteract deviant labels, remains a topic for future exploration.

ENDNOTES

[1] Although instructive, an integration of the medical, psychological, and sociocultural perspectives on eating disorders is beyond the scope of this paper.

[2] Exceptions to the neglect of sociocultural factors are discussions of sex-role socialization in the development of eating disorders. Anorexics' girlish appearance has been interpreted as a rejection of femininity and womanhood (Bruch 1981; Orbach 1979, 1985). In contrast, bulimics have been characterized as overconforming to traditional female sex roles (Boskind-Lodahl 1976).

[3] Although a group experience for self-defined bulimics has been reported (Boskind-Lodahl 1976), the researcher, from the outset, focused on Gestalt and behaviorist techniques within a feminist orientation.

[4] One explanation for fewer anorexics than bulimics in the sample is that, in the general population, anorexics are outnumbered by bulimics at 8 or 10 to 1 (Lawson, as reprinted in American Anorexia and Bulimia Association Newsletter 1985:1). The proportion of bulimics to anorexics in the sample is 6.5 to 1. In addition, compared to bulimics, anorexics may be less likely to attend a self-help group as they have a greater tendency to deny the existence of an eating problem (Humphries et al. 1982). However, the four anorexics in the present study were among the members who attended the meetings most often.

[5] Interactions in the families of anorexics and bulimics might seem deviant in being inordinately close. However, in the larger societal context, the family members epitomize the norms of family cohesiveness. Perhaps unusual in their occurrence, these families are still within the realm of conformity. Humphries and colleagues (1982) refer to the "highly enmeshed and protective" family as part of the "idealized family myth" (p. 202).

REFERENCES

American Anorexia / Bulimia Association. 1983, April. Correspondence.

American Anorexia / Bulimia Association Newsletter. 1985. 8(3).

Becker, Howard S. 1973. *Outsiders*. New York: Free Press.

Boskind-Lodahl, Marlene. 1976. "Cinderella's Stepsisters: A Feminist Perspective on Anorexia Nervosa and Bulimia." *Signs, Journal of Women in Culture and Society* 2:342–56.

Boskind-White, Marlene. 1985. "Bulimarexia: A Sociocultural Perspective." Pp. 113–26 in *Theory and Treatment of Anorexia Nervosa and Bulimia: Biomedical, Sociocultural and Psychological Perspectives*, edited by S. W. Emmett. New York: Brunner / Mazel.

Branch, C. H. Hardin and Linda J. Eurman. 1980. "Social Attitudes toward Patients with Anorexia Nervosa." *American Journal of Psychiatry* 137:631–32.

Bruch, Hilda. 1981. "Developmental Considerations of Anorexia Nervosa and Obesity." *Canadian Journal of Psychiatry* 26:212–16.

Chernin, Kim. 1981. *The Obsession: Reflections on the Tyranny of Slenderness*. New York: Harper & Row.

Crisp, A. H. 1977. "The Prevalence of Anorexia Nervosa and Some of Its Associations in the General Population." *Advances in Psychosomatic Medicine* 9:38–47.

Crisp, A. H., R. L. Palmer, and R. S. Kalucy. 1976. "How Common Is Anorexia Nervosa? A Prevalence Study." *British Journal of Psychiatry* 128:549–54.

DeJong, William. 1980. "The Stigma of Obesity: The Consequences of Naive Assumptions Concerning the Causes of Physical Deviance." *Journal of Health and Social Behavior* 21:75–87.

Fox, K. C. and N. McI. James. 1976. "Anorexia Nervosa: A Study of 44 Strictly Defined Cases." *New Zealand Medical Journal* 84:309–12.

Garner, David M., Paul E. Garfinkel, Donald Schwartz, and Michael Thompson. 1980. "Cultural Expectations of Thinness in Women." *Psychological Reports* 47:483–91.

Goffman, Erving. 1963. *Stigma.* Englewood Cliffs, NJ: Prentice-Hall.

Halmi, Katherine A., James R. Falk, and Estelle Schwartz. 1981. "Binge-Eating and Vomiting: A Survey of a College Population." *Psychological Medicine* 11:697–706.

Herzog, David B. 1982. "Bulimia: The Secretive Syndrome." *Psychosomatics* 23:481–83.

Hughes, Everett C. 1958. *Men and Their Work.* New York: Free Press.

Humphries, Laurie L., Sylvia Wrobel, and H. Thomas Wiegert. 1982. "Anorexia Nervosa." *American Family Physician* 26:199–204.

Johnson, Craig L., Marilyn K. Stuckey, Linda D. Lewis, and Donald M. Schwartz. 1982. "Bulimia: A Descriptive Survey of 316 Cases." *International Journal of Eating Disorders* 2(1):3–16.

Kalucy, R. S., A. H. Crisp, and Britta Harding. 1977. "A Study of 56 Families with Anorexia Nervosa." *British Journal of Medical Psychology* 50:381–95.

Lacey, Hubert J., Sian Coker, and S. A. Birtchnell. 1986. "Bulimia: Factors Associated with Its Etiology and Maintenance." *International Journal of Eating Disorders* 5:475–87.

Lemert, Edwin M. 1951. *Social Pathology.* New York: McGraw-Hill.

———. 1967. *Human Deviance, Social Problems and Social Control.* Englewood Cliffs, NJ: Prentice-Hall.

Minuchin, Salvador, Bernice L. Rosman, and Lester Baker. 1978. *Psychosomatic Families: Anorexia Nervosa in Context.* Cambridge, MA: Harvard University Press.

Orbach, Susie. 1979. *Fat Is a Feminist Issue.* New York: Berkeley.

———. 1985. "Visibility/Invisibility: Social Considerations in Anorexia Nervosa—a Feminist Perspective." Pp. 127–38 in *Theory and Treatment of Anorexia Nervosa and Bulimia: Biomedical, Sociocultural and Psychological Perspectives,* edited by S. W. Emmett. New York: Brunner/Mazel.

Ritenbaugh, Cheryl. 1982. "Obesity As a Culture-Bound Syndrome." *Culture, Medicine and Psychiatry* 6:347–61.

Russell, Gerald. 1979. "Bulimia Nervosa: An Ominous Variant of Anorexia Nervosa." *Psychological Medicine* 9:429–48.

Schlesier-Stropp, Barbara. 1984. "Bulimia: A Review of the Literature." *Psychological Bulletin* 95:247–57.

Schur, Edwin M. 1971. *Labeling Deviant Behavior.* New York: Harper & Row.

———. 1979. *Interpreting Deviance: A Sociological Introduction.* New York: Harper & Row.

———. 1984. *Labeling Women Deviant: Gender, Stigma, and Social Control.* New York: Random House.

Schwartz, Donald M. and Michael G. Thompson. 1981. "Do Anorectics Get Well? Current Research and Future Needs." *American Journal of Psychiatry* 138:319–23.

Schwartz, Donald M., Michael G. Thompson, and Craig L. Johnson. 1982. "Anorexia Nervosa and Bulimia: The Socio-Cultural Context." *International Journal of Eating Disorders* 1(3):20–36.

Selvini-Palazzoli, Mara. 1978. *Self-Starvation: From Individual to Family Therapy in the Treatment of Anorexia Nervosa.* New York: Jason Aronson.

Stangler, Ronnie S. and Adolph M. Printz. 1980. "DSM-III: Psychiatric Diagnosis in a University Population." *American Journal of Psychiatry* 137:937–40.

Theander, Sten. 1970. "Anorexia Nervosa." *Acta Psychiatrica Scandinavica Supplement* 214:24–31.

Thompson, Michael G. and Donald M. Schwartz. 1982. "Life Adjustment of Women with Anorexia Nervosa and Anorexic-like Behavior." *International Journal of Eating Disorders* 1(2):47–60.

Willi, Jurg and Samuel Grossman. 1983. "Epidemiology of Anorexia Nervosa in a Defined Region of Switzerland." *American Journal of Psychiatry* 140:564–67.

21

IN SEARCH OF RESPECT
Selling Crack in El Barrio

PHILIPPE BOURGOIS

One type of social deviance, according to sociologists, is crime. If deviance is the violation of a social norm, then a *crime* is the violation of social norms that have been made into laws. One type of crime that sociologists have long studied is illegal drug use. Why do segments of the population use and abuse illegal drugs? How can we explain the growing underground economy of illegal drugs? In this selection, taken from *In Search of Respect: Selling Crack in El Barrio* (1995), Philippe Bourgois takes us inside the crack economy in East Harlem, New York City. Bourgois, professor and chair of anthropology at the San Francisco Urban Institute, spent three and a half years living in "El Barrio," where he came to know the residents and their day-to-day struggles for economic survival. Bourgois' ethnographic account of life and social marginalization in this inner-city neighborhood reveals that many social factors lead people to deal illegal drugs and that other social barriers prevent them from reentering the legal economy.

I was forced into crack against my will. When I first moved to East Harlem—"El Barrio"—as a newlywed in the spring of 1985, I was looking for an inexpensive New York City apartment from which I could write about the experience of poverty and ethnic segregation in the heart of one of

From *In Search of Respect: Selling Crack in El Barrio* by Philippe Bourgois. Copyright © 1995 by Cambridge University Press. Reprinted with the permission of Cambridge University Press.

the most expensive cities in the world. I was interested in the political economy of inner-city street culture. I wanted to probe the Achilles' heel of the richest industrialized nation in the world by documenting how it imposes racial segregation and economic marginalization on so many of its Latino/a and African American citizens.

My original subject was the entire underground (untaxed) economy, from curbside car repairing and baby-sitting to unlicensed off-track betting and drug dealing. I had never even heard of crack when I first arrived in the neighborhood—no one knew about this particular substance yet, because this brittle compound of cocaine and baking soda processed into efficiently smokable pellets was not yet available as a mass-marketed product. By the end of the year, however, most of my friends, neighbors and acquaintances had been swept into the multibillion-dollar crack cyclone: selling it, smoking it, fretting over it. I followed them, and I watched the murder rate in the projects opposite my crumbling tenement apartment spiral into one of the highest in Manhattan.

But this essay is not about crack, or drugs, per se. Substance abuse in the inner city is merely a symptom—and a vivid symbol—of deeper dynamics of social marginalization and alienation. Of course, on an immediately visible personal level, addiction and substance abuse are among the most immediate, brutal facts shaping daily life on the street. Most important, however, the two dozen street dealers and their families that I befriended were not interested in talking primarily about drugs. On the contrary, they wanted me to learn all about their daily struggles for subsistence and dignity at the poverty line.

Through the 1980s and 1990s, slightly more than one in three families in El Barrio have received public assistance. Female heads of these impoverished households have to supplement their meager checks in order to keep their children alive. Many are mothers who make extra money by baby-sitting their neighbors' children, or by housekeeping for a paying boarder. Others may bartend at one of the half-dozen social clubs and after-hours dancing spots scattered throughout the neighborhood. Some work "off the books" in their living rooms as seamstresses for garment contractors. Finally, many also find themselves obliged to establish amorous relationships with men who are willing to make cash contributions to their household expenses.

Male income-generating strategies in the underground economy are more publicly visible. Some men repair cars on the curb; others wait on stoops for unlicensed construction subcontractors to pick them up for fly-by-night demolition jobs or window renovation projects. Many sell "numbers"—the street's version of off-track betting. The most visible cohorts hawk "nickels and dimes" of one illegal drug or another. They are part of the most robust, multibillion-dollar sector of the booming underground economy. Cocaine and crack, in particular during the mid-1980s and through the early 1990s, followed by heroin in the mid-1990s, have become the fastest-growing—if not the only—equal-opportunity employers of men in Harlem.

Retail drug sales easily outcompete other income-generating opportunities, whether legal or illegal.

Why should these young men and women take the subway to work minimum-wage jobs—or even double-minimum-wage jobs—in downtown offices when they can usually earn more, at least in the short run, by selling drugs on the street corner in front of their apartment or schoolyard? In fact, I am always surprised that so many inner-city men and women remain in the legal economy and work nine-to-five plus overtime, barely making ends meet. According to the 1990 Census of East Harlem, 48 percent of all males and 35 percent of females over 16 were employed in officially reported jobs, compared with a citywide average of 64 percent for men and 49 percent for women. In the census tracts surrounding my apartment, 53 percent of all men over 16 years of age (1,923 out of 3,647) and 28 percent of all women over 16 (1,307 out of 4,626) were working legally in officially censused jobs. An additional 17 percent of the civilian labor force was unemployed but actively looking for work, compared with 16 percent for El Barrio as a whole, and 9 percent for all of New York City.

"If I Was Working Legal . . ."

Street dealers tend to brag to outsiders and to themselves about how much money they make each night. In fact, their income is almost never as consistently high as they report it to be. Most street sellers, like my friend Primo (who, along with other friends and co-workers, allowed me to tape hundreds of hours of conversation with him over five years), are paid on a piece-rate commission basis. When converted into an hourly wage, this is often a relatively paltry sum. According to my calculations, the workers in the Game Room crackhouse, for example, averaged slightly less than double the legal minimum wage—between 7 and 8 dollars an hour. There were plenty of exceptional nights, however, when they made up to ten times minimum wage—and these are the nights they remember when they reminisce. They forget about all the other shifts when they were unable to work because of police raids, and they certainly do not count as forfeited working hours the nights they spent in jail.

This was brought home to me symbolically one night as Primo and his co-worker Caesar were shutting down the Game Room. Caesar unscrewed the fuses in the electrical box to disconnect the video games. Primo had finished stashing the leftover bundles of crack vials inside a hollowed-out live electrical socket and was counting the night's thick wad of receipts. I was struck by how thin the handful of bills was that he separated out and folded neatly into his personal billfold. Primo and Caesar then eagerly lowered the iron riot gates over the Game Room's windows and snapped shut the heavy

Yale padlocks. They were moving with the smooth, hurried gestures of workers preparing to go home after an honest day's hard labor. Marveling at the universality in the body language of workers rushing at closing time, I felt an urge to compare the wages paid by this alternative economy. I grabbed Primo's wallet out of his back pocket, carefully giving a wide berth to the fatter wad in his front pocket that represented Ray's share of the night's income—and that could cost Primo his life if it were waylaid. Unexpectedly, I pulled out fifteen dollars' worth of food stamps along with two $20 bills. After an embarrassed giggle, Primo stammered that his mother had added him to her food-stamp allotment.

> Primo: *I gave my girl, Maria, half of it. I said, "Here take it, use it if you need it for whatever." And then the other half I still got it in my wallet for emergencies.*
>   *Like that, we always got a couple of dollars here and there, to survive with. Because tonight, straight cash, I only got garbage. Forty dollars! Do you believe that?*

At the same time that wages can be relatively low in the crack economy, working conditions are often inferior to those in the legal economy. Aside from the obvious dangers of being shot, or of going to prison, the physical work space of most crackhouses is usually unpleasant. The infrastructure of the Game Room, for example, was much worse than that of any legal retail outfit in East Harlem: There was no bathroom, no running water, no telephone, no heat in the winter and no air conditioning in the summer. Primo occasionally complained:

> *Everything that you see here* [sweeping his arm at the scratched and dented video games, the walls with peeling paint, the floor slippery with litter, the filthy windows pasted over with ripped movie posters] *is fucked up. It sucks, man* [pointing at the red 40-watt bare bulb hanging from an exposed fixture in the middle of the room and exuding a sickly twilight].

Indeed, the only furnishings besides the video games were a few grimy milk crates and bent aluminum stools. Worse yet, a smell of urine and vomit usually permeated the locale. For a few months Primo was able to maintain a rudimentary sound system, but it was eventually beaten to a pulp during one of Caesar's drunken rages. Of course, the deficient infrastructure was only one part of the depressing working conditions.

> Primo: *Plus I don't like to see people fucked up* [handing over three vials to a nervously pacing customer]. *This is fucked-up shit. I don't like this crack dealing. Word up.*
>   [gunshots in the distance] *Hear that?*

In private, especially in the last few years of my residence, Primo admitted that he wanted to go back to the legal economy.

Primo: *I just fuck up the money here. I rather be legal.*

Philippe: *But you wouldn't be the head man on the block with so many girlfriends.*

Primo: *I might have women on my dick right now but I would be much cooler if I was working legal. I wouldn't be drinking and the coke wouldn't be there every night.*

Plus if I was working legally I would have women on my dick too, because I would have money.

Philippe: *But you make more money here than you could ever make working legit.*

Primo: *O.K. So you want the money but you really don't want to do the job.*

I really hate it, man. Hate it! I hate the people! I hate the environment! I hate the whole shit, man! But it's like you get caught up with it. You do it, and you say, "Ay, fuck it today!" Another day, another dollar. [pointing at an emaciated customer who was just entering] *But I don't really, really think that I would have hoped that I can say I'm gonna be richer one day. I can't say that. I think about it, but I'm just living day to day.*

If I was working legal, I wouldn't be hanging out so much. I wouldn't be treating you. [pointing to the 16-ounce can of Colt 45 in my hand] *In a job, you know, my environment would change . . . totally. Cause I'd have different friends. Right after work I'd go out with a co-worker, for lunch, for dinner. After work I may go home; I'm too tired for hanging out—I know I gotta work tomorrow.*

After working a legal job, I'm pretty sure I'd be good.

Burned in the FIRE Economy

The problem is that Primo's good intentions do not lead anywhere when the only legal jobs he can compete for fail to provide him with a livable wage. None of the crack dealers were explicitly conscious of the links between their limited options in the legal economy, their addiction to drugs and their dependence on the crack economy for economic survival and personal dignity. Nevertheless, all of Primo's colleagues and employees told stories of rejecting what they considered to be intolerable working conditions at entry-level jobs.

Most entered the legal labor market at exceptionally young ages. By the time they were 12, they were bagging and delivering groceries at the supermarket for tips, stocking beer off the books in local bodegas, or running errands. Before reaching 21, however, virtually none had fulfilled their early childhood dreams of finding stable, well-paid legal work.

The problem is structural: From the 1950s through the 1980s, second-generation inner-city Puerto Ricans were trapped in the most vulnerable niche of a factory-based economy that was rapidly being replaced by service industries. Between 1950 and 1990, the proportion of factory jobs in New York City decreased approximately threefold at the same time that service-sector jobs doubled. The Department of City Planning calculates that more than 800,000 industrial jobs were lost from the 1960s through the early 1990s, while the total number of jobs in all categories remained more or less constant at 3.5 million.

Few scholars have noted the cultural dislocations of the new service economy. These cultural clashes have been most pronounced in the office-work service jobs that have multiplied because of the dramatic expansion of the finance, insurance and real estate (FIRE) sector in New York City. Service work in professional offices is the most dynamic place for ambitious inner-city youths to find entry-level jobs if they aspire to upward mobility. Employment as mailroom clerks, photocopiers and messengers in the high-rise office corridors of the financial district propels many into a wrenching cultural confrontation with the upper-middle-class white world. Obedience to the norms of high-rise, office-corridor culture is in direct contradiction to street culture's definitions of personal dignity, especially for males who are socialized not to accept public subordination.

Most of the dealers have not completely withdrawn from the legal economy. On the contrary—they are precariously perched on its edge. Their poverty remains their only constant as they alternate between street-level crack dealing and just-above-minimum-wage legal employment. The working-class jobs they manage to find are objectively recognized to be among the least desirable in U.S. society; hence the following list of just a few of the jobs held by some of the Game Room regulars during the years I knew them: unlicensed asbestos remover, home attendant, street-corner flier distributor, deep-fat fry cook and night-shift security guard on the violent ward at the municipal hospital for the criminally insane.

The stable factory-worker incomes that might have allowed Caesar and Primo to support families have largely disappeared from the inner city. Perhaps if their social network had not been confined to the weakest sector of manufacturing in a period of rapid job loss, their teenage working-class dreams might have stabilized them long enough to enable them to adapt to the restructuring of the local economy. Instead, they find themselves propelled headlong into an explosive confrontation between their sense of cultural dignity versus the humiliating interpersonal subordination of service work.

Workers like Caesar and Primo appear inarticulate to their professional supervisors when they try to imitate the language of power in the workplace; they stumble pathetically over the enunciation of unfamiliar words. They cannot decipher the hastily scribbled instructions—rife with mysterious abbreviations—that are left for them by harried office managers on diminutive

Post-its. The "common sense" of white-collar work is foreign to them; they do not, for example, understand the logic in filing triplicate copies of memos or for postdating invoices. When they attempt to improvise or show initiative, they fail miserably and instead appear inefficient—or even hostile—for failing to follow "clearly specified" instructions.

In the high-rise office buildings of midtown Manhattan or Wall Street, newly employed inner-city high school dropouts suddenly realize they look like idiotic buffoons to the men and women for whom they work. But people like Primo and Caesar have not passively accepted their structural victimization. On the contrary, by embroiling themselves in the underground economy and proudly embracing street culture, they are seeking an alternative to their social marginalization. In the process, on a daily level, they become the actual agents administering their own destruction and their community's suffering.

Both Primo and Caesar experienced deep humiliation and insecurity in their attempts to penetrate the foreign, hostile world of high-rise office corridors. Primo had bitter memories of being the mailroom clerk and errand boy at a now-defunct professional trade magazine. The only time he explicitly admitted to having experienced racism was when he described how he was treated at that particular work setting.

> Primo: *I had a prejudiced boss. . . . When she was talking to people she would say, "He's illiterate," as if I was really that stupid that I couldn't understand what she was talking about.*
>
> *So what I did one day—you see they had this big dictionary right there on the desk, a big heavy motherfucker—so what I just did was open up the dictionary, and I just looked up the word, "illiterate." And that's when I saw what she was calling me.*
>
> *So she's saying that I'm stupid or something. I'm stupid!* [pointing to himself with both thumbs and making a hulking face] *"She doesn't know shit."*

In contrast, in the underground economy Primo never had to risk this kind of threat to his self-worth.

> Primo: *Ray would never disrespect me that way; he wouldn't tell me that because he's illiterate too, plus I've got more education than him. I almost got a G.E.D.*

The contemporary street sensitivity to being dissed immediately emerges in these memories of office humiliation. The machismo of street culture exacerbates the sense of insult experienced by men because the majority of office supervisors at the entry level are women. In the lowest recesses of New York City's FIRE sector, tens of thousands of messengers, photocopy machine operators and security guards serving the Fortune 500 companies are brusquely ordered about by young white executives—often female—who sometimes make bimonthly salaries superior to their underlings' yearly wages. The extraordinary wealth of Manhattan's financial district exacerbates the sense of sexist-racist insult associated with performing just-above-minimum-wage labor.

"I Don't Even Got a Dress Shirt"

Several months earlier, I had watched Primo drop out of a "motivational training" employment program in the basement of his mother's housing project, run by former heroin addicts who had just received a multimillion-dollar private sector grant for their innovative approach to training the "unemployable." Primo felt profoundly disrespected by the program, and he focused his discontent on the humiliation he faced because of his inappropriate wardrobe. The fundamental philosophy of such motivational job-training programs is that "these people have an attitude problem." They take a boot-camp approach to their unemployed clients, ripping their self-esteem apart during the first week in order to build them back up with an epiphanic realization that they want to find jobs as security guards, messengers and data-input clerks in just-above-minimum-wage service-sector positions. The program's highest success rate had been with middle-aged African American women who wanted to terminate their relationship to welfare once their children leave home.

I originally had a "bad attitude" toward the premise of psychologically motivating and manipulating people to accept boring, poorly paid jobs. At the same time, however, the violence and self-destruction I was witnessing at the Game Room were convincing me that it is better to be exploited at work than to be outside the legal labor market. In any case, I persuaded Primo and a half-dozen of his Game Room associates to sign up for the program. Even Caesar was tempted to join.

None of the crack dealers lasted for more than three sessions. Primo was the first to drop out, after the first day. For several weeks he avoided talking about the experience. I repeatedly pressed him to explain why he "just didn't show up" at the sessions. Only after repeated badgering on my part did he finally express the deep sense of shame and vulnerability he experienced whenever he attempted to venture into the legal labor market.

> Philippe: *Yo, Primo, listen to me. I worry that there's something taking place that you're not aware of, in terms of yourself. Like the coke that you be sniffing all the time; it's like every night.*
> Primo: *What do you mean?*

Philippe: *Like not showing up at the job training. You say it's just procrasti-*
nation, but I'm scared it's something deeper that you're not dealing with. Like
wanting to be partying all night, and sniffing. Maybe that's why you never
went back.

Primo: *The truth though—listen, Felipe—my biggest worry was the dress*
code, 'cause my gear is limited. I don't even got a dress shirt, I only got one
pair of shoes, and you can't wear sneakers at that program. They wear ties
too—don't they? Well, I ain't even got ties—I only got the one you lent me.

   I would've been there three weeks in the same gear. T-shirt and jeans. Es-
toy jodido como un bón! [I'm all fucked up like a bum!]

Philippe: *What the fuck kinda bullshit excuse are you talking about? Don't*
tell me you were thinking that shit. No one notices how people are dressed.

Primo: *Yo, Felipe, this is for real! Listen to me! I was thinking about that*
shit hard. Hell yeah!

   Hell yes they would notice, because I would notice if somebody's wearing a
fucked-up tie and shirt.

   I don't want to be in a program all abochornado *[bumlike]. I probably*
won't even concentrate, getting dissed, like . . . and being looked at like a
sucker. Dirty jeans . . . or like old jeans, because I would have to wear jeans,
'cause I only got one slack. Word though! I only got two dress shirts and one of
them is missing buttons.

   I didn't want to tell you about that because it's like a poor excuse, but that
was the only shit I was really thinking about. At the time I just said, "Well, I
just don't show up."

   And Felipe, I'm a stupid [very] skinny nigga'. So I have to be careful how
I dress, otherwise people will think I be on the stem [a crack addict who
smokes out of a glass-stem pipe].

Philippe: [nervously] *Oh shit. I'm even skinnier than you. People must*
think I'm a total drug addict.

Primo: *Don't worry. You're white.*

Obviously, the problem is deeper than not having enough money to buy
straight-world clothes. Racism and the other subtle badges of symbolic
power are expressed through wardrobes and body language. Ultimately,
Primo's biggest problem was that he had no idea of what clothes might be appropriate in the professional, service sector context. Like Caesar, he feared he
might appear to be a buffoon on parade on the days when he was trying to
dress up. He admitted that the precipitating factor in his decision not to go
back to the job training program was when he overheard someone accus-
ing Candy of "looking tacky" after she proudly inaugurated her new fancy
clothes at the first class. As a matter of fact, Primo had thought she had
looked elegant in her skintight, yellow jumpsuit when she came over to his
apartment to display her new outfit proudly to him and his mother before going to class.

Isolating oneself in inner-city street culture removes any danger of having to face the humiliations Candy, Caesar, or Primo inevitably confront when they venture out of their social circle to try to find legal employment. . . .

Conclusion

Ooh, Felipe! You make us sound like such sensitive crack dealers.
— CAESAR [COMMENTING ON THE MANUSCRIPT]

There is no panacea for the suffering and self-destruction of the protagonists in these pages. Solutions to inner-city poverty and substance abuse framed in terms of public policy often appear naive or hopelessly idealistic. Given the dimensions of structural oppression in the United States, it is atheoretical to expect isolated policy initiatives, or even short-term political reforms, to remedy the plight of the poor in U.S. urban centers in the short or medium term. Racism and class segregation in the United States are shaped in too complex a mesh of political-economic structural forces, historical legacies, cultural imperatives, and individual actions to be susceptible to simple solutions.

There are also the inevitable limits of political feasibility. For a number of complicated historical and ideological reasons the United States simply lacks the political will to address poverty in any concerted manner. Nevertheless, I hope my presentation of the experience of social marginalization in El Barrio, as seen through the struggles for dignity and survival of Ray's crack dealers and their families, contributes on a concrete practical level to calling attention to the tragedy of persistent poverty and racial segregation in the urban United States. I cannot resign myself to the terrible irony that the richest industrialized nation on earth, and the greatest world power in history, confines so many of its citizens to poverty and to prison. . . .

The increasing material and political powerlessness of the working poor in the United States needs to become a central concern. The concentration of poverty, substance abuse, and criminality within inner-city enclaves such as East Harlem is the product of state policy and free market forces that have inscribed spatially the rising levels of social inequality discussed earlier. More subtly, this urban decay expresses itself in the growing polarization around street culture in North America, giving rise to what some observers call a "crisis in U.S. race relations." Middle-class society and its elites increasingly have been able to disassociate themselves from the ethnically distinct, urban-based working poor and unemployed who inhabit the inner city. Budget cuts and fiscal austerity have accelerated the trend toward public sector breakdown in impoverished urban neighborhoods, while services improve, or at least stay the same, in Anglo-dominated, wealthy suburban communities.

The psychological-reductionist and cultural-essentialist analyses of social marginalization that pass for common sense in the United States frame solutions to racism and poverty around short-term interventions that target the "bad attitude" of individuals. The biggest sociological unit for most poverty policy intervention, for example, is the nuclear family. Job training programs emphasize attitude and personal empowerment. Seminars designed to promote multicultural sensitivity are fashionable in both public and private sector institutions. While these initiatives are not harmful, and might even help superficially on the margins, it is the institutionalized expression of racism—America's de facto apartheid and inner-city public sector breakdown—that government policy and private sector philanthropy need to address if anything is ever to change significantly in the long run.

In other words, to draw on a classic metaphor from sports, the United States needs to level its playing field. Concretely, this means that the garbage needs to be picked up, schools have to teach, and laws must be enforced, as effectively in Latino/a, African American, Asian, and Native American communities as they are in white, middle-class suburbs. There is nothing particularly complicated or subtle about remedying the unequal provision of public funds and services across class and ethnic lines. Hundreds of short-term policy and legal reforms immediately jump to mind: from tax reform—namely, taxing the home mortgages of the upper middle class and exempting the federal and state transfer benefits of the poor—to streamlining access to social welfare benefits and democratizing educational institutions—namely, universal affordable health care coverage, free day care, equalizing per capita funding for schools and universities, and so on.

One message the crack dealers communicated clearly to me is that they are not driven solely by simple economic exigency. Like most humans on earth, in addition to material subsistence, they are also searching for dignity and fulfillment. In the Puerto Rican context, this incorporates cultural definitions of *respeto* built around a personal concern for autonomy, self-assertion, and community within constantly changing social hierarchies of statuses based on kinship, age, and gender. Complex cultural and social dimensions that extend far beyond material and logistical requirements have to be addressed by poverty policies if the socially marginal in the United States are ever going to be able to demand, and earn, the respect that mainstream society needs to share with them for its own good. Specifically, this means evaluating how public policy initiatives and the more impersonal political economy forces of the larger society interact with rapidly changing cultural definitions of gender and family. Women, children, and the elderly constitute most of the poor in the United States. Public policy intervention consequently should prioritize the needs of women and children instead of marginalizing them. Most important, poor women should not be forced to seek desperate alliances with men in order to stay sheltered, fed, clothed, and healthy. Current welfare policy explicitly encourages mothers to seek men with unreported illegal income. . . .

The painful symptoms of inner-city apartheid will continue to produce record numbers of substance abusers, violent criminals, and emotionally disabled and angry youths if nothing is done to reverse the trends in the United States since the late 1960s around rising relative poverty rates and escalating ethnic and class segregation.

Given the bleak perspectives for policy reform at the federal level, on the one hand, or for political mobilization in the U.S. inner city, on the other, my most immediate goal in this research is to humanize the public enemies of the United States without sanitizing or glamorizing them. In documenting the depths of personal pain that are inherent to the experience of persistent poverty and institutional racism, I hope to contribute to our understanding of the fundamental processes and dynamics of oppression in the United States. More subtly, I also want to place drug dealers and street-level criminals into their rightful position within the mainstream of U.S. society. They are not "exotic others" operating in an irrational netherworld. On the contrary, they are "made in America." Highly motivated, ambitious inner-city youths have been attracted to the rapidly expanding, multibillion-dollar drug economy during the 1980s and 1990s precisely because they believe in Horatio Alger's version of the American Dream.

Like most other people in the United States, drug dealers and street criminals are scrambling to obtain their piece of the pie as fast as possible. In fact, in their pursuit of success they are even following the minute details of the classical Yankee model for upward mobility. They are aggressively pursuing careers as private entrepreneurs; they take risks, work hard, and pray for good luck. They are the ultimate rugged individualists braving an unpredictable frontier where fortune, fame, and destruction are all just around the corner, and where the enemy is ruthlessly hunted down and shot. In the specifically Puerto Rican context, resistance to mainstream society's domination and pride in street culture identity resonates with a reinvented vision of the defiant *jíbaro* who refused to succumb to elite society's denigration under Spanish and U.S. colonialism. The hyper-urban reconstruction of a hip-hop version of the rural *jíbaro* represents the triumph of a newly constituted Puerto Rican cultural assertion among the most marginalized members of the Puerto Rican diaspora. The tragedy is that the material base for this determined search for cultural respect is confined to the street economy.

At the same time, there is nothing exotically Puerto Rican about the triumphs and failures of the protagonists of this study. On the contrary, "mainstream America" should be able to see itself in the characters presented on these pages and recognize the linkages. The inner city represents the United States' greatest domestic failing, hanging like a Damocles sword over the larger society. Ironically, the only force preventing this suspended sword from falling is that drug dealers, addicts, and street criminals internalize their rage and desperation. They direct their brutality against themselves and their immediate community rather than against their structural oppressors. From a comparative perspective, and in a historical context, the painful and prolonged self-destruction of people like Primo, Caesar, Candy, and their children is cruel and unnecessary. There is no technocratic solution. Any long-term paths out of the quagmire will have to address the structural and political economic roots, as well as the ideological and cultural roots of social marginalization. The first step out of the impasse, however, requires a fundamental ethical and political reevaluation of basic socioeconomic models and human values.

22

FRATERNITIES AND RAPE ON CAMPUS

PATRICIA YANCEY MARTIN • ROBERT A. HUMMER

Conflict theory suggests that, in our society, who and what the label "deviant" is placed on is based primarily on relative power. Those who have more authority and control define what is "normal" and what is deviant. Moreover, conflict theorists argue that social norms, including laws, generally reflect the interests of the rich and powerful. Thus, historically, we have property laws to protect against the theft of property of the land-owning classes and domestic laws that protect the status of men, as patriarchs, within the family. The reading by Patricia Yancey Martin and Robert A. Hummer, originally published in 1989, exemplifies this process, in which the privileged attempt to socially construct deviance and crime to their advantage. In particular, Martin, a professor of sociology at Florida State University, and Hummer, an associate professor of sociology at University of Texas at Austin, analyze the social norms and rituals of male fraternities that contribute to the high incidence of violence against women on many college campuses.

R apes are perpetrated on dates, at parties, in chance encounters, and in specially planned circumstances. That group structure and processes, rather than individual values or characteristics, are the impetus for many rape episodes was documented by Blanchard (1959) [40] years ago (also see Geis 1971), yet sociologists have failed to pursue this theme (for an exception, see Chancer 1987). A review of research (Muehlenhard and Linton 1987) on sexual violence, or rape, devotes only a few pages to the situational

From *Gender & Society* 3, No. 4 (December 1989):457–73. Copyright © 1989 by Sociologists for Women in Society. Reprinted with the permission of Sage Publications, Inc.

contexts of rape events, and these are conceptualized as potential risk factors for individuals rather than qualities of rape-prone social contexts.

Many rapes, far more than come to the public's attention, occur in fraternity houses on college and university campuses, yet little research has analyzed fraternities at American colleges and universities as rape-prone contexts (cf. Ehrhart and Sandler 1985). Most of the research on fraternities reports on samples of individual fraternity men. One group of studies compares the values, attitudes, perceptions, family socioeconomic status, psychological traits (aggressiveness, dependence), and so on, of fraternity and nonfraternity men (Bohrnstedt 1969; Fox, Hodge, and Ward 1987; Kanin 1967; Lemire 1979; Miller 1973). A second group attempts to identify the effects of fraternity memberships over time on the values, attitudes, beliefs, or moral precepts of members (Hughes and Winston 1987; Marlowe and Auvenshine 1982; Miller 1973; Wilder, Hoyt, Doren, Hauck, and Zettle 1978; Wilder, Hoyt, Shurbeck, Wilder, and Carney 1986). With minor exceptions, little research addresses the group and organizational context of fraternities or the social construction of fraternity life (for exceptions, see Letchworth 1969; Longino and Kart 1973; Smith 1964).

Gary Tash, writing as an alumnus and trial attorney in his fraternity's magazine, claims that over 90 percent of all gang rapes on college campuses involve fraternity men (1988:2). Tash provides no evidence to substantiate this claim, but students of violence against women have been concerned with fraternity men's frequently reported involvement in rape episodes (Adams and Abarbanel 1988). Ehrhart and Sandler (1985) identify over 50 cases of gang rape on campus perpetrated by fraternity men, and their analysis points to many of the conditions that we discuss here. Their analysis is unique in focusing on conditions in fraternities that make gang rapes of women by fraternity men both feasible and probable. They identify excessive alcohol use, isolation from external monitoring, treatment of women as prey, use of pornography, approval of violence, and excessive concern with competition as precipitating conditions to gang rape (also see Merton 1985; Roark 1987).

The study reported here confirmed and complemented these findings by focusing on both conditions and processes. We examined dynamics associated with the social construction of fraternity life, with a focus on processes that foster the use of coercion, including rape, in fraternity men's relations with women. Our examination of men's social fraternities on college and university campuses as groups and organizations led us to conclude that fraternities are a physical and sociocultural context that encourages the sexual coercion of women. We make no claim that all fraternities are "bad" or that all fraternity men are rapists. Our observations indicated, however, that rape is especially probable in fraternities because of the kinds of organizations they are, the kinds of members they have, the practices their members engage in, and a virtual absence of university or community oversight. Analyses that lay blame for rapes by fraternity men on "peer pressure" are, we feel, overly simplistic (cf. Burkhart 1989; Walsh 1989). We suggest, rather, that fraternities create a sociocultural context in which the use of coercion in sexual relations with women is normative and in which the mechanisms to keep this pattern of behavior in check are minimal at best and absent at worst. We conclude that unless fraternities change in fundamental ways, little improvement can be expected.

Methodology

Our goal was to analyze the group and organizational practices and conditions that create in fraternities an abusive social context for women. We developed a conceptual framework from an initial case study of an alleged gang rape at Florida State University that involved four fraternity men and an 18-year-old coed. The group rape took place on the third floor of a fraternity house and ended with the "dumping" of the woman in the hallway of a neighboring fraternity house. According to newspaper accounts, the victim's blood-alcohol concentration, when she was discovered, was .349 percent, more than three times the legal limit for automobile driving and an almost lethal amount. One law enforcement officer reported that sexual intercourse occurred during the time the victim was unconscious: "She was in a life-threatening situation" (*Tallahassee Democrat* 1988b). When the victim was found, she was comatose and had suffered multiple scratches and abrasions. Crude words and a fraternity symbol had been written on her thighs (*Tampa Tribune* 1988). When law enforcement officials tried to investigate the case, fraternity members refused to cooperate. This led, eventually, to a five-year ban of the fraternity from campus by the university and by the fraternity's national organization.

In trying to understand how such an event could have occurred, and how a group of over 150 members (exact figures are unknown because the fraternity refused to provide a membership roster) could hold rank, deny knowledge of the event, and allegedly lie to a grand jury, we analyzed newspaper articles about the case and conducted open-ended interviews with a variety of respondents about the case and about fraternities, rapes, alcohol use, gender relations, and sexual activities on campus. Our data included over 100 newspaper articles on the initial gang rape case; open-ended interviews with Greek (social fraternity and sorority) and non-Greek (independent) students (N = 20); university administrators (N = 8, five men, three women); and alumni advisers to Greek organizations (N = 6). Open-ended interviews were held also with judges, public and private defense attorneys, victim advocates, and state prosecutors regarding the processing of sexual assault cases. Data were analyzed using the grounded theory method (Glaser 1978; Martin and Turner 1986). In the following analysis, concepts generated from the data analysis are integrated with the literature on men's social fraternities, sexual coercion, and related issues.

Fraternities and the Social Construction of Men and Masculinity

Our research indicated that fraternities are vitally concerned—more than with anything else—with masculinity (cf. Kanin 1967). They work hard to create a macho image and context and try to avoid any suggestion of "wimpishness," effeminacy, and homosexuality. Valued members display, or are willing to go along with, a narrow conception of masculinity that stresses competition, athleticism, dominance, winning, conflict, wealth, material possessions, willingness to drink alcohol, and sexual prowess vis-à-vis women.

Valued Qualities of Members

When fraternity members talked about the kind of pledges they prefer, a litany of stereotypical and narrowly masculine attributes and behaviors was recited and feminine or women-associated qualities and behaviors expressly denounced (cf. Merton 1985). Fraternities seek men who are "athletic," "big guys," good in intramural competition, "who can talk college sports." Males "who are willing to drink alcohol," "who drink socially," or "who can hold their liquor" are sought. Alcohol and activities associated with the recreational use of alcohol are cornerstones of fraternity social life. Nondrinkers are viewed with skepticism and rarely selected for membership.[1]

Fraternities try to avoid "geeks," nerds, and men said to give the fraternity a "wimpy" or "gay" reputation. Art, music, and humanities majors, majors in traditional women's fields (nursing, home economics, social work, education), men with long hair, and those whose appearance or dress violate current norms are rejected. Clean-cut, handsome men who dress well (are clean, neat, conforming, fashionable) are preferred. One sorority woman commented that "the top-ranking fraternities have the best-looking guys."

One fraternity man, a senior, said his fraternity recruited "some big guys, very athletic" over a two-year period to help overcome its image of wimpiness. His fraternity had won the interfraternity competition for highest grade-point average several years running but was looked down on as "wimpy, dancy, even gay." With their bigger, more athletic recruits, "our reputation improved; we're a much more recognized fraternity now." Thus a fraternity's reputation and status depends on members' possession of stereotypically masculine qualities. Good grades, campus leadership, and community service are "nice," but masculinity dominance—for example, in athletic events, physical size of members, athleticism of members—counts most.

Certain social skills are valued. Men are sought who "have good personalities," are friendly, and "have the ability to relate to girls" (cf. Longino and Kart 1973). One fraternity man, a junior, said: "We watch a guy [a potential pledge] talk to women. . . . We want guys who can relate to girls." Assessing a pledge's ability to talk to women is, in part, a preoccupation with homosexuality and a conscious avoidance of men who seem to have effeminate manners or qualities. If a member is suspected of being gay, he is ostracized and informally drummed out of the fraternity. A fraternity with a reputation as wimpy or tolerant of gays is ridiculed and shunned by other fraternities. Militant heterosexuality is frequently used by men as a strategy to keep each other in line (Kimmel 1987).

Financial affluence or wealth, a male-associated value in American culture, is highly valued by fraternities. In accounting for why the fraternity involved in the gang rape that precipitated our research project had been recognized recently as "the best fraternity chapter in the United States," a university official said: "They were good-looking, a big fraternity, had lots of BMWs [expensive, German-made automobiles]." After the rape, newspaper stories described the fraternity members' affluence, noting the high number of members who owned expensive cars (*St. Petersburg Times* 1988).

The Status and Norms of Pledgeship

A pledge (sometimes called an associate member) is a new recruit who occupies a trial membership status for a specific period of time. The pledge period (typically ranging from 10 to 15 weeks) gives fraternity brothers an opportunity to assess and socialize new recruits. Pledges evaluate the fraternity also and decide if they want to become brothers. The socialization experience is structured partly through assignment of a Big Brother to each pledge. Big Brothers are expected to teach pledges how to become a brother and to support them as they progress through the trial membership period. Some pledges are repelled by the pledging experience, which can entail physical abuse; harsh discipline; and demands to be subordinate, follow orders, and engage in demeaning routines and activities, similar to those used by the military to "make men out of boys" during boot camp.

Characteristics of the pledge experience are rationalized by fraternity members as necessary to help pledges unite into a group, rely on each other, and join together against outsiders. The process is highly masculinist in execution as well as conception. A willingness to submit to authority, follow orders, and do as one is told is viewed as a sign of loyalty, togetherness, and unity. Fraternity pledges who find the pledge process offensive often drop out. Some do this by openly quitting, which can subject them to ridicule by brothers and other pledges, or they may deliberately fail to make the grades necessary for initiation or transfer schools and decline to reaffiliate with the fraternity on the new campus. One fraternity pledge who quit the fraternity he had pledged described the experience during pledgeship as follows:

> This one guy was always picking on me. No matter what I did, I was wrong. One night after dinner, he and two other guys called me and two other pledges into the chapter room. He said, "Here X, hold this 25 pound bag of ice at arms' length 'til I tell you to stop." I did it even though my arms and hands were killing me.

When I asked if I could stop, he grabbed me around the throat and lifted me off the floor. I thought he would choke me to death. He cussed me and called me all kinds of names. He took one of my fingers and twisted it until it nearly broke. . . . I stayed in the fraternity for a few more days, but then I decided to quit. I hated it. Those guys are sick. They like seeing you suffer.

Fraternities' emphasis on toughness, withstanding pain and humiliation, obedience to superiors, and using physical force to obtain compliance contributes to an interpersonal style that deemphasizes caring and sensitivity but fosters intragroup trust and loyalty. If the least macho or most critical pledges drop out, those who remain may be more receptive to, and influenced by, masculinist values and practices that encourage the use of force in sexual relations with women and the covering up of such behavior (cf. Kanin 1967).

Norms and Dynamics of Brotherhood

Brother is the status occupied by fraternity men to indicate their relations to each other and their membership in a particular fraternity organization or group. Brother is a male-specific status; only males can become brothers, although women can become "Little Sisters," a form of pseudomembership. "Becoming a brother" is a rite of passage that follows the consistent and often lengthy display by pledges of appropriately masculine qualities and behaviors. Brothers have a quasi-familial relationship with each other, are normatively said to share bonds of closeness and support, and are sharply set off from nonmembers. Brotherhood is a loosely defined term used to represent the bonds that develop among fraternity members and the obligations and expectations incumbent upon them (cf. Marlowe and Auvenshine [1982] on fraternities' failure to encourage "moral development" in freshman pledges).

Some of our respondents talked about brotherhood in almost reverential terms, viewing it as the most valuable benefit of fraternity membership. One senior, a business-school major who had been affiliated with a fairly high-status fraternity throughout four years on campus, said:

Brotherhood spurs friendship for life, which I consider its best aspect, although I didn't see it that way when I joined. Brotherhood bonds and unites. It instills values of caring about one another, caring about community, caring about ourselves. The values and bonds [of brotherhood] continually develop over the four years [in college] while normal friendships come and go.

Despite this idealization, most aspects of fraternity practice and conception are more mundane. Brotherhood often plays itself out as an overriding concern with masculinity and, by extension, femininity. As a consequence, fraternities comprise collectivities of highly masculinized men with attitudinal qualities and behavior norms that predispose them to sexual coercion of women (cf. Kanin 1967; Merton 1985; Rapaport and Burkhart 1983). The norms of masculinity are complemented by conceptions of women and femininity that are equally distorted and stereotyped and that may enhance the probability of women's exploitation (cf. Ehrhart and Sandler 1985; Sanday 1981, 1986).

Practices of Brotherhood

Practices associated with fraternity brotherhood that contribute to the sexual coercion of women include a preoccupation with loyalty, group protection and secrecy, use of alcohol as a weapon, involvement in violence and physical force, and an emphasis on competition and superiority.

Loyalty, Group Protection, and Secrecy   Loyalty is a fraternity preoccupation. Members are reminded constantly to be loyal to the fraternity and to their brothers. Among other ways, loyalty is played out in practices of group protection and secrecy. The fraternity must be shielded from criticism. Members are admonished to avoid getting the fraternity into trouble and to bring all problems "to the chapter" (local branch of a national social fraternity) rather than to outsiders. Fraternities try to protect themselves from close scrutiny and criticism by the Interfraternity Council (a quasi-governing body composed of representatives from all social fraternities on campus), their fraternity's national office, university officials, law enforcement, the media, and the public. Protection of the fraternity often takes precedence over what is procedurally, ethically, or legally correct. Numerous examples were related to us of fraternity brothers' lying to outsiders to "protect the fraternity."

Group protection was observed in the alleged gang rape with which we began our study. Except for one brother, a rapist who turned state's evidence, the entire remaining fraternity membership was accused by university and criminal justice officials of lying to protect the fraternity. Members consistently failed to cooperate even though the alleged crimes were felonies, involved only four men (two of whom were not even members of the local chapter), and the victim of the crime nearly died. According to a grand jury's findings, fraternity officers repeatedly broke appointments with law enforcement officials, refused to provide police with a list of members, and refused to cooperate with police and prosecutors investigating the case (*Florida Flambeau* 1988).

Secrecy is a priority value and practice in fraternities, partly because full-fledged membership is premised on it (for confirmation, see Ehrhart and Sandler 1985; Longino and Kart 1973; Roark 1987). Secrecy is also a boundary-maintaining mechanism, demarcating in-group from out-group, us from them. Secret rituals, handshakes, and mottoes are revealed to pledge brothers as they are initiated into full brotherhood. Since only brothers are supposed to know a fraternity's secrets, such knowledge affirms membership in the fraternity and separates a brother from others. Extending secrecy tactics from protection of private knowledge to protection of the fraternity from criticism is a predictable development. Our interviews indicated that individual members knew the difference between right and wrong, but fraternity norms that emphasize loyalty, group protection, and secrecy often overrode standards of ethical correctness.

Alcohol as Weapon   Alcohol use by fraternity men is normative. They use it on weekdays to relax after class and on weekends to "get drunk," "get crazy," and "get laid." The use of alcohol to obtain sex from women is pervasive— in other words, it is used as a weapon against sexual reluctance. According to several fraternity men whom we interviewed, alcohol is the major tool used to gain sexual mastery over women (cf. Adams and Abarbanel 1988; Ehrhart and Sandler 1985). One fraternity man, a 21-year-old senior, de- scribed alcohol to gain sex as follows: "There are girls that you know will fuck, then some you have to put some effort into it. . . . You have to buy them drinks or find out if she's drunk enough."

A similar strategy is used collectively. A fraternity man said that at par- ties with Little Sisters: "We provide them with 'hunch punch' and things get wild. We get them drunk and most of the guys end up with one." "'Hunch punch,'" he said, "is a girls' drink made up of overproof alcohol and pow- dered Kool-Aid, no water or anything, just ice. It's very strong. Two cups will do a number on a female." He had plans in the next academic term to sur- reptitiously give hunch punch to women in a "prim and proper" sorority be- cause "having sex with prim and proper sorority girls is definitely a goal." These women are a challenge because they "won't openly consume alcohol and won't get openly drunk as hell." Their sororities have "standards com- mittees" that forbid heavy drinking and easy sex.

In the gang rape case, our sources said that many fraternity men on cam- pus believed the victim had a drinking problem and was thus an "easy make." According to newspaper accounts, she had been drinking alcohol on the evening she was raped; the lead assailant is alleged to have given her a bottle of wine after she arrived at his fraternity house. Portions of the rape occurred in a shower, and the victim was reportedly so drunk that her assailants had difficulty holding her in a standing position (*Tallahassee Democrat* 1988a). While raping her, her assailants repeatedly told her they were members of another fraternity under the apparent belief that she was too drunk to know the difference. Of course, if she was too drunk to know who they were, she was too drunk to consent to sex (cf. Allgeier 1986; Tash 1988).

One respondent told us that gang rapes were wrong and can get one ex- pelled, but he seemed to see nothing wrong in sexual coercion one-on-one. He seemed unaware that the use of alcohol to obtain sex from a woman is grounds for a claim that a rape occurred (cf. Tash 1988). Few women on cam- pus (who also may not know these grounds) report date rapes, however; so the odds of detection and punishment are slim for fraternity men who use al- cohol for "seduction" purposes (cf. Byington and Keeter 1988; Merton 1985).

Violence and Physical Force   Fraternity men have a history of violence (Ehr- hart and Sandler 1985; Roark 1987). Their record of hazing, fighting, property destruction, and rape has caused them problems with insurance companies (Bradford 1986; Pressley 1987). Two university officials told us that fraterni- ties "are the third riskiest property to insure behind toxic waste dumps and amusement parks." Fraternities are increasingly defendants in legal actions brought by pledges subjected to hazing (Meyer 1986; Pressley 1987) and by women who were raped by one or more members. In an alleged gang rape incident at another Florida university, prosecutors failed to file charges but the victim filed a civil suit against the fraternity nevertheless (*Tallahassee Democrat* 1989).

Competition and Superiority   Interfraternity rivalry fosters in-group identification and out-group hostility. Fraternities stress pride of membership and superiority over other fraternities as major goals. Interfraternity rivalries take many forms, including competition for desirable pledges, size of pledge class, size of membership, size and appearance of fraternity house, superiority in intramural sports, highest grade-point averages, giving the best parties, gaining the best or most campus leadership roles, and, of great importance, attracting and displaying "good looking women." Rivalry is particularly intense over members, intramural sports, and women (cf. Messner 1989).

Fraternities' Commodification of Women

In claiming that women are treated by fraternities as commodities, we mean that fraternities knowingly, and intentionally, *use* women for their benefit. Fraternities use women as bait for new members, as servers of brothers' needs, and as sexual prey.

Women as Bait   Fashionable attractive women help a fraternity attract new members. As one fraternity man, a junior, said, "They are good bait." Beautiful, sociable women are believed to impress the right kind of pledges and give the impression that the fraternity can deliver this type of woman to its members. Photographs of shapely, attractive coeds are printed in fraternity brochures and videotapes that are distributed and shown to potential pledges. The women pictured are often dressed in bikinis, at the beach, and are pictured hugging the brothers of the fraternity. One university official says such recruitment materials give the message: "Hey, they're here for you, you can have whatever you want," and "We have the best-looking women. Join us and you can have them too." Another commented: "Something's wrong when males join an all-male organization as the best place to meet women. It's so illogical."

Fraternities compete in promising access to beautiful women. One fraternity man, a senior, commented that "the attraction of girls [i.e., a fraternity's success in attracting women] is a big status symbol for fraternities." One university official commented that the use of women as a recruiting tool is so well entrenched that fraternities that might be willing to forgo it say they cannot afford to unless other fraternities do so as well. One fraternity man said, "Look, if we don't have Little Sisters, the fraternities that do will get all the good pledges." Another said, "We won't have as good a rush [the period during which new members are assessed and selected] if we don't have these women around."

In displaying good-looking, attractive, skimpily dressed, nubile women to potential members, fraternities implicitly, and sometimes explicitly, promise sexual access to women. One fraternity man commented that "part of what being in a fraternity is all about is the sex" and explained how his fraternity uses Little Sisters to recruit new members:

> We'll tell the sweetheart [the fraternity's term for Little Sister], "You're gorgeous; you can get him." We'll tell her to fake a scam and she'll hang all over him during a rush party, kiss him, and he thinks he's done wonderful and wants to join. The girls think it's great too. It's flattering for them.

Women as Servers   The use of women as servers is exemplified in the Little Sister program. Little Sisters are undergraduate women who are rushed and selected in a manner parallel to the recruitment of fraternity men. They are affiliated with the fraternity in a formal but unofficial way and are able, indeed required, to wear the fraternity's Greek letters. Little Sisters are not full-fledged fraternity members, however; and fraternity national offices and most universities do not register or regulate them. Each fraternity has an officer called Little Sister Chairman who oversees their organizations and activities. The Little Sisters elect officers among themselves, pay monthly dues to the fraternity, and have well-defined roles. Their dues are used to pay for the fraternity's social events, and Little Sisters are expected to attend and hostess fraternity parties and hang around the house to make it a "nice place to be." One fraternity man, a senior, described Little Sisters this way: "They are very social girls, willing to join in, be affiliated with the group, devoted to the fraternity." Another member, a sophomore, said: "Their sole purpose is social— attend parties, attract new members, and 'take care' of the guys."

Our observations and interviews suggested that women selected by fraternities as Little Sisters are physically attractive, possess good social skills, and are willing to devote time and energy to the fraternity and its members. One undergraduate woman gave the following job description for Little Sisters to a campus newspaper:

> It's not just making appearances at all the parties but entails many more responsibilities. You're going to be expected to go to all the intramural games to cheer the brothers on, support and encourage the pledges, and just be around to bring some extra life to the house. [As a Little Sister] you have to agree to take on a new responsibility other than studying to maintain your grades and managing to keep your checkbook from bouncing. You have to make time to be a part of the fraternity and support the brothers in all they do. (*The Tomahawk* 1988)

The title of Little Sister reflects women's subordinate status; fraternity men in a parallel role are called Big Brothers. Big Brothers assist a sorority primarily with the physical work of sorority rushes, which, compared to fraternity rushes, are more formal, structured, and intensive. Sorority rushes take place in the daytime and fraternity rushes at night so fraternity men are free to help. According to one fraternity member, Little Sister status is a benefit to women because it gives them a social outlet and "the protection of the brothers." The gender-stereotypic conceptions and obligations of these Little Sister and Big Brother statuses indicate that fraternities and sororities promote a gender hierarchy on campus that fosters subordination and dependence in women, thus encouraging sexual exploitation and the belief that it is acceptable.

Women as Sexual Prey   Little Sisters are a sexual utility. Many Little Sisters do not belong to sororities and lack peer support for refraining from unwanted sexual relations. One fraternity man (whose fraternity has 65 members and 85 Little Sisters) told us they had recruited "wholesale" in the prior year to "gets lots of new women." The structural access to women that the Little Sister program provides and the absence of normative supports for refusing fraternity members' sexual advances may make women in this program particularly susceptible to coerced sexual encounters with fraternity men.

Access to women for sexual gratification is a presumed benefit of fraternity membership, promised in recruitment materials and strategies and through brothers' conversations with new recruits. One fraternity man said: "We always tell the guys you get sex all the time, there's always new girls. . . . After I became a Greek, I found out I could be with females at will." A university official told us that, based on his observations, "no one [i.e., fraternity men] on this campus wants to have 'relationships.' They just want to have fun [i.e., sex]." Fraternity men plan and execute strategies aimed at obtaining sexual gratification, and this occurs at both individual and collective levels.

Individual strategies include getting a woman drunk and spending a great deal of money on her. As for collective strategies, most of our undergraduate interviewees agreed that fraternity parties often culminate in sex and that this outcome is planned. One fraternity man said fraternity parties often involve sex and nudity and can "turn into orgies." Orgies may be planned in advance, such as the Bowery Ball party held by one fraternity. A former fraternity member said of this party:

> *The entire idea behind this is sex. Both men and women come to the party wearing little or nothing. There are pornographic pinups on the walls and usually porno movies playing on the TV. The music carries sexual overtones. . . . They just get schnockered [drunk] and, in most cases, they also get laid.*

When asked about the women who come to such a party, he said: "Some Little Sisters just won't go. . . . The girls who do are looking for a good time, girls who don't know what it is, things like that."

Other respondents denied that fraternity parties are orgies but said that sex is always talked about among the brothers and they all know "who each other is doing it with." One member said that most of the time, guys have sex with their girlfriends "but with socials, girlfriends aren't allowed to come and it's their [members'] big chance [to have sex with other women]." The use of alcohol to help get women into bed is a routine strategy at fraternity parties.

Conclusions

In general, our research indicated that the organization and membership of fraternities contribute heavily to coercive and often violent sex. Fraternity houses are occupied by same-sex (all men) and same-age (late teens, early 20s) peers whose maturity and judgment are often less than ideal. Yet fraternity houses are private dwellings that are mostly off-limits to, and away from scrutiny of, university and community representatives, with the result that fraternity house events seldom come to the attention of outsiders. Practices associated with the social construction of fraternity brotherhood emphasize a macho conception of men and masculinity, a narrow, stereotyped conception of women and femininity, and the treatment of women as commodities. Other practices contributing to coercive sexual relations and the cover-up of rapes include excessive alcohol use, competitiveness, and normative support for deviance and secrecy (cf. Bogal-Allbritten and Allbritten 1985; Kanin 1967).

Some fraternity practices exacerbate others. Brotherhood norms require "sticking together" regardless of right or wrong; thus rape episodes are unlikely to be stopped or reported to outsiders, even when witnesses disapprove. The ability to use alcohol without scrutiny by authorities and alcohol's frequent association with violence, including sexual coercion, facilitates rape in fraternity houses. Fraternity norms that emphasize the value of maleness and masculinity over femaleness and femininity and that elevate the status of men and lower the status of women in members' eyes undermine perceptions and treatment of women as persons who deserve consideration and care (cf. Ehrhart and Sandler 1985; Merton 1985).

Androgynous men and men with a broad range of interests and attributes are lost to fraternities through their recruitment practices. Masculinity of a narrow and stereotypical type helps create attitudes, norms, and practices that predispose fraternity men to coerce women sexually, both individually and collectively (Allgeier 1986; Hood 1989; Sanday 1981, 1986). Male athletes on campus may be similarly disposed for the same reasons (Kirshenbaum 1989; Telander and Sullivan 1989).

Research into the social contexts in which rape crimes occur and the social constructions associated with these contexts illumine rape dynamics on campus. Blanchard (1959) found that group rapes almost always have a leader who pushes others into the crime. He also found that the leader's latent homosexuality, desire to show off to his peers, or fear of failing to prove himself a man are frequently an impetus. Fraternity norms and practices contribute to the approval and use of sexual coercion as an accepted tactic in relations with women. Alcohol-induced compliance is normative, whereas, presumably, use of a knife, gun, or threat of bodily harm would not be because the woman who "drinks too much" is viewed as "causing her own rape" (cf. Ehrhart and Sandler 1985).

Our research led us to conclude that fraternity norms and practices influence members to view the sexual coercion of women, which is a felony crime, as sport, a contest, or a game (cf. Sato 1988). This sport is played not between men and women but between men and men. Women are the pawns or prey in the interfraternity rivalry game; they prove that a fraternity is successful or prestigious. The use of women in this way encourages fraternity men to see women as objects and sexual coercion as sport. Today's societal norms support young women's right to engage in sex at their discretion, and coercion is unnecessary in a mutually desired encounter. However, nubile young women say they prefer to be "in a relationship" to have sex while young men say they prefer to "get laid" without a commitment (Muehlenhard and Linton 1987). These differences may reflect, in part, American puritanism and men's fears of sexual intimacy or perhaps intimacy of any kind. In a fraternity context, getting sex without giving emotionally demonstrates "cool" masculinity. More important, it poses no threat to the bonding and loyalty of the fraternity brotherhood (cf. Farr 1988). Drinking large quantities of alcohol before having sex suggests that "scoring" rather than intrinsic sexual pleasure is a primary concern of fraternity men.

Unless fraternities' compositions, goals, structures, and practices change in fundamental ways, women on campus will continue to be sexual prey for fraternity men. As all-male enclaves dedicated to opposing faculty and administration and to cementing in-group ties, fraternity members eschew any hint of homosexuality. Their version of masculinity transforms women, and men with womanly characteristics, into the out-group. "Womanly men" are ostracized; feminine women are used to demonstrate members' masculinity. Encouraging renewed emphasis on their founding values (Longino and Kart 1973), service orientation and activities (Lemire 1979), or members' moral development (Marlowe and Auvenshine 1982) will have little effect on fraternities' treatment of women. A case for or against fraternities cannot be made by studying individual members. The fraternity qua group and organization is at issue. Located on campus along with many vulnerable women, embedded in a sexist society, and caught up in masculinist goals, practices, and values, fraternities' violation of women—including forcible rape—should come as no surprise.

ENDNOTE

[1] Recent bans by some universities on open-keg parties at fraternity houses have resulted in heavy drinking before coming to a party and an increase in drunkenness

among those who attend. This may aggravate, rather than improve, the treatment of women by fraternity men at parties.

REFERENCES

Adams, Aileen and Gail Abarbanel. 1988. *Sexual Assault on Campus: What Colleges Can Do.* Santa Monica, CA: Rape Treatment Center.

Allgeier, Elizabeth. 1986. "Coercive versus Consensual Sexual Interactions." G. Stanley Hall Lecture to American Psychological Association Annual Meeting, Washington, DC, August.

Blanchard, W. H. 1959. "The Group Process in Gang Rape." *Journal of Social Psychology* 49:259–66.

Bogal-Allbritten, Rosemarie B. and William L. Allbritten. 1985. "The Hidden Victims: Courtship Violence among College Students." *Journal of College Student Personnel* 43:201–204.

Bohrnstedt, George W. 1969. "Conservatism, Authoritarianism and Religiosity of Fraternity Pledges." *Journal of College Student Personnel* 27:36–43.

Bradford, Michael. 1986. "Tight Market Dries Up Nightlife at University." *Business Insurance*, March 2, pp. 2, 6

Burkhart, Barry. 1989. Comments in Seminar on Acquaintance/Date Rape Prevention: A National Video Teleconference, February 2.

Burkhart, Barry R. and Annette L. Stanton. 1985. "Sexual Aggression in Acquaintance Relationships." Pp. 43–65 in *Violence in Intimate Relationships,* edited by G. Russell. Englewood Cliffs, NJ: Spectrum.

Byington, Diane B. and Karen W. Keeter. 1988. "Assessing Needs of Sexual Assault Victims on a University Campus." Pp. 23–31 in *Student Services: Responding to Issues and Challenges.* Chapel Hill: University of North Carolina Press.

Chancer, Lynn S. 1987. "New Bedford, Massachusetts, March 6, 1983–March 22, 1984: The 'Before and After' of a Group Rape." *Gender & Society* 1:239–60.

Ehrhart, Julie K. and Bernice R. Sandler. 1985. *Campus Gang Rape: Party Games?* Washington, DC: Association of American Colleges.

Farr, K. A. 1988. "Dominance Bonding through the Good Old Boys Sociability Network." *Sex Roles* 18:259–77.

Florida Flambeau. 1988. "Pike Members Indicted in Rape," May 19, pp. 1, 5.

Fox, Elaine, Charles Hodge, and Walter Ward. 1987. "A Comparison of Attitudes Held by Black and White Fraternity Members." *Journal of Negro Education* 56:521–34.

Geis, Gilbert. 1971. "Group Sexual Assaults." *Medical Aspects of Human Sexuality* 5:101–13.

Glaser, Barney G. 1978. *Theoretical Sensitivity: Advances in the Methodology of Grounded Theory.* Mill Valley, CA: Sociology Press.

Hood, Jane. 1989. "Why Our Society Is Rape-Prone." *New York Times,* May 16.

Hughes, Michael J. and Roger B. Winston, Jr. 1987. "Effects of Fraternity Membership on Interpersonal Values." *Journal of College Student Personnel* 45:405–11.

Kanin, Eugene J. 1967. "Reference Groups and Sex Conduct Norm Violations." *The Sociological Quarterly* 8:495–504.

Kimmel, Michael, ed. 1987. *Changing Men: New Directions in Research on Men and Masculinity.* Newbury Park, CA: Sage.

Kirshenbaum, Jerry. 1989. "Special Report, an American Disgrace: A Violent and Unprecedented Lawlessness Has Arisen among College Athletes in All Parts of the Country." *Sports Illustrated,* February 27, pp. 16–19.

Lemire, David. 1979. "One Investigation of the Stereotypes Associated with Fraternities and Sororities." *Journal of College Student Personnel* 37:54–57.

Letchworth, G. E. 1969. "Fraternities Now and in the Future." *Journal of College Student Personnel* 10:118–22.

Longino, Charles F., Jr. and Cary S. Kart. 1973. "The College Fraternity: An Assessment of Theory and Research." *Journal of College Student Personnel* 31:118–25.

Marlowe, Anne F. and Dwight C. Auvenshine. 1982. "Greek Membership: Its Impact on the Moral Development of College Freshmen." *Journal of College Student Personnel* 40:53–57.

Martin, Patricia Yancey and Barry A. Turner. 1986. "Grounded Theory and Organizational Research." *Journal of Applied Behavioral Science* 22:141–57.

Merton, Andrew. 1985. "On Competition and Class: Return to Brotherhood." *Ms,* September, pp. 60–65, 121–22.

Messner, Michael. 1989. "Masculinities and Athletic Careers." *Gender & Society* 3: 71–88.

Meyer, T. J. 1986. "Fight against Hazing Rituals Rages on Campuses." *Chronicle of Higher Education,* March 12, pp. 34–36.

Miller, Leonard D. 1973. "Distinctive Characteristics of Fraternity Members." *Journal of College Student Personnel* 31:126–28.

Muehlenhard, Charlene L. and Melaney A. Linton. 1987. "Date Rape and Sexual Aggression in Dating Situations: Incidence and Risk Factors." *Journal of Counseling Psychology* 34:186–96.

Pressley, Sue Anne. 1987. "Fraternity Hell Night Still Endures." *Washington Post,* August 11, p. B1.

Rapaport, Karen and Barry R. Burkhart. 1983. "Personality and Attitudinal Characteristics of Sexually Coercive College Males." *Journal of Abnormal Psychology* 93: 216–21.

Roark, Mary L. 1987. "Preventing Violence on College Campuses." *Journal of Counseling and Development* 65:367–70.

St. Petersburg Times. 1988. "A Greek Tragedy," May 29, pp. 1F, 6F.

Sanday, Peggy Reeves. 1981. "The Socio-Cultural Context of Rape: A Cross-Cultural Study." *Journal of Social Issues* 37:5–27.

———. 1986. "Rape and the Silencing of the Feminine." Pp. 84–101 in *Rape,* edited by S. Tomaselli and R. Porter. Oxford: Basil Blackwell.

Sato, Ikuya. 1988. "Play Theory of Delinquency: Toward a General Theory of 'Action.'" *Symbolic Interaction* 11:191–212.

Smith, T. 1964. "Emergence and Maintenance of Fraternal Solidarity." *Pacific Sociological Review* 7:29–37.

Tallahassee Democrat. 1988a. "FSU Fraternity Brothers Charged," April 27, pp. 1A, 12A.

———. 1988b. "FSU Interviewing Students about Alleged Rape," April 24, p. 1D.

———. 1989. "Woman Sues Stetson in Alleged Rape," March 19, p. 3B.

Tampa Tribune. 1988. "Fraternity Brothers Charged in Sexual Assault of FSU Coed," April 27, p. 6B.

Tash, Gary B. 1988. "Date Rape." *The Emerald of Sigma Pi Fraternity* 75(4):1–2.

Telander, Rick and Robert Sullivan. 1989. "Special Report, You Reap What You Sow." *Sports Illustrated,* February 27, pp. 20–34.

The Tomahawk. 1988. "A Look Back at Rush, a Mixture of Hard Work and Fun," April/May, p. 3D.

Walsh, Claire. 1989. Comments in Seminar on Acquaintance/Date Rape Prevention: A National Video Teleconference, February 2.

Wilder, David H., Arlyne E. Hoyt, Dennis M. Doren, William E. Hauck, and Robert D. Zettle. 1978. "The Impact of Fraternity and Sorority Membership on Values and Attitudes." *Journal of College Student Personnel* 36:445–49.

Wilder, David H., Arlyne E. Hoyt, Beth Shuster Shurbeck, Janet C. Wilder, and Patricia Imperatrice Carney. 1986. "Greek Affiliation and Attitude Change in College Students." *Journal of College Student Personnel* 44:510–19.

PART VI

Social Inequality

23

WHO RULES AMERICA?
The Corporate Community and the Upper Class

G. WILLIAM DOMHOFF

In the following four selections, we investigate social inequality that results from social class membership. *Social class* refers to categories of people who share common economic interests in a stratification system. Sociologists utilize various indicators to measure social class. For example, *socioeconomic status* (SES) is calculated using income, educational attainment, and occupational status. Sociologists also employ subjective indicators of social class, such as attitudes and values, class identification, and consumption patterns. This selection is by G. William Domhoff, a professor emeritus of psychology at the University of California, Santa Cruz, and it is taken from his 1998 book, *Who Rules America Now? Power and Politics in the Year 2000*. Using both objective and subjective indicators of social class status, Domhoff finds that in addition to wealth, the upper class shares a distinctive lifestyle through participation in various social institutions. Domhoff argues not only that there is a cohesive upper class in the United States, but also that the upper class has a disproportionate share of power through its control over economic and political decision making in this country.

Most Americans do not like the idea that there are social classes. Classes imply that people have relatively fixed stations in life. They fly in the face of beliefs about equality of opportunity and seem to ignore the evidence of upward social mobility. Even more, Americans tend to deny that social classes are based in wealth and occupational roles but then

From *Who Rules America: Power and Politics in the Year 2000*, Third Edition, by G. William Domhoff. Copyright © 1998 by Mayfield Publishing Company. Reprinted by permission of the publisher.

belie that denial through a fascination with rags-to-riches stories and the trappings of wealth. . . .

If there is an American upper class, it must exist not merely as a collection of families who feel comfortable with each other and tend to exclude outsiders from their social activities. It must exist as a set of interrelated social institutions. That is, there must be patterned ways of organizing the lives of its members from infancy to old age that create a relatively unique style of life, and there must be mechanisms for socializing both the younger generation and new adult members who have risen from lower social levels. If the class is a reality, the names and faces may change somewhat over the years, but the social institutions that underlie the upper class must persist with remarkably little change over several generations. This emphasis on the institutionalized nature of the upper class, which reflects a long-standing empirical tradition in studies of it, is compatible with the theoretical focus of the "new institutionalists" within sociology and political science.

Four different types of empirical studies establish the existence of an interrelated set of social institutions, organizations, and social activities. They are historical case studies, quantitative studies of biographical directories, open-ended surveys of knowledgeable observers, and interview studies with members of the upper-middle and upper classes. . . .

Prepping for Power

From infancy through young adulthood, members of the upper class receive a distinctive education. This education begins early in life in preschools that frequently are attached to a neighborhood church of high social status. Schooling continues during the elementary years at a local private school called a day school. During the adolescent years the student may remain at day school, but there is a strong chance that at least one or two years will be spent away from home at a boarding school in a quiet rural setting. Higher education will take place at one of a small number of heavily endowed private colleges and universities. Large and well-known Ivy League schools in the East and Stanford in the West head the list, followed by smaller Ivy League schools in the East and a handful of other small private schools in other parts of the country. Although some upper-class children may attend public high school if they live in a secluded suburban setting, or go to a state university if there is one of great esteem and tradition in their home state, the system of formal schooling is so insulated that many upper-class students never see the inside of a public school in all their years of education.

This separate educational system is important evidence for the distinctiveness of the mentality and lifestyle that exists within the upper class because schools play a large role in transmitting the class structure to their students. Surveying and summarizing a great many studies on schools in general, sociologist Randall Collins concludes: "Schools primarily teach vocabulary and inflection, styles of dress, aesthetic tastes, values and manners."[1] His statement takes on greater significance for studies of the upper class when it is added that only 1 percent of American teenagers attend independent private high schools of an upper-class nature.[2]

The training of upper-class children is not restricted to the formal school setting, however. Special classes, and even tutors, are a regular part of their extracurricular education. This informal education usually begins with dancing classes in the elementary years, which are seen as important for learning proper manners and the social graces. Tutoring in a foreign language may begin in the elementary years, and there are often lessons in horseback riding and music as well. The teen years find the children of the upper class in summer camps or on special travel tours, broadening their perspectives and polishing their social skills.

The linchpins in the upper-class educational system are the dozens of boarding schools founded in the last half of the nineteenth and the early part of the twentieth centuries. Baltzell concludes that these schools became "surrogate families" that played a major role "in creating an upper-class subculture on almost a national scale in America."[3] The role of boarding schools in providing connections to other upper-class social institutions is also important. As one informant explained to Ostrander in her interview study of upper-class women: "Where I went to boarding school, there were girls from all over the country, so I know people from all over. It's helpful when you move to a new city and want to get invited into the local social club."[4]

It is within these few hundred schools that are consciously modeled after their older and more austere British counterparts that a distinctive style of life is inculcated through such traditions as the initiatory hazing of beginning students, the wearing of school blazers or ties, compulsory attendance at chapel services, and participation in esoteric sports such as squash and crew. Even a different terminology is adopted to distinguish these schools from public schools. The principal is a headmaster or rector, the teachers are sometimes called masters, and the students are in forms, not grades. Great emphasis is placed on the building of "character." The role of the school in preparing the future leaders of America is emphasized through the speeches of the headmaster and the frequent mention of successful alumni. Thus, boarding schools are in many ways the kind of highly effective socializing agent that sociologist Erving Goffman calls "total institutions," isolating their members from the outside world and providing them with a set of routines and traditions that encompass most of their waking hours.[5] The end result is a feeling of separateness and superiority that comes from having survived a rigorous education. As a retired business leader told one of my research assistants: "At school we were made to feel somewhat better [than other people] because of our class. That existed, and I've always disliked it intensely. Unfortunately, I'm afraid some of these things rub off on one."[6]

Almost all graduates of private secondary schools go on to college, and almost all do so at prestigious universities. Graduates of the New England boarding schools, for example, historically found themselves at one of four large Ivy League universities: Harvard, Yale, Princeton, and Columbia. . . . Now many upper-class students attend a select handful of smaller private liberal arts colleges, most of which are in the East, but there are a few in the South and West as well.

Graduates of private schools outside of New England most frequently attend a prominent state university in their area, but a significant minority go to Eastern Ivy League and top private universities in other parts of the country. . . . A majority of private school graduates pursue careers in business, finance, or corporate law. For example, a classification of the occupations of a sample of the graduates of four private schools—St. Mark's, Groton, Hotchkiss, and Andover—showed that the most frequent occupation for all but the Andover graduates was some facet of finance and banking. Others became presidents of medium-size businesses or were partners in large corporate law firms. A small handful went to work as executives for major national corporations.[7] . . .

Although finance, business, and law are the most typical occupations of upper-class males, there is no absence of physicians, architects, museum officials, and other professional occupations. This fact is demonstrated most systematically in Baltzell's study of Philadelphia: 39 percent of the Philadelphia architects and physicians listed in *Who's Who* for the early 1940s were also listed in the *Social Register,* as were 35 percent of the museum officials. These figures are close to the 51 percent for lawyers and the 42 percent for businessmen, although they are far below the 75 percent for bankers— clearly the most prestigious profession in Philadelphia at that time.[8] . . .

From kindergarten through college, then, schooling is very different for members of the upper class and it teaches them to be distinctive in many ways. In a country where education is highly valued and nearly everyone attends public schools, this private system benefits primarily members of the upper class and provides one of the foundations for the old-boy and old-girl networks that will be with them throughout their lives.

Social Clubs

Just as private schools are a pervasive feature in the lives of upper-class children, so, too, are private social clubs a major point of orientation in the lives of upper-class adults. These clubs also play a role in differentiating members of the upper class from other members of society. According to Baltzell, "the club serves to place the adult members of society and their families within the social hierarchy." He quotes with approval the suggestion by historian Crane Brinton that the club "may perhaps be regarded as taking the place of those extensions of the family, such as the clan and the brotherhood, which have disappeared from advanced societies."[9] Conclusions similar to Baltzell's resulted from an interview study in Kansas City: "Ultimately, say upper-class Kansas Citians, social standing in their world reduces to one issue: where does an individual or family rank on the scale of private club memberships and informal cliques?"[10]

The clubs of the upper class are many and varied, ranging from family-oriented country clubs and downtown men's and women's clubs to highly specialized clubs for yacht owners, gardening enthusiasts, and fox hunters. Many families have memberships in several different types of clubs, but the days when most of the men by themselves were in a half dozen or more clubs faded before World War II. Downtown men's clubs originally were places for having lunch and dinner, and occasionally for attending an evening performance or a weekend party. But as upper-class families deserted the city for large suburban estates, a new kind of club, the country club, gradually took over some of these functions. The downtown club became almost entirely a luncheon club, a site to hold meetings, or a place to relax on a free afternoon. The country club, by contrast, became a haven for all members of the family. It offered social and sporting activities ranging from dances, parties, and banquets to golf, swimming, and tennis. Special group dinners were often arranged for all members on Thursday night—the traditional maid's night off across the United States.

Sporting activities are the basis for most of the specialized clubs of the upper class. The most visible are the yachting and sailing clubs, followed by the clubs for lawn tennis or squash. The most exotic are the several dozen fox hunting clubs. They have their primary strongholds in rolling countrysides from southern Pennsylvania down into Virginia, but they exist in other parts of the country as well. Riding to hounds in scarlet jackets and black boots, members of the upper class sustain over 130 hunts under the banner of the Masters of Fox Hounds Association. The intricate rituals and grand feasts accompanying the event, including the Blessing of the Hounds by an Episcopal bishop in the Eastern hunts, go back to the eighteenth century in the United States.[11]

Initiation fees, annual dues, and expenses vary from a few thousand dollars in downtown clubs to tens of thousands of dollars in some country clubs, but money is not the primary barrier in gaining membership to a club. Each club has a very rigorous screening process before accepting new members. Most require nomination by one or more active members, letters of recommendation from three to six members, and interviews with at least some members of the membership committee. Names of prospective members are sometimes posted in the clubhouse, so all members have an opportunity to make their feelings known to the membership committee. Negative votes by two or three members of what is typically a ten- to twenty-person committee often are enough to deny admission to the candidate. The carefulness with which new members are selected extends to a guarding of club membership lists, which are usually available only to club members. Older membership lists are sometimes given to libraries by members or their surviving spouses, but for most clubs there are no membership lists in the public domain.

Not every club member is an enthusiastic participant in the life of the club. Some belong out of tradition or a feeling of social necessity. One woman told Ostrander the following about her country club: "We don't feel we should withdraw our support even though we don't go much." Others mentioned a feeling of social pressure: "I've only been to [the club] once this year. I'm really a loner, but I feel I have to go and be pleasant even though I don't want to." Another volunteered: "I think half the members go because they like it and half because they think it's a social necessity." [12]

People of the upper class often belong to clubs in several cities, creating a nationwide pattern of overlapping memberships. These overlaps provide evidence for social cohesion within the upper class. An indication of the nature and extent of this overlapping is revealed by sociologist Philip Bonacich's study of membership lists for twenty clubs in several major cities across the country, including the Links in New York, the Century Association in New York, the Duquesne in Pittsburgh, the Chicago in Chicago, the Pacific Union in San Francisco, and the California in Los Angeles. Using his own original clustering technique based on Boolean algebra, his study revealed there was sufficient overlap among eighteen of the twenty clubs to form three regional groupings and a fourth group that provided a bridge between the two largest regional groups. The several dozen men who were in three or more of the clubs—most of them very wealthy people who also sat on several corporate boards—were especially important in creating the overall pattern. At the same time, the fact that these clubs often have from 1,000 to 2,000 members makes the percentage of overlap within this small number of clubs relatively small, ranging from as high as 20 to 30 percent between clubs in the same city to as low as 1 or 2 percent in clubs at opposite ends of the country. [13]

The overlap of this club network with corporate boards of directors provides evidence for the intertwining of the upper class and corporate community. In one study, the club memberships of the chairs and outside directors of the twenty largest industrial corporations were counted. The overlaps with upper-class clubs in general were ubiquitous, but the concentration of directors in a few clubs was especially notable. At least one director from twelve of the twenty corporations was a member of the Links Club, which Baltzell calls "the New York rendezvous of the national corporate establishment." [14] Seven of General Electric's directors were members, as were four from Chrysler, four from Westinghouse, three from IBM, and two from U.S. Steel. In addition to the Links, several other clubs had directors from four or more corporations. A study I did using membership lists from eleven prestigious clubs in different parts of the country confirmed and extended these findings. A majority of the top twenty-five corporations in every major sector of the economy had directors in at least one of these clubs, and several had many more. . . .

There seems to be a great deal of truth to the earlier-cited suggestion by Crane Brinton that clubs may function within the upper class the way that the clan or brotherhood does in tribal societies. With their restrictive membership policies, initiatory rituals, private ceremonials, and great emphasis on tradition, clubs carry on the heritage of primitive secret societies. They create among their members an attitude of prideful exclusiveness that contributes greatly to an in-group feeling and a sense of fraternity within the upper class.

In concluding this discussion of . . . [social clubs and] the intersection of the upper class and corporate community, it needs to be stressed that the [social club] is not a place of power. No conspiracies are hatched there, nor anywhere else. Instead, it is a place where powerful people relax, make new acquaintances, and enjoy themselves. It is primarily a place of social bonding. The main sociological function of . . . [social] clubs is stated by sociologist Thomas Powell, based on his own interview study of members in upper-class clubs:

> The clubs are a repository of the values held by the upper-level prestige groups in the community and are a means by which these values are transferred to the business environment. The clubs are places in which the beliefs, problems, and values of the industrial organization are discussed and related to the other elements in the larger community. Clubs, therefore, are not only effective vehicles of informal communication, but also valuable centers where views are presented, ideas are modified, and new ideas emerge. Those in the interview sample were appreciative of this asset; in addition, they considered the club as a valuable place to combine social and business contacts.[15]

The Female Half of the Upper Class

During the late nineteenth and early twentieth centuries, women of the upper class carved out their own distinct roles within the context of male domination in business, finance, and law. They went to separate private schools, founded their own social clubs, and belonged to their own volunteer associations. As young women and party goers, they set the fashions for society. As older women and activists, they took charge of the nonprofit social welfare and cultural institutions of the society, serving as fund-raisers, philanthropists, and directors in a manner parallel to what their male counterparts did in business and politics. To prepare themselves for their leadership roles, in 1901 they created the Junior League to provide internships, role models, mutual support, and training in the management of meetings.

Due to the general social changes of the 1960s—and in particular the revival of the feminist movement—the socialization of wealthy young women has changed somewhat in recent decades. Many private schools are now co-educational. Their women graduates are encouraged to go to major four-year colleges rather than finishing schools. Women of the upper class are more likely to have careers; there are already two or three examples of women who have risen to the top of their family's business. They are also more likely to serve on corporate boards. Still, due to its emphasis on tradition, there may be even less gender equality in the upper class than there is in the professional stratum; it is not clear how much more equality will be attained.

The female half of the upper class has been studied by several sociologists. Their work provides an important window into the upper class and class consciousness in general as well as a portrait of the socialization of well-born women. But before focusing on their work, it is worthwhile to examine one unique institution of the upper class that has not changed very much in its long history—the debutante party that announces a young woman's coming of age and eligibility for marriage. It contains general lessons on class consciousness and the difficulties of maintaining traditional socializing institutions in a time of social unrest.

The Debutante Season

The debutante season is a series of parties, teas, and dances that culminates in one or more grand balls. It announces the arrival of young women of the upper class into adult society with the utmost of formality and elegance. These highly expensive rituals—in which great attention is lavished on every detail of the food, decorations, and entertainment—have a long history in the upper class. They made their first appearance in Philadelphia in 1748 and Charleston, South Carolina, in 1762, and they vary only slightly from city to city across the country. They are a central focus of the Christmas social season just about everywhere, but in some cities debutante balls are held in the spring as well.

Dozens of people are involved in planning the private parties that most debutantes have before the grand ball. Parents, with the help of upper-class women who work as social secretaries and social consultants, spend many hours with dress designers, caterers, florists, decorators, bandleaders, and champagne importers, deciding on just the right motif for their daughter's coming out. Most parties probably cost between $25,000 and $75,000, but sometimes the occasion is so extraordinary that it draws newspaper attention. Henry Ford II spent $250,000 on a debutante party for one of his daughters, hiring a Paris designer to redo the Country Club of Detroit in an eighteenth-century chateau motif and flying in 2 million magnolia boughs from Mississippi to cover the walls of the corridor leading to the reception room. A Texas oil and real estate family chartered a commercial jet airliner for a party that began in Dallas and ended with an all-night visit to the clubs in the French Quarter of New Orleans.[16]

The debutante balls themselves are usually sponsored by local social clubs. Sometimes there is an organization whose primary purpose is the selection of debutantes and the staging of the ball, such as the Saint Cecelia Society in Charleston, South Carolina, or the Allegro Club in Houston, Texas. Adding to the solemnity of the occasion, the selection of the season's debutantes is often made by the most prominent upper-class males in the city, often through such secret societies as the Veiled Prophet in St. Louis or the Mardi Gras krewes in New Orleans.

Proceeds from the balls are usually given to a prominent local charity sponsored by members of the upper class. "Doing something for charity makes the participants feel better about spending," explains Mrs. Stephen Van Rensselear Strong, a social press agent in New York and herself a member of the upper class.[17] It also makes at least part of the expense of the occasion tax deductible.

Evidence for the great traditional importance attached to the debut is to be found in the comments Ostrander received from women who thought the whole process unimportant but made their daughters go through it anyhow: "It think it's passé, and I don't care about it, but it's just something that's done," explained one woman. Another commented: "Her father wanted her to do it. We do have a family image to maintain. It was important to the grandparents, and I felt it was an obligation to her family to do it." When people begin to talk about doing something out of tradition or to uphold an image, Ostrander suggests, then the unspoken rules that dictate class-oriented behavior are being revealed through ritual behavior.[18]

Despite the great importance placed on the debut by upper-class parents, the debutante season came into considerable disfavor among young women as the social upheavals of the late 1960s and early 1970s reached their climax. This decline reveals that the reproduction of the upper class as a social class is an effort that must be made with each new generation. Although enough young women participated to keep the tradition alive, a significant minority refused to participate, which led to the cancellation of some balls and the curtailment of many others. Stories appeared on the women's pages across the country telling of debutantes who thought the whole process was "silly" or that the money should be given to a good cause. By 1973, however, the situation began to change again, and by the mid-1970s things were back to normal.[19]

The decline of the debutante season and its subsequent resurgence in times of domestic tranquility reveal very clearly that one of its latent functions is to help perpetuate the upper class from generation to generation. When the underlying values of the class were questioned by a few of its younger members, the institution went into decline. Attitudes toward such social institutions as the debutante ball are one indicator of whether adult members of the upper class have succeeded in insulating their children from the rest of society.

The Role of Volunteer

The most informative and intimate look at the adult lives of traditional upper-class women is provided in three different interview and observation studies, one on the East Coast, one in the Midwest, and one on the West

Coast. They reveal the women to be both powerful and subservient, playing decision-making roles in numerous cultural and civic organizations but also accepting traditional roles at home vis-à-vis their husbands and children. By asking the women to describe a typical day and to explain which activities were most important to them, sociologists Arlene Daniels, Margot McLeod, and Susan Ostrander found that the role of community volunteer is a central preoccupation of upper-class women, having significance as a family tradition and as an opportunity to fulfill an obligation to the community. One elderly woman involved for several decades in both the arts and human services told Ostrander: "If you're privileged, you have a certain responsibility. This was part of my upbringing; it's a tradition, a pattern of life that my brothers and sisters do too." [20]

This volunteer role is institutionalized in the training programs and activities of a variety of service organizations, especially the Junior League, which is meant for women between 20 and 40 years of age, including some upwardly mobile professional women. "Volunteerism is crucial and the Junior League is the quintessence of volunteer work," said one woman. "Everything the League does improves the situation but doesn't rock the boat. It fits into existing institutions." [21]

Quite unexpectedly, Ostrander found that many of the women serving as volunteers, fund-raisers, and board members for charitable and civic organizations viewed their work as a protection of the American way of life against the further encroachment of government into areas of social welfare. Some even saw themselves as bulwarks against socialism. "There must always be people to do volunteer work," one said. "If you have a society where no one is willing, then you may as well have communism where it's all done by the government." Another commented: "It would mean that the government would take over, and it would all be regimented. If there are no volunteers, we would live in a completely managed society which is quite the opposite to our history of freedom." Another equated government support with socialism: "You'd have to go into government funds. That's socialism. The more we can keep independent and under private control, the better it is." [22]

Despite this emphasis on volunteer work, the women placed high value on family life. They arranged their schedules to be home when children came home from school (thirty of the thirty-eight in Ostrander's study had three or more children), and they emphasized that their primary concern was to provide a good home for their husbands. Several wanted to have greater decision-making power over their inherited wealth, but almost all wanted to take on the traditional roles of wife and mother, at least until their children were grown.

In recent years, thanks to the pressures on corporations from the women's movement, upper-class women have expanded their roles to include corporate directorships. A study of women in the corporate community by former sociologist Beth Ghiloni, now a corporate executive, found that 26 percent of all women directors had upper-class backgrounds, a figure very similar to overall findings for samples of predominantly male directors. The figure was even higher, about 71 percent, for the one-fifth of directors who described themselves as volunteers before joining corporate boards. Many of these women told Ghiloni that their contacts with male corporate leaders on the boards of women's colleges and cultural organizations led to their selection as corporate directors.[23]

Women of the upper class are in a paradoxical position. They are subordinate to male members of their class, but they nonetheless exercise important class power in some institutional arenas. They may or may not be fully satisfied with their ambiguous power status, but they bring an upper-class, antigovernment perspective to their exercise of power. There is thus class solidarity between men and women toward the rest of society. Commenting on the complex role of upper-class women, feminist scholar Catherine Stimson draws the following stark picture: "First they must do to class what gender has done to their work—render it invisible. Next, they must maintain the same class structure they have struggled to veil."[24]

Marriage and Family Continuity

The institution of marriage is as important in the upper class as it is in any level of American society, and it does not differ greatly from other levels in its patterns and rituals. Only the exclusive site of the occasion and the lavishness of the reception distinguish upper-class marriages. The prevailing wisdom within the upper class is that children should marry someone of their own social class. The women interviewed by Ostrander, for example, felt that marriage was difficult enough without differences in "interests" and "background," which seemed to be the code words for class in discussions of marriage. Marriages outside the class were seen as likely to end in divorce.[25]

The original purpose of the debutante season was to introduce the highly sheltered young women of the upper class to eligible marriage partners. It was an attempt to corral what Baltzell calls "the democratic whims of romantic love," which "often play havoc with class solidarity."[26] But the day when the debut could play such a role was long past, even by the 1940s. The function of directing romantic love into acceptable channels was taken over by fraternities and sororities, singles-only clubs, and exclusive summer resorts.

However, in spite of parental concerns and institutionalized efforts to provide proper marriage partners, some upper-class people marry members of the upper-middle and middle classes. Although there are no completely satisfactory studies, and none that are very recent, what information is available suggests that members of the upper class are no more likely to marry within their class than people of other social levels. The most frequently cited evidence on upper-class marriage patterns appears as part of biographical studies of prominent families. Though these studies demonstrate that a great many marriages take place within the class—and often between scions of very large fortunes—they also show that some marriages are to sons and daughters of middle-class professionals and managers. No systematic conclusions can be drawn from these examples.

Wedding announcements that appear in major newspapers provide another source of evidence on this question. In a study covering prominent wedding stories on the society pages on Sundays in June for two different years one decade apart, it was found that 70 percent of the grooms and 84 percent of the brides had attended a private secondary school. Two-thirds of the weddings involved at least one participant who was listed in the *Social Register,* with both bride and groom listed in the *Social Register* in 24 percent of the cases.[27] However, those who marry far below their station may be less likely to have wedding announcements prominently displayed, so such studies must be interpreted with caution.

A study that used the *Social Register* as its starting point may be indicative of rates of intermarriage within the upper class, but it is very limited in its scope and therefore can only be considered suggestive. It began with a compilation of all the marriages listed in the Philadelphia *Social Register* for 1940 and 1960. Since the decision to list these announcements may be a voluntary one, a check of the marriage announcements in the *Philadelphia Bulletin* for those years was made to see if there were any marriages involving listees in the *Social Register* that had not been included, but none was found. One in every three marriages for 1940 and one in five for 1961 involved partners who were both listed in the *Social Register.* When private-school attendance and social club membership as well as the *Social Register* were used as evidence for upper-class standing, the rate of intermarriage averaged 50 percent for the two years. This figure is very similar to that for other social levels.[28]

The general picture for social class and marriage in the United States is suggested in a statistical study of neighborhoods and marriage patterns in the San Francisco area. Its results are very similar to those of the Philadelphia study using the *Social Register.* Of eighty grooms randomly selected from the highest-level neighborhoods, court records showed that 51 percent married brides of a comparable level. The rest married women from middle-level neighborhoods; only one or two married women from lower-level residential areas. Conversely, 63 percent of eighty-one grooms from the lowest-level neighborhoods married women from comparable areas, with under 3 percent having brides from even the lower end of the group of top neighborhoods. Completing the picture, most of the eighty-two men from middle-level areas married women from the same types of neighborhoods, but about 10 percent married into higher-level neighborhoods. Patterns of intermarriage, then, suggest both stability and some upward mobility through marriage into the upper class.[29]

Turning now to the continuity of the upper class, there is evidence that it is very great from generation to generation. This finding conflicts with the oft-repeated folk wisdom that there is a large turnover at the top of the American social ladder. Once in the upper class, families tend to stay there even as they are joined in each generation by new families and by middle-class brides and grooms who marry into their families. One study demonstrating this point began with a list of twelve families who were among the top wealthholders in Detroit for 1860, 1892, and 1902. After demonstrating their high social standing as well as their wealth, it traced their Detroit-based descendants to 1970. Nine of the twelve families still had members in the Detroit upper class; members from six of the families were directors of top corporations in the city. The study cast light on some of the reasons why the continuity is not even greater. One of the top wealthholders of 1860 had only one child, who in turn had no children. Another family dropped out of sight after the six children of the original 1860 wealthholder's only child went to court to divide the dwindling estate of $250,000 into six equal parts. A third family persisted into a fourth generation of four great-granddaughters, all of whom married outside of Detroit.[30] . . .

Tracing the families of the steel executives into the twentieth century, John Ingham determined that most were listed in the *Social Register*, were members of the most exclusive social clubs, lived in expensive neighborhoods, and sent their children to Ivy League universities. He concludes that "there has been more continuity than change among the business elites and upper classes in America," and he contrasts his results with the claims made by several generations of impressionistic historians that there has been a decline of aristocracy, the rise of a new plutocracy, or a passing of the old order.[31] . . .

It seems likely, then, that the American upper class is a mixture of old and new members. There is both continuity and social mobility, with the newer members being assimilated into the lifestyle of the class through participation in the schools, clubs, and other social institutions described [here]. There may be some tensions between those newly arrived and those of established status—as novelists and journalists love to point out—but what they have in common soon outweighs their differences.[32]

ENDNOTES

[1] Randall Collins, "Functional and Conflict Theories of Educational Stratification," *American Sociological Review* 36 (1971):1010.

[2] "Private Schools Search for a New Role," *National Observer* (August 26, 1968), p. 5. For an excellent account of major boarding schools, see Peter Cookson and Caroline Hodge Persell, *Preparing for Power: America's Elite Boarding Schools* (New York: Basic Books, 1985).

[3] E. Digby Baltzell, *Philadelphia Gentlemen: The Making of a National Upper Class* (Glencoe, IL: Free Press, 1958), p. 339.

[4] Susan Ostrander, *Women of the Upper Class* (Philadelphia: Temple University Press, 1984), p. 85.

[5] Erving Goffman, *Asylums* (Chicago: Aldine, 1961).

[6] Interview conducted for G. William Domhoff by research assistant Deborah Samuels, February 1975; see also Gary Tamkins, "Being Special: A Study of the Upper Class" (Ph.D. Dissertation, Northwestern University, 1974).

[7] Steven Levine, "The Rise of the American Boarding Schools" (Senior Honors Thesis, Harvard University, 1975), pp. 128–30.

[8] Baltzell, *Philadelphia Gentlemen*, pp. 51–65.

[9] Baltzell, *Philadelphia Gentlemen*, p. 373.

[10] Richard P. Coleman and Lee Rainwater, *Social Standing in America* (New York: Basic Books, 1978), p. 144.

[11] Sophy Burnham, *The Landed Gentry* (New York: G. P. Putnam's Sons, 1978).

[12] Ostrander, *Women of the Upper Class*, p. 104.

[13] Philip Bonacich and G. William Domhoff, "Latent Classes and Group Membership," *Social Networks* 3 (1981).

[14] G. William Domhoff, *Who Rules America?* (Englewood Cliffs, NJ: Prentice-Hall, 1967), p. 26; E. Digby Baltzell, *The Protestant Establishment*, op. cit., p. 371.

[15] Thomas Powell, *Race, Religion, and the Promotion of the American Executive* (Columbus: Ohio State University Press, 1969), p. 50.

[16] Gay Pauley, "Coming-Out Party: It's Back in Style," *Los Angeles Times*, March 13, 1977, section 4, p. 22; "Debs Put Party on Jet," *San Francisco Chronicle*, December 18, 1965, p. 2.

[17] Pauley, "Coming-Out Party."

[18] Ostrander, "Upper-Class Women: Class Consciousness As Conduct and Meaning," *Women of the Upper Class*, pp. 93–94; Ostrander, *Women of the Upper Class*, pp. 89–90.

[19] "The Debut Tradition: A Subjective View of What It's All About," *New Orleans Times-Picayune*, August 29, 1976, section 4, p. 13; Tia Gidnick, "On Being 18 in '78: Deb Balls Back in Fashion," *Los Angeles Times*, November 24, 1978, part 4, p. 1; Virginia Lee Warren, "Many Young Socialites Want Simpler Debutante Party, or None," *New York Times*, July 2, 1972, p. 34; Mary Lou Loper, "The Society Ball: Tradition in an Era of Change," *Los Angeles Times*, October 28, 1973, part 4, p. 1.

[20] Ostrander, *Women of the Upper Class*, pp. 128–29. For three other fine accounts of the volunteer work of upper-class women, see Arlene Daniels, *Invisible Careers* (Chicago: University of Chicago Press, 1988); Margot MacLeod, "Influential Women Volunteers" (paper presented to the meetings of the American Sociological Association, San Antonio, August 1984); and Margot MacLeod, "Older Generation, Younger Generation: Transition in Women Volunteers' Lives" (unpublished manuscript, 1987). For women's involvement in philanthropy and on the boards of nonprofit organizations, see Teresa Odendahl, *Charity Begins at Home: Generosity and Self-Interest among the Philanthropic Elite* (New York: Basic Books, 1990), and Teresa Odendahl and Michael O'Neill, eds., *Women and Power in the Nonprofit Sector* (San Francisco: Jossey-Bass, 1994). For in-depth interviews of both women and men philanthropists, see Francie Ostrower, *Why the Wealthy Give: The Culture of Elite Philanthropy* (Princeton, NJ: Princeton University Press, 1995).

[21] Ostrander, *Women of the Upper Class*, pp. 113, 115.

[22] Ostrander, "Upper-Class Women," p. 84; Ostrander, *Women of the Upper Class*, pp. 132–37.

[23] Beth Ghiloni, "New Women of Power" (Ph.D. Dissertation, University of California, Santa Cruz, 1986), pp. 122, 159.

[24] Daniels, *Invisible Careers*, p. x.

[25] Ostrander, *Women of the Upper Class*, pp. 85–88.

[26] Baltzell, *Philadelphia Gentlemen*, p. 26.

[27] Paul M. Blumberg and P. W. Paul, "Continuities and Discontinuities in Upper-Class Marriages," *Journal of Marriage and the Family*, vol. 37, no. 1 (February 1975): 63–77; David L. Hatch and Mary A. Hatch, "Criteria of Social Status As Derived from Marriage Announcements in the *New York Times*," *American Sociological Review* 12 (August 1947):396–403.

[28] Lawrence Rosen and Robert R. Bell, "Mate Selection in the Upper Class," *Sociological Quarterly* 7 (Spring 1966):157–66. I supplemented the original study by adding the information on schools and clubs.

[29] Robert C. Tryon, "Identification of Social Areas by Cluster Analysis: A General Method with an Application to the San Francisco Bay Area," *University of California Publications in Psychology* 8 (1955); Robert C. Tryon, "Predicting Group Differences in Cluster Analysis: The Social Areas Problem," *Multivariate Behavioral Research* 2 (1967):453–75.

[30] T. D. Schuby, "Class Power, Kinship, and Social Cohesion: A Case Study of a Local Elite," *Sociological Focus* 8, no. 3 (August 1975):243–55; Donald Davis, "The Price of Conspicuous Production: The Detroit Elite and the Automobile Industry, 1900–1933," *Journal of Social History* 16 (1982):21–46.

[31] John Ingham, *The Iron Barons* (Westport, CT: Greenwood Press, 1978), pp. 230–31. For the continuity of a more general sample of wealthy families, see Michael Allen, *The Founding Fortunes* (New York: Truman Talley Books, 1987).

[32] For further evidence of the assimilation of new members into the upper class, see the study of the social affiliations and attitudes of the successful Jewish business owners who become part of the upper class by Richard L. Zweigenhaft and G. William Domhoff, *Jews in the Protestant Establishment* (New York: Praeger, 1982).

24

BLACK WEALTH/WHITE WEALTH
A New Perspective on Racial Inequality

MELVIN L. OLIVER • THOMAS M. SHAPIRO

As G. William Domhoff argues in the previous selection, social classes do exist in America, and class distinctions can be observed through a variety of objective and subjective indicators. To understand social class relationships fully, however, sociologists also must examine racial-ethnic differences in the indicators of socioeconomic status. For example, data show persistent

Copyright © 1995 Routledge, Inc. From *Black Wealth/White Wealth* by Melvin L. Oliver and Thomas M. Shapiro. Reproduced by permission of Routledge, Inc. part of the Taylor & Francis Group.

wealth discrepancies between African Americans and European Americans with similar achievements and credentials. Sociologists Melvin L. Oliver and Thomas M. Shapiro examine this racial inequality in wealth in their book *Black Wealth/White Wealth: A New Perspective on Racial Inequality* (1995). In the excerpt that follows, Oliver and Shapiro analyze state policies that currently and historically have curtailed opportunities for wealth accumulation among African Americans.

A frican Americans are vastly overrepresented among those Americans whose lives are the most economically and socially distressed. As William Julius Wilson has argued in *The Truly Disadvantaged*, "the most disadvantaged segments of the black urban community" have come to make up the majority of "that heterogeneous grouping of families and individuals who are outside the mainstream of the American occupational system," and who are euphemistically called the underclass.[1] With little or no access to jobs, trapped in poor areas with bad schools and little social and economic opportunity, members of the underclass resort to crime, drugs, and other forms of aberrant behavior to make a living and eke some degree of meaning out of their materially impoverished existence. Douglas Massey and Nancy Denton's *American Apartheid* has reinforced in our minds the crucial significance of racial segregation, which Lawrence Bobo calls the veritable "structural linchpin" of American racial inequality.[2]

These facts should not be in dispute. What is in dispute is our understanding of the source of such resounding levels of racial inequality. What factors were responsible for their creation and what are the sources of their continuation? Sociologists and social scientists have focused on either race or class or on some combination or interaction of the two as overriding factors responsible for racial inequality.

A focus on race suggests that race has had a unique cultural meaning in American society wherein blacks have been oppressed in such a way as to perpetuate their inferiority and second-class citizenship. Race in this context has a socially constructed meaning that is acted on by whites to purposefully limit and constrain the black population. The foundation of this social construction is the ideology of racism. Racism is a belief in the inherent inferiority of one race in relation to another. Racism both justifies and dictates the actions and institutional decisions that adversely affect the target group.[3]

Class explanations emphasize the relational positioning of blacks and whites in society and the differential access to power that accrues to the status of each group. Those classes with access to resources through the ownership or control of capital (in the Marxian variant) or through the occupational hierarchy (in the Weberian variant) are able to translate these resources into policies and structures through their access to power. In some cases this can be seen in the way in which those who control the economy also control the polity. In other cases it can be observed in the way in which institutional elites control institutions. In any case the class perspective emphasizes the relative positions of blacks and whites with respect to the ownership and control of the means of production and to access to valued occupational niches, both historically and contemporaneously. Because blacks have traditionally had access to few of these types of valued resources, they share an interest with the other have-nots. As Raymond Franklin notes in *Shadows of Race and Class*, "Ownership carries with it domination; its absence leads to subordination."[4] The subordinated and unequal status of African Americans, in the class perspective, grows out of the structured class divisions between blacks and a small minority of resource-rich and powerful whites.

Each of these perspectives has been successfully applied to understanding racial inequality. However, each also has major failings. The emphasis on race creates problems of evidence. Especially in the contemporary period, as William Wilson notes in *The Declining Significance of Race*, it is difficult to trace the enduring existence of racial inequality to an articulated ideology of racism. The trail of historical evidence proudly left in previous periods is made less evident by heightened sensitivity to legal sanctions and racial civility in language. Thus those who still emphasize race in the modern era speak of covert racism and use as evidence racial disparities in income, jobs, and housing. In fact, however, impersonal structural forces whose racial motivation cannot be ascertained are often the cause of the black disadvantage that observers identify. Likewise, class perspectives usually wash away any reference to race.[5] Moreover, the class-based analysis that blacks united with low-income white workers and other disadvantaged groups would be the most likely source of collective opposition to current social economic arrangements has given way to continued estrangement between these groups.[6] The materialist perspective that policy should address broad class groups as opposed to specific racial groups leaves the unique historical legacy of race untouched.

Despite these weaknesses it is imperative that race and class factors be taken into consideration in any attempt to understand contemporary racial inequality. It is clear, however, that a singular focus on one as opposed to another is counterproductive. Take, for example, earnings inequality. As economists assert, earnings are affected today more by class than by racial factors. Human capital attributes (such as education, experience, skills, etc.) that may result from historical disadvantages play an important role in the earnings gap between blacks and whites. But because of the unique position of black Americans, earnings must be viewed in relation to joblessness. If you do not have a job, you have no earnings. Here it is clear that race and class are important. As structural changes in the economy have occurred, blacks have been disproportionately disadvantaged. Such structural changes as the movement of entry-level jobs outside of the central city, the change in the economy from goods to service production, and the shift to higher skill levels have created a jobless black population.[7] Furthermore, increasing numbers of new entrants into the labor market find low-skill jobs below poverty wages that do not support a family. Nevertheless, race is important as well. Evidence from employers shows that negative racial attitudes about black workers are still motivating their hiring practices, particularly in reference to central-city blacks and in the service economy. In service jobs nonblacks are preferred over blacks, particularly black men, a preference that contributes to the low wages blacks earn, to high rates of joblessness, and thus to earnings inequality.[8]

Because of the way in which they reveal the effect of historical factors on contemporary processes, racial differences in wealth provide an important means of combining race and class arguments about racial inequality. We therefore turn to a theoretical discussion of wealth and race that develops aspects of traditional race and class arguments in an attempt to illuminate the processes that have led to wealth disparities between black and white Americans.

Toward a Sociology of Race and Wealth

A sociology of race and wealth must go beyond the traditional analysis of wealth that economists have elaborated. Economists begin with the assumption that wealth is a combination of inheritance, earnings, and savings and is enhanced by prudent consumption and investment patterns over a person's lifetime. Of course, individual variability in any of these factors depends on a whole set of other relationships that are sociologically relevant. Obviously one's inheritance depends on the family into which one is born. If one's family of origin is wealthy, one's chances of accumulating more wealth in a lifetime are greater. Earnings, the economists tell us, are a function of the productivity of our human capital: our education, experience, and skills. Since these are, at least in part, dependent on an investment in training activities, they can be acquired by means of inherited resources. Savings are a function of both our earning power and our consumption patterns. Spendthrifts will have little or no disposable income to save, while those who are frugal can find ways to put money aside. Those with high levels of human capital, who socially interact in the right circles, and who have knowledge of investment opportunities, will increase their wealth substantially more during their lifetime, than will those who are only thrifty. And since money usually grows over time, the earlier one starts and the longer one's money is invested, the more wealth one will be able to amass. Economists therefore explain differences in wealth accumulation by pointing to the lack of resources that blacks inherit compared to whites, their low investment in human capital, and their extravagant patterns of consumption.

Sociologists do not so much disagree with the economists' emphasis on these three factors and their relationship to human capital in explaining black-white differences in wealth; rather, they are concerned that economists have not properly appreciated the social context in which the processes in question take place. Quite likely, formal models would accurately predict wealth differences. However, in the real world, an emphasis on these factors isolated from the social context misses the underlying reasons for why whites and blacks have displayed such strong differences in their ability to generate wealth. The major reason that blacks and whites differ in their ability to accumulate wealth is not only that they come from different class backgrounds or that their consumption patterns are different or that they fail to save at the same rate but that the structure of investment opportunity that blacks and whites face has been dramatically different. Work and wages play a smaller role in the accumulation of wealth than the prevailing discourse admits.

Blacks and whites have faced an opportunity to create wealth that has been structured by the intersection of class and race. Economists rightly note that blacks' lack of desirable human capital attributes places them at a disadvantage in the wealth accumulation process. However, those human capital deficiencies can be traced, in part, to barriers that denied blacks access to quality education, job training opportunities, jobs, and other work-related factors. Below we develop three concepts—the racialization of the state, the economic detour, and the sedimentation of racial inequality—to help us situate the distinct structures of investment opportunity that blacks and whites have faced in their attempts to generate wealth.

Racialization of the State

The context of one's opportunity to acquire land, build community, and generate wealth has been structured particularly by state policy. Slavery itself, the most constricting of social systems, was a result of state policy that gave blacks severely limited economic rights. Slaves were by law not able to own property or accumulate assets.[9] In contrast, no matter how poor whites were, they had the right—if they were males, that is—if not the ability, to buy land, enter into contracts, own businesses, and develop wealth assets that could build equity and economic self-sufficiency for themselves and their families. Some argue that it was the inability to participate in and develop a habit of savings during slavery that directly accounts for low wealth development among blacks today. Using a cultural argument, they assert that slaves developed a habit of excessive consumerism and not one of savings and thrift. This distorts the historical reality, however. While slaves were legally not able to amass wealth they did, in large numbers, acquire assets through thrift, intelligence, industry, and their owners' liberal paternalism. These assets were used to buy their own and their loved ones' freedom, however, and thus did not form the core of a material legacy that could be passed from generation to generation. Whites could use their wealth for the future; black slaves' savings could only buy the freedom that whites took for granted.

Slavery was only one of the racialized state policies that have inhibited the acquisition of assets for African Americans. . . . The homestead laws that opened up the East during colonial times and West during the nineteenth century created vastly different opportunities for black and white settlers. One commentator even suggests land grants "allowed three-fourths of America's colonial families to own their own farms."[10] Black settlers in California, the "Golden State," found that their claims for homestead status were not legally enforceable. Thus African Americans were largely barred from taking advantage of the nineteenth-century federal land-grant program.[11]

A centerpiece of the New Deal social legislation and a cornerstone of the modern welfare state, the old-age insurance program of the Social Security Act of 1935 virtually excluded African Americans and Latinos, for it exempted agricultural and domestic workers from coverage and marginalized low-wage workers.[12] As Gwendolyn Mink shows in "The Lady and the Tramp," men's benefits were tied to wages, military service, and unionism rather than to need or any notion of equality. Thus blacks were disadvantaged in New Deal legislation because they were historically less well paid, less fully employed, disproportionately ineligible for military service, and less fully unionized than white men. Minority workers were covered by social security and New Deal labor policies if employed in eligible occupations and if they earned the minimum amount required. Because minority wages were so low, minority workers fell disproportionately below the threshold for coverage in comparison to whites. In 1935, for example, 42 percent of black workers in occupations covered by social insurance did not earn enough to qualify for benefits compared to 22 percent for whites.[13]

Not only were blacks initially disadvantaged in their eligibility for social security, but they have disproportionately paid more into the system and received less. Because social security contributions are made on a flat rate and black workers earn less, as Jill Quadagno explains in *The Color of Welfare,* "black men were taxed on 100 percent of their income, on average, while white men earned a considerable amount of untaxed income." Black workers also earn lower retirement benefits. And benefits do not extend as long as for whites because their life span is shorter. Furthermore, since more black women are single, divorced, or separated, they cannot look forward to sharing a spouse's benefit. As Quadagno notes, again, the tax contributions of black working women "subsidize the benefits of white housewives."[14] In many ways social security is a model state program that allows families to preserve assets built over a lifetime. For African Americans, however, it is a different kind of model of state bias. Initially built on concessions made to white racial privilege in the South, the social security program today is a system in which blacks pay more to receive less. It is a prime example of how the political process and state policy build opportunities for asset accumulation sharply skewed along racial lines.

We now turn to three other instruments of state policy that we feel have been central to creating structured opportunities for whites to build assets while significantly curtailing access to those same opportunities among blacks. Sometimes the aim was blatantly racial; sometimes the racial intention was not clear. In both instances, however, the results have been explicitly racial. They are the Federal Housing Authority; the Supplementary Social Security Act, which laid the foundation for our present day Aid to Families with Dependent Children (AFDC); and the United States tax code. In each case, state policies have created differential opportunities for blacks and whites to develop disposable income and to generate wealth.

FHA

As noted in earlier research, the development of low-interest, long-term mortgages backed by the federal government marked the appearance of a crucial opportunity for the average American family to generate a wealth stake. The purchase of a home has now become the primary mechanism for generating wealth. However, the FHA's conscious decision to channel loans away from the central city and to the suburbs has had a powerful effect on the creation of segregated housing in post–World War II America. George Lipsitz reports in "The Possessive Investment in Whiteness" that in the Los Angeles area of Boyle Heights, FHA appraisers denied home loans to prospective buyers because the neighborhood was "a melting pot area literally honeycombed with diverse and subversive elements." [15] Official government policy supported the prejudiced attitudes of private finance companies, realtors, appraisers, and a white public resistant to sharing social space with blacks.

The FHA's official handbook even went so far as to provide a model "restrictive covenant" that would pass court scrutiny to prospective white homebuyers. Such policies gave support to white neighborhoods like those in East Detroit in 1940. Concerned that blacks would move in, the Eastern Detroit Realty Association sponsored a luncheon on "the benefits of an improvement association" where the speaker, a lawyer, lectured on how "to effect legal restrictions against the influx of colored residents into white communities." [16] He went on to present the elements needed to institute a legally enforceable restrictive covenant for "a district of two miles square." Such a task was too much for one man and would require an "organization" that could mobilize and gain the cooperation of "everyone in a subdivision." Imagine the hurdles that are placed in the path of blacks' attempts to move into white neighborhoods when communities, realtors, lawyers, and the federal government are all wholly united behind such restrictions!

Restrictive covenants and other "segregation markers" have been ruled unconstitutional in a number of important court cases. But the legacy of the FHA's contribution to racial residential segregation lives on in the inability of blacks to incorporate themselves into integrated neighborhoods in which the equity and demand for their homes is maintained. This is seen most clearly in the fact that black middle-class homeowners end up with less valuable homes even when their incomes are similar to those of whites. When black middle-class families pursue the American Dream in white neighborhoods adjacent to existing black communities, a familiar process occurs. As one study explains it:

> White households will begin to move out and those neighborhoods will tend to undergo complete racial transition or to "tip." Typically, when the percentage of blacks in a neighborhood increases to a relatively small amount, 10 to 20 percent, white demand for housing in the neighborhood will fall off and the neighborhood will tip toward segregation.[17]

Even though the neighborhood initially has high market value generated by the black demand for houses, as the segregation process kicks in, housing values rise at a slower rate. By the end of the racial transition, housing prices have declined as white homeowners flee. Thus middle-class blacks encounter lower rates of home appreciation than do similar middle-class whites in all-white communities. As Raymond Franklin notes in *Shadows of Race and Class*, this is an example of how race and class considerations are involved in producing black-white wealth differentials. The "shadow" of class creates a situation of race. To quote Franklin:

> In sum, because there is a white fear of being inundated with lower-class black "hordes" who lack market capacities, it becomes necessary to prevent the entry of middle-class black families who have market capacities. In this way, middle-class blacks are discriminated against for purely racial reasons. . . . Given the "uncertainty inherent in racial integration and racial transition," white families—unwilling to risk falling property values—leave the area. This, of course, leads to falling prices, enabling poorer blacks' to enter the neighborhood "until segregation becomes complete."[18]

The impact of race and class is also channeled through institutional mechanisms that help to destabilize black communities. Insurance redlining begins to make it difficult and/or expensive for homes and businesses to secure coverage. City services begin to decline, contributing to blight. As the community declines, it becomes the center for antisocial activities: drug dealing, hanging out, and robbery and violence.[19] In this context the initial investment that the middle-class black family makes either stops growing or grows at a rate that is substantially lower than the rate at which a comparable investment made by a similarly well-off, middle-class white in an all-white community would gain in value. Racialized state policy contributed to this pattern, and the pattern continues unabated today.

AFDC

Within the public mind and according to the current political debate, AFDC has become synonymous with "welfare," even though it represents less than 10 percent of all assistance for the poor.[20] The small sums paid to women and their children are designed not to provide families a springboard for their future but to help them survive in a minimal way from day to day. When the initial legislation for AFDC was passed, few of its supporters envisioned a program that would serve large numbers of African American women and their children; the ideal recipient, according to Michael Katz in *In the Shadow of the Poor House,* "was a white widow and her young children." Until the mid-1960s, states enforced this perception through the establishment of eligibility requirements that disproportionately excluded black women and their children. Southern states routinely deemed black women and their children as "unsuitable" for welfare by way of demeaning home inspections and searches. Northern states likewise created barriers that were directly targeted at black-female-headed families. They participated in "midnight raids" to discover whether a "man was in the house" or recomputed budgets to find clients ineligible and keep them off the rolls. Nonetheless, by the mid-1960s minorities were disproportionately beneficiaries of AFDC, despite intentions to the contrary. In 1988 while blacks and Hispanics made up only 44 percent of all women who headed households, they constituted 55 percent of all AFDC recipients.[21]

In exchange for modest and sometimes niggardly levels of income support, women must go through an "assets test" before they are eligible. Michael Sherraden describes it this way in his *Assets and the Poor:*

> The assets test requires that recipients have no more than minimal assets (usually $1,500, with home equity excluded) in order to become or remain eligible for the program. The asset test effectively prohibits recipients from accumulating savings.[22]

As a consequence, women enter welfare on the economic edge. They deplete almost all of their savings in order to become eligible for a program that will not provide more than a subsistence living. What little savings remain are usually drawn down to meet routine shortfalls and emergencies. The result is that AFDC has become for many women, especially African American women, a state-sponsored policy to encourage and maintain asset poverty.

To underscore the impact of AFDC's strictures, let us draw the distinction between this program and Supplementary Security Income (SSI), a program that provides benefits for women and children whose spouses have died or become disabled after paying into social security. In contrast to AFDC benefits, SSI payments are generous. More important perhaps, eligibility for SSI does not require drawing down a family's assets as part of a "means test." The result, which is built into the structure of American welfare policy, is that "means tested" programs like AFDC and "non-means tested" social insurance programs like social security and SSI, in Michael Katz's words, have "preserved class distinctions" and "in no way redistribute income."[23] It is also an example of how the racialization of the state preserves and broadens the already deep wealth divisions between black and white.

The Internal Revenue Code

A substantial portion of state expenditures take the form of tax benefits, or "fiscal welfare." These benefits are hidden in the tax code as taxes individuals do not have to pay because the government has decided to encourage certain types of activity and behavior and not others. In *America: Who Really Pays the Taxes?* Donald Barlett and James Steele write that one of the most cherished privileges of the very rich and powerful resides in their ability to influence the tax code for their own benefit by protecting capital assets. Tax advantages may come in the form of different rates on certain types of income, tax deferral, or deductions, exclusions, and credits. Many are asset-based: if you own certain assets, you receive a tax break. In turn, these tax breaks directly help people accumulate financial and real assets. They benefit not only the wealthy but the broad middle class of homeowners and pension holders as well. More important, since blacks have fewer assets to begin with, the effect of the tax code's "fiscal welfare" is to limit the flow of tax relief to blacks and to redirect it to those who already have assets. The seemingly race-neutral tax code thus generates a racial effect that deepens rather than equalizes the economic gulf between blacks and whites.

Two examples will illustrate how the current functioning of the tax code represents yet another form of the "racialization of state policy." The *lower tax rates on capital gains* and the *deduction for home mortgages and real estate taxes,* we argue, flow differentially to blacks and whites because of the fact that blacks generally have fewer and different types of assets than whites with similar incomes.

For most of our nation's tax history, the Internal Revenue Code has encouraged private investment by offering lower tax rates for income gained through "capital assets." This policy exists to encourage investment and further asset accumulation, not to provide more spendable income. In 1994, earned income in the top bracket was taxed at 39.6 percent, for example, while capital gains were taxed at 24 percent, a figure that can go as low as 14 percent. One has to be networked with accountants, tax advisers, investors, partners, and friends knowledgeable about where to channel money to take advantage of these breaks. Capital gains may be derived from the sale of stocks, bonds, commodities, and other assets. In 1989 the IRS reported that $150.2 billion in capital gains income was reported by taxpayers.[24] While this sounds like a lot of capital gains for everyone to divvy up, the lion's share (72 percent) went to individuals and families earning more than $100,000 yearly. These families represented only 1 percent of all tax filers. The remaining $42 billion in capital gains income was reported by only 7.2 million people with incomes of under $100,000 per year. This group represented only 6 percent of tax filers. Thus for more than nine of every ten tax filers (93 percent) no capital gains income was reported. Clearly then, the tax-reduction benefits on capital gains income are highly concentrated among the nation's wealthiest individuals and families. Thus it would follow that blacks, given their lower incomes and fewer assets, would be much less likely than whites to gain the tax advantage associated with capital gains. The black disadvantage becomes most obvious when one compares middle-class and higher-income blacks to whites at a similar level of earnings. Despite comparable incomes, middle-class blacks have fewer of their wealth holdings in capital-producing assets than similarly situated whites. Our data show that among high-earning families ($50,000 a year or more) 17 percent of whites' assets are in stocks, bonds, and mortgages versus 5.4 percent for blacks. Thus while race-neutral in intent, the current tax policy on capital gains provides disproportionate benefits to high-income whites, while limiting a major tax benefit to practically all African Americans.

Accessible to a larger group of Americans are those tax deductions, exclusions, and deferrals that the IRS provides to homeowners. Four IRS-mandated benefits can flow from home ownership: (1) the home mortgage interest deduction; (2) the deduction for local real estate taxes; (3) the avoidance of taxes on the sale of a home when it is "rolled over" into another residence; and (4) the one-time permanent exclusion of up to $125,000 of profit on the sale of a home after the age of fifty-five. Put quite simply, since blacks are less likely to own homes, they are less likely to be able to take advantage of these benefits. Furthermore, since black homes are on average less expensive than white homes, blacks derive less benefit than whites when they do utilize these tax provisions. And finally, since most of the benefits in question here are available only when taxpayers itemize their deductions, there is a great deal of concern that many black taxpayers may not take advantage of the tax breaks they are eligible for because they file the short tax form. The stakes here are very high. The subsidy that goes to homeowners in the form of tax deductions for mortgage interest and property taxes alone comes to $54 billion, about $20 billion of which goes to the top 5 percent of taxpayers.[25]

These examples illustrate how the U.S. tax code channels benefits and encourages property and capital asset accumulation differentially by race. They are but a few of several examples that could have been used. Tax provisions pertaining to inheritance, gift income, alimony payments, pensions and Keogh accounts, and property appreciation, along with the marriage tax and the child-care credit, on their face are not color coded, yet they carry with them the potential to channel benefits away from most blacks and toward some whites. State policy has racialized the opportunities for the development of wealth, creating and sustaining the existing patterns of wealth inequality and extending them into the future. . . .

The Sedimentation of Racial Inequality

The disadvantaged status of contemporary African Americans cannot be divorced from the historical processes that undergird racial inequality. The past has a living effect on the present. We argue that the best indicator of this sedimentation of racial inequality is wealth. Wealth is one indicator of material disparity that captures the historical legacy of low wages, personal and organizational discrimination, and institutionalized racism. The low levels of wealth accumulation evidenced by current generations of black Americans best represent the position of blacks in the stratificational order of American society.

Each generation of blacks generally began life with few material assets and confronted a world that systematically thwarted any attempts to economically better their lives. In addition to the barriers that we have just described in connection with the racialization of state policy and the economic detour, blacks also faced other major obstacles in their quest for economic security. In the South, for example, as W. E. B. Du Bois notes in *Black Reconstruction in America,* blacks were tied to a system of peonage that kept them in debt virtually from cradle to grave. Schooling was segregated and unequally funded. Blacks in the smokestack industries of the North and the South were paid less and assigned to unskilled and dirty jobs.[26] The result was that generation after generation of blacks remained anchored to the lowest economic status in American society. The effect of this "generation after generation" of poverty and economic scarcity for the accumulation of wealth has been to "sediment" this kind of inequality into the social structure.

The sedimentation of inequality occurred because blacks had barriers thrown up against them in their quest for material self-sufficiency. Whites in general, but well-off whites in particular, were able to amass assets and use their secure economic status to pass their wealth from generation to generation. What is often not acknowledged is that the accumulation of wealth for some whites is ultimately tied to the poverty of wealth for most blacks.[27] Just as blacks have had "cumulative disadvantages," whites have had "cumulative advantages." Practically, every circumstance of bias and discrimination against blacks has produced a circumstance and opportunity of positive gain for whites. When black workers were paid less than white workers, white workers gained a benefit; when black businesses were confined to the segregated black market, white businesses received the benefit of diminished competition; when FHA policies denied loans to blacks, whites were the beneficiaries of the spectacular growth of good housing and housing equity in the suburbs. The cumulative effect of such a process has been to sediment blacks at the bottom of the social hierarchy and to artificially raise the relative position of some whites in society.

To understand the sedimentation of racial inequality, particularly with respect to wealth, is to acknowledge the way in which structural disadvantages have been layered one upon the other to produce black disadvantage and white privilege. Returning again to the Federal Housing Act of 1934, we may recall that the federal government placed its credit behind private loans to homebuyers, thus putting home ownership within the reach of millions of citizens for the first time. White homeowners who had taken advantage of FHA financing policies saw the value of their homes increase dramatically, especially during the 1970s when housing prices tripled.[28] As previously noted, the same FHA policies excluded blacks and segregated them into all-black areas that either were destroyed during urban renewal in the sixties or benefited only marginally from the inflation of the 1970s. Those who were locked out of the housing market by FHA policies and who later sought to become first-time homebuyers faced rising housing costs that curtailed their ability to purchase the kind of home they desired. The postwar generation of whites whose parents gained a foothold in the housing market through the FHA will harvest a bounteous inheritance in the years to come.[29] Thus the process of asset accumulation that began in the 1930s has become layered over and over by social and economic trends that magnify inequality over time and across generations.

ENDNOTES

[1] Wilson (1987:8).
[2] Bobo (1989:307).
[3] See Omi and Winant (1986).
[4] Franklin (1991:xviii).
[5] See Baran and Sweezy (1966) and Cox (1948).
[6] See Hill (1977) and Jacobson (1968).
[7] See Johnson and Oliver (1992); Kasarda (1988); and Wilson (1987).
[8] See Kirschenman and Neckerman (1991).
[9] See Butler (1991); Light (1972); and Myrdal (1944).
[10] Anderson (1994:123).
[11] See Beasley (1919).
[12] See Quadagno (1994:20–24).
[13] Quadagno (1994:161).
[14] Ibid., p. 162.
[15] Lipsitz (1995).
[16] Thomas (1992:140).
[17] Mieszkowski and Syron (1979:35).
[18] Franklin (1991:126).
[19] See Skogan (1990).
[20] See Rank (1994) and Stack (1974).
[21] Sherraden (1991:63).
[22] Ibid., p. 64.
[23] See Katz (1986:247).
[24] See Barlett and Steele (1992).
[25] See Jackman and Jackman (1980); Ong and Grigsby (1988); and Horton and Thomas (1993).
[26] See Jaynes (1986) and Lieberson (1980); Bloch (1969) and Bonacich (1976).
[27] See Blauner (1972); Lipsitz (1995); and Thurow (1975).
[28] See Adams (1988) and Stutz and Kartman (1982).
[29] See Levy and Michel (1996).

REFERENCES

Adams, John. 1988. "Growth of U.S. Cities and Recent Trends in Urban Real Estate Values." Pp. 108–45 in *Cities and Their Vital Systems,* edited by J. H. Ausubel and R. Herman. Washington, DC: National Academy Press.

Anderson, Claud. 1994. *Black Labor, White Wealth: The Search for Power and Economic Justice.* Edgewood, MD: Duncan and Duncan.

Baran, Paul A. and Paul M. Sweezy. 1966. *Monopoly Capital.* New York: Monthly Review Press.

Barlett, Donald L. and James B. Steele. 1992. *America: What Went Wrong?* Kansas City: Andrews and McMeel.

———. 1994. *America: Who Really Pays the Taxes?* New York: Touchstone.

Beasley, Delilah. 1919. *Negro Trail Blazers of California.* Los Angeles: Times Mirror Print and Binding House.

Blauner, Bob. 1972. *Racial Oppression in America.* New York: Harper.

Bloch, Herman David. 1969. *The Circle of Discrimination: An Economic and Social Study of the Black Man in New York.* New York: New York University Press.

Bobo, Lawrence. 1989. "Keeping the Linchpin in Place: Testing the Multiple Sources of Opposition to Residential Integration." *Revue Internationale de Psychologie Sociale* 2:306–23.

Bonacich, Edna. 1976. "Advanced Capitalism and Black-White Relations in the United States: A Split Labor Market Interpretation." *American Sociological Review* 37:547–59.

Butler, John Sibley. 1991. *Entrepreneurship and Self-Help among Black Americans: A Reconsideration of Race and Economics.* Albany: State University of New York Press.

Cox, Oliver C. 1948. *Caste, Race, and Class.* New York: Modern Reader Paperback.

Du Bois, W. E. B. 1935. *Black Reconstruction in America.* New York: Harcourt, Brace.

Franklin, Raymond S. 1991. *Shadows of Race and Class.* Minneapolis: University of Minnesota Press.

Hill, Herbert. 1977. *Black Labor and the American Legal System: Race, Work, and the Law.* Madison: University of Wisconsin Press.

Horton, Hayward Derrick and Melvin E. Thomas. 1993. "Race, Class, and Family Structure: Differences in Housing Values for Black and White Homeowners." Unpublished manuscript.

Jackman, Mary R. and Robert W. Jackman. 1980. "Racial Inequalities in Home Ownership." *Social Forces* 58:1221–33.

Jacobson, Julius, ed. 1968. *The Negro and the American Labor Movement.* New York: Anchor.

Jaynes, Gerald D. 1986. *Branches without Roots: Genesis of the Black Working Class in the American South, 1862–1882.* New York: Oxford University Press.

Johnson, James H. and Melvin L. Oliver. 1992. "Structural Changes in the U.S. Economy and Black Male Joblessness: A Reassessment." Pp. 113–47 in *Urban Labor Markets and Job Opportunity,* edited by George Peterson and Wayne Vroman. Washington, DC: Urban Institute Press.

Kasarda, John D. 1988. "Jobs, Migration, and Emerging Urban Mismatches." Pp. 148–98 in *Urban Change and Poverty,* edited by M. G. H. McGeary and L. E. Lynn, Jr. Washington, DC: National Academy Press.

Katz, Michael. 1986. *In the Shadow of the Poor House: A Social History of Welfare in America.* New York: Basic Books.

Kirschenman, Joleen and Katherine Neckerman. 1991. "'We'd Love to Hire Them But': The Meaning of Race for Employers." Pp. 203–32 in *The Urban Underclass,* edited by Christopher Jencks and Paul Peterson. Washington, DC: Brookings Institution.

Levy, Frank S. and Richard Michel. 1996. "An Economic Bust for the Baby Boom." *Challenge*, March/April: 33–39.

Lieberson, Stanley. 1980. *A Piece of the Pie*. Berkeley: University of California Press.

Light, Ivan. 1972. *Ethnic Enterprise in America*. Berkeley: University of California Press.

Lipsitz, George. 1995. "The Possessive Investment in Whiteness: The 'White' Problem in American Studies." *American Quarterly*, Fall.

Massey, Douglas S. and Nancy A. Denton. 1993. *American Apartheid: Segregation and the Making of the Underclass*. Cambridge, MA: Harvard University Press.

Mieszkowski, Peter and Richard F. Syron. 1979. "Economic Explanations for Housing Segregation." *New England Economic Review*, November/December: 33–34.

Mink, Gwendolyn. 1990. "The Lady and the Tramp: Gender, Race, and the Origins of the American Welfare State." Pp. 92–122 in *Women, the State, and Welfare*, edited by Linda Gordon. Madison: University of Wisconsin Press.

Myrdal, Gunnar. 1944. *An American Dilemma*. New York: Harper.

Omi, Michael and Howard Winant. 1986. *Racial Formation in the United States: From the 1960s to the 1980s*. New York: Routledge.

Ong, Paul and Eugene Grigsby, III. 1988. "Race and Life Cycle Effects on Home Ownership in Los Angeles, 1970 to 1980." *Urban Affairs Quarterly* 23:601–15.

Quadagno, Jill. 1994. *The Color of Welfare*. New York: Oxford University Press.

Rank, Mark R. 1994. *Living on the Edge: The Realities of Welfare in America*. New York: Columbia University Press.

Sherraden, Michael. 1991. *Assets and the Poor: A New American Welfare Policy*. New York: Sharpe.

Skogan, Wesley G. 1990. *Disorder and Decline: Crime and the Spiral of Decay in American Neighborhoods*. New York: Free Press.

Stack, Carol. 1974. *All Our Kin*. New York: Harper.

Stutz, Fred and A. E. Kartman. 1982. "Housing Affordability and Spatial Price Variation in the United States." *Economic Geography* 58:221–35.

Thomas, Richard Walter. 1992. *Life for Us Is What We Make It: Building Black Community in Detroit, 1915–1945*. Bloomington: Indiana University Press.

Thurow, Lester C. 1975. *Generating Inequality: Mechanisms of Distribution in the U.S. Economy*. New York: Basic Books.

Wilson, William J. 1978. *The Declining Significance of Race*. Chicago: University of Chicago Press.

———. 1987. *The Truly Disadvantaged*. Chicago: University of Chicago Press.

25

POSITIVE FUNCTIONS OF THE UNDESERVING POOR
Uses of the Underclass in America

HERBERT J. GANS

As the previous reading by Oliver and Shapiro demonstrated, the American dream and the accumulation of wealth have been difficult to obtain for African Americans. They also have been impossible goals for the poor. Instead, the indigent struggle to meet the economic requirements of everyday survival. This 1994 article by Herbert J. Gans provides a functional analysis of poverty. Contrary to the conflict theory views presented in the readings by Domhoff and by Oliver and Shapiro, where power is the central characteristic of class relations, the *functionalist* view of social class is concerned with how stratification may benefit society. Utilizing this perspective, Gans outlines the benefits or functions that the poor serve in our society. An important point to remember is that Gans is *not* arguing that poverty is inherently acceptable but, rather, that a functionalist perspective analyzes how poverty benefits the social system as a whole; that is to say, he is trying to explain why poverty persists.

I. Introduction

Poverty, like any other social phenomenon, can be analyzed in terms of the *causes* which initiate and perpetuate it, but once it exists, it can also be studied in terms of the consequences or *functions* which follow. These functions can be both *positive* and *negative*, adaptive and destructive, depending on their nature and the people and interests affected.

Poverty has many negative functions (or dysfunctions), most for the poor themselves, but also for the nonpoor. Among those of most concern to both populations, perhaps the major one is that a small but visible proportion of poor people is involved in activities which threaten their physical safety, for example street crime, or which deviate from important norms claimed to be "mainstream," such as failing to work, bearing children in adolescence and out of wedlock, and being "dependent" on welfare. In times of high un-

From *Koelner Zeitschrift für Soziologie und Sozialpsychologie,* Sonderheft No. 32, 48–62. Copyright © 1992 by Westdeutscher Verlag GmbH. Reprinted by permission from Westdeutscher Verlag GmbH.

employment, illegal and even legal immigrants are added to this list for endangering the job opportunities of native-born Americans.

Furthermore, many better-off Americans believe that the number of poor people who behave in these ways is far larger than it actually is. More important, many think that poor people act as they do because of moral shortcomings that express themselves in lawlessness or in the rejection of mainstream norms. Like many other sociologists, however, I argue that the behavior patterns which concern the more fortunate classes are *poverty-related*, because they are, and have historically been, associated with poverty. After all, mugging is only practiced by the poor. They are in fact caused by poverty, although a variety of other causes must also be at work since most poor people are not involved in any of these activities, including mugging.

Because their criminal or disapproved behavior is ascribed to moral shortcomings, the poor people who resort to it are often classified as unworthy or *undeserving*. For example, even though the failure of poor young men (or women) to work may be the effect of a lack of jobs, they are frequently accused of laziness, and then judged undeserving. Likewise, even though poor young mothers may decide not to marry the fathers of their children, because they, being jobless, cannot support them, the women are still accused of violating conventional familial norms, and also judged undeserving. Moreover, once judged to be undeserving, poor people are then no longer thought to be deserving of public aid that is financially sufficient and secure enough to help them escape poverty.

Judgments of the poor as undeserving are not based on evidence, but derive from a stereotype, even if, like most others, it is a stereotype with a "kernel of truth" (e.g., the monopolization of street crime by the poor). . . . It is not difficult to understand why people, poor and more fortunate, are fearful of street crime committed by poor people, and even why the jobless poor and welfare recipients, like paupers before them, may be perceived as economic threats for not working and drawing on public funds, at least in bad economic times. Also, one can understand why other forms of poverty-related behavior, such as the early sexual activity of poor youngsters and the dramatic number of poor single-parent families, are viewed as moral threats, since they violate norms thought to uphold the two-parent nuclear family and related normative bases of the social order. However, there would seem to be no inherent reason for exaggerating these threats, for example, in the case of welfare recipients who obtain only a tiny proportion of governmental expenditures, or more generally, by stereotyping poor people as undeserving without evidence of what they have and have not done, and why.

One reason, if not the only one, for the exaggeration and the stereotyping, and for the continued attractiveness of the concept of the undeserving poor itself, is that undeservingness has a number of *positive* functions for the better-off population. Some of these functions, or uses, are positive for everyone who is not poor, but most are positive for only some people, interest groups, and institutions, ranging from moderate income to wealthy ones.

Needless to say, that undeservingness has uses for some people does not justify it; the existence of functions just helps to explain why it persists.

My notion of function, or empirically observable adaptive consequence, is adapted from the classic conceptual scheme of Robert K. Merton.[1] My analysis will concentrate on those positive functions which Merton conceptualized as *latent*, which are unrecognized and/or unintended, but with the proviso that the functions which are identified as latent would probably not be abolished once they were widely recognized. Positive functions are, after all, also benefits, and people are not necessarily ready to give up benefits, including unintended ones, even if they become aware of them.[2]

The rest of this article deals only with the functions of the poor labeled undeserving. It can also be read as a sequel to an earlier article, in which I analyzed the positive functions of poverty without distinguishing between the deserving and undeserving poor.[3]

II. Functions of the Undeserving Poor[4]

I will discuss five sets of positive functions: microsocial, economic, normative-cultural, political, and macrosocial, which I divide into 13 specific functions, although the sets are arbitrarily chosen and interrelated, and I could add many more functions. The functions are not listed in order of importance, for such a listing is not possible without empirical research on the various beneficiaries of undeservingness.

Two Microsocial Functions

1. *Risk reduction.* Perhaps the primary use of the idea of the undeserving poor, primary because it takes place at the microsocial scale of everyday life, is that it distances the labeled from those who label them. By stigmatizing people as undeserving, labelers protect themselves from the responsibility of having to associate with them, or even to treat them like moral equals, which reduces the risk of being hurt or angered by them. Risk reduction is a way of dealing with actual or imagined threats to physical safety, for example from people who might be muggers, or cultural threats attributed to poor youngsters or normative ones imagined to come from welfare recipients. All pejorative labels and stereotypes serve this function, which may help to explain why there are so many such labels.

2. *Scapegoating and displacement.* By being thought undeserving, the stigmatized poor can be blamed for virtually any shortcoming of everyday life which can be credibly ascribed to them—violations of the laws of logic or social causation notwithstanding. Faulting the undeserving poor can also support the desire for revenge and punishment. In a society in which punishment is reserved for legislative, judicial, and penal institutions, *feelings* of revenge and punitiveness toward the undeserving poor supply at least some emotional satisfaction.

Since labeling poor people undeserving opens the door for nearly un-limited scapegoating, the labeled are also available to serve what I call the displacement function. Being too weak to object, the stigmatized poor can be accused of having caused social problems which they did not actually cause and can serve as cathartic objects on which better-off people can unload their own problems, as well as those of the economy, the polity, or of any other in-stitution, for the shortcomings of which the poor can be blamed.

Whether societywide changes in the work ethic are displaced on to "shift-lessness," or economic stagnation on to "welfare dependency," the poor can be declared undeserving for what ails the more affluent. This may also help to explain why the national concern with poor Black unmarried mothers, al-though usually ascribed to the data presented in the 1965 Moynihan Report, did not gather steam until the beginning of the decline of the economy in the mid-1970s. Similarly, the furor about poor "babies having babies" waited for the awareness of rising adolescent sexual activity among the better-off classes in the 1980s—at which point rates of adolescent pregnancy among the poor had already declined. But when the country became ambivalent about the desirability of abortions, the issue was displaced on the poor by making it al-most impossible for them to obtain abortions. . . .

Three Economic Functions

3. *Economic banishment and the reserve army of labor.* People who have success-fully been labeled as undeserving can be banished from the formal labor mar-ket. If young people are designated "school dropouts," for example, they can also be thought to lack the needed work habits, such as proper adherence to the work ethic, and may not be offered jobs to begin with. Often, they are effectively banished from the labor market before entering it because em-ployers imagine them to be poor workers simply because they are young, male, and Black.[5] Many ex-convicts are declared unemployable in similar fashion, and some become recidivists because they have no other choice but to go back to their criminal occupations.

Banishing the undeserving also makes room for immigrant workers, who may work for lower wages, are more deferential, and are more easily exploitable by being threatened with deportation. In addition, banishment helps to reduce the official jobless rate, a sometimes useful political function, especially if the banished drop so completely out of the labor force that they are not even available to be counted as "discouraged workers."

The economic banishment function is in many ways a replacement for the old reserve army of labor function, which played itself out when the un-deserving poor could be hired as strikebreakers, as defense workers in the case of sudden wartime economic mobilization, as "hypothetical workers," who by their very presence could be used to depress the wages of other workers, or to put pressure on the unions not to make wage and other de-mands. Today, however, with a plentiful supply of immigrants, as well as a constantly growing number of banished workers who are becoming surplus labor, a reserve army is less rarely needed—and when needed, can be recruited from sources other than the undeserving poor.[6]

Welfare recipients may, however, turn out to continue to be a part of the reserve army. Currently, they are encouraged to stay out of the labor market by remaining eligible for the Medicaid benefits they need for their children only if they remain on welfare.[7] Should the Clinton administration welfare reform program become reality, however, welfare recipients, who will be required to work for the minimum wage or less, could exert pressure on the wages of the employed, thus bringing them right back into the reserve army.

4. *Supplying illegal goods.* The undeserving poor who are banished from other jobs remain eligible for work in the manufacture and sale of illegal goods, including drugs. Although it is estimated that 80 percent of all illegal drugs are sold to Whites who are not poor, the sellers are often people banished from the formal labor market.[8] Other suppliers of illegal goods include the illegal immigrants, considered undeserving in many American communities, who work for garment industry sweatshops manufacturing clothing under illegal conditions.

5. *Job creation.* Perhaps the most important economic function of the undeserving poor today is that their mere presence creates jobs for the better-off population, including professional ones. Since the undeserving poor are thought to be dangerous or improperly socialized, either their behavior has to be modified so that they act in socially approved ways, or they have to be isolated from the deserving sectors of society. The larger the number of people who are declared undeserving, the larger also the number of people needed to modify and isolate as well as control, guard, and care for them. Among these are the social workers, teachers, trainers, mentors, psychiatrists, doctors and their support staffs in juvenile training centers, "special" schools, drug treatment centers, and penal behavior modification institutions, as well as the police, prosecutors, defense attorneys, judges, court officers, probation personnel and others who constitute the criminal courts, and the guards and others who run the prisons.

Jobs created by the presence of the undeserving poor also include the massive bureaucracy of professionals, investigators, and clerks who administer welfare. Other jobs go to the officials who seek out poor fathers for child support monies they may or may not have, as well as the welfare office personnel needed to take recipients in violation of welfare rules off the rolls, and those needed to put them back on the rolls when they reapply. In fact, one can argue that some of the rules for supervising, controlling, and punishing the undeserving poor are more effective at performing the latent function of creating clerical and professional jobs for the better-off population than the manifest function of achieving their official goals.

More jobs are created in the social sciences and in journalism for conducting research about the undeserving poor and producing popular books, articles, and TV documentaries for the more fortunate who want to learn about them. The "job chain" should also be extended to the teachers and others who train those who serve, control, and study the undeserving poor.

In addition, the undeserving poor make jobs for what I call the salvation industries, religious, civil, or medical, which also try to modify the behavior of those stigmatized as undeserving. Not all such jobs are paid, for the undeserving poor also provide occasional targets for charity and thus offer volunteer jobs for those providing it—and paid jobs for the professional fund-raisers who obtain most of the charitable funds these days. Among the most visible volunteers are the members of "cafe" and "high" society who organize and contribute to these benefits.[9]

Three Normative Functions

6. *Moral legitimation.* Undeservingness justifies the category of deservingness and thus supplies moral and political legitimacy, almost by definition, to the institutions and social structures that include the deserving and exclude the undeserving.[10] Of these structures, the most important is undoubtedly the class hierarchy, for the existence of an undeserving class or stratum legitimates the deserving classes, if not necessarily all of their class-related behavior.[11] The alleged immorality of the undeserving also gives a moral flavor to, and justification for, the class hierarchy, which may help to explain why upward mobility itself is so praiseworthy.[12]

7. *Norm reinforcement.* By violating, or being imagined as violating, a number of mainstream behavioral patterns and values, the undeserving poor help to reaffirm and reinforce the virtues of these patterns—and to do so visibly, since the violations by the undeserving are highly publicized. As Emile Durkheim pointed out nearly a century ago, norm violations and their punishments also provide an opportunity for preserving and reaffirming the norms. This is not insignificant, for norms sometimes disparaged as "motherhood" values gain new moral power when they are violated, and their violators are stigmatized.

If the undeserving poor can be imagined to be lazy, they help to reaffirm the Protestant work ethic; if poor single-parent families are publicly condemned, the two-parent family is once more legitimated as ideal. In the 1960s, middle-class morality was sometimes criticized as culturally parochial and therefore inappropriate for the poor, but since the 1980s, mainstream values have once more been regarded as vital sources of behavioral guidance for them.[13]

Enforcing the norms also contributes further to preserving them in another way, for one of the standard punishments of the undeserving poor for misbehaving—as well as a standard obligation in exchange for help—is practicing the mainstream norms, including those that the members of the mainstream may only be preaching, and that might die out if the poor were not required to incorporate them in their behavior. Old work rules that can no longer be enforced in the rest of the economy can be maintained in the regulations for workfare; old-fashioned austerity and thrift are built into the consumption patterns expected of welfare recipients. Economists like to argue that if the poor want to be deserving, they should take any kind of job, regardless of its low pay or demeaning character, reflecting a work ethic which economists themselves have never practiced.

Similarly, welfare recipients may be removed from the rolls if they are found to be living with a man—but the social worker who removes them has every right to cohabit and not lose his or her job. In most states, welfare recipients must observe rules of housecleaning and child care that middle-class people are free to ignore without being punished. While there are many norms and laws governing child care, only the poor are monitored to see if they obey these. Should they use more physical punishment on their children than social workers consider desirable, they can be charged with child neglect or abuse and can lose their children to foster care.[14]

The fact is that the defenders of such widely preached norms as hard work, thrift, monogamy, and moderation need people who can be accused, accurately or not, of being lazy, spendthrift, promiscuous, and immoderate. One reason that welfare recipients are a ready target for punitive legislation is that politicians, and most likely some of their constituents, imagine them to be enjoying leisure and an active sex life at public expense. Whether or not very many poor people actually behave in the ways that are judged undeserving is irrelevant if they can be imagined as doing so. Once imagining and stereotyping are allowed to take over, then judgments of undeservingness can be made without much concern for empirical accuracy. For example, in the 1990s, the idea that young men from poor single-parent families were highly likely to commit street crimes became so universal that the news media no longer needed to quote experts to affirm the accuracy of the charge.

Actually, most of the time most of the poor are as law abiding and observant of mainstream norms as are other Americans. Sometimes they are even more observant; thus the proportion of welfare recipients who cheat is always far below the percentage of taxpayers who do so.[15] Moreover, survey after survey has shown that the poor, including many street criminals and drug sellers, want to hold respectable jobs like everyone else, hope someday to live in the suburbs, and generally aspire to the same American dream as most moderate and middle-income Americans.[16]

8. *Supplying popular culture villains.* The undeserving poor have played a long-term role in supplying American popular culture with villains, allowing the producers of the culture both to reinforce further mainstream norms and to satisfy audience demands for revenge, notably by showing that crime and other norm violations do not pay. Street criminals are shown dead or alive in the hands of the police on local television news virtually every day, and more dramatically so in the crime and action movies and television series.

For many years before and after World War II, the criminal characters in Hollywood movies were often poor immigrants, frequently of Sicilian origin. Then they were complemented for some decades by communist spies and other Cold War enemies who were not poor, but even before the end of the Cold War, they were being replaced by Black and Hispanic drug dealers and gang leaders.

At the same time, however, the popular culture industry has also supplied music and other materials offering marketable cultural and political protest which does not reinforce mainstream norms, or at least not directly. Some of the creators and performers come from poor neighborhoods, however, and it may be that some rap music becomes commercially successful by displacing on ghetto musicians the cultural and political protest of record buyers from more affluent classes.[17]

Three Political Functions

9. *Institutionalized scapegoating.* The scapegoating of the undeserving poor mentioned in Function 2 above also extends to institutions which mistreat them. As a result, some of the responsibility for the existence of poverty, slums, unemployment, poor schools, and the like is taken off the shoulders of elected and appointed officials who are supposed to deal with these problems. For example, to the extent that educational experts decide that the children of the poor are learning disabled or that they are culturally or genetically inferior in intelligence, attempts to improve the schools can be put off or watered down.

To put it another way, the availability of institutional scapegoats both personalizes and exonerates social systems. The alleged laziness of the jobless and the anger aimed at beggars take the heat off the failure of the economy, and the imagined derelictions of slum dwellers and the homeless, off the housing industry. In effect, the undeserving poor are blamed both for their poverty and also for the absence of "political will" among the citizenry to do anything about it.

10. *Conservative power shifting.* Once poor people are considered undeserving, they also lose their political legitimacy and whatever little political influence they had before they were stigmatized. Some cannot vote, and many do not choose to vote or mobilize because they know politicians do not listen to their demands. Elected officials might ignore them even if they voted or mobilized, because these officials and the larger polity cannot easily satisfy their demands for economic and other kinds of justice.[18] As a result, the political system is able to pay additional attention to the demands of more affluent constituents. It can therefore shift to the "right."

The same shift to the right also takes place ideologically. Although injustices of poverty help justify the existence of liberals and the more radical left, the undeserving poor themselves provide justification and opportunities for conservatives to attack their ideological enemies on their left. When liberals can be accused of favoring criminals over victims, their accusers can launch and legitimate incursions on the civil liberties and rights of the undeserving poor, and concurrently on the liberties and rights of defenders of the poor.

Moreover, the undeservingness of the poor can be used to justify attacks on the welfare state. Charles Murray understood the essence of this ideological function when he argued that other welfare state legislation for the poor only increased the number of poor people.[19]

11. *Spatial purification.* Stigmatized populations are often used, deliberately or not, to stigmatize the areas in which they live, making such areas eligible for various kinds of purification. As a result, "underclass areas" can be torn down and their inhabitants moved to make room for more affluent residents or higher taxpayers.

However, such areas can also be used to isolate stigmatized poor people and facilities by selecting them as locations for homeless shelters, halfway houses for the mentally ill or for ex-convicts, drug treatment facilities, and even garbage dumps, which have been forced out of middle- and working-class areas following NIMBY (not in my backyard) protests. Drug dealers and other sellers of illegal goods also find a haven in areas stigmatized as underclass areas, partly because these supply some customers, but also because police protection in such areas is usually minimal enough to allow illegal activities without significant interference from the law.[20] In fact, municipalities would face major economic and political obstacles to their operations without stigmatized areas in which stigmatized people and activities can be located.

Two Macrosocial Functions

12. *Reproduction of stigma and the stigmatized.* For centuries now, undeservingness has given rise to policies and agencies which are manifestly set up to help the poor economically and otherwise to become deserving, but which actually prevent the undeserving poor from being freed of their stigma, and which also manage, unwittingly, to see to it that their children face the same obstacles.[21] In some instances, this process works so speedily that the children of the stigmatized face "anticipatory stigmatization," among them the children of welfare recipients who are frequently predicted to be unable to learn, to work, and to remain on the right side of the law even before they have been weaned.

If this outcome were planned deliberately, one could argue that politically and culturally dominant groups are reluctant to give up an easily accessible and always available scapegoat. In actuality, however, the reproduction function results unwittingly from other intended and seemingly popular practices. For example, the so-called War on Drugs, which has unsuccessfully sought to keep hard drugs out of the United States, but has meanwhile done little to provide drug treatment to addicts who want it, thereby aids the continuation of addiction, street crime, and a guaranteed prison population, not to mention the various disasters that visit the families of addicts and help to keep them poor.

The other major source of reproducing stigma and the stigmatized is the routine activities of the organizations which service welfare recipients, the homeless, and other stigmatized poor, and end up mistreating them.[22]

For one thing, such agencies, whether they exist to supply employment to the poor or to help the homeless, are almost certain to be underfunded because of the powerlessness of their clientele. No organization has ever had the funds or power to buy, build, or rehabilitate housing for the homeless in sufficient number. Typically, they have been able to fund or carry out small demonstration projects.

In addition, organizations which serve stigmatized people often attract less well-trained and qualified staff than those with high-status clients, and if the clients are deemed undeserving, competence may become even less important in choosing staff.[23] Then too, helping organizations generally reflect the societal stratification hierarchy, which means that organizations with poor, low-status clients frequently treat them as undeserving. If they also fear some of their clients, they may not only withhold help, but attack the clients on a preemptive strike basis. Last but not least, the agencies that serve the undeserving poor are bureaucracies which operate by rules and regulations that routinize the work, encourage the stability and growth of the organizations, and serve the needs of their staffs before those of their clients.

When these factors are combined, as they often are, and become cumulative, as they often do, it should not be surprising that the organizations cut off escape routes from poverty not only for the clients, but in doing so, also make sure that some of their children remain poor as well.

13. *Extermination of the surplus.* In earlier times, when the living standards of all poor people were at or below subsistence, many died at an earlier age than the better off, thus performing the set of functions for the latter forever associated with Thomas Malthus. Standards of living, even for the very poor, have risen considerably in the last century, but even today, morbidity and mortality rates remain much higher among the poor than among moderate-income people. To put it another way, various social forces combine to do away with some of the people who have become surplus labor and are no longer needed by the economy.

Several of the killing illnesses and pathologies of the poor change over time; currently, they include AIDS, tuberculosis, hypertension, heart attacks, and cancer, as well as psychosis, substance abuse, street crime, injury and death during participation in the drug trade and other underworld activities, and intraclass homicide resulting from neighborhood conflicts over turf and "respect." Whether the poor people whose only problem is being unfairly stereotyped and stigmatized as undeserving die earlier than other poor people is not known.[24]

Moreover, these rates can be expected to remain high or even to rise as rates of unemployment—and of banishment from the labor force—rise, especially for the least skilled. Even the better-off jobless created by the downsizing of the 1990s blame themselves for their unemployment if they cannot eventually find new jobs, become depressed, and in some instances begin the same process of being extruded permanently from the labor market experienced by the least skilled of the jobless.

In effect, contemporary advanced capitalism may well have created the conditions for a new Malthusian hypothesis. In any case, the early departure of poor people from an economy and society which do not need them is useful for those who remain. Since the more fortunate classes have already developed a purposive blindness to the structural causes of unemployment and to the poverty-related causes of pathology and crime that follow, those who benefit from the current job erosion and the possible extermination of the surplus labor may not admit it consciously either. Nonetheless, those left over to compete for scarce jobs and other resources will have a somewhat easier time in the competition, thus assigning undeservingness a final positive function for the more fortunate members of society.[25]

III. Conclusion

I have described thirteen of the more important functions of the undeserving poor, enough to support my argument that both the idea of the undeserving poor and the stigmas with which some poor people are thus labeled may persist in part because they are useful in a variety of ways to the people who are not poor.

This analysis does not imply that undeservingness will or should persist. Whether it *will* persist is going to be determined by what happens to poverty in America. If it declines, poverty-related crime should also decline, and then fewer poor people will probably be described as undeserving. If poverty worsens, so will poverty-related crime, as well as the stereotyping and stigmatization of the poor, and any worsening of the country's economy is likely to add to the kinds and numbers of undeserving poor, if only because they make convenient and powerless scapegoats.

The functions that the undeserving poor play cannot, by themselves, perpetuate either poverty or undeservingness, for as I noted earlier, functions are not causes. For example, if huge numbers of additional unskilled workers should be needed, as they were for the World War II war effort, the undeserving poor will be welcomed back into the labor force, at least temporarily. Of course, institutions often try to survive once they have lost both their reasons for existence and their functions. Since the end of the Cold War, parts of the military-industrial establishment both in the United States and Russia have been campaigning for the maintenance of some Cold War forces and weapons to guarantee their own futures, but these establishments also supply jobs to their national economies, and in the United States, for the constituents of elected officials. Likewise, some of the institutions and interest groups that benefit from the existence of undeservingness, or from controlling the undeserving poor, may try to maintain undeservingness and its stigma. They may not even need to, for if Emile Durkheim was right, the decline of undeservingness would lead to the criminalization, or at least stigmatization, of new behavior patterns.

Whether applying the label of undeservingness to the poor *should* persist is a normative question which ought to be answered in the negative. Although people have a right to judge each other, that right does not extend to judging large numbers of people as a single group, with one common moral fault, or to stereotyping them without evidence either about their behavior or their values. Even if a case could be made for judging large cohorts of people as undeserving, these judgments should be distributed up and down the socioeconomic hierarchy, requiring Americans also to consider whether and how people in the working, middle, and upper classes are undeserving.

The same equality should extend to the punishment of crimes. Today, many Americans and courts still treat white-collar and upper-class criminals more leniently than poor ones. The public excuse given is that the street crime of the undeserving poor involves violence and thus injury or death, but as many students of white-collar and corporate crime have pointed out, these also hurt and kill people, and often in larger numbers, even if they do so less directly and perhaps less violently.

Changes also need to be made in the American conception of deviance, which like that of other countries, conflates people whose behavior is *different* with those whose behavior is socially *harmful*. Bearing children without marriage is a long-standing tradition among the poor. Born of necessity rather than preference, it is a poverty-related practice, but it is not, by itself, harmful, or at least not until it can be shown that either the children—or the moral sensibilities of the people who oppose illegitimacy—are significantly hurt. Poor single-parent families are hardly desirable, but as the lack of condemnation of more affluent single-parent families should suggest, the major problem of such families is not the number of parents, actual or surrogate, in the family, but its poverty.

Finally, because many of the poor are stereotyped unjustly as undeserving, scholars, writers, journalists, and others should launch a systematic and public effort to deconstruct and delegitimate the notion of the undeserving poor. This effort, which is necessary to make effective antipoverty programs politically acceptable again, should place the following five ideas on the public agenda and encourage discussion as well as dissemination of available research.

The five ideas, all discussed earlier in this article, are that (1) the criminal and deviant behavior among the poor is largely poverty related rather than the product of free choice based on distinctive values; (2) the undeservingness of the poor is an ancient stereotype, and like all stereotypes, it vastly exaggerates the actual dangers that stem from the poor; (3) poverty-related deviance is not necessarily harmful just because it does not accord with mainstream norms; (4) the notion of undeservingness survives in part because of the positive functions it has for the better-off population; and (5) the only certain way to eliminate both this notion and the functions is to eliminate poverty.[26]

ENDNOTES

Author's Note: This is a revised version of an article first published in the *Koelner Zeitschrift für Soziologie und Sozialpsychologie,* Sonderheft No. 32, 1992, 48–62. It appears with the permission of the original publisher, Westdeutscher Verlag Gmbh, Opladen. I am grateful to Allan Silver for helpful comments on an earlier draft of this article.

[1] Robert K. Merton, "Manifest and Latent Functions," in his *Social Theory and Social Structure: Toward the Codification of Social Research* (Glencoe, IL, 1949), chap. 1.

[2] Actually, some of the functions that follow may in fact have been intended by some interest groups in society, but neither intended nor recognized by others, adding an interesting conceptual variation—and empirical question—to Merton's dichotomy.

[3] Herbert J. Gans, "The Positive Functions of Poverty," *American Journal of Sociology* 78, no. 2 (1972):275–89. That article also had another purpose, to show that functional analysis could come to liberal or radical conclusions, to counter the charge commonly launched against functional analysis that it is inherently conservative or supportive of the status quo. That article, like its present complement, was a straightforward analysis, written sans irony, even though the analysis of latent functions often becomes a debunking exercise that can take on an unintentionally ironic tone.

[4] For brevity's sake, I will hereafter refer to the undeserving poor instead of the poor labeled undeserving, but I always mean the latter.

[5] Kathryn M. Neckerman and Joleen Kirschenman, "Hiring Strategies, Racial Bias and Inner-City Workers," *Social Problems* 38, no. 4 (1991):433–47.

[6] Dahrendorf has suggested, surely with Marx's *Lumpenproletariat* in mind, that when the very poor are excluded from full citizenship, they can become "a reserve army for demonstrations . . . including soccer violence, race riots, and running battles with the police." Ralf Dahrendorf, *Law and Order* (London: Stevens, 1985), 107. He is writing with Europe in mind, however.

[7] Consequently, they are part of the reserve army only if and when they also work off-the-books and in the informal economy. For the argument that recipients are permanently part of the reserve army, see Frances F. Piven and Richard A. Cloward, *Regulating the Poor: The Functions of Public Welfare,* 2d ed. (New York: Pantheon, 1993).

[8] Ron Harris, "Blacks Feel Brunt of Drug War," *Los Angeles Times,* April 22, 1990, p. 1.

[9] While most charity benefits target the deserving poor, they are also held for poor AIDS victims and the homeless, who are considered undeserving, at least by some members of the better-off classes. The undeserving poor who are served by these charities thus help to justify the continued existence of these upper-class "societies."

[10] Since political legitimacy is involved here, these functions could also be listed among the political ones below.

[11] That many of the undeserving poor, and literally those of the underclass, are also thought to be *déclassé,* adds to the moral and political legitimacy of the rest of the class system.

[12] Although Marxists might have been expected to complain that the notion of the undeserving poor enables the higher classes to create a split in the lower ones, instead Marxist theory creates a mirror image of the capitalist pattern. In declaring undeserving the owners of the means of production, and sometimes the entire bourgeoisie, the theorists ennobled the working class and the poor together with it. Nonetheless, Marx found it necessary to make room for the *Lumpenproletariat,* although for him if not all of his successors, its moral failures were largely determined

by the needs of Marxist ideology, just as those of the undeserving poor were shaped by capitalist ideology.

[13] See Isabel Sawhill, "The Underclass: An Overview," *The Public Interest*, no. 96 (1989):3–15. For a contrary analysis, which finds and criticizes the acceptance of poverty-related deviance as normal, see Daniel P. Moynihan, "Defining Deviancy Down," *American Scholar* 62, no. 1 (1993):17–30.

[14] Poor immigrants who still practice old-country discipline norms are particularly vulnerable to being accused of child abuse.

[15] Teresa Funiciello, *Tyranny of Kindness: Dismantling the Welfare System to End Poverty in America* (New York: Atlantic Monthly Press, 1993), 60.

[16] See Mark R. Rank, *Living on the Edge: The Realities of Welfare in America* (New York: Columbia University Press, 1994), 93.

[17] A sizable proportion of the blues, country music, cowboy songs, and jazz of earlier eras was originally composed and played in prisons, brothels, and slum area taverns. It is probably not coincidental that as far back as the eighteenth century, at least, English "actors, fencers, jugglers, minstrels, and in fact all purveyors of amusements to common folk," were thought undeserving by the higher classes. Webb and Webb, *English Poor Law History*, 354.

[18] In addition, the undeserving poor make a dangerous constituency. Politicians who say kind words about them or who act to represent their interests are likely to be attacked for their words and actions. Jesse Jackson was hardly the first national politician to be criticized for being too favorable to the poor.

[19] Charles Murray, *Losing Ground: American Social Policy, 1950–1980* (New York: Basic Books, 1984). Myron Magnet went him one step better, blaming the increase in undeservingness also on various unnamed radicals associated with the conservative image of the 1960s. Myron Magnet, *The Dream and the Nightmare: The Sixties' Legacy to the Underclass* (New York: Morrow, 1993).

[20] Since even middle-class drug buyers are willing to travel to underclass areas for drugs, neighborhoods convenient to expressways and bridges that serve the suburbs often become major shopping centers for hard drugs.

[21] It is well known that many policies and agencies reproduce the positions and statuses of the people they are asked to raise, notably the public schools.

[22] For some examples of the literature on client mistreatment, see Michael B. Katz, *In the Shadow of the Poor House: A Social History of Welfare in America* (New York: Basic Books, 1986); Michael Lipsky, *Street Level Bureaucracy: Dilemmas of the Individual in Public Services* (New York: Russell Sage Foundation, 1980); Piven and Cloward, *Regulating the Poor*, chaps. 4 and 5; and for mistreatment of the homeless, Elliot Liebow, *Tell Them Who I Am: The Lives of Homeless Women* (New York: Free Press, 1993), chap. 4.

[23] They may also attract young professionals with reforming or missionary impulses, but many of them either burn out or leave for financial reasons when they begin to raise families.

[24] Poor Blacks and members of some racial minorities pay additional "health penalties" for being non-White.

[25] Killing off the undeserving poor may conflict with the prior function (see Function 12) of reproducing them, but functional analysis describes consequences which do not have to be logically consistent. Moreover, since turning poor people into undeserving ones can be a first step toward eliminating them, Functions 12 and 13 may even be logically consistent.

[26] A fuller discussion of policy proposals will appear in my forthcoming book, *Ending the War against the Poor*.

26

MAKING ENDS MEET
How Single Mothers Survive on a Welfare Check

KATHRYN EDIN • LAURA LEIN

Many Americans commonly assume that people on welfare are abusing the system by refusing to go to work and by having additional children in order to receive more welfare benefits. The reality is actually quite different, as Kathryn Edin, an associate professor of sociology at the University of Pennsylvania, and Laura Lein, a senior lecturer at the University of Texas at Austin, demonstrate in this reading. This selection, taken from their book *Making Ends Meet: How Single Mothers Survive Welfare and Low-Wage Work* (1997), shows how women spend their welfare checks each month. In this comprehensive study of impoverished women in four U.S. cities (Boston, Charleston, Chicago, and San Antonio), Edin and Lein interviewed 379 single mothers who were either welfare recipients or nonrecipients who held low-wage jobs. The selection that follows focuses on the 214 welfare-reliant mothers and their struggles to sustain their families each month.

Along Minnesota's Highway 72—which runs between the Canadian border town of Rainy River and Bemidji, Minnesota—a large, crudely lettered billboard greets the southbound traveler:

WELCOME TO MINNESOTA
LAND OF 10,000 TAXES
BUT WELFARE PAYS GOOD

Antiwelfare sentiment is common among Minnesotans, who live in a state with high personal income taxes and cash welfare benefits substantially above the national median. But even in southern states, where cash welfare benefits are very low and taxes modest, citizens are likely to denigrate welfare. In 1990, about 40 percent of respondents in each region told interviewers from the National Opinion Research Center that the United States spends too much on welfare.[1] In 1994, another nationally representative survey found that 65 percent of Americans believed welfare spending was too high (Blendon et al. 1995).

From *Making Ends Meet,* © 1997 Russell Sage Foundation, New York, New York. Reprinted with permission from the publisher.

Legislators recognize welfare's unpopularity. In the first half of the 1990s, several states cut benefits, and all let their value lag behind inflation. In addition, most states applied for federal waivers to experiment with benefit limitations or sanctions not allowed by the old federal rules. Some states established a "family cap," which denied additional cash to mothers who had another child while receiving welfare. In other states, mothers whose children were truant from school lost a portion of their cash grant. Furthermore, under the new federal rules, all states must limit the amount of time a mother spends on welfare to five years.

Public dissatisfaction with welfare persists despite the fact that cash benefits to welfare recipients have declined by more than 40 percent in real terms since the mid-1970s (Blank 1994:179). The reasons for the continuing public discontent throughout this period are complex, but probably rest on the widespread belief that the federal welfare entitlement perpetuated laziness and promiscuity (Bobo and Smith 1994; Page and Shapiro 1992).[2] Lazy women had babies to get money from the welfare system, the story went, and then let lazy boyfriends share their beds and live off their benefits. These lazy and immoral adults then raised lazy and immoral children, creating a vicious cycle of dependency.

Those who have promoted this view include the news media and talk show hosts, but social scientists also have contributed. The most widely known "scientific" argument was developed by Charles Murray, who in 1984 claimed that welfare actually makes the poor worse off. Federal welfare became too generous during the 1960s and 1970s, Murray argued, and began to reward unwed motherhood and indolence over marriage and jobs (Murray 1984). Social scientists spent much of the late 1980s attempting to discover whether Murray was right. Typically, economists judged the merits of the claim by estimating the disincentive effects of more or less generous state welfare benefits on work (for a review of this literature, see Moffitt 1992). Other researchers attempted to measure the effect of varying state benefits on marriage, divorce, and remarriage (Bane and Ellwood 1994).

The task we set for ourselves in this [article] is a more fundamental one. In order to assess whether any welfare program is too generous, one must compare its benefits to the cost of living faced by that program's recipients. An obvious starting point is to ask how much families headed by single mothers spend each month to make ends meet, and how that income compares with what they receive from welfare.

How Much Do Welfare-Reliant Mothers Spend?

In 1992, Donna Carson, a forty-year-old African American mother of two living in San Antonio, characterized herself as "ambitious and determined." She had spent most of her adult life playing by the rules. After high school graduation, she got a job and got married. She conceived her first child at age twenty-five, but her husband left before the child was born. Soon after her son's birth, she arranged for her mother to take care of him and went back to work. Because she did not have to pay for child care, her wages from her nurse's aide job combined with the child support she received from her ex-husband were enough to pay the bills. Ten years later, when she turned thirty-six, she had a second child. This time she was not married to the father. Carson's mother was willing to watch this child as well, so again she returned to work. Shortly thereafter, Carson's father's diabetes worsened and both of his legs were amputated. Her mother was overwhelmed by the tragedy and checked herself into a psychiatric hospital, leaving Carson to care for her two children and her disabled father alone. Seeing no other way out, she quit her job and turned to welfare. That was 1989.

Three years later, when we were talking with her, Carson was still on welfare, and her budget was tight. Her typical monthly expenditures were about $920 a month. One-third of that amount went to rent and utilities, another third went to food, and the rest went to cover her children's clothing, their school supplies, her transportation, and all the other things the family needed. Her combined monthly benefits from AFDC and food stamps, however, came to only $477.

Some months, she received a "pass through" child support payment of $50 from the father of her first child, who was legally obligated to pay. Although this payment did not reduce her AFDC benefits, her food stamps did go down by about $15 every time she received it. The father of her second child bypassed the formal child support system and paid her $60 directly each month. To get the rest of the money she needed, Carson took care of a working neighbor's child during the day. This neighbor could pay only $100 a month, but gave her the money in cash so that Carson's welfare caseworker could not detect the earnings and reduce her check. She got the rest of the money she needed from her father, who paid her $250 in cash each month to care for him.

Though Carson had more personal tragedy than most, her budget was similar to that of most other welfare recipients we talked with. Table 26.1 gives the monthly expenses of the 214 welfare-reliant mothers we interviewed (and their 464 children). It shows that our respondents averaged $213 a month on housing, $262 on food, $336 on other necessary expenses, and $64 on items that were arguably not essential—a total of $876 for an average family of 3.17 people.[3]

Housing Expenses

The housing expenses of welfare-reliant families varied substantially. This variation depended on whether recipients paid market rent, had a housing subsidy in a public housing project or a private building (Section 8), or shared housing with a relative or friend. Donna Carson paid market rent, which in San Antonio was quite low but still higher than what most mothers pay in

TABLE 26.1 Monthly Expenses of 214 AFDC Recipients:
Means and Standard Deviations

	Mean	SD
Housing costs	$213	$187
Food costs	262	112
Other necessities	336	176
Medical	18	43
Clothing	69	62
Transportation	62	83
Child care	7	32
Phone	31	35
Laundry/toiletries/cleaning supplies	52	31
Baby care	18	32
School supplies and fees	14	48
Appliance and furniture	17	39
Miscellaneous	47	59
Nonessentials	64	63
Entertainment	20	31
Cable TV	6	14
Cigarettes and alcohol	22	30
Eat out	13	27
Lottery costs	3	16
TOTAL EXPENSES	$876	$283

Source: Authors' calculations using Edin and Lein survival strategies data.
Note: The mean family size is 3.17 people. Numbers do not total due to rounding.

subsidized units. However, apartments that meet the physical criteria required for Section 8 tended to be in neighborhoods with less access to public transportation than the neighborhoods where housing projects were generally located, so these families usually had to maintain an automobile. Consequently, while public housing and Section 8 residents paid roughly the same amount for housing, Section 8 families spent far more for transportation.

In most cases, the welfare-reliant families who shared housing with a friend or relative were able to split the rent, utilities, telephone bill, and other household expenses. Thus, their expenses for rent and these other items were relatively low. About half of those who shared housing lived with one or both parents. The other half lived with siblings or friends. Mothers who lived with a parent usually made only token contributions toward the rent and took some portion of the responsibility for utilities and household maintenance. Most lived with their parents precisely because they could not afford to maintain their own households. Those who lived with a sibling or friend usually paid half of the household expenses. Sometimes, however, mothers "rented" only a portion of the living space (a single room, for example) and paid only a quarter or a third of the household costs.[4]

Food Expenses

Food expenditures averaged $262 a month for the welfare-reliant families we interviewed. This means that these mothers spent $19 per person on food in a typical week. This amount is nearly identical to the federal government's cheap food plan (the "thrifty food budget"), which uses as its base what poor mothers bought for their families in the 1950s and adjusts the prices in that "basket" for inflation each year (Ruggles 1990; Schwarz and Volgy 1992). The average weekly food stamp allotment for the families we interviewed, however, was slightly lower than this amount—$16 per person. This is because we oversampled mothers with housing subsidies to try to find mothers who could live on their benefits alone, and they do not qualify for the maximum amount of food stamps (food stamps are adjusted for living costs). This meant that the average mother had to cover $40 of food expenses each month with income from some source other than food stamps.[5]

Food stamp benefits also varied with family income, including cash welfare. In the lowest AFDC benefit states, therefore, families could receive up to $292 a month in food stamps for a family of three, or $21 per person per week in 1991, and families in these sites who reported no outside income received this maximum. Most found it sufficient to cover the bulk of their food expenditures. Families in states that paid more generous welfare benefits received roughly 30 cents less in food stamps for each additional dollar in cash welfare benefits. Because of this, hardly anyone who lived outside the South could pay their food bills with food stamps alone.[6] In San Antonio, food stamps covered 99 percent of respondents' average food expenditures; in Charleston, 88 percent; in Chicago, 80 percent; and in high-benefit Boston, only 65 percent.

Other Expenses

Besides housing and food, clothing took the next biggest bite out of the average family's monthly budget, followed by transportation, laundry and toiletries, telephone charges, medical expenses, baby care, and appliance and furniture costs. On average, welfare-reliant mothers spent $69 a month on clothing. This means that the mothers with whom we spoke typically purchased $261 worth of shoes, coats, and other apparel for each family member in a year. Most of this was for their children, since children continually grow out of their clothing.

Welfare-reliant mothers employed a number of strategies to contain their clothing expenditures. Virtually all purchased some of their clothing at thrift or second-hand stores, and most scoured neighborhood yard sales. During our interviews, many mothers proudly showed us their second-hand buys: a barely worn pair of name-brand jeans or a winter coat that was practically new and only a bit too small. A mother's largest expense in the clothing category was for children's shoes. Children not only went through two or more pairs of shoes a year, but shoes in children's sizes and in good condition were seldom available at neighborhood thrift stores. Winter coats, hats, mittens, and boots were also expensive, and most children grew out of them every other winter. Thus in the winter months, clothing needs could become an added hardship. One mother told us,

> *In the winter months, I have had to keep my children at home on the really cold days because I didn't have warm enough clothes to dress them. I have learned to swallow my pride, though, and go to the second-hand shops and try to get the right kind of winter clothes for the boys.*

The welfare-reliant mothers we interviewed felt that second-hand clothing was acceptable for younger children, whose peers were still largely unconcerned with appearance. One mother told us,

> *For shopping I go to yard sales and the Salvation Army for Jay's clothes. Fortunately, he isn't the type of kid who always has to have Nike sneakers or he won't go to school. I get him K-Mart ones, or I go to the used clothes store [on] Belmont [Avenue]. I probably spend $200 a season on new clothes for him, but some of those he can wear from season to season.*

Other mothers reported that their older children—especially high school boys—felt they could not maintain their self-respect or the respect of their peers while wearing K-Mart shoes to school. Some mothers felt that if they did not purchase name-brand sneakers, an athletic jacket, or other popular items for their teenagers, their children might be lured into criminal activity so they could buy these items themselves:

> *My boy, he sees these kids that sell drugs. They can afford to buy these [tennis shoes] and he can't. So I have my little side-job and [I buy them for him]. You got to do it to keep them away from drugs, from the streets.*

One mother told us that in order to buy her child a $50 pair of tennis shoes, she ate only one meal a day for a month. The savings in her food bill were enough to cover the purchase of the shoes. Most mothers in her neighborhood did not feel it was necessary to go hungry to meet their children's clothing needs, because they could generate the extra cash in other ways, which we discuss later.

Mothers who bought new clothing generally had to put the clothing on layaway. They paid a small portion of the purchase price each month. Some others found professional shoplifters who would note the children's sizes, shoplift the clothing, and sell it for a fraction of the ticket price to the mother.

Transportation cost the average welfare-reliant family $62 a month. Families living in Charleston (where there was little access to public transportation) and families living outside central cities spent more because they had to maintain automobiles or pay for taxis. At the time of our interviews, welfare rules limited the value of a family's automobile to $2,500. This meant that mothers had older cars, which generally required more frequent repair and got poorer gas mileage. All of the states we studied had mandatory insurance laws, and respondents told us that minimum insurance coverage cost at least $40 a month. In addition, Chicago and metropolitan Boston required that families purchase city stickers to park on the street, and South Carolina taxed the value of a family's car each year.

Although mothers who had access to public transportation spent less than those mothers who maintained cars, bus and subway transportation cost the average mother who used it more than $60 a month. Few mothers lived in areas where they could walk to the laundromat or the grocery store. In neighborhoods that provided these amenities, rents were higher. Since few mothers could afford child care, a shopping trip required that mothers bring their children with them and pay the bus or subway fares for the older children as well (younger children often ride free).

Laundry, toiletries, and cleaning supplies also constituted a significant proportion of monthly expenses. Some mothers washed their clothing in the bathtub and let it air-dry in their apartment or outside. This is a time-consuming task, however, and mothers complained that their clothes did not get as clean as machine-washed clothing. A few mothers owned or rented their own washers and dryers, but most used local laundromats. Because most families' clothing stock was slim (for example, two or three pairs of pants for each person was typical), mothers usually washed their clothing once each week or more. Laundromat prices varied, but mothers seldom spent less than $6 for coin machines each time they visited the laundromat, for roughly three loads.

All told, the welfare-reliant mothers had to spend $23 in a typical month to wash and dry their clothing and an additional $29 on toiletries and cleaning supplies. Food stamps could not be used to purchase toiletries or cleaning supplies, so mothers had to pay for sponges, cleaning fluids, dishwashing liquid, hand and laundry soap, bleach, toilet paper, hair care products, deodorant, disposable razors, and feminine products with cash.

Ninety-two percent of our sample had telephone service for at least part of the year. On average, families spent $31 monthly on telephone charges. Twenty-six percent of the welfare recipients had their phone disconnected at least once during the past year because of nonpayment. When mothers ran short of money, they were usually more willing to do without a phone than to neglect rent, utilities, food, clothing, transportation, or other essentials. Basic service charges also varied widely by site. In San Antonio, where basic local service cost about $12 a month, families spent only $18 a month for phone-related costs. In all other sites, comparable service ranged from $20 to $25 a month, and families spent much more. These costs included not only charges for local and long-distance calls but connection and reconnection charges as well. Although not strictly necessary for a family's material well-being, mothers without telephones had a difficult time maintaining contact with welfare caseworkers and their children's schools. It was also more difficult to apply for jobs because prospective employers could not reach them to set up an interview. Some solved this dilemma by sharing a phone with a neighbor; messages left with neighbors, however, were not always promptly forwarded.

Medicaid, the government's health insurance program for low-income families, offered free emergency care and routine physician care. All the households in our welfare-reliant sample were covered by Medicaid. Over-the-counter medicines and other medical services, however, were not covered and constituted another $18 of the average welfare-reliant mother's monthly budget. These expenses included routine drugstore costs, such as those for pain relievers, cough syrup, adhesive bandages, vitamin tablets, or other medicines families frequently used. In addition, few state Medicaid programs pay for prescription birth control pills, abortions, antidepressants, or other mental health drugs. Nor do most Medicaid plans pay for dental care, except for emergency oral surgery.

Diapers and other baby care products cost an average welfare-reliant family $18 a month (37 percent of the welfare recipients in our sample had babies in diapers). Welfare-reliant mothers with infants and young toddlers typically received formula, milk, eggs, and cheese from WIC (Women's, Infants', and Children's nutritional program). Most mothers told us, however, that they were usually one or two cans short of formula each month and had to purchase them at the grocery store. In addition, WIC does not provide disposable diapers, which constituted roughly 80 percent of the cash welfare-reliant mothers had to spend on baby care. Only a tiny minority of the mothers we interviewed used cloth diapers; although cheaper than disposables, cloth diapering was not practicable for mothers who relied on laundromats. In addition, mothers who used cloth diapers reported substantial up-front costs (they had to buy the diapers), and these mothers spent substantially more for laundry supplies than other mothers. Mothers also averaged $14 a month on school-related expenses and $7 a month on child care.

Appliances and furniture cost the typical family another $17 a month. Generally mothers purchased both new and used furniture and appliances with installment payments. Because they could not get bank credit, these mothers would often arrange credit at local thrift shops and "rent-to-own" furniture stores. Although local thrift stores did not generally apply finance charges to mothers' purchases (they usually held the item until it was fully paid for), rent-to-own furniture stores did. Because the latter stores charged very high interest rates and allowed long repayment periods, mothers sometimes ended up paying two to three times the actual value of the item. Meanwhile, mothers who missed a payment could have the furniture repossessed, losing whatever equity they had built up.

Miscellaneous items in the families' budgets included check-cashing fees and fees for money orders, debt service, burial insurance, and haircuts. These items totaled $47 in the average month.

Nonessentials

Entertainment cost the typical family $20 each month and was usually limited to video rentals; occasionally it included movies, trips to amusement parks, and travel (mothers sometimes sent their children to relatives during the summer). Mothers spent an average of $22 for cigarettes and alcohol each month, mostly on cigarettes. Mothers seldom bought their own alcohol, and those who drank depended on boyfriends, friends, and family members to pay for their drinks. This was also true for most mothers who used marijuana or other drugs. In addition, mothers spent an average of $3 a month for the lottery, $6 a month for cable television, and $13 a month to eat out. All told, the typical welfare-reliant family spent $64 a month on these unnecessary items, or about 7 percent of their total budget.[7] Although not physical necessities, the items met crucial psychological needs.

Although the mothers in our sample worried about day-to-day material survival, most saw survival as having broader "psychological" and "social" dimensions. One mother commented:

> *You know, we live in such a materialistic world. Our welfare babies have needs and wants too. They see other kids going to the circus, having toys and stuff like that. You gotta do what you gotta do to make your kid feel normal. There is no way you can deprive your child.*

This woman's statement captures a common sentiment among the welfare recipients we interviewed: children need to have an occasional treat, and mothers who refuse them may deprive their offspring of normalcy. Even among Mexican American mothers in San Antonio, who spent less than any of the other welfare-reliant mothers, one family in six paid a small monthly fee for a basic cable subscription. These mothers told us they saw the cable subscription as a cheap way of keeping their kids off the streets and out of trouble.

The mothers themselves needed an occasional boost too. Many reported that by spending small amounts on soda pop, cosmetics, cigarettes, alcohol, or the lottery, they avoided feeling like they were "completely on the bottom," or that their lives were "completely hopeless." When we asked respondents if they could do without them, they replied that these items gave them some measure of self-respect, and without them they would lose hope of bettering their situations:

> *I never buy for myself, only for my son. Well, I take that back. I allow myself two of what I guess you would call luxuries. Well, I guess three. First, I buy soda pop. I do not eat meals hardly ever, but I always have to have a can of Pepsi in my hand. I drink Pepsi nonstop. My boyfriend, he buys it for me by the case 'cause*

he knows how much I like it, and I guess it's the pop that gives me my energy for dealing with my son—you know, the sugar and caffeine and stuff.

And then I treat myself to the cigarettes. Without the smoking, I would just worry all the time about how we was going to eat and would never relax. I feel like I deserve some little pleasure, you know, and so those cigarettes keep me up, keep me feeling that things aren't so bad.

And the other thing is, I buy my cosmetics. I mean, I go around feeling so low all the time, and the makeup makes me feel, you know, better about myself. I feel like I'm not so poor when I can buy myself some cosmetics at the discount house.

The few respondents who spent money on alcohol reported similar sentiments:

Oh, sometimes, you know, just to relax or somethin', I just go out and have a few. And when I'm really low, I sometimes go out and tie one on, if you know what I mean. Sometimes I think I'll go crazy all day in the house if I can't get out once in a while. I just couldn't take it.

Although few mothers played the lottery with any regularity, those who did also viewed it as a sort of escape:

I just can't afford not to buy some tickets when the pot gets real big. I sometimes buy five tickets if I can afford it. I like to plan what I'm going to do with it, you know, fantasize and stuff—dream of what it would be like to own nice things and such. . . .

Only one of our 214 mothers—an extremely frugal, publicly housed Boston-area resident—was able to meet her expenses with her welfare benefits. She made ends meet because she lived in an unusually generous state and spent nothing whatsoever on entertainment, alcohol, cigarettes, or the lottery; nothing on child care; nothing on school supplies (what the school did not provide, her son did not get); and nothing on furniture or appliances (she scavenged broken-down furniture from alleys). She spent nothing on transportation, since all her friends lived in the projects and she walked nearly everywhere she needed to go. She also spent very little on laundry because she washed clothes in the bathtub and let them air-dry. She spent little on clothing because she purchased the majority of the family's clothes (the few there were) at thrift stores. Finally, she spent nothing for Christmas, birthdays, or any other special occasion. No other respondent in *any* site made ends meet on so little. Since her child frequently went hungry, had only one change of clothes, and often missed school because he lacked adequate winter clothing, several of this woman's neighbors (whom we interviewed) had reported her to child protective services for neglect.

How Do Welfare-Reliant Mothers Make Ends Meet?

No one without substantial assets can spend more than they take in for long. The welfare-reliant women we interviewed had few savings, no IRA accounts, no stocks or bonds, and no valuable assets. If they had and if their caseworkers had known, they would have been ineligible for welfare. When they ran out of cash and food stamps, those who did not have a generous parent or boyfriend worked at regular or informal jobs. They also had to "work" the system, making sure that neither their earnings nor the contributions they received came to the attention of the welfare department. If they reported such income, their welfare checks would soon be reduced by almost the full amount of this income, leaving them as poor as before.

Table 26.2 shows that, on average, cash welfare, food stamps, and SSI covered only about three-fifths of welfare-reliant mothers' expenses.[8] A small amount also came from the earned income tax credit (EITC) for wages earned in the prior year. From our conversations with mothers, we learned that they made up the remaining gap by generating extra cash, garnering in-kind contributions, and purchasing stolen goods at below market value. We found it difficult to estimate, however, how much each mother saved by using the latter two techniques. Therefore, we present figures only for those strategies that generated extra cash.

Earnings from reported work, unreported work (off the books or under a false identity), or work in the underground economy (selling sex, drugs, or stolen goods) made up 15 percent of welfare-reliant mothers' total monthly income.[9] Another chunk (17 percent) came from members of their personal networks and went unreported. Agency-based contributions—usually cash contributions, direct payment of mothers' bills, or the portion of student grants and loans that could be squeezed for extra household cash after paying for tuition and books—covered the last 4 percent of the average welfare-reliant mother's budget.

To get a clearer sense of how welfare-reliant mothers generated extra income, Table 26.2 also shows the degree to which mothers relied on various sources of income each month. By definition, all the mothers we coded as welfare-reliant received something from the AFDC program. Table 26.2 shows that almost all of them also received food stamps (95 percent), compared with 87 percent of welfare recipients nationwide (U.S. House of Representatives 1993:711).[10] Nine percent of the sample received SSI or payments for the care of foster children. Seven percent received money from the EITC because they reported income from work during the previous calendar year.

Table 26.2 gives further detail on how mothers' earnings from work contributed to their family budgets. Five percent worked in the formal economy at reported jobs, compared with 6 percent nationally (U.S. House of Representatives 1993:696). Others were also working and not reporting it. Approximately two-fifths (39 percent) worked off the books or under a false

TABLE 26.2   Survival Strategies of 214 Welfare-Reliant Mothers

Variable	Amount of Income Generated Through Each Survival Strategy	Percentage of Total Budget	Percent of Mothers Engaging in Each Survival Strategy[a]
TOTAL EXPENSES	$876	100%	N/A
Housing costs	213	24	N/A
Food costs	262	30	N/A
Other necessities	336	39	N/A
Nonessentials	64	7	N/A
Welfare benefits	565	64	N/A
AFDC	307	35	100%
Food Stamps	222	25	95
SSI	36	4	9
EITC	3	2	7
Work-based strategies	128	15	46
Reported work	19	2	5
Unreported work	90	10	39
Underground work	19	2	8
Network-based strategies	151	17	77
Family and friends	62	7	46
Men	95	11	52
Boyfriends	56	6	29
Absent fathers	39	4	33
Covert system	33	4	23
Formal system	7	1	14
Agency-based strategies	37	4	31
TOTAL INCOME	$883	100%	N/A

[a] The sum of the percentages exceeds the total because some mothers engaged in more than one strategy.
Source: Authors' calculations using Edin and Lein survival strategies data.
Note: These income-generating strategies do not include in-kind contributions or purchasing goods illegally because these figures were difficult to estimate. Columns do not total due to rounding.

identity to generate additional income, and 8 percent worked in the underground economy selling sex, drugs, or stolen goods. (The percentages do not sum to 46 percent because some mothers engaged in more than one strategy.) Table 26.2 also shows that 77 percent of mothers were currently receiving covert contributions from family, boyfriends, or absent fathers in order to make ends meet.[11] Nearly half (46 percent) of welfare-reliant mothers relied on family and friends for financial help each month. Even more, 52 percent, received help from a man: 29 percent from boyfriends on a regular basis, 14 percent through the formal child support collection system, and 23 percent from the fathers of their children on a covert basis. In addition, 31 percent received cash, voucher, or direct assistance in paying a bill from a community group, charity, or student aid program.

Critics of welfare programs often suspect that low-income families cause their material poverty through poor money management (Heclo 1994). By comparing the expenses that our mothers reported, however, with those of the poorest income group in the Consumer Expenditure Survey (CES), we show that our welfare-reliant mothers spent substantially less than most American households in the early 1990s.[12] . . .

Surviving on Welfare

Americans have long worried that welfare benefits are too generous. Many hear about high rates of out-of-wedlock births among the poor and conclude that welfare contributes to the problem. A more fundamental question is how do individual welfare recipients actually use the government support they receive? What standard of living do welfare benefits afford single mothers?

We have attempted to answer this question by interviewing 214 welfare-reliant mothers about what they spent to keep their families together. We also examined the level of welfare benefits available to the mothers. We found that for most welfare-reliant mothers food and shelter alone cost almost as much as these mothers received from the government. For more than one-third, food and housing costs exceeded their cash benefits, leaving no extra money for uncovered medical care, clothing, and other household expenses. When we added the costs of other necessities to the mothers' budgets, it was evident that virtually all welfare-reliant mothers experienced a wide gap between what they could get from welfare and what they needed to support their families. In fact, with only one exception, we met no welfare mother who was making ends meet on her government check alone. Mothers filled the gap through reported and unreported work and through handouts from family, friends, and agencies. . . . Finally, we asked the difficult question of whether welfare-reliant mothers' expenditures were truly necessary. We found that our mothers' budgets were far below the household budgets collected by the Consumer Expenditure Survey in 1991 for single-parent families. Our welfare-reliant mothers also spent less than the lowest income group the CES interviewed. Our conclusion is that the vast majority of our welfare-reliant mothers' expenses were at the very low end of widely shared national consumption norms.

Despite spending far more than their welfare benefits, many of the families we interviewed experienced serious material hardship. Variations in benefit levels had real consequences for welfare-reliant single mothers and their children. Lower benefits substantially increased material hardship as did having larger families. Life on welfare, it seems, was an exceedingly tenuous affair.[13] An articulate Chicago respondent put it this way:

> *I don't understand why [Public Aid is] punishing people who are poor if you want to mainstream them. If indeed, the idea is to segregate, to be biased, to create a widening gap between the haves and the have-nots, then the welfare system is working. If it is to provide basic needs, not just the financial but the psychological and social needs of every human being, then the system fails miserably.*

ENDNOTES

[1] In 1994, 49 percent of Americans thought that welfare programs discouraged people from working, and two-thirds believed that welfare encouraged women to have more children than they would have had if welfare were not available (Blendon et al. 1995).

[2] These responses were gathered during the center's General Social Survey.

[3] Due to rounding, these estimates do not total $876.

[4] We did not include any teenage mothers living at home. Mothers under age eighteen constitute only a tiny portion of all mothers on the welfare rolls (U.S. House of Representatives 1995, table 10-27). We did interview seventeen teenage mothers and found that they paid almost none of their own bills because most of them lived rent-free with their mothers while they tried to finish school. Therefore, these teenage mothers could not construct a household budget.

[5] Nor could families with housing subsidies, disability income, or reported outside income buy all of their food with food stamps.

[6] There is a reduction in food stamp benefits as cash benefits rise.

[7] In terms of nonnecessary spending, more than a third of families spent nothing whatsoever on entertainment during the previous year; two-thirds never ate out; nearly half had spent nothing on cigarettes or alcohol during the year; and four-fifths had gone without cable television.

[8] Four percent of all welfare-reliant families received either SSI or survivor's benefits (U.S. House of Representatives 1993, p. 719).

[9] For those mothers who sold illegal drugs, a small personal supply was sometimes an in-kind benefit of the job.

[10] These small differences are due to the fact that we did not interview any teenage recipients, who often lived with better-off family members and were thus not eligible for food stamps.

[11] Fourteen percent had received payments through the Child Support Enforcement system in the last year, which was slightly above the national average of 12 percent for welfare recipients (U.S. Department of Health and Human Services 1990, p. 43).

[12] This poorest income group included individuals and families reporting household incomes of less than $5,000 a year. Of course, this group spent far more than their reported income, and the CES could not account for the discrepancy.

[13] Whereas Charles Murray (1984) portrayed an overly generous welfare system that kept the poor in poverty because it rewarded their indolence, mothers saw welfare as a stingy and punishing system that placed them and their children in a desperate economic predicament.

REFERENCES

Bane, Mary Jo and David T. Ellwood. 1994. *Welfare Realities: From Rhetoric to Reform.* Cambridge, MA: Harvard University Press.

Blank, Rebecca M. 1994. "The Employment Strategy: Public Policies to Increase Work and Earnings." In *Confronting Poverty,* edited by Sheldon H. Danziger, Gary D. Sandefur, and Daniel H. Weinberg. Cambridge, MA: Harvard University Press; New York: Russell Sage Foundation.

Blendon, Robert J., Drew E. Altman, John Benson, Mollyann Brodie, Matt James, and Gerry Chervinsky. 1995. "The Public and the Welfare Reform Debate." *Archives of Pediatric and Adolescent Medicine* 149:1065–69.

Bobo, Lawrence and Ryan A. Smith. 1994. "Antipoverty Policy, Affirmative Action, and Racial Attitudes." In *Confronting Poverty,* edited by Sheldon H. Danziger, Gary D. Sandefur, and Daniel H. Weinberg. Cambridge, MA: Harvard University Press; New York: Russell Sage Foundation.

Heclo, Hugh. 1994. "Poverty Politics." In *Confronting Poverty,* edited by Sheldon H. Danziger, Gary D. Sandefur, and Daniel H. Weinberg. Cambridge, MA: Harvard University Press; New York: Russell Sage Foundation.

Moffitt, Robert. 1992. "Incentive Effects of the U.S. Welfare System: A Review." *Journal of Economic Literature* 30 (March):1–61.

Murray, Charles A. 1984. *Losing Ground: American Social Policy.* New York: Basic Books.

Page, Benjamin I. and Robert Y. Shapiro. 1992. *The Rational Public: Fifty Years of Trends in Americans' Policy Preferences.* Chicago: University of Chicago Press.

Ruggles, Patricia. 1990. *Drawing the Line: Alternative Poverty Measures and Their Implications.* Washington, DC: Urban Institute Press.

Schwarz, John E. and Thomas J. Volgy. 1992. "Social Support for Self-Reliance: The Politics of Making Work Pay." *American Prospect* 9 (Spring):67–73.

U.S. Department of Health and Human Services. 1990. *Child Support Enforcement.* Annual Report to Congress 92-3301. Washington, DC: U.S. Government Printing Office.

U.S. House of Representatives, Committee on Ways and Means. 1993. Overview of Entitlement Programs (Green Block). Washington, DC: U.S. Government Printing Office.

U.S. House of Representatives, Committee on Ways and Means. 1995. Overview of Entitlement Programs (Green Block). Washington, DC: U.S. Government Printing Office.

27

GENDER AS STRUCTURE

BARBARA RISMAN

Gender stratification, examined in the next four selections, refers to those social systems in which socioeconomic resources and political power are distributed on the basis of one's sex and gender. In any social system, we can measure the gendered distribution of resources and rewards to see whether men or women have a higher social status. Objective indices of gender inequality include income, educational attainment, wealth, occupational status, mortality rates, and access to social institutions. In the selection that follows, Barbara Risman, a professor of sociology at North Carolina State University, examines four theories that attempt to explain why gender stratification exists.

There are three distinct theoretical traditions that help us to understand sex and gender, and a fourth is now taking shape. The first tradition focuses on gendered selves, whether sex differences are biological or social in origin. The second tradition . . . focuses on how the social structure (as opposed to biology or individual learning) creates gendered behavior. The third tradition . . . emphasizes contextual issues and how doing gender re-creates inequality during interaction. The fourth, multilevel approach treats gender itself as built in to social life via socialization, interaction, and institutional organization. This new perspective integrates the previous ones; it is formed on the assumption that each viewpoint sheds different light on the same question. . . .

Gendered Selves

There are numerous theoretical perspectives within this tradition, but all share the assumption that maleness and femaleness are, or become, properties of individuals. . . . Research questions in this tradition focus on the development of sex differences and their relative importance for behavior. . . .

Risman, Barbara. 1998. "Gender as Structure." Pp. 13–31 in *Gender Vertigo: American Families in Transition.* New Haven: Yale University Press. Reprinted by permission from Yale University Press.

Sociobiologists have argued that such behaviors as male aggressiveness and female nurturance result from natural selection. Biosociologists stress the infant care skills in which females appear to excel. Their perspective has been criticized for its ethnocentrism and its selective use of biological species as evidence. . . .

More recent biosocial theories have posited complex interactions between environment and biological predispositions, with attention to explaining intrasex differences. This new version of biosociology may eventually help to identify the biological parameters that, in interaction with environmental stimuli, affect human behavior. . . .

Sex-role theory suggests that early childhood socialization is an influential determinant of later behavior, and research has focused on how societies create feminine women and masculine men. There is an impressive variety of sex-role explanations for gender-differentiated behavior in families. Perhaps the most commonly accepted explanation is reinforcement theory (e.g., Bandura and Walters 1963, Mischel 1966, and Weitzman 1979). Reinforcement theory suggests, for example, that girls develop nurturant personalities because they are given praise and attention for their interest in dolls and babies, and that boys develop competitive selves because they are positively reinforced for winning, whether at checkers or football. Although much literature suggests that the socialization experiences of boys and girls continue to differ dramatically, it is clearly the case that most girls raised in the 1990s have received ambiguous gender socialization: they have been taught to desire domesticity (dolls remain a popular toy for girls), as well as to pursue careers. For generations, African American girls have been socialized for both motherhood and paid work (Collins 1990).

Nancy Chodorow's (1978, 1989) feminist psychoanalytic analysis approach has also been influential, particularly in feminist scholarship. Chodorow develops an object-relations psychoanalytic perspective to explain how gendered personalities develop as a result of exclusively female mothering. . . . Chodorow notices . . . that mothers are responsible for young children almost universally. She argues that mothers relate to their boy and girl infants differently, fusing identities with their daughters while relating to their sons as separate and distinct. As a result, according to this feminist version of psychoanalysis, girls develop selves based on connectedness and relationships while boys develop selves based on independence and autonomy. In addition, boys must reject their first love-object (mother) in order to adopt masculinity, and they do this by rejecting and devaluing what is feminine in themselves and in society. Thus, we get nurturant women and independent men in a society dominated by men and which values independence. Many feminist studies have incorporated this psychoanalytic view of gender as an underlying assumption (Keller 1985; L. Rubin 1982; Williams 1989). . . .

Other feminist theorists, such as Ruddick (1989, 1992) and Aptheker (1989), build on the notion that the constant nature of mothering creates a certain kind of thinking, what Ruddick calls "maternal thinking." The logic of this argument does not depend on a psychoanalytic framework, but it implicitly uses one: through nurturing their children, women develop psychological frameworks that value peace and justice. Therefore, if women (or men who mothered children) were powerful political actors, governments would use more peaceful conflict resolution strategies and value social justice more highly.

All individualist theories, including sex-role socialization and psychoanalytic thought, posit that by adulthood most men and women have developed very different personalities. Women have become nurturant, person oriented, and child centered. Men have become competitive and work oriented. According to individualist theorists, there are limits to flexibility. Intensely held emotions, values, and inclinations developed during childhood coalesce into a person's self-identity. Although these theorists do not deny that social structures influence family patterns, nor that notions of gender meaning are always evolving . . . they focus on how culturally determined family patterns and sex-role socialization create gendered selves, which then provide the motivations for individuals to fill their socially appropriate roles.

Historically, sex-role theorists have assumed that men and women behave differently because gender resides primarily in personality. This approach has several serious conceptual weaknesses. . . . First, such theories usually presume behavioral continuity throughout the life course. In fact, women socialized for nurturance are capable of competitive and aggressive behavior, and men raised without any expectation of taking on primary responsibility can "mother" when they need to (Bielby and Bielby 1984; Gerson 1985, 1993; Risman 1987). Another weakness of these individualist-oriented theories is their oversocialized conception of human behavior—that once we know how an individual has been raised, the training is contained primarily inside his or her head (cf. Wrong 1961). Such theories might suggest, for example, that women do not revolt and are not necessarily unhappy with their subordinate status because they have been so well trained for femininity. . . .

This overdependence on internalization of culture and socialization leads to the most serious problem with sex-role theory: its depoliticization of gender inequality. Although sex-role socialization and revisionist psychoanalytic theorists often have explicitly feminist goals, their focus on sex differences has legitimated a dualistic conception of gender that relies on a reified male/female dichotomy. The very notion of comparing all men to all women without regard for diversity within groups presumes that gender is primarily about individual differences between biological males and biological females, downplaying the role of interactional expectations and the social structure.

The sex-role socialization theory is an application of a normative role theory for human behavior. It assumes that social stability is motivated primarily by beliefs and values acquired during socialization. Individuals are assumed to use whatever resources are available to realize these values and to maintain their identities. As Stokes and Hewitt (1976) have argued, social-ization cannot serve as the fundamental link between culture and action. In-deed, studies of intergenerational shifts in values suggest that economic and political conditions produce beliefs, attitudes, and preferences for action that overcome those acquired during childhood (Inglehart 1977, 1981; Lesthaeghe 1980). We cannot assume that internalization of norms—through psychoan-alytic processes or sex-role socialization—is the primary means by which so-ciety organizes human conduct. . . .

Structure vs. Personality

The overreliance on gendered selves as the primary explanation for sexual stratification led many feminist sociologists—myself included—to argue that what appear to be sex differences are really, in Epstein's terms, "decep-tive distinctions" (Epstein 1988; Kanter 1977; Risman and Schwartz 1989). Although empirically documented sex differences do occur, structuralists like me have argued that men and women behave differently because they fill different positions in institutional settings, work organizations, or families. That is, the previous structural perspectives on gender assume that work and family structures create empirically distinct male and female behavior. . . . Within this perspective, men and women in the same structural slots are ex-pected to behave identically. Epstein's (1988) voluminous review of the multi-disciplinary research on gender and sex differences is perhaps the strongest and most explicit support for a social-structural explanation of gendered behavior. She suggests that there are perhaps no empirically documented differences that can be traced to the predispositions of males and females. Instead, the deceptive differences reflect women's lack of opportunity in a male-dominated society.

Gender relations in the labor force have received far more of this sort of structural analysis than have gender relations in intimate settings. Kanter's classic work *Men and Women of the Corporation* (1977) introduced this kind of structural perspective on gender in the workplace. Kanter showed that when women had access to powerful mentors, interactions with people like them-selves, and the possibility for upward mobility, they behaved like others— regardless of sex—with similar advantages. These social network variables could explain success at work far better than could assumptions of mascu-line versus feminine work styles. Women were less often successful because they were more often blocked from network advantages, not because they feared success or had never developed competitive strategies. Men who lacked such opportunities did not advance, and they behaved with stereo-typical feminine work styles. Kanter argued persuasively that structural sys-tem properties better explain sex differences in workplace behavior than does sex-role socialization. . . .

The application of a structural perspective to gender within personal relationships has been less frequent. . . . In a series of studies (Risman 1986, 1987, 1988), I tested whether apparent sex differences in parenting styles are better attributed to sex-role socialization or to the structural contingencies of adult life. The question I asked was "Can men mother?" The answer is yes, but only if they do not have women to do it for them. The lack of sex-role socialization for nurturance did not inhibit the development of male mothering when structural contingencies demanded it. This is an important part of the story, but not all of it. . . .

While applications of structural perspectives both to workplaces and to intimate relationships have furthered the sociological understanding of gender, there is a fundamental flaw in the logic of these arguments. . . .

Several studies (Williams 1992; Yoder 1991; Zimmer 1988) found that Kanter's hypotheses about the explanatory power of social structural variables such as relative numbers, access to mentors, and upward mobility are not, in fact, gender neutral. That is, Kanter's hypotheses are supported empirically only when societally devalued groups enter traditionally white male work environments. When white males enter traditionally female work environments, they do not hit the glass ceiling, they ride glass elevators. Reskin (1988) has suggested that we have so accepted these "structural" arguments that we sometimes forget that sexism itself stratifies our labor force. Evidence similarly points to continued existence of gendered behavior in family settings. Hertz reported that in her 1986 study of couples in which husbands and wives held equivalent, high-status corporate jobs and brought similar resources to their marriages, the wives continued to shoulder more responsibility for family work (even if that means hiring and supervising help). Despite the importance of structural variables in explaining behavior in families, the sex category itself remains a powerful predictor of who does what kind of family work (Brines 1994; South and Spitz 1994). Gender stratification remains even when other structural aspects of work or of family life are divorced from sex category. The interactionist theory discussed below helps us to understand why.

Doing Gender

This approach to gender was best articulated by West and Zimmerman in their 1987 article "Doing Gender." . . . West and Zimmerman suggest that once a person is labeled a member of a sex category, she or he is morally accountable for behaving as persons in that category do. That is, the person is expected to "do gender"; the ease of interaction depends on it. One of the groundbreaking aspects in this argument is that doing gender implies legitimating inequality. The authors suggest that, by definition, what is female in a patriarchal society is devalued. Within this theoretical framework, the very belief that biological males and females are essentially different (apart from their reproductive capabilities) exists to justify male dominance.

The tradition of doing gender has been well accepted in feminist sociology (West and Zimmerman's article was cited in journals more than one hundred times by 1995). West and Zimmerman articulated an insight whose time had come—that gender is not what we are but something that we do. Psychologists Deaux and Major (1990) . . . argue that interactional contexts take priority over individual traits and personality differences; others' expectations create the self-fulfilling prophecies that lead all of us to do gender. . . . They suggest that actual behavior depends on the interaction of participants' self-definitions, the expectations of others, and the cultural expectations attached to the context itself. I agree. The weakness in the doing-gender approach is that it undertheorizes the pervasiveness of gender inequality in organizations and gendered identities.

Although gender is always present in our interaction, it is not present only in interaction. We must have a theoretical link from material constraints to what we do now, to who we think we are. I suggest that the doing-gender perspective is incomplete because it slights the institutional level of analysis and the links among institutional gender stratification, situational expectations, and gendered selves.

West and Fenstermaker (1995) have extended the argument from doing gender to "doing difference." They suggest that just as we create inequality when we create gender during interaction, so we create race and class inequalities when we interact in daily life. Race does not generally hold the biologically based assumption of dichotomy (as sex category does), yet in American society we constantly use race categories to guide our interactional encounters. This extension of theoretical ideas from gender to the analysis of inequalities is perhaps the most important direction gender theorizing has taken in the past decade. . . .

Gender as Social Structure

The sex-differences literature, the doing-gender contextual analyses, and the structural perspectives are not necessarily incompatible, although I, as well as others, have portrayed them as alternatives (e.g., Epstein 1988, Ferree 1990, Kanter 1977, Risman 1987, Risman and Schwartz 1989). . . . My view of gender as a social structure incorporates each level of analysis. . . .

Lorber (1994) argues that gender is an entity in and of itself that establishes patterns of expectations for individuals, orders social processes of everyday life, and is built into all other major social organizations of society. She goes further, however, to argue that gender difference is *primarily* a means to justify sexual stratification. Gender is so ubiquitous because unless we see difference, we cannot justify inequality. Lorber provides much cross-

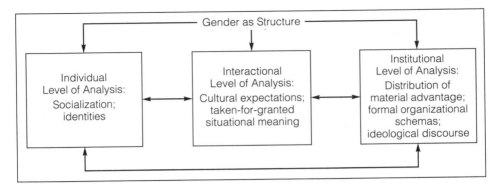

FIGURE 27.1   Gender as Structure

cultural, literary, and scientific evidence to show that gender difference is socially constructed and yet is universally used to justify stratification. She writes that "the continuing purpose of gender as a modern social institution is to construct women as a group to be subordinate to men as a group" (p. 33).

I build on this notion that gender is an entity in and of itself and has consequences at every level of analysis. And I share the concern that the very creation of difference is the foundation on which inequality rests. In my view, it is most useful to conceptualize gender as a structure that has consequences for every aspect of society. . . .

Gender itself must be considered a structural property of society. It is not manifested just in our personalities, our cultural rules, or other institutions. Gender is deeply embedded as a basis for stratification, differentiating opportunities and constraints. This differentiation has consequences on three levels: (1) at the individual level, for the development of gendered selves; (2) at the interactional level, for men and women face different expectations even when they fill the identical structural position; and (3) at the institutional level, for rarely will women and men be given identical positions. Differentiation at the institutional level is based on explicit regulations or laws regarding resource distribution, whether resources be defined as access to opportunities or actual material goods. (See Figure 27.1 for a schematic summary of the argument thus far.)

While the *gender structure* clearly affects selves, cultural rules, and institutions, far too much explanatory power is presumed to rest in the motivation of gendered selves. We live in a very individualistic society that teaches us to make our own choices and take responsibility for our own actions. What this has meant for theories about gender is that a tremendous amount of energy is spent on trying to understand why women and men "choose" to devote their life energies to such different enterprises. The distinctly sociological contribution to the explanation hasn't had enough attention: even when individual women and men do *not* desire to live gendered lives or to support male dominance, they often find themselves compelled to do so by the logic of gendered choices. That is, interactional pressures and institutional design create gender and the resultant inequality, even in the absence of individual desires. . . .

Choices often assumed to be based on personalities and individual preferences (e.g., consequences of the gender structure at the individual level) are better understood as social constructions based on institutionally constrained opportunities and the limited availability of nongendered cognitive images. . . .

Even if individuals are capable of change and wish to eradicate male dominance from their personal lives, the influence of gendered institutions and interactional contexts persists. These contexts are organized by gender stratification at the institutional level, which includes the distribution of material resources organized by gender, the ways by which formal organizations and institutions themselves are gendered, and gendered ideological discourse. For example, in a society in which girls are not taught to read, we could never find a young woman who would be considered a potential international leader. Nor would men denied access to jobs with "family wages" be seen by middle-class American women as good catches for husbands.

At this moment in American society, cultural rules and cognitive images that operate at the interactional level are particularly important in the persistence of gender stratification in families. It is not that sex-role socialization or early childhood experience is trivial; gender structure creates gendered selves. But, at this point in history, sex-role socialization itself is ambivalent. In addition, it is clear that even women with feminist worldviews and substantial incomes are constrained by gender structures.

In spite of the removal of some gender discrimination in both law and organizations, gender stratification remains. That is, formal access to opportunities may be gender neutral, yet equality of results may not ensue. Therefore, neither the individual-level explanations nor those based solely on institutional discrimination can explain continued gender stratification in families. Instead, the cognitive images to which we must respond during interaction are the engines that drive continued gender stratification when individuals desire egalitarian relationships and the law allows them (cf. Ridgeway 1997). . . .

The social structure clearly constrains gendered action even as it makes it possible. Wives, even those who have no motivation to provide domestic service to their husbands, are constrained to do so by social expectations. A husband who has a disheveled appearance reflects poorly on his wife's domestic abilities (in real life as well as "ring around the collar"' commercials). A wife will be sanctioned by friends and family for keeping a cluttered and dusty home; a husband will not be. Husbands' behaviors are constrained as well. A husband who is content with a relatively low-wage, low-stress occupation may be pressured (by his wife, among others) to provide more for his family. Few wives, however, are pressured into higher-stress, higher-wage occupations by their families. The expectations we face during ongoing interaction often push us to behave as others want us to (Heiss 1981).

Cultural images within marriage also make gendered action possible. Husbands are not free to work long hours in order to climb the career ladder or increase income unless they are superordinate partners in a system in which wives provide them the "leisure" (i.e., freedom from responsibility for self-care or family care) to do so. Some married women may leave jobs they dislike because the position of domestic wife is open to them. A husband and father unable to keep a job has few other options for gaining self-esteem and identity.

Individuals often act in a structurally patterned fashion, without much thought. Routine is taken for granted even when the action re-creates the inequitable social structure. A woman may choose to change her name upon marriage simply because it seems easier. (Some women may not even know they are making a choice, as name change is so routine in their social circle.) Yet by changing her name a woman implicitly supports and re-creates a reflective definition of wifehood. She does gender. Similarly, when a woman assents to her children carrying her husband's surname (even when she herself has retained her own), she is recreating a patrilineal system by which family identity is traced primarily through the male line. In both these examples, a couple's intention may be to create a nuclear family identity and to avoid the awkwardness of hyphenated names for children. Whatever the intention, the structure has constrained the possible choices available to them. Their purposive actions may provide them with both the desired consequences (one family name) *and* the unintended consequence of re-creating a gender structure based on reflective female identity and patrilineal family names.

REFERENCES

Aptheker, Bettina. 1989. *Tapestries of Life: Women's Work, Women's Consciousness, and the Meaning of Daily Experience*. Amherst: University of Massachusetts Press.

Bandura, Albert and Richard H. Walters. 1963. *Social Learning and Personality*. New York: Holt, Rinehart and Winston.

Bielby, Denise D. and William T Bielby. 1984. "Work Commitment and Sex-Role Attitudes." *American Sociological Review* 49:234–47.

Brines, Julie. 1994. "Economic Dependency and the Division of Labor." *American Journal of Sociology* 100(3):652–88.

Chodorow, Nancy. 1978. *The Reproduction of Mothering*. Berkeley: University of California Press.

———. 1989. *Feminism and Psychoanalytic Theory*. New Haven, CT: Yale University Press.

Collins, Patricia Hill. 1990. *Black Feminist Thought: Knowledge, Consciousness, and the Politics of Empowerment*. Boston: Unwin, Hyman.

Deaux, Kay and Brenda Major. 1990. "A Social–Psychological Model of Gender." In *Theoretical Perspectives on Sexual Difference*, edited by Deborah Rhode. New Haven, CT: Yale University Press.

Epstein, Cynthia Fuchs. 1988. *Deceptive Distinctions: Sex, Gender, and the Social Order.* New Haven, CT: Yale University Press.

Ferree, Myra Marx. 1990. "Beyond Separate Spheres: Feminism and Family Research." *Journal of Marriage and the Family* 53(4):866–84.

Gerson, Kathleen. 1985. *Hard Choices.* Berkeley: University of California Press.

———. 1993. *No Man's Land.* New York: Basic Books.

Heiss, Jerold. 1981. "Social Rules." In *Social Psychology: Sociological Perspectives,* edited by Morris Rosenberg and Ralph H. Turner. New York: Basic Books.

Hertz, Rosanna. 1986. *More Equal Than Others: Women and Men in Dual-Career Marriages.* Berkeley: University of California Press.

Inglehart, Ronald. 1977. *The Silent Revolution: Changing Values and Political Styles among Western Publics.* Princeton, NJ: Princeton University Press.

———. 1981. "Post-Materialism in an Environment of Insecurity." *American Political Science Review* 75:880–900.

Kanter, Rosabeth. 1977. *Men and Women of the Corporation.* New York: Harper and Row.

Keller, Evelyn Fox. 1985. *Reflections on Gender and Science.* New Haven, CT: Yale University Press.

Lesthaeghe, Ron. 1980. "On the Social Control of Human Reproduction." *Population and Development Review* 4:427–548.

Lorber, Judith. 1994. *Paradoxes of Gender.* New Haven, CT: Yale University Press.

Mischel, Walter. 1966. "A Social Learning View of Sex Differences in Behavior." Pp. 56–81 in *The Development of Sex Differences,* edited by Eleanor Maccoby. Stanford, CA: Stanford University Press.

Reskin, Barbara. 1988. "Bringing the Men Back In: Sex Differentiation and the Devaluation of Women's Work." *Gender and Society* 2:58–81.

Ridgeway, Cecilia. 1997. "Interaction and the Conservation of Gender Inequality: Considering Employment." *American Sociological Review* 62:218–35.

Risman, Barbara. 1986. "Can Men 'Mother'?: Life as a Single Father." *Family Relations* 35:95–102.

———. 1987. "Intimate Relationships from a Microstructural Perspective: Mothering Men." *Gender and Society* 1:6–32.

———. 1988. "Just the Two of Us: Parent–Child Relationships in Single Parent Homes." *Journal of Marriage and the Family* 50:1049–62.

Risman, Barbara and Pepper Schwartz. 1989. *Gender in Intimate Relationships.* Belmont, CA: Wadsworth.

Rubin, Lillian. 1982. *Intimate Strangers.* New York: Harper and Row.

Ruddick, Sara. 1989. *Maternal Thinking.* Boston: Beacon Press.

———. 1992. "Thinking About Fathers." In *Rethinking the Family: Some Feminist Questions,* edited by Barrie Thorne. Boston: Northeastern University Press.

South, Scott J. and Glenna Spitz. 1994. "Housework in Marital and Nonmarital Households." *American Sociological Review* 59:327–47.

Stokes, Randall and John Hewitt. 1976. "Aligning Actions." *American Sociological Review* 41:838–49.

Weitzman, Lenore Jacqueline. 1979. *Sex Role Socialization: A Focus on Women.* Palo Alto, CA: Mayfield.

West, Candace and Don H. Zimmerman. 1987. "Doing Gender." *Gender and Society* 1(2):125–51.

West, Candace and Sarah Fenstermaker. 1995. "Doing Difference." *Gender and Society* 9:8–37.

Williams, Christine. 1989. *Gender Differences at Work.* Berkeley: University of California Press.

———. 1992. "The Glass Escalator: Hidden Advantages for Men in the 'Female' Professions." *Social Problems* 39:253–67.

Wrong, Dennis H. 1961. "The Oversocialized Conception of Man in Modern Sociol-
  ogy." *American Sociological Review* 26:183–93.
Yoder, Janice. 1991. "Rethinking Tokenism: Looking Beyond Numbers." *Social Prob-
  lems* 5:178–92.
Zimmer, Lynn. 1988. "Tokenism and Women in the Workplace: The Limits of Gender-
  Neutral Theory." *Social Problems* 35:64–77.

28

THE GLASS ESCALATOR
Hidden Advantages for Men
in the "Female" Professions

CHRISTINE L. WILLIAMS

Sociologists argue that individuals learn gender roles and gender stereotyping through socialization. Gender role socialization often reinforces gender
inequality because men and women are expected to fulfill different family
and occupation roles. Thus, in U.S. society, women traditionally are assigned
the roles of homemaker, nurse, teacher, and secretary, which typically have
less social status and lower salaries than male occupational roles. This 1992
article by Christine L. Williams is an analysis of what happens when men enter traditionally defined "female" occupations. Williams, a professor of sociology at the University of Texas at Austin, has researched gender issues for
a number of years, especially society's treatment of men and the changing
cultural definitions of masculinity. The study excerpted here utilizes in-
depth interviews to reveal the advantages and disadvantages experienced
by male nurses, teachers, librarians, and social workers.

The sex segregation of the U.S. labor force is one of the most perplex-
ing and tenacious problems in our society. Even though the proportion
of men and women in the labor force is approaching parity (particularly for younger cohorts of workers) (U.S. Department of Labor 1991:18),
men and women are still generally confined to predominantly single-sex

From *Social Problems* 39, no. 3 (August 1992):253–67. © 1992 by The Society for the
Study of Social Problems. Reprinted by permission from University of California
Press.

occupations. Forty percent of men or women would have to change major occupational categories to achieve equal representation of men and women in
all jobs (Reskin and Roos 1990:6), but even this figure underestimates the
true degree of sex segregation. It is extremely rare to find specific jobs where
equal numbers of men and women are engaged in the same activities in the
same industries (Bielby and Baron 1984).

Most studies of sex segregation in the workforce have focused on
women's experiences in male-dominated occupations. Both researchers and
advocates for social change have focused on the barriers faced by women
who try to integrate predominantly male fields. Few have looked at the "flip
side" of occupational sex segregation: the exclusion of men from predominantly female occupations (exceptions include Schreiber 1979; Williams 1989;
Zimmer 1988). But the fact is that men are less likely to enter female sex-
typed occupations than women are to enter male-dominated jobs (Jacobs
1989). Reskin and Roos, for example, were able to identify 33 occupations in
which female representation increased by more than nine percentage points
between 1970 and 1980, but only three occupations in which the proportion
of men increased as radically (1990:20–21).

In this paper, I examine men's underrepresentation in four predominantly female occupations—nursing, librarianship, elementary school teaching, and social work. Throughout the twentieth century, these occupations
have been identified with "women's work"—even though prior to the Civil
War, men were more likely to be employed in these areas. These four occupations, often called the female "semi-professions" (Hodson and Sullivan
1990), today range from 5.5 percent male (in nursing) to 32 percent male (in
social work). These percentages have not changed substantially in decades.
In fact, two of these professions—librarianship and social work—have experienced declines in the proportions of men since 1975. Nursing is the only
one of the four experiencing noticeable changes in sex composition, with the
proportion of men increasing 80 percent between 1975 and 1990. Even so,
men continue to be a tiny minority of all nurses. . . .

Methods

I conducted in-depth interviews with 76 men and 23 women in four occupations from 1985 to 1991. Interviews were conducted in four metropolitan
areas: San Francisco/Oakland, California; Austin, Texas; Boston, Massachusetts; and Phoenix, Arizona. These four areas were selected because they show
considerable variation in the proportions of men in the four professions.
For example, Austin has one of the highest percentages of men in nursing
(7.7 percent), whereas Phoenix's percentage is one of the lowest (2.7 percent)
(U.S. Bureau of the Census 1980). The sample was generated using "snow-
balling" techniques. Women were included in the sample to gauge their feelings and responses to men who enter "their" professions. . . .

Discrimination in Hiring

Contrary to the experience of many women in the male-dominated professions, many of the men and women I spoke to indicated that there is a *preference* for hiring men in these four occupations. A Texas librarian at a junior high school said that his school district "would hire a male over a female."

> I: Why do you think that is?
>
> R: *Because there are so few, and the . . . ones that they do have, the library directors seem to really . . . think they're doing great jobs. I don't know, maybe they just feel they're being progressive or something, [but] I have had a real sense that they really appreciate having a male, particularly at the junior high. . . . As I said, when seven of us lost our jobs from the high schools and were redistributed, there were only four positions at junior high, and I got one of them. Three of the librarians, some who had been here longer than I had with the school district, were put down in elementary school as librarians. And I definitely think that being male made a difference in my being moved to the junior high rather than an elementary school.*

Many of the men perceived their token status as males in predominantly female occupations as an *advantage* in hiring and promotions. I asked an Arizona teacher whether his specialty (elementary special education) was an unusual area for men compared to other areas within education. He said,

> *Much more so. I am extremely marketable in special education. That's not why I got into the field. But I am extremely marketable because I am a man.*

In several cases, the more female-dominated the specialty, the greater the apparent preference for men. For example, when asked if he encountered any problem getting a job in pediatrics, a Massachusetts nurse said,

> *No, no, none. . . . I've heard this from managers and supervisory-type people with men in pediatrics: "It's nice to have a man because it's such a female-dominated profession."*

However, there were some exceptions to this preference for men in the most female-dominated specialties. In some cases, formal policies actually barred men from certain jobs. This was the case in some rural Texas school districts, which refused to hire men in the youngest grades (K–3). Some nurses also reported being excluded from positions in obstetrics and gynecology wards, a policy encountered more frequently in private Catholic hospitals.

But often the pressures keeping men out of certain specialties were more subtle than this. Some men described being "tracked" into practice areas within their professions which were considered more legitimate for men. For example, one Texas man described how he was pushed into administration and planning in social work, even though "I'm not interested in writing policy; I'm much more interested in research and clinical stuff." A nurse who is interested in pursuing graduate study in family and child health in Boston said he was dissuaded from entering the program specialty in favor of a concentration in "adult nursing." A kindergarten teacher described the difficulty of finding a job in his specialty after graduation: "I was recruited immediately to start getting into a track to become an administrator. And it was men who recruited me. It was men that ran the system at that time, especially in Los Angeles."

This tracking may bar men from the most female-identified specialties within these professions. But men are effectively being "kicked upstairs" in the process. Those specialties considered more legitimate practice areas for men also tend to be the most prestigious, better-paying ones. A distinguished kindergarten teacher, who had been voted citywide "Teacher of the Year," told me that even though people were pleased to see him in the classroom, "there's been some encouragement to think about administration, and there's been some encouragement to think about teaching at the university level or something like that, or supervisory-type position." That is, despite his aptitude and interest in staying in the classroom, he felt pushed in the direction of administration.

The effect of this "tracking" is the opposite of that experienced by women in male-dominated occupations. Researchers have reported that many women encounter a "glass ceiling" in their efforts to scale organizational and professional hierarchies. That is, they are constrained by invisible barriers to promotion in their careers, caused mainly by sexist attitudes of men in the highest positions (Freeman 1990). In contrast to the "glass ceiling," many of the men I interviewed seem to encounter a "glass escalator." Often, despite their intentions, they face invisible pressures to move up in their professions. As if on a moving escalator, they must work to stay in place.

A public librarian specializing in children's collections (a heavily female-dominated concentration) described an encounter with this "escalator" in his very first job out of library school. In his first six-months' evaluation, his supervisors commended him for his good work in storytelling and related activities, but they criticized him for "not shooting high enough."

> *Seriously. That's literally what they were telling me. They assumed that because I was a male—and they told me this—and that I was being hired right out of graduate school, that somehow I wasn't doing the kind of management-oriented work that they thought I should be doing. And as a result, really they had a lot of bad marks, as it were, against me on my evaluation. And I said I couldn't believe this!*

Throughout his 10-year career, he has had to struggle to remain in children's collections.

The glass escalator does not operate at all levels. In particular, men in academia reported some gender-based discrimination in the highest positions due to their universities' commitment to affirmative action. Two nursing professors reported that they felt their own chances of promotion to deanships were nil because their universities viewed the position of nursing dean as a guaranteed female appointment in an otherwise heavily male-dominated administration. One California social work professor reported his university canceled its search for a dean because no minority male or female candidates had been placed on their short list. It was rumored that other schools on campus were permitted to go forward with their searches—even though they also failed to put forward names of minority candidates—because the higher administration perceived it to be "easier" to fulfill affirmative action goals in the social work school. The interviews provide greater evidence of the "glass escalator" at work in the lower levels of these professions.

Of course, men's motivations also play a role in their advancement to higher professional positions. I do not mean to suggest that the men I talked to all resented the informal tracking they experienced. For many men, leaving the most female-identified areas of their professions helped them resolve internal conflicts involving their masculinity. One man left his job as a school social worker to work in a methadone drug treatment program not because he was encouraged to leave by his colleagues, but because "I think there was some macho shit there, to tell you the truth, because I remember feeling a little uncomfortable there . . . ; it didn't feel right to me." Another social worker, employed in the mental health services department of a large urban area in California, reflected on his move into administration:

> *The more I think about it, through our discussion, I'm sure that's a large part of why I wound up in administration. It's okay for a man to do the administration. In fact, I don't know if I fully answered a question that you asked a little while ago about how did being male contribute to my advancing in the field. I was saying it wasn't because I got any special favoritism as a man, but . . . I think . . . because I'm a man, I felt a need to get into this kind of position. I may have worked harder toward it, may have competed harder for it, than most women would do, even women who think about doing administrative work.*

Elsewhere I have speculated on the origins of men's tendency to define masculinity through single-sex work environments (Williams 1989). Clearly, personal ambition does play a role in accounting for men's movement into more "male-defined" arenas within these professions. But these occupations also structure opportunities for males independent of their individual desires or motives.

The interviews suggest that men's underrepresentation in these professions cannot be attributed to discrimination in hiring or promotions. Many of the men indicated that they received preferential treatment because they were men. Although men mentioned gender discrimination in the hiring process, for the most part they were channeled into the more "masculine" specialties within these professions, which ironically meant being "tracked" into better-paying and more prestigious specialties.

Supervisors and Colleagues: The Working Environment

Researchers claim that subtle forms of workplace discrimination push women out of male-dominated occupations (Jacobs 1989; Reskin and Hartmann 1986). In particular, women report feeling excluded from informal leadership and decision-making networks, and they sense hostility from their male co-workers, which makes them feel uncomfortable and unwanted (Carothers and Crull 1984). Respondents in this study were asked about their relationships with supervisors and female colleagues to ascertain whether men also experienced "poisoned" work environments when entering gender atypical occupations.

A major difference in the experience of men and women in nontraditional occupations is that men in these situations are far more likely to be supervised by a member of their own sex. In each of the four professions I studied, men are overrepresented in administrative and managerial capacities, or, as is the case of nursing, their positions in the organizational hierarchy are governed by men (Grimm and Stern 1974; Phenix 1987; Schmuck 1987; Williams 1989; York, Henley, and Gamble 1987). Thus, unlike women who enter "male fields," the men in these professions often work under the direct supervision of other men.

Many of the men interviewed reported that they had good rapport with their male supervisors. Even in professional school, some men reported extremely close relationships with their male professors. For example, a Texas librarian described an unusually intimate association with two male professors in graduate school:

> I can remember a lot of times in the classroom there would be discussions about a particular topic or issue, and the conversation would spill over into their office hours, after the class was over. And even though there were . . . a couple of the other women that had been in on the discussion, they weren't there. And I don't know if that was preferential or not. . . . It certainly carried over into personal life as well. Not just at the school and that sort of thing. I mean, we would get together for dinner. . . .

Other men reported similar closeness with their professors. A Texas psychotherapist recalled his relationships with his male professors in social work school:

> I made it a point to make a golfing buddy with one of the guys that was in administration. He and I played golf a lot. He was the guy who kind of ran the research training, the research part of the master's program. Then there was a sociologist who ran the other part of the research program. He and I developed a good friendship.

This close mentoring by male professors contrasts with the reported experience of women in nontraditional occupations. Others have noted a lack of solidarity among women in nontraditional occupations. Writing about military academies, for example, Yoder (1989) describes the failure of token women to mentor succeeding generations of female cadets. She argues that women attempt to play down their gender difference from men because it is the source of scorn and derision.

> Because women felt unaccepted by their male colleagues, one of the last things they wanted to do was to emphasize their gender. Some women thought that, if they kept company with other women, this would highlight their gender and would further isolate them from male cadets. These women desperately wanted to be accepted as cadets, not as *women* cadets. Therefore, they did everything from not wearing skirts as an option with their uniforms to avoiding being a part of a group of women. (P. 532)

Men in nontraditional occupations face a different scenario—their gender is construed as a *positive* difference. Therefore, they have an incentive to bond together and emphasize their distinctiveness from the female majority. . . .

Openly gay men may encounter less favorable treatment at the hands of their supervisors. For example, a nurse in Texas stated that one of the physicians he worked with preferred to staff the operating room with male nurses exclusively—as long as they weren't gay. Stigma associated with homosexuality leads some men to enhance, or even exaggerate, their "masculine" qualities and may be another factor pushing men into more "acceptable" specialties for men.

Not all men who work in these occupations are supervised by men. Many of the men interviewed who had female bosses also reported high levels of acceptance—although levels of intimacy with women seemed lower than with other men. In some cases, however, men reported feeling shut out from decision making when the higher administration was constituted entirely by women. I asked an Arizona librarian whether men in the library profession were discriminated against in hiring because of their sex:

> *Professionally speaking, people go to considerable lengths to keep that kind of thing out of their [hiring] deliberations. Personally, is another matter. It's pretty common around here to talk about the "old girl network." This is one of the few libraries that I've had any intimate knowledge of which is actually controlled by women. . . . Most of the department heads and upper-level administrators are women. And there's an "old girl network" that works just like the "old boy network," except that the important conferences take place in the women's room rather than on the golf course. But the political mechanism is the same, the exclusion of the other sex from decision making is the same. The reasons are the same. It's somewhat discouraging. . . .*

Although I did not interview many supervisors, I did include 23 women in my sample to ascertain their perspectives about the presence of men in their professions. All of the women I interviewed claimed to be supportive of their male colleagues, but some conveyed ambivalence. For example, a social work professor said she would like to see more men enter the social work profession, particularly in the clinical specialty (where they are underrepresented). Indeed, she favored affirmative action hiring guidelines for men in the profession. Yet, she resented the fact that her department hired "another white male" during a recent search. . . .

Even outside work, most of the men interviewed said they felt fully accepted by their female colleagues. They were usually included in informal socializing occasions with the women—even though this frequently meant attending baby showers or Tupperware parties. Many said that they declined offers to attend these events because they were not interested in "women's things," although several others claimed to attend everything: The minority men I interviewed seemed to feel the least comfortable in these informal contexts. One social worker in Arizona was asked about socializing with his female colleagues:

> I: So in general, for example, if all the employees were going to get together to have a party, or celebrate a bridal shower or whatever, would you be invited along with the rest of the group?
>
> R: *They would invite me, I would say, somewhat reluctantly. Being a black male, working with all white females, it did cause some outside problems. So I didn't go to a lot of functions with them. . . .*
>
> I: You felt that there was some tension there on the level of your acceptance . . . ?
>
> R: *Yeah. It was OK working, but on the outside, personally, there was some tension there. It never came out, that they said, "Because of who you are we can't invite you" (laughs), and I wouldn't have done anything anyway. I would have probably respected them more for saying what was on their minds. But I never felt completely in with the group.*

Some single men also said they felt uncomfortable socializing with married female colleagues because it gave the "wrong impression." But in general, the men said that they felt very comfortable around their colleagues and described their workplaces as very congenial for men. It appears unlikely, therefore, that men's underrepresentation in these professions is due to hostility toward men on the part of supervisors or women workers.

Discrimination from "Outsiders"

The most compelling evidence of discrimination against men in these professions is related to their dealings with the public. Men often encounter negative stereotypes when they come into contact with clients or "outsiders"—people they meet outside of work. For instance, it is popularly assumed that male nurses are gay. Librarians encounter images of themselves as "wimpy" and asexual. Male social workers describe being typecast as "feminine" and "passive." Elementary school teachers are often confronted by suspicions that they are pedophiles. One kindergarten teacher described an experience that occurred early in his career, which was related to him years afterward by his principal:

> He indicated to me that parents had come to him and indicated to him that they had a problem with the fact that I was a male. . . . I recall almost exactly what he said. There were three specific concerns that the parents had: One parent said, "How can he love my child; he's a man." The second thing that I recall, he said the parent said, "He has a beard." And the third thing was, "Aren't you concerned about homosexuality?"

Such suspicions often cause men in all four professions to alter their work behavior to guard against sexual abuse charges, particularly in those specialties requiring intimate contact with women and children.

Men are very distressed by these negative stereotypes, which tend to undermine their self-esteem and to cause them to second-guess their motivations for entering these fields. A California teacher said,

> If I tell men that I don't know, that I'm meeting for the first time, that that's what I do, . . . sometimes there's a look on their faces that, you know, "Oh, couldn't get a real job?"

When asked if his wife, who is also an elementary school teacher, encounters the same kind of prejudice, he said,

> No, it's accepted because she's a woman. . . . I think people would see that as a . . . step up, you know. "Oh, you're not a housewife, you've got a career. That's great . . . that you're out there working. And you have a daughter, but you're still out there working. You decided not to stay home, and you went out there and got a job." Whereas for me, it's more like I'm supposed to be out working anyway, even though I'd rather be home with [my daughter].

Unlike women who enter traditionally male professions, men's movement into these jobs is perceived by the "outside world" as a step down in status. This particular form of discrimination may be most significant in explaining why men are underrepresented in these professions. Men who otherwise might show interest in and aptitudes for such careers are probably discouraged from pursuing them because of the negative popular stereotypes associated with the men who work in them. This is a crucial difference from the experience of women in nontraditional professions: "My daughter, the physician," resonates far more favorably in most people's ears than "my son, the nurse."

Many of the men in my sample identified the stigma of working in a female-identified occupation as the major barrier to more men entering their professions. However, for the most part, they claimed that these negative stereotypes were not a factor in their own decisions to join these occupations. Most respondents didn't consider entering these fields until well into adulthood, after working in some related occupation. Several social workers and librarians even claimed they were not aware that men were a minority in their chosen professions. Either they had no well-defined image or stereotype, or their contacts and mentors were predominantly men. For example, prior to entering library school, many librarians held part-time jobs in university libraries, where there are proportionally more men than in the profession generally. Nurses and elementary school teachers were more aware that mostly women worked in these jobs, and this was often a matter of some concern to them. However, their choices were ultimately legitimized by mentors, or by encouraging friends or family members who implicitly reassured them that entering these occupations would not typecast them as feminine. In some cases, men were told by recruiters there were special advancement opportunities for men in these fields, and they entered them expecting rapid promotion to administrative positions.

> I: Did it ever concern you when you were making the decision to enter nursing school, the fact that it is a female-dominated profession?
>
> R: *Not really. I never saw myself working on the floor. I saw myself pretty much going into administration, just getting the background and then getting a job someplace as a supervisor and then working, getting up into administration.*

Because of the unique circumstances of their recruitment, many of the respondents did not view their occupational choices as inconsistent with a male gender role, and they generally avoided the negative stereotypes directed against men in these fields.

Indeed, many of the men I interviewed claimed that they did not encounter negative professional stereotypes until they had worked in these fields for several years. Popular prejudices can be damaging to self-esteem and probably push some men out of these professions altogether. Yet, ironically, they sometimes contribute to the "glass escalator" effect I have been describing. Men seem to encounter the most vituperative criticism from the public when they are in the most female-identified specialties. Public concerns sometimes result in their being shunted into more "legitimate" positions for men. A librarian formerly in charge of a branch library's children's collection, who now works in the reference department of the city's main library, describes his experience:

> R: *Some of the people [who frequented the branch library] complained that they didn't want to have a man doing the storytelling scenario. And I got transferred here to the central library in an equivalent job. . . . I thought that I did a good job. And I had been told by my supervisor that I was doing a good job.*

I: Have you ever considered filing some sort of lawsuit to get that other job back?

R: *Well, actually, the job I've gotten now . . . well, it's a reference librarian; it's what I wanted in the first place. I've got a whole lot more authority here. I'm also in charge of the circulation desk. And I've recently been promoted because of my new stature, so . . . no, I'm not considering trying to get that other job back.*

The negative stereotypes about men who do "women's work" can push men out of specific jobs. However, to the extent that they channel men into more "legitimate" practice areas, their effects can actually be positive. Instead of being a source of discrimination, these prejudices can add to the "glass escalator effect" by pressuring men to move *out* of the most female-identified areas and *up* to those regarded more legitimate and prestigious for men.

Author's Note: This research was funded in part by a faculty grant from the University of Texas at Austin. I also acknowledge the support of the sociology departments of the University of California, Berkeley; Harvard University; and Arizona State University. I would like to thank Judy Auerbach, Martin Button, Robert Nye, Teresa Sullivan, Debra Umberson, Mary Waters, and the reviewers at *Social Problems* for their comments on earlier versions of this paper.

REFERENCES

Bielby, William T. and James N. Baron. 1984. "A Woman's Place Is with Other Women: Sex Segregation within Organizations." Pp. 27–55 in *Sex Segregation in the Workplace: Trends, Explanations, Remedies,* edited by Barbara Reskin. Washington, DC: National Academy Press.

Carothers, Suzanne C. and Peggy Crull. 1984. "Contrasting Sexual Harassment in Female-Dominated and Male-Dominated Occupations." Pp. 220–27 in *My Troubles Are Going to Have Trouble with Me: Everyday Trials and Triumphs of Women Workers,* edited by Karen B. Sacks and Dorothy Remy. New Brunswick, NJ: Rutgers University Press.

Freeman, Sue J. M. 1990. *Managing Lives: Corporate Women and Social Change.* Amherst: University of Massachusetts Press.

Grimm, James W. and Robert N. Stern. 1974. "Sex Roles and Internal Labor Market Structures: The Female Semi-Professions." *Social Problems* 21:690–705.

Hodson, Randy and Teresa Sullivan. 1990. *The Social Organization of Work.* Belmont, CA: Wadsworth Publishing Co.

Jacobs, Jerry. 1989. *Revolving Doors: Sex Segregation and Women's Careers.* Stanford, CA: Stanford University Press.

Phenix, Katherine. 1987. "The Status of Women Librarians." *Frontiers* 9:36–40.

Reskin, Barbara and Heidi Hartmann. 1986. *Women's Work, Men's Work: Sex Segregation on the Job.* Washington, DC: National Academy Press.

Reskin, Barbara and Patricia Roos. 1990. *Job Queues, Gender Queues: Explaining Women's Inroads into Male Occupations.* Philadelphia: Temple University Press.

Schmuck, Patricia A. 1987. "Women School Employees in the United States." Pp. 75–97 in *Women Educators: Employees of Schools in Western Counties,* edited by Patricia A. Schmuck. Albany: State University of New York Press.

Schreiber, Carol. 1979. *Men and Women in Transitional Occupations.* Cambridge, MA: MIT Press.

U.S. Bureau of the Census. 1980. *Detailed Population Characteristics,* vol. 1, chap. D. Washington, DC: Government Printing Office.

U.S. Department of Labor. Bureau of Labor Statistics. 1991. *Employment and Earnings.* Washington, DC: Government Printing Office.

Williams, Christine L. 1989. *Gender Differences at Work: Women and Men in Nontraditional Occupations.* Berkeley: University of California Press.

Yoder, Janice D. 1989. "Women at West Point: Lessons for Token Women in Male-Dominated Occupations." Pp. 523–37 in *Women: A Feminist Perspective,* edited by Jo Freeman. Mountain View, CA: Mayfield Publishing Company.

York, Reginald O., H. Carl Henley, and Dorothy N. Gamble. 1987. "Sexual Discrimination in Social Work: Is It Salary or Advancement?" *Social Work* 32:336–40.

Zimmer, Lynn. 1988. "Tokenism and Women in the Workplace." *Social Problems* 35:64–77.

29

THE RACIAL CONSTRUCTION OF ASIAN AMERICAN WOMEN AND MEN

YEN LE ESPIRITU

Gender inequality has enormous consequences for women, men, and society. Gender inequality reinforces and perpetuates *sexism,* which is prejudice and discrimination against a person on the basis of his or her sex. The costs and consequences of sexism are extensive and include the wage gap, the feminization of poverty, high rates of female victimization as a result of male violence, and psychological and physical health problems in both women and men. This selection by Yen Le Espiritu, taken from *Asian American Women and Men: Labor, Laws, and Love* (1997), reveals the rampant sexism and racism within the institution of the media, both historically and currently. Specifically, Espiritu, a professor of ethnic studies at the University of California, San Diego, examines the interaction between race, social class, and gender in the treatment of Asian American women and men by the media and by the dominant culture. She finds that the cultural images of Asian Americans often contain sexual stereotypes, which are both racist and sexist, and they reinforce racial, patriarchal, and social class domination.

Yen Le Espiritu, *Asian American Women and Men: Labor, Laws, and Love,* pp. 86–88, 90–102, 106–107, copyright © 1997 by Sage Publications, Inc. Reprinted by permission of Sage Publications, Inc.

The slit-eyed, bucktooth Jap thrusting his bayonet, thirsty for blood. The in-
scrutable, wily Chinese detective with his taped eyelids and wispy moustache.
The childlike, indolent Filipino houseboy. Always giggling. Bowing and scrap-
ing. Eager to please, but untrustworthy. The sexless, hairless Asian male. The
servile, oversexed Asian female. The Geisha. The sultry, sarong-clad, South
Seas maiden. The serpentine, cunning Dragon Lady. Mysterious and evil,
eager to please. Effeminate. Untrustworthy. Yellow Peril. Fortune Cookie Psy-
chic. Savage. Dogeater. Invisible. Mute. Faceless peasants breeding too many
children. Gooks. Passive Japanese Americans obediently marching off to "relo-
cation camps" during the Second World War.

—JESSICA HAGEDORN (1993:XXII)

ocusing on the material lives of Asian Americans, . . . [earlier research
explored] . . . how racist and gendered immigration policies and labor
conditions have worked in tandem to keep Asian Americans in an assigned, subordinate place. But as is evident from the stereotypes listed above,
besides structural discrimination, Asian American men and women have
been subject to ideological assaults. Focusing on the ideological dimension of
Asian American oppression, this [article] examines the cultural symbols—or
what Patricia Hill Collins (1991) called "controlling images" (pp. 67–68)—
generated by the dominant group to help justify the economic exploitation
and social oppression of Asian American men and women over time. Writing on the objectification of black women, Collins (1991) observed that the
exercise of political-economic domination by racial elites "always involves
attempts to objectify the subordinate group" (p. 69). Transmitted through
cultural institutions owned, controlled, or supported by various elites, these
"controlling images" naturalize racism, sexism, and poverty by branding
subordinate groups as alternatively inferior, threatening, or praiseworthy.
These controlling images form part of a larger system of what Donald G.
Baker (1983) referred to as "psychosocial dominance" (p. 37). Along with the
threat and occasional use of violence, the psychosocial form of control conditions the subject minority to become the stereotype, to "live it, talk it, embrace it, measure group and individual worth in its terms, and believe it"
(Chin and Chan 1972:66–67). In so doing, minority members reject their own
individual and group identity and accept in its stead "a white supremacist
complex that establishes the primacy of Euro-American cultural practices
and social institutions" (Hamamoto 1994:2). But the objectification of Asian
Americans as the exotic and inferior "other" has never been absolute. Asian
Americans have always, but particularly since the 1960s, resisted race, class,
and gender exploitation not only through political and economic struggles
but also through cultural activism. My goal is to understand how the internalization and renunciation of these stereotypes have shaped sexual and gender politics within Asian America. In particular, I explore the conflicting politics of gender between Asian American men and women as they negotiate

the difficult terrain of cultural nationalism—the construction of an antias-
similationist, native Asian American subject—and gender identities.

Yellow Peril, Charlie Chan, and Suzie Wong

A central aspect of racial exploitation centers on defining people of color as
"the other" (Said 1979). The social construction of Asian American "otherness"—through such controlling images as the Yellow Peril, the model minority, the Dragon Lady, and the China Doll—is "the precondition for their
cultural marginalization, political impotence, and psychic alienation from
mainstream American society" (Hamamoto 1994:5). As indicated by these
stereotypes, representations of gender and sexuality figure strongly in the articulation of racism. These racist stereotypes collapse gender and sexuality:
Asian men have been constructed as hypermasculine, in the image of the
"Yellow Peril," but also as effeminate, in the image of the "model minority,"
and Asian women have been depicted as superfeminine, in the image of the
"China Doll," but also as castrating, in the image of the "Dragon Lady"
(Mullings 1994:279–80; Okihiro 1995). As Mary Ann Doane (1991) suggested, sexuality is "indissociable from the effects of polarization and differentiation, often linking them to structures of power and domination" (p. 217).
In the Asian American case, the gendering of ethnicity—the process whereby
white ideology assigns selected gender characteristics to various ethnic
"others"—cast Asian American men and women as simultaneously masculine and feminine but also as neither masculine nor feminine. On the one
hand, as part of the Yellow Peril, Asian American men and women have
been depicted as a *masculine* threat that needs to be contained. On the other
hand, both sexes have been skewed toward the female side: an indication of
the group's marginalization in U.S. society and its role as the compliant
"model minority" in contemporary U.S. cultural ideology. Although an apparent disjunction, both the feminization and masculinization of Asian men
and women exist to define and confirm the white man's superiority (Kim
1990). . . .

The Racial Construction of Asian American Manhood

Like other men of color, Asian American men have been excluded from
white-based cultural notions of the masculine. Whereas white men are depicted both as virile and as protectors of women, Asian men have been characterized both as asexual *and* as threats to white women. It is important to
note the historical contexts of these seemingly divergent representations of
Asian American manhood. The racist depictions of Asian men as "lascivious
and predatory" were especially pronounced during the nativist movement
against Asians at the turn of the century (Frankenberg 1993:75–76). The exclusion of Asian women from the United States and the subsequent estab-

lishment of bachelor societies eventually reversed the construction of Asian masculinity from "hypersexual" to "asexual" and even "homosexual." The contemporary model-minority stereotype further emasculates Asian American men as passive and malleable. Disseminated and perpetuated through the popular media, these stereotypes of the emasculated Asian male construct a reality in which social and economic discrimination against these men appears defensible. As an example, the desexualization of Asian men naturalized their inability to establish conjugal families in pre–World War II United States. Gliding over race-based exclusion laws that banned the immigration of most Asian women and antimiscegenation laws that prohibited men of color from marrying white women, these dual images of the eunuch and the rapist attributed the "womanless households" characteristic of prewar Asian America to Asian men's lack of sexual prowess and desirability.

A popular controlling image applied to Asian American men is that of the sinister Oriental—a brilliant, powerful villain who plots the destruction of Western civilization. Personified by the movie character of Dr. Fu Manchu, this Oriental mastermind combines Western science with Eastern magic and commands an army of devoted assassins (Hoppenstand 1983: 178). Though ruthless, Fu Manchu lacks masculine heterosexual prowess (Wang 1988:19), thus privileging heterosexuality. Frank Chin and Jeffrey Chan (1972), in a critique of the desexualization of Asian men in Western culture, described how the Fu Manchu character undermines Chinese American virility:

> Dr. Fu, a man wearing a long dress, batting his eyelashes, surrounded by muscular black servants in loin cloths, and with his habit of caressingly touching white men on the leg, wrist, and face with his long fingernails is not so much a threat as he is a frivolous offense to white manhood. (P. 60)

In another critique that glorifies male aggression, Frank Chin (1972) contrasted the neuterlike characteristics assigned to Asian men to the sexually aggressive images associated with other men of color: "Unlike the white stereotype of the evil black stud, Indian rapist, Mexican macho, the evil of the evil Dr. Fu Manchu was not sexual, but homosexual" (p. 66). However, Chin failed to note that as a homosexual, Dr. Fu (and by extension, Asian men) threatens and offends white masculinity—and therefore needs to be contained ideologically and destroyed physically.[1]

Whereas the evil Oriental stereotype marks Asian American men as the white man's enemy, the stereotype of the sexless Asian sidekick—Charlie Chan, the Chinese laundryman, the Filipino houseboy—depicts Asian men as devoted and impotent, eager to please. William Wu (1982) reported that the Chinese servant "is the most important single image of the Chinese immigrants" in American fiction about Chinese Americans between 1850 and 1940 (p. 60). More recently, such diverse television programs as *Bachelor Father*

(1957–1962), *Bonanza* (1959–1973), *Star Trek* (1966–1969), and *Falcon Crest* (1981–1990) all featured the stock Chinese bachelor domestic who dispenses sage advice to his superiors in addition to performing traditional female functions within the household (Hamamoto 1994:7). By trapping Chinese men (and by extension, Asian men) in the stereotypical "feminine" tasks of serving white men, American society erases the figure of the Asian "masculine" plantation worker in Hawaii or railroad construction worker in the western United States, thus perpetuating the myth of the androgynous and effeminate Asian man (Goellnicht 1992:198). This feminization, in turn, confines Asian immigrant men to the segment of the labor force that performs women's work.

The motion picture industry has been key in the construction of Asian men as sexual deviants. In a study of Asians in the U.S. motion pictures, Eugene Franklin Wong maintained that the movie industry filmically castrates Asian males to magnify the superior sexual status of white males (1978:27). As on-screen sexual rivals of whites, Asian males are neutralized, unable to sexually engage Asian women and prohibited from sexually engaging white women. By saving the white woman from sexual contact with the racial "other," the motion picture industry protects the Anglo-American, bourgeois male establishment from any challenges to its hegemony (Marchetti 1993:218). At the other extreme, the industry has exploited one of the most potent aspects of the Yellow Peril discourses—the sexual danger of contact between the races—by concocting a sexually threatening portrayal of the licentious and aggressive Yellow Man lusting after the White Woman (Marchetti 1993:3). Heedful of the larger society's taboos against Asian male-white female sexual union, white male actors donning "yellowface"—instead of Asian male actors—are used in these "love scenes." Nevertheless, the message of the perverse and animalistic Asian male attacking helpless white women is clear (Wong 1978). Though depicting sexual aggression, this image of the rapist, like that of the eunuch, casts Asian men as sexually undesirable. As Wong (1978) succinctly stated, in Asian male-white female relations, "There can be rape, but there cannot be romance" (p. 25). Thus, Asian males yield to the sexual superiority of the white males who are permitted filmically to maintain their sexual dominance over both white women and women of color. A young Vietnamese American man describes the damaging effect of these stereotypes on his self-image:

> Every day I was forced to look into a mirror created by white society and its media. As a young Asian man, I shrank before white eyes. I wasn't tall, I wasn't fair, I wasn't muscular, and so on. Combine that with the enormous insecurities any pubescent teenager feels, and I have no difficulty in knowing now why I felt naked before a mass of white people. (Nguyen 1990:23)

White cultural and institutional racism against Asian males is also reflected in the motion picture industry's preoccupation with the death of

Asians—a filmic solution to the threats of the Yellow Peril. In a perceptive analysis of Hollywood's view of Asians in films made from the 1930s to the 1960s, Tom Engelhardt (1976) described how Asians, like Native Americans, are seen by the movie industry as inhuman invaders, ripe for extermination. He argued that the theme of the nonhumanness of Asians prepares the audience to accept, without flinching, "the levelling and near-obliteration of three Asian areas in the course of three decades" (Engelhardt 1976:273). The industry's death theme, though applying to all Asians, is mainly focused on Asian males, with Asian females reserved for sexual purposes (Wong 1978:35). Especially in war films, Asian males, however advantageous their initial position, inevitably perish at the hands of the superior white males (Wong 1978:34).

The Racial Construction of Asian American Womanhood

Like Asian men, Asian women have been reduced to one-dimensional caricatures in Western representation. The condensation of Asian women's multiple differences into gross character types—mysterious, feminine, and nonwhite—obscures the social injustice of racial, class, and gender oppression (Marchetti 1993:71). Both Western film and literature promote dichotomous stereotypes of the Asian woman: She is either the cunning Dragon Lady or the servile Lotus Blossom Baby (Tong 1994:197). Though connoting two extremes, these stereotypes are interrelated: Both eroticize Asian women as exotic "others"—sensuous, promiscuous, but untrustworthy. Whereas American popular culture denies "manhood" to Asian men, it endows Asian women with an excess of "womanhood," sexualizing them but also impugning their sexuality. In this process, both sexism and racism have been blended together to produce the sexualization of white racism (Wong 1978:260). Linking the controlling images of Asian men and women, Elaine Kim (1990) suggested that Asian women are portrayed as sexual for the same reason that men are asexual: "Both exist to define the white man's virility and the white man's superiority" (p. 70).

As the racialized exotic "others," Asian American women do not fit the white-constructed notions of the feminine. Whereas white women have been depicted as chaste and dependable, Asian women have been represented as promiscuous and untrustworthy. In a mirror image of the evil Fu Manchu, the Asian woman was portrayed as the castrating Dragon Lady who, while puffing on her foot-long cigarette holder, could poison a man as easily as she could seduce him. "With her talon-like six-inch fingernails, her skin-tight satin dress slit to the thigh," the Dragon Lady is desirable, deceitful, and dangerous (Ling 1990:11). In the 1924 film *The Thief of Baghdad*, Anna May Wong, a pioneer Chinese American actress, played a handmaid who employed treachery to help an evil Mongol prince attempt to win the hand of the Princess of Baghdad (Tajima 1989:309). In so doing, Wong unwittingly popularized a common Dragon Lady social type: treacherous women who are partners in crime with men of their own kind. The publication of *Daughter of Fu Manchu* (1931) firmly entrenched the Dragon Lady image in white consciousness. Carrying on her father's work as the champion of Asian hegemony over the white race, Fah Lo Sue exhibited, in the words of American studies scholar William F. Wu, "exotic sensuality, sexual availability to a white man, and a treacherous nature" (cited in Tong 1994:197). A few years later, in 1934, Milton Caniff inserted into his adventure comic strip *Terry and the Pirates* another version of the Dragon Lady who "combines all the best features of past moustache twirlers with the lure of the handsome wench" (Hoppenstand 1983:178). As such, Caniff's Dragon Lady fuses the image of the evil male Oriental mastermind with that of the Oriental prostitute first introduced some 50 years earlier in the dime novels.

At the opposite end of the spectrum is the Lotus Blossom stereotype, reincarnated throughout the years as the China Doll, the Geisha Girl, the War Bride, or the Vietnamese prostitute—many of whom are the spoils of the last three wars fought in Asia (Tajima 1989:309). Demure, diminutive, and deferential, the Lotus Blossom Baby is "modest, tittering behind her delicate ivory hand, eyes downcast, always walking ten steps behind her man, and, best of all, devot[ing] body and soul to serving him" (Ling 1990:11). Interchangeable in appearance and name, these women have no voice; their "nonlanguage" includes uninterpretable chattering, pidgin English, giggling, or silence (Tajima 1989). These stereotypes of Asian women as submissive and dainty sex objects not only have impeded women's economic mobility but also have fostered an enormous demand for X-rated films and pornographic materials featuring Asian women in bondage, for "Oriental" bathhouse workers in U.S. cities, and for Asian mail-order brides (Kim 1984:64).

Sexism, Racism, and Love

The racialization of Asian manhood and womanhood upholds white masculine hegemony. Cast as sexually available, Asian women become yet another possession of the white man. In motion pictures and network television programs, interracial sexuality, though rare, occurs principally between a white male and an Asian female. A combination of sexism and racism makes this form of miscegenation more acceptable: Race mixing between an Asian male and a white female would upset not only racial taboos but those that attend patriarchal authority as well (Hamamoto 1994:39). Whereas Asian men are depicted as either the threatening rapist or the impotent eunuch, white men are endowed with the masculine attributes with which to sexually attract the Asian women. Such popular television shows as *Gunsmoke* (1955–1975) and *How the West Was Won* (1978–1979) clearly articulate the theme of Asian female sexual possession by the white male. In these shows, only white males have the prerogative to cross racial boundaries and to choose freely from among women of color as sex partners. Within a system of racial and gender oppression, the sexual possession of women and men of color by white men becomes yet another means of enforcing unequal power relations (Hamamoto 1994:46).

The preference for white male-Asian female is also prevalent in contemporary television news broadcasting, most recently in the 1993–1995 pairing of Dan Rather and Connie Chung as co-anchors of the *CBS Evening News.* Today, virtually every major metropolitan market across the United States has at least one Asian American female newscaster (Hamamoto 1994:245). While female Asian American anchorpersons—Connie Chung, Tritia Toyota, Wendy Tokuda, and Emerald Yeh—are popular television news figures, there is a nearly total absence of Asian American men. Critics argue that this is so because the white male hiring establishment, and presumably the larger American public, feels more comfortable (i.e., less threatened) seeing a white male sitting next to a minority female at the anchor desk than the reverse. Stephen Tschida of WDBJ-TV (Roanoke, Virginia), one of only a handful of male Asian American television news anchors, was informed early in his career that he did not have the proper "look" to qualify for the anchorperson position. Other male broadcast news veterans have reported being passed over for younger, more beauteous, female Asian Americans (Hamamoto 1994:245). This gender imbalance sustains the construction of Asian American women as more successful, assimilated, attractive, and desirable than their male counterparts.

To win the love of white men, Asian women must reject not only Asian men but their entire culture. Many Hollywood narratives featuring romances between Anglo American men and Asian women follow the popular Pocahontas mythos: The Asian woman, out of devotion for her white American lover, betrays her own people and commits herself to the dominant white culture by dying, longing for, or going to live with her white husband in his country. For example, in the various versions of *Miss Saigon,* the contemporary version of *Madame Butterfly,* the tragic Vietnamese prostitute eternally longs for the white boy soldier who has long abandoned her and their son (Hagedorn 1993:xxii). These tales of interracial romance inevitably have a tragic ending. The Asian partner usually dies, thus providing a cinematic resolution to the moral lapse of the Westerner. The Pocahontas paradigm can be read as a narrative of salvation; the Asian woman is saved either spiritually or morally from the excesses of her own culture, just as she physically saves her Western lover from the moral degeneracy of her own people (Marchetti 1993:218). For Asian women, who are marginalized not only by gender but also by class, race, or ethnicity, the interracial romance narratives promise "the American Dream of abundance, protection, individual choice, and freedom from the strictures of a traditional society in the paternalistic name of heterosexual romance" (Marchetti 1993:91). These narratives also carry a covert political message, legitimizing a masculinized Anglo American rule over a submissive, feminized Asia. The motion picture *China Gate* (1957) by Samuel Fuller and the network television program *The Lady from Yesterday* (1985), for example, promote an image of Vietnam that legitimizes American rule. Seduced by images of U.S. abundance, a feminized Vietnam sacrifices herself for the possibility of future incorporation into America, the land of individual freedom and economic opportunities. Thus, the interracial tales function not only as a romantic defense of traditional female roles within the patriarchy but also as a political justification of American hegemony in Asia (Marchetti 1993:108).

Fetishized as the embodiment of perfect womanhood and genuine exotic femininity, Asian women are pitted against their more modern, emancipated Western sisters (Tajima 1989). In two popular motion pictures, *Love Is a Many-Splendored Thing* (1955) and *The World of Suzie Wong* (1960), the white women remain independent and potentially threatening, whereas both Suyin and Suzie give up their independence in the name of love. Thus, the white female characters are cast as calculating, suffocating, and thoroughly undesirable, whereas the Asian female characters are depicted as truly "feminine"—passive, subservient, dependent, and domestic. Implicitly, these films warn white women to embrace the socially constructed passive Asian beauty as the feminine ideal if they want to attract and keep a man. In pitting white women against Asian women, Hollywood affirms white male identity against the threat of emerging feminism and the concomitant changes in gender relations (Marchetti 1993:115–16). As Robyn Wiegman (1991) observed, the absorption of women of color into gender categories traditionally reserved for white women is "part of a broader program of hegemonic recuperation, a program that has as its main focus the reconstruction of white masculine power" (p. 320). It is also important to note that as the racialized exotic "other," Asian women do not replace but merely substitute for white women, and thus will be readily dismissed once the "real" mistress returns.

The controlling images of Asian men and Asian women, exaggerated out of all proportion in Western representation, have created resentment and tension between Asian American men and women. Given this cultural milieu, many American-born Asians do not think of other Asians in sexual terms (Fung 1994:163). In particular, due to the persistent desexualization of the Asian male, many Asian females do not perceive their ethnic counterparts as desirable marriage partners (Hamamoto 1992:42). In so doing, these women unwittingly enforce the Eurocentric gender ideology that objectifies both sexes and racializes all Asians (see Collins 1990:185–86). In a column to *Asian Week*, a weekly Asian American newspaper, Daniel Yoon (1993) reported that at a recent dinner discussion hosted by the Asian American Students Association at his college, the Asian American women in the room proceeded, one after another, to describe how "Asian American men were too passive, too weak, too boring, too traditional, too abusive, too domineering, too ugly, too greasy, too short, too . . . Asian. Several described how they preferred white men, and how they never had and never would date an Asian man" (p. 16). Partly as a result of the racist constructions of Asian American womanhood and manhood and their acceptance by Asian Americans, intermarriage patterns are high, with Asian American women intermarrying at a much higher rate than Asian American men.[2] Moreover, Asian women involved in intermarriage have usually married white partners (Agbayani-Siewert & Revilla 1995:156; Min 1995:22; Nishi 1995:128). In part, these intermarriage patterns reflect the sexualization of white racism that constructs white men as the most desirable sexual partners, frowns on Asian male-white women relations, and fetishizes Asian women as the embodiment of perfect womanhood. Viewed in this light, the high rate of outmarriage for Asian American women is the "material outcome of an interlocking system of sexism and racism" (Hamamoto 1992:42).[3]

Cultural Resistance: Reconstructing Our Own Images

"One day/I going to write/about you," wrote Lois-Ann Yamanaka (1993) in "Empty Heart" (p. 548). And Asian Americans did write—"to inscribe our faces on the blank pages and screens of America's hegemonic culture" (Kim 1993:xii). As a result, Asian Americans' objectification as the exotic aliens who are different from, and other than, Euro-Americans has never been absolute. Within the confines of race, class, and gender oppression, Asian Americans have maintained independent self-definitions, challenging controlling images and replacing them with Asian American standpoints. The civil rights and ethnic studies movements of the late 1960s were training grounds for Asian American cultural workers and the development of oppositional projects. Grounded in the U.S. black power movement and in anticolonial struggles of Third World countries, Asian American antihegemonic projects have been unified by a common goal of articulating cultural resistance. Given the historical distortions and misrepresentations of Asian Americans in mainstream media, most cultural projects produced by Asian American men and women perform the important tasks of correcting histories, shaping legacies, creating new cultures, constructing a politics of resistance, and opening spaces for the forcibly excluded (Fung 1994:165; Kim 1993:xiii).

Fighting the exoticization of Asian Americans has been central in the ongoing work of cultural resistance. As discussed above, Asian Americans, however rooted in this country, are represented as recent transplants from Asia or as bearers of an exotic culture. . . . Asian American cultural workers simply do not accept the exotic, one-dimensional caricatures of themselves in U.S. mass media. . . . Asian American cultural projects also deconstruct the myth of the benevolent United States promised to women and men from Asia. . . . To reject the myth of a benevolent United States is also to refute ideological racism: the justification of inequalities through a set of controlling images that attribute physical and intellectual traits to racially defined groups (Hamamoto 1994:3). . . . Finally, Asian American cultural workers re-ject the narrative of salvation: the myth that Asian women (and a feminized Asia) are saved, through sexual relations with white men (and a masculin-ized United States), from the excesses of their own culture. Instead, they un-derscore the considerable potential for abuse in these inherently unequal re-lationships. . . .

Conclusion

Ideological representations of gender and sexuality are central in the exer-cise and maintenance of racial, patriarchal, and class domination. In the Asian American case, this ideological racism has taken seemingly contrasting forms: Asian men have been cast as both hypersexual and asexual, and Asian women have been rendered both superfeminine and masculine. Although in apparent disjunction, both forms exist to define, maintain, and justify white male supremacy. The racialization of Asian American manhood and wom-anhood underscores the interconnections of race, gender, and class. As cate-gories of difference, race and gender relations do not parallel but intersect and confirm each other, and it is the complicity among these categories of dif-ference that enables U.S. elites to justify and maintain their cultural, social, and economic power. Responding to the ideological assaults on their gender identities, Asian American cultural workers have engaged in a wide range of oppositional projects to defend Asian American manhood and womanhood. In the process, some have embraced a masculinist cultural nationalism, a stance that marginalizes Asian American women and their needs. Though sensitive to the emasculation of Asian American men, Asian American fem-inists have pointed out that Asian American nationalism insists on a fixed masculinist identity, thus obscuring gender differences. Though divergent, both the nationalist and feminist positions advance the dichotomous stance of man or woman, gender or race or class, without recognizing the complex relationality of these categories of oppression. It is only when Asian Ameri-cans recognize the intersections of race, gender, and class that we can trans-form the existing hierarchical structure.

ENDNOTES

[1] I thank Mary Romero for pointing this out to me.

[2] Filipino Americans provide an exception in that Filipino American men tend to in-termarry as frequently as Filipina American women. This is partly so because they are more Americanized and have a relatively more egalitarian gender-role orienta-tion than other Asian American men (Agbayani-Siewert & Revilla 1995:156).

[3] In recent years, Asian Americans' rising consciousness, coupled with their phenom-enal growth in certain regions of the United States, has led to a significant increase in inter-Asian marriages (e.g., Chinese Americans to Korean Americans). In a compar-

ative analysis of the 1980 and 1990 Decennial Census, Larry Hajimi Shinigawa and Gin Young Pang (forthcoming) found a dramatic decrease of interracial marriages and a significant rise of inter-Asian marriages. In California (where 39% of all Asian Pacific Americans reside), inter-Asian marriages increased from 21.1% in 1980 to 64% in 1990 of all intermarriages for Asian American husbands, and from 10.8% to 45% for Asian American wives during the same time period.

REFERENCES

Agbayani-Siewart, Pauline and Linda Revilla. 1995. "Filipino Americans." Pp. 134–68 in *Asian Americans: Contemporary Trends and Issues,* edited by P. G. Min. Thousand Oaks, CA: Sage.

Baker, Donald G. 1983. *Race, Ethnicity, and Power: A Comparative Study.* New York: Routledge.

Chin, Frank. 1972. "Confessions of the Chinatown Cowboy." *Bulletin of Concerned Asian Scholars* 4(3):66.

Chin, Frank and Jeffrey P. Chan. 1972. "Racist Love." Pp. 65–79 in *Seeing through Shuck,* edited by R. Kostelanetz. New York: Ballantine.

Collins, Patricia Hill. 1990. *Black Feminist Thought: Knowledge, Consciousness, and the Politics of Empowerment.* New York: Routledge.

Doane, Mary Ann. 1991. *Femme Fatales: Feminism, Film Theory, Psychoanalysis.* New York: Routledge.

Engelhardt, Tom. 1976. "Ambush at Kamikaze Pass." Pp. 270–79 in *Counterpoint: Perspectives on Asian America,* edited by E. Gee. Los Angeles: University of California at Los Angeles, Asian American Studies Center.

Frankenberg, Ruth. 1993. *White Women, Race Matters: The Social Construction of Whiteness.* Minneapolis: University of Minnesota Press.

Fung, R. 1994. "Seeing Yellow: Asian Identities in Film and Video." Pp. 161–71 in *The State of Asian America,* edited by K. Aguilar-San Juan. Boston: South End Press.

Goellnicht, D. C. 1992. "Tang Ao in America: Male Subject Positions in *China Men.*" Pp. 191–212 in *Reading the Literatures of Asian America,* edited by S. G. Lim and A. Ling. Philadelphia: Temple University Press.

Hagedorn, J. 1993. "Introduction: 'Role of Dead Man Require Very Little Acting.'" Pp. xxi–xxx in *Charlie Chan Is Dead: An Anthology of Contemporary Asian American Fiction,* edited by J. Hagedorn. New York: Penguin.

Hamamoto, D. Y. 1992. "Kindred Spirits: The Contemporary Asian American Family on Television." *Amerasia Journal* 18(2):35–53.

———. 1994. *Monitored Peril: Asian Americans and the Politics of Representation.* Minneapolis: University of Minnesota Press.

Hoppenstand, G. 1983. "Yellow Devil Doctors and Opium Dens: A Survey of the Yellow Peril Stereotypes in Mass Media Entertainment." Pp. 171–85 in *The Popular Culture Reader,* edited by C. D. Geist and J. Nachbar. Bowling Green, OH: Bowling Green University Press.

Kim, E. 1984. "Asian American Writers: A Bibliographical Review." *American Studies International* 22:2.

———. 1990. "'Such Opposite Creatures': Men and Women in Asian American Literature." *Michigan Quarterly Review* 29:68–93.

———. 1993. "Preface." Pp. vii–xiv in *Charlie Chan Is Dead: An Anthology of Contemporary Asian American Fiction,* edited by J. Hagedorn. New York: Penguin.

Ling, A. 1990. *Between Worlds: Women Writers of Chinese Ancestry.* New York: Pergamon.

Marchetti, G. 1993. *Romance and the "Yellow Peril": Race, Sex, and Discursive Strategies in Hollywood Fiction.* Berkeley: University of California Press.

Min, P. G. 1995. "Korean Americans." Pp. 199–231 in *Asian Americans: Contemporary Trends and Issues,* edited by P. G. Min. Thousand Oaks, CA: Sage.

Mullings, L. 1994. "Images, Ideology, and Women of Color." Pp. 265–89 in *Women of Color in U.S. Society,* edited by M. B. Zinn and B. T. Dill. Philadelphia: Temple University Press.

Nguyen, V. 1990. "Growing Up in White America." *Asian Week,* December 7, p. 23.

Nishi, S. M. 1995. "Japanese Americans." Pp. 95–133 in *Asian Americans: Contemporary Trends and Issues,* edited by P. G. Min. Thousand Oaks, CA: Sage.

Okihiro, G. Y. 1995. "Reading Asian Bodies, Reading Anxieties." Paper presented at the University of California, San Diego Ethnic Studies Colloquium, La Jolla, CA. November.

Said, E. 1979. *Orientalism.* New York: Random House.

Tajima, R. 1989. "Lotus Blossoms Don't Bleed: Images of Asian Women." Pp. 308–17 in *Making Waves: An Anthology of Writings by and about Asian American Women,* edited by Asian Women United of California. Boston: Beacon.

Tong, B. 1994. *Unsubmissive Women: Chinese Prostitutes in Nineteenth-Century San Francisco.* Norman: University of Oklahoma Press.

Wang, A. 1988. "Maxine Hong Kingston's Reclaiming of America: The Birthright of the Chinese American Male." *South Dakota Review* 26:18–29.

Wiegman, Robin. 1991. "Black Bodies/American Commodities: Gender, Race, and the Bourgeois Ideal in Contemporary Film." Pp. 308–28 in *Unspeakable Images: Ethnicity and the American Cinema,* edited by L. D. Friedman. Urbana: University of Illinois Press.

Wong, Eugene Franklin. 1978. *On Visual Media Racism: Asians in the American Motion Pictures.* New York: Arno.

Wu, William F. 1982. *The Yellow Peril: Chinese Americans in American Fiction, 1850–1940.* Hamden, CT: Archon.

Yamanaka, Lois-Ann. 1993. "Empty Heart." Pp. 544–50 in *Charlie Chan Is Dead: An Anthology of Contemporary Asian American Fiction,* edited by J. Hagedorn. New York: Penguin.

Yoon, D. D. 1993. "Asian American Male: Wimp or What?" *Asian Week,* November 26, p. 16.

30

_____

WHITE PRIVILEGE AND MALE PRIVILEGE
A Personal Account of Coming to See
Correspondences through Work
in Women's Studies

PEGGY McINTOSH

When sociologists examine social inequality, they try to understand how different types of inequality interact with and affect each other. For example, it is difficult to understand social class inequality without also examining racial and gender inequality. Similarly, it is difficult to understand gender oppression without also looking at the experiences of women and men in different social classes and racial-ethnic groups. In this selection, Peggy McIntosh argues that she was better able to understand the racial privileges of being white after she applied her understanding from Women's Studies about the gender privileges of being male. The typology she presents can be adapted to any form of social inequality. Higher status groups receive more privileges while lower status groups face more barriers.

Through work to bring materials and perspectives from Women's Studies into the rest of the curriculum, I have often noticed men's unwillingness to grant that they are overprivileged in the curriculum, even though they may grant that women are disadvantaged. Denials that amount to taboos surround the subject of advantages that men gain from women's disadvantages. These denials protect male privilege from being fully recognized, acknowledged, lessened, or ended.

Thinking through unacknowledged male privilege as a phenomenon with a life of its own, I realized that since hierarchies in our society are interlocking, there was most likely a phenomenon of white privilege that was similarly denied and protected, but alive and real in its effects. As a white person, I realized I had been taught about racism as something that puts others at a disadvantage, but had been taught not to see one of its corollary aspects, white privilege, which puts me at an advantage.

I think whites are carefully taught not to recognize white privilege, as males are taught not to recognize male privilege. So I have begun in an

_____

Working Paper #189, "White Privilege and Male Privilege: A Personal Account of Coming to See Correspondences Through Work in Women's Studies." Copyright © 1988 by Peggy McIntosh. May not be reprinted without permission from the author, Wellesley College Center for Research on Women, Wellesley, MA 02481-8208, (781) 283-2522, Fax (781) 283-2504.

untutored way to ask what it is like to have white privilege. This paper is a partial record of my personal observations and not a scholarly analysis. It is based on my daily experiences within my particular circumstances.

I have come to see white privilege as an invisible package of unearned assets that I can count on cashing in each day, but about which I was "meant" to remain oblivious. White privilege is like an invisible weightless knapsack of special provisions, assurances, tools, maps, guides, codebooks, passports, visas, clothes, compass, emergency gear, and blank checks.

Since I have had trouble facing white privilege, and describing its results in my life, I saw parallels here with men's reluctance to acknowledge male privilege. Only rarely will a man go beyond acknowledging that women are disadvantaged to acknowledging that men have unearned advantage, or that unearned privilege has not been good for men's development as human beings, or for society's development, or that privilege systems might ever be challenged and *changed*.

I will review here several types or layers of denial that I see at work protecting, and preventing awareness about, entrenched male privilege. Then I will draw parallels, from my own experience, with the denials that veil the facts of white privilege. Finally, I will list forty-six ordinary and daily ways in which I experience having white privilege, by contrast with my African American colleagues in the same building. This list is not intended to be generalizable. Others can make their own lists from within their own life circumstances.

Writing this paper has been difficult, despite warm receptions for the talks on which it is based.[1] For describing white privilege makes one newly accountable. As we in Women's Studies work to reveal male privilege and ask men to give up some of their power, so one who writes about having white privilege must ask, "Having described it, what will I do to lessen or end it?"

The denial of men's overprivileged state takes many forms in discussions of curriculum change work. Some claim that men must be central in the curriculum because they have done most of what is important or distinctive in life or in civilization. Some recognize sexism in the curriculum but deny that it makes male students seem unduly important in life. Others agree that certain *individual* thinkers are male oriented but deny that there is any *systemic* tendency in disciplinary frameworks or epistemology to overempower men as a group. Those men who do grant that male privilege takes institutionalized and embedded forms are still likely to deny that male hegemony has opened doors for them personally. Virtually all men deny that male overreward alone can explain men's centrality in all the inner sanctums of our most powerful institutions. Moreover, those few who will acknowledge that male privilege systems have overempowered them usually end up doubting that we could dismantle these privilege systems. They may say they will work to improve women's status, in the society or in the university, but they can't or won't support the idea of lessening men's. In curricular terms, this is the point at which they say that they regret they cannot use any of the interesting new scholarship on women because the syllabus is full. When the talk turns to giving men less cultural room, even the most thoughtful and fair-minded of the men I know will tend to reflect, or fall back on, conservative assumptions about the inevitability of present gender relations and distributions of power, calling on precedent or sociobiology and psychobiology to demonstrate that male domination is natural and follows inevitably from evolutionary pressures. Others resort to arguments from "experience" or religion or social responsibility or wishing and dreaming.

After I realized, through faculty development work in Women's Studies, the extent to which men work from a base of unacknowledged privilege, I understood that much of their oppressiveness was unconscious. Then I remembered the frequent charges from women of color that white women whom they encounter are oppressive. I began to understand why we are justly seen as oppressive, even when we don't see ourselves that way. At the very least, obliviousness of one's privileged state can make a person or group irritating to be with. I began to count the ways in which I enjoy unearned skin privilege and have been conditioned into oblivion about its existence, unable to see that it put me "ahead" in any way, or put my people ahead, overrewarding us and yet also paradoxically damaging us, or that it could or should be changed.

My schooling gave me no training in seeing myself as an oppressor, as an unfairly advantaged person, or as a participant in a damaged culture. I was taught to see myself as an individual whose moral state depended on her individual moral will. At school, we were not taught about slavery in any depth; we were not taught to see slaveholders as damaged people. Slaves were seen as the only group at risk of being dehumanized. My schooling followed the pattern which Elizabeth Minnich has pointed out: whites are taught to think of their lives as morally neutral, normative, and average, and also ideal, so that when we work to benefit others, this is seen as work that will allow "them" to be more like "us." I think many of us know how obnoxious this attitude can be in men.

After frustration with men who would not recognize male privilege, I decided to try to work on myself at least by identifying some of the daily effects of white privilege in my life. It is crude work, at this stage, but I will give here a list of special circumstances and conditions I experience that I did not earn but that I have been made to feel are mine by birth, by citizenship, and by virtue of being a conscientious law-abiding "normal" person of goodwill. I have chosen those conditions that I think in my case *attach somewhat more to skin-color privilege* than to class, religion, ethnic status, or geographic location, though these other privileging factors are intricately intertwined. As far as I can see, my Afro-American co-workers, friends, and acquaintances with whom I come into daily or frequent contact in this particular time, place, and line of work cannot count on most of these conditions.

1. I can, if I wish, arrange to be in the company of people of my race most of the time.

2. I can avoid spending time with people whom I was trained to mistrust and who have learned to mistrust my kind or me.

3. If I should need to move, I can be pretty sure of renting or purchasing housing in an area which I can afford and in which I would want to live.

4. I can be reasonably sure that my neighbors in such a location will be neutral or pleasant to me.

5. I can go shopping alone most of the time, fairly well assured that I will not be followed or harassed by store detectives.

6. I can turn on the television or open to the front page of the paper and see people of my race widely and positively represented.

7. When I am told about our national heritage or about "civilization," I am shown that people of my color made it what it is.

8. I can be sure that my children will be given curricular materials that testify to the existence of their race.

9. If I want to, I can be pretty sure of finding a publisher for this piece on white privilege.

10. I can be fairly sure of having my voice heard in a group in which I am the only member of my race.

11. I can be casual about whether or not to listen to another woman's voice in a group in which she is the only member of her race.

12. I can go into a book shop and count on finding the writing of my race represented, into a supermarket and find the staple foods that fit with my cultural traditions, into a hairdresser's shop and find someone who can deal with my hair.

13. Whether I use checks, credit cards, or cash, I can count on my skin color not to work against the appearance that I am financially reliable.

14. I could arrange to protect our young children most of the time from people who might not like them.

15. I did not have to educate our children to be aware of systemic racism for their own daily physical protection.

16. I can be pretty sure that my children's teachers and employers will tolerate them if they fit school and workplace norms; my chief worries about them do not concern others' attitudes toward their race.

17. I can talk with my mouth full and not have people put this down to my color.

18. I can swear, or dress in secondhand clothes, or not answer letters, without having people attribute these choices to the bad morals, the poverty, or the illiteracy of my race.

19. I can speak in public to a powerful male group without putting my race on trial.

20. I can do well in a challenging situation without being called a credit to my race.

21. I am never asked to speak for all the people of my racial group.

22. I can remain oblivious to the language and customs of persons of color who constitute the world's majority without feeling in my culture any penalty for such oblivion.
23. I can criticize our government and talk about how much I fear its policies and behavior without being seen as a cultural outsider.
24. I can be reasonably sure that if I ask to talk to "the person in charge," I will be facing a person of my race.
25. If a traffic cop pulls me over or if the IRS audits my tax return, I can be sure I haven't been singled out because of my race.
26. I can easily buy posters, postcards, picture books, greeting cards, dolls, toys, and children's magazines featuring people of my race.
27. I can go home from most meetings of organizations I belong to feeling somewhat tied in, rather than isolated, out of place, outnumbered, unheard, held at a distance, or feared.
28. I can be pretty sure that an argument with a colleague of another race is more likely to jeopardize her chances for advancement than to jeopardize mine.
29. I can be fairly sure that if I argue for the promotion of a person of another race, or a program centering on race, this is not likely to cost me heavily within my present setting, even if my colleagues disagree with me.
30. If I declare there is a racial issue at hand, or there isn't a racial issue at hand, my race will lend me more credibility for either position than a person of color will have.
31. I can choose to ignore developments in minority writing and minority activist programs, or disparage them, or learn from them, but in any case, I can find ways to be more or less protected from negative consequences of any of these choices.
32. My culture gives me little fear about ignoring the perspectives and powers of people of other races.
33. I am not made acutely aware that my shape, bearing, or body odor will be taken as a reflection on my race.
34. I can worry about racism without being seen as self-interested or self-seeking.
35. I can take a job with an affirmative action employer without having my co-workers on the job suspect that I got it because of my race.
36. If my day, week, or year is going badly, I need not ask of each negative episode or situation whether it has racial overtones.
37. I can be pretty sure of finding people who would be willing to talk with me and advise me about my next steps, professionally.
38. I can think over many options, social, political, imaginative, or professional, without asking whether a person of my race would be accepted or allowed to do what I want to do.
39. I can be late to a meeting without having the lateness reflect on my race.

40. I can choose public accommodation without fearing that people of my race cannot get in or will be mistreated in the places I have chosen.
41. I can be sure that if I need legal or medical help, my race will not work against me.
42. I can arrange my activities so that I will never have to experience feelings of rejection owing to my race.
43. If I have low credibility as a leader, I can be sure that my race is not the problem.
44. I can easily find academic courses and institutions that give attention only to people of my race.
45. I can expect figurative language and imagery in all of the arts to testify to experiences of my race.
46. I can choose blemish cover or bandages in "flesh" color and have them more or less match my skin.

I repeatedly forgot each of the realizations on this list until I wrote it down. For me, white privilege has turned out to be an elusive and fugitive subject. The pressure to avoid it is great, for in facing it I must give up the myth of meritocracy. If these things are true, this is not such a free country; one's life is not what one makes it; many doors open for certain people through no virtues of their own. These perceptions mean also that my moral condition is not what I had been led to believe. The appearance of being a good citizen rather than a troublemaker comes in large part from having all sorts of doors open automatically because of my color.

A further paralysis of nerve comes from literary silence protecting privilege. My clearest memories of finding such analysis are in Lillian Smith's unparalleled *Killers of the Dream* and Margaret Andersen's review of Karen and Mamie Fields' *Lemon Swamp*. Smith, for example, wrote about walking toward black children on the street and knowing they would step into the gutter; Andersen contrasted the pleasure that she, as a white child, took on summer driving trips to the south with Karen Fields' memories of driving, in a closed car stocked with all necessities lest, in stopping, her black family should suffer "insult, or worse." Adrienne Rich also recognizes and writes about daily experiences of privilege, but in my observation, white women's writing in this area is far more often on systemic racism than on our daily lives as light-skinned women.[2]

In unpacking this invisible knapsack of white privilege, I have listed conditions of daily experience that I once took for granted, as neutral, normal, and universally available to everybody, just as I once thought of a male-focused curriculum as the neutral or accurate account that can speak for all. Nor did I think of any of these perquisites as bad for the holder. I now think that we need a more finely differentiated taxonomy of privilege, for some of these varieties are only what one would want for everyone in a just society, and others give license to be ignorant, oblivious, arrogant, and destructive. Before proposing some more finely tuned categorization, I will make some observations about the general effects of these conditions on my life and expectations.

In this potpourri of examples, some privileges make me feel at home in the world. Others allow me to escape penalties or dangers that others suffer. Through some, I escape fear, anxiety, insult, injury, or a sense of not being welcome, not being real. Some keep me from having to hide, to be in disguise, to feel sick or crazy, to negotiate each transaction from the position of being an outsider or, within my group, a person who is suspected of having too close links with a dominant culture. Most keep me from having to be angry.

I see a pattern running through the matrix of white privilege, a pattern of assumptions that were passed on to me as a white person. There was one main piece of cultural turf; it was my own turf, and I was among those who could control the turf. I could measure up to the cultural standards and take advantage of the many options I saw around me to make what the culture would call a success of my life. *My skin color was an asset for any move I was educated to want to make.* I could think of myself as "belonging" in major ways and of making social systems work for me. I could freely disparage, fear, neglect, or be oblivious to anything outside of the dominant cultural forms. Being of the main culture, I could also criticize it fairly freely. My life was reflected back to me frequently enough so that I felt, with regard to my race, if not to my sex, like one of the real people.

Whether through the curriculum or in the newspaper, the television, the economic system, or the general look of people in the streets, I received daily signals and indications that my people counted and that others *either didn't exist or must be trying, not very successfully, to be like people of my race.* I was given cultural permission not to hear voices of people of other races or a tepid cultural tolerance for hearing or acting on such voices. I was also raised not to suffer seriously from anything that darker-skinned people might say about my group, "protected," though perhaps I should more accurately say *prohibited,* through the habits of my economic class and social group, from living in racially mixed groups or being reflective about interactions between people of differing races.

In proportion as my racial group was being made confident, comfortable, and oblivious, other groups were likely being made unconfident, uncomfortable, and alienated. Whiteness protected me from many kinds of hostility, distress, and violence, which I was being subtly trained to visit in turn upon people of color.

For this reason, the word "privilege" now seems to me misleading. Its connotations are too positive to fit the conditions and behaviors which "privilege systems" produce. We usually think of privilege as being a favored state, whether earned, or conferred by birth or luck. School graduates are reminded they are privileged and urged to use their (enviable) assets well. The word "privilege" carries the connotation of being something everyone must want. Yet some of the conditions I have described here work to systemically overempower certain groups. Such privilege simply *confers dominance,* gives permission to control, because of one's race or sex. The kind of privilege that gives license to some people to be, at best, thoughtless and, at worst, murderous should not continue to be referred to as a desirable attribute. Such "privilege" may be widely desired without being in any way beneficial to the whole society.

Moreover, though "privilege" may confer power, it does not confer moral strength. Those who do not depend on conferred dominance have traits and qualities that may never develop in those who do. Just as Women's Studies courses indicate that women survive their political circumstances to lead lives that hold the human race together, so "underprivileged" people of color who are the world's majority have survived their oppression and lived survivors' lives from which the white global minority can and must learn. In some groups, those dominated have actually become strong through *not* having all of these unearned advantages, and this gives them a great deal to teach the others. Members of so-called privileged groups can seem foolish, ridiculous, infantile, or dangerous by contrast.

I want, then, to distinguish between earned strength and unearned power conferred systemically. Power from unearned privilege can look like strength when it is, in fact, permission to escape or to dominate. But not all of the privileges on my list are inevitably damaging. Some, like the expectation that neighbors will be decent to you, or that your race will not count against you in court, should be the norm in a just society and should be considered as the entitlement of everyone. Others, like the privilege not to listen to less powerful people, distort the humanity of the holders as well as the ignored groups. Still others, like finding one's staple foods everywhere, may be a function of being a member of a numerical majority in the population. Others have to do with not having to labor under pervasive negative stereotyping and mythology.

We might at least start by distinguishing between positive advantages that we can work to spread, to the point where they are not advantages at all but simply part of the normal civic and social fabric, and negative types of advantage that unless rejected will always reinforce our present hierarchies. For example, the positive "privilege" of belonging, the feeling that one belongs within the human circle, as Native Americans say, fosters development and should not be seen as privilege for a few. It is, let us say, an entitlement that none of us should have to earn; ideally it is an *unearned entitlement.* At present, since only a few have it, it is an *unearned advantage* for them. The negative "privilege" that gave me cultural permission not to take darker-skinned Others seriously can be seen as arbitrarily conferred dominance and should not be desirable for anyone. This paper results from a process of coming to see that some of the power that I originally saw as attendant on being a human being in the United States consisted in *unearned advantage* and *conferred dominance,* as well as other kinds of special circumstance not universally taken for granted.

In writing this paper I have also realized that white identity and status (as well as class identity and status) give me considerable power to choose whether to broach this subject and its trouble. I can pretty well decide whether to disappear and avoid and not listen and escape the dislike I may engender in other people through this essay, or interrupt, answer, interpret, preach, correct, criticize, and control to some extent what goes on in reaction to it. Being white, I am given considerable power to escape many kinds of danger or penalty as well as to choose which risks I want to take.

There is an analogy here, once again, with Women's Studies. Our male colleagues do not have a great deal to lose in supporting Women's Studies, but they do not have a great deal to lose if they oppose it either. They simply have the power to decide whether to commit themselves to more equitable distributions of power. They will probably feel few penalties whatever choice they make; they do not seem, in any obvious short-term sense, the ones at risk, though they and we are all at risk because of the behaviors that have been rewarded in them.

Through Women's Studies work I have met very few men who are truly distressed about systemic, unearned male advantage and conferred dominance. And so one question for me and others like me is whether we will be like them, or whether we will get truly distressed, even outraged, about unearned race advantage and conferred dominance and if so, what we will do to lessen them. In any case, we need to do more work in identifying how they actually affect our daily lives. We need more down-to-earth writing by people about these taboo subjects. We need more understanding of the ways in which white "privilege" damages white people, for these are not the same ways in which it damages the victimized. Skewed white psyches are an inseparable part of the picture, though I do not want to confuse the kinds of damage done to the holders of special assets and to those who suffer the deficits. Many, perhaps most, of our white students in the United States think that racism doesn't affect them because they are not people of color; they do not see "whiteness" as a racial identity. Many men likewise think that Women's Studies does not bear on their own existences because they are not female; they do not see themselves as having gendered identities. Insisting on the universal "effects" of "privilege" systems, then, becomes one of our chief tasks, and being more explicit about the *particular* effects in particular contexts is another. Men need to join us in this work.

In addition, since race and sex are not the only advantaging systems at work, we need to similarly examine the daily experience of having age advantage, or ethnic advantage, or physical ability, or advantage related to nationality, religion, or sexual orientation. Professor Marnie Evans suggested to me that in many ways the list I made also applies directly to heterosexual privilege. This is a still more taboo subject than race privilege: the daily ways in which heterosexual privilege makes some persons comfortable or powerful, providing supports, assets, approvals, and rewards to those who live or expect to live in heterosexual pairs. Unpacking that content is still more difficult, owing to the deeper imbeddedness of heterosexual advantage and dominance and stricter taboos surrounding these.

But to start such an analysis I would put this observation from my own experience: the fact that I live under the same roof with a man triggers all kinds of societal assumptions about my worth, politics, life, and values and triggers a host of unearned advantages and powers. After recasting many elements from the original list I would add further observations like these:

1. My children do not have to answer questions about why I live with my partner (my husband).
2. I have no difficulty finding neighborhoods where people approve of our household.
3. Our children are given texts and classes that implicitly support our kind of family unit and do not turn them against my choice of domestic partnership.
4. I can travel alone or with my husband without expecting embarrassment or hostility in those who deal with us.
5. Most people I meet will see my marital arrangements as an asset to my life or as a favorable comment on my likability, my competence, or my mental health.
6. I can talk about the social events of a weekend without fearing most listeners' reactions.
7. I will feel welcomed and "normal" in the usual walks of public life, institutional and social.
8. In many contexts, I am seen as "all right" in daily work on women because I do not live chiefly with women.

Difficulties and dangers surrounding the task of finding parallels are many. Since racism, sexism, and heterosexism are not the same, the advantages associated with them should not be seen as the same. In addition, it is hard to isolate aspects of unearned advantage that derive chiefly from social class, economic class, race, religion, region, sex, or ethnic identity. The oppressions are both distinct and interlocking, as the Combahee River Collective statement of 1977 continues to remind us eloquently.[3]

One factor seems clear about all of the interlocking oppressions. They take both active forms that we can see and embedded forms that members of the dominant group are taught not to see. In my class and place, I did not see myself as racist because I was taught to recognize racism only in individual acts of meanness by members of my group, never in invisible systems conferring racial dominance on my group from birth. Likewise, we are taught to think that sexism or heterosexism is carried on only through intentional, individual acts of discrimination, meanness, or cruelty, rather than in invisible systems conferring unsought dominance on certain groups. Disapproving of the systems won't be enough to change them. I was taught to think that racism could end if white individuals changed their attitudes; many men think sexism can be ended by individual changes in daily behavior toward women. But a man's sex provides advantage for him whether or not he approves of the way in which dominance has been conferred on his group. A "white" skin in the United States opens many doors for whites whether or not we approve of the way dominance has been conferred on us. Individual acts can palliate, but cannot end, these problems. To redesign social systems, we need first to acknowledge their colossal unseen dimensions. The silences and denials surrounding privilege are the key political tool here. They keep the thinking about equality or equity incomplete, protecting unearned advantage and conferred dominance by making these taboo subjects. Most talk by whites about equal opportunity seems to me now to be about equal opportunity to try to get into a position of dominance while denying that *systems* of dominance exist.

Obliviousness about white advantage, like obliviousness about male advantage, is kept strongly inculturated in the United States so as to maintain the myth of meritocracy, the myth that democratic choice is equally available to all. Keeping most people unaware that freedom of confident action is there for just a small number of people props up those in power and serves to keep power in the hands of the same groups that have most of it already. Though systemic change takes many decades, there are pressing questions for me, and I imagine for some others like me, if we raise our daily consciousness on the privileges of being light-skinned. What will we do with such knowledge? As we know from watching men, it is an open question whether we will choose to use unearned advantage to weaken invisible privilege systems and whether we will use any of our arbitrarily awarded power to try to reconstruct power systems on a broader base.

ENDNOTES

[1] This paper was presented at the Virginia Women's Studies Association conference in Richmond in April 1986 and the American Educational Research Association conference in Boston in October 1986, and discussed with two groups of participants in the Dodge seminars for Secondary School Teachers in New York and Boston in the spring of 1987.

[2] Margaret Andersen, "Race and the Social Science Curriculum: A Teaching and Learning Discussion," *Radical Teacher*, November 1984, pp. 17–20. Lillian Smith, *Killers of the Dream* (New York: W. W. Norton, 1949).

[3] The Combahee River Collective, "A Black Feminist Statement," in *All the Women Are White, All the Blacks Are Men, But Some of Us Are Brave: Black Women's Studies*, ed. G. Hull, P. Scott, and B. Smith (Old Westbury, NY: The Feminist Press, 1982).

31

THE PROBLEM OF
THE TWENTIETH CENTURY IS
THE PROBLEM OF THE COLOR LINE

W. E. B. Du BOIS

Race and ethnicity are the topics explored in the next four selections. The first reading is by W. E. B. Du Bois (1868–1963), a leading social theorist on race issues in the United States, and his study, *The Philadelphia Negro* (1899), is considered a classic empirical sociological work. Another of his works, *Souls of Black Folk* (1903), stirred up controversy within the African American community. Du Bois went on to organize the Niagara Movement (1905–1910), which developed into the NAACP, and he also was active in the Pan-African movement. Du Bois moved to Ghana in 1961, where he died on August 27, 1963, the day of the civil rights march on Washington, D.C.

The reading excerpted here, "The Problem of the Twentieth Century Is the Problem of the Color Line," describes the U.S. system of racial apartheid. Du Bois wrote the first essay based on that title in 1901. In this selection, written in 1950, Du Bois analyzes the changing patterns of racial relations since the turn of the century. Even though some progress had been made in 50 years, Du Bois concludes that the color line is still visible in everyday life in the United States.

We are just finishing the first half of the twentieth century. I remember its birth in 1901. There was the usual discussion as to whether the century began in 1900 or 1901; but, of course, 1901 was correct. We expected great things . . . peace; the season of war among nations had passed; progress was the order . . . everything going forward to bigger and better things. And then, not so openly expressed, but even more firmly believed, the rule of white Europe and America over black, brown, and yellow peoples.

I was 32 years of age in 1901, married, and a father, and teaching at Atlanta University with a program covering a hundred years of study and investigation into the condition of American Negroes. Our subject of study at

From *Pittsburgh Courier* (January 14, 1950). Copyright © 1950 by the Pittsburgh Courier Publishing Co. Reprinted with permission of the Estate of W. E. B. Du Bois.

that time was education: the college-bred Negro in 1900, the Negro common school in 1901. My own attitude toward the twentieth century was expressed in an article which I wrote in the *Atlantic Monthly* in 1901. It said:

> The problem of the Twentieth Century is the problem of the color-line. . . . I have seen a land right merry with the sun, where children sing, and rolling hills lie like passioned women wanton with harvest. And there in the King's Highway sat, and sits, a figure veiled and bowed, by which the Traveler's footsteps hasten as they go. On the tainted air broods fair. Three centuries' thought have been the raising and unveiling of that bowed human soul; and now behold, my fellows, a century now for the duty and the deed! The problem of the Twentieth Century is the problem of the color-line.

This is what we hoped, to this we Negroes looked forward; peace, progress and the breaking of the color line. What has been the result? We know it all too well . . . war, hate, the revolt of the colored peoples and the fear of more war.

In the meantime, where are we; those 15,000,000 citizens of the United States who are descended from the slaves, brought here between 1600 and 1900? We formed in 1901, a separate group because of legal enslavement and emancipation into caste conditions, with the attendant poverty, ignorance, disease, and crime. We were an inner group and not an integral part of the American nation; but we were exerting ourselves to fight for integration.

The burden of our fight was in seven different lines. We wanted education; we wanted particularly the right to vote and civil rights; we wanted work with adequate wage; housing, without segregation or slums; a free press to fight our battles, and (although in those days we dare not say it) social equality.

In 1901 our education was in perilous condition, despite what we and our white friends had done for 30 years. The Atlanta University Conference said in its resolutions of 1901:

> We call the attention of the nation to the fact that less than one million of the three million Negro children of school age are at present regularly attending school, and these attend a session which lasts only a few months. We are today deliberately rearing millions of our citizens in ignorance and at the same time limiting the rights of citizenship by educational qualifications. This is unjust.

More particularly in civil rights, we were oppressed. We not only did not get justice in the courts, but we were subject to peculiar and galling sorts of injustice in daily life. In the latter half of the nineteenth century, where we first get something like statistics, no less than 3,000 Negroes were lynched without trial. And in addition to that we were subject continuously to mob violence and judicial lynching.

In political life we had, for 25 years, been disfranchised by violence, law, and public opinion. The 14th and 15th amendments were deliberately violated and the literature of the day in book, pamphlet, and daily press, was widely of opinion that the Negro was not ready for the ballot, could not use it intelligently, and that no action was called for to stop his political power from being exercised by Southern whites like Tillman and Vardaman.

We did not have the right or opportunity to work at an income which would sustain a decent and modern standard of life. Because of a past of chattel slavery, we were for the most part common laborers and servants, and a very considerable proportion were still unable to leave the plantations where they worked all their lives for next to nothing.

There were a few who were educated for the professions and we had many good artisans; that number was not increasing as it should have been, nor were new artisans being adequately trained. Industrial training was popular, but funds to implement it were too limited, and we were excluded from unions and the new mass industry.

We were housed in slums and segregated districts where crime and disease multiplied, and when we tried to move to better and healthier quarters we were met by segregation ordinance if not by mobs. We not only had no social equality, but we did not openly ask for it. It seemed a shameful thing to beg people to receive us as equals and as human beings; that was something we argued "that came and could not be fetched." And that meant not simply that we could not marry white women or legitimize mulatto bastards, but we could not stop in a decent hotel, nor eat in a public restaurant nor attend the theater, nor accept an invitation to a private white home, nor travel in a decent railway coach. When the "public" was invited, this did not include us and admission to colleges often involved special consideration if not blunt refusal.

Finally we had poor press . . . a few struggling papers with little news and inadequately expressed opinion, with small circulation or influence and almost no advertising.

This was our plight in 1901. It was discouraging, but not hopeless. There is no question but that we had made progress, and there also was no doubt but what that progress was not enough to satisfy us or to settle our problems.

We could look back on a quarter century of struggle which had its results. We had schools; we had teachers; a few had forced themselves into the leading colleges and were tolerated if not welcomed. We voted in Northern cities, owned many decent homes and were fighting for further progress. Leaders like Booker Washington had perceived wide popular approval and a Negro literature had begun to appear.

But what we needed was organized effort along the whole front, based on broad lines of complete emancipation. This came with the Niagara Movement in 1906 and the NAACP in 1909. In 1910 came the *Crisis* magazine and the real battle was on.

What have we gained and accomplished? The advance has not been equal on all fronts, nor complete on any. We have not progressed with closed ranks like a trained army, but rather with severed and broken ranks, with wide gaps and even temporary retreats. But we have advanced. Of that there can be no atom of doubt.

First of all in education; most Negro children today are in school and most adults can read and write. Unfortunately this literacy is not as great as the census says. The draft showed that at least a third of our youth are illiterate. But education is steadily rising. Six thousand bachelor degrees are awarded to Negroes each year and doctorates in philosophy and medicine are not uncommon. Nevertheless as a group, American Negroes are still in the lower ranks of learning and adaptability to modern conditions. They do not read widely, their travel is limited and their experience through contact with the modern world is curtailed by law and custom.

Secondly, in civil rights, the Negro has perhaps made his greatest advance. Mob violence and lynching have markedly decreased. Three thousand Negroes were lynched in the last half of the nineteenth century and five hundred in the first half of the twentieth. Today lynching is comparatively rare. Mob violence also has decreased, but is still in evidence, and summary and unjust court proceedings have taken the place of open and illegal acts. But the Negro has established, in the courts, his legal citizenship and his right to be included in the Bill of Rights. The question still remains of "equal but separate" public accommodations, and that is being attacked. Even the institution of "jim-crow" in travel is tottering. The infraction of the marriage situation by law and custom is yet to be brought before the courts and public opinion in a forcible way.

Third, the right to vote on the part of the Negro is being gradually established under the 14th and 15th amendments. It was not really until 1915 that the Supreme Court upheld this right of Negro citizens and even today the penalties of the 14th amendment have never been enforced. There are 7,000,000 possible voters among American Negroes and of these it is a question if more than 2,000,000 actually cast their votes. This is partly from the national inertia, which keeps half of all American voters away from the polls; but even more from the question as to what practical ends the Negro shall cast his vote.

He is thinking usually in terms of what he can do by voting to better his condition and he seldom gets a chance to vote on this matter. On the wider implications of political democracy he has not yet entered; particularly he does not see the economic foundations of present civilization and the necessity of his attacking the rule of corporate wealth in order to free the labor group to which he belongs.

Fourth, there is the question of occupation. There are our submerged classes of farm labor and tenants: our city laborers, washerwomen and scrubwomen and the mass of lower-paid servants. These classes still form a majority of American Negroes and they are on the edge of poverty, with the ignorance, disease, and crime that always accompany such poverty.

If we measure the median income of Americans, it is $3,000 for whites and $2,000 for Negroes. In Southern cities, seven percent of the white families and 30 percent of the colored families receive less than $1,000 a year. On the other hand, the class differentiation by income among Negroes is notable: the number of semiskilled and skilled artisans has increased or will as membership in labor unions. Professional men have increased, especially teachers and less notably, physicians, dentists, and lawyers.

The number of Negroes in business has increased; mostly in small retail businesses, but to a considerable extent in enterprises like insurance, real estate and small banking, where the color line gives Negroes certain advantages and where, too, there is a certain element of gambling. Also beyond the line of gambling, numbers of Negroes have made small fortunes in antisocial enterprises. All this means that there has arisen in the Negro group a distinct stratification from poor to rich. Recently I polled 450 Negro families belonging to a select organization 45 years old. Of these families, 127 received over $10,000 a year and a score of these over $25,000; 200 families received from $5,000 to $10,000 a year and 86 less than $5,000.

This is the start of a tendency which will grow; we are beginning to follow the American pattern of accumulating individual wealth and of considering that this will eventually settle the race problem. On the other hand, the whole trend of the thought of our age is toward social welfare; the prevention of poverty by more equitable distribution of wealth, and business for general welfare rather than private profit. There are few signs that these ideals are guiding Negro development today. We seem to be adopting increasingly the ideal of American culture.

Housing has, of course, been a point of bitter pressure among Negroes, because the attempt to segregate the race in its living conditions has not only kept the more fortunate ones from progress, but it has confined vast numbers of Negro people to the very parts of cities and country districts where they have fewest opportunities and least social contacts. They must live largely in slums, in contact with criminals and with fewest of the social advantages of government and human contact. The fight against segregation has been carried on in the courts and shows much progress against city ordinances, against covenants which make segregation hereditary.

Literature and art have made progress among Negroes, but with curious handicaps. An art expression is normally evoked by the conscious and unconscious demand of people for portrayal of their own emotion and experience. But in the case of the American Negroes, the audience, which embodies the demand and which pays sometimes enormous price for satisfaction, is not the Negro group, but the white group. And the pattern of what the white group wants does not necessarily agree with the natural desire of Negroes.

The whole of Negro literature is therefore curiously divided. We have writers who have written, not really about Negroes, but about the things which white people, and not the highest class of whites, like to hear about Negroes. And those who have expressed what the Negro himself thinks and feels, are those whose books sell to few, even of their own people; and whom most folk do not know. This has not made for the authentic literature which the early part of this century seemed to promise. To be sure, it can be said that American literature today has a considerable amount of Negro expression and influence, although not as much as once we hoped.

Despite all this we have an increasing number of excellent Negro writers who make the promise for the future great by their real accomplishment. We have done something in sculpture and painting, but in drama and music we have markedly advanced. All the world listens to our singers, sings our music, and dances to our rhythms.

In science, our handicaps are still great. Turner, a great entomologist, was worked to death for lack of laboratory, just never had the recognition he richly deserved; and Carver was prisoner of his inferiority complex. Notwithstanding this, our real accomplishment in biology and medicine; in history and law; and in the social sciences has been notable and widely acclaimed. To this in no little degree is due our physical survival, our falling death rate, and our increased confidence in our selves and in our destiny.

The expression of Negro wish and desire through a free press has greatly improved as compared with 1900. We have a half dozen large weekly papers with circulations of a hundred thousand or more. Their news coverage is immense, even if not discriminating. But here again, the influence of the American press on us has been devastating. The predominance of advertising over opinion, the desire for income rather than literary excellence and the use of deliberate propaganda, has made our press less of a power than it could be, and leaves wide chance for improvement in the future.

In comparison with other institutions, the Negro church during the twentieth century has lost ground. It is no longer the dominating influence that it used to be, the center of social activity and of economic experiment. Nevertheless, it is still a powerful institution in the lives of a numerical majority of American Negroes if not upon the dominant intellectual classes. There has been a considerable increase in organized work for social progress through the church, but there has also been a large increase of expenditure for buildings, furnishings, and salaries; and it is not easy to find any increase in moral stamina or conscientious discrimination within church circles.

The scandal of deliberate bribery in election of bishops and in the holding of positions in the churches without a hierarchy has been widespread. It is a critical problem now as to just what part in the future the church among Negroes is going to hold.

Finally there comes the question of social equality, which, despite efforts on the part of thinkers, white and black, is after all the main and fundamental problem of race in the United States. Unless a human being is going to have all human rights, including not only work, but friendship, and if mutually desired, marriage and children, unless these avenues are open and free, there can be no real equality and no cultural integration.

It has hitherto seemed utterly impossible that any such solution of the Negro problem in America could take place. The situation was quite similar to the problem of the lower classes of laborers, serfs and servants in European nations during the sixteenth, seventeenth, and eighteenth centuries. All nations had to consist of two separate parts and the only relations between them was employment and philanthropy.

That problem has been partly solved by modern democracy, but modern democracy cannot succeed unless the peoples of different races and religions are also integrated into the democratic whole. Against this, large numbers of Americans have always fought and are still fighting, but the progress despite this has been notable. There are places in the United States, especially in large cities like New York and Chicago, where the social differences between the races has, to a large extent, been nullified and there is a meeting on terms of equality which would have been thought impossible a half century ago.

On the other hand, in the South, despite religion, education, and reason, the color line, although perhaps shaken, still stands, stark and unbending, and to the minds of most good people, eternal. Here lies the area of the last battle for the complete rights of American Negroes.

Within the race itself today there are disquieting signs. The effort of Negroes to become Americans of equal status with other Americans is leading them to a state of mind by which they not only accept what is good in America, but what is bad and threatening so long as the Negro can share equally. This is peculiarly dangerous at this epoch in the development of world culture.

After two world wars of unprecedented loss of life, cruelty, and destruction, we are faced by the fact that the industrial organization of our present civilization has in it something fundamentally wrong. It went to pieces in the first world war because of the determination of certain great powers excluded from world rule to share in that rule, by acquisition of the labor and materials of colonial peoples. The attempt to recover from the cataclysm resulted in the collapse of our industrial system, and a second world war.

In spite of the propaganda which has gone on, which represents America as the leading democratic state, we Negroes know perfectly well, and ought to know even better than most, that America is not a successful democracy and that until it is, it is going to drag down the world. This nation is ruled by corporate wealth to a degree which is frightening. One thousand persons own the United States and their power outweighs the voice of the mass of American citizens. This must be cured, not by revolution, not by war and violence, but by reason and knowledge.

Most of the world is today turning toward the welfare state; turning against the idea of production for individual profit toward the idea of production for use and for the welfare of the mass of citizens. No matter how difficult such a course is, it is the only course that is going to save the world and this we American Negroes have got to realize.

We may find it easy now to get publicity, reward, and attention by going along with the reactionary propaganda and war hysteria which is convulsing this nation, but in the long run America will not thank its black children if they help it go the wrong way, or retard its progress.

32

"IS THIS A WHITE COUNTRY, OR WHAT?"

LILLIAN B. RUBIN

In this reading, Lillian B. Rubin presents her findings of racial hostility among working-class white ethnics. Rubin, a senior research fellow at the Institute for the Study of Social Change at the University of California, Berkeley, finds that the "color line" has been redefined to include immigrants and all people of color. Using interviews and document analysis, Rubin compares the anti-immigrant, racist beliefs of her respondents with actual demographic data on immigration and social opportunities in the United States. This excerpt is taken from Rubin's 1994 book, *Families on the Fault Line: America's Working Class Speaks about the Family, the Economy, Race, and Ethnicity.*

"They're letting all these coloreds come in and soon there won't be any place left for white people," broods Tim Walsh, a 33-year-old white construction worker. "It makes you wonder: Is this a white country, or what?"

It's a question that nags at white America, one perhaps that's articulated most often and most clearly by the men and women of the working class. For it's they who feel most vulnerable, who have suffered the economic contractions of recent decades most keenly, who see the new immigrants most clearly as direct competitors for their jobs.

It's not whites alone who stew about immigrants. Native-born blacks, too, fear the newcomers nearly as much as whites—and for the same economic reasons. But for whites the issue is compounded by race, by the fact that the newcomers are primarily people of color. For them, therefore, their economic anxieties have combined with the changing face of America to create a profound uneasiness about immigration—a theme that was sounded by nearly 90 percent of the whites I met, even by those who are themselves first-generation, albeit well-assimilated, immigrants.

Sometimes they spoke about this in response to my questions; equally often the subject of immigration arose spontaneously as people gave voice to their concerns. But because the new immigrants are predominantly people of color, the discourse was almost always cast in terms of race as well as immigration, with the talk slipping from immigration to race and back again as

From *Families on the Fault Line: America's Working Class Speaks about the Family, the Economy, Race, and Ethnicity,* pp. 172–75 and 176–87. Copyright © 1994 by Lillian B. Rubin. Reprinted with the permission of Rhoda Weyr Literary Agency.

if these are not two separate phenomena. "If we keep letting all them for-eigners in, pretty soon there'll be more of them than us and then what will this country be like?" Tim's wife, Mary Anne, frets. "I mean, this is *our* coun-try, but the way things are going, white people will be the minority in our own country. Now, does that make any sense?"

Such fears are not new. Americans have always worried about the strangers who came to our shores, fearing that they would corrupt our soci-ety, dilute our culture, debase our values. So I remind Mary Anne, "When your ancestors came here, people also thought we were allowing too many foreigners into the country. Yet those earlier immigrants were successfully in-tegrated into the American society. What's different now?"

"Oh, it's different, all right," she replies without hesitation. "When my people came, the immigrants were all white. That makes a big difference."

"Why do you think that's so?"

"I don't know; it just is, that's all. Look at the black people; they've been here a long time, and they still don't live like us—stealing and drugs and having all those babies."

"But you were talking about immigrants. Now you're talking about blacks, and they're not immigrants."

"Yeah, I know," she replies with a shrug. "But they're different, and there's enough problems with them, so we don't need any more. With all these other people coming here now, we just have more trouble. They don't talk English; and they think different from us, things like that."

Listening to Mary Anne's words, I was reminded again how little we Americans look to history for its lessons, how impoverished is our historical memory. For, in fact, being white didn't make "a big difference" for many of those earlier immigrants. The dark-skinned Italians and the eastern Euro-pean Jews who came in the late nineteenth and early twentieth centuries didn't look very white to the fair-skinned Americans who were here then. Indeed, the same people we now call white—Italians, Jews, Irish—were seen as another race at that time. Not black or Asian, it's true, but an alien other, a race apart, although one that didn't have a clearly defined name. Moreover, the racist fears and fantasies of native-born Americans were far less con-tained then than they are now, largely because there were few social con-straints on their expression.

When, during the nineteenth century, for example, some Italians were taken for blacks and lynched in the South, the incidents passed virtually un-noticed. And if Mary Anne and Tim Walsh, both of Irish ancestry, had come to this country during the great Irish immigration of that period, they would have found themselves defined as an inferior race and described with the same language that was used to characterize blacks: "low-browed and sav-age, grovelling and bestial, lazy and wild, simian and sensual."[1] Not only during that period but for a long time afterward as well, the U.S. Census Bu-reau counted the Irish as a distinct and separate group, much as it does today with the category it labels "Hispanic."

But there are two important differences between then and now, differences that can be summed up in a few words: the economy and race. Then, a growing industrial economy meant that there were plenty of jobs for both immigrant and native workers, something that can't be said for the contracting economy in which we live today. True, the arrival of the immigrants, who were more readily exploitable than native workers, put Americans at a disadvantage and created discord between the two groups. Nevertheless, work was available for both.

Then, too, the immigrants—no matter how they were labeled, no matter how reviled they may have been—were ultimately assimilable, if for no other reason than that they were white. As they began to lose their alien ways, it became possible for native Americans to see in the white ethnics of yesteryear a reflection of themselves. Once this shift in perception occurred, it was possible for the nation to incorporate them, to take them in, chew them up, digest them, and spit them out as Americans—with subcultural variations not always to the liking of those who hoped to control the manners and mores of the day, to be sure, but still recognizably white Americans.

Today's immigrants, however, are the racial other in a deep and profound way. It's true that race is not a fixed category, that it's no less an *idea* today than it was yesterday. And it's also possible, as I have already suggested, that we may be witness to social transformation from race to ethnicity among some of the most assimilated—read: middle-class—Asians and Latinos. But even if so, there's a long way to go before that metamorphosis is realized. Meanwhile, the immigrants of this era not only bring their own language and culture, they are also people of color—men, women, and children whose skin tones are different and whose characteristic features set them apart and justify the racial categories we lock them into.[2] And integrating masses of people of color into a society where race consciousness lies at the very heart of our central nervous system raises a whole new set of anxieties and tensions.

It's not surprising, therefore, that racial dissension has increased so sharply in recent years. What is surprising, however, is the passion for ethnicity and the preoccupation with ethnic identification among whites that seems suddenly to have burst upon the public scene. . . .

What does being German, Irish, French, Russian, Polish mean to someone who is an American? It's undoubtedly different for recent immigrants than for those who have been here for generations. But even for a relative newcomer, the inexorable process of becoming an American changes the meaning of ethnic identification and its hold on the internal life of the individual. Nowhere have I seen this shift more eloquently described than in a recent op-ed piece published in the *New York Times*. The author, a Vietnamese refugee writing on the day when Vietnamese either celebrate or mourn the fall of Saigon, depending on which side of the conflict they were on, writes:

Although I sometimes mourn the loss of home and land, it's the American landscape and what it offers that solidify my hyphenated identity. . . .

Assimilation, education, the English language, the American 'I'—these have carried me and many others further from that beloved tropical country than the C-130 ever could. . . . When did this happen? Who knows? One night, America quietly seeps in and takes hold of one's mind and body, and the Vietnamese soul of sorrows slowly fades away. In the morning, the Vietnamese American speaks a new language of materialism: his vocabulary includes terms like career choices, down payment, escrow, overtime.[3]

A new language emerges, but it lives, at least for another generation, alongside the old one; Vietnamese, yes, but also American, with a newly developed sense of self and possibility—an identity that continues to grow stronger with each succeeding generation. It's a process we have seen repeated throughout the history of American immigration. The American world reaches into the immigrant communities and shapes and changes the people who live in them.[4] By the second generation, ethnic identity already is attenuated; by the third, it usually has receded as a deeply meaningful part of life.

Residential segregation, occupational concentration, and a common language and culture—these historically have been the basis for ethnic solidarity and identification. As strangers in a new land, immigrants banded together, bound by their native tongue and shared culture. The sense of affinity they felt in these urban communities was natural; they were a touch of home, of the old country, of ways they understood. Once within their boundaries, they could feel whole again, sheltered from the ridicule and revulsion with which they were greeted by those who came before them. For whatever the myth about America's welcoming arms, nativist sentiment has nearly always been high and the anti-immigrant segment of the population large and noisy.

Ethnic solidarity and identity in America, then, were the consequence of the shared history each group brought with it, combined with the social and psychological experience of establishing themselves in the new land. But powerful as these were, the connections among the members of the group were heightened and sustained by the occupational concentration that followed—the Irish in the police departments of cities like Boston and San Francisco, for example, the Jews in New York City's garment industry, the east central Europeans in the mills and mines of western Pennsylvania.[5]

As each ethnic group moved into the labor force, its members often became concentrated in a particular occupation, largely because they were helped to find jobs there by those who went before them. For employers, this ethnic homogeneity made sense. They didn't have to cope with a babel of different languages, and they could count on the older workers to train the newcomers and keep them in line. For workers, there were advantages as well. It meant that they not only had compatible workmates, but that they weren't alone as they faced the jeers and contempt of their American-born counterparts. And perhaps most important, as more and more ethnic peers filled the available jobs, they began to develop some small measure of control in the workplace.

The same pattern of occupational concentration that was characteristic of yesterday's immigrant groups exists among the new immigrants today, and for the same reasons. The Cubans in Florida and the Dominicans in New York,[6] the various Asian groups in San Francisco, the Koreans in Los Angeles and New York—all continue to live in ethnic neighborhoods; all use the networks established there to find their way into the American labor force.[7]

For the white working-class ethnics whose immigrant past is little more than part of family lore, the occupational, residential, and linguistic chain has been broken. This is not to say that white ethnicity has ceased to be an observable phenomenon in American life. Cities like New York, Chicago, and San Francisco still have white ethnic districts that influence their culture, especially around food preferences and eating habits. But as in San Francisco's North Beach or New York's Little Italy, the people who once created vibrant neighborhoods, where a distinct subculture and language remained vividly alive, long ago moved out and left behind only the remnants of the commercial life of the old community. As such transformations took place, ethnicity became largely a private matter, a distant part of the family heritage that had little to do with the ongoing life of the family or community.

What, then, are we to make of the claims to ethnic identity that have become so prominent in recent years? Herbert Gans has called this identification "symbolic ethnicity"—that is, ethnicity that's invoked or not as the individual chooses.[8] Symbolic ethnicity, according to Gans, has little impact on a person's daily life and, because it is not connected to ethnic structures or activities—except for something like the wearing of the green on St. Patrick's Day—it makes no real contribution to ethnic solidarity or community.

The description is accurate. But it's a mistake to dismiss ethnic identification, even if only symbolic, as relatively meaningless. Symbols, after all, become symbolic precisely because they have meaning. In this case, the symbol has meaning at two levels: One is the personal and psychological, the other is the social and political.

At the personal level, in a nation as large and diverse as ours—a nation that defines itself by its immigrant past, where the metaphor for our national identity has been the melting pot—defining oneself in the context of an ethnic group is comforting. It provides a sense of belonging to some recognizable and manageable collectivity—an affiliation that has meaning because it's connected to the family where, when we were small children, we first learned about our relationship to the group. As Vilma Janowski, a 24-year-old first-generation Polish American who came here as a child put it: "Knowing there's other people like you is really nice. It's like having a big family, even if you don't ever really see them. It's just nice to know they're there. Besides, if I said I was American, what would it mean? Nobody's just American."

Which is true. Being an American is different from being French or Dutch or any number of other nationalities because, except for Native Americans, there's no such thing as an American without a hyphen somewhere in the past. To identify with the front end of that hyphen is to maintain a connection—however tenuous, illusory, or sentimentalized—with our roots. It sets us apart from others, allows us the fantasy of uniqueness—a quest given particular urgency by a psychological culture that increasingly emphasizes the development of the self and personal history. Paradoxically, however, it also gives us a sense of belonging—of being one with others like ourselves—that helps to overcome some of the isolation of modern life.

But these psychological meanings have developed renewed force in recent years because of two significant sociopolitical events. The first was the civil rights movement with its call for racial equality. The second was the change in the immigration laws, which, for the first time in nearly half a century, allowed masses of immigrants to enter the country.

It was easy for northern whites to support the early demands of the civil rights movement when blacks were asking for the desegregation of buses and drinking fountains in the South. But supporting the black drive to end discrimination in jobs, housing, and education in the urban North was quite another matter—especially among those white ethnics whose hold on the ladder of mobility was tenuous at best and with whom blacks would be most likely to compete, whether in the job market, the neighborhood, or the classroom. As the courts and legislatures around the country began to honor some black claims for redress of past injustices, white hackles began to rise.

It wasn't black demands alone that fed the apprehensions of whites, however. In the background of the black civil rights drive, there stood a growing chorus of voices, as other racial groups—Asian Americans, Latinos, and Native Americans—joined the public fray to seek remedy for their own grievances. At the same time that these home-grown groups were making their voices heard and, not incidentally, affirming their distinctive cultural heritages and calling for public acknowledgment of them, the second great wave of immigration in this century washed across our shores.

After having closed the gates to mass immigration with the National Origins Act of 1924, Congress opened them again when it passed the Immigration Act of 1965.[9] This act, which was a series of amendments to the McCarran-Walter Act of 1952, essentially jettisoned the national origins provisions of earlier law and substituted overall hemisphere caps. The bill, according to immigration historian Roger Daniels, "changed the whole course of American immigration history" and left the door open for a vast increase in the numbers of immigrants.[10]

More striking than the increase in numbers has been the character of the new immigrants. Instead of the large numbers of western Europeans whom the sponsors had expected to take advantage of the new policy, it has been the people of Asia, Latin America, and the Caribbean who rushed to the boats. "It is doubtful if any drafter or supporter of the 1965 act envisaged this result," writes Daniels.[11] In fact, when members of Lyndon Johnson's administration, under whose tenure the bill became law, testified before Congress, they assured the legislators and the nation that few Asians would come in under the new law.[12]

This is a fascinating example of the unintended consequences of a political act. The change in the law was sponsored by northern Democrats who sought to appeal to their white ethnic constituencies by opening the gates to their countrymen once again—that is, to the people of eastern and southern Europe whom the 1924 law had kept out for nearly half a century. But those same white ethnics punished the Democratic Party by defecting to the Republicans during the Reagan-Bush years, a defection that was at least partly related to their anger about the new immigrants and the changing racial balance of urban America.

During the decade of the 1980s, 2.5 million immigrants from Asian countries were admitted to the United States, an increase of more than 450 percent over the years between 1961 and 1970, when the number was slightly less than half a million. In 1990 alone, nearly as many Asian immigrants—one-third of a million—entered the country as came during the entire decade of the 1960s. Other groups show similarly noteworthy increases. Close to three-quarters of a million documented Mexicans crossed the border in the single year of 1990, compared to less than half a million during all of the 1960s. Central American immigration, too, climbed from just under one hundred thousand between 1961 and 1970 to more than triple that number during the 1980s. And immigrants from the Caribbean, who numbered a little more than half a million during the 1960s, increased to over three-quarters of a million in the years between 1981 and 1989.[13]

Despite these large increases and the perception that we are awash with new immigrants, it's worth noting that they are a much smaller proportion of the total population today, 6.2 percent, than they were in 1920, when they were a hefty 13.2 percent of all U.S. residents.[14] But the fact that most immigrants today are people of color gives them greater visibility than ever before.

Suddenly, the nation's urban landscape has been colored in ways unknown before. In 1970, the California cities that were the site of the original research for *Worlds of Pain* were almost exclusively white. Twenty years later, the 1990 census reports that their minority populations range from 54 to 69 percent. In the nation at large, the same census shows nearly one in four Americans with African, Asian, Latino, or Native American ancestry, up from one in five in 1980.[15] So dramatic is this shift that whites of European descent now make up just over two-thirds of the population in New York State, while in California they number only 57 percent. In cities like New York, San Francisco, and Los Angeles whites are a minority—accounting for 38, 47, and 37 percent of residents, respectively. Twenty years ago the white population in all these cities was over 75 percent.[16]

The increased visibility of other racial groups has focused whites more self-consciously than ever on their own racial identification. Until the new immigration shifted the complexion of the land so perceptibly, whites didn't think of themselves as white in the same way that Chinese know they're Chinese and African Americans know they're black. Being white was simply a fact of life, one that didn't require any public statement, since it was the definitive social value against which all others were measured. "It's like everything's changed and I don't know what happened," complains Marianne Bardolino. "All of a sudden you have to be thinking all the time about these race things. I don't remember growing up thinking about being white like I think about it now. I'm not saying I didn't know there was coloreds and whites; it's just that I didn't go along thinking, *Gee, I'm a white person.* I never thought about it at all. But now with all the different colored people around, you have to think about it because they're thinking about it all the time."

"You say you feel pushed now to think about being white, but I'm not sure I understand why. What's changed?" I ask.

"I told you," she replies quickly, a small smile covering her impatience with my question. "It's because they think about what they are, and they want things their way, so now I have to think about what I am and what's good for me and my kids." She pauses briefly to let her thoughts catch up with her tongue, then continues. "I mean, if somebody's always yelling at you about being black or Asian or something, then it makes you think about being white. Like, they want the kids in school to learn about their culture, so then I think about being white and being Italian and say: What about my culture? If they're going to teach about theirs, what about mine?"

To which America's racial minorities respond with bewilderment. "I don't understand what white people want," says Gwen Tomalson. "They say if black kids are going to learn about black culture in school, then white people want their kids to learn about white culture. I don't get it. What do they think kids have been learning about all these years? It's all about white people and how they live and what they accomplished. When I was in school you wouldn't have thought black people existed for all our books ever said about us."

As for the charge that they're "thinking about race all the time," as Marianne Bardolino complains, people of color insist that they're forced into it by a white world that never lets them forget. "If you're Chinese, you can't forget it, even if you want to, because there's always something that reminds you," Carol Kwan's husband, Andrew, remarks tartly. "I mean, if Chinese kids get good grades and get into the university, everybody's worried and you read about it in the papers."

While there's little doubt that racial anxieties are at the center of white concerns, our historic nativism also plays a part in escalating white alarm. The new immigrants bring with them a language and an ethnic culture that's vividly expressed wherever they congregate. And it's this also, the constant reminder of an alien presence from which whites are excluded, that's so troublesome to them.

The nativist impulse isn't, of course, given to the white working class alone. But for those in the upper reaches of the class and status hierarchy—those whose children go to private schools, whose closest contact with public transportation is the taxicab—the immigrant population supplies a source of cheap labor, whether as nannies for their children, maids in their households, or workers in their businesses. They may grouse and complain that "nobody speaks English anymore," just as working-class people do. But for the people who use immigrant labor, legal or illegal, there's a payoff for the inconvenience—a payoff that doesn't exist for the families in this study but that sometimes costs them dearly.[17] For while it may be true that American workers aren't eager for many of the jobs immigrants are willing to take, it's also true that the presence of a large immigrant population—especially those who come from developing countries where living standards are far below our own—helps to make these jobs undesirable by keeping wages depressed well below what most American workers are willing to accept.[18]

Indeed, the economic basis of our immigration policies too often gets lost in the lore that we are a land that says to the world, "Give me your tired, your poor, your huddled masses, yearning to breathe free."[19] I don't mean to suggest that our humane impulses are a fiction, only that the reality is far more complex than Emma Lazarus' poem suggests. The massive immigration of the nineteenth and early twentieth centuries didn't just happen spontaneously. America may have been known as the land of opportunity to the Europeans who dreamed of coming here—a country where, as my parents once believed, the streets were lined with gold. But they believed these things because that's how America was sold by the agents who spread out across the face of Europe to recruit workers—men and women who were needed to keep the machines of our developing industrial society running and who, at the same time, gave the new industries a steady supply of hungry workers willing to work for wages well below those of native-born Americans.

The enormous number of immigrants who arrived during that period accomplished both those ends. In doing so, they set the stage for a long history of antipathy to foreign workers. For today, also, one function of the new immigrants is to keep our industries competitive in a global economy. Which simply is another way of saying that they serve to depress the wages of native American workers.

It's not surprising, therefore, that working-class women and men speak so angrily about the recent influx of immigrants. They not only see their jobs and their way of life threatened, they feel bruised and assaulted by an environment that seems suddenly to have turned color and in which they feel like strangers in their own land. So they chafe and complain: "They come here to take advantage of us, but they don't really want to learn our ways," Beverly Sowell, a 33-year-old white electronics assembler, grumbles irritably. "They live different than us; it's like another world how they live. And they're so clannish. They keep to themselves, and they don't even *try* to learn English. You go on the bus these days and you might as well be in a foreign country; everybody's talking some other language, you know, Chinese or Spanish or something. Lots of them have been here a long time, too, but they don't care; they just want to take what they can get."

But their complaints reveal an interesting paradox, an illuminating glimpse into the contradictions that beset native-born Americans in their relations with those who seek refuge here. On the one hand, they scorn the immigrants; on the other, they protest because they "keep to themselves." It's the same contradiction that dominates black–white relations. Whites refuse to integrate blacks but are outraged when they stop knocking at the door, when they move to sustain the separation on their own terms—in black theme houses on campuses, for example, or in the newly developing black middle-class suburbs.

I wondered, as I listened to Beverly Sowell and others like her, why the same people who find the lifeways and languages of our foreign-born population offensive also care whether they "keep to themselves."

"Because like I said, they just shouldn't, that's all," Beverly says stubbornly. "If they're going to come here, they should be willing to learn our ways—you know what I mean, be real Americans. That's what my grandparents did, and that's what they should do."

"But your grandparents probably lived in an immigrant neighborhood when they first came here, too," I remind her.

"It was different," she insists. "I don't know why; it was. They wanted to be Americans; these here people now, I don't think they do. They just want to take advantage of this country."

She stops, thinks for a moment, then continues, "Right now it's awful in this country. Their kids come into the schools, and it's a big mess. There's not enough money for our kids to get a decent education, and we have to spend money to teach their kids English. It makes me mad. I went to public school, but I have to send my kids to Catholic school because now on top of the black kids, there's all these foreign kids who don't speak English. What kind of an education can kids get in a school like that? Something's wrong when plain old American kids can't go to their own schools.

"Everything's changed, and it doesn't make sense. Maybe you get it, but I don't. We can't take care of our own people and we keep bringing more and more foreigners in. Look at all the homeless. Why do we need more people here when our own people haven't got a place to sleep?"

"Why do we need more people here?"—a question Americans have asked for two centuries now. Historically, efforts to curb immigration have come during economic downturns, which suggests that when times are good, when American workers feel confident about their future, they're likely to be more generous in sharing their good fortune with foreigners. But when the economy falters, as it did in the 1990s, and workers worry about having to compete for jobs with people whose standard of living is well below their own, resistance to immigration rises. "Don't get me wrong; I've got nothing against these people," Tim Walsh demurs. "But they don't talk English, and they're used to a lot less, so they can work for less money than guys like me can. I see it all the time; they get hired and some white guy gets left out."

It's this confluence of forces—the racial and cultural diversity of our new immigrant population; the claims on the resources of the nation now being made by those minorities who, for generations, have called America their home; the failure of some of our basic institutions to serve the needs of our people; the contracting economy, which threatens the mobility aspirations of working-class families—all these have come together to leave white workers feeling as if everyone else is getting a piece of the action while they get nothing. "I feel like white people are left out in the cold," protests Diane Johnson, a 28-year-old white single mother who believes she lost a job as a bus driver to a black woman. "First it's the blacks; now it's all those other colored people, and it's like everything always goes their way. It seems like a white person doesn't have a chance anymore. It's like the squeaky wheel gets the grease, and they've been squeaking and we haven't," she concludes angrily.

Until recently, whites didn't need to think about having to "squeak"—at least not specifically as whites. They have, of course, organized and squeaked at various times in the past—sometimes as ethnic groups, sometimes as workers. But not as whites. As whites they have been the dominant group, the favored ones, the ones who could count on getting the job when people of color could not. Now suddenly there are others—not just individual others but identifiable groups, people who share a history, a language, a culture, even a color—who lay claim to some of the rights and privileges that formerly had been labeled "for whites only." And whites react as if they've been betrayed, as if a sacred promise has been broken. They're white, aren't they? They're *real* Americans, aren't they? This is their country, isn't it?

ENDNOTES

[1] David R. Roediger, *The Wages of Whiteness* (New York: Verso, 1991), p. 133.

[2] I'm aware that many Americans who have none of the characteristic features associated with their African heritage are still defined as black. This is one reason why I characterize race as an idea, not a fact. Nevertheless, the main point I am making here still holds—that is, the visible racial character of a people makes a difference in whether white Americans see them as assimilable or not.

[3] *New York Times,* April 30, 1993.

[4] For an excellent historical portrayal of the formation of ethnic communities among the east central European immigrants in Pennsylvania, the development of ethnic identity, and the process of Americanization, see Ewa Morawska, *For Bread with Butter* (New York: Cambridge University Press, 1985).

[5] Ibid.

[6] Alejandro Portes and Ruben G. Rumbaut, *Immigrant America* (Berkeley: University of California Press, 1990).

[7] One need only walk the streets of New York to see the concentration of Koreans in the corner markets and the nail care salons that dot the city's landscape.

In San Francisco the Cambodians now own most of the donut shops in the city. It all started when, after working in such a shop, an enterprising young Cambodian combined the family resources and opened his own store and bakery. He now has 20 shops and has been instrumental in helping his countrymen open more, all of them buying their donuts from his bakery.

[8] Herbert Gans, "Symbolic Ethnicity: The Future of Ethnic Groups and Cultures in America," *Ethnic and Racial Studies* 2 (1979):1–18.

[9] Despite nativist protests, immigration had proceeded unchecked by government regulation until the end of the nineteenth century. The first serious attempt to restrict immigration came in 1882 when, responding to the clamor about the growing immigration of Chinese laborers to California and other western states, Congress passed the Chinese Exclusion Act. But European immigration remained unimpeded. In the years between 1880 and 1924, twenty-four million newcomers arrived on these shores, most of them eastern and southern Europeans, all bringing their own language and culture, and all the target of pervasive bigotry and exploitation by native-born Americans. By the early part of the twentieth century, anti-immigration sentiments grew strong enough to gain congressional attention once again. The result was the National Origins Act of 1924, which established the quota system that sharply limited immigration, especially from the countries of southern and eastern Europe.

[10] Roger Daniels, *Coming to America: A History of Immigration and Ethnicity in American Life* (New York: HarperCollins, 1990), pp. 338–44.

[11] Daniels, *Coming to America,* p. 341, writes further, "In his Liberty Island speech Lyndon Johnson stressed the fact that he was redressing the wrong done [by the McCarran-Walter Act] to those 'from southern or eastern Europe,' and although he did mention 'developing continents,' there was no other reference to Asian or Third World immigration."

[12] For a further review of the Immigration Act of 1965, see chapter 13 (pp. 328–49) of *Coming to America.*

[13] *Statistical Abstract,* U.S. Bureau of the Census (1992), Table 8, p. 11.

[14] *Statistical Abstract,* U.S. Bureau of the Census (1992), Table 45, p. 42.

[15] *Statistical Abstract,* U.S. Bureau of the Census (1992), Table 18, p. 18, and Table 26, p. 24.

[16] U.S. Bureau of the Census, *Population Reports,* 1970 and 1990. Cited in Mike Davis, "The Body Count," *Crossroads* (June 1993). The difference in the racial composition of New York and San Francisco explains, at least in part, why black–white tensions are so much higher in New York City than they are in San Francisco. In New York, 38 percent of the population is now white, 30 percent black, 25 percent Hispanic, and 7 percent Asian. In San Francisco, whites make up 47 percent of the residents, blacks 11 percent, Hispanics 14 percent, and Asians 29 percent. Thus, blacks in New York reflect the kind of critical mass that generally sparks racial prejudices, fears, and conflicts. True, San Francisco's Asian population—three in ten of the city's residents—also form that kind of critical and noticeable mass. But whatever the American prejudice against Asians, and however much it has been acted out in the past, Asians do not stir the same kind of fear and hatred in white hearts as do blacks.

[17] Zoë Baird, the first woman ever to be nominated to be attorney general of the United States, was forced to withdraw when it became known that she and her husband had hired an illegal immigrant as a nanny for their three-year-old child. The public indignation that followed the revelation came largely from people who were furious that, in a time of high unemployment, American workers were bypassed in favor of cheaper foreign labor.

[18] This is now beginning to happen in more skilled jobs as well. In California's Silicon Valley, for example, software programmers and others are being displaced by Indian workers, people who are trained in India and recruited to work here because they are willing to do so for lower wages than similarly skilled Americans (*San Francisco Examiner,* February 14, 1993).

[19] From Emma Lazarus' "The New Colossus," inscribed at the base of the Statue of Liberty in New York's harbor, the gateway through which most of the immigrants from Europe passed as they came in search of a new life.

33

BLUE DREAMS
Korean Americans and the Los Angeles Riots

NANCY ABELMANN • JOHN LIE

Race is a creation of culture that reflects social distinctions and power. To say that race is a social construction, however, does not mean that race is not real. Many people believe in the existence of discrete biological racial categories. Sociologists are concerned not only with how race and ethnicity are defined but also with the consequences of those distinctions. One important aspect in the social construction of race and ethnicity is how the media defines and frames race-ethnicity and racial problems. The following reading by Nancy Abelmann and John Lie, both professors at the University of Illinois, Urbana-Champaign, examines how the media "framed" the 1992 Los Angeles riots as an interethnic conflict between Korean Americans and African Americans. Their analysis shows how problematic these media frames of race issues are for race relations in the United States. This selection is excerpted from Abelmann and Lie's 1995 book, *Blue Dreams: Korean Americans and the Los Angeles Riots.*

As the complex realities of the multiethnic L.A. riots came to the surface, the media fixated on the conflict between African Americans and Korean Americans.[1] Their mutual animosity became an article of faith. The *Los Angeles Business Journal* reported: "The feelings of many in the black community toward Koreans had become comparable to that of a vanquished populace to the occupying army" (McNelis-Ahern 1992:4). Simultaneously, as Harold Meyerson (1992) explained: "Many within the Korean community conceal a raging anti-black animus behind a wafer-thin

From *Blue Dreams: Korean Americans and the Los Angeles Riots* by Nancy Abelmann and John Lie, pp. 148–149, 159–165, 175–180. © 1995 by the President and Fellows of Harvard College. Reprinted by permission of Harvard University Press.

veneer of peace rhetoric" (p. 2). The looming "race war" prompted Jeff Yang (1992) to observe: "The broadest barrage turned the L.A. riots into a sensationalistic Tale of Two Tapes: Rodney King versus Soon Ja Du, the 'killer Korean shopkeeper'" (p. 47). Instances of the "Black–Korean conflict" beyond Los Angeles, ranging from episodes in Spike Lee's film *Do the Right Thing* to the well-publicized boycott of a Korean American grocer in Flatbush, New York, suggested that it might be a nationwide phenomenon.

Here we criticize the "Black–Korean conflict" frame of the L.A. riots and examine its ideological context. We realize that challenging its explanatory power or noting its ideological construction does not fully explain particular instances of African American–Korean American tension. The reality of individual anger and passionate prejudices held by some African Americans and Korean Americans toward each other cannot be denied. Nor do we wish to dismiss vitriolic expressions of dislike and distrust broadcast in the media simply as articulations of dominant ideologies. Nonetheless, we advance two interrelated arguments against the "Black–Korean conflict." First, we argue that it reifies both African Americans and Korean Americans, and the instances of conflict between them. In other words, it homogenizes diverse peoples and phenomena and thus elides alternative interpretations. Second, and more important, we trace the ideological currents that bolster the "Black–Korean conflict" as a depiction of the two groups as antipodal minorities: the Asian American model minority epitomized by Korean entrepreneurial success and the urban underclass represented by the impoverished African American community. These two portraits constitute flip sides of the same ideological coin, which presumes that the United States is an open society with no systematic barriers to success. The same constellation of factors—culture, attitudes, and family structure—is used to explain the success and failure of each group. We locate the sources of this ideology in the conservative climate of the 1980s in particular and in the idea of the American dream in general. The ideological construction and constitution of the "Black–Korean conflict" should alert us to the dangers of emphasizing this interethnic conflict. . . .

The Reification of the Interethnic Conflict

Before we explore the ideological roots of the "Black–Korean conflict," let us consider its descriptive and explanatory problems. The "Black–Korean conflict" reifies both African Americans and Korean Americans and the conflict itself. In so doing, the interethnic conflict becomes a ready-made explanation for diverse phenomena and diverts our attention from other events and explanations.

The media disseminates ready-made stereotypes as truths about the two groups. All African Americans are not poor, nor do they constitute a homogeneous or cohesive group. Similarly, neither are all Korean Americans shopkeepers nor do they constitute a unified community, even within the narrow perimeters of Koreatown. Multiethnic South Central Los Angeles and Koreatown belie simple ethnic generalizations. We must, therefore, beware of presuming widespread interethnic animosity from individual expressions of anger and prejudice by people in particular social positions.

Beyond promoting overgeneralizations concerning each group, the frame reifies the conflict itself. Uncritical acceptance of the frame leads to descriptive and explanatory errors. In narrating a set scenario depicting warring factions of Korean American merchants against African American residents, distinct events, with different causes and characteristics, become instantiations of the same conflict. In effect, the "Black–Korean conflict" frame acts as an ex post facto explanation; disparate events are treated under the same rubric. Consider, for example, a 1990 boycott in New York. Although ostensibly a case of "Black–Korean conflict," the reality in Brooklyn was not the same as that in South Central Los Angeles. The initial conflict arose between recent Haitian immigrants and a Korean American shopkeeper (Rieder 1990). Although long-term African American residents of South Central Los Angeles and recent Haitian immigrants in Brooklyn are both black within the American racial framework, it would be a mistake to consider them in the same category. In this regard, we should note that in Miami, for instance, people speak of the "Black–Haitian conflict" (Portes and Stepick 1993:190–92).

The interethnic conflict frame leads to explanations, which, in keeping with the prior reifications of each group, locate the conflict's cause in each group's characteristics. Rather than focusing on the broader political economic context, the presumed interethnic conflict pits one homogenized group against another. Consider the hypothetical case of a Korean American shopkeeper who fires an African American employee. In the dominant media frame, the individual case may stimulate a narrative about the "Black–Korean conflict" and explanations based on different interpersonal interaction styles or cultural characteristics. Yet the case may be nothing more than an employer laying off an employee—a product of capitalist social relations rather than interethnic conflict.

The presumed existence of the "Black–Korean conflict" blinds us to a number of inconvenient facts. If there were seething hatred between the two groups, then one might have expected some instances of interethnic killing during the riots. Yet there were no such documented cases. More crucially, the ground zero of the 1992 upheaval was the verdict in the Rodney King beating. African Americans' anger was primarily directed against white racism and the attack on the "black body" (Turner 1993:207–208). Most immediate reactions as well as later reflections by African American writers rarely mentioned Korean Americans (Alan-Williams 1994:169–73; Cleage 1993:123–27; Wiley 1993:82–91). During the riots: "People took up chants proposing alternative targets. 'Beverly Hills!' shouted one cluster. 'Parker Center' (Los Angeles Police Department headquarters), yelled another" (Meyerson 1992:2; see also Ward 1992). Pamela Franklin told the *New York Times:* "The looting and violence was the only way angry blacks in Los Angeles had left to express their bitterness to whites. She said the destruction should be carried to Beverly Hills" (Marriott 1992:A11). Rioters and looters were unable to go to Beverly Hills because of police protection and logistical difficulties, not lack of intention. Hence Korean Americans focused not on African American rioting or looting but, rather, on the state's abandonment of Koreatown and South Central Los Angeles during the riots.

The "Black–Korean conflict" also averts our gaze from interethnic conflicts that have *prima facie* plausibility. African Americans and Latinos, especially recent Central American immigrants, compete for employment, housing, and political power. Thus one might expect a potent interethnic conflict between African Americans and Latinos—the so-called "Black–Brown conflict" (Miles 1992; Oliver and Johnson 1984:75–84; Skerry 1993:83–86). Korean Americans, in contrast, do not generally compete with African Americans, particularly in South Central Los Angeles, for manufacturing or service jobs. Very few Korean Americans live in South Central Los Angeles, and therefore they do not vie for existing housing stock or struggle over political power and representation.

Alternatively, we might have expected more media coverage of the "Korean–Latino conflict," especially given that so many Latinos work for Korean American businesses and industries. As we have noted, the majority of rioters and looters arrested were Latinos; recall the second-generation Korean American's shock over the looting in Koreatown carried out by his Latino neighbors and acquaintances.

Our intention is not to initiate discourses on the "Black–Latino conflict" or the "Korean–Latino conflict" but to question the salience of the "Black–Korean conflict." Indeed, we might ask why the media did not seize on the "Korean–white conflict," given that European Americans also looted Koreatown stores. The African American novelist Ishmael Reed (1993) queries: "Why doesn't the looting and burning of Korean stores by whites in Koreatown—which was witnessed by Pacifica Radio's Kwazi Nkrumah—indicate a bias of whites toward Koreans?" (p. 44).

The Antipodal Minorities

Why should the "Black–Korean conflict" emerge as a central phenomenon in the reporting on the 1992 L.A. riots? We argue that the "Black–Korean conflict" is deeply rooted in American ideologies.

Media reports on the "Black–Korean conflict" often highlight different customs and interpersonal interaction styles as the source of friction between Korean American merchants and African American customers (Cheng and Espiritu 1989:525–28; Stewart 1989, 1993). Korean American merchants are said to avoid eye contact, slam the change on the countertop, fail to make small talk, and, in general, refuse to assimilate to American cultural norms.[2] The journalist C. Connie Kang explains: "In the Confucian-steeped Korean culture, a smile is reserved for family members and close friends. . . . Expressions such as 'thank you' and 'excuse me' are used sparingly."[3] A source even more likely than Confucian legacies, however, is the experience of living in Seoul, which, as one of the world's most densely populated and rapidly urbanized cities, has not been congenial to refined manners. At worst, Korean American merchants are depicted as rude, racist, and rapacious. In turn, African American customers are said not to understand Korean cultural norms and to act in such a way as to offend Korean American merchants. H. Andrew Kim writes: "Blacks have little understanding of Korean merchants, who are in constant fear of being robbed or shot, while going through the massive readjustment to a strange culture, customs and language" (*Korea Times* 1992:6).

The concept of culture generally denotes a constellation of attributes, transient and intransigent, that distinguishes one group from another—for example, the French from the German. Cultural characteristics may be easily transferable—a Korean may become inordinately fond of truffles, a French person may acquire a taste for *kimch'i*, a spicy Korean dish—or more intransigent: values and world views often do not translate or transplant well across cultures. Both the transient and the intransigent aspects of culture are used to characterize the conflict between African Americans and Korean Americans.

The focus on transient aspects of culture mandates cosmetic changes in order to achieve interethnic reconciliation. From this perspective, better understanding, promoted through mutual recognition and interethnic interaction, would solve the problem. The stress on transient cultural attributes leads the *New York Times* to celebrate New York's "admirable example" (that is, its lack of rioting and looting after the L.A. riots) as the result of the Human Rights Commission's providing "sensitivity training to Korean merchants and the black community on how to prevent tensions and what to do when problems occur."[4] Seminars, furthermore, teach Korean American merchants to "smile more frequently" and African American leaders are invited on tours of South Korea (Martin 1993). Though commendable, these steps provide superficial solutions. After all, smiling Korean American merchants and understanding African American customers leave both groups in the same place they were in to begin with: Korean Americans as merchants and African Americans as customers.

Many commentators therefore seek deeper causes of the conflict and argue that the two groups manifest contrasting values, attitudes, and behavior—intransigent cultural differences. Accounts emphasizing intransigent aspects of culture highlight Korean Americans' education, hard work, and family solidarity as corollaries of the Confucian ethos and their supposed corresponding absence among African Americans. These contrasting cultural constructs are used to explain the different success rates of Korean Americans and African Americans.

At the heart of the interethnic contrast lies the Korean American entrepreneur—independent and diligent—who embodies the promise of capitalism and the free enterprise system. The *Economist* writes: "The Koreans have
a remarkable business bent. . . . They are also capitalists. In short, they are
model American citizens" (Grimond 1982). Edward Norden (1992) waxes enthusiastic about a Korean American shop owner, Roy Kim: "Kim's story . . .
was the usual one for [Korean Americans] who had set up in South-Central.
He stepped off the plane with $100 in his pocket, and by mobilizing his fam-
ily, joining a *kye* [rotating credit association], and working fifteen-hour days
for fifteen years, put enough money aside to buy a mortgaged house in the
suburbs" (p. 33).

In contrast to the entrepreneurial heroism of Korean Americans, African
Americans cut a pathetic figure in this ideological fabric. Norden (1992) is
indignant about an African American activist who faults the larger society:
"So why not found bigger, stronger, more aggressive black banks with the
black money out there, or the black version of the *kye*, the hybrid lottery and
savings-and-loan scheme to which masses of KAs [Korean Americans] belong? . . . Or why not mobilize families . . . to run mom-and-pop shops for
fifteen hours a day in place of KAs [Korean Americans]?" (p. 38). The contrast
is drawn more starkly regarding their relationship to welfare. "It's rare for
Korean immigrants to go on the dole, even in the beginning. For these people
[after the riots] it was shameful to have to prove, in triplicate, not only that
the livelihoods they had created had been destroyed, but that they had no
savings, no insurance, and no close relatives working" (p. 35). Korean Americans, in this line of argument, are exemplary for not relying on welfare.[5]

According to these accounts, not only do Korean American merchants
exhibit the virtues of rugged individualism and make a mockery of racism
and welfare, but they rely on familial and communal resources. Jim Sleeper
proclaims:

> Many of the Koreans get their business going because they have a sense
> of responsibility to each other. They pool their limited resources to
> "stake" one another—in a way we don't see happening even with these
> African Americans who make it out of the ghettos. . . . It's just so obvious
> that family units are critical to success. Inner-city black communities do
> not have the social structure to sustain the bonds of trust that are needed
> to "stake" one another and sustain that kind of family output.[6]

In these accounts, Korean Americans and African Americans are polar
opposites.

The contrast is most insistently articulated by conservative commentators.

[It] was permissible to explain black antagonism toward Koreans in Los
Angeles in terms of "anger" over Soon Ja Du, the Korean shopkeeper who,

having shot and killed a 15-year-old black girl named Latasha Harlins who had assaulted her, was then released by a judge. But it was impermissible to note that 25 Korean merchants had been murdered in the ghetto in the last two years. It was permissible to mention that blacks were "frustrated" by Korean economic success. It was impermissible to specify that this rise was based on 14-hour work days, personal sacrifice often approaching indenture, and family solidarity. (*Heterodoxy* 1992:10)

In lionizing the Korean American shopkeepers, the polemic simultaneously belittles African American charges of racism and discrimination: "The Koreans had given the lie to fantasies about racism and its discontents on which black leadership has come to depend. . . . They were a living refutation, right there in South Central Los Angeles, of the notion that job equals chump, an argument against the narcotic of self-pity and the whine of victimhood which has become the elevator music of the ghetto."[7]

In these narratives, Korean American entrepreneurs personify the values of individual responsibility and family solidarity, while African Americans stand for welfare dependence and family dissolution. These views appear to be widespread. Neil Saari (1992) wrote to *Time* that "the intense attacks directed at the Koreans were unmistakably racist. Instead of burning them out, Los Angeles' African Americans would do well to study and copy the Koreans' work ethic and family solidarity" (p. 10). Or, as one "white man" told the *Los Angeles Times:* "I'm so goddamn mad. Let these people burn their own stuff down. If you don't like the Koreans, why don't you go get your own grocery store, mister?" (*Los Angeles Times* 1992, pt. iii, p. 6). Max Kerstein (1992), publisher of the *Beverage Bulletin,* wrote: "It is a sad commentary when honest, hard-working citizens of our city face criminals within our society bent on destruction, injury, death and hate. Of all the people who suffered those terrible losses [during the riots], the Korean community felt the devastation and ruin more than anyone else" (p. 18).

In summary, many accounts depict African Americans and Korean Americans as antipodal minorities. The comparison highlights the contrasting portrait of each group in the 1980s: Korean Americans as a model minority and African Americans as an urban underclass. . . .

The American Dream: Capitalism, Race, and Community

The celebration of the model minority and the denigration of the urban underclass reflected and basked in the conservative climate of the 1980s, a decade of both greed and denial, during which the rich grew richer and the poor grew poorer (Mattera 1990). Kevin Phillips (1991) writes: "The 1980s were the triumph of upper America—an ostentatious celebration of wealth, the political ascendancy of the richest third of the population and a glorification of capitalism, free markets and finance" (p. xvii). The unfettered pursuit of profit became fashionable; capitalist theologians such as George Gilder and Charles Murray celebrated the entrepreneurial spirit of U.S. capitalism and simultaneously absolved the system of any problems. Concomitant with the unleashing of the greed motive was the denial of its costs. As Haynes Johnson (1991) entitled his book on the Reagan years, the United States seemed to be "sleepwalking through history."[8] While the United States was gradually losing its claim as the premier economic power in the world, the momentary euphoria of the Gulf War victory symbolized, while the Rodney King beating epitomized the underside of, the decade of self-congratulation.[9]

It is in this context that we need to understand the popularity of the underclass thesis, as well as its foil, the successful model minority. The underlying message is that people succeed or fail in spite of external constraints and contexts. The self-evident successes of Asian Americans, in the absence of government support, supposedly controvert the claim that more welfare or antiracist remedies are necessary to alleviate inner-city poverty.

The categories of the model minority and the urban underclass became ubiquitous in the 1980s because of their affinity with the dominant ideological movement. Their popularity, however, is not a temporary aberration. Rather, the archaeology of the dominant ideological current in the United States suggests their venerable provenance—the ideal of the American dream. Its principal tenet is that the United States is essentially an open society in which everyone can achieve her or his dream. A corollary of the belief is a series of assumptions about the nature of the economy, race, and community in the United States. . . .

The American dream denotes a belief in the United States as a land of opportunity in which no major obstacles exist to individual success. Unlike in the Old World or the Third World, individuals are liberated and unleashed from their pre-American fetters to pursue their vision of happiness.[10] Inequalities and divides of class, gender, and race are ultimately meaningless; rugged individualism reigns supreme in this social view. Put simply, people with talent and who work hard succeed, while others do not. Those who fail, then, have no one to blame but themselves.[11]

The American dream is an individualistic ideology. The projected economic order is *laissez-faire* capitalism, in which sovereign individuals compete with one another to pursue material gains. In this vision, the entrepreneur, relying essentially on ingenuity and hard work, represents the iconic figure of success.[12] In turn, social welfare programs are never legitimate except as expressions of collective "charity" to the "truly needy." Michael Katz comments in *The Undeserving Poor* (1989) that there is a long tradition of sequestering the comfortable middle-class "us" from the morally inferior and impoverished "them." The moral primacy of work and its flip side, the ethical castigation of the "lazy" poor, is a deeply ingrained Americanism, a civilization founded on the rejection of European aristocrats and the denigration of African slaves (Shklar 1991, chap. 2; see also Rodgers 1978). In this line of thought, people on welfare are, almost by definition, morally suspect; the very concept of social welfare carries a pejorative connotation. When the Reagan and Bush administrations castigated the moral standing of welfare recipients, they were expressing a conservative reading of the American dream ideology.[13] In 1987 Reagan said of welfare: "It is time to reform this outdated social dinosaur and finally break the poverty trap."[14]

The celebration of the individual often entails the neglect of the collective and systematic constraints. Class is eschewed in public discourse.[15] Racism, sexism, or other forms of systematic discrimination neither explain nor justify existing inequalities. The refutation of racism constitutes, as we have suggested, one of the appeals of the model minority thesis.[16] One terminus of the denial of racism is universal "ethnicization." In effect, everyone becomes an "ethnic" in the United States. Richard Alba (1990) argues: "The thrust of European-American identity is to defend the individualistic view of the American system, because it portrays the system as open to those who are willing to work hard and pull themselves over barriers of poverty and discrimination" (p. 317). Charges of racism lose force if all ethnicities are considered to have struggled their way toward equality and prosperity under the same conditions.[17]

Finally, the American dream offers a particular social vision (Baritz 1989). The outline of a good society is constituted by two pillars: the family as a "haven in a heartless world" and the community that upholds the individualist ethos. In this vision, "home" is the nurturing environment, while the larger "community" protects the "home." The family is a sacred institution in the ideal of the American dream. Essentially, the home is a "haven" where individuals are nourished and protected; it is an incubator and protector of individuality.[18] The community is inseparable from the family.[19] Reagan, for example, spoke of America's "bedrock, its communities where neighbors help one another" (Reich 1991:277). In turn, the idealized environment of the ideal family in modern America is suburbia. "The central symbol of the nearly perfected America . . . was the suburban family. Suburbia meant more than physical comfort; it embodied a long-held American dream of a happy, secure family life" (Skolnick 1991:2). "Bourgeois utopias" of American suburbia became the ideal community (Fishman 1987; see also Hayden 1984 and Jackson 1985). In contrast, urban life represents an undesirable ideal. The city, with its disorders and dangers, represents a demonized environment. In the cacophony and heterogeneity of city life, deviant social relations and institutions proliferate.[20] More prosaically, the city is where the "community," understood in all its suburban splendor, breaks down; in cities, strange languages, foods, and peoples coexist. The city is, moreover, racialized and poor. Instead of individual achievement, there is sloth and dependence (on government welfare); instead of family values, there is deviance; instead of suburban *communitas,* there is urban anomie; and, finally, instead of "real" Americans, there are minorities.[21] The city—particularly the inner city—is the racialized "other" of the American dream.

The American dream thus projects a vision of the United States where individual initiatives and efforts determine success and failure, racism is not a serious affliction, and the family and the community exist to nurture sovereign individuals.

The social reality of the contemporary United States contradicts the idealized vision of the American dream. The world of entrepreneurial capitalism, for example, occupies a relatively small, if surprisingly persistent, part of the contemporary United States economy. The global economy of the late twentieth century is dominated by large corporations and large governments. It is via corporations and professions, not classical entrepreneurship, that most Americans seek material comfort in affluent suburbs. The free market ideology, however, celebrates nineteenth-century entrepreneurial capitalism, while ignoring the reality of twentieth-century corporate capitalism.[22] To be sure, instances of individual success continue to exist, but it would be egregious to deny the predominance of large corporations in the contemporary economy.

The individualism articulated in the American dream downplays systemic barriers to individual success, such as racism. Such a view misses not only racism's historical ferocity against African Americans—Jim Crow laws that rendered them virtually an "untouchable" caste into the 1960s in some regions of the United States—but also its contemporary, albeit weakening, force.[23]

The ideal of the nuclear family, similarly, diverges from the reality of most U.S. households. Many people of all ethnicities live in a variety of "nontraditional" households.[24] In addition, a generation of women's movements and feminist writings have noted the dysfunctions of the patriarchal nuclear family (Thorne 1992). Similarly, in spite of the celebration of the suburbs and the denigration of the city, people's concrete living patterns and ideals complicate this simple dichotomy. One principal trend, for example, has been the gentrification and renewal of urban centers (Zukin 1991). More important, many people abhor the isolation, anomie, and homogeneity of suburbs. Most American suburbs are not places, in Reagan's idealized imagery, "where neighbors help one another," but instead resemble the stereotyped cold and impersonal city.

The American dream presents a problematic ideal of individual life and community. More crucially for our purpose, however, the constellation of attitudes and institutions that constitutes the American dream has found a powerful articulation in the contrast between the model minority and the urban underclass: Korean Americans embody the American dream, while African Americans betray its promise. The ideological constitution and construction of the "Black–Korean conflict" should alert us not only to the importance of the broader political economy but also to the necessity of rethinking dominant American ideologies.

We cannot make sense of the heterogeneous voices of both conflict and cooperation, racism and solidarity, unless we see that they are the very ground on which ideologies work. In particular, an attempt to understand Korean American responses to the riots and the "Black–Korean conflict" requires us to consider their transnational context and their heterogeneity. In so doing, we place American ideologies on trial. The complexities and contradictions of Korean American responses—indeed, the gritty reality of individual immigrant lives—require nothing less than an appreciation of themes at the heart of this research.

ENDNOTES

1 There is by now a growing literature on the "Black–Korean conflict"; see, for example, E. Chang (1990, 1993a, 1993b); Abelmann (1991); Ahn (1991); Chen (1991); S. Kim (1991); P. G. Min (1991); Yi (1992); S. K. Cho (1985); and E. H. Kim (1993). For literary works, see Lew (1993) and K. Min (1994).

2 Eui-Young Yu (1990) notes: "Korean shoppers think that non-Korean markets are more courteous, less expensive, carry more fresh vegetables, and have more choices" (p. 106).

3 Shaw (1990:A31). Edward Chang (1990) asserts that Korean Americans "tend to be very cold toward people they do not know" and hence "there is a tendency . . . to disrespect their black customers" (p. 244).

4 *New York Times* (1992a). One effort forces individuals to crystallize and articulate "a compilation of negative, false stereotypes" about others (Njeri 1993:22).

5 Charles Murray (1992) states: "The rhetoric had always proclaimed that affirmative action was needed to help minorities who were disadvantaged by the white majority. But Asians refused to exhibit the symptoms of disadvantage" (p. 32).

6 In *Tikkun* (1992:42). In *The Closest of Strangers*, Sleeper (1990) writes: "Yet one 'means' never mentioned [by African American activists] is the recruitment and training of a few hundred young blacks prepared to work fifteen hours a day at low wages and in close family units, as the Koreans do, in order to pay their debts to immigrant lending societies [rotating credit associations]" (p. 208).

7 *Heterodoxy* (1992:10). In a similar vein, Midge Decter (1992) charges that the "refusal of empathy with the Los Angeles Koreans on the part of America's liberal publicists has very deep roots," which include their advocacy of social welfare: "Assuming responsibility for one's life, for one's everyday choices as well as for one's moral conduct, is a practice that has been eroding in American life for a long, long time" (pp. 21–22).

8 On Reagan, see the indispensable work by Wills (1987). The best metaphor of denial comes from neurophysiologist Oliver Sachs: "Aphasiacs . . . experience an elevated understanding of . . . the quality of speech that communicates an inner meaning rather than the mere assemblage of words. One cannot lie to an aphasiac because he cannot comprehend your words, and so is not deceived by them. . . . An aphasiac perceives the verisimilitude of a speaker's voice and cannot suspend disbelief. Reagan's 'grimaces, the histrionisms, the false gestures, and above all, the false tones and cadences of the voice . . . rang false for these immensely sensitive patients.' . . . Normal audiences, 'aided doubtless by our wish to be fooled, were indeed well and truly fooled.' The president's cunning and 'deceptive' use of words and tones assured that 'only the brain-damaged remained intact, undeceived'" (Schaller 1992:59).

9 See, for example, Shapiro (1992). Stephen Graubard (1992) polemicizes: "The United States has become a victim of years of self-neglect, self-delusion, and self-praise.

Once a quintessential model of a progressive society, it has become dowdy and old-fashioned, losing appreciation of its one remaining substantial resource—the heterogeneity of its people" (p. 187).

[10] Kluegel and Smith (1986) conclude their survey of ordinary Americans' beliefs about inequality thus: "A clear majority of the American population subscribes, largely undeservedly, to the characterization of America as the 'land of opportunity'" (p. 52).

[11] "The belief that all men, in accordance with certain rules, but exclusively by their own efforts, can make of their own lives what they will has been widely popularized for well over a century" (Weiss 1969:3). See also Lipset (1979:2).

[12] Bellah and his colleagues (1985) note: "The self-sufficient entrepreneur, competitive, tough, and freed by wealth from external constraints, was one new American character" (p. 44).

[13] As Piven and Cloward (1993, chap. 11) argue, the anti-welfare ideology also functions to discipline workers.

[14] Schwarz and Volgy (1992:133). Although the transformation of social welfare into a social evil marked a tremendous shift in the terrain of political debate from the 1960s and 1970s, when Great Society programs and the alleviation of poverty were nearly consensual goals for U.S. citizens, the moral-philosophical foundation of social welfare in the United States remains less than secure and legitimate (see Katz 1989, chap. 3). Indeed, what Theodore Marmor and his colleagues call the "opportunity-insurance" state, which U.S. citizens broadly support, suffers from its conflation with the maligned welfare state (Marmor, Mashaw, and Harvey 1990:49).

[15] Benjamin DeMott (1990) writes: "America as a classless society is, finally, a deceit, and today, as yesterday, the deceit causes fearful moral and social damage" (p. 12). Americans may be, however, class conscious in some ways; see Vanneman and Cannon (1987).

[16] Indeed, neoconservative writers, especially in the 1980s, were emphatic on this point: to blame the lack of progress by some African Americans on racism was not only empirically wrong but morally objectionable. In so doing, they attempted to stem the tide of progressive "racial" legislation initiated by the civil rights movement of the 1950s and 1960s. Two African American intellectuals particularly influential in the 1980s articulated the ultimate irrelevance of race. Denying the impact of racism, the economist Thomas Sowell (1981b) notes: "The presence of Jewish and Japanese Americans at the top of the income rankings must undermine any simplistic theory that discrimination is an overwhelming determinant of socioeconomic position" (p. 126). In his best-selling book *Ethnic America,* Sowell (1981a) argues further that "perhaps the most striking difference among ethnic groups is in their attitudes toward learning and self-improvement" (p. 280). In other words, racism explains little of the disproportionate poverty experienced by African Americans. In another version of this argument, Shelby Steele (1990) highlights the fault with explaining African American problems with reference to racism. He writes: "Hard work, education, individual initiative, stable family life, property ownership—those have always been the means by which ethnic groups have moved ahead in America" (p. 108).

[17] Universal ethnicity also accentuates the irreducible import of culture in the sense that Michael Novak (1972) wrote: "Emotions, instincts, memory, imagination, passions, and ways of perceiving are passed on to us in ways we do not choose, and in ways so thick with life that they lie far beyond the power of consciousness (let alone of analytical and verbal reason) thoroughly to master, totally to alter. We are, in a word, ineffably ethnic in our values and our actions" (p. xvi). Our "ineffably ethnic" self exists as a crucial precondition for the cultural explanation of ethnic groups' success and failure.

[18] The shift from the older patriarchal norm to the new individualist ideal occurred as early as the late eighteenth century. Helena Wall (1990) writes: "Colonial society began by deferring to the needs of the community and ended by deferring to the rights of the individual" (p. vii). The new ideal "was understood to be affectionate, voluntaristic, and private" (p. 138).

[19] Claude Fischer (1991) writes: "Americans of the Left and of the Right esteem the local community. It rests in the pantheon of American civil religion paradoxically close to that supreme value, individualism. In our ideology, the locality is, following the family, the premier locus for 'community,' in the fullest sense of solidarity, commitment, and intimacy" (p. 79). See also Gans (1988:64).

[20] Lewis Lapham (1992) notes: "The idea of a great city never has occupied a comfortable place in the American imagination. Much of the country's political and literary history suggests that the city stands as a metaphor for depravity—the port of entry for things foreign and obnoxious" (p. 4). See also White and White (1962).

[21] The political scientist Edward Banfield (1974) writes: "The most conspicuous fact of life in the city is racial division. . . . The residential suburbs are mostly white—often 'lily-white'; the central cities, especially their older, more deteriorated parts, and above all their slums, are predominantly or entirely black" (p. 77).

[22] "Voices still trumpeting the nineteenth-century medley of stable independence and dynamic entrepreneurship have a patently disingenuous ring. The largest conglomerates regularly advertise their similarity to small business" (Berthoff 1980: 42–43).

[23] See, for example, Burstein (1985:1). As Cornel West (1991) describes: "The chronic refusal of most Americans to understand the sheer absurdity that confronts human beings of African descent in this country—the incessant assaults on black intelligence, beauty, character, and possibility—is not simply a matter of defending white-skin privilege. It also bespeaks a reluctance to look squarely at the brutal side and tragic dimension of the American past and present" (p. 35). See also Gould (1992); T. Morrison (1992); Shklar (1991); and Sundquist (1993).

[24] Arlene Skolnick (1991) writes: "Contrary to the homogeneous, idealized family portrayed in the sitcoms, the most distinctive feature of American family life has always been its diversity" (p. 3). She also notes that the 1950s was in fact the "deviant decade" (pp. 51–54). See also Coontz (1992).

REFERENCES

Abelmann, Nancy. 1991. "Transgressing Headlines: Reporting Race in the African American/Korean American Conflicts." Paper presented at the Association for Asian Studies meeting, New Orleans, LA.

Ahn, Choong Sik. 1991. "An Alternative Approach to the Racial Conflict between Korean Small Business Owners and the Black-American Community in the New York Area." Pp. 49–55 in *The Korean-American Community*, edited by Tae-Hwan Kwak and Seong Hyong Lee.

Alan-Williams, Gregory. 1994. *A Gathering of Heroes: Reflections on Rage and Responsibility—a Memoir of the Los Angeles Riots*. Chicago: Academy Chicago.

Alba, Richard. 1990. *Ethnic Identity: The Transformation of White America*. New Haven, CT: Yale University Press.

Banfield, Edward C. 1974. *The Unheavenly City Revisited*. Boston: Little, Brown.

Baritz, Loren. 1989. *The Good Life: The Meaning of Success for the American Middle Class*. New York: Knopf.

Bellah, Robert, et al. 1985. *Habits of the Heart: Individualism and Commitment in American Life*. Berkeley: University of California Press.

Berthoff, Rowland. 1980. "Independence and Enterprise: Small Business in the American Dream." Pp. 28–48 in *Small Business in American Life,* edited by Stuart W. Bruchey. New York: Columbia University Press.

Burstein, Paul. 1985. *Discrimination, Jobs, and Politics: The Struggle for Equal Employment Opportunity in the United States since the New Deal.* Chicago: University of Chicago Press.

Chang, Edward T. 1990. "New Urban Crisis: Korean–Black Conflicts in Los Angeles." Ph.D. dissertation, University of California, Berkeley.

———. 1993a. *Hug'in: Kudul un nugunji* [Blacks: Who Are They?]. Seoul: Han'guk Kyongje Sinmunsa.

———. 1993b. "America's First Multiethnic 'Riots.'" Pp. 101–17 in *The State of Asian America,* edited by Karin Aguilar-San Juan. Boston: South End Press.

Chen, Elsa Y. 1991. "Black-Led Boycotts of Korean-Owned Grocery Stores." B.A. Thesis, Princeton University.

Cheng, Lucie and Yen Espiritu. 1989. "Korean Businesses in Black and Hispanic Neighborhoods: A Study of Intergroup Relations." *Sociological Perspectives* (32):521–34.

Cho, Soon Kyong. 1985. "The Labor Process and Capital Mobility: The Limits of the New International Division of Labor." *Politics and Society* (14):185–22.

Cleage, Pearl. 1993. *Deals with the Devil and Other Reasons to Riot.* New York: Harper and Row.

Coontz, Stephanie. 1992. *The Way We Never Were: American Families and the Nostalgia Trap.* New York: Basic Books.

Decter, Midge. 1992. "How the Rioters Won." *Commentary,* July, pp. 17–22.

DeMott, Benjamin. 1990. *The Imperial Middle: Why Americans Can't Think Straight about Class.* New York: William Morrow.

Fischer, Claude S. 1991. "Ambivalent Communities: How Americans Understand Their Localities." Pp. 79–90 in *America at Century's End,* edited by Alan Wolfe. Berkeley: University of California Press.

Fishman, Robert. 1987. *Bourgeois Utopias: The Rise and Fall of Suburbia.* New York: Basic Books.

Gans, Herbert J. 1988. *Middle American Individualism: The Future of Liberal Democracy.* New York: Free Press.

Gould, Mark. 1992. "The New Racism in the United States Society." Pp. 154–74 in *The Dynamics of Social Systems,* edited by P. Colomy. London: Sage.

Graubard, Stephen R. 1992. *Mr. Bush's War: Adventures in the Politics of Illusion.* New York: Hill and Wang.

Grimond, John. 1982. "Somewhere Serious: Los Angeles—a Survey." *Economist,* April 3, special survey section.

Hayden, Delores. 1984. *Redesigning the American Dream: The Future of Housing, Work, and Family Life.* New York: Norton.

Heterodoxy. 1992. June.

Jackson, Kenneth T. 1985. *Crabgrass Frontier: The Suburbanization of the United States.* New York: Oxford University Press.

Johnson, Haynes. 1991. *Sleepwalking through History: America in the Reagan Years.* New York: Norton.

Katz, Michael B. 1989. *The Undeserving Poor: From the War on Poverty to the War on Welfare.* New York: Pantheon.

Kerstein, Max. 1992. "Rebuilding Anew." *KAGRO Newsletter* 3(5/6):18.

Kim, Elaine H. 1993. "Creating a Third Space." *Bay Guardian,* March 10, pp. 31ff.

Kim, Shin. 1991. "Conceptualization of Inter-minority Group Conflict: Conflict between Korean Entrepreneurs and Black Local Residents." Pp. 29–48 in *The Korean-American Community,* edited by Tae-Hwan Kwak and Seong Hyong Lee.

Kluegel, James R. and Eliot R. Smith. 1986. *Beliefs about Inequality: Americans' Views of What Is and What Ought to Be.* New York: Aldine de Gruyter.

Korea Times. 1992. "Letters to Ted Koppel." May 11, p. 7.

Lapham, Lewis. 1992. "Notebook: City Lights." *Harper's Magazine,* July, pp. 4–6.

Lew, Walter. 1993. "Black Korea." Pp. 230–35 in *Charlie Chan Is Dead,* edited by J. Hagedorn. New York: Penguin.

Lipset, Seymour Martin. 1979. *The First New Nation: The United States in Historical and Comparative Perspective.* 2d ed. New York: Norton.

Los Angeles Times. 1992. "Understanding the Riots," parts 1–5. May 11–16.

Marmor, Theodore R., Jerry L. Mashaw, and Philip L. Harvey. 1990. *America's Misunderstood Welfare State: Persistent Myths, Enduring Realities.* New York: Basic Books.

Marriott, Michael. 1992. "Fire of Anguish and Rage as Random Violence Spreads across Los Angeles." *New York Times,* May 1, p. A11.

Martin, Douglas. 1993. "Seeking New Ties and Clout, Korean Grocers Join Voices." *New York Times,* March 22, pp. A1ff.

Mattera, Philip. 1990. *Prosperity Lost: How a Decade of Greed Has Eroded Our Standard of Living and Endangered Our Children's Future.* Reading, MA: Addison-Wesley.

McNelis-Ahern, Margaret. 1992. "Agenda for Action." Pp. 12–15 in *Beyond the Ashes,* edited by the *Los Angeles Business Journal.*

Meyerson, Harold. 1992. "Casualties of the Los Angeles Riot." *In These Times,* May 13–19, p. 2.

Miles, Jack. 1992. "Blacks vs. Browns." *Atlantic,* October, pp. 41–61.

Min, Katherine. 1994. "K-Boy and 2 Bad." *TriQuarterly* (89):38–51.

Min, Pyong Gap. 1991. "Korean Immigrants' Small Business Activities and Korean–Black Interracial Conflicts." Pp. 13–28 in *The Korean-American Community,* edited by Tae-Hwan Kwak and Seong Hyong Lee.

Morrison, Toni. 1992. *Playing in the Dark: Whiteness and the Literary Imagination.* Cambridge, MA: Harvard University Press.

Murray, Charles. 1992. "Causes, Root Causes, and Cures." *National Review,* June 8, pp. 30–32.

Njeri, Itabara. 1993. "The Conquest of Hate." *Los Angeles Times Magazine,* April 25, pp. 20–21.

Norden, Edward. 1992. "South-Central Korea: Post-Riot L.A." *American Spectator,* September, pp. 33–40.

Novak, Michael. 1972. *The Rise of the Unmeltable Ethnics: Politics and Culture in the Seventies.* New York: Macmillan.

Oliver, Melvin L., and James H. Johnson, Jr. 1984. "Inter-Ethnic Conflict in an Urban Ghetto: The Case of Blacks and Latinos in Los Angeles." *Research in Social Movements, Conflict, and Change* (6):57–94.

Phillips, Kevin. 1991. *The Politics of Rich and Poor: Wealth and the American Electorate in the Reagan Aftermath.* 2d ed. New York: Harper Perennial.

Piven, Frances Fox and Richard A. Cloward. 1993. *Regulating the Poor: The Functions of Public Welfare.* Updated ed. New York: Vintage.

Portes, Alejandro and Alex Stepick. 1993. *City on the Edge: The Transformation of Miami.* Berkeley: University of California Press.

Reed, Ishmael. 1993. *Airing Dirty Laundry.* Reading, MA: Addison-Wesley.

Reich, Robert B. 1991. *The Work of Nations: Preparing Ourselves for Twenty-First Century Capitalism.* New York: Knopf.

Rieder, Jonathan. 1990. "Trouble in Store." *New Republic,* July 2, pp. 16–20.

Rodgers, Daniel. 1978. *The Work Ethic in Industrial America, 1850–1920.* Chicago: University of Chicago Press.

Saari, Neil. 1992. "Letter." *Time,* June 1, p. 10.

Schaller, Michael. 1992. *Reckoning with Reagan: America and Its President in the 1980s.* New York: Oxford University Press.

Schwarz, John E. and Thomas J. Volgy. 1992. *The Forgotten Americans: Thirty Million Working Poor in the Land of Opportunity.* New York: Norton.

Shapiro, Andrew L. 1992. *We're Number One.* New York: Vintage.

Shaw, David. 1990. "Asian-Americans Chafe against Stereotype of 'Model Citizen.'" *Los Angeles Times,* Dec. 11, p. A31.

Shklar, Judith N. 1991. *American Citizenship: The Quest for Inclusion.* Cambridge, MA: Harvard University Press.

Skerry, Peter. 1993. *Mexican-Americans: The Ambivalent Minority.* New York: Free Press.

Skolnick, Arlene. 1991. *Embattled Paradise: The American Family in an Age of Uncertainty.* New York: Basic Books.

Sleeper, Jim. 1990. *The Closest of Strangers: Liberalism and the Politics of Race in New York.* New York: Norton.

Sowell, Thomas. 1981a. *Ethnic America: A History.* New York: Basic Books.

———. 1981b. *Markets and Minorities.* New York: Basic Books.

Steele, Shelby. 1990. *The Content of Our Character: A New Vision of Race in America.* New York: St. Martin's Press.

Stewart, Ellen. 1989. "Ethnic Cultural Diversity: An Interpretive Study of Cultural Differences and Communication Styles between Korean Merchants/Employees and Black Patrons in South Los Angeles." M.A. Thesis, California State University, Los Angeles.

———. 1993. "Communication between African Americans and Korean Americans: Before and after the Los Angeles Riots." *Amerasia Journal* 19(2):23–53.

Sundquist, Eric J. 1993. *To Wake the Nations: Race in the Making of American Literature.* Cambridge, MA: Harvard University Press.

Thorne, Barrie. 1992. "Feminism and the Family: Two Decades of Thought." Pp. 3–30 in *Rethinking the Family: Some Feminist Questions,* rev. ed., edited by Barrie Thorne and Marilyn Yalom. Boston: Northeastern University Press.

Tikkun. 1992. "Roundtable: Domestic Social Policy after the L.A. Uprising." July/ August, pp. 39–44, 74–75.

Turner, Patricia A. 1993. *I Heard It through the Grapevine: Rumor in African-American Culture.* Berkeley: University of California Press.

Vanneman, Reeve and Lynn Weber Cannon. 1987. *The American Perception of Class.* Philadelphia: Temple University Press.

Wall, Helena M. 1990. *Fierce Communion: Family and Community in Early America.* Cambridge, MA: Harvard University Press.

Ward, Arvli. 1992. "Twenty-Four Hours in the Life of the Rebellion." *Nommo,* May/June, pp. 18ff.

Weiss, Richard. 1969. *The American Myth of Success: From Horatio Alger to Norman Vincent Peale.* New York: Basic Books.

West, Cornel. 1991. "On Black Rage." *Village Voice,* September 17, pp. 35–36.

White, Morton and Lucia White. 1962. *The Intellectual versus the City: From Thomas Jefferson to Frank Lloyd Wright.* Cambridge, MA: Harvard University Press.

Wiley, Ralph. 1993. *What Black People Should Do Now: Dispatches from Near the Vanguard.* New York: Ballantine.

Wills, Garry. 1987. *Reagan's America: Innocents at Home.* Garden City, NY: Doubleday.

Yang, Jeff. 1992. "Shooting Back." *Village Voice,* May 19, pp. 47–48.

Yi, Jeongduk. 1992. "Social Order and Protest: Black Boycotts against Korean Shopkeepers in Poor New York City Neighborhoods." Paper presented at the meeting of the American Anthropological Association, Chicago, IL.

Yu, Eui-Young. 1990. *Korean Community Profile: Life and Consumer Patterns.* Los Angeles: Korea Times.

Zukin, Sharon. 1991. "Hollow Center: U.S. Cities in the Global Era." Pp. 245–61 in *America at Century's End,* edited by Alan Wolfe. Berkeley: University of California Press.

34

NAVIGATING PUBLIC PLACES

JOE R. FEAGIN • MELVIN P. SIKES

Racism is any prejudice or discrimination against an individual or a group based on their race, ethnicity, or some other perceived difference. The following reading by Joe R. Feagin, a professor of sociology at the University of Florida, and Melvin P. Sikes, a clinical psychologist and consultant, documents the common and everyday discrimination that middle-class African Americans experience. Utilizing research based on over 200 interviews, Feagin and Sikes find that their respondents encounter a disturbing and extensive amount of both individual and institutional discrimination. Moreover, they report that because discrimination often involves racial stereotyping, verbal harassment, and even the threat or occurrence of violence, the consequences of discrimination on the individual are enormous. This excerpt is from Feagin and Sike's 1994 book, *Living with Racism: The Black Middle-Class Experience.*

Titl II of the most important civil rights act of this century, the 1964 Civil Rights Act, stipulates that "all persons shall be entitled to the full and equal enjoyment of the goods, services, facilities, privileges, advantages, and accommodations of any place of public accommodation . . . without discrimination or segregation on the ground of race, color, religion, or national origin." Yet, as we approach the twenty-first century, this promise of full and equal enjoyment of the public places and accommodations of the United States is far from reality for African Americans.

Not long ago Debbie Allen, a movie star and television producer, recounted a painful experience with discrimination at a Beverly Hills jewelry store. A white clerk, possibly stereotyping Allen as poor or criminal, refused to show her some jewelry. Allen was so incensed that she used the incident as the basis for an episode on a television show. Across the country in Tamarac, Florida, a 20-year-old black man, wearing a Syracuse University cap and hoping to invest his savings, visited a branch of Great Western Bank seeking information. After stopping at other banks, he returned to Great Western, got more information, and then went to his car to review the materials. There he was surrounded by sheriff's deputies with guns drawn, handcuffed, and read

From *Living with Racism* by Joe R. Feagin and Melvin P. Sikes. © 1994 by Joe R. Feagin and Melvin P. Sikes. Reprinted by permission of Beacon Press, Boston.

his rights. The deputies questioned him for some time before dismissing the report of white bank employees that the black man looked like a bank robber.[1]

Discrimination in Public Accommodations

In this chapter the middle-class respondents challenge us to reflect on their experiences with discrimination as they move into traditionally white public accommodations, such as upscale restaurants and department stores, and through public streets once the territory only of whites. They frequently report that their middle-class resources and status provide little protection against overt discrimination. Although there are, at least in principle, some social restraints on hostile white behavior in public accommodations, African Americans often experience hostility and mistreatment when they venture into spaces where many whites question the presence of a black person.

In the authors' experience, many middle-class African Americans can relate several recent stories of being treated poorly by whites in public accommodations officially made hospitable by decades of civil rights laws. In our respondents' accounts restaurants are one site of hostile treatment, as are stores, hotels, and places of amusement. A black minister in a predominantly white denomination described his experience at a restaurant near a southern religious camp:

> *We were refused service, because they said they didn't serve black folk. It was suggested that if we stayed there any longer, that there was a possibility that our tires would be slashed. We finally stayed long enough for them to say, "Well, I'll tell you what. We will serve you something to go, but you cannot come inside. We refuse that." And it was a situation that—I was not prepared for that. I was angry. I was humiliated, and I wanted to do something. I wanted to kick some ass.[2]*

Given the threat of violence, he did not respond aggressively to this exclusion, but internalized his anger. Such encounters are not isolated events for many middle-class black Americans. The minister described yet another incident in a southern metropolis:

> *I was at this place called Joe's restaurant. I had to go into Joe's because I came up in that community. Joe's is a barbecue place that is right by the auto plant, so all of the executives from the plant would come there for lunch. I went there with a guy who was successful. [I] thought I was a decent black person, came in wearing a suit and tie, sat down, and I noticed that, you know, these white boys kept coming in, and the waitress kept on looking over me. And I eventually said to her, "Ma'am, I'd like to order." She said, "Well, you're going to have to wait." And I complained to the owner and he proceeded to cuss me out. Told me that I*

didn't have "no goddamn business" in that restaurant telling them who they ought to serve and when they ought to serve them. Told me that. I came up in the neighborhood, been eating there for years, and it suddenly dawned on me that white folk will take your money, but to them in their minds you're still a nigger. They're able to separate economics from dealing with relationships between them and black folk. He challenged me to a fight, and this was another source of humiliation. I said to myself, "If I fought this man in his restaurant with there being a hundred white boys that'll substantiate whatever story he told, they could lynch me and say that I hung myself, you know." I left. I've never gone back to that place. But I've always thought about burning it down.

In spite of the 1964 Civil Rights Act black customers today encounter poor service or are refused service. Even with the growth of black economic resources, there seems to be some conflict within many white business owners between taking the dollars blacks can spend and recoiling from dealing with blacks.

In such events the person being rudely treated or ignored is usually quite conscious of the historical context of the interaction, as can be seen in the minister's allusion to lynching. In another account, a black news director at a television station described an incident in which she and her boyfriend responded very differently to an act of discrimination and the anger it provoked in them:

He was waiting to be seated. . . . He said, "You go to the bathroom and I'll get the table. . . ." He was standing there when I came back; he continued to stand there. The restaurant was almost empty. There were waiters, waitresses, and no one seated. And when I got back to him, he was ready to leave, and said, "Let's go." I said, "What happened to our table?" He wasn't seated. So I said, "No, we're not leaving, please." And he said, "No, I'm leaving." So we went outside, and we talked about it. And what I said to him was, you have to be aware of the possibilities that this is not the first time that this has happened at this restaurant or at other restaurants, but this is the first time it has happened to a black news director here or someone who could make an issue of it, or someone who is prepared to make an issue of it.

So we went back inside after I talked him into it and, to make a long story short, I had the manager come. I made most of the people who were there (while conducting myself professionally the whole time) aware that I was incensed at being treated this way. . . . I said, "Why do you think we weren't seated?" And the manager said, "Well, I don't really know." And I said, "Guess." He said, "Well, I don't know, because you're black?" I said, "Bingo. Now isn't it funny that you didn't guess that I didn't have any money (and I opened up my purse and I said, because I certainly have money). And isn't it odd that you didn't guess that it's because I couldn't pay for it because I've got two American Express cards and a Master Card right here. I think it's just funny that you would have assumed that it's because I'm black." . . . And then I took out my [business]

card and gave it to him and said, "If this happens again, or if I hear of this hap-
pening again, I will bring the full wrath of an entire news department down on
this restaurant." And he just kind of looked at me. "Not [just] because I am per-
sonally offended. I am. But because you have no right to do what you did, and as
a people we have lived a long time with having our rights abridged."

There were probably three or four sets of diners in the restaurant and maybe
five waiters/waitresses. They watched him [her boyfriend] standing there wait-
ing to be seated. His reaction to it was that he wanted to leave. I understood why
he would have reacted that way, because he felt that he was in no condition to be
civil. He was ready to take the place apart and . . . sometimes it's appropriate to
behave that way. We hadn't gone the first step before going on to the next step.
He didn't feel that he could comfortably and calmly take the first step, and I did.
So I just asked him to please get back in the restaurant with me, and then you
don't have to say a word, and let me handle it from there. It took some convinc-
ing, but I had to appeal to his sense of, this is not just you, this is not just for you.
We are finally in a position as black people where there are some of us who can
genuinely get their attention. And if they don't want to do this because it's right
for them to do it, then they'd better do it because they're afraid to do otherwise.
If it's fear, then fine, instill the fear.

Discrimination here was not the "No Negroes" exclusion of the recent past,
but rejection in the form of poor service. Again a black person's skin color
took precedence over money. The black response has changed too, since the
1950s and 1960s, from deference to indignant, vigorous confrontation. Here
the assertive black response and the white backtracking are typical of "negotiation" that can occur in racial confrontations today.

In recounting this incident, this black professional mentions black
"rights" several times. Clearly embedded in her response is a theory of rights
that she, like many African Americans, holds as a part of her worldview. Her
response signals the impact of the tradition of civil rights struggle, and civil
rights laws, on the life perspective of African Americans. Also of interest
here is her mention of her credit cards and other middle-class resources. A
quick reading of her statement, and that of other black middle-class people
who mention similar trappings of success, might lead to the conclusion that
middle-class blacks expect to be treated better than poorer blacks because
they have worked hard and have money. But this does not seem to be the
meaning of such references. Instead, this woman is outraged that the obvious
evidence of hard work and achievements does not protect her from racial discrimination. She has achieved certain elements of the American dream, but
they are not sufficient.

A close look at the experience of middle-class African Americans is important to understand the racial backwardness of contemporary U.S. society,
for it confirms that no amount of hard work, money, and success can protect
a black person from the destructive impact of racial stereotyping and discrimination. In this [article] we show that middle-class black Americans, just

like other black Americans, have terrible experiences with everyday racism. But we show much more than that. We also demonstrate that racial stereotyping and discrimination operate independently of the real identities and achievements of specifically targeted black individuals.

The ability of middle-class African Americans to act forcefully against discrimination by whites marks a change from a few decades ago when very few had the resources to fight back successfully. Black Americans have always fought against discrimination, but in earlier decades such fights were usually doomed to failure if not injury. In this account, the woman's ability as a professional to bring a television news team to the restaurant enabled her to take assertive action. This example also underscores the complexity of the interaction in some situations of discrimination, for not only is there a confrontation with a white manager over mistreatment but also a negotiation between the black individuals over how to respond.

It is an effective antidiscrimination strategy on the part of black Americans to make the confrontations public. An executive at a financial institution in an East Coast city recounted his experience with a pattern of poor service in a restaurant, explaining his decision to confront the discriminators:

I took the staff here to a restaurant that had recently opened in the prestigious section of the city, and we waited while other people got waited on, and decided that after about a half hour that these people don't want to wait on us. I happened to have been in the same restaurant a couple of evenings earlier, and it took them about 45 minutes before they came to wait on me and my guest. So, on the second incident, I said, this is not an isolated incident, this is a pattern, because I had spoken with some other people who had not been warmly received in the restaurant. So, I wrote a letter to the owners . . . and sent copies to the city papers. That's my way of expressing myself and letting the world know. You have to let people, other than you and the owner know. You have to let others know you're expressing your dismay at the discrimination or the barrier that's presented to you. I met with the owners. Of course, they wanted to meet with their attorneys with me, because they wanted to sue me. I told them they're welcome to do so. I don't have a thing, but fine they can do it. It just happens that I knew their white attorney. And he more or less vouched that if I had some concern that it must have been legitimate in some form. When the principals came in, one of the people who didn't wait on me was one of the owners who happened to be waiting on everybody else. We resolved the issue by them inviting me to come again, and if I was fairly treated, or if I would come on several occasions and if I was fairly treated I would write a statement of retraction. I told them I would not write a retraction, I would write a statement with regard to how I was treated. Which I ultimately did. And I still go there today, and they speak to me, and I think the pattern is changed to a great degree.

The time- and energy-consuming aspects of publicly confronting discrimination are apparent in this account. The respondent invested much of himself in a considered response to a recurring problem. Forcing whites to renegotiate, especially by using negative publicity, can bring about changes. The arrival on the restaurant scene of middle-class black Americans with substantial resources has at least created situations that force whites into explicit negotiating.

Whites often enter into this "bargaining" situation with tacit assumptions and cultural expectations about black powerlessness. In the two previous examples we see the black professionals establishing "power credibility," as the whites decide that they are not bluffing. It is important to note that the whites here are not just the blue-collar whites often said to be the primary source of whatever bigotry remains in the United States. Those doing the discrimination include middle-class whites, a fact that signals the importance of race over class in much racial interaction.

That discrimination against black customers and employees in white-owned restaurants is widespread has become evident in several court suits filed since 1990 against national chains, including Denny's, Shoney's, and the International House of Pancakes (IHOP). In December 1991, for example, several groups of black college students were reportedly turned away from a Milwaukee IHOP restaurant and told that it was closed, while white customers were allowed in. In 1993 a federal judge ordered the restaurant to pay a settlement for the discrimination. Also in 1993, the Denny's chain, found to have a pattern of discrimination by the U.S. Justice Department, reached an agreement with the Department in which executives promised to train employees in nondiscriminatory behavior and to include more minorities in its advertising. This settlement did not affect a class-action discrimination suit by 32 black customers who reportedly had suffered discrimination in several Denny's restaurants in California. Moreover, in mid-1993 six black secret service agents also sued the chain, alleging discrimination at a Denny's in Annapolis, Maryland. The black agents reported that while they waited for service for nearly an hour, white agents and other white patrons were promptly served.[3] After much bad publicity, Denny's joined in an important agreement with the NAACP to work to end discrimination in its restaurants.[4]

As revealed in the court cases, restaurant discrimination has recently included long waits while whites are served, special cover fees applied only to blacks, and prepayment requirements only for black customers.[5] In the Shoney's case, the chain was sued over discrimination against black employees. According to the *St. Petersburg Times,* top officers in the white-run firm were well known for their antiblack views, and local managers were discouraged from hiring black employees. In a 1992 landmark agreement the company agreed to pay $115 million, the most ever, to employees who could prove racial discrimination.[6]

Restaurants are only one site of discrimination. Daily life inevitably involves contact with clerks and managers in various retail and grocery stores. A utility company executive in an eastern city described how her family was treated in a small store:

> *I can remember one time my husband had picked up our son . . . from camp; and he'd stopped at a little store in the neighborhood near the camp. It was hot, and he was going to buy him a snowball. . . . This was a very old, white neighborhood, and it was just a little sundry store. But the proprietor had a little window where people could come up and order things. Well, my husband and son had gone into the store. And he told them, "Well, I can't give it to you here, but if you go outside to the window, I'll give it to you." And there were other people in the store who'd been served [inside]. So, they just left and didn't buy anything.*

The old white neighborhood in which this episode occurred exemplifies the racial-territorial character of many cities even today. The poor service here seems a throwback to the South of the 1950s, where deferential blacks were served only at the back of a store. This man chose not to confront the white person nor to acquiesce abjectly but rather to leave. Here the effect on the white man was probably inconsequential because there was no confrontation and interracial negotiation. The long-run importance of a service site may well affect a black person's choice of how to respond to such discrimination. The store in this example was not important to the black family just passing through the area. The possibility of returning might have generated a more confrontational response.

Another problem that black shoppers face, especially in department and grocery stores, is the common white assumption that they are likely shop-lifters. This is true in spite of the fact that national crime statistics show that most shoplifters are white. For several months in late 1991, a news team at KSTP-TV in Minneapolis conducted a field study of discrimination against black shoppers in several local department stores. Members of the team took jobs as security personnel in the stores, and black and white shoppers were sent into the stores in order to observe the reactions of white security personnel. The ensuing television report, "Who's Minding the Store?" showed how many black customers became the targets of intensive surveillance from white security guards, who neglected white shoppers when black shoppers were in the stores. As a result of the documentary, local black leaders called for a boycott of one of the store chains. Soon a number of the local stores changed their surveillance and security procedures.[7] Excessive surveillance of black customers in department and other stores was reported by some we interviewed. A black professional in the North commented on how she deals with whites who harass her with excessive surveillance and other acts of rejection:

> *[I have faced] harassment in stores, being followed around, being questioned about what are you going to purchase here. . . . I was in an elite department store just this past Saturday and felt that I was being observed while I was window shopping. I, in fact, actually ended up purchasing something, but felt the entire time I was there—I was in blue jeans and sneakers, that's how I dress on a Saturday—I felt that I was being watched in the store as I was walking through the*

store—what business did I have there, what was I going to purchase, that kind
of thing. . . . There are a few of those white people that won't put change in your
hand, touch your skin. That doesn't need to go on. [Do you tell them that?] Oh,
I do, I do. That is just so obvious. I usually [speak to them] if they're rude in the
manner in which they deal with people. [What do they say about that?] Oh, stuff
like, "Oh, excuse me," and some who are really unconscious about it, say "Ex-
cuse me," and put the change in your hand. That's happened. But I've watched
other people be rude, and I've been told to mind my own business. [But you still
do it?] Oh, sure, because for the most part I think that people do have to learn
to think for themselves, and demand respect for themselves. . . . I find my best
weapon of defense is to educate them, whether it's in the store, in a line, at the
bank, any situation, I teach them. And you take them by surprise because you
tell them and show them what they should be doing, and what they should be
saying, and how they should be thinking. And they look at you because they
don't know how to process you. They can't process it because you've just shown
them how they should be living, and the fact that they are cheating themselves,
really, because the racism is from fear. The racism is from lack of education.

A number of racial stereotypes are evident in this account. Whites with images of black criminality engage in excessive surveillance, and whites with
images of black dirtiness will not touch black hands or skin. Black shoppers
at all income levels report being ignored when in need of service and the unwillingness of some whites even to touch their hands. Why such a reaction to
black bodies? In a speculative Freudian analysis of white racism, Joel Kovel
has argued that for centuries whites have irrationally connected blackness,
and black bodies, with fecal matter and dirt. In his view, whites are somehow
projecting onto the darkness of the black outgroup personal inclinations, desires, and fears that cannot be openly and honestly acknowledged.[8]

A common black response to contemporary discrimination is evident
here. Rather than withdrawing when facing such discrimination, this professional sometimes protracts the interaction with verbal confrontation. She
notes the surprise effect of calling whites on the carpet for discrimination,
which she sees as grounded in fear and ignorance. Interrupting the normal
flow of an interaction to change a one-way experience into a two-way experience forces whites into unaccustomed situations in which they are unsure
how to respond.

Middle-class African Americans enter many settings where few blacks
have been before. A news anchorperson for an East Coast television station
reported on an incident at a luxury automobile dealer:

I knew I wanted to buy a Porsche, but I didn't know which model. So, on my
day off, I went into a Porsche dealership in the city I used to work in. . . . And I
was dressed like I normally do when I'm off. I'm into working out a lot, so I'm
in sweatsuits, baseball caps, sunglasses quite a bit. So I dashed into this place
dressed like that, and I must have walked around the show room floor for 20 min-
utes. No salesperson ever walked up to me and asked me, "Can I help you? Can

I give you some information?" Nothing. I got the impression, the opinion, that they generally thought that this person, being black, being dressed in a sweat-suit, cannot hardly afford to be in here buying a Porsche. He's wasting my time, so I'm not even going to bother. And I knew that. So I specifically, the next day on my lunch hour, dressed in my work clothes, having just come off the air, I walked into that showroom. And I said, "Can I see the general manager?" And they got the general manager for me. And I said to the general manager, "I was in here yesterday." Well, I said, "First of all, I want to buy that Porsche there, the most expensive one on the floor." And I also told him, "Just yesterday I was in here, I was looking in, and I was hoping I could get some information, and oddly none of your sales people ever asked me if they could help me." . . . And there is prejudice, discrimination and racism, and things like that go on. Once they found out who I was, they bent over backward [to wait on me].

White salespeople apparently took the cue from this man's color and cloth-ing and stereotyped him as moneyless, an assumption that the victim chal-lenged the next day when he engaged in an unexpected confrontation. This chronic mistreatment by white salespeople, while white shoppers are gener-ally treated with greater respect, is infuriating for black customers. It is clear from our interviews that African Americans must prepare themselves for this sort of encounter, for they never know when they will be shown normal respect and courtesy as customers or when they must "front" (dress in a cer-tain way, talk in a certain way) in order to receive the treatment accorded a comparable white customer.

Among several respondents who discussed discrimination at retail stores, the manager of a career development organization, who found that discrimination by clerks is common, had a repertoire of responses for deal-ing with it:

If you're in a store—and let's say the person behind the counter is white—and you walk up to the counter, and a white person walks up to the counter, and you know you were there before the white customer, the person behind the counter knows you were there first, and it never fails, they always go, "Who's next." OK. And what I've done, if they go ahead and serve the white person first, then I will immediately say, "Excuse me, I was here first, and we both know I was here first." . . . If they get away with it once, they're going to get away with it more than once, and then it's going to become something else. And you want to make sure that folks know that you're not being naive, that you really see through what's happening. Or if it's a job opportunity or something like that, too, same thing. You first try to get a clear assessment of what's really going on and sift through that information, and then . . . go from there.

In discussions with middle-class black Americans across the nation, both our respondents and a variety of informants and journalists, we heard many similar accounts of white clerks "looking through" black customers and only "seeing" whites farther back in line. Such incidents suggest that much of the hostility manifest in white actions is based on a deep-lying, perhaps even subconscious or half-conscious, aversion to black color and persona. This executive also spoke of her coping process, one that begins with sifting information before deciding on action. Frequently choosing immediate action, she forces whites to face the reality of their behavior.

The dean of a black college who travels in various parts of the United States described the often complex process of evaluating and responding to the mistreatment that has plagued him in public accommodations:

> *When you're in a restaurant and . . . you notice that blacks get seated near the kitchen. You notice that if it's a hotel, your room is near the elevator, or your room is always way down in a corner somewhere. You find that you are getting the undesirable rooms. And you come there early in the day and you don't see very many cars on the lot and they'll tell you that this is all we've got. Or you get the room that's got a bad television set. You know that you're being discriminated against. And of course you have to act accordingly. You have to tell them, "Okay, the room is fine, [but] this television set has got to go. Bring me another television set." So in my personal experience, I simply cannot sit and let them get away with it and not let them know that I know that that's what they are doing. . . .*
>
> *When I face discrimination, first I take a long look at myself and try to determine whether or not I am seeing what I think I'm seeing in 1989, and if it's something that I have an option [about]. In other words, if I'm at a store making a purchase, I'll simply walk away from it. If it's at a restaurant where I'm not getting good service, I first of all let the people know that I'm not getting good service, then I [may] walk away from it. But the thing that I have to do is to let people know that I know that I'm being singled out for separate treatment. And then I might react in any number of ways—depending on where I am and how badly I want whatever it is that I'm there for.*

These recurring incidents in public accommodations illustrate the cumulative nature of discrimination. The dean first takes care to assess the incident and avoid jumping to conclusions. One must be constantly prepared on everyday excursions to assess accurately what is happening and then to decide on an appropriate response. What is less obvious here is the degree of pain and emotional drain that such a constant defensive stance involves.

ENDNOTES

[1] Lena Williams, "When Blacks Shop, Bias Often Accompanies a Sale," *New York Times*, April 30, 1991, pp. A1, A9.

[2] Names and places in interview quotes have been disguised or eliminated to protect anonymity. Some quotes have been lightly edited for grammar and to delete excessive pause phrases like "you know" and "uh."

[3] National Public Radio, "Weekend Edition," May 29, 1993.

[4] Associated Press, "Denny's to Monitor Treatment of Blacks," *Gainesville Sun*, May 30, 1993, p. 7A.

[5] Judy Pasternak, "Service Still Skin Deep for Blacks," *Los Angeles Times,* April 1, 1993, p. A1.

[6] Martin Dyckman, "Lawyers Can Be Heroes Too," *St. Petersburg Times,* April 11, 1993, p. 3D.

[7] Bill McAuliffe, "Black Leaders Call for Boycott of Local Carsons Stores," *Star Tribune,* December 10, 1991, p. 1B.

[8] Joel Kovel, *White Racism.* Rev. ed. (New York: Columbia University Press, 1984).

PART VII

Social Institutions

35

THE POWER ELITE

C. WRIGHT MILLS

Who really governs in the United States? In this selection, C. Wright Mills argues that the most important decisions in this country are made by a cohesive "power elite." This *power elite* consists of the top leaders in three areas: The corporate elite is made up of the executives from large companies; the military elite is the senior officers; and the small political elite includes the president and top officials in the executive and legislative branches. According to Mills' argument, these elite officials all know each other and act in unison when critical decisions must be made. This selection, originally published in 1956, is the first of three addressing power and politics.

The powers of ordinary men are circumscribed by the everyday worlds in which they live, yet even in these rounds of job, family, and neighborhood they often seem driven by forces they can neither understand nor govern. "Great changes" are beyond their control, but affect their conduct and outlook nonetheless. The very framework of modern society confines them to projects not their own, but from every side, such changes now press upon the men and women of the mass society, who accordingly feel that they are without purpose in an epoch in which they are without power.

But not all men are in this sense ordinary. As the means of information and of power are centralized, some men come to occupy positions in American society from which they can look down upon, so to speak, and by their decisions mightily affect, the everyday worlds of ordinary men and women. They are not made by their jobs; they set up and break down jobs for thou-

From *The Power Elite* New Edition. Copyright © 1956, 2000 by Oxford University Press. Reprinted with the permission of Oxford University Press, Inc..

sands of others; they are not confined by simple family responsibilities; they can escape. They may live in many hotels and houses, but they are bound by no one community. They need not merely "meet the demands of the day and hour"; in some part, they create these demands and cause others to meet them. Whether or not they profess their power, their technical and political experience of it far transcends that of the underlying population. What Jacob Burckhardt [a German historian, 1818–1897] said of "great men," most Americans might well say of their elite: "They are all that we are not."

The power elite is composed of men whose positions enable them to transcend the ordinary environments of ordinary men and women; they are in positions to make decisions having major consequences. Whether they do or do not make such decisions is less important than the fact that they do occupy such pivotal positions: Their failure to act, their failure to make decisions, is itself an act that is often of greater consequence than the decisions they do make. For they are in command of the major hierarchies and organizations of modern society. They rule the big corporations. They run the machinery of the state and claim its prerogatives. They direct the military establishment. They occupy the strategic command posts of the social structure, in which are now centered the effective means of the power and the wealth and the celebrity which they enjoy.

The power elite are not solitary rulers. Advisers and consultants, spokesmen and opinion makers are often the captains of their higher thought and decision. Immediately below the elite are the professional politicians of the middle levels of power, in the Congress and in the pressure groups, as well as among the new and old upper classes of town and city and region. Mingling with them, in curious ways which we shall explore, are those professional celebrities who live by being continually displayed but are never, so long as they remain celebrities, displayed enough. If such celebrities are not at the head of any dominating hierarchy, they do often have the power to distract the attention of the public or afford sensations to the masses, or, more directly, to gain the ear of those who do occupy positions of direct power. More or less unattached, as critics of morality and technicians of power, as spokesmen of God and creators of mass sensibility, such celebrities and consultants are part of the immediate scene in which the drama of the elite is enacted. But that drama itself is centered in the command posts of the major institutional hierarchies.

The truth about the nature and the power of the elite is not some secret which men of affairs know but will not tell. Such men hold quite various theories about their own roles in the sequence of event and decision. Often they are uncertain about their roles, and even more often they allow their fears and their hopes to affect their assessment of their own power. No matter how great their actual power, they tend to be less acutely aware of it than of the resistances of others to its use. Moreover, most American men of affairs have learned well the rhetoric of public relations, in some cases even to the point of using it when they are alone, and thus coming to believe it. The personal awareness of the actors is only one of the several sources one must examine in order to understand the higher circles. Yet many who believe that there is no elite, or at any rate none of any consequence, rest their argument upon what men of affairs believe about themselves, or at least assert in public.

There is, however, another view: Those who feel, even if vaguely, that a compact and powerful elite of great importance does now prevail in America often base that feeling upon the historical trend of our time. They have felt, for example, the domination of the military event, and from this they infer that generals and admirals, as well as other men of decision influenced by them, must be enormously powerful. They hear that the Congress has again abdicated to a handful of men decisions clearly related to the issue of war or peace. They know that the bomb was dropped over Japan in the name of the United States of America, although they were at no time consulted about the matter. They feel that they live in a time of big decisions; they know that they are not making any. Accordingly, as they consider the present as history, they infer that at its center, making decisions or failing to make them, there must be an elite of power.

On the one hand, those who share this feeling about big historical events assume that there is an elite and that its power is great. On the other hand, those who listen carefully to the reports of men apparently involved in the great decisions often do not believe that there is an elite whose powers are of decisive consequence.

Both views must be taken into account, but neither is adequate. The way to understand the power of the American elite lies neither solely in recognizing the historic scale of events nor in accepting the personal awareness reported by men of apparent decision. Behind such men and behind the events of history, linking the two, are the major institutions of modern society. These hierarchies of state and corporation and army constitute the means of power; as such they are now of a consequence not before equaled in human history—and at their summits, there are now those command posts of modern society which offer us the sociological key to an understanding of the role of the higher circles in America.

Within American society, major national power now resides in the economic, the political, and the military domains. Other institutions seem off to the side of modern history, and, on occasion, duly subordinated to these. No family is as directly powerful in national affairs as any major corporation; no church is as directly powerful in the external biographies of young men in America today as the military establishment; no college is as powerful in the shaping of momentous events as the National Security Council. Religious, educational, and family institutions are not autonomous centers of national power; on the contrary, these decentralized areas are increasingly shaped by the big three, in which developments of decisive and immediate consequence now occur.

Families and churches and schools adapt to modern life; governments and armies and corporations shape it; and, as they do so, they turn these lesser institutions into means for their ends. Religious institutions provide chaplains to the armed forces where they are used as a means of increasing the effectiveness of its morale to kill. Schools select and train men for their jobs in corporations and their specialized tasks in the armed forces. The extended family has, of course, long been broken up by the industrial revolution, and now the son and the father are removed from the family, by compulsion if need be, whenever the army of the state sends out the call. And the symbols of all these lesser institutions are used to legitimate the power and the decisions of the big three.

The life-fate of the modern individual depends not only upon the family into which he was born or which he enters by marriage, but increasingly upon the corporation in which he spends the most alert hours of his best years; not only upon the school where he is educated as a child and adolescent, but also upon the state which touches him throughout his life; not only upon the church in which on occasion he hears the word of God, but also upon the army in which he is disciplined.

If the centralized state could not rely upon the inculcation of nationalist loyalties in public and private schools, its leaders would promptly seek to modify the decentralized educational system. If the bankruptcy rate among the top 500 corporations were as high as the general divorce rate among the 37 million married couples, there would be economic catastrophe on an international scale. If members of armies gave to them no more of their lives than do believers to the churches to which they belong, there would be a military crisis.

Within each of the big three, the typical institutional unit has become enlarged, has become administrative, and, in the power of its decisions, has become centralized. Behind these developments there is a fabulous technology, for as institutions, they have incorporated this technology and guide it, even as it shapes and paces their developments.

The economy—once a great scatter of small productive units in autonomous balance—has become dominated by two or three hundred giant corporations, administratively and politically interrelated, which together hold the keys to economic decisions.

The political order, once a decentralized set of several dozen states with a weak spinal cord, has become a centralized, executive establishment which has taken up into itself many powers previously scattered, and now enters into each and every cranny of the social structure.

The military order, once a slim establishment in a context of distrust fed by state militia, has become the largest and most expensive feature of government, and, although well-versed in smiling public relations, now has all the grim and clumsy efficiency of a sprawling bureaucratic domain.

In each of these institutional areas, the means of power at the disposal of decision makers have increased enormously; their central executive powers have been enhanced; within each of them modern administrative routines have been elaborated and tightened up.

As each of these domains becomes enlarged and centralized, the consequences of its activities become greater, and its traffic with the others increases. The decisions of a handful of corporations bear upon military and political as well as upon economic developments around the world. The decisions of the military establishment rest upon and grievously affect political life as well as the very level of economic activity. The decisions made within the political domain determine economic activities and military programs. There is no longer, on the one hand, an economy, and, on the other hand, a political order containing a military establishment unimportant to politics and to money making. There is a political economy linked, in a thousand ways, with military institutions and decisions. On each side of the world-split running through central Europe and around the Asiatic rimlands, there is an ever-increasing interlocking of economic, military, and political structures. If there is government intervention in the corporate economy, so is there corporate intervention in the governmental process. In the structural sense, this triangle of power is the source of the interlocking directorate that is most important for the historical structure of the present.

The fact of the interlocking is clearly revealed at each of the points of crisis of modern capitalist society—slump, war, and boom. In each, men of decision are led to an awareness of the interdependence of the major institutional orders. In the nineteenth century, when the scale of all institutions was smaller, their liberal integration was achieved in the automatic economy, by an autonomous play of market forces, and in the automatic political domain, by the bargain and the vote. It was then assumed that out of the imbalance and friction that followed the limited decisions then possible a new equilibrium would in due course emerge. That can no longer be assumed, and it is not assumed by the men at the top of each of the three dominant hierarchies.

For given the scope of their consequences, decisions—and indecisions—in any one of these ramify into the others, and hence top decisions tend either to become coordinated or to lead to a commanding indecision. It has not always been like this. When numerous small entrepreneurs made up the economy, for example, many of them could fail and the consequences still remain local; political and military authorities did not intervene. But now, given political expectations and military commitments, can they afford to allow key units of the private corporate economy to break down in slump? Increasingly, they do intervene in economic affairs, and as they do so, the controlling decisions in each order are inspected by agents of the other two, and economic, military, and political structures are interlocked.

At the pinnacle of each of the three enlarged and centralized domains, there have arisen those higher circles which make up the economic, the political, and the military elites. At the top of the economy, among the corporate rich, there are the chief executives; at the top of the political order, the members of the political directorate; at the top of the military establishment, the elite of soldier-statesmen clustered in and around the Joint Chiefs of Staff and the upper echelon. As each of these domains has coincided with the others, as decisions tend to become total in their consequence, the leading men in each of the three domains of power—the warlords, the corporation chieftains, the political directorate—tend to come together, to form the power elite of America.

The higher circles in and around these command posts are often thought of in terms of what their members possess: They have a greater share than other people of the things and experiences that are most highly valued. From this point of view, the elite are simply those who have the most of what there is to have, which is generally held to include money, power, and prestige—as well as all the ways of life to which these lead. But the elite are not simply those who have the most, for they could not "have the most" were it not for their positions in the great institutions. For such institutions are the necessary bases of power, of wealth, and of prestige, and at the same time, the chief means of exercising power, of acquiring and retaining wealth, and of cashing in the higher claims for prestige.

By the powerful we mean, of course, those who are able to realize their will, even if others resist it. No one, accordingly, can be truly powerful unless he has access to the command of major institutions, for it is over these institutional means of power that the truly powerful are, in the first instance, powerful. Higher politicians and key officials of government command such institutional power; so do admirals and generals, and so do the major owners and executives of the larger corporations. Not all power, it is true, is anchored in and exercised by means of such institutions, but only within and through them can power be more or less continuous and important.

Wealth also is acquired and held in and through institutions. The pyramid of wealth cannot be understood merely in terms of the very rich; for the great inheriting families, as we shall see, are now supplemented by the corporate institutions of modern society: Every one of the very rich families has been and is closely connected—always legally and frequently managerially as well—with one of the multimillion-dollar corporations.

The modern corporation is the prime source of wealth, but, in latter-day capitalism, the political apparatus also opens and closes many avenues to wealth. The amount as well as the source of income, the power over consumer's goods as well as over productive capital, are determined by position within the political economy. If our interest in the very rich goes beyond their lavish or their miserly consumption, we must examine their relations to modern forms of corporate property as well as to the state; for such relations now determine the chances of men to secure big property and to receive high income.

Great prestige increasingly follows the major institutional units of the social structure. It is obvious that prestige depends, often quite decisively, upon access to the publicity machines that are now a central and normal feature of all the big institutions of modern America. Moreover, one feature of these hierarchies of corporation, state, and military establishment is that their top positions are increasingly interchangeable. One result of this is the accumulative nature of prestige. Claims for prestige, for example, may be initially based on military roles, then expressed in and augmented by an educational institution run by corporate executives, and cashed in, finally, in the political order, where, for General Eisenhower and those he represents, power and prestige finally meet at the very peak. Like wealth and power, prestige tends to be cumulative: The more of it you have, the more you can get. These values also tend to be translatable into one another: The wealthy find it easier than the poor to gain power; those with status find it easier than those without it to control opportunities for wealth.

If we took the one hundred most powerful men in America, the one hundred wealthiest, and the one hundred most celebrated away from the institutional positions they now occupy, away from their resources of men and women and money, away from the media of mass communication that are now focused upon them—then they would be powerless and poor and uncelebrated. For power is not of a man. Wealth does not center in the person of the wealthy. Celebrity is not inherent in any personality. To be celebrated, to be wealthy, to have power requires access to major institutions, for the institutional positions men occupy determine in large part their chances to have and to hold these valued experiences.

The people of the higher circles may also be conceived as members of a top social stratum, as a set of groups whose members know one another, see one another socially and at business, and so, in making decisions, take one another into account. The elite, according to this conception, feel themselves to be, and are felt by others to be, the inner circle of "the upper social classes." They form a more or less compact social and psychological entity; they have become self-conscious members of a social class. People are either accepted into this class or they are not, and there is a qualitative split, rather than merely a numerical scale, separating them from those who are not elite. They are more or less aware of themselves as a social class, and they behave toward one another differently from the way they do toward members of other classes. They accept one another, understand one another, marry one another, tend to work and to think if not together at least alike.

Now, we do not want by our definition to prejudge whether the elite of the command posts are conscious members of such a socially recognized class, or whether considerable proportions of the elite derive from such a clear and distinct class. These are matters to be investigated. Yet in order to be able to recognize what we intend to investigate, we must note something that all biographies and memoirs of the wealthy and the powerful and the eminent make clear: No matter what else they may be, the people of these higher circles are involved in a set of overlapping "crowds" and intricately connected "cliques." There is a kind of mutual attraction among those who "sit on the same terrace"—although this often becomes clear to them, as well as to others, only at the point at which they feel the need to draw the line; only when, in their common defense, they come to understand what they have in common, and so close their ranks against outsiders.

The idea of such ruling stratum implies that most of its members have similar social origins, that throughout their lives they maintain a network of informal connections, and that to some degree there is an interchangeability of position between the various hierarchies of money and power and celebrity. We must, of course, note at once that if such an elite stratum does exist, its social visibility and its form, for very solid historical reasons, are quite different from those of the noble cousinhoods that once ruled various European nations.

That American society has never passed through a feudal epoch is of decisive importance to the nature of the American elite, as well as to American society as a historic whole. For it means that no nobility or aristocracy, established before the capitalist era, has stood in tense opposition to the higher bourgeoisie. It means that this bourgeoisie has monopolized not only wealth but prestige and power as well. It means that no set of noble families has commanded the top positions and monopolized the values that are generally held in high esteem; and certainly that no set has done so explicitly by inherited right. It means that no high church dignitaries or court nobilities, no entrenched landlords with honorific accouterments, no monopolists of high army posts have opposed the enriched bourgeoisie and in the name of birth and prerogative successfully resisted its self-making.

But this does *not* mean that there are no upper strata in the United States. That they emerged from a "middle class" that had no recognized aristocratic superiors does not mean they remained middle class when enormous increases in wealth made their own superiority possible. Their origins and their newness may have made the upper strata less visible in America than elsewhere. But in America today there are in fact tiers and ranges of wealth and power of which people in the middle and lower ranks know very little and may not even dream. There are families who, in their well-being, are quite insulated from the economic jolts and lurches felt by the merely prosperous and those farther down the scale. There are also men of power who in quite small groups make decisions of enormous consequence for the underlying population.

36
───────

DOLLARS AND VOTES
How Business Campaign
Contributions Subvert Democracy

DAN CLAWSON • ALAN NEUSTADTL • MARK WELLER

Sociological research supports the thesis that a power elite exists in this country. A point of debate is the degree of interconnection among the three groups—the corporate, military, and political elite. Nonetheless, current social research still indicates that power is concentrated among a few social groups and institutions, as shown in a 1998 study discussed in this selection by Dan Clawson, Alan Neustadtl, and Mark Weller. After investigating 309 corporate political action committees (PACs), the authors conclude that PACs, which represent corporate interests, ensure that the concerns of Big Business are heard on Capitol Hill.

The Money Primary

Imagine the November election is just a few weeks away, and your friend Sally Robeson is seriously considering running for Congress two years from now. This year the incumbent in your district, E. Chauncey DeWitt III, will (again!) be reelected by a substantial margin, but you and Sally hate Chauncey's positions on the issues and are convinced that with the right campaign he can be beaten. Sally is capable, articulate, well informed, respected in the community, politically and socially connected, charming, good at talking to many kinds of people, and highly telegenic. She has invited you and several other politically active friends to meet with her immediately after the election to determine what she would need to do to become a viable candidate.

The meeting that takes place covers a host of topics: What are the key issues? On which of these are Sally's stands popular, and on which unpopular? What attacks, and from what quarters, will be launched against her? What individuals or groups can she count on for support? How, why, and where is the incumbent vulnerable? But lurking in the background is the question that

───────

From *Dollars and Votes: How Business Campaign Contributions Subvert Democracy* by Dan Clawson, Alan Neustadtl, and Mark Weller, pp. 1–12, 21–24, 26–28. Copyright © 1998 Temple University. Reprinted by permission of Temple University Press.

cannot be ignored: *Can Sally (with the help of her friends and backers) raise enough money to be a contender?*

This is the *money primary, the first, and, in many instances, the most important round of the contest.* It eliminates more candidates than any other hurdle. Because it eliminates them so early and so quietly, its impact is often unobserved. To make it through, candidates don't have to come in first, but they do need to raise enough money to be credible contenders. Although having the most money is no guarantee of victory, candidates who don't do well in the money primary are no longer serious contenders. Certainly, plenty of well-funded candidates lose—Michael Huffington spent $25 million of his own money in an unsuccessful 1994 race for the Senate. But in order to be viable, a candidate needs to raise a substantial minimum.

How much is needed? If Sally hopes to win, rather than just put up a good fight, she, you, and the rest of her supporters will need to raise staggering amounts. (At least they are staggering from the perspective of most Americans; Ross Perot, Steve Forbes, or Michael Huffington may view the matter differently.) In order to accumulate the *average* amount for major-party congressional candidates in the general election, you will collectively need to raise $4,800 next week. And the week after. And *every* week for the next two years.

But even that is not enough. The average amount includes many candidates who were never "serious"; that is, they didn't raise enough to have a realistic hope of winning. If you and your friends want to raise the average amount spent by a *winning* candidate for the House, you'll have to come up with $6,730 next week and every single week until the election, two years away.

Well, you say, your candidate is hardly average. She is stronger, smarter, more politically appealing, and more viable than the "average" challenger. You think she can win even if she doesn't raise $6,730 a week. Let's use past experience—the results of the 1996 elections—to consider the likelihood of winning for challengers, based on how much money they raised. In 1996 more than 360 House incumbents were running for reelection; only 23 of them were beaten by their challengers. The average successful challenger spent $1,045,361—that is, he or she raised an average of over $10,000 every week for two years. What were the chances of winning without big money? Only one winning challenger spent less than $500,000, 12 spent between a half-a-million and a million dollars, and 10 spent more than a million dollars. Furthermore, 13 of the 23 winning challengers outspent the incumbent. A House challenger who can't raise at least a half-million dollars doesn't have a one percent chance of winning; the key primary is the money primary. The *Boston Globe* reported that "House candidates who headed into the final three weeks with the most in combined spending and cash on hand won 93 percent of the time."[1] What about that one low-spending winner? She is Carolyn Cheeks Kilpatrick, who won election by beating an incumbent in the primary and then having a walkover in the general election; the district, in Detroit, is the fourth poorest in the nation and consistently votes more than 80 percent Democratic. Although Kilpatrick spent only $174,457, few other districts make possible a similar election strategy.

In the Senate, even more money is needed. Suppose your candidate were going to run for the Senate, and started fundraising immediately after an election, giving her six years to prepare for the next election. How much money would she need to raise each and every week for those *six* years? The average winning Senate candidate raised approximately $15,000 per week.

For presidential candidates, the stakes are, of course, much higher: "The prevailing view is that for a politician to be considered legitimate, he or she must collect at least $20 million by the first of January 2000."[2] Presumably any candidate who does not do so is "illegitimate" and does not belong in the race. . . .

Coming up with the money is a major hassle; even for incumbents, it requires constant effort. *National Journal,* probably the single most authoritative source on the Washington scene, reports that "there is widespread agreement that the congressional money chase has become an unending marathon, as wearying to participants as it is disturbing to spectators," and quoted an aide to a Democratic senator as observing, "During hearings of Senate committees, you can watch senators go to phone booths in the committee rooms to dial for dollars." Just a few years ago—in 1990, the date of this statement— soliciting funds from federal property, whether Congress or the White House, was routine, openly discussed, and not regarded as problematic. The activity had always been technically illegal, but only in 1997 did it become an issue, with President Clinton and (especially) Vice President Gore singled out as if they were the only offenders. . . .

Not only is it necessary to raise lots of money; it is important—for both incumbents and challengers—to raise it early. Senator Rudy Boschwitz, Republican of Minnesota, was clear about this as a strategy. He spent $6 million getting reelected in 1984 and had raised $1.5 million of it by the beginning of the year, effectively discouraging the most promising Democratic challengers. After the election he wrote, and typed up himself, a secret evaluation of his campaign strategy:

> "Nobody in politics (except me!) likes to raise money, so I thought the best way of discouraging the toughest opponents from running was to have a few dollars in the sock. *I believe it worked. . . . From all forms of fundraising I raised $6 million plus and got 3 or 4 (maybe even 5) stories and cartoons that irked me,"* he said. "In retrospect, I'm glad I had the money."[3]

Similarly, in March 1996 Bill Paxon, chair of the House Republican campaign committee, said, "We've been pounding on members to raise more money by the filing deadline; if they show a good balance, that could ward off opponents."[4]

The Contributors' Perspective

Candidates need money, lots of it, if they are to have any chance of winning. The obvious next question, and in some sense the focus of [our research], is who gives, why, and what they expect for it.

Contributions are made for many different reasons. The candidate's family and friends chip in out of loyalty and affection. Others contribute because they are asked to do so by someone who has done favors for them. People give because they agree with the candidate's stand on the issues, either on a broad ideological basis or on a specific issue. Sometimes these donations are portrayed as a form of voting—people show that they care by putting their money where their mouth is, anyone can contribute, and the money raised reflects the wishes of the people. Even for these contributions, however, if voting with dollars replaces voting at the ballot box, then the votes will be very unequally distributed: the top 1 percent of the population by wealth will have more "votes" than the bottom 90 percent of the population. In the 1996 elections, less than one-fourth of one percent of the population gave contributions of $200 or more to a federal candidate.[5] PACs and large contributors provide most of the money, however; small contributors accounted for under one-third of candidate receipts.[6]

It is not just that contributions come from the well-to-do. Most contributors have a direct material interest in what the government does or does not do. Their contributions, most of them made directly or indirectly by business, provide certain people a form of leverage and "access" not available to the rest of us. The chair of the political action committee at one of the twenty-five largest manufacturing companies in the United States explained to us why his corporation has a PAC:

> The PAC gives you access. It makes you a player. These congressmen, in particular, are constantly fundraising. Their elections are very expensive, and getting increasingly expensive each year. So they have an ongoing need for funds.
>
> It profits us in a sense to be able to provide some funds because in the provision of it you get to know people, you help them out. There's no real quid pro quo. There is nobody whose vote you can count on, not with the kind of money we are talking about here. But the PAC gives you access. Puts you in the game.
>
> You know, some congressman has got X number of ergs of energy and here's a person or a company who wants to come see him and give him a thousand dollars, and here's another one who wants to just stop by and say hello. And he only has time to see one. Which one? So the PAC's an attention getter.

So-called soft money, where the amount of the contribution is unlimited, might appear to be an exception: Isn't $100,000 enough to buy a guaranteed outcome? We will argue that it is *not*, at least not in any simple and straightforward way. PAC contributions are primarily for members of Congress; they are for comparatively small amounts, but enough to gain access to individual members of Congress. The individual member, however, has limited power. Soft money donations are best thought of as a way of gaining access to the president, top party leaders, and the executive branch. These individuals are more powerful than ordinary members of Congress, so access to them comes at a higher price. That privileged access is invaluable, but, as we will try to show, it does not—and is not expected to—*guarantee* a quid pro quo. The following example illustrates how corporations benefit from this "access" and how they use it to manipulate the system.

Why Does the Air Stink?

Everybody wants clean air. Who could oppose it? "I spent seven years of my life trying to stop the Clean Air Act," explained the vice president of a major corporation that is a heavy-duty polluter. Nonetheless, he was perfectly willing to make campaign contributions to members who voted for the act:

> How a person votes on the final piece of legislation often is not representative of what they have done. Somebody will do a lot of things during the process. How many guys voted against the Clean Air Act? But during the process some of them were very sympathetic to some of our concerns.

In the world of Congress and political action committees things are not always what they seem. Members of Congress all want to vote for clean air, but they also want to get campaign contributions from corporations, and they want to pass a law that business will accept as "reasonable." The compromise solution is to gut the bill by crafting dozens of loopholes. These are inserted in private meetings or in subcommittee hearings that don't get much (if any) attention in the press. Then the public vote on the final bill can be nearly unanimous. Members of Congress can reassure both their constituents and their corporate contributors: constituents, that they voted for the final bill; corporations, that they helped weaken it in private. [Our research] analyzes how this happens; clean air, and especially the Clean Air Act of 1990, can serve as an introduction to the kind of process we try to expose.

The public strongly supports clean air and is unimpressed when corporate officials and apologists trot out their normal arguments—"corporations are already doing all they reasonably can to improve environmental quality," "we need to balance the costs against the benefits," "people will lose their jobs if we make controls any stricter." The original Clean Air Act was passed in 1970, revised in 1977, and not revised again until 1990. Although the initial goal was to have us breathing clean air by 1975, the deadline has been repeatedly extended—and the 1990 legislation provides a new set of deadlines to be reached sometime in the distant future.

Corporations control the production process unless the government specifically intervenes. Therefore, any delay in government action leaves corporations free to do as they choose; business often prefers a weak, ineffective, and unenforceable law. The laws have not only been slow to come, but corporations have also fought to delay or subvert implementation. The 1970 law ordered the Environmental Protection Agency (EPA) to regulate the hundreds of poisonous chemicals that are emitted by corporations, but, as William Greider notes, "In twenty years of stalling, dodging, and fighting off court orders, the EPA has managed to issue regulatory standards for a total of seven toxics."[7]

Corporations have done exceptionally well politically, given the problem they face: The interests of business are diametrically opposed to those of the public. Clean air laws and amendments have been few and far between, enforcement is ineffective, and the penalties minimal. On the one hand, corporations *have* had to pay *billions* for cleanups; on the other, the costs to date are a small fraction of what would be needed to actually clean up the environment.

This corporate struggle for the right to pollute has taken place on many fronts. The most visible is public relations: the Chemical Manufacturers Association took out a two-page Earth Day ad in the *Washington Post* to demonstrate its concern; coincidentally, the names of many of the corporate signers of this ad appear on the EPA's list of high-risk producers.[8] Another front is expert studies that delay action while more information is gathered. The federally funded National Acid Precipitation Assessment Program took ten years and $600 million to figure out whether acid rain was in fact a problem. Both business and the Reagan administration argued that nothing should be done until the study was completed.[9] Ultimately, the study was discredited: The "summary of findings" minimized the impact of acid rain, even though this did not accurately represent the expert research in the report. But the key site of struggle was Congress. For years, corporations successfully defeated legislation. In 1987 utility companies were offered a compromise bill on acid rain, but they "were very adamant that they had beat the thing since 1981 and they could always beat it," according to Representative Edward Madigan (Republican–Illinois).[10] The utilities beat back all efforts at reform through the 1980s, but their intransigence probably hurt them when revisions finally came to be made.

The stage was set for a revision of the Clean Air Act when George Bush, "the environmental president," was elected, and George Mitchell, a strong supporter of environmentalism, became the Senate majority leader. But what sort of clean air bill would it be? "What we wanted," said Richard Ayres, head of the environmentalists' Clean Air Coalition, "is a health based standard—one-in-1-million cancer risk," a standard that would require corporations to clean up their plants until the cancer risk from their operations was reduced to 1 in a million. "The Senate bill still has the requirement," Ayres

said, "but there are forty pages of extensions and exceptions and qualifications and loopholes that largely render the health standard a nullity." [11]
Greider reports, for example, "According to the EPA, there are now twenty-six
coke ovens that pose a cancer risk greater than 1 in 1000 and six where the
risk is greater than 1 in 100. Yet the new clean-air bill will give the steel industry another thirty years to deal with the problem." [12]

This change from what the bill was supposed to do to what it did do
came about through what corporate executives like to call the "access"
process. The principal aim of most corporate campaign contributions is to
help corporate executives gain "access" to key members of Congress and
their staffs. In these meetings, corporate executives (and corporate PAC
money) work to persuade the member of Congress to accept a predesigned
loophole that will sound innocent but effectively undercut the stated intention of the bill. Representative John D. Dingell (Democrat–Michigan), who
was chair of the House committee, is a strong industry supporter; one of the
people we interviewed called him "the point man for the Business Roundtable on clean air." Representative Henry A. Waxman (Democrat–California),
chair of the subcommittee, is an environmentalist. Observers had expected a
confrontation and contested votes on the floor of the Congress.

The problem for corporations was that, as one Republican staff aide
said, "If any bill has the blessing of Waxman and the environmental groups,
unless it is totally in outer space, who's going to vote against it?" [13] But corporations successfully minimized public votes. Somehow, Waxman was
persuaded to make behind-the-scenes compromises with Dingell so members, during an election year, didn't have to side publicly with business
against the environment. Often the access process leads to loopholes that
protect a single corporation, but for "clean" air most of the special deals
targeted not specific companies but entire industries. The initial bill, for example, required cars to be able to use carefully specified, cleaner fuels. But
the auto industry wanted the rules loosened, and Congress eventually incorporated a variant of a formula suggested by the head of General Motors'
fuels and lubricants department.

Nor did corporations stop fighting even after they gutted the bill through
amendments. Business pressed the EPA for favorable regulations to implement the law: "The cost of this legislation could vary dramatically, depending on how EPA interprets it," said William D. Fay, vice president of the
National Coal Association, who headed the hilariously misnamed Clean Air
Working Group, an industry coalition that fought to weaken the legislation. [14]
As one EPA aide working on acid rain regulations reported, "We're having a
hard time getting our work done because of the number of phone calls we're
getting" from corporations and their lawyers.

Corporations trying to get federal regulators to adopt the "right" regulations don't rely exclusively on the cogency of their arguments. They often exert pressure on a member of Congress to intervene for them at the EPA or
other agency. Senators and representatives regularly intervene on behalf of

constituents and contributors by doing everything from straightening out a social security problem to asking a regulatory agency to explain why it is pressuring a company. This process—like campaign finance—usually follows rules of etiquette. In addressing a regulatory agency, the senator does not say: "Lay off my campaign contributors or I'll cut your budget." One standard phrasing for letters asks regulators to resolve the problem "as quickly as possible within applicable rules and regulations."[15] No matter how mild and careful the inquiry, the agency receiving the request is certain to give it extra attention; only after careful consideration will they refuse to make any accommodation.

Soft money—unregulated megabuck contributions—also shaped what happened to air quality. Archer Daniels Midland argued that increased use of ethanol would reduce pollution from gasoline; coincidentally, ADM controls a majority of the ethanol market. To reinforce its arguments, in the 1992 election ADM gave $90,000 to Democrats and $600,000 to Republicans, the latter supplemented with an additional $200,000 as an individual contribution from the company head, Dwayne Andreas. Many environmentalists were skeptical about ethanol's value in a clean air strategy, but President Bush issued regulations promoting wider use of ethanol; we presume he was impressed by the force of ADM's 800,000 Republican arguments. Bob Dole, the 1996 Republican presidential candidate, helped pass and defend special breaks for the ethanol industry; he not only appreciated ADM's Republican contributions, but presumably approved of the more than $1 million they gave to the American Red Cross during the period when it was headed by his wife, Elizabeth Dole.[16] What about the post-1994 Republican-controlled Congress, defenders of the free market and opponents of government giveaways? Were they ready to end this subsidy program, cracking down on corporate welfare as they did on people welfare? Not a chance. In 1997, the Republican chair of the House Ways and Means Committee actually attempted to eliminate the special tax breaks for ethanol. Needless to say, he was immediately put in his place by other members of the Republican leadership, including Speaker Newt Gingrich and most of the Senate, with the subsidy locked in place for years to come,[17] in spite of a General Accounting Office report that "found that the ethanol subsidy justifies none of its political boasts."[18] The Center for Responsive Politics calculated that ADM, its executives and PAC, made more than $1 million in campaign contributions of various types; the only thing that had changed was that in 1996, with a Democratic president, this money was "divided more or less evenly between Republicans and Democrats."[19]

The disparity in power between business and environmentalists looms large during the legislative process, but it is enormous afterward. When the Clean Air Act passed, corporations and industry groups offered positions, typically with large pay increases, to congressional staff members who wrote the law. The former congressional staff members who now work for corporations both know how to evade the law and can persuasively claim to EPA that they know what Congress intended. Environmental organizations pay substantially less than Congress and can't afford large staffs. They are seldom able to become involved in the details of the administrative process or to influence implementation and enforcement.[20]

Having pushed Congress and the Environmental Protection Agency to allow as much pollution as possible, business then went to the Quayle council for rules allowing even more pollution. Vice President J. Danforth Quayle's council, technically known as the "Council on Competitiveness," was created by President Bush specifically to help reduce regulations on business. Quayle told the *Boston Globe* "that his council has an 'open door' to business groups and that he has a bias against regulations."[21] During the Bush administration, this council reviewed, and could override, all regulations, including those by the EPA setting the limits at which a chemical was subject to regulation. The council also recommended that corporations be allowed to increase their polluting emissions if a state did not object within seven days of the proposed increase. Corporations thus have multiple opportunities to win. If they lose in Congress, they can win at the regulatory agency; if they lose there, they can try again at the Quayle council (or later equivalent). If they lose there, they can try to reduce the money available to enforce regulations, or tie the issue up in the courts, or plan on accepting a minimal fine.

The operation of the Quayle council would probably have received little publicity, but reporters discovered that the executive director of the council, Allan Hubbard, had a clear conflict of interest. Hubbard chaired the biweekly White House meetings on the Clean Air Act. He owned half of World Wide Chemical, received an average of more than $1 million a year in profits from it while directing the Quayle council, and continued to attend quarterly stockholder meetings. According to the *Boston Globe*, "Records on file with the Indianapolis Air Pollution Control Board show that World Wide Chemical emitted 17,000 to 19,000 pounds of chemicals into the air" in 1991.[22] At that time the company did "not have the permit required to release the emissions," was "putting out nearly four times the allowable emissions without a permit, and could be subject to a $2,500-a-day penalty" according to David Jordan, director of the Indianapolis Air Pollution Board.[23]

This does not, however, mean that business always gets exactly what it wants. In 1997, the Environmental Protection Agency proposed tough new rules for soot and smog. Business fought hard to weaken or eliminate the rules: hiring experts (from pro-business think tanks) to attack the scientific studies supporting the regulations and putting a raft of lobbyists ("many of them former congressional staffers," the *Washington Post* reported[24]) to work securing the signatures of 250 members of Congress questioning the standards. But the late 1990s version of these industry mobilizations adds a new twist—creating a pseudo-grassroots campaign. For example, business, operating under a suitably disguised name (Foundation for Clean Air Progress), paid for television ads telling farmers that the EPA rules would prohibit them from plowing on dry windy days, with other ads predicting the EPA rules "would lead to forced carpooling or bans on outdoor barbecues—claims the EPA dismisses as ridiculous."[25] Along with the ads, industry worked to mobilize local politicians and business executives in what business groups called a "grass tops" campaign.

Despite a massive industry campaign, EPA head Carol Browner remained firm, and President Clinton was persuaded to go along. Of course, industry immediately began working on ways to undercut the regulations with congressional loopholes and exceptions—but business had suffered a defeat, and proponents of clean air (that is, most of the rest of us) had won at least a temporary and partial victory. And who leads the struggles to overturn or uphold these regulations? Just as before, Dingell and Waxman; Republicans "are skittish about challenging" the rules publicly, "so they gladly defer to Dingell as their surrogate."[26] Dingell's forces have more than 130 cosponsors (about one-third of them Democrats) for a bill to, in effect, override the EPA standards.

In business–government relations, most attention becomes focused on instances of scandal. The real issue, however, is not one or another scandal or conflict of interest, but rather the *system* of business–government relations, and especially of campaign finance, that offers business so many opportunities to craft loopholes, undermine regulations, and subvert enforcement. Still worse, many of these actions take place beyond public scrutiny. . . . [Our research] focuses on business and the way it uses money and power to subvert the democratic process. . . .

What Is Power?

Our analysis is based on an understanding of power that differs from that usually articulated by both business and politicians. The corporate PAC directors we interviewed insisted that they have no power.

> *If you were to ask me what kind of access and influence do we have, being roughly the 150th largest PAC, I would have to tell you that on the basis of our money we have zero. . . . If you look at the level of our contributions, we know we're not going to buy anybody's vote, we're not going to rent anybody, or whatever the clichés have been over the years. We know that.*

The executives who expressed these views clearly meant these words sincerely. Their statements are based on roughly the same understanding of "power" that is current within political science, which is also the way the term was defined by Max Weber, the classical sociological theorist. Power, in this common conception, is the ability to make someone do something against their will. If that is what power means, then corporations rarely have any in relation to members of Congress, nor does soft money give the donor power over presidents. As one senior vice president said to us: "You certainly aren't going to be able to buy anybody for $500 or $1,000 or $10,000—it's a joke." . . . In this regard we agree with the corporate officials we interviewed:

A corporation is not in a position to say to a member of Congress, "Either you vote for this bill or we will defeat your bid for reelection." Rarely do they even say: "You vote for this bill or you won't get any money from us."

The definition of power as the ability to make someone do something against their will is what Steven Lukes calls a "one-dimensional" view of power.[27] A two-dimensional view recognizes the existence of nondecisions: A potential issue never gets articulated or, if articulated by someone somewhere, never receives serious consideration. For example, in 1989 and 1990 one of the major political battles, and a focus of great effort by corporate PACs, was the Clean Air Act. Yet twenty or thirty years earlier, before the rise of the environmental movement, pollution was a nonissue: it simply was not considered, although its effects were, in retrospect, of great importance. In one of the Sherlock Holmes stories, the key clue is that the dog didn't bark.[28] A two-dimensional view of power makes the same point: The most important clue in some situation may be that no one noticed power was exercised—because there was no overt conflict.

Even this model of power is too restrictive, however, because it still focuses on discrete decisions and nondecisions. Tom Wartenberg . . . argues, instead, for a "field theory" of power that analyzes social power as a force similar to a magnetic field. A magnetic field alters the motion of objects susceptible to magnetism. Similarly, the mere presence of a powerful social agent alters the social space for others and causes them to orient themselves toward the powerful agent.[29] For example, one of the executives we interviewed took it for granted that "if we go see the congressman who represents [a city where the company has a major plant], where 10,000 of our employees are also his constituents, we don't need a PAC to go see him." The corporation is so important in that area that the member has to orient himself in relation to the corporation and its concerns. In a different sense, the very act of accepting a campaign contribution changes the way a member relates to a PAC, creating a sense of obligation, a need to reciprocate. The PAC contribution has altered the member's social space, his or her awareness of the company and wish to help it, even if no explicit commitments have been made.

Business Is Different

Power, we would argue, is not just the ability to force someone to do something against their will; it is most effective (and least recognized) when it shapes the field of action. Moreover, business's vast resources, influence on the economy, and general legitimacy place it on a different footing from other campaign contributors. Every day a member of Congress accepts a $1,000 donation from a corporate PAC, goes to a committee hearing, proposes "minor" changes in a bill's wording, and has those changes accepted without discussion or examination. The changes "clarify" the language of the bill, legalizing higher levels of pollution for a specific pollutant, or exempting the company from some tax. The media do not report this change and no one speaks against it. . . .

Even groups with great social legitimacy encounter more opposition and controversy than business faces for proposals that are virtually without public support. One example is the contrast between the largely unopposed commitment of tens or hundreds of billions of dollars for the savings and loan bailout, compared to the sharp debate, close votes, and defeats for the rights of men and women to take *unpaid* parental leaves. The classic term for something noncontroversial that everyone must support is "a motherhood issue," and while it costs little to guarantee every woman the right to an *unpaid* parental leave, this measure nonetheless generated intense scrutiny and controversy—going down to defeat under President Bush, passing under President Clinton, and then again becoming a focus of attack after the 1994 Republican takeover of Congress. Few indeed are the people publicly prepared to defend pollution or tax evasion. Nonetheless, business is routinely able to win pollution exemptions and tax loopholes. Although cumulatively some vague awareness of these provisions may trouble people, most are allowed individually to pass without scrutiny. *No* analysis of corporate political activity makes sense unless it begins with a recognition of this absolutely vital point. The PAC is a vital element of corporate power, but it does not operate by itself. The PAC donation is always backed by the wider power and influence of business.

Corporations are unlike other "special interest" groups not only because business has far more resources, but also because of its acceptance and legitimacy. When people feel that "the system" is screwing them, they tend to blame politicians, the government, the media—but rarely business. In terms of campaign finance, while much of the public is outraged at the way money influences elections and public policy, the issue is almost always posed in terms of politicians, what they do or don't do. This is part of a pervasive double standard that largely exempts business from criticism. We, however, believe it is vital to scrutinize business as well. . . .

The Limits to Business Power

We have argued that power is more than winning an open conflict and that business is different from other groups because its pervasive influence on our society shapes the social space for all other actors. These two arguments, however, are joined with a third: a recognition—in fact an insistence—on the limits to business power. Though we stress the power of business, business does not feel powerful. As one executive said to us:

> I really wish that our PAC in particular, and our lobbyists, had the influence that is generally perceived by the general population. If you see it written in the press, and you talk to people, they tell you about all that influence that you've got, and

frankly I think that's far overplayed, as far as the influence goes. Certainly you can get access to a candidate, and certainly you can get your position known; but as far as influencing that decision, the only way you influence it is by the providing of information.

Executives believe that corporations are constantly under attack, primarily because government simply doesn't understand that business is crucial to everything the society does, but can easily be crippled by well-intentioned but unrealistic government policies. A widespread view among the people we interviewed is, "Far and away the vast majority of things that we do are literally to protect ourselves from public policy that is poorly crafted and nonresponsive to the needs and realities and circumstances of our company." These misguided policies, they feel, can come from many sources: labor unions, environmentalists, the pressure of unrealistic public interest groups, the government's constant need for money or the weight of its oppressive bureaucracy. Therefore, simply to stay even requires a pervasive effort. If attention slips for even a minute, an onerous regulation will be imposed or a precious resource taken away. To some extent such a view is an obvious consequence of the position of the people we interviewed: If business could be sure of always winning, the government relations unit (and thus the jobs of its members) would be unnecessary; if it is easy to win, PAC directors deserve little credit for company victories and much blame for defeats. But evidently the corporation agrees with them, since it devotes significant resources to political action of many kinds, including the awareness and involvement of top officials. Chief executive officers and members of the board of directors repeatedly express similar views. . . .

. . . Once upon a time, perhaps, business could simply make its wishes known and receive what it wanted; today, corporations must form PACs, give soft money, actively lobby, make their case to the public, run advocacy ads, and engage in a whole range of costly and degrading activities that they wish were unnecessary. From the outside, we are impressed with their high success rates over a wide range of issues and with the absence of a credible challenge to the general authority of business. From the inside, corporations are impressed with the serious consequences of their occasional losses and with the unremitting effort needed to maintain their privileged position.

ENDNOTES

[1] *Boston Globe,* November 8, 1996, p. A26.

[2] *New York Times,* September 3, 1997, p. A18.

[3] Boschwitz, quoted in Brooks Jackson, *Honest Graft: Big Money and the American Political Process* (New York: Knopf, 1988), pp. 251–52. Emphasis in book. (Obviously, the secret memo didn't stay secret.) Boschwitz's 1990 strategy backfired. He discouraged the most "promising" Democratic candidates, but Paul Wellstone—a true long shot by all accounts—beat him, despite Boschwitz's 4 to 1 spending advantage. In the 1996 rematch between the two candidates, Wellstone outspent Boschwitz and won handily.

[4] Quoted in Elizabeth Drew, *Whatever it Takes: The Real Struggle for Political Power in America* (New York: Viking, 1997), pp. 19–20.

[5] David Donnelly, Janice Fine, and Ellen S. Miller, "Going Public," *Boston Review,* April–May 1997. Larry Makinson, "The Big Picture: Money Follows Power Shift on Capitol Hill" (Washington, D.C.: Center for Responsive Politics, 1997, www.crp.org).

[6] www.fec.gov.

[7] William Greider, "Whitewash: Is Congress Conning Us on Clean Air?" *Rolling Stone,* June 14, 1990, p. 40.

[8] Greider, "Whitewash,"p. 40.

[9] Margaret E. Kriz, "Dunning the Midwest," *National Journal,* April 14, 1990, p. 895.

[10] Kriz, "Dunning the Midwest," p. 895.

[11] Quoted in Greider, "Whitewash," p. 40.

[12] Greider, "Whitewash," p. 41.

[13] Margaret E. Kriz, "Politics at the Pump," *National Journal,* June 2, 1990, p. 1328.

[14] Why can't industry just come out and name its groups "Polluters for Profit" or the "Coalition for Acid Rain Preservation" (CARP)? All quotes in this paragraph are from Carol Matlack, "It's Round Two in Clean Air Fight," *National Journal,* January 26, 1991, p. 226.

[15] *Washington Post,* January 16, 1991, p. A17.

[16] *New York Times,* April 16, 1996, p. A16.

[17] *New York Times,* June 22, 1997, p. 17.

[18] *Wall Street Journal,* June 6, 1997.

[19] *New York Times,* June 22, 1997, p. 17.

[20] Matlack, "It's Round Two," p. 227.

[21] *Boston Globe,* November 21, 1991, p. 17.

[22] *Boston Globe,* November 21, 1991, p. 17.

[23] *Boston Globe,* November 20, 1991, p. 4.

[24] *Washington Post,* June 17, 1997, p. A1.

[25] *Washington Post,* June 17, 1997, p. A1.

[26] Richard E. Cohen, "Two Dems Are on Familiar Battlefield," *National Journal,* September 6, 1997, p. 1742.

[27] Steven Lukes, *Power: A Radical View* (New York: Macmillan, 1974).

[28] Theodore J. Eismeier and Philip H. Pollock III, "The Retreat from Partisanship: Why the Dog Didn't Bark in the 1984 Election." In *Business Strategy and Public Policy,* ed. Alfred A. Marcus, Allen M. Kaufman, and David R. Beam (Westport, Conn.: Quorum Books, 1987), pp. 137–47.

[29] Thomas Wartenberg, *The Forms of Power: From Domination to Transformation* (Philadelphia: Temple University Press, 1990), p. 74.

37

THE MASS MEDIA
AS A POWER INSTITUTION

MARTIN N. MARGER

This selection by Martin N. Marger, an associate professor of sociology at Michigan State University, also exemplifies C. Wright Mills' notion of the power elite. As Marger argues, even though Mills recognized 45 years ago that the mass media could be an effective tool of manipulation, Mills could not have imagined how powerful the institution of the mass media would become. In fact, Marger situates the media alongside the government and the economy as one of the most dominant institutions in society. Marger explains the magnitude of the mass media's authority by analyzing the ownership and control of media industries, the content of media information, and the effects the mass media have on public opinion and political awareness.

In contemporary societies, the two major institutions of power—government and economy—must be joined by a third—the mass media—to complete any scheme of societal power. Although not formally a part of either government or the economy, the mass media are integrally tied to both, and both rely on the mass media to function as they do. Moreover, the mass media have substantial independent resources that make them a formidable institution of power in their own right.

The Societal Role of the Mass Media

The mass media are of two types: print and electronic. Print media are books, magazines, and newspapers; electronic media are television, radio, and films. To refer to them as *mass* media implies that their communicative realm is extremely broad, often encompassing the entire society. In modern societies, the mass media serve several vital functions. They are agents of socialization, instructing people in the norms and values of their society and generally transmitting the society's culture. They are sources of information, supplying

From *Power in Modern Societies* by Marvin Olsen and Martin Marger. Copyright © 1996 by Westview Press, Inc. Reprinted by permission of Westview Press, a member of Perseus Books, L.L.C.

citizens with knowledge about their society and especially about the political economy. They function as propaganda mechanisms through which powerful units of the government and economy seek to persuade the public either to support their policies (government) or to buy their consumer products (corporations). Finally, they serve as agents of legitimacy, generating mass belief in (and acceptance of) dominant political and economic institutions.

Given these vital functions, three queries are of fundamental importance in examining the mass media's power in modern societies. The first concerns their control and accessibility: Who owns or controls the mass media, and how much access to them is afforded individuals and groups in the society? The second question pertains to their content: What do the media present to the public, and who makes decisions regarding that content? The third question concerns the effects of mass media on public opinion and political awareness: To what extent do the mass media shape people's views of events and personalities in their society and the world, and how do the media transmit ideology?

Most media research during the past several decades has focused on the United States. The following discussion, therefore, pertains to the power of the mass media primarily in American society. Most of the patterns and tendencies apparent in the United States, however, are increasingly characteristic of the mass media in other industrial societies.

Media Control and Accessibility

Control and accessibility of the mass media in the United States and increasingly in other industrial societies are determined primarily by the economic context within which the media function and by their place in the political economy.

In the United States, the mass media operate almost entirely as privately owned enterprises. In most other industrial societies, newspapers are privately owned but television and radio are at least partially public corporations that compete within a mixed public-private system. Television and radio in Canada, for example, are dominated by the state-run Canadian Broadcasting Corporation (CBC), although there are also several privately owned television and radio networks. A similar system exists in Britain, where the electronic media are a mixture of public and commercial corporations. Only in autocratic societies like China are the media fully state controlled; in these societies, the media are organized and operated to implement the government's social and political policies (Wright 1986). In recent years, there has been a movement in most societies toward the dominance of privately owned and operated electronic media, although the United States remains unique in the extent of private ownership and control. Moreover, although the electronic media are nominally regulated by government, they operate with far fewer restrictions in the United States than in other societies. Meanwhile, a global trend toward convergence of national networks and companies into transnational units is increasingly evident (Schiller 1989).

The mass media are huge corporations (or parts of corporate conglomerates) whose primary objective, like all enterprises in a capitalist economy, is to maximize their profits. Like most industries in the American political economy, the mass media are concentrated in a few giant corporate units and thus constitute an oligopoly. Vast multifaceted companies composed of newspaper chains, radio and television stations, and recording, motion-picture, and publishing units dominate the media industry. Among the 1,600 United States daily newspapers, about a dozen corporations control more than half the circulation. The Knight-Ridder chain, for example, owns newspapers throughout the United States with three million in daily circulation, including the *Detroit Free Press,* the *Miami Herald,* the *Philadelphia Inquirer,* and numerous smaller dailies. Gannett owns *USA Today* as well as 88 other dailies with six million in circulation. Although 11,000 individual magazine titles are published in the United States, a handful of corporations derive most of the magazine revenue (Time-Warner alone controls more than 40 percent of magazine business), and among more than 2,500 book publishing companies, a half-dozen corporations sell most books. Three major studios control most of the movie business, and three corporations draw most of the audience and revenue of the television industry (Bagdikian 1989). Edward Herman and Noam Chomsky have identified 24 media giants that basically control the industry. Twenty-three of these companies had assets in excess of $1 billion in 1986, and three-quarters of them earned after-tax profits of over $100 million (Herman and Chomsky 1988).

One must also consider the scope and diversity of these companies' media holdings and activities. Time-Warner, for example, is made up of Warner Brothers Pictures (movies), dozens of popular mass circulation magazines (including *Time* and *Life*), cable television companies, and book companies. NBC is part of the RCA Corporation, which, in turn, is part of General Electric. CBS and Capital Cities/ABC are massive media conglomerates that own numerous television and radio stations, cable television networks, and magazine, recording, book publishing, and motion-picture companies.

Topping off this narrow media concentration are the wire service companies, which accumulate news stories. A large proportion of the items appearing in every mass circulation newspaper in the United States comes from the wires of the Associated Press (AP) or United Press International (UPI). Newspapers subscribe to these services, which become the major source of stories. A few of the larger newspaper companies operate their own wire services and also supply other smaller papers. Thus, in the coverage of national or international news, the difference from one newspaper to another is ordinarily slight. Radio and television news, to a lesser degree, also rely on these wire services.

It is apparent, then, that in the United States, as in most industrial societies, ownership and control of the mass media are extremely concentrated. This concentration parallels the tendency of all political and economic institutions in modern societies to converge into fewer and more powerful units. All other aspects of media power, including their content and effects, are colored by this fact.

In modern societies, to publicly communicate views or ideas requires use of the media. A critical concern, therefore, is not only who owns or controls the media but also who has access to them. In modern societies, only government and big business have the resources—money, authority, and influence—to employ the media regularly and effectively.

As privately owned enterprises, the major goal of the various media is to generate revenue. This objective requires that the media cater primarily to those who can pay to put their views on the air or into print: the major corporations, which use the media primarily to create demand for their products and services through advertising. Consider that a 30-second television commercial on Super Bowl Sunday in 1992 cost $850,000; or that Procter and Gamble spends almost $1.5 billion each year on media advertising. Advertising not only serves to create demand but also provides corporations with a means of creating a positive public image. General Electric, for example, tells the public that "we bring good things to life." Most corporations convey similar messages in which they are portrayed not as profit-seeking enterprises but as compassionate, publicly responsible citizens.

Government access to the media is founded not on financial power but on the fact that the media are closely interwoven with government, particularly at the national level. Put simply, the relationship between government and media is symbiotic; neither can function effectively without the other. As a regulated industry in the United States, the media must take into account the interests of government elites. More importantly, however, the media are heavily dependent on government elites as their major source of political information, which is the core of news. In fact, it is the actions of government elites that dominate news as presented by both print and electronic media. Moreover, much of the news transmitted by the mass media is prepared by government agencies. Studies have indicated that not only are government officials the source of most news but most news stories are drawn from situations over which newsmakers "have either complete or substantial control" (Sigal 1973).

Power elites, particularly those in the realm of government, can easily gain access to the mass media simply because they possess credibility among the public as well as among the media elite. Their accounts of events and policies are more likely to be accepted and thus become part of the news format than accounts and interpretations provided by other sources (Gans 1979). Moreover, in gathering information, the mass media ordinarily follow the path of least resistance; this means relying on official sources for information. As Herman and Chomsky (1988) have noted, "Taking information from sources that may be presumed credible reduces investigative expense, whereas material from sources that are not prima facie credible, or that will elicit criticism and threats, requires careful checking and costly research" (p. 19).

Government elites, however, are equally dependent on the mass media. This dependency stems from their need to employ the media to convey their messages to the public and thus shape and influence public opinion. Political leaders today rarely engage in face-to-face communication with the masses. Instead, they speak primarily through the electronic media in sound bites and project their images through photo opportunities. Political dialogue, particularly at the national level, is increasingly reduced to creating impressions (Postman 1985). This process reaches a high point in the orchestration of pseudo-events, that is, carefully scripted and staged events that are designed to create favorable public images but that have little basis in reality (Boorstin 1961).

Mass Media Content

The mass media exercise considerable power independently of both government and business. This power is particularly significant in their role as gatekeepers of political, economic, and social information—what is ordinarily termed "news." As information gatekeepers, it is the media who define what news is or what is socially significant. As suppliers of vital information, the mass media in modern societies are unequaled. They have become our window on the world, and it is through them that we learn about key events, personalities, and other so-called news. The media, in other words, have become a source of reality itself. As Ben Bagdikian (1971) has put it: "For most of the people of the world, for most of the events of the world, what the news systems do not transmit did not happen. To that extent, the world and its inhabitants are what the news media say they are" (pp. xii–xiii).

Given the media's strong influence on the molding of political, economic, and social reality, a key power issue concerns the decision-making process of news selection and presentation. Like critical decisions of government and the economy, this process is essentially an elite function. Events become newsworthy, and thus of importance to the society, only after they have been selected by the communications elite—editors, journalists, and media executives (Cohen and Young 1973; Epstein 1974; Gans 1979; Tuchman 1978). It is the media elite, therefore, who are largely responsible for molding the public's conception of political, economic, and social events and conditions. The media elite must therefore be added to corporate and governmental elites as top decision makers in the United States and other modern societies.

What are the consequences of this concentration of control over the shaping of sociopolitical reality? Here we must consider the political-economic context of the mass media in the United States and most other modern societies. First, because the major media operate as business enterprises, the media elite, when making content decisions, must take into account the interests of the dominant economic groups—the large corporations—that supply them with revenue. Second, given their symbiotic relationship with government, these decisions must be weighed against the interests of political elites. The result is that ideas or movements outside the political and economic mainstream receive little attention. In U.S. elections, for example, minor parties and candidates are generally treated by the mass media as curiosities, not as legitimate contenders. Hence, political debate is narrowly limited to the two major parties in the mainstream political arena, parties that rarely differ fundamentally on policy or philosophical issues. In short, ruling business and political elites are best situated to exercise influence over the content of the mass media.

With maximum access to the mass media as well as the ability to shape news, elites of the political economy are able not only to place their issues on the political agenda but also to define them in ways "likely to influence their resolution" (Bennett 1988:96). Parties, organizations, and individuals who advocate serious economic or political change but lack financial and political resources have a very difficult time communicating their messages through the mass media. It is true that challenges to established authority are often given attention by newspaper and, particularly, television journalism. But this is due primarily to the fact that "the logic of audience maintenance favors conflict between easily recognizable groups" (Epstein 1974:269). Coverage is not provided in acknowledgment of the legitimacy of challenging groups or to present the substance of their protest (Gitlin 1980).

The emphasis on official perspectives results in limited public understanding of the nature of political, economic, and social problems and how they might be resolved. Rarely do the mass media subject the dominant political economy to serious scrutiny and criticism. "The political world," Lance Bennett (1988) has explained, "becomes a caricature drawn out of unrealistic stereotypes, predictable political postures, and superficial images" (p. 96). Moreover, even when attention is drawn to societal shortcomings by public affairs or news programs or investigative journalists, it is done in the spirit of the dominant ideology. That is, problems are presented as the products of deviant individuals or groups within the context of an otherwise healthy social system. The *systemic* origins of chronic problems are rarely explained or even acknowledged. As David Paletz and Robert Entman (1981) have observed, "The mass media have never given powerless Americans the necessary information to link the ubiquitous rotten apples to the structure of the barrel" (p. 167). Questioning the structure and functioning of dominant political and economic institutions is clearly beyond the capabilities of the mass media (Gans 1979; Gitlin 1980; Parenti 1986).

The bias of mass media content toward the dominant system should not be seen, however, as the result of government and economic elites conspiring with media editors, journalists, and executives. The media elite express dominant values largely unconsciously: They see themselves as objective news commentators, not bearers of opinion. As Herbert Gans (1979) has noted, "The values in the news are rarely explicit and must be found between the lines—in what actors and activities are reported or ignored, and in how they are described" (pp. 39–40). Political objectivity, therefore, is not political neutrality. Critical information presented by the media, in the form of news and public affairs, is framed by dominant values and shaped by power elites, no matter how seemingly objective the presentation may be (Iyengar and Kinder 1987). Moreover, the very notion of objectivity among the media is illusory. As Paletz and Entman (1981) have explained, "To edit is to interpret, to speak is to define, to communicate is to structure reality" (p. 22). Hence, the media, by, their very nature, cannot be objective.

The inability of the mass media to present issues to the public in a thorough and critical manner is largely a result of their commercial imperatives. News, like other aspects of mass media, must be sold as a consumer product. This requires that it be presented in an entertainment format and, as Bennett (1988) has explained, be personalized, dramatized, fragmented, and normalized. It is personalized in the sense that it "gives preference to the individual actors and human-interest angles in events while downplaying institutional and political considerations that establish the social contexts for those events" (p. 26). Similarly, the media seek out dramatic events and personalities to which viewers and readers can relate, rather than events and personalities that may be more politically significant though less glamorous and fascinating. The entertainment format of news forces it to be presented in unrelated bits and pieces rather than as a meaningful whole. As a result, news becomes a series of what Neil Postman (1985) has called "decontextualized facts," comparable to background music. Finally, information presented as news is filtered through traditional themes and images of the society, thereby assuring the viewer or reader of the merit of dominant institutions and discrediting challenges to them.

In short, although they may engage in social criticism, the mass media frame their presentations in a way that legitimizes the prevailing political economy. Although there is no blatant censorship of media content in the United States as there is in a totalitarian society, an implicit understanding exists on the part of the media elite regarding their role in upholding the status quo. Self-censorship by the media is reinforced when they anticipate the reactions of political and economic elites and alter their presentations in advance. At times, of course, more blatant attempts at censorship may arise, as when corporate advertisers exert direct pressure to influence the content of the media or when government elites pressure the media to "toe the line" (Gans 1979). Although the media elite may resist these pressures, more often their ideological perspectives are fully compatible with those of political and economic elites, and they may therefore have little inclination to follow a path not basically in line with those views. Moreover, although the media commonly present opposing sides of social and political issues, the two perspectives are only narrowly divergent and the issues are presented in ideologically safe stereotypes. The irony of modern communications systems is that despite the profusion of messages with which the citizenry is bombarded daily, the absence of a thorough exploration of issues by the mass media results in an increasingly uninformed public.

It is also important to consider the essentially passive role of the citizenry in the communications system of most modern societies. In essence, political communication flows only in one direction. The media are virtually unchallenged by consumers. There is little effective feedback from those who read newspapers and especially from those who watch television. Thus, as Mills (1956) explained [over] four decades ago, there is a growing tendency for mass media to be tools of manipulation rather than channels for the interchange of opinion: "In the primary public the competition of opinions goes on between people holding views in the service of their interests and their reasoning. But in the mass society of media markets, competition, if any, goes on between the manipulators with their mass media on the one hand, and the people receiving their propaganda on the other" (p. 305).

Although viewers and readers, as consumers, can choose not to buy a newspaper or watch a television program, the mass media operate in an oligopolistic market domestically and, increasingly, in an integrated international market. Hence, consumer choices are limited and, in the end, it is the producers—in this case the newspapers and television networks—who make critical decisions about the product and who exercise control over its supply and demand.

Media Effects

Concentrated media power, in the form of constricted ownership and control of content, does not necessarily guarantee to the users of the media—primarily government and big business—that the effects they desire, that is, public acceptance and internalization of their messages, will be produced. To what extent are the media effective in molding public opinion and shaping people's versions of political and social reality?

Although sociologists and communications experts are not certain about the precise effects of the mass media on socialization or how the media modify the influences of other socializers like the family and the school (Comstock 1980; Gerbner 1967), it appears that the media are becoming the chief means through which people construct their versions of social reality. Well before the advent of television, Walter Lippmann (1922) explained how the mass media, by selectively reporting and interpreting events and personalities, determine the pictures in our heads (stereotypes, as he referred to them) that shape our social worlds. With the predominance of television, this "reality-shaping" function of the mass media has become much more complete. Television serves increasingly in this capacity because few can escape its influence. Only sleep and work occupy more of Americans' time than television viewing. Most important, the mass media serve as the primary organs of political communication, setting the framework of public discourse, solidifying the legitimacy of powerful institutions and elites, and transmitting the society's dominant ideology.

The mediated version of social reality presented by television, newspapers, and other media is most evident in the communication of news. "News," as has been suggested, is hardly a complete or precise picture of societal or world events. Rather, it is a picture constructed by the media elite who select and interpret events, processes, and personalities. From an almost infinite number of happenings that occur each day, only a few are chosen for transmission as news. Beyond the realm of our personal lives, the issues that concern us are therefore the issues defined for us by the media elite as important and worthy of our attention.

In the early years of research on the effects of mass media on public attitudes and beliefs, the prevalent view was that media had a direct and significant influence. Starting in the 1940s, research seemed to reverse this view, concluding instead that the power of the mass media had been exaggerated. The new perspective held that viewers and readers were not to be seen as a "mass," but rather as individual consumers whose interpretations of media presentations were modified by social class, ethnicity, religion, and other social variables (Lazarsfeld, Berelson, and Gaudet 1948). People exposed themselves to the media selectively, it was suggested, so that media messages generally had the effect of simply reaffirming people's prior beliefs and views. V. O. Key (1964) warned against overestimating the effectiveness of the mass media in conveying the same messages to all people: "The flow of the messages of the mass media," he wrote, "is rather like dropping a handful of confetti from the rim of the Grand Canyon with the object of striking a man astride a burro on the canyon floor. In some measure chance determines which messages reach what targets" (p. 357). This "minimal-effects" view remains today among some media observers. Albert Gollin (1988), for example, has written that "People bring to their encounters with the mass media a formidable array of established habits, motives, social values and perceptual defenses that screen out, derail the intent or limit the force of media messages. The media certainly do affect people in obvious and subtle ways. But no simple 1:1 relationship exists between content or intent and effects" (p. 43).

More recently, researchers have pointed out that the minimal-effects view was based on perceived changes, brought about by the media, in attitudes about political issues. What was overlooked, however, was the impact of mass media on creating a public *awareness* of issues. This has become known as the "agenda-setting function" of the mass media (McCombs and Shaw 1972). Communications researchers have explained that although television and other mass media may not be overly effective in telling us *what* to think, they are extremely effective in telling us what and whom to think *about* (Iyengar and Kinder 1987; Shaw and McCombs 1977). Issues emphasized by the media become the issues regarded by viewers and readers as significant. As the media shift their emphasis to new issues, public perceptions change correspondingly. Moreover, Iyengar and Kinder (1987) have suggested a kind of media power that goes one step beyond agenda setting, which they call "priming." Priming refers to changes in the standards that people use in making political choices and judgments. As news, especially television news, shifts its attention from one issue to another, governments and political leaders are judged on their performance regarding those issues. Thus, by drawing attention to some aspects of political life at the expense of others, television helps bring to mind certain bits of political memory while others are ignored.

The mass media not only transmit descriptions of events and personalities but, more importantly, they convey the society's dominant ideology. It is in this sense that the media are agents of social control, used by power elites not only to communicate and legitimize their policies and actions but to stabilize the political and economic systems by generating allegiance among the public. As Todd Gitlin (1980) has explained:

> The media bring a manufactured public world into private space. From within their private crevices, people find themselves relying on the media for concepts, for images of their heroes, for guiding information, for emotional charges, for a recognition of public values, for symbols in general, even for language. Of all the institutions of daily life, the media specialize in orchestrating everyday consciousness—by virtue of their pervasiveness, their accessibility, their centralized symbolic capacity. They name the world's parts, they certify reality *as* reality—and when their certifications are doubted and opposed, as they surely are, it is those same certifications that limit the terms of effective opposition. To put it simply: the mass media have become core systems for the distribution of ideology. (Pp. 1–2)

We should not assume that the presentation of news is the mass media's only way of creating support for the society's dominant ideology and institutions. In modern societies, news and public affairs represent only a small portion of all media fare, particularly of television. The remaining entertainment, and especially the advertising that constantly accompanies it, is no less reflective and supportive of the society's prevailing value system (Bagdikian 1983; Goldsen 1977; Parenti 1986).

In recognizing the enormous power of mass media in modern societies to portray a particular version of reality, it should be understood that this is not consummate power. The ability of the media to propagate dominant values and shape political reality is by no means absolute. More specialized media (i.e., non–mass media), especially books and magazines, regularly present alternative and dissenting views. Moreover, dissident views are given coverage by the mass media once those views have gained at least some credibility. Nor can the media create problems that are nonexistent or conceal those that do exist (Iyengar and Kinder 1987).

Acknowledging the less-than-total power of mass media to influence people's social and political worlds, however, should not lead to an underestimation of the power of this institution. In all modern societies, control of information is critical: Whoever controls the means of communication has great power. Marx posited that those who control the society's means of material production are the most powerful. It might be claimed that in modern societies, great power hinges on control of the means of information—the media. This is the reason that political and economic elites make great efforts to dominate the media and to control the flow of information. Those who exert significant control over the media or who can freely gain access to them are able to exercise great influence in determining the views, images, and ideas that will become part of the public consciousness.

REFERENCES

Bagdikian, Ben. 1971. *The Information Machines.* New York: Harper & Row.

———. 1983. *The Media Monopoly.* Boston: Beacon.

———. 1989. "Missing from the News." *The Progressive* 53 (August): 32–34.

Bennett, W. Lance. 1988. *News: The Politics of Illusion.* 2d ed. New York: Longman.

Boorstin, Daniel J. 1961. *The Image: A Guide to Pseudo-Events in America.* New York: Harper & Row.

Cohen, Stanley and Jock Young, eds. 1973. *The Manufacture of News.* London: Constable.

Comstock, George. 1980. "The Impact of Television on American Institutions." Pp. 28–44 in *Readings in Mass Communication: Concepts and Issues in the Mass Media,* edited by Michael Emery and Ted Curtis Smythe. 4th ed. Dubuque, IA: Wm. C. Brown.

Epstein, Edwin Jay. 1974. *News from Nowhere.* New York: Vintage.

Gans, Herbert J. 1979. *Deciding What's News.* New York: Pantheon.

Gerbner, G. 1967. "An Institutional Approach to Mass Communications Research." Pp. 429–51 in *Communication: Theory and Research,* edited by L. Thayer. Springfield, IL: Charles C. Thomas.

Gitlin, Todd. 1980. *The Whole World Is Watching.* Berkeley: University of California Press.

Goldsen, Rose K. 1977. *The Show and Tell Machine: How Television Works and Works You Over.* New York: Dell.

Gollin, Albert E. 1988. "Media Power: On Closer Inspection, It's Not That Threatening." Pp. 41–44 in *Impacts of Mass Media,* edited by Ray Eldon Hiebert and Carol Reuss. 2d ed. New York: Longman.

Herman, Edward S. and Noam Chomsky. 1988. *Manufacturing Consent: The Political Economy of the Mass Media.* New York: Pantheon.

Iyengar, Shanto and Donald R. Kinder. 1987. *News That Matters: Television and American Opinion.* Chicago: University of Chicago Press.

Key, V. O., Jr. 1964. *Public Opinion and American Democracy.* New York: Knopf.

Lazarsfeld, Paul, Bernard Berelson, and H. Gaudet. 1948. *The People's Choice.* New York: Columbia University Press.

Lippmann, Walter. 1922. *Public Opinion.* New York: Macmillan.

McCombs, Maxwell and Donald Shaw. 1972. "The Agenda-Setting Function of Mass Media." *Public Opinion Quarterly* 36:176–87.

Mills, C. Wright. 1956. *The Power Elite.* New York: Oxford University Press.

Paletz, David L. and Robert M. Entman. 1981. *Media Power Politics.* New York: Free Press.

Parenti, Michael. 1986. *Inventing Reality: The Politics of the Mass Media.* New York: St. Martin's.

Postman, Neil. 1985. *Amusing Ourselves to Death: Public Discourse in the Age of Show Business.* New York: Penguin.

Schiller, Herbert I. 1989. *Culture, Inc.: The Corporate Takeover of Public Expression.* New York: Oxford University Press.

Shaw, Donald L. and Maxwell E. McCombs. 1977. *The Emergence of American Political Issues: The Agenda-Setting Function of the Press.* St. Paul, MN: West Publishers.

Sigal, Leon V. 1973. *Reporters and Officials: The Organization and Politics of News Reporting.* Lexington, MA: Heath.

Tuchman, Gaye. 1978. *Making News.* New York: Free Press.

Wright, Charles R. 1986. *Mass Communication: A Sociological Perspective.* 3d ed. New York: Random House.

THE ECONOMY AND WORK

38

MANIFESTO OF THE COMMUNIST PARTY

KARL MARX • FRIEDRICH ENGELS

The economy and work are the focus of the next three readings. The first selection in this group is an excerpt from the classic "Manifesto of the Communist Party," written by Karl Marx and Friedrich Engels in 1848. Students often are surprised to discover the currency of many of the topics discussed by Marx (1818–1883) and Engels (1820–1895). Specifically, Marx and Engels foresaw the rise of global capitalism. They also accurately described exploitive industrial conditions and the oppositional interests of workers and capitalists. Even though Marx and Engels are criticized for not foreseeing the rise of other social agents (such as the middle class, the government, and

English translation by Friedrich Engels, 1888.

unions) in mediating the conflict between capitalists and workers, their theory of class struggle and revolution is still provocative and a source for worldwide social change.

T he history of all hitherto existing society is the history of class struggles.

Freeman and slave, patrician and plebeian, lord and serf, guild-master and journeyman, in a word, oppressor and oppressed, stood in constant opposition to one another, carried on an uninterrupted, now hidden, now open fight, a fight that each time ended, either in a revolutionary reconstitution of society at large, or in the common ruin of the contending classes.

In the earlier epochs of history, we find almost everywhere a complicated arrangement of society into various orders, a manifold gradation of social rank. In ancient Rome we have patricians, knights, plebeians, slaves; in the Middle Ages, feudal lords, vassals, guild-masters, journeymen, apprentices, serfs; in almost all of these classes, again, subordinate gradations.

The modern bourgeois society that has sprouted from the ruins of feudal society has not done away with class antagonisms. It has but established new classes, new conditions of oppression, new forms of struggle in place of the old ones.

Our epoch, the epoch of the bourgeoisie, possesses, however, this distinctive feature: It has simplified the class antagonisms. Society as a whole is more and more splitting up into two great hostile camps, into two great classes directly facing each other: Bourgeoisie and Proletariat.

From the serfs of the Middle Ages sprang the chartered burghers of the earliest towns. From these burgesses the first elements of the bourgeoisie were developed.

The discovery of America, the rounding of the Cape, opened up fresh ground for the rising bourgeoisie. The East-Indian and Chinese markets, the colonization of America, trade with the colonies, the increase in the means of exchange and in commodities generally, gave to commerce, to navigation, to industry, an impulse never before known, and thereby, to the revolutionary element in the tottering feudal society, a rapid development.

The feudal system of industry, under which industrial production was monopolized by closed guilds, now no longer sufficed for the growing wants of the new markets. The manufacturing system took its place. The guild-masters were pushed on one side by the manufacturing middle class; division of labour between the different corporate guilds vanished in the face of division of labour in each single workshop.

Meantime the markets kept ever growing, the demand ever rising. Even manufacture no longer sufficed. Thereupon, steam and machinery revolutionized industrial production. The place of manufacture was taken by the giant, Modern Industry, the place of the industrial middle class, by industrial millionaires, the leaders of whole industrial armies, the modern bourgeois.

Modern industry has established the world-market, for which the discovery of America paved the way. This market has given an immense development to commerce, to navigation, to communication by land. This development has, in its turn, reacted on the extension of industry; and in proportion as industry, commerce, navigation, railways extended, in the same proportion the bourgeoisie developed, increased its capital, and pushed into the background every class handed down from the Middle Ages.

We see, therefore, how the modern bourgeoisie is itself the product of a long course of development, of a series of revolutions in the modes of production and of exchange.

Each step in the development of the bourgeoisie was accompanied by a corresponding political advance of that class. An oppressed class under the sway of the feudal nobility, an armed and self-governing association in the mediaeval commune; here independent urban republic (as in Italy and Germany), there taxable "third estate" of the monarchy (as in France), afterwards, in the period of manufacture proper, serving either the semi-feudal or the absolute monarchy as a counterpoise against the nobility, and, in fact, corner-stone of the great monarchies in general, the bourgeoisie has at last, since the establishment of Modern Industry and of the world-market, conquered for itself, in the modern representative State, exclusive political sway. The execution of the modern State is but a committee for managing the common affairs of the whole bourgeoisie.

The bourgeoisie, historically, has played a most revolutionary part.

The bourgeoisie, wherever it has got the upper hand, has put an end to all feudal, patriarchal, idyllic relations. It has pitilessly torn asunder the motley feudal ties that bound man to his "natural superiors," and has left remaining no other nexus between man and man than naked self-interest, than callous "cash payment." It has drowned the most heavenly ecstasies of religious fervor, of chivalrous enthusiasm, of philistine sentimentalism, in the icy water of egotistical calculation. It has resolved personal worth into exchange value and, in place of the numberless indefeasible chartered freedoms, has set up that single, unconscionable freedom—Free Trade. In one word, for exploitation, veiled by religious and political illusions, it has substituted naked, shameless, direct, brutal exploitation.

The bourgeoisie has stripped of its halo every occupation hitherto honored and looked up to with reverent awe. It has converted the physician, the lawyer, the priest, the poet, the man of science, into its paid wage-labourers.

The bourgeoisie has torn away from the family its sentimental veil, and has reduced the family relation to a mere money relation.

The bourgeoisie has disclosed how it came to pass that the brutal display of vigor in the Middle Ages, which Reactionists so much admire, found its fitting complement in the most slothful indolence. It has been the first to show what man's activity can bring about. It has accomplished wonders far surpassing Egyptian pyramids, Roman aqueducts, and Gothic cathedrals; it has conducted expeditions that put in the shade all former Exoduses of nations and crusades.

The bourgeoisie cannot exist without constantly revolutionizing the instruments of production, and thereby the relations of production, and with them the whole relations of society. Conservation of the old modes of production in unaltered form, was, on the contrary, the first condition of existence for all earlier industrial classes. Constant revolutionizing of production, uninterrupted disturbance of all social conditions, everlasting uncertainty and agitation distinguish the bourgeois epoch from all earlier ones. All fixed, fast-frozen relations, with their train of ancient and venerable prejudices and opinions, are swept away, all new-formed ones become antiquated before they can ossify. All that is solid melts into air, all that is holy is profaned, and man is at last compelled to face with sober senses, his real conditions of life, and his relations with his kind.

The need of a constantly expanding market for its products chases the bourgeoisie over the whole surface of the globe. It must nestle everywhere, settle everywhere, establish connections everywhere.

The bourgeoisie has through its exploitation of the world-market given a cosmopolitan character to production and consumption in every country. To the great chagrin of Reactionists, it has drawn from under the feet of industry the national ground on which it stood. All old-established national industries have been destroyed or are daily being destroyed. They are dislodged by new industries, whose introduction becomes a life and death question for all civilized nations, by industries that no longer work up indigenous raw material, but raw material drawn from the remotest zones; industries whose products are consumed, not only at home, but in every quarter of the globe. In place of the old wants, satisfied by the productions of the country, we find new wants, requiring for their satisfaction the products of distant lands and climes. In place of the old local and national seclusion and self-sufficiency, we have intercourse in every direction, universal inter-dependence of nations. And as in material, so also in intellectual production. The intellectual creations of individual nations become common property. National one-sidedness and narrow-mindedness become more and more impossible, and from the numerous national and local literatures, there arises a world literature.

The bourgeoisie, by the rapid improvement of all instruments of production, by the immensely facilitated means of communication, draws all, even the most barbarian, nations into civilization. The cheap prices of its commodities are the heavy artillery with which it batters down all Chinese walls, with which it forces the barbarians' intensely obstinate hatred of foreigners to capitulate. It compels all nations, on pain of extinction, to adopt the bourgeois mode of production; it compels them to introduce what it calls civilization into their midst, *i.e.,* to become bourgeois themselves. In one word, it creates a world after its own image.

The bourgeoisie has subjected the country to the rule of the towns. It has created enormous cities, has greatly increased the urban population as compared with the rural, and has thus rescued a considerable part of the population from the idiocy of rural life. Just as it has made the country dependent on the towns, so it has made barbarian and semi-barbarian countries dependent on the civilized ones, nations of peasants on nations of bourgeois, the East on the West.

The bourgeoisie keeps more and more doing away with the scattered state of the population, of the means of production, and of property. It has agglomerated population, centralized means of production, and has concentrated property in a few hands. The necessary consequence of this was political centralization. Independent, or but loosely connected provinces, with separate interests, laws, governments and systems of taxation, became lumped together into one nation, with one government, one code of laws, one national class-interest, one frontier and one customs-tariff.

The bourgeoisie, during its rule of scarce one hundred years, has created more massive and more colossal productive forces than have all preceding generations together. Subjection of Nature's forces to man, machinery, application of chemistry to industry and agriculture, steam-navigation, railways, electric telegraphs, clearing of whole continents for cultivation, canalization of rivers, whole populations conjured out of the ground—what earlier century had even a presentiment that such productive forces slumbered in the lap of social labour?

We see then: the means of production and of exchange, on whose foundation the bourgeoisie built itself up, were generated in feudal society. At a certain stage in the development of these means of production and of exchange, the conditions under which feudal society produced and exchanged, the feudal organization of agriculture and manufacturing industry, in one word, the feudal relations of property became no longer compatible with the already developed productive forces; they became so many fetters. They had to be burst asunder; they were burst asunder.

Into their place stepped free competition, accompanied by a social and political constitution adapted to it, and by the economical and political sway of the bourgeois class.

A similar movement is going on before our own eyes. Modern bourgeois society with its relations of production, of exchange and of property, a society that has conjured up such gigantic means of production and of exchange, is like the sorcerer, who is no longer able to control the powers of the nether world whom he has called up by his spells. For many a decade past the history of industry and commerce is but the history of the revolt of modern productive forces against modern conditions of production, against the property relations that are the conditions for the existence of the bourgeoisie and of its rule. It is enough to mention the commercial crises that by their periodical return put on its trial, each time more threateningly, the existence of the entire bourgeois society. In these crises a great part not only of the existing products, but also of the previously created productive forces, are periodically destroyed. In these crises there breaks out an epidemic that, in all earlier epochs, would have seemed an absurdity—the epidemic of over-production. Society suddenly finds itself put back into a state of momentary barbarism; it appears as if a famine, a universal war of devastation had cut off the supply of every means of subsistence; industry and commerce seem to be destroyed; and why? Because there is too much civilization, too much means of subsistence, too much industry, too much commerce. The productive forces at the disposal of society no longer tend to further the development of the conditions of bourgeois property; on the contrary, they have become too powerful for these conditions, by which they are fettered, and so soon as they overcome these fetters, they bring disorder into the whole of bourgeois society, endanger the existence of bourgeois property. The conditions of bourgeois society are too narrow to comprise the wealth created by them. And how does the bourgeoisie get over these crises? On the one hand by enforced destruction of a mass of productive forces; on the other, by the conquest of new markets, and by the more thorough exploitation of the old ones. That is to say, by paving the way for more extensive and more destructive crises, and by diminishing the means whereby crises are prevented.

The weapons with which the bourgeoisie felled feudalism to the ground are now turned against the bourgeoisie itself.

But not only has the bourgeoisie forged the weapons that bring death to itself; it has also called into existence the men who are to wield those weapons—the modern working class—the proletarians.

In proportion as the bourgeoisie, *i.e.,* capital, is developed, in the same proportion is the proletariat, the modern working class, developed—a class of labourers, who live only so long as they find work and who find work only so long as their labour increases capital. These labourers, who must sell themselves piece-meal, are a commodity, like every other article of commerce, and are consequently exposed to all the vicissitudes of competition, to all the fluctuations of the market.

Owing to the extensive use of machinery and to division of labour, the work of the proletarians has lost all individual character and, consequently, all charm for the workman. He becomes an appendage of the machine, and it is only the most simple, most monotonous, and most easily acquired knack that is required of him. Hence, the cost of production of a workman is restricted, almost entirely, to the means of subsistence that he requires for his maintenance and for the propagation of his race. But the price of a commodity, and therefore also of labour, is equal to its cost of production. In proportion, therefore, as the repulsiveness of the work increases, the wage decreases. Nay more, in proportion as the use of machinery and division of labour increases, in the same proportion the burden of toil also increases, whether by prolongation of the working hours, by increase of the work exacted in a given time, or by increased speed of the machinery, etc.

Modern industry has converted the little workshop of the patriarchal master into the great factory of the industrial capitalist. Masses of labourers, crowded into the factory, are organised like soldiers. As privates of the industrial army they are placed under the command of a perfect hierarchy of officers and sergeants. Not only are they slaves of the bourgeois class and of the bourgeois State; they are daily and hourly enslaved by the machine, by the over-looker, and, above all, by the individual bourgeois manufacturer himself. The more openly this despotism proclaims gain to be its end and aim, the more petty, the more hateful and the more embittering it is.

The less the skill and exertion of strength implied in manual labour, in other words, the more modern industry becomes developed, the more is the labour of men superseded by that of women. Differences of age and sex have no longer any distinctive social validity for the working class. All are instruments of labour, more or less expensive to use, according to their age and sex.

No sooner is the exploitation of the labourer by the manufacturer, so far, at an end, that he receives his wages in cash, than he is set upon by the other portions of the bourgeoisie, the landlord, the shopkeeper, the pawnbroker, etc.

39

WHEN WORK DISAPPEARS
The World of the New Urban Poor

WILLIAM JULIUS WILSON

This reading is an excerpt from William Julius Wilson's 1996 book, *When Work Disappears: The World of the New Urban Poor.* Wilson, a sociologist, is the Malcolm Wiener Professor of Social Policy at the John F. Kennedy School of Government, Harvard University. Here, Wilson examines the effects jobless-ness and declining wages have had on inner-city neighborhoods in Chicago. Economic changes related to deindustrialization, the globalization of capi-talism, and especially the decline of blue-collar jobs have contributed to the

From *When Work Disappears* by William Julius Wilson. Copyright © 1996 by William Julius Wilson. Reprinted by permission of Alfred A. Knopf, Inc., a division of Random House, Inc.

concentration of poverty in urban ghettos. In addition, Wilson analyzes other structural factors, such as residential segregation, demographic changes in the population, and local and federal policies that have contributed to the ghettoization of inner-city neighborhoods.

T he disappearance of work in many inner-city neighborhoods is partly related to the nationwide decline in the fortunes of low-skilled workers. Although the growing wage inequality has hurt both low-skilled men and women, the problem of declining employment has been concentrated among low-skilled men. In 1987–89, a low-skilled male worker was jobless eight and a half weeks longer than he would have been in 1967–69. Moreover, the proportion of men who "permanently" dropped out of the labor force was more than twice as high in the late 1980s than it had been in the late 1960s. A precipitous drop in real wages—that is, wages adjusted for inflation—has accompanied the increases in joblessness among low-income workers. If you arrange all wages into five groups according to wage percentile (from highest to lowest), you see that men in the bottom fifth of this income distribution experienced more than a 30 percent drop in real wages between 1970 and 1989.

Even the low-skilled workers who are consistently employed face problems of economic advancement. Job ladders—opportunities for promotion within firms—have eroded, and many less-skilled workers stagnate in dead-end, low-paying positions. This suggests that the chances of improving one's earnings by changing jobs have declined: if jobs inside a firm have become less available to the experienced workers in that firm, they are probably even more difficult for outsiders to obtain.

But there is a paradox here. Despite the increasing economic marginality of low-wage workers, unemployment dipped below 6 percent in 1994 and early 1995, many workers are holding more than one job, and overtime work has reached a record high. Yet while tens of millions of new jobs have been created in the past two decades, men who are well below retirement age are working less than they did two decades ago—and a growing percentage are neither working nor looking for work. The proportion of male workers in the prime of their life (between the ages of 22 and 58) who worked in a given decade full-time, year-round, in at least eight out of ten years declined from 79 percent during the 1970s to 71 percent in the 1980s. While the American economy saw a rapid expansion in high technology and services, especially advanced services, growth in blue-collar factory, transportation, and construction jobs, traditionally held by men, has not kept pace with the rise in the working-age population. These men are working less as a result.

The growth of a nonworking class of prime-age males along with a larger number of those who are often unemployed, who work part-time, or who work in temporary jobs is concentrated among the poorly educated, the school dropouts, and minorities. In the 1970s, two-thirds of prime-age male workers with less than a high school education worked full-time, year-round, in eight out of ten years. During the 1980s, only half did so. Prime-age black men experienced a similar sharp decline. Seven out of ten of all black men worked full-time, year-round, in eight out of ten years in the 1970s, but only half did so in the 1980s. The figures for those who reside in the inner city are obviously even lower. . . .

Joblessness and declining wages are . . . related to the recent growth in ghetto poverty. The most dramatic increases in ghetto poverty occurred between 1970 and 1980, and they were mostly confined to the large industrial metropolises of the Northeast and Midwest, regions that experienced massive industrial restructuring and loss of blue-collar jobs during that decade. But the rise in ghetto poverty was not the only problem. Industrial restructuring had devastating effects on the social organization of many inner-city neighborhoods in these regions. The fate of the West Side black community of North Lawndale vividly exemplifies the cumulative process of economic and social dislocation that has swept through Chicago's inner city.

After more than a quarter century of continuous deterioration, North Lawndale resembles a war zone. Since 1960, nearly half of its housing stock has disappeared; the remaining units are mostly run-down or dilapidated. Two large factories anchored the economy of this West Side neighborhood in its good days—the Hawthorne plant of Western Electric, which employed over 43,000 workers; and an International Harvester plant with 14,000 workers. The world headquarters for Sears, Roebuck and Company was located there, providing another 10,000 jobs. The neighborhood also had a Copenhagen snuff plant, a Sunbeam factory, and a Zenith factory, a Dell Farm food market, an Alden's catalog store, and a U.S. Post Office bulk station. But conditions rapidly changed. Harvester closed its doors in the late 1960s. Sears moved most of its offices to the Loop in downtown Chicago in 1973; a catalog distribution center with a workforce of 3,000 initially remained in the neighborhood but was relocated outside of the state of Illinois in 1987. The Hawthorne plant gradually phased out its operations and finally shut down in 1984.

The departure of the big plants triggered the demise or exodus of the smaller stores, the banks, and other businesses that relied on the wages paid by the large employers. "To make matters worse, scores of stores were forced out of business or pushed out of the neighborhoods by insurance companies in the wake of the 1968 riots that swept through Chicago's West Side after the assassination of Dr. Martin Luther King, Jr. Others were simply burned or abandoned. It has been estimated that the community lost 75 percent of its business establishments from 1960 to 1970 alone." In 1986, North Lawndale, with a population of over 66,000, had only one bank and one supermarket; but it was also home to forty-eight state lottery agents, fifty currency exchanges, and ninety-nine licensed liquor stores and bars.

The impact of industrial restructuring on inner-city employment is clearly apparent to urban blacks. The UPFLS [Chicago Urban Poverty and

Family Life Survey] survey posed the following question: "Over the past five or ten years, how many friends of yours have lost their jobs because the place where they worked shut down—would you say none, a few, some, or most?" Only 26 percent of the black residents in our sample reported that none of their friends had lost jobs because their workplace shut down. Indeed, both black men and black women were more likely to report that their friends had lost jobs because of plant closings than were the Mexicans and the other ethnic groups in our study. Moreover, nearly half of the employed black fathers and mothers in the UPFLS survey stated that they considered themselves to be at high risk of losing their jobs because of plant shutdowns. Significantly fewer Hispanic and white parents felt this way.

Some of the inner-city neighborhoods have experienced more visible job losses than others. But residents of the inner city are keenly aware of the rapid depletion of job opportunities. A 33-year-old unmarried black male of North Lawndale who is employed as a clerical worker stated: "Because of the way the economy is structured, we're losing more jobs. Chicago is losing jobs by the thousands. There just aren't any starting companies here and it's harder to find a job compared to what it was years ago."

A similar view was expressed by a 41-year-old black female, also from North Lawndale, who works as a nurse's aide:

> *Chicago is really full of peoples. Everybody can't get a good job. They don't have enough good jobs to provide for everybody. I don't think they have enough jobs period. . . . And all the factories and the places, they closed up and moved out of the city and stuff like that, you know. I guess it's one of the reasons they haven't got too many jobs now, 'cause a lot of the jobs now, factories and business, they're done moved out. So that way it's less jobs for lot of peoples.*

Respondents from other neighborhoods also reported on the impact of industrial restructuring. According to a 33-year-old South Side janitor:

> *The machines are putting a lot of people out of jobs. I worked for* Time *magazine for seven years on a videograph printer and they come along with the Abedic printer, it cost them half a million dollars: they did what we did in half the time, eliminated two shifts.*

"Jobs were plentiful in the past," stated a 29-year-old unemployed black male who lives in one of the poorest neighborhoods on the South Side.

> *You could walk out of the house and get a job. Maybe not what you want but you could get a job. Now, you can't find anything. A lot of people in this neighborhood, they want to work but they can't get work. A few, but a very few, they just don't want to work. The majority they want to work but they can't find work.*

Finally, a 41-year-old hospital worker from another impoverished South Side neighborhood associated declining employment opportunities with decreasing skill levels:

Well, most of the jobs have moved out of Chicago. Factory jobs have moved out. There are no jobs here. Not like it was 20, 30 years ago. And people aren't skilled enough for the jobs that are here. You don't have enough skilled and educated people to fill them.

The increasing suburbanization of employment has accompanied industrial restructuring and has further exacerbated the problems of inner-city joblessness and restricted access to jobs. "Metropolitan areas captured nearly 90 percent of the nation's employment growth; much of this growth occurred in booming 'edge cities' at the metropolitan periphery. By 1990, many of these 'edge cities' had more office space and retail sales than the metropolitan downtowns." Over the last two decades, 60 percent of the new jobs created in the Chicago metropolitan area have been located in the northwest suburbs of Cook and Du Page counties. African Americans constitute less than 2 percent of the population in these areas.

In *The Truly Disadvantaged* (1987), I maintained that one result of these changes for many urban blacks has been a growing mismatch between the suburban location of employment and minorities' residence in the inner city. Although studies based on data collected before 1970 showed no consistent or convincing effects on black employment as a consequence of this spatial mismatch, the employment of inner-city blacks relative to suburban blacks has clearly deteriorated since then. Recent research, conducted mainly by urban and labor economists, strongly shows that the decentralization of employment is continuing and that employment in manufacturing, most of which is already suburbanized, has decreased in central cities, particularly in the Northeast and Midwest. As Farrell Bloch, an economic and statistical consultant, points out, "Not only has the number of manufacturing jobs been decreasing, but new plants now tend to locate in the suburbs to take advantage of cheap land, access to highways, and low crime rates; in addition, businesses shun urban locations to avoid buying land from several different owners, paying high demolition costs for old buildings, and arranging parking for employees and customers."

Blacks living in central cities have less access to employment, as measured by the ratio of jobs to people and the average travel time to and from work, than do central-city whites. Moreover, unlike most other groups of workers across the urban/suburban divide, less educated central-city blacks receive lower wages than suburban blacks who have similar levels of education. And the decline in earnings of central-city blacks is related to the decentralization of employment—that is, the movement of jobs from the cities to the suburbs—in metropolitan areas.

But are the differences in employment between city and suburban blacks mainly the result of changes in the location of jobs? It is possible that in recent years the migration of blacks to the suburbs has become much more selective than in earlier years, so much so that the changes attributed to job location are actually caused by this selective migration. The pattern of black migration to the suburbs in the 1970s was similar to that of whites during the 1950s and 1960s in the sense that it was concentrated among the better-educated and younger city residents. However, in the 1970s this was even more true for blacks, creating a situation in which the education and income gaps between city and suburban blacks seemed to expand at the same time that the differences between city and suburban whites seemed to contract. Accordingly, if one were to take into account differences in education, family background, and so on, how much of the employment gap between city and suburbs would remain?

This question was addressed in a study of the Gautreaux program in Chicago. The Gautreaux program was created under a 1976 court order resulting from a judicial finding of widespread discrimination in the public housing projects of Chicago. The program has relocated more than 4,000 residents from public housing into subsidized housing in neighborhoods throughout the Greater Chicago area. The design of the program permitted the researchers, James E. Rosenbaum and Susan J. Popkin, to contrast systematically the employment experiences of a group of low-income blacks who had been assigned private apartments in the suburbs with the experience of a control group with similar characteristics and histories who had been assigned private apartments in the city. Their findings support the spatial mismatch hypothesis. After taking into account the personal characteristics of the respondents (including family background, family circumstances, levels of human capital, motivation, length of time since the respondent first enrolled in the Gautreaux program), Rosenbaum and Popkin found that those who moved to apartments in the suburbs were significantly more likely to have a job after the move than those placed in the city. When asked what makes it easier to obtain employment in the suburbs, nearly all the suburban respondents mentioned the high availability of jobs.

The African Americans surveyed in the UPFLS clearly recognized a spatial mismatch of jobs. Both black men and black women saw greater job prospects outside the city. For example, only one-third of black fathers from areas with poverty rates of at least 30 percent reported that their best opportunities for employment were to be found in the city. Nearly two-thirds of whites and Puerto Ricans and over half of Mexicans living in similar neighborhoods felt this way. Getting to suburban jobs is especially problematic for the jobless individuals in the UPFLS because only 28 percent have access to an automobile. This rate falls even further to 18 percent for those living in the ghetto areas.

Among two-car middle-class and affluent families, commuting is accepted as a fact of life; but it occurs in a context of safe school environments for children, more available and accessible day care, and higher incomes to support mobile, away-from-home lifestyles. In a multitiered job market that requires substantial resources for participation, most inner-city minorities must rely on public transportation systems that rarely provide easy and quick access to suburban locations. A 32-year-old unemployed South Side welfare mother described the problem this way:

> *There's not enough jobs. I thinks Chicago's the only city that does not have a lot of opportunities opening in it. There's not enough factories, there's not enough work. Most all the good jobs are in the suburbs. Sometimes it's hard for the people in the city to get to the suburbs, because everybody don't own a car. Everybody don't drive.*

After commenting on the lack of jobs in his area, a 29-year-old unemployed South Side black male continued:

> *You gotta go out in the suburbs, but I can't get out there. The bus go out there but you don't want to catch the bus out there, going two hours each ways. If you have to be at work at eight that mean you have to leave for work at six, that mean you have to get up at five to be at work at eight. Then when wintertime come you be in trouble.*

Another unemployed South Side black male had this to say: "Most of the time . . . the places be too far and you need transportation and I don't have none right now. If I had some I'd probably be able to get one [a job]. If I had a car and went way into the suburbs, 'cause there ain't none in the city." This perception was echoed by an 18-year-old unemployed West Side black male:

> *They are most likely hiring in the suburbs. Recently, I think about two years ago, I had a job but they say that I need some transportation and they say that the bus out in the suburbs run at a certain time. So I had to pass that job up because I did not have no transport.*

An unemployed unmarried welfare mother of two from the West Side likewise stated:

> *Well, I'm goin' to tell you: most jobs, more jobs are in the suburbs. It's where the good jobs and stuff is but you gotta have transportation to get there and it's hard to be gettin' out there in the suburbs. Some people don't know where the suburbs is, some people get lost out there. It is really hard, but some make a way.*

One employed factory worker from the West Side who works a night shift described the situation this way:

> *From what I, I see, you know, it's hard to find a good job in the inner city 'cause so many people moving, you know, west to the suburbs and out of state. . . . Some people turn jobs down because they don't have no way of getting out there. . . . I just see some people just going to work—and they seem like they the type who just used to—they coming all the way from the city and go on all the way to the suburbs and, you know, you can see 'em all bundled and—catching one bus and the next bus. They just used to doing that.*

But the problem is not simply one of transportation and the length of commuting time. There is also the problem of the travel expense and of whether the long trek to the suburbs is actually worth it in terms of the income earned—after all, owning a car creates expenses far beyond the purchase price, including insurance, which is much more costly for city dwellers than it is for suburban motorists. "If you work in the suburbs you gotta have a car," stated an unmarried welfare mother of three children who lives on Chicago's West Side, "then you gotta buy gas. You spending more getting to the suburbs to work, than you is getting paid, so you still ain't getting nowhere."

Indeed, one unemployed 36-year-old black man from the West Side of Chicago actually quit his suburban job because of the transportation problem. "It was more expensive going to work in Naperville, transportation and all, and it wasn't worth it. . . . I was spending more money going to work than I earned working."

If transportation poses a problem for those who have to commute to work from the inner city to the suburbs, it can also hinder poor ghetto residents' ability to travel to the suburbs just to seek employment. For example, one unemployed man who lives on the South Side had just gone to O'Hare Airport looking for work with no luck. His complaint: "The money I spent yesterday, I coulda kept that in my pocket—I coulda kept that. 'Cause you know I musta spent $7 or somethin'. I coulda kept that."

Finally, in addition to enduring the search-and-travel costs, inner-city black workers often confront racial harassment when they enter suburban communities. A 38-year-old South Side divorced mother of two children who works as a hotel cashier described the problems experienced by her son and his co-worker in one of Chicago's suburbs:

> *My son, who works in Carol Stream, an all-white community, they've been stopped by a policeman two or three times asking them why they're in the community. And they're trying to go to work. They want everyone to stay in their own place. That's what society wants. And they followed them all the way to work to make sure. 'Cause it's an all-white neighborhood. But there're no jobs in the black neighborhoods. They got to go way out there to get a job.*

These informal observations on the difficulties and cost of travel to suburban employment are consistent with the results of a recent study by the labor economists Harry J. Holzer, Keith R. Ihlandfeldt, and David L. Sjoquist (1994). In addition to finding that the lack of automobile ownership among inner-city blacks contributed significantly to their lower wages and lower rate of employment, these authors also reported that African Americans "spend more time traveling to work than whites," that "the time cost per mile traveled is . . . significantly higher for blacks," and that the resulting gains are relatively small. Overall, their results suggest that the amount of time and money spent in commuting, when compared with the actual income that accrues to inner-city blacks in low-skill jobs in the suburbs, acts to discourage poor people from seeking employment far from their own neighborhoods. Holzer and his colleagues concluded that it was quite rational for blacks to reject these search-and-travel choices when assessing their position in the job market.

Changes in the industrial and occupational mix, including the removal of jobs from urban centers to suburban corridors, represent external factors that have helped to elevate joblessness among inner-city blacks. But important social and demographic changes within the inner city are also associated with the escalating rates of neighborhood joblessness, and we shall consider these next.

The increase in the proportion of jobless adults in the inner city is also related to changes in the class, racial, and age composition of such neighborhoods—changes that have led to greater concentrations of poverty. Concentrated poverty is positively associated with joblessness. That is, when the former appears, the latter is found as well. As stated previously, poor people today are far more likely to be unemployed or out of the labor force than in previous years. In *The Truly Disadvantaged* (1987), I argue that in addition to the effects of joblessness, inner-city neighborhoods have experienced a growing concentration of poverty for several other reasons, including (1) the outmigration of nonpoor black families; (2) the exodus of nonpoor white and other nonblack families; and (3) the rise in the number of residents who have become poor while living in these areas. Additional research on the growth of concentrated poverty suggests another factor: the movement of poor people into a neighborhood (inmigration). And one more factor should be added to this mix: changes in the age structure of the community.

I believe that the extent to which any one factor is significant in explaining the decrease in the proportion of nonpoor individuals and families depends on the poverty level and racial or ethnic makeup of the neighborhood at a given time. . . .

One of the important demographic shifts that had an impact on the upturn in the jobless rate has been the change in the age structure of inner-city ghetto neighborhoods. Let us . . . examine the three Bronzeville neighborhoods of Douglas, Grand Boulevard, and Washington Park. . . . [T]he proportion of those in the age categories (20–64) that roughly approximate the prime-age workforce has declined in all three neighborhoods since 1950, whereas the proportion in the age category 65 and over has increased. Of the adults aged 20 and over, the proportion in the prime-age categories declined by 17 percent in Grand Boulevard, 16 percent in Douglas, and 12 percent in Washington Park between 1950 and 1990. The smaller the percentage of prime-age adults in a population, the lower the proportion of residents who are likely to be employed. The proportion of residents in the age category 5–19 increased sharply in each neighborhood from 1950 to 1990, suggesting that the growth in the proportion of teenagers also contributed to the rise in the jobless rate. However, if we consider the fact that male employment in these neighborhoods declined by a phenomenal 46 percent between 1950 and 1960, these demographic changes obviously can account for only a fraction, albeit a significant fraction, of the high proportion of the area's jobless adults.

The rise in the proportion of jobless adults in the Bronzeville neighborhoods has been accompanied by an incredible depopulation—a decline of 66 percent in the three neighborhoods combined—that magnifies the problems of the new poverty neighborhoods. As the population drops and the proportion of nonworking adults rises, basic neighborhood institutions are more difficult to maintain: stores, banks, credit institutions, restaurants, dry cleaners, gas stations, medical doctors, and so on lose regular and potential patrons. Churches experience dwindling numbers of parishioners and shrinking resources; recreational facilities, block clubs, community groups, and other informal organizations also suffer. As these organizations decline, the means of formal and informal social control in the neighborhood become weaker. Levels of crime and street violence increase as a result, leading to further deterioration of the neighborhood.

The more rapid the neighborhood deterioration, the greater the institutional disinvestment. In the 1960s and 1970s, neighborhoods plagued by heavy abandonment were frequently "redlined" (identified as areas that should not receive or be recommended for mortgage loans or insurance); this paralyzed the housing market, lowered property values, and further encouraged landlord abandonment. The enactment of federal and state community reinvestment legislation in the 1970s curbed the practice of open redlining. Nonetheless, "prudent lenders will exercise increased caution in advancing mortgages, particularly in neighborhoods marked by strong indication of owner disinvestment and early abandonment."

As the neighborhood disintegrates, those who are able to leave depart in increasing numbers; among these are many working- and middle-class families. The lower population density in turn creates additional problems. Abandoned buildings increase and often serve as havens for crack use and other illegal enterprises that give criminals footholds in the community. Precipitous declines in density also make it even more difficult to sustain or develop a sense of community. The feeling of safety in numbers is completely lacking in such neighborhoods.

Although changes in the economy (industrial restructuring and reorganization) and changes in the class, racial, and demographic composition of inner-city ghetto neighborhoods are important factors in the shift from institutional to jobless ghettos since 1970, we ought not to lose sight of the fact that this process actually began immediately following World War II.

The federal government contributed to the early decay of inner-city neighborhoods by withholding mortgage capital and by making it difficult for urban areas to retain or attract families able to purchase their own homes. Spurred on by massive mortgage foreclosures during the Great Depression, the federal government in the 1940s began underwriting mortgages in an effort to enable citizens to become homeowners. But the mortgage program was selectively administered by the Federal Housing Administration (FHA), and urban neighborhoods considered poor risks were redlined—an action that excluded virtually all the black neighborhoods and many neighborhoods with a considerable number of European immigrants. It was not until the 1960s that the FHA discontinued its racial restrictions on mortgages.

By manipulating market incentives, the federal government drew middle-class whites to the suburbs and, in effect, trapped blacks in the inner cities. Beginning in the 1950s, the suburbanization of the middle class was also facilitated by a federal transportation and highway policy, including the building of freeway networks through the hearts of many cities, mortgages for veterans, mortgage-interest tax exemptions, and the quick, cheap production of massive amounts of tract housing.

In the nineteenth and early twentieth centuries, with the offer of municipal services as an inducement, cities tended to annex their suburbs. But the relations between cities and suburbs in the United States began to change following a century-long influx of poor migrants who required expensive services and paid relatively little in taxes. Annexation largely ended in the mid-twentieth century as suburbs began to resist incorporation successfully. Suburban communities also drew tighter boundaries through the manipulation of zoning laws and discriminatory land-use controls and site-selection practices, making it difficult for inner-city racial minorities to penetrate.

As separate political jurisdictions, suburbs exercised a great deal of autonomy in their use of zoning, land-use policies, covenants, and deed restrictions. In the face of mounting pressures calling for integration in the 1960s, "suburbs chose to diversify by race rather than class. They retained zoning and other restrictions that allowed only affluent blacks (and, in some instances, Jews) to enter, thereby intensifying the concentration and isolation of the urban poor."

Other government policies also contributed to the growth of jobless ghettos, both directly and indirectly. Many black communities were uprooted by urban renewal and forced migration. The construction of freeway and highway networks through the hearts of many cities in the 1950s produced the most dramatic changes, as many viable low-income communities were destroyed. These networks not only encouraged relocation from the cities to the suburbs, "they also created barriers between the sections of the cities, walling off poor and minority neighborhoods from central business districts. Like urban renewal, highway and expressway construction also displaced many poor people from their homes."

Federal housing policy also contributed to the gradual shift to jobless ghettos. Indeed, the lack of federal action to fight extensive segregation against African Americans in urban housing markets and acquiescence to the opposition of organized neighborhood groups to the construction of public housing in their communities have resulted in massive segregated housing projects. The federal public housing program evolved in two policy stages that represented two distinct styles. The Wagner Housing Act of 1937 initiated the first stage. Concerned that the construction of public housing might depress private rent levels, groups such as the U.S. Building and Loan League and the National Association of Real Estate Boards successfully lobbied Congress to require, by law, that for each new unit of public housing one "unsafe or un-sanitary" unit of public housing be destroyed. As Mark Condon (1991) points out, "This policy increased employment in the urban construction market while insulating private rent levels by barring the expansion of the housing stock available to low-income families."

The early years of the public housing program produced positive results. Initially, the program mainly served intact families temporarily displaced by the Depression or in need of housing after the end of World War II. For many of these families, public housing was the first step on the road toward eco-nomic recovery. Their stay in the projects was relatively brief. The economic mobility of these families "contributed to the sociological stability of the first public housing communities, and explains the program's initial success."

The passage of the Housing Act of 1949 marked the beginning of the sec-ond policy stage. It instituted and funded the urban renewal program de-signed to eradicate urban slums. "Public housing was now meant to collect the ghetto residents left homeless by the urban renewal bulldozers." A new, lower-income ceiling for public housing residency was established by the federal Public Housing Authority, and families with incomes above that ceil-ing were evicted, thereby restricting access to public housing to the most eco-nomically disadvantaged segments of the population.

This change in federal housing policy coincided with the mass migration of African Americans from the rural South to the cities of the Northeast and Midwest. Since smaller suburban communities refused to permit the con-struction of public housing, the units were overwhelmingly concentrated in the overcrowded and deteriorating inner city ghettos—the poorest and least socially organized sections of the city and the metropolitan area. "This grow-ing population of politically weak urban poor was unable to counteract the desires of vocal middle- and working-class whites for segregated housing," housing that would keep blacks out of white neighborhoods. In short, public housing represents a federally funded institution that has isolated families by race and class for decades, and has therefore contributed to the growing concentration of jobless families in the inner-city ghettos in recent years.

Also, since 1980, a fundamental shift in the federal government's support for basic urban programs has aggravated the problems of joblessness and so-cial organization in the new poverty neighborhoods. The Reagan and Bush administrations—proponents of the New Federalism—sharply cut spend-ing on direct aid to cities, including general revenue sharing, urban mass transit, public service jobs and job training, compensatory education, social service block grants, local public works, economic development assistance, and urban development action grants. In 1980, the federal contribution to city budgets was 18 percent; by 1990 it had dropped to 6.4 percent. In addition, the economic recession which began in the Northeast in 1989 and lasted until the early 1990s sharply reduced those revenues that the cities themselves generated, thereby creating budget deficits that resulted in further cutbacks in basic services and programs along with increases in local taxes.

For many cities, especially the older cities of the East and Midwest, the combination of the New Federalism and the recession led to the worst fiscal and service crisis since the Depression. Cities have become increasingly underserviced, and many have been on the brink of bankruptcy. They have therefore not been in a position to combat effectively three unhealthy social conditions that have emerged or become prominent since 1980: (1) the prevalence of crack-cocaine addiction and the violent crime associated with it; (2) the AIDS epidemic and its escalating public health costs; and (3) the sharp rise in the homeless population not only for individuals but for whole families as well.

Although drug addiction and its attendant violence, AIDS and its toll on public health resources, and homelessness are found in many American communities, their impact on the ghetto is profound. These communities, whose residents have been pushed to the margins of society, have few resources with which to combat these social ills that arose in the 1980s. Fiscally strapped cities have watched helplessly as these problems—exacerbated by the new poverty, the decline of social organization in the jobless neighborhoods, and the reduction of social services—have made the city at large seem a dangerous and threatening place in which to live. Accordingly, working- and middle-class urban residents continue to relocate in the suburbs. Thus, while joblessness and related social problems are on the rise in inner-city neighborhoods, especially in those that represent the new poverty areas, the larger city has fewer and fewer resources with which to combat them.

Finally, policymakers indirectly contributed to the emergence of jobless ghettos by making decisions that have decreased the attractiveness of low-paying jobs and accelerated the relative decline in wages for low-income workers. In particular, in the absence of an effective labor-market policy, they have tolerated industry practices that undermine worker security, such as the reduction in benefits and the rise of involuntary part-time employment, and they have "allowed the minimum wage to erode to its second-lowest level in purchasing power in 40 years." After adjusting for inflation, "the minimum wage is 26 percent below its average level in the 1970s." Moreover, they virtually eliminated AFDC benefits for families in which a mother is employed at least half-time. In the early 1970s, a working mother with two children whose wages equaled 75 percent of the amount designated as the poverty line could receive AFDC benefits as a wage supplement in forty-nine states; in 1995 only those in three states could. . . . [E]ven with the expansion of the earned income tax credit (a wage subsidy for the working poor) such policies make it difficult for poor workers to support their families and protect their children. The erosion of wages and benefits forces many low-income workers in the inner city to move or remain on welfare.

REFERENCES

Condon, Mark. 1991. "Public Housing, Crime, and the Urban Labor Market: A Study of Black Youths in Chicago." Working paper series, Malcolm Wiener Center for Social Policy, John F. Kennedy School of Government, Harvard University, March, no. H-91-3.

Holzer, Harry J., Keith R. Ihlanfeldt, and David L. Sjoquist. 1994. "Work, Search and Travel among White and Black Youth." *Journal of Urban Economics* 35:320–45.

Wilson, William Julius. 1987. *The Truly Disadvantaged: The Inner City, the Underclass, and Public Policy.* Chicago: University of Chicago Press.

40

OVER THE COUNTER
McDonald's

ROBIN LEIDNER

Robin Leidner's 1993 case study, "Over the Counter: McDonald's," takes us inside one employment organization and reveals what it is like to work there. Leidner, an associate professor of sociology at the University of Pennsylvania, shows how McDonald's employees are intensively socialized. She also illustrates how the work is reduced to simple steps, and therefore routinized, so that managers and owners can maintain the most control over their product and over their employees. This process of increased routinization in the workplace has a long history in industrialization, especially within factory work. Many social analysts, including Karl Marx (1818–1883), have argued that the routinization of work leads to workers' feeling alienated from their products and from their sense of self.

Organizations have many ways of obtaining the cooperation of participants, ranging from persuasion and enticement to force and curtailment of options. All organizations "hope to make people want to do what the organization needs done" (Biggart 1989:128), but when they cannot count on success in manipulating people's desires they can do their best to compel people to act in the organization's interests.

From *Fast Food, Fast Talk: Service Work and the Routinization of Everyday Life,* pp. 44–46, 47–48, 49–52, 53–55, 60, 65, 72–76, 82–85. Copyright © 1993 by The Regents of the University of California. Reprinted with the permission of University of California Press.

Organizations choose strategies that rely on socialization and social control in varying mixtures that are determined by the aims of the organization, the constraints set by the organizational environment and the nature of the work, and the interests and resources of the parties involved. In service-providing organizations, upper-level management must concern itself with the wishes and behavior of service recipients and various groups of workers.[1] For each group, service organizations try to find the most effective and least costly ways to get people to act in the organizations' interests, proffering various carrots and sticks, making efforts to win hearts and minds, closing off choices.

Organizations that routinize work exert control primarily by closing off choices. There is much room for variation, however, in what aspects of the work organizations will choose to routinize, how they go about it, and how much freedom of decision making remains. Moreover, even when routines radically constrain choice, organizations still must socialize participants and set up systems of incentives and disincentives to ensure the compliance of workers and customers.

. . . McDonald's . . . take[s] routinization to extremes . . . includ[ing] predetermination of action and transformation of character. . . . McDonald's stresses minute specification of procedures, eliminating most decision making for most workers, although it does make some efforts to standardize operations by transforming the characters of its store-level managers. . . .

This . . . [selection] show[s] how the compan[y's] approaches to routinizing the work of those who interact with customers depend largely on the predictability of service recipients' behavior, which in turn depends on the kinds of resources the organizations have available to channel consumer behavior. . . . At McDonald's . . . the routines sharply limit the workers' autonomy without giving them much leverage over customers.

McDonald's

No one ever walks into a McDonald's and asks, "So, what's good today?" except satirically. The heart of McDonald's success is its uniformity and predictability. Not only is the food supposed to taste the same every day everywhere in the world, but McDonald's promises that every meal will be served quickly, courteously, and with a smile. Delivering on that promise over 20 million times a day in 54 countries is the company's colossal challenge (*McDonald's Annual Report* 1990:2). Its strategy for meeting that challenge draws on scientific management's most basic tenets: Find the One Best Way to do every task and see that the work is conducted accordingly.[2]

To ensure that all McDonald's restaurants serve products of uniform quality, the company uses centralized planning, centrally designed training programs, centrally approved and supervised suppliers, automated machinery and other specially designed equipment, meticulous specifications, and systematic inspections. To provide its customers with a uniformly pleasant "McDonald's experience," the company also tries to mass produce friendliness, deference, diligence, and good cheer through a variety of socialization and social control techniques. Despite sneers from those who equate uniformity with mediocrity, the success of McDonald's has been spectacular.

McFacts

By far the world's largest fast-food company, McDonald's has over 11,800 stores worldwide (*McDonald's Annual Report* 1990:1), and its 1990 international sales surpassed those of its three largest competitors combined (Berg 1991 sec. 3:6).[3] In the United States, consumer familiarity with McDonald's is virtually universal: The company estimates that 95 percent of U.S. consumers eat at a McDonald's at least once a year (Koepp 1987:58). McDonald's 1990 profits were $802.3 million, the third highest profits of any retailing company in the world (*Fortune* 1991:179). At a time when the ability of many U.S. businesses to compete on the world market is in question, McDonald's continues to expand around the globe—most recently to Morocco—everywhere remaking consumer demand in its own image.

As politicians, union leaders, and others concerned with the effects of the shift to a service economy are quick to point out, McDonald's is a major employer. McDonald's restaurants in the United States employ about half a million people (Bertagnoli 1989:33), including one out of 15 first-time job seekers (Wildavsky 1989:30). The company claims that 7 percent of all current U.S. workers have worked for McDonald's at some time (Koepp 1987:59). Not only has McDonald's directly influenced the lives of millions of workers, but its impact has also been extended by the efforts of many kinds of organizations, especially in the service sector, to imitate the organizational features they see as central to McDonald's success. . . .

The relentless standardization and infinite replication that inspire both horror and admiration are the legacy of Ray Kroc, a salesman who got into the hamburger business in 1954, when he was 52 years old, and created a worldwide phenomenon.[4] His inspiration was a phenomenally successful hamburger stand owned by the McDonald brothers of San Bernardino, California. He believed that their success could be reproduced consistently through carefully controlled franchises, and his hamburger business succeeded on an unprecedented scale. The basic idea was to serve a very few items of strictly uniform quality at low prices. Over the years, the menu has expanded somewhat and prices have risen, but the emphasis on strict, detailed standardization has never varied. . . .

Enforcement of McDonald's standards has been made easier over the years by the introduction of highly specialized equipment. Every company-owned store in the United States now has an "in-store processor," a computer system that calculates yields and food costs, keeps track of inventory and cash, schedules labor, and breaks down sales by time of day, product, and worker (*McDonald's Annual Report* 1989:29). In today's McDonald's, lights and buzzers tell workers exactly when to turn burgers or take fries out of the fat, and technologically advanced cash registers, linked to the computer system, do much of the thinking for window workers. Specially designed ketchup dispensers squirt exactly the right amount of ketchup on each burger in the approved flower pattern. The french-fry scoops let workers fill a bag and set it down in one continuous motion and help them gauge the proper serving size.

The extreme standardization of McDonald's products, and its workers, is closely tied to its marketing. The company advertises on a massive scale—in 1989, McDonald's spent $1.1 billion systemwide on advertising and promotions (*McDonald's Annual Report* 1989:32). In fact, McDonald's is the single most advertised brand in the world (*Advertising Age* 1990:6).[5] The national advertising assures the public that it will find high standards of quality, service, and cleanliness at every McDonald's store. The intent of the strict quality-control standards applied to every aspect of running a McDonald's outlet, from proper cleaning of the bathrooms to making sure the hamburgers are served hot, is to help franchise owners keep the promises made in the company's advertising.[6]

The image of McDonald's outlets promoted in the company's advertising is one of fun, wholesomeness, and family orientation. Kroc was particularly concerned that his stores not become teenage hangouts, since that would discourage families' patronage. To minimize their attractiveness to teenage loiterers, McDonald's stores do not have jukeboxes, video games, or even telephones. Kroc initially decided not to hire young women to work behind McDonald's counters for the same reason: "They attracted the wrong kind of boys" (Boas and Chain 1976:19).

You Deserve a Break Today: Conditions of Employment

Although McDonald's does not want teenagers to hang out on its premises, it certainly does want them to work in the stores. Almost half of its U.S. employees are under 20 years old (Wildavsky 1989:30). In recent years, as the McDonald's chain has grown faster than the supply of teenagers, the company has also tried to attract senior citizens and housewives as workers. What people in these groups have in common is a preference or need for part-time work, and therefore a dearth of alternative employment options. Because of this lack of good alternatives, and because they may have other means of support for themselves and their dependents, many people in these groups are willing to accept jobs that provide less than subsistence wages.

Traditionally, McDonald's has paid most of its employees the minimum wage, although labor shortages have now forced wages up in some parts of the country, raising the average hourly pay of crew people to $4.60 by 1989

(Gibson and Johnson 1989:B1). Benefits such as health insurance and sick days are entirely lacking for crew people at most franchises. In fact, when the topic of employee benefits was introduced in a class lecture at McDonald's management training center, it turned out to refer to crew meetings, individual work-evaluation sessions, and similar programs to make McDonald's management seem accessible and fair.

The lack of more tangible benefits is linked to the organization of employment at McDonald's as part-time work. According to the manager of the franchise I studied, all McDonald's hourly employees are officially part-time workers, in that no one is guaranteed a full work week. The company's labor practices are designed to make workers bear the costs of uncertainty based on fluctuation in demand. McDonald's places great emphasis on having no more crew people at work at any time than are required by customer flow at that period, as measured in half-hour increments. Most workers therefore have fluctuating schedules, and they are expected to be flexible about working late or leaving early depending on the volume of business.

Not surprisingly, McDonald's employee-turnover rates are extremely high. Turnover averaged 153 percent in 1984, and 205 percent in 1985 (training center lecture). These high rates are partly attributable to the large percentage of teenage workers, many of whom took the job with the intention of working for only a short time. However, the limited job rewards, both financial and personal, of working at McDonald's are certainly crucial contributing factors.

Some argue that the conditions of employment at McDonald's are unproblematic to the workers who take them. If we assume that most McDonald's workers are teenagers who are in school and are not responsible for supporting themselves or others, then many of the features of McDonald's work do not seem so bad. Fringe benefits and employment security are relatively unimportant to them, and the limited and irregular hours of work may actually be attractive (see Greenberger and Steinberg 1986). These arguments are less persuasive when applied to other McDonald's employees, such as mothers of young children, and retirees, although those workers might similarly appreciate the part-time hours, and access to other forms of income and benefits could make McDonald's employment conditions acceptable, if not desirable. Employment security would not be important to the many people who choose to work at McDonald's as a stopgap or for a limited period.[7] Many of the workers at the franchise I studied had taken their jobs with the intention of holding them only temporarily, and many were being supported by their parents. However, other workers there were trying to support themselves and their dependents on earnings from McDonald's, sometimes in combination with other low-paying jobs. . . .

McDonald's wants both managers and workers to dedicate themselves to the values summed up in its three-letter corporate credo, "QSC." Quality, service, and cleanliness are the ends that the company's thousands of rules and specifications are intended to achieve. Kroc promised his customers QSC,[8] and he believed firmly that if, at every level of the organization, McDonald's workers were committed to providing higher-quality food, speedier service, and cleaner surroundings than the competition, the success of the enterprise was assured. McDonald's extraordinarily elaborate training programs are designed both to teach McDonald's procedures and standards and to instill and enforce corporate values.

Kroc approached his business with a zeal and dedication that even he regarded as religious: "I've often said that *I believe in God, family, and McDonald's—and in the office that order is reversed*" (Kroc with Anderson 1977:124 [emphasis in original]). Throughout the organization, Kroc is still frequently quoted and held up as a model, and nowhere is his ongoing influence more apparent than at Hamburger University.

Taking Hamburgers Seriously: Training Managers

McDonald's main management training facility is located on 80 beautifully landscaped acres in Oak Brook, Illinois, a suburb of Chicago. Its name, Hamburger University, captures the thoroughness and intensity with which McDonald's approaches management training, and it also suggests the comic possibilities of immersion in McDonald's corporate world.[9] The company tries to produce managers "with ketchup in their veins," a common McDonald's phrase for people who love their work, take pride in it, and are extraordinarily hardworking, competitive, and loyal to McDonald's. A line I heard frequently at Hamburger U. was, "We take hamburgers very seriously here." Nothing I saw called this fixity of purpose into doubt.

Ensuring uniformity of service and products in its far-flung empire is a major challenge for McDonald's. In each McDonald's store, in regional training centers, and at Hamburger University, crew people, managers, and franchisees learn that there is a McDonald's way to handle virtually every detail of the business and that doing things differently means doing things wrong. Training begins in the stores, where crew people are instructed using materials provided by the corporation and where managers prepare for more advanced training. Management trainees and managers seeking promotion work with their store managers to learn materials in manuals and workbooks provided by the corporation. When they have completed the manual for the appropriate level, they are eligible for courses taught in regional training centers and at Hamburger University: the Basic Operations Course, the Intermediate Operations Course, the Applied Equipment Course, and, finally, the Advanced Operations Course, taught only at Hamburger University. Altogether, the full training program requires approximately six hundred to one thousand hours of work. It is required of everyone who wishes to own a McDonald's store, and it is strongly recommended for all store managers. By the time trainees get to Hamburger University for the Advanced Operations Course, they have already put in considerable time working in a McDonald's store—two to three and a half years, on average—and have acquired much detailed knowledge about McDonald's workings.

Hamburger University sometimes offers special programs and seminars in addition to the regular training courses. For example, a group of McDonald's office workers attended Hamburger University during my visit; a training manager told me that they had been brought in to get "a little shot of ketchup and mustard." [10]

The zeal and competence of franchisees and managers are of special concern to McDonald's, since they are the people responsible for daily enforcement of corporate standards. Their training therefore focuses as much on building commitment and motivation as on extending knowledge of company procedures. In teaching management skills, McDonald's also works on the personalities of its managers, encouraging both rigid adherence to routines and, somewhat paradoxically, personal flexibility. Flexibility is presented as a virtue both because the company wants to minimize resistance to adopting McDonald's ways of doing things and to frequent revision of procedures, and because managers must provide whatever responsiveness to special circumstances the system has, since crew people are allowed virtually no discretion. Hamburger University therefore provides a large dose of personal-growth cheerleading along with more prosaic skills training. . . .

The curriculum of the Advanced Operating Course includes inculcation with pride in McDonald's. Sessions are devoted to McDonald's history and McDonald's dedication to ever-improving QSC. Lectures are sprinkled with statistics attesting to McDonald's phenomenal success. Students hear the story of Ray Kroc's rise to wealth and prominence, based on his strength of character and willingness to work hard, and are assigned his autobiography, *Grinding It Out* (Kroc with Anderson 1977). Kroc is quoted frequently in lectures, and students are encouraged to model themselves on him. They are told repeatedly that they have all proven themselves "winners" by getting as far as they have at McDonald's. The theme throughout is "We're the best in the world, we know exactly what we're doing, but our success depends on the best efforts of every one of you." [11]

About 3,500 students from all over the world attend classes at Hamburger University each year, most of them taking the Advanced Operations Course (Rosenthal 1989). Those who complete the course receive diplomas proclaiming them Doctors of Hamburgerology. As late as 1978 or 1979, a training manager told me, most classes included only one or two women, but women now comprise 40–60 percent of the students, and women and minorities now make up 54 percent of McDonald's franchisees (Bertagnoli 1989:33). In my homeroom, however, the proportion of women was much smaller, and there was just a handful of minority students.

The course lasts two weeks and is extremely rigorous. Class time is about evenly divided between work in the labs and lectures on store operations and personnel management. In the labs, trainees learn the mechanics of ensuring that McDonald's food is of consistent quality and its stores in good working order. They learn to check the equipment and maintain it properly so that fries cook at precisely the right temperature, shakes are mixed to just the right consistency, and ice cubes are uniform. "Taste of Quality" labs reinforce McDonald's standards for food quality. For instance, in a Condiments Lab, trainees are taught exactly how to store vegetables and sauces, what the shelf lives of these products are, and how they should look and taste. Samples of "McDonald's quality" Big Mac Special Sauce are contrasted with samples that have been left too long unrefrigerated and should be discarded. The importance of serving only food that meets McDonald's standards is constantly emphasized and, a trainer pointed out, "McDonald's has standards for everything, down to the width of the pickle slices." . . .

The training at Hamburger University combines a sense of fun with dead seriousness about keeping McDonald's on top in the hamburger business through relentless quality control and effective management of workers and customers. It is up to the owners and managers of individual McDonald's stores to make that happen. . . .

Learning the Job

As a manager at Hamburger University explained to me, the crew training process is how McDonald's standardization is maintained, how the company ensures that Big Macs are the same everywhere in the world. The McDonald's central administration supplies franchisees with videotapes and other materials for use in training workers to meet the company's exacting specifications. The company produces a separate videotape for each job in the store, and it encourages franchisees to keep their tape libraries up-to-date as product specifications change. The Hamburger University professor who taught the Advanced Operating Course session on training said that, to keep current, franchisees should be buying 10 or 12 tapes a year. For each work station in the store, McDonald's also has a "Station Operation Checklist" (SOC), a short but highly detailed job description that lays out exactly how the job should be done: how much ketchup and mustard go on each kind of hamburger, in what sequence the products customers order are to be gathered, what arm motion is to be used in salting a batch of fries, and so on. . . .

The Routine

McDonald's had routinized the work of its crews so thoroughly that decision making had practically been eliminated from the jobs. As one window worker told me, "They've tried to break it down so that it's almost idiot-proof." Most of the workers agreed that there was little call for them to use their own judgment on the job, since there were rules about everything. If an unusual problem arose, the workers were supposed to turn it over to a manager.

Many of the noninteractive parts of the window workers' job had been made idiot-proof through automation.[12] The soda machines, for example, automatically dispensed the proper amount of beverage for regular, medium, and large cups. Computerized cash registers performed a variety of functions handled elsewhere by human waitresses, waiters, and cashiers, making some kinds of skill and knowledge unnecessary. As a customer gave an order, the window worker simply pressed the cash register button labeled with the name of the selected product. There was no need to write the orders down, because the buttons lit up to indicate which products had been selected. Nor was there any need to remember prices, because the prices were programmed into the machines. Like most new cash registers, these added the tax automatically and told workers how much change customers were owed, so the window crew did not need to know how to do those calculations. The cash registers also helped regulate some of the crew's interactive work by reminding them to try to increase the size of each sale. For example, when a customer ordered a Big Mac, large fries, and a regular Coke, the cash register buttons for cookies, hot apple pies, ice cream cones, and ice cream sundaes would light up, prompting the worker to suggest dessert. It took some skill to operate the relatively complicated cash register, as my difficulties during my first work shift made clear, but this organizationally specific skill could soon be acquired on the job.

In addition to doing much of the workers' thinking for them, the computerized cash registers made it possible for managers to monitor the crew members' work and the store's inventory very closely.[13] For example, if the number of Quarter Pounder with Cheese boxes gone did not match the number of Quarter Pounders with Cheese sold or accounted for as waste, managers might suspect that workers were giving away or taking food. Managers could easily tell which workers had brought in the most money during a given interval and who was doing the best job of persuading customers to buy a particular item. The computerized system could also complicate what would otherwise have been simple customer requests, however. For example, when a man who had not realized the benefit of ordering his son's food as a Happy Meal came back to the counter to ask whether his little boy could have one of the plastic beach pails the Happy Meals were served in, I had to ask a manager what to do, since fulfilling the request would produce a discrepancy between the inventory and the receipts.[14] Sometimes the extreme systematization can induce rather than prevent idiocy, as when a window worker says she cannot serve a cup of coffee that is half decaffeinated and half regular because she would not know how to ring up the sale.[15]

The interactive part of window work is routinized through the Six Steps of Window Service and also through rules aimed at standardizing attitudes and demeanors as well as words and actions. The window workers were taught that they represented McDonald's to the public and that their attitudes were therefore an important component of service quality. Crew people could be reprimanded for not smiling, and often were. The window workers were supposed to be cheerful and polite at all times, but they were also told to be themselves while on the job. McDonald's does not want its workers to seem like robots, so part of the emotion work asked of the window crew is that they act naturally. "Being yourself" in this situation meant behaving in a way that did not seem stilted. Although workers had some latitude to go beyond the script, the short, highly schematic routine obviously did not allow much room for genuine self-expression.

Workers were not the only ones constrained by McDonald's routines, of course. The cooperation of service recipients was crucial to the smooth functioning of the operation. In many kinds of interactive service work . . . constructing the compliance of service recipients is an important part of the service worker's job. The routines such workers use may be designed to maximize the control each worker has over customers. McDonald's window workers' routines were not intended to give them much leverage over customers' behavior, however. The window workers interacted only with people who had already decided to do business with McDonald's and who therefore did not need to be persuaded to take part in the service interaction. Furthermore, almost all customers were familiar enough with McDonald's routines to know how they were expected to behave. For instance, I never saw a customer who did not know that she or he was supposed to come up to the counter rather than sit down and wait to be served. This customer training was accomplished through advertising, spatial design, customer experience, and the example of other customers, making it unnecessary for the window crew to put much effort into getting customers to fit into their work routines.[16]

McDonald's ubiquitous advertising trains consumers at the same time that it tries to attract them to McDonald's. Television commercials demonstrate how the service system is supposed to work and familiarize customers with new products. Additional cues about expected customer behavior are provided by the design of the restaurants. For example, the entrances usually lead to the service counter, not to the dining area, making it unlikely that customers will fail to realize that they should get in line, and the placement of waste cans makes clear that customers are expected to throw out their own trash. Most important, the majority of customers have had years of experience with McDonald's, as well as with other fast-food restaurants that have similar arrangements. The company estimates that the average customer visits a McDonald's 20 times a year (Koepp 1987:58), and it is not uncommon for a customer to come in several times per week. For many customers, then, ordering at McDonald's is as routine an interaction as it is for the window worker. Indeed, because employee turnover is so high, steady customers may be more familiar with the work routines than the workers serving them are. Customers who are new to McDonald's can take their cue from more experienced customers.[17]

Not surprisingly, then, most customers at the McDonald's I studied knew what was expected of them and tried to play their part well. They sorted themselves into lines and gazed up at the menu boards while waiting to be served. They usually gave their orders in the conventional sequence: burgers or other entrees, french fries or other side orders, drinks, and desserts. Hurried customers with savvy might order an item "only if it's in the bin," that is, ready to be served. Many customers prepared carefully so that they could give their orders promptly when they got to the counter. This preparation sometimes became apparent when a worker interrupted to ask, "What kind of dressing?" or "Cream and sugar?", flustering customers who could not deliver their orders as planned.

McDonald's routines, like those of other interactive service businesses, depend on the predictability of customers, but these businesses must not grind to a halt if customers are not completely cooperative. Some types of deviations from standard customer behavior are so common that they become routine themselves, and these can be handled through subroutines (Stinchcombe 1990:39). McDonald's routines work most efficiently when all customers accept their products exactly as they are usually prepared; indeed, the whole business is based on this premise. Since, however, some people give special instructions for customized products, such as "no onions," the routine allows for these exceptions.[18] At the franchise I studied, workers could key the special requests into their cash registers, which automatically printed out "grill slips" with the instructions for the grill workers to follow. Under this system, the customer making the special order had to wait for it to be prepared, but the smooth flow of service for other customers was not interrupted. Another type of routine difficulty was customer dissatisfaction with food quality. Whenever a customer had a complaint about the food — cold fries, dried-out burger — window workers were authorized to supply a new product immediately without consulting a supervisor.[19]

These two kinds of difficulties—special orders and complaints about food—were the only irregularities window workers were authorized to handle. The subroutines increased the flexibility of the service system, but they did not increase the workers' discretion, since procedures were in place for dealing with both situations. All other kinds of demands fell outside the window crew's purview. If they were faced with a dispute about money, an extraordinary request, or a furious customer, workers were instructed to call a manager; the crew had no authority to handle such problems.

Given the almost complete regimentation of tasks and preemption of decision making, does McDonald's need the flexibility and thoughtfulness of human workers? As the declining supply of teenagers and legislated increases in the minimum wage drive up labor costs, it is not surprising that McDonald's is experimenting with electronic replacements. So far, the only robot in use handles behind-the-scenes work rather than customer interactions. ARCH (Automated Restaurant Crew Helper) works in a Minnesota McDonald's where it does all the frying and lets workers know when to prepare sandwich buns, when supplies are running low, and when fries are no longer fresh enough to sell. Other McDonald's stores (along with Arby's and Burger King units) are experimenting with a touch-screen computer system that lets customers order their meals themselves, further curtailing the role of the window worker. Although it requires increased customer socialization and cooperation, early reports are that the system cuts service time by 30 seconds and increases sales per window worker 10–20 percent (Chaudhry 1989:F61).

Overview

McDonald's pioneered the routinization of interactive service work and remains an exemplar of extreme standardization. Innovation is not discouraged at McDonald's; the company favors experimentation, at least among managers and franchisees. Ironically, though, "the object is to look for new, innovative ways to create an experience that is exactly the same no matter what McDonald's you walk into, no matter where it is in the world" (Rosenthal 1989:12). Thus, when someone in the field comes up with a good idea— and such McDonald's success stories as the Egg McMuffin and the Big Mac were store-level inspirations (Koepp 1987:60)—the corporation experiments, tests, and refines the idea and finally implements it in a uniform way systemwide. One distinctive feature of McDonald's-style routinization is that there, to a great extent, uniformity is a goal in itself. . . .

McDonald's . . . does promise uniform products and consistent service, and to provide them the company has broken down virtually every task required to run a store into detailed routines with clear instructions and standards. For those routines to run smoothly, conditions must be relatively predictable, so McDonald's tries to control as many contingencies as possible, including the attitudes and behavior of workers, managers, and customers. The company uses a wide array of socialization and control techniques to ensure that these people are familiar with McDonald's procedures and willing to comply with them.

Most McDonald's work is organized as low-paying, low-status, part-time jobs that give workers little autonomy. Almost every decision about how to do crew people's tasks has been made in advance by the corporation, and many of the decisions have been built into the stores' technology. Why use human workers at all, if not to take advantage of the human capacity to respond to circumstances flexibly? McDonald's does want to provide at least a simulacrum of the human attributes of warmth, friendliness, and recognition. For that reason, not only workers' movements but also their words, demeanor, and attitudes are subject to managerial control.

Although predictability is McDonald's hallmark, not all factors can be controlled by management. One of the most serious irregularities that store management must deal with is fluctuation in the flow of customers, both expected and unexpected. Since personnel costs are the most manipulable variable affecting a store's profitability, managers want to match labor power to consumer demand as exactly as possible. They do so by paying all crew people by the hour, giving them highly irregular hours based on expected sales—sometimes including split shifts—and sending workers home early or keeping them late as conditions require. In other words, the costs of uneven demand are shifted to workers whenever possible. Since most McDonald's crew people cannot count on working a particular number of hours at precisely scheduled times, it is hard for them to make plans based on how much money they will earn or exactly what times they will be free. Workers are pressured to be flexible in order to maximize the organization's own flexibility in staffing levels. In contrast, of course, flexibility in the work process itself is minimized.

Routinization has not made the crew people's work easy. Their jobs, although highly structured and repetitive, are often demanding and stressful. Under these working conditions, the organization's limited commitment to workers, as reflected in job security, wages, and benefits, makes the task of maintaining worker motivation and discipline even more challenging. A variety of factors, many orchestrated by the corporation, keeps McDonald's crew people hard at work despite the limited rewards. Socialization into McDonald's norms, extremely close supervision (both human and electronic), individual and group incentives, peer pressure, and pressure from customers all play their part in getting workers to do things the McDonald's way.

Because franchisees and store-level managers are responsible for enforcing standardization throughout the McDonald's system, their socialization includes a more intensive focus on building commitment to and pride in the organization than does crew training. In fact, it is the corporate attempt at transforming these higher-level McDonald's people by making them more loyal, confident, flexible, and sensitive to others, as well as more knowledgeable about company procedures, that makes the extreme rigidity of the crew training workable. The crew people do not have to be trusted with decision-making authority, because all unusual problems are referred to managers. Their more extensive training gives them the knowledge and attitudes to make the kinds of decisions the corporation would approve. . . . In addition to thorough socialization, McDonald's managers and franchisees are subjected to close corporate oversight. Every aspect of their stores' operations is rated by corporate staff, and they are sanctioned accordingly.

Despite elaborate socialization and social controls, McDonald's stores do not, of course, carry out every corporate directive exactly as recommended. In the store I studied, managers did not always provide their workers with the mandated support and encouragement, crew trainers did not always follow the four-step training system, and window workers did not always carry out the Six Steps of Window Service with the required eye contact and smile. There were many kinds of pressures to deviate from corporate standards. Nonetheless, the benefits of standardization should not be underestimated. As every Durkheimian knows, clear rules and shared standards provide support and coherence as well as constraint. Although some aspects of the routines did strike the participants as overly constraining, undignified, or silly, the approved routines largely worked. In all of these examples of deviation, the routines would have produced more efficient and pleasant service, and those that apply to management and training would have benefited workers as well as customers.

Obtaining the cooperation of workers and managers is not enough to ensure the smooth functioning of McDonald's relatively inflexible routines. Customers must be routinized as well. Not only do customers have to understand the service routine and accept the limited range of choices the company offers, they also must be willing to do some kinds of work that are done for them in conventional restaurants, including carrying food to the table and throwing out their trash. Experience, advertising, the example set by other customers, and clear environmental cues familiarize customers with McDonald's routines, and most want to cooperate in order to speed service. For these reasons, McDonald's interactive service workers do not have to direct most customers, and window workers' routines are therefore not designed to give them power over customers.

ENDNOTES

[1] Suppliers, competitors, and other parties outside of the organization are also relevant actors, but organizational efforts to control their behavior will not be considered here (see Prus 1989).

[2] The 1990s may bring unprecedented changes to McDonald's. Although its overseas business continues to thrive, domestic sales have been declining. To overcome the challenges to profitability presented by the economic recession, lower-priced competitors, and changes in consumer tastes, CEO Michael Quinlan has instituted experimental changes in the menu, in pricing strategy, and even in the degree of flexibility granted to franchisees (see *Advertising Age* 1991; Berg 1991; *McDonald's Annual Report* 1990; Therrien 1991).

[3] McDonald's restaurants are generally referred to as "stores" by McDonald's staff. The company's share of the domestic fast-food market has declined from 18.7 percent in 1985 to 16.6 percent in 1990 (Therrien 1991).

[4] Information about McDonald's history comes primarily from Boas and Chain 1976; Kroc with Anderson 1977; Love 1986; Luxenberg 1985; and McDonald's training materials. Reiter's (1991) description of Burger King reveals numerous parallels in the operation of the two companies, although Burger King, unlike McDonald's, is a subsidiary of a multinational conglomerate.

[5] In addition to paid advertising, McDonald's bolsters its public image with promotional and philanthropic activities such as an All-American High School Basketball Game, essay contests and scholarship programs for black and Hispanic students, and Ronald McDonald Houses where outpatient children and their families and the parents of hospitalized children can stay at minimal cost.

[6] Conversely, details of the routines are designed with marketing in mind. The bags that hold the regular-size portions of french fries are shorter than the french fries are, so that when workers fill them with their regulation french-fry scoops, the servings seem generous, overflowing the packaging. The names of the serving sizes also are intended to give customers the impression that they are getting a lot for their money: French fries come in regular and large sizes, sodas in regular, medium, and large cups. I was quickly corrected during a work shift when I inadvertently referred to an order for a "small" drink.

[7] Some commentators fall into the trap of assuming that workers' preferences are determinative of working conditions, a mistake they do not make when discussing higher-status workers such as faculty who must rely on a string of temporary appointments.

[8] Actually, Kroc usually spoke of QSCV—quality, service, cleanliness, and value (see Kroc with Anderson 1977)—but QSC was the term used in most McDonald's training and motivational materials at the time of my research. The company cannot enforce "value" because antitrust restrictions prevent McDonald's from dictating prices to its franchisees (Love 1986:145). Nevertheless, recent materials return to the original four-part pledge of QSC & V (see, e.g., *McDonald's Annual Report* 1989:i).

[9] Branches of Hamburger University now operate in London, Munich, and Tokyo (*McDonald's Annual Report* 1989:28). Burger King University is similar in many respects (Reiter 1991).

[10] The effort to involve corporate employees in the central mission of the organization extends beyond such special programs. McDonald's prides itself on keeping its corporate focus firmly on store-level operations, and it wants all its employees to have a clear idea of what it takes to make a McDonald's restaurant work. Therefore, all McDonald's employees, from attorneys to data-entry clerks, spend time working in a McDonald's restaurant.

[11] Biggart (1989:143–47) shows that both adulation of a charismatic founder and repeated characterization of participants as winners are common in direct-sales organizations. Like McDonald's, such organizations face the problem of motivating people who are widely dispersed geographically and who are not corporate employees.

[12] The in-store processors similarly affected managers' work. A disaffected McDonald's manager told Garson, "There is no such thing as a McDonald's manager. The computer manages the store" (Garson 1988:39).

[13] Garson (1988) provides an extended discussion of this point.

[14] The manager gave him the pail but had to ring it up on the machine as if he had given away a whole Happy Meal.

[15] Thanks to Charles Bosk for this story.

[16] Mills (1986) elaborates on "customer socialization." Environmental design as a factor in service provision is discussed by Wener (1985) and Normann (1984).

[17] The importance of customer socialization becomes apparent when people with very different consumer experiences are introduced to a service system. When the first McDonald's opened in the Soviet Union in 1990, Moscow's citizens did not find the system immediately comprehensible. They had to be persuaded to get on the shortest lines at the counter, since they had learned from experience that desirable goods were available only where there are long lines (Goldman 1990).

[18] Burger King's "Have it your way" campaign virtually forced McDonald's to allow such customized service.

[19] The defective food or its container was put into a special waste bin. Each shift, one worker or manager had the unenviable task of counting the items in the waste bin so that the inventory could be reconciled with the cash intake.

REFERENCES

Advertising Age. 1990. "Adman of the Decade: McDonald's Fred Turner: Making All the Right Moves," January 1, p. 6.

———. 1991. "100 Leading National Advertisers: McDonald's," September 25, pp. 49–50.

Berg, Eric N. 1991. "An American Icon Wrestles with a Troubled Future." *New York Times*, May 12, sec. 3, pp. 1, 6.

Bertagnoli, Lisa. 1989. "McDonald's: Company of the Quarter Century." *Restaurants and Institutions*, July 10, pp. 32–60.

Biggart, Nicole Woolsey. 1989. *Charismatic Capitalism: Direct Selling Organizations in America*. Chicago: University of Chicago Press. Pp. 128, 143–47.

Boas, Max and Steve Chain. 1976. *Big Mac: The Unauthorized Story of McDonald's*. New York: New American Library. P. 19.

Chaudhry, Rajan. 1989. "Burger Giants Singed by Battle." *Nation's Restaurant News*, August 7, p. F61.

"Fortune Global Service 500: The 50 Largest Retailing Companies." 1991. *Fortune*, August 26, p. 179.

Garson, Barbara. 1988. *The Electronic Sweatshop: How Computers Are Transforming the Office of the Future into the Factory of the Past*. New York: Simon and Schuster. P. 39.

Gibson, Richard and Robert Johnson. 1989. "Big Mac Plots Strategy to Regain Sizzle." *Wall Street Journal*, September 29, p. B1.

Goldman, Marshall. 1990. Presentation at colloquium on Reforming the Soviet Economy, University of Pennsylvania, May 17.

Greenberger, Ellen and Laurence Steinberg. 1986. *When Teenagers Work: The Psychological and Social Costs of Adolescent Employment*. New York: Basic Books.

Koepp, Stephen. 1987. "Big Mac Strikes Back." *Time*, April 13, p. 60.

Kroc, Ray with Robert Anderson. 1977. *Grinding It Out: The Making of McDonald's*. Chicago: Contemporary Books. P. 124.

Love, John F. 1986. *McDonald's: Behind the Arches*. New York: Bantam Books. P. 145.

Luxenberg, Stan. 1985. *Roadside Empires: How the Chains Franchised America*. New York: Viking.

McDonald's Annual Report. 1989. Oak Brook, Illinois. Pp. i, 28, 29, 32.

———. 1990. Oak Brook, Illinois. Pp. 1–2.

Mills, Peter K. 1986. *Managing Service Industries: Organizational Practices in a Post-Industrial Economy*. Cambridge, MA: Ballinger.

Normann, Richard. 1984. *Service Management: Strategy and Leadership in Service Businesses*. Chichester, England: Wiley.

Prus, Robert. 1989. *Pursuing Customers: An Ethnography of Marketing Activities*. Newbury Park, CA: Sage.

Reiter, Ester. 1991. *Making Fast Food: From the Frying Pan into the Fryer*. Montreal: McGill-Queen's University Press.

Rosenthal, Herman M. 1989. "Inside Big Mac's World." *Newsday*, June 4, p. 12.

Stinchcombe, Arthur L. 1990. *Information and Organizations*. Berkeley: University of California Press. P. 39.

Therrien, Lois. 1991. "McRisky." *Business Week*, October 21, pp. 114–22.

Wener, Richard E. 1985. "The Environmental Psychology of Service Encounters." Pp. 101–12 in *The Service Encounter: Managing Employee/Customer Interaction in Service Businesses*, edited by John A. Czepiel, Michael R. Solomon, and Carol F. Surprenant. Lexington, MA: Lexington Books.

Wildavsky, Ben. 1989. "McJobs: Inside America's Largest Youth Training Program." *Policy Review* 49:30–37.

RELIGION

41

THE PROTESTANT ETHIC
AND THE SPIRIT OF CAPITALISM

MAX WEBER

The institution of religion is the topic of the following three selections. Sociologists have long studied how religion affects the social structure and the
personal experience of individuals in society. Max Weber (1858–1917), for
example, often placed the institution of religion at the center of his social
analyses. Weber was particularly concerned with how changes in the institution of religion influenced changes in other social institutions, especially
the economy. The selection excerpted here is from Weber's definitive and
most famous study, *The Protestant Ethic and the Spirit of Capitalism* (1905). In
his analysis of capitalism, Weber argues that the early Protestant worldviews of Calvinism and Puritanism were the primary factors in influencing
the development of a capitalist economic system. Without the Protestant
Reformation and a change in societal values toward rationality, capitalism
would not have evolved as we know it today.

A product of modern European civilization, studying any problem of
universal history, is bound to ask himself to what combination of circumstances the fact should be attributed that in Western civilization,
and in Western civilization only, cultural phenomena have appeared which
(as we like to think) lie in a line of development having *universal* significance
and value. . . . All over the world there have been merchants, wholesale and
retail, local and engaged in foreign trade. . . .

But in modern times the Occident has developed, in addition to this, a
very different form of capitalism which has appeared nowhere else: the rational capitalistic organization of (formally) free labour. Only suggestions of
it are found elsewhere. Even the organization of unfree labour reached a
considerable degree of rationality only on plantations and to a very limited
extent in the *Ergasteria* of antiquity. In the manors, manorial workshops, and

---

From *The Protestant Ethic and the Spirit of Capitalism* by Max Weber, © 1958 Prentice-
Hall, Inc. Reprinted by permission of Prentice-Hall, Inc., Upper Saddle River, NJ.

domestic industries on estates with serf labour it was probably somewhat less developed. Even real domestic industries with free labour have definitely been proved to have existed in only a few isolated cases outside the Occident. . . .

Rational industrial organization, attuned to a regular market, and neither to political nor irrationally speculative opportunities for profit, is not, however, the only peculiarity of Western capitalism. The modern rational organization of the capitalistic enterprise would not have been possible without two other important factors in its development: the separation of business from the household, which completely dominates modern economic life, and closely connected with it, rational bookkeeping. . . .

Hence in a universal history of culture the central problem for us is not, in the last analysis, even from a purely economic view-point, the development of capitalistic activity as such, differing in different cultures only in form: the adventurer type, or capitalism in trade, war, politics, or administration as sources of gain. It is rather the origin of this sober bourgeois capitalism with its rational organization of free labour. Or in terms of cultural history, the problem is that of the origin of the Western bourgeois class and of its peculiarities, a problem which is certainly closely connected with that of the origin of the capitalistic organization of labour, but is not quite the same thing. For the bourgeois as a class existed prior to the development of the peculiar modern form of capitalism, though, it is true, only in the Western hemisphere.

Now the peculiar modern Western form of capitalism has been, at first sight, strongly influenced by the development of technical possibilities. Its rationality is today essentially dependent on the calculability of the most important technical factors. But this means fundamentally that it is dependent on the peculiarities of modern science, especially the natural sciences based on mathematics and exact and rational experiment. On the other hand, the development of these sciences and of the technique resting upon them now receives important stimulation from these capitalistic interests in its practical economic application. It is true that the origin of Western science cannot be attributed to such interests. Calculation, even with decimals, and algebra have been carried on in India, where the decimal system was invented. But it was only made use of by developing capitalism in the West, while in India it led to no modern arithmetic or book-keeping. Neither was the origin of mathematics and mechanics determined by capitalistic interests. But the *technical* utilization of scientific knowledge, so important for the living conditions of the mass of people, was certainly encouraged by economic considerations, which were extremely favourable to it in the Occident. But this encouragement was derived from the peculiarities of the social structure of the Occident. We must hence ask, from *what* parts of that structure was it derived, since not all of them have been of equal importance?

Among those of undoubted importance are the rational structures of law and of administration. For modern rational capitalism has need, not only of the technical means of production, but of a calculable legal system and of administration in terms of formal rules. Without it adventurous and speculative trading capitalism and all sorts of politically determined capitalisms are possible, but no rational enterprise under individual initiative, with fixed capital and certainty of calculations. Such a legal system and such administration have been available for economic activity in a comparative state of legal and formalistic perfection only in the Occident. We must hence inquire where that law came from. Among other circumstances, capitalistic interest have in turn undoubtedly also helped, but by no means alone nor even principally, to prepare the way for the predominance in law and administration of a class of jurists specially trained in rational law. But these interests did not themselves create that law. Quite different forces were at work in this development. And why did not the capitalistic interests do the same in China or India? Why did not the scientific, the artistic, the political, or the economic development there enter upon that path of rationalization which is peculiar to the Occident?

For in all the above cases it is a question of the specific and peculiar rationalism of Western culture. . . . It is hence our first concern to work out and to explain genetically the special peculiarity of Occidental rationalism, and within this field that of the modern Occidental form. Every such attempt at explanation must, recognizing the fundamental importance of the economic factor, above all take account of the economic conditions. But at the same time the opposite correlation must not be left out of consideration. For though the development of economic rationalism is partly dependent on rational technique and law, it is at the same time determined by the ability and disposition of men to adopt certain types of practical rational conduct. When these types have been obstructed by spiritual obstacles, the development of rational economic conduct has also met serious inner resistance. The magical and religious forces, and the ethical ideas of duty based upon them, have in the past always been among the most important formative influences on conduct. In the studies collected here we shall be concerned with these forces.

Two older essays have been placed at the beginning which attempt, at one important point, to approach the side of the problem which is generally most difficult to grasp: the influence of certain religious ideas on the development of an economic spirit, or the *ethos* of an economic system. In this case we are dealing with the connection of the spirit of modern economic life with the rational ethics of ascetic Protestantism. Thus we treat here only one side of the causal chain. . . .

. . . [T]hat side of English Puritanism which was derived from Calvinism gives the most consistent religious basis for the idea of the calling. . . . For the saints' everlasting rest is in the next world; on earth man must, to be certain of his state of grace, "do the works of him who sent him, as long as it is yet day." Not leisure and enjoyment, but only activity serves to increase the glory of God according to the definite manifestations of His will.

Waste of time is thus the first and in principle the deadliest of sins. The span of human life is infinitely short and precious to make sure of one's own election. Loss of time through sociability, idle talk, luxury, even more sleep than is necessary for health, six to at most eight hours, is worthy of absolute moral condemnation. It does not yet hold, with Franklin, that time is money, but the proposition is true in a certain spiritual sense. It is infinitely valuable because every hour lost is lost to labour for the glory of God. Thus inactive contemplation is also valueless, or even directly reprehensible if it is at the expense of one's daily work. . . .

[T]he same prescription is given for all sexual temptation as is used against religious doubts and a sense of moral unworthiness: "Work hard in your calling." But the most important thing was that even beyond that labour came to be considered in itself the end of life, ordained as such by God. St. Paul's "He who will not work shall not eat" holds unconditionally for everyone. Unwillingness to work is symptomatic of the lack of grace.

Here the difference from the mediæval viewpoint becomes quite evident. Thomas Aquinas also gave an interpretation of that statement of St. Paul. But for him labour is only necessary *naturali ratione* for the maintenance of individual and community. Where this end is achieved, the precept ceases to have any meaning. Moreover, it holds only for the race, not for every individual. It does not apply to anyone who can live without labour on his possessions, and of course contemplation, as a spiritual form of action in the Kingdom of God, takes precedence over the commandment in its literal sense. Moreover, for the popular theology of the time, the highest form of monastic productivity lay in the increase of the *Thesaurus eccleslice* through prayer and chant.

. . . For everyone without exception God's Providence has prepared a calling, which he should profess and in which he should labour. And this calling is not, as it was for the Lutheran, a fate to which he must submit and which he must make the best of, but God's commandment to the individual to work for the divine glory. This seemingly subtle difference had far-reaching psychological consequences, and became connected with a further development of the providential interpretation of the economic order which had begun in scholasticism.

It is true that the usefulness of a calling, and thus its favour in the sight of God, is measured primarily in moral terms, and thus in terms of the importance of the goods produced in it for the community. But a further, and, above all, in practice the most important, criterion is found in private profitableness. For if that God, whose hand the Puritan sees in all the occurrences of life, shows one of His elect a chance of profit, he must do it with a purpose. Hence the faithful Christian must follow the call by taking advantage of the opportunity. "If God show you a way in which you may lawfully get more than in another way (without wrong to your soul or to any other), if you refuse this, and choose the less gainful way, you cross one of the ends of your calling, and you refuse to be God's steward, and to accept His gifts and use them for Him when He requireth it: you may labour to be rich for God, though not for the flesh and sin.". . . .

The superior indulgence of the *seigneur* and the parvenu ostentation of the *nouveau riche* are equally detestable to asceticism. But, on the other hand, it has the highest ethical appreciation of the sober, middle-class, self-made man. "God blesseth His trade" is a stock remark about those good men who had successfully followed the divine hints. The whole power of the God of the Old Testament, who rewards His people for their obedience in this life, necessarily exercised a similar influence on the Puritan who . . . compared his own state of grace with that of the heroes of the Bible. . . . .

Although we cannot here enter upon a discussion of the influence of Puritanism in all . . . directions, we should call attention to the fact that the toleration of pleasure in cultural goods, which contributed to purely aesthetic or athletic enjoyment, certainly always ran up against one characteristic limitation: They must not cost anything. Man is only a trustee of the goods which have come to him through God's grace. He must, like the servant in the parable, give an account of every penny entrusted to him, and it is at least hazardous to spend any of it for a purpose which does not serve the glory of God but only one's own enjoyment. What person, who keeps his eyes open, has not met representatives of this viewpoint even in the present? The idea of a man's duty to his possessions, to which he subordinates himself as an obedient steward, or even as an acquisitive machine, bears with chilling weight on his life. The greater the possessions the heavier, if the ascetic attitude toward life stands the test, the feeling of responsibility for them, for holding them undiminished for the glory of God and increasing them by restless effort. The origin of this type of life also extends in certain roots, like so many aspects of the spirit of capitalism, back into the Middle Ages. But it was in the ethic of ascetic Protestantism that it first found a consistent ethical foundation. Its significance for the development of capitalism is obvious.

This worldly Protestant asceticism, as we may recapitulate up to this point, acted powerfully against the spontaneous enjoyment of possessions; it restricted consumption, especially of luxuries. On the other hand, it had the psychological effect of freeing the acquisition of goods from the inhibitions of traditionalistic ethics. It broke the bonds of the impulse of acquisition in that it not only legalized it, but (in the sense discussed) looked upon it as directly willed by God. . . .

As far as the influence of the Puritan outlook extended, under all circumstances—and this is, of course, much more important than the mere encouragement of capital accumulation—it favoured the development of a rational bourgeois economic life; it was the most important, and above all the only consistent influence in the development of that life. It stood at the cradle of the modern economic man.

To be sure, these Puritanical ideals tended to give way under excessive pressure from the temptations of wealth, as the Puritans themselves knew very well. With great regularity we find the most genuine adherents of Puritanism among the classes which were rising from a lowly status, the small bourgeois and farmers while the *beati possidentes,* even among Quakers, are often found tending to repudiate the old ideals. It was the same fate which again and again befell the predecessor of this worldly asceticism, the monastic asceticism of the Middle Ages. In the latter case, when rational economic activity had worked out its full effects by strict regulation of conduct and limitation of consumption, the wealth accumulated either succumbed directly to the nobility, as in the time before the Reformation, or monastic discipline threatened to break down, and one of the numerous reformations became necessary.

In fact the whole history of monasticism is in a certain sense the history of a continual struggle with the problem of the secularizing influence of wealth. The same is true on a grand scale of the worldly asceticism of Puritanism. The great revival of Methodism, which preceded the expansion of English industry toward the end of the eighteenth century, may well be compared with such a monastic reform. We may hence quote here a passage from John Wesley himself which might well serve as a motto for everything which has been said above. For it shows that the leaders of these ascetic movements understood the seemingly paradoxical relationships which we have here analysed perfectly well, and in the same sense that we have given them. He wrote:

> I fear, wherever riches have increased, the essence of religion has decreased in the same proportion. Therefore I do not see how it is possible, in the nature of things, for any revival of true religion to continue long. For religion must necessarily produce both industry and frugality, and these cannot but produce riches. But as riches increase, so will pride, anger, and love of the world in all its branches. How then is it possible that Methodism, that is, a religion of the heart, though it flourishes now as a green bay tree, should continue in this state? For the Methodists in every place grow diligent and frugal; consequently they increase in goods. Hence they proportionately increase in pride, in anger, in the desire of the flesh, the desire of the eyes, and the pride of life. So, although the form of religion remains, the spirit is swiftly vanishing away. Is there no way to prevent this—this continual decay of pure religion? We ought not to prevent people from being diligent and frugal; *we must exhort all Christians to gain all they can, and to save all they can; that is, in effect, to grow rich.*

As Wesley here says, the full economic effect of those great religious movements, whose significance for economic development lay above all in their ascetic educative influence, generally came only after the peak of the purely religious enthusiasm was past. Then the intensity of the search for the Kingdom of God commenced gradually to pass over into sober economic virtue; the religious roots died out slowly, giving way to utilitarian worldliness. Then, as Dowden puts it, as in *Robinson Crusoe,* the isolated economic man who carries on missionary activities on the side takes the place of the lonely spiritual search for the Kingdom of Heaven of Bunyan's pilgrim, hurrying through the market-place of Vanity. . . .

A specifically bourgeois economic ethic had grown up. With the consciousness of standing in the fullness of God's grace and being visibly blessed by Him, the bourgeois business man, as long as he remained within the bounds of formal correctness, as long as his moral conduct was spotless and the use to which he put his wealth was not objectionable, could follow his pecuniary interests as he would and feel that he was fulfilling a duty in doing so. The power of religious asceticism provided him in addition with sober, conscientious, and unusually industrious workmen, who clung to their work as to a life purpose willed by God.

Finally, it gave him the comforting assurance that the unequal distribution of the goods of this world was a special dispensation of Divine Providence, which in these differences, as in particular grace, pursued secret ends unknown to men. . . .

One of the fundamental elements of the spirit of modern capitalism, and not only of that but of all modern culture: Rational conduct on the basis of the idea of the calling, was born—that is what this discussion has sought to demonstrate—from the spirit of Christian asceticism. One has only to reread the passage from Franklin, quoted at the beginning of this essay, in order to see that the essential elements of the attitude which was there called the spirit of capitalism are the same as what we have just shown to be the content of the Puritan worldly asceticism, only without the religious basis, which by Franklin's time had died away. . . .

Since asceticism undertook to remodel the world and to work out its ideals in the world, material goods have gained an increasing and finally an inexorable power over the lives of men as at no previous period in history. Today the spirit of religious asceticism—whether finally, who knows?—has escaped from the cage. But victorious capitalism, since it rests on mechanical foundations, needs its support no longer. The rosy blush of its laughing heir, the Enlightenment, seems also to be irretrievably fading, and the idea of duty in one's calling prowls about in our lives like the ghost of dead religious beliefs. Where the fulfilment of the calling cannot directly be related to the highest spiritual and cultural values, or when, on the other hand, it need not be felt simply as economic compulsion, the individual generally abandons the attempt to justify it at all. In the field of its highest development, in the United States, the pursuit of wealth, stripped of its religious and ethical meaning, tends to become associated with purely mundane passions, which often actually give it the character of sport.

No one knows who will live in this cage in the future, or whether at the end of this tremendous development entirely new prophets will arise, or there will be a great rebirth of old ideas and ideals, or, if neither, mechanized petrification, embellished with a sort of convulsive self-importance. For of the last stage of this cultural development, it might well be truly said: "Specialists without spirit, sensualists without heart; this nullity imagines that it has attained a level of civilization never before achieved."

But this brings us to the world of judgments of value and of faith, with which this purely historical discussion need not be burdened. . . .

Here we have only attempted to trace the fact and the direction of its influence to their motives in one, though a very important point. But it would also further be necessary to investigate how Protestant Asceticism was in turn influenced in its development and its character by the totality of social conditions, especially economic. The modern man is in general, even with the best will, unable to give religious ideas a significance for culture and national character which they deserve. But it is, of course, not my aim to substitute for a one-sided materialistic an equally one-sided spiritualistic causal interpretation of culture and of history. Each is equally possible, but each, if it does not serve as the preparation, but as the conclusion of an investigation, accomplishes equally little in the interest of historical truth.

42

WHY "MAINLINE" DENOMINATIONS DECLINE

ROGER FINKE • RODNEY STARK

Sociologists who study the institution of religion are documenting the changes occurring within this social institution. One current debate is whether religiosity is growing in the United States or if it is declining due to increasing secularization. In this reading, Roger Finke and Rodney Stark investigate why mainline American denominations have declined since the eighteenth century, while newer sects are increasing in membership. They also examine four recent religious eruptions and discuss the impacts they have had on the institution of religion in America. Their findings, reported here, were first published in the 1992 book *The Churching of America, 1776–1990: Winners and Losers in Our Religious Economy.*

From *The Churching of America, 1776–1990* by Roger Finke and Rodney Stark. Copyright © 1992 by Roger Finke and Rodney Stark. Reprinted by permission of Rutgers University Press.

Since at least 1776 the upstart sects have grown as the mainline American denominations have declined. And this trend continues unabated, as new upstarts continue to push to the fore. Consider that the Church of God in Christ (3.7 million members) is already substantially larger than the United Church of Christ (1.7 million), the Presbyterian Church, U.S.A. (2.9 million), the Episcopal Church (2.4 million), and the American Baptist Churches in the U.S.A. (1.6 million). The Assemblies of God now number 2.2 million, and the Churches of Christ enroll 1.6 million. As for the Latter-day Saints, their American membership now trails only that of the Roman Catholics, Southern Baptists, United Methodists, and the newly merged Evangelical Lutheran Church in America.

These historical trends are not oddities of the American religious economy or of recent history—they are not new things under the sun. Rather, they reflect basic social forces that first cause successful religious firms to compromise their "errand into the wilderness" and then to lose their organizational vigor, eventually to be replaced by less worldly groups, whereupon the process is repeated. That is, the *sect-church process is always under way*, and the less regulated the religious economy, the more rapidly and thoroughly the process will occur.

Our view is not shared by most sociologists of religion, let alone most church historians. Most scholars interested in the subject see the religious condition of the United States, and of societies generally, as the product of unique, if periodic, cultural crises and eruptions. Thus, the preference is for *ad hoc* explanations that often amount to little more than identifying some eras as periods of religious excitement and others as periods of lethargy. . . .

To open this [reading] we shall examine claims about four major eruptions in American religion during the twentieth century and show that these too are mainly in the eyes of the beholders. Then we will more fully develop the proposition that *religious organizations are stronger to the degree that they impose significant costs in terms of sacrifice and even stigma upon their members*. Herein lies the key to the trends noted throughout [our research]. People tend to value religion on the basis of how costly it is to belong—the more one must sacrifice in order to be in good standing, the more valuable the religion. A major reason people rate religion this way is that as religious bodies ask less of their members their ability to reward their members declines proportionately. Thus, in terms of real costs and benefits, the more "mainline" the church (in the sense of being regarded as "respectable" and "reasonable"), the lower the value of belonging to it, and this eventually results in widespread defection. . . .

Four Recent Religious Eruptions That Didn't Happen

The literature on cult[1] and sect formation in contemporary America is saturated with the belief that we have recently been living through strange times—through an interrelated set of cultural crises that have resulted in four major religious eruptions. The first of these is sometimes known as a "Consciousness Reformation" and refers to an "eruption" of cult formation and religious novelty during the sixties and early seventies (Glock and Bellah 1976; Wuthnow 1976, 1978). The second concerns an eruption within an eruption; the sudden influx of Eastern, and especially Indian, faiths, during the cult eruption of the sixties and early seventies. The third eruption involves the transformation of many of the Eastern teachings that came to the fore during the late sixties and early seventies into the New Age Movement of more recent years. Popularized by actress Shirley MacLaine and others, the movement has received a great deal of press coverage and has generated serious concern and organized opposition from evangelical Protestant groups. The fourth eruption is the "explosion" of evangelical Protestantism and the corresponding decline of mainline denominations over the past several decades. This conservative eruption is often seen as a reactionary response to the same cultural crises that produced the religious novelties of the sixties (Berger 1982; Marsden 1982; Marty 1979; Tipton 1982).

Real social crises often do have real consequences for religious culture, and the greater the degree of suffering and social disorganization, the greater the likelihood that radical changes will occur in the religious sphere (Stark 1991, 1992; Stark and Bainbridge 1987). Nevertheless, such moments are very rare and play no role in the birth or death of most religious movements. Indeed, we argue that whether or not there have been cultural crises in recent times, they did not prompt significant religious reactions—because the alleged eruptions of cult and sect activity never took place. We argue instead that the recent history of cults and sects is far better characterized by stability and continuity. Although significant changes have occurred, or at least have been recently recognized, they were the result not of sudden eruptions but of gradual, long-term, linear shifts.

The Mystical Sixties

Everyone knows that the latter part of the sixties turned into a "magical mystery tour" during which an explosion of cult formation and importation took place and that, for the first time, the cultural climate was right for faiths from the East, and especially from India, to make significant headway. That these perceptions are accurate seems obvious. Nevertheless, we believe that these, like many other seemingly self-evident assertions about American religion, are mainly myths. That is, we intend to show that there was nothing unusual about the number of cults that formed in this era and that the sudden surge in Indian religious influence had mundane causes having little or nothing to do with deeper cultural matters.

Let us first examine the claim that the sixties were a period when there was an unusual outburst of cult formation. Consider the number of cult movements founded per year for each of the four decades, 1950–1989 (see

TABLE 42.1   Formation Rate of Cult Movements, 1950–1989

	1950–1959	1960–1969	1970–1979	1980–1989[a]
Number of groups founded per year	8.6	16.4	20.6	20.2
Number of groups founded per million population	0.52	0.84	0.95	0.85
Percentage Eastern	7.0	17.1	18.6	11.8

Source: Melton (1988). Based on the files of the Institute for the Study of American Religion, University of California at Santa Barbara.
[a]Projected from 1980–1985 data.

Table 42.1).[2] At first glance it would seem that there was a dramatic shift between the fifties and the sixties in terms of the number of foundings, but, as will be explained shortly, this is probably an illusion. In any event, the sixties did not stand out from either the seventies or the eighties in terms of cult formation. It also seems reasonable to take population growth into account (on the assumption that the larger the population, the greater the absolute number available for recruitment). In terms of the number of cult movements founded during a decade per million population (at mid-decade), the sixties exceed only the fifties.

What these data really show is great stability over the entire period. This stability becomes even more evident when it is realized that the data for the fifties were not assembled until the late sixties and early seventies. Many obscure and short-lived groups, having failed to leave sufficient traces so that reliable data about them could be gathered a decade or two later, would necessarily have been missed. For example, about 20 percent of the groups included in the rate for the sixties are defunct today, and little if any information would be recovered about them by a data collection campaign inaugurated now. We believe that the actual cult formation rate for the fifties was probably about the same as for the other decades.[3] For those determined to remember the fifties as the quiet and conformist decade of Eisenhowerism, it may be worth pointing out that Scientology was founded in 1954, that Elizabeth Clare Prophet's Church Universal and Triumphant was founded in 1958,[4] and that the first American converts to the Unification Church were gathered in Eugene, Oregon, during 1959.

That an unusual number of new cults did not appear during the sixties does not rule out the possibility that far *more people actually participated* in such movements during this brief era. Were that the case, then the eruption thesis is salvaged. But there seems to be no support for this alternative. Rather, what is striking is how poorly contemporary cult movements have done in gaining converts when compared with movements from earlier times. With the exception of Transcendental Meditation—which represented nothing more than a brief experiment in self-improvement for all but the tiniest portion of those who encountered it (Stark and Bainbridge 1985)—no cult movement of the sixties or early seventies seems ever to have attracted more than a few thousand American members, and most of even the well-publicized groups counted their true membership in the hundreds, not the thousands. For example, after more than thirty years of missionizing, it is estimated that there have never been more than 5,000 followers of the Unification Church (the Moonies) in the United States, some of whom are from abroad. After more than twenty years of operations, the membership of ISKCON (the Hare Krishnas) is estimated at 3,000 (Melton 1989). In 1984 a Toronto magazine estimated that there were 10,000 Hare Krishna members in that city. But when Irving Hexham, Raymond Currie, and Joan Townsend (1985) checked on the matter, they found that the correct total was 80.

In 1990 Barry A. Kosmin (1991) and his colleagues at the City University of New York conducted the largest survey ever devoted to American religious affiliation. All told, 113,000 randomly sampled Americans were interviewed about their religious preference. Because such an immense sample yields very stable statistics, Kosmin projected his distributions back to the total adult population of the forty-eight contiguous states. Kosmin projected a nationwide total of 8,000 members of Wiccan groups and, nearly forty years after their founding, 45,000 Scientologists (or about 1 percent of the number of members claimed by the group in 1978).

In contrast, the Mormons grew from six members in 1830 to more than 30,000 a decade later, more than 60,000 by 1850, and more than 80,000 by 1860. In similar fashion, Christian Science grew from 27 members in 1880 to 8,724 in 1890, 65,717 in 1906, and 202,098 by 1926. Moreover, the Mormons and Christian Scientists achieved their rapid growth from a far smaller population base than has been available to recent movements.

These data are utterly at variance with the perception that an eruption of cults took place in the late sixties and early seventies. How is it possible for informed opinion to be so wrong? As we have already seen, misperceptions, even ones of this magnitude, are common in the histories of American religion. When quantitative claims are involved, the opinions of people who fail to count, shouldn't count. It is also possible that cult movements were more prominent on campuses during the sixties than had been the case earlier and therefore attracted more notice. Young adults are always the primary source of converts for such movements, and probably no cohort of young people was ever so overreported and overinterpreted as the baby-boomers, whose antics *were* the sixties.

The Eastern Aspect

In their foreword to Part I of *The New Religious Consciousness*, Charles Y. Glock and Robert N. Bellah (1976:1) noted: "One of the most striking characteristics of the counterculture [of the sixties] and of the movements growing out of it is the influence of Asian religions. Of course, Americans have been interested in Asian religions for over a century, but the present period seems to differ from earlier ones both quantitatively and qualitatively . . . . Most important of all was the fact that Asian religions were attracting not only the curiosity of educated youth but also serious devotion and commitment."

That same year Harvey Cox stressed the same points in his book *Turning East: The Promise and Peril of the New Orientalism.* Cox wanted to explain this phenomenon. Why was it happening? What did it all mean? In a 1983 interview he commented that Americans embraced Eastern faiths because "they've been maddened by a consumer culture." Cox (1983) continued: "In American society, I believe we're now in the late phase, the most deteriorated, decadent phase, of consumer capitalism. When I say 'consumer capitalism,' I don't mean simply the form of our economic life; I mean our whole culture. . . . People's primal energies are fixated on commodities that are supposed to bring satisfaction of inner hungers. Through the suggestive and hypnotic power of the advertising industry, a direct connection is made from very basic and underlying needs and fears to material commodities which are touted as things which satisfy those needs; but of course they do not" (p. 42). In conclusion, Cox noted a great irony, that though many critics charge that "vulnerable kids . . . are picked off the streets and brainwashed into the cults," it is only those who have not yet been brainwashed into the "existing distorted values of society" who are clear-headed enough to be "open to other life-patterns."

Underneath Cox's polemics one can detect a very common belief about the phenomenon in question: Indian religions arrived here in a sudden eruption and therefore they *must* reflect a serious cultural crisis. But such crises are, in fact, rare and have little, if anything, to do with the instance at hand.

Glock and Bellah were correct to note that there had been substantial interest in Indian and other Asian religions for more than a century. Gordon Melton (1987) has sketched the extensive involvements of Harvard professors and various proper Bostonians in Eastern religions during the latter part of the nineteenth century. The Boston Unitarian Church was responsible for the initial visits by Hindu teachers to the United States. According to Melton, the first of these was Protap Chundar Mozoomdar. In 1883 he gave his first American lecture in the Concord living room of the widow of Ralph Waldo Emerson. Other gurus soon followed.

In the wake of World War I, however, Congress passed very restrictive immigration laws that effectively excluded all Asians and thereby limited authentic Eastern religious teachers to brief visits on tourist visas. Thenceforth, Americans interested in exploring Eastern religion had to rely on books, travel abroad, or depend upon American teachers—some of whom pretended to be authentic Indians.[5]

In 1965 the exclusionary rules against Asian immigration were quietly dropped.[6] Before the year was out Swami Bhaktivedanta, founder of ISKCON, had become a resident of New York. Many other teachers of Eastern religion quickly followed, and some succeeded in attracting a following. It is their success that Cox and others were trying to explain. But it seems to us that there is much less here than meets the eye.

Given the existence of a sizable audience for books and periodicals dealing with "Eastern wisdom," it does not seem surprising that when talented gurus finally arrived and offered direct teaching they had little trouble finding at least some followers. Put another way, it was not so much that Eastern faiths suddenly struck a responsive chord in the American counterculture as that their growth had been artificially thwarted until then. With the barrier removed, normalization occurred. Given the structure of guru-based religions (Shinn 1985), virtually each new guru who came to the United States founded a *separate* movement. Thus it took only a relatively small number of American converts to Hinduism to generate a substantial total of Hindu-based cult movements. Herein lies the explanation of the fact that an unusual number of the cult movements founded in the late sixties were of the Hindu variety. The bottom row in Table 42.1 indicates this increase. Only 7 percent of the groups founded during the fifties were based on Eastern faiths, but 17.1 percent of those founded during the sixties and 18.6 of those formed in the seventies were of the Eastern variety. Notice, too, that this has declined in the eighties—which supports the notion that the surge was simply a normalization of "frustrated" demand. The ability of a sudden influx of Eastern and Indian religious teachers to collectively round up a few thousand followers in the vast American religious economy was at most a blip, not an eruption.

The New Age

The term "New Age" is an old one, as is the practice of "channeling." In 1881 and 1882 John Ballou Newbrough, a New York spiritualist, "channeled" a manuscript later published as *Oahspe: A New Age Bible.* The phrase "New Age" was recurrent in the Theosophical Society at the turn of the century and was commonly used by followers of Vedanta and the Rosicrucian Fellowship. During the 1950s, when "flying saucer cults" were popular, many spoke and wrote about the New Age that would begin when the "brothers from outer space" revealed themselves to the world. It was in the 1980s, however, that the term became widely known, largely owing to the publicity given to channelers such as J. Z. Knight and Kevin Ryerson by Shirley MacLaine (Melton 1990).

Most observers of the American religious scene regard the New Age movement as the truly important and lasting legacy of the earlier eruptions of new mysticisms (Babbie 1990; Burrows 1987; Robbins and Anthony 1990). In this they have been much abetted by the news media, for both the print and the electronic media uncritically pass along New Age press releases claiming that hundreds of thousands (perhaps millions) of Americans are sleeping in homemade pyramids and attending channeling classes. And judging from the shelf space devoted to anti–New Age materials in most Christian bookstores, the New Age is *the* cult threat of the moment.

Once again, we dissent. We believe that most people who can in any way be said to have responded to the New Age movement regard it as more of an amusement than a religion. Most are no more than casual dabblers in the various pseudo-scientific activities and techniques promoted as New Age. Indeed, we suspect that for all but a handful of committed participants, the New Age movement is an audience cult (Stark and Bainbridge 1985) and reflects interest levels on a par with reading astrology columns.

A recent report suggests how tiny the New Age movement is. Based on Barry Kosmin's (1991) survey, discussed above, it can be estimated that 20,000 Americans regard their religious preference as New Age. Admittedly, some people who reported themselves to be Baptists or Lutherans take part in the New Age *audience*. But audiences do not constitute movements. And even this audience is probably not all that large. For example, the *New Age Journal* claimed an average circulation of fewer than 150,000 copies for 1990. It seems to us that the New Age is no more potent or relatively popular today than it was in the heyday of Theosophical Society, which claimed a total membership of 6,780 in 1926.

The Evangelical Eruption

In 1972 Dean M. Kelley, an executive of the National Council of Churches, provoked a storm of controversy, especially among religious liberals, with his book *Why Conservative Churches Are Growing*. His first sentence noted: "In the latter years of the 1960s something remarkable happened in the United States: for the first time in the nation's history most of the major church groups stopped growing and began to shrink." Kelley was among the very first to attempt to explain what Martin Marty (1979:10) would later describe as a "seismic shift" in American religion: the sudden and very steep membership declines that began to hit the mainline denominations during the sixties. Summing up the evidence of a series of graphs showing membership figures for a number of major denominations, Kelley (1972) noted that in the sixties the "strong upward curve weakens, falters, and tilts downward like a spent skyrocket" (p. 2). As the title of his book revealed, however, not *all* denominations had hit the skids. The evangelical Protestant bodies were still growing—many of them quite rapidly.

What was going on? According to Marty (1976) it was another cultural crisis: "mainline churches always have the advantage . . . [when] the official culture is secure and expansive . . . [but they] suffer in times of cultural crisis and disintegration, when they receive blame for what goes wrong in society but are bypassed when people look for new ways to achieve social identity and location. So they looked good in the 1950s as they looked bad in the 1970s" (p. 71). Kelley disagreed. He claimed that the mainline bodies were failing to offer credible religion, that they had become so accommodated to the secular culture that people could no longer satisfy their need for the sacred by attending services at their local Methodist, Congregationalist, Episcopalian, or Presbyterian church.

As much as we admire Kelley's book, and his courage in writing it, we think the whole discussion of the sudden decline of the liberal denominations and the sudden "resurgence" of evangelical groups is based on a distorted historical perspective. Like Marty, Kelley was still trying to explain why this "sudden change took place in the 60s." Several years later Kelley (1984) expressed continued confidence in his explanation of why the "conservatives" grew (as the "liberals" declined), but he confessed he was "less satisfied" that he had explained "why it happened at this particular time in history [the 1960s]" (p. 89).

But did anything akin to an eruption take place? Kelley's skyrocket image to the contrary, what is involved here is a gradual trend that has been going on for at least two centuries. The notion of a "seismic shift" is based on the fact that it was only in the sixties that this trend was finally noticed. If we are correct, all efforts by Marty and others to link the fate of the liberal churches to the "cultural crisis of the 1960s" (Marsden 1982:156) are falsified by the inability of consequences to precede their causes in time.

The general consensus of church historians (and most sociologists) is that the decline of the liberal Protestant churches was a product of the sixties. For example, Winthrop S. Hudson (1981) claimed that the declines which "had begun in the 1960s . . . constituted a marked reversal after a century and a half of steady growth" (p. 439). Likewise, Marty (1979) noted: "From the birth of the republic until around 1965, as is well known, the churches now called mainline Protestant tended to grow with every census or survey" (1979). But in light of the two centuries of church statistics we have examined, it is obvious that a group can add members and still fail to keep pace with the growth of the population and of other religious firms.

Social scientists who mistakenly accepted that an eruption of cult activities took place in the sixties can rightly claim that appropriate numerical estimates have been very hard to come by. But those who think there has been a "recent" surge of evangelical growth lack such a defense. Consider Table 42.2. The mainline denominations do not qualify as rockets that suddenly ran out of fuel in the sixties—their market shares were falling in the forties and fifties too, and throughout the century. In contrast, the evangelical groups—some of them rapidly becoming the new upstart sects of our era—do look like rockets. So much, then, for perceptions of a "seismic shift" or a sudden response to a cultural crisis. The speed of conservative growth and liberal decline will no doubt change from time to time, but the general trend has remained consistent for more than two centuries of American history. Thus, while it is true, as Hudson and Marty claim, that the total number of members of these mainline bodies increased regularly until the 1960s, each year they represented a smaller fraction of total church membership.

TABLE 42.2   Market Shares of Mainline, Evangelicals, and Catholics per 1,000
Church Members, 1940–1985

Denomination	1940	1960	1985	Percentage loss or gain
MAINLINE				
United Methodists	124.7	93.0	64.3	−48%
Presbyterian, U.S.A.	41.7	36.4	21.3	−49%
Episcopal	30.9	28.6	19.2	−38%
Christian (Disciples)	25.7	15.7	7.8	−70%
United Church of Christ (Congregationalists)	26.5	19.6	11.8	−56%
EVANGELICALS				
Southern Baptists	76.7	85.0	101.3	+32%
Assemblies of God	3.1	4.4	14.6	+371%
Church of the Nazarene	2.6	2.7	3.7	+42%
Church of God (Cleveland, Tenn.)	1.0	1.5	3.6	+260%
ROMAN CATHOLICS	330.0	367.9	368.4	+12%

Source: Calculated from *Yearbook of American and Canadian Churches* (1988).

Even those without the slightest awareness of market share cannot long ignore an actual decline in numbers. And by the seventies the numbers were falling fast. Attempts to dismiss these declines as purely demographic (cf. Hoge and Roozen 1979) or as symptomatic of the general decline in religiousness produced by modernity fall apart when it is noted that *only some* religious bodies were losing out. And indeed, as Dean Kelley bravely noted, the "conservative" Protestant bodies were still growing.

There have been many attempts to explain this "unwelcome" fact away. Carl Bangs (1972) charged Kelley with using "deceptive statistics." Others suggested that Kelley had fallen into the trap of confusing quantity with quality—that though the evangelicals grow rapidly by "herding insecure and frightened masses together into a superficial conformity," it is the liberal churches who are the "faithful remnant of God's people whose prophetic courage and lifestyle will truly point the way" (Miller 1978:257). Others claimed that the growth of evangelical Protestant bodies was nothing but inflated membership roles caused by people who frequently hop from one sect to another, thus being counted again and again (Bibby and Brinkerhoff 1973, 1983). Some even suggest that it was all a function of disparities in absolute size, because it is easy for small evangelical sects to have high percentage rates of growth, but virtually impossible for large denominations to keep growing rapidly (Nelson and Bromley 1988). This excuse not only ignored the fact that the nation's largest Protestant body, the Southern Baptist Convention, was among those growing rapidly, but also ignored the huge potential for growth that actually exists in the American religious economy.

Two cases are illustrative. Between 1960 and 1970 the Assemblies of God grew by 22.9 percent to reach a total membership of 625,027. This was one of the "small" groups, thereby able to grow fast, cited by Kelley's critics. Meanwhile, the United Church of Christ (formerly the Congregationalists) declined by 12.5 percent, to 1,960,608 members, between 1960 and 1970. In 1987 the Assemblies of God numbered 2,160,667 members and the United Church of Christ had only 1,662,568. Does anyone really think that the advantage currently rests with the U.C.C., now that it has become the smaller group? It seems clear that the decline of the Protestant mainline is a long, steady trend. It is pointless to search the 1960s for the causes of a phenomenon that was far along by the War of 1812. But the question persists: why do mainline faiths fail and why do the sects always overtake them? . . .

Rational Models of Religious Belief and Sacrifice

. . .The inevitable dilemma is clear. On the one hand, a congregational structure that relies on the collective action of numerous volunteers is needed to make the religion credible and potent. On the other hand, unless these volunteers are mobilized to a high level of participation, that same congregational structure threatens to undermine the level of commitment and contributions needed to make a religion viable.

Costly demands offer a solution to the dilemma. That is, the level of stigma and sacrifice demanded by religious groups will be positively correlated with levels of member participation.

Religious stigmas consist of all aspects of social deviance that attach to membership in the group. A group may prohibit some activities deemed normal in the external society (dancing, for example) and require other activities deemed abnormal by the world (speaking in tongues, for example). By meeting these expectations of the group, members deviate from the norms of surrounding society. In the extreme case, when the state attempts to sustain a religious monopoly, membership alone in a dissenting group can be an immense stigma.

Sacrifices consist of investments (material and human) required to gain and retain membership in the group. The requirements of some religious groups involve stigma and sacrifice simultaneously, in that stigmatized persons must often forgo rewards such as career opportunities.

On the surface it would seem that increased costs must always make a religion less attractive. And indeed the economists' law of demand predicts just that, *other things remaining equal*. But it turns out that other things *do not* remain equal when religions impose these sorts of costs on their members. To the contrary, costly demands strengthen a religious group by mitigating "free rider" problems and by increasing the production of collective religious commodities.

When high costs create a barrier to group entry, potential members can no longer reap the benefits of attendance or membership without first incurring substantial costs. To take part at all a prospective member must qualify by accepting the stigmas and sacrifices demanded for everyone. Laurence R. Iannaccone (1989) explains: "Potential members are forced to choose: participate fully or not at all. The seductive middle-ground of free riding and low participation is eliminated" (p. 9). High costs serve to *screen out* potential members whose commitment and participation would otherwise be low. The costs act as nonrefundable registration fees which, as in secular markets, measure seriousness of interest in the product. As a result, the demanding sects speak of "conversions," "being born again," and "submitting their lives to the Lord." The less demanding churches refer to affiliations that are seldom life-altering events. Sectarian members are either in or out; they must follow the demands of the group or withdraw. The "seductive middle-ground" is lost.

For those who do join, high costs increase their level of involvement because it makes activities outside of the group more costly. Group members find that the temptation to free-ride is weaker, not because their human nature has somehow been transformed, but because the opportunities to free-ride have been reduced and the flow of rewards for displaying high levels of commitment has been substantially increased. Looked at another way, prohibiting an activity effectively increases its price, because the full cost now includes the cost of discovery and, often, the price of concealment. As the increased price of the prohibited activity reduces demand for it, the demand for substitutes rises. If we may not attend dances or movies, play cards, go to taverns, or join fraternal organizations, we will probably look forward rather eagerly to the social activities at church.

Finally, it must be noted that the higher the costs of membership, the greater the material and social, as well as religious, benefits of membership.

At first glance it seems paradoxical that when the cost of membership increases the net gains of membership increase too. This is necessarily the case, however, when the commodity involved is collectively produced and when increased costs result in increased levels of participation in collective action, for this results in a greater supply of collective goods. An individual's positive experience in a worship service increases to the degree that the church is full, members enthusiastically participate (everyone sings and recites prayers, for example), and others express their positive evaluations of what is going on. Thus, as each individual member pays the cost of high levels of commitment, each benefits from the higher average level of participation thereby generated by the group. In similar fashion, people will value the otherworldly rewards of religion more highly to the extent that those around them do so. Or, to leave the realm of the immaterial, because Mormons are asked to contribute not only 10 percent of their income but 10 percent of their time to the church, they are able to lavish social services upon one another. Thus are the rewards of Mormon membership made tangible.

Membership in strict religions is, for many people, a "good bargain" in terms of a conventional cost-benefit analysis. We should acknowledge, however, that there are limits to the amount of sacrifice or the level of stigma people are willing to endure. Requiring members to withdraw from all secular opportunities, as some communes do, will clearly limit the growth of the organization. But most churches and sects do not increase sacrifice and stigma over time. As the circuit rider Peter Cartwright complained of the Methodists in 1856, the recurring trend over the past two hundred years has been for "expensive" sects gradually to lower the costs of membership and, by doing so, to reduce the benefits of membership as well. Thus our attention must focus on why and how the reduction of tensions with the surrounding culture weakens religious organizations.

ENDNOTES

[1] We use the term "cult" in a technical rather than a pejorative sense. A sect is a new organization of a conventional faith (conventional, that is, in the society under observation); a cult is an unconventional religion. Cults can occur because someone succeeds in attracting followers to a movement based on a new religious culture. They can also occur by importation from another society. Thus a religious group can be a cult in one society while being a conventional faith in another—Hinduism is a cult in the United States and Christianity is a cult in India. For a full discussion, see Stark and Bainbridge (1985,1987).

[2] We removed atheist and adventist groups on the grounds that they were not cults, and we removed purely mail-order organizations on the grounds that they were neither cults nor sects. As it turned out, the results were unchanged by these omissions.

[3] We note that Melton interprets these same data as a gradually accelerating curve— that cult formation is slowly increasing. While we disagree, Melton's interpretation is as incompatible as ours with the sixties eruption thesis.

[4] Under the name of Summit Lighthouse.

[5] The popular mail-order guru Yogi Ramacharaka was actually an American named William Walker Atkinson (Melton 1987).

[6] In 1965 there were 467 immigrants from India, in 1966 there were 2,293, and Indian immigration now runs at about 25,000 a year.

REFERENCES

Babbie, Earl. 1990. "Channels to Elsewhere." In *In Gods We Trust,* 2d ed., edited by Thomas Robbins and Dick Anthony. New Brunswick, NJ: Transaction Publishers.

Bangs, Carl. 1972. "Deceptive Statistics." *Christian Century* 89:852–53.

Berger, Peter. 1982. "From the Crisis of Religion to the Crisis of Secularity." In Mary Bibby, Reginald W., and Merlin B. Brinkerhoff. 1973. "The Circulation of the Saints." *Journal for the Scientific Study of Religion* 12:273–83.

Bibby, Reginald W. and Merlin B. Brinkerhoff. 1973. "The Circulation of the Saints." *Journal for the Scientific Study of Religion* 12:273–83.

———. 1983. "Circulation of the Saints Revisited." *Journal for the Scientific Study of Religion* 22:253–62.

Burrows, Robert. 1987. "A Christian Critiques the New Age." *Christianity Today* 16.

Cox, Harvey. 1977. *Turning East: The Promise and Peril of the New Orientalism.* New York: Simon and Schuster.

———. 1983. "Interview." In *Hare Krishna, Hare Krishna,* edited by Steven J. Gelberg. New York: Grove Press.

Glock, Charles Y., and Robert N. Bellah, eds. 1976. *The New Religious Consciousness.* Berkeley: University of California Press.

Hexham, Irving, Raymond F. Currie, and Joan B. Townsend, 1985. "New Religious Movements." In *The Canadian Encyclopedia.* Edmonton: Hurtig.

Hoge, Dean R. and David A. Roozen, eds. 1979. *Understanding Church Growth and Decline, 1950–1978.* New York: Pilgrim Press.

Hudson, Winthrop S. 1981. *Religion in America.* 3d ed. New York: Charles Scribner's Sons.

Iannaccone, Laurence R. 1989. "Why Strict Churches Are Strong." Presented at the annual meeting of the Society for the Scientific Study of Religion, Salt Lake City, UT.

Kelley, Dean. 1972. *Why Conservative Churches Are Growing.* New York: Harper and Row.

Kosmin, Barry A. 1991. *Research Report: The National Survey of Religious Identification.* New York: CUNY Graduate Center.

———. 1984. "Why Conservative Churches Are Still Growing." In *Religion: North American Style,* edited by Patrick H. McNamara. Belmont, CA: Wadsworth.

Marsden, George M. 1982. "Preachers of Paradox: The Religious New Right in Historical Perspective." In *Religion and America: Spirituality in a Secular Age.* Boston: Beacon Press.

Marty, Martin E. 1976. *A Nation of Behavers.* Chicago: University of Chicago Press.

———. 1979. "Foreword." In *Understanding Church Growth and Decline, 1950–1978.* edited by Dean R. Hoge and David A. Roozen. New York: Pilgrim Press.

Melton, J. Gordon. 1987. "How New Is New? The Flowering of the 'New' Religious Consciousness since 1965." In *The Future of New Religious Movements,* edited by David G. Bromley and Phillip E. Hammond. Macon, GA: Mercer University Press.

———. 1988. "Testing the Truisms about the 'Cults': Toward a New Perspective on Nonconventional Religion." Presented at the annual meeting of the American Academy of Religion, Chicago.

———. 1989. *The Encyclopedia of American Religions.* 3d ed. Detroit: Gale Research.

———. 1990. *New Age Encyclopedia.* Detroit: Gale Research.

Miller, Paul M. 1978. "Yes, Dean Kelly [*sic*], There Has Been Growth." *Gospel Herald,* March 28.

Nelson, Lynn D. and David G. Bromley. 1988. "Another Look at Conversion and Defection in Conservative Churches." In *Falling from the Faith,* edited by David G. Bromley. Newbury Park, CA: Sage.

Robbins, Thomas and Dick Anthony, eds. 1990. "Introduction." In *In Gods We Trust,* 2d ed. New Brunswick, NJ: Transaction Publishers.

Shinn, Larry D. 1985. "Conflicting Networks: Guru and Friend in ISKCON." In *Religious Movements: Genesis, Exodus, and Numbers,* edited by Rodney Stark. New York: Paragon.

Stark, Rodney. 1991. "Antioch as the Social Situation for Matthew's Gospel." In *Social History of the Matthean Community: Cross-Disciplinary Approaches to an Open Question,* edited by David L. Balch, Minneapolis: Augsburg-Fortress.

———. 1992. "Epidemics, Networks, and the Rise of Christianity." *Semeia* (issue edited by L. Michael White).

Stark, Rodney and William Sims Bainbridge. 1985. *The Future of Religion: Secularization, Revival, and Cult Formation.* Berkeley: University of California Press.

———. 1987. *A Theory of Religion.* New York and Bern: Peter Lang.

Tipton, Steven M. 1982. "The Moral Logic of Alternative Religions." In *Religion and America: Spirituality in a Secular Age,* edited by Mary Douglas and Steven M. Tipton, Boston: Beacon Press.

Wuthnow, Robert. 1976. *The Consciousness Reformation.* Berkeley: University of California Press.

————. 1978. *Experimentation in American Religion.* Berkeley: University of California Press.

43

BARING OUR SOULS
TV Talk Shows and the Religion of Recovery

KATHLEEN S. LOWNEY

Kathleen S. Lowney, professor of sociology, anthropology, and criminal justice at Valdosta State University in Georgia, is interested in the socio-cultural study of religion, especially the history and growth of civil religions in the popular culture of the United States. In this reading, Lowney examines how television talk shows have come to be modern forms of religious revivals, using the religion of recovery and the pop psychology of the self-help movement to obtain converts and spectators. What follows is a fascinating sociological analysis of television talk shows and their limited potential for social change. This excerpt is taken from Lowney's 1999 book, *Baring Our Souls: TV Talk Shows and the Religion of Recovery.*

I confess—I watch television talk shows. I can't even remember when I first watched one, which is evidence that it was quite a while ago. Over the years I have had various favorite shows, depending on which shows my local stations broadcast and on how I felt about the host or the topics being covered. Occasionally today I will intensely focus on a show, but more often it serves as background "noise" while I change clothes after work, read the mail, and begin dinner. The shows and their hosts become companions as I unwind from teaching. At times they have made me laugh out loud at the outrageousness of the stories being told, at times they have made me cry, and

Reprinted with permission from Kathleen S. Lowney, author. New York, Aldine de Gruyter. Copyright © 1999 Walter de Gruyter, Inc., New York.

a few times they have made me angry. And yes, I have talked—okay, I admit it, even yelled—back at the screen, telling guests, Oprah Winfrey, Phil Donahue, Sally Jessy Raphael, or Montel Williams what's what. My guess is that most of us have had these same experiences—we *feel* as we watch talk shows. That is what the shows are hoping for; they want us to become caught up in the stories that are being shared that day, and the next and the next. But in the past 2 years, I have begun to contemplate talk shows and the feelings they try to evoke in their audiences even more. What kinds of emotions do they produce? Do they help us search for explanations of and solutions to some of our nation's most pressing social problems? Alas, I don't think that they are as useful as they can or should be, given their popularity. This [reading] will explain why I am concerned about talk shows and the kind of moral code they promote. But I want to make it clear, I am critiquing talk shows as a viewer as well as a scholar. This is a friendly critique, but a critique nonetheless.

I'm a member of the television generation. I've grown up watching it. Born in 1958, I can't remember living without at least one television set, often more. I have marked the passage of time, both in my life and in the life of our nation, with television clips. . . .

So I'm not ashamed to say that I watch television and that I watch talk shows. I am not alone. During the week of July 7–13, 1997, between 3 and 6 million households watched each of the top seven rated syndicated talk shows.[1] Why do people watch these shows? Like me, many people watch them for fun. They are recreational escapes from our often-harried lives. For others, such shows are sources of information. People see a variety of illnesses or problems on the shows and recognize parallels to their own lives or the lives of their loved ones. Important issues might be debated on these shows, such as when presidential candidates appeared on some shows during the 1996 campaign. Other episodes are a way to "see how the other half lives." We might never have experienced having "embryos . . . stolen and given to another family,"[2] or having a teenage daughter who is "in love with a 76-year-old"[3] or having "had sex with [my] husband and my ex-husband on [the] same day—result, twins with different dads,"[4] but it can be exhilarating, in a vicarious sort of way, to see what kinds of problems other people have. Sometimes watching these shows, I think what a normal life I have had, overall. My problems seem much smaller, more mundane, after an hour of Oprah, Phil, Geraldo, Sally, or Montel! . . .

Yes Virginia, There *Is* Morality on Daytime Talk Shows: Explaining the Present by Looking to the Past

In this [reading] I want to explore the normative order on talk shows by examining the shows themselves. Having just written this sentence, I took a bit of a break and watched *The Jerry Springer Show*.[5] It was wild, and on one level could be used as a perfect illustration of the immorality of talk shows. The show focused on just one family, albeit a very unusual one. Amber was introduced first; she was 12 years old and had been dating, with her parents' approval, a 24-year-old guy named Glenn, who was another one of the guests. Amber admitted that she and Glenn had sexual intercourse on their first date, but only that one time, because she "didn't want Glenn to get into trouble." Her parents knew of the sexual encounter, she said. This was confirmed during the show: both parents admitted to their knowledge of the sexual relationship between their preteen daughter and Glenn. As Jerry talked with Amber, the story grew more and more complicated: her mother, Pam (the third guest) was dating Glenn and wanted to marry him. It was obvious that Amber felt betrayed and hurt by this turn of events. About 20 minutes into the show, Amber's father, Frank, came out on the stage. He promptly threatened Glenn with bodily harm, and they both had to be restrained by well-muscled male guards who worked for Springer. As the show progressed, emotions became extremely intense. Pam told her daughter that it was time that her own needs came first and her daughter would have to cope with Glenn as her new stepfather or else Amber would just have to get lost. The mother went on to say more hurtful and embarrassing things about her daughter, such as the fact that she smelled due to poor hygiene. This was the last straw for Jerry, who launched into a vehement denunciation of Pam, chastising her over and over again for being a lousy mother. He repeatedly uttered that a "good" mother always put a child's needs over her own (selfish) ones. The audience chimed in with applause and a standing ovation when he was finished.

On the surface, this show could be an excellent typifying example of what critics mean when they say that talk shows are destroying America's moral fabric. One whole television hour was devoted to discussing the sexual appetites of a 12-year-old girl and her mother. At first glance, it is hard to see how any of the guests would feel better after appearing on the show. Glenn discovered that Pam thought that he was "stupid and slow"; Pam admitted to prostitution (she said that Frank "put her on the street" and would do the same with Amber), a drug habit, and serving time in prison; Frank sort of admitted to having a violent relationship with Pam (they have been separated for 10 years, but never divorced, although they live across the street from each other); Pam called Amber lots of names (many were bleeped out), including "slut"; and Amber in turn told Pam that she no longer thought of her as a mother, because she hated her. All this in 48 minutes of airtime! It wasn't totally clear how the audience was uplifted by such a show. I'll admit that I heard a lot more than I cared to about this family. In fact, at times the show was positively painful to watch. I felt sorry for Amber, angry with her parents, especially her mother, and frustrated with Glenn's inability to see why having sex with a preteen was wrong. Sometimes I felt all these things simultaneously. My guess is many others who watched shared my reactions.

But there was more to the show. The host, Jerry Springer, played a significant role. He was constantly interrupting the guests, especially Pam, and most interruptions communicated one of two emotions. The first was incredulity—that a mother would say such hurtful, selfish things to her daughter. The second emotion was sarcasm. Jerry made pointed comments about Pam and Frank's parenting skills, Glenn's decision-making capabilities, and even Amber's choices (though he was careful to say repeatedly that she was a child and children make mistakes and that she shouldn't be judged too harshly). Jerry definitely was grounding his remarks in a moral code that I think Bill Bennett would have approved of: children should not be having sex and should definitely not be having sex with a 24-year-old, and parents should protect their children, even if it means putting the needs of the children above those of the parents. As Jerry frequently told Pam—"it is just what you do as a parent." Near the end of the show, a male psychologist joined the family on stage. He promptly added his critical voice by telling Glenn to leave this family alone. He told Pam to start acting like a mother to her daughter, not a rival, and told both parents to start loving their daughter more if they wanted her to have any self-esteem. All of the psychological advice centered on what was best for Amber, the most vulnerable member of this family.

Clearly there was a quite strong moral message to this show. It didn't come only at the end of the show; Springer wove it throughout the program. The morality was hard to ignore. In addition to Jerry's sarcasm and his outrage, the audience was there, booing and hissing Pam, Glenn, and even Frank. They clapped wildly when Springer moralized; when he finished a 3-minute harangue against Pam, the audience gave him a standing ovation. Jerry Springer, the audience, and the psychologist reiterated time and again a moral code that valued sexual restraint and honoring commitments to others (such as mother to daughter). Still, critics such as Bennett would probably say that this is all well and good, but why does such an upstanding moral message need to be couched in the public humiliation of a 12-year-old girl? The viewing public now knows about her promiscuity and her troubled family life, and for what? What did that show cost Amber, her family, and perhaps our nation's very soul? . . .

Secular Fun: The Circus As Entertainment

. . . The roots of the modern-day talk shows lie in the nineteenth century's carnivals and revivals. The parallels are striking. The talk show and the carnival both tempt us to watch portrayals of otherness. We see behaviors that are neither common nor publicly discussed suddenly exhibited for all to see. Just as the circus performers were displayed one dimensionally, so are talk show guests. "What does characterize the bulk of the [talk show participants], despite the diversity, is that some feature of their lifestyles, personalities, or life histories is considered abnormal or deviant to various degrees by society. Indeed, this atypical or deviant position was what generally earned them an invitation to appear on the show."[6] And it is the talk show host, like the circus ringmaster of old, who identifies the guests' particular deviance for us from the outset, just in case those in the audience missed it. A person's complex life becomes summarized in a simplistic, made-for-TV label just as freaks were publicized for their unique characteristics on circus handbills. These labels are reinforced throughout the program by subtitles shown just under guests' faces. But this facile labeling distorts the guests' life histories, their social location, so that the "deviant labels come to be seen by 'normals' [the in-studio and at-home audiences] as *the* defining feature, taking precedence over the other characteristics a marginalized group member may have."[7] Just this one aspect of the guests' lives is lifted up for moral judgment.

Carnivals, circuses, and talk shows highlight behavior that falls outside the realm of normality for society. Most of us do not traipse on high wires, work with animal acts, or read the future, neither are we "mothers who covered up their daughters' pregnancies,"[8] or "high-powered women derailed by menopause,"[9] or a "father who abused all four of us sisters,"[10] and so on. It seems unlikely that any one of us can personally relate to more than a small percentage of show topics. So why then do we watch? In the circus act, the performance was fraught with risk; we knew the "definition of the situation" was tenuous. We knew that no matter how practiced a performer might be, he or she was always flirting with injury, possibly even death. Amusement was a second away from possible peril. Their risk taking was part of our vicarious thrill. Likewise, guests on talk shows take risks. They expose their lives in ways that some of us might fantasize about and others might find repellant. They can disclose—and cause—wounds. We know that secrets are a moment away from being spilled. Anxiously we watch both the carnival and the talk show "acts," always aware of the precariousness of the situation. Talk shows become glimpses into the pain (much less often the joy) that is life. Watching deviant persons suffer can make us rejoice at the life that we have while at the same time they can remind us of the need for a morality that binds people together. These shows do, then, feature a moral discourse.

Talk shows do not just entertain us—they are also a site for American revivalism, of a novel sort. They provide an "electronic tent" under which we can gather together and watch sinners confess, sometimes receiving absolution from the people whom they have hurt, and be reinstated into the moral community. The hosts are contemporary preachers, cajoling guests, studio audiences, and those of us at home to obey the normative order. Hosts take this responsibility quite seriously; "being a talk show host is more than a job, they suggest, it's a calling."[11] And any good preacher knows that an excellent technique to facilitate conversion is to offer oneself as an exemplar of a sinner now redeemed. Talk show hosts make good use of this rhetorical strategy; thus audiences know about Oprah Winfrey's and Ricki Lake's weight loss,

Sally Jessy Raphael's daughter's drug use and subsequent death, Oprah's shame over and healing from sexual abuse, Phil Donahue's divorce and admission of being a less-than-adequate father to his children in their early years, and Geraldo Rivera's numerous sexual dalliances. These admissions of failing are used to establish a parasocial sense of solidarity between host, guest, and even audience members.[12] This parasocial connection is exhibited when the public thinks that we "know" all about celebrities even though we haven't met them—and probably never will. And hosts manipulate this parasocial relationship.

> People feel more at ease telling secrets, and can better trust advice they hear, when talking with someone who knows what it's like. As a result, the hosts need to establish a common bond with guests and viewers. And that bond is based on mutual suffering. . . . The hosts establish a standard of behavior that fosters the kind of disclosures that ultimately benefit their shows.[13]

The hosts' life stories, so well known to viewers due in part to repeated disclosures on the shows, invite others to share their pain. And boy, do the guests talk and talk and talk some more about their troubles. We see them shamed by the host, audience, and other guests and we are reminded of what is (considered) right and wrong in our society. The hosts are pop cultural moralists and the audience accepts them in that role.

Therefore, talk shows parallel nineteenth-century Protestant revivals. The host is the visiting preacher bent on offering salvation to all those who seek it. The guests are primarily sinners—some penitent, others petulant and unwilling to change, and the audience is the ardent congregation goading, chastising, and cajoling the sinners, and celebrating their repentance. Guests not in need of conversion are the aggrieved victims, demanding change in the sinner-guest's behavior before they even will contemplate offering forgiveness. All the televisual attention is directed toward creating a conversion experience—toward sinner-guests turning from the destructive toward the good. The music, the staging techniques, and the pace of the show all parallel the structure of revivals: longer introductory segments that build tension as the sinners testify and then culminate in a segment in which the sinner is forced to make a choice—to continue to sin or move toward the good.[14]

What mattered under the revivalist's tent is also what matters under the electronic tent of the talk shows, that people convert to a moral lifestyle. Turning away from sin is not a one-time event but something that has to happen every minute of every day. In the nineteenth century, the moral community of the local church was there for the former sinner. On talk shows, the host and the psychological expert, who appears at the end of many shows, share the conversion duties. The host and audience members diagnose and emotional experts certify the moral failings of the sinner-guests so that the audience can display a type of sympathy by the end of the show. But the sinner-guests do not automatically receive this sympathy. Sympathy is interactionally constructed on these shows: sinner-guests must earn our sympathy by admitting to sin and guilt *and* by agreeing to a process that will solidify their new status of convert. The experts show the way: therapy. Guests are chided until they agree to enter therapy or go to a 12-step program or some other support group. Like the sinners on the anxious bench, conversion on talk shows is understood as tenuous; backsliding is always a possibility. It is with the support of and the interaction with a primary group of "ex-es" that the now ex-sinners can walk the straight and narrow, the moral path. Recovery is still an individual experience, yet is shared with others who are "working the (same) program." Many talk shows now have full-time staff members whose primary responsibility is to put guests in contact with counselors in their local communities. These staff experts will "follow-up" with guests to see how they are doing, etc. The audience is assured that the staff will "be there" for the guests (common terminology on these shows) long after the studio lights have dimmed.

What Kind of Morality Is the Religion of Recovery?

We have come full circle—it is inaccurate to claim that there isn't morality on talk shows. Hosts, audiences, and experts all have a moral perspective that shapes their performance. Conservative critics have missed this point. The question is not whether there ought to be a moral code on talk shows, but *whose* morality it should be. Talk shows are frequent visitors in American homes. We can be enveloped in their "electronic tents" 24 hours a day if we want to, for just about any time of the day some channel is carrying one. But when we watch, to what altar, to use revivalists' language, are the guests—and ultimately the viewers—being called? I think it is important that we understand this newest form of American civil religion.[15] What kind of moral code is being internalized by the viewers? Other analysts have already commented on this:

> Attention is paid to "therapy" not solid change. The 12-step therapeutic model permeates the popular literature on addiction "treatment." . . . It has become the ideology of the new television talk shows.[16]

> Talk shows . . . never leave things hanging. They work . . . toward hour's end to bring out, insist upon, and reinforce through "expert" testimony by therapists and authors, the ultimate solution to all personal problems: the Recovery Movement as doctrine and practice. . . . Results matter here and the preferred result is that those most confused and unstable be routed to the official place of treatment: the 12 step movement.[17]

> The growing prevalence of this kind of [therapeutic] language on talk shows is the dynamic that works most profoundly to establish the Recovery Movement as a kind of common sense religion.[18]

Earlier religious revivals persuaded converts to join or rejoin the local church and act responsibly. From that foundation of moral behavior, a significant portion of Protestant and Roman Catholic believers then chose to act in and on the world, trying to help others who were less fortunate.[19] However, this newest kind of revivalism found on television talk shows encourages people to turn inward to a psychological or pseudo-psychological belief system, expressed through attendance at therapy sessions or support groups. But such a belief system rarely encourages a turn outward to help the poor or the needy; healing one's inner child becomes more important than healing the world. Converts are

> encouraged to "come to believe," as the 12 steps put it, that their troubles are internal rather than socially determined; that their cures are to be found in private and spiritual, not social or political arenas; and that their time, as parents, friends, wives, lovers, and even workers, is best spent in spreading the word, in sponsoring and supporting more and more hurting people in 12 step activities.[20]

Perhaps the clearest statement of this Recovery Movement theology was an exchange between Oprah Winfrey and Marianne Williamson, a "New Age guru" and author. The exchange begins with Oprah stating "that the root of all problems in mankind and womankind is that people don't feel a sense of value for themselves."[21] Several minutes later they return to the same conversational thread:

> Oprah Winfrey: *So when you see a child murdered or children molested or all the other things going on in the world, because you have no real value for your own self and soul.*
>
> Ms. Williamson: *You're desensitized.*
>
> Oprah Winfrey: *. . . you can't extend it to other people.*
>
> Ms. Williamson: *Right.*
>
> Oprah Winfrey: *So you can talk about it, because intellectually you know you should care . . .*
>
> Ms. Williamson: *Right.*
>
> Oprah Winfrey: *. . . that children are being murdered.*
>
> Ms. Williamson: *Right.*
>
> Oprah Winfrey: *But you don't. There's not enough of that in you to make you get up and do something about it.*
>
> Ms. Williamson: *Right. That's why wounded people who are not themselves healed are the most dangerous. Because they are—they are lacking sensitivity to other people's pain because they haven't addressed their own.*
>
> Oprah Winfrey: *Mm-hmm.*
>
> Ms. Williamson: *That's why the work of personal growth and personal recovery and spiritual work on ourselves is the most important work of all.*[22]

Think of the ethical message Williamson promulgates—care for self is the most important human task. Television talk shows' new revivalism encourages people to convert to a psychological or pseudo-psychological belief system. Such a belief system rarely encourages a person to turn outward to help the poor or the suffering. Instead, one is required to work on oneself. Healing one's inner child, sadly, becomes more important than healing even one citizen of the real world.

This is not the same morality that social conservatives like Bill Bennett want to see advocated on talk shows. But this self-absorbed morality does not seem to concern them much. They abhor the sexy and violent show topics, and miss what I feel is the more substantial moral issue, the religion of self that is sanctioned on these talk shows. I wonder why, for there are significant social and moral questions that need to be asked about a civil religion based on the Recovery Movement. What kind of a society can be constructed based on these 12-step prescriptions? Will it be one that can better tolerate others different than ourselves? Will it be a society that will create new solutions to long-term social problems such as racism, sexism, or poverty? Or will it be a society so self-focused that the only time we talk to our neighbors in need will be to invite them to the next 12-step meeting? . . .

Recovery sells. Books, tapes, and workshops are big business. In particular, the production norms of talk shows make this industry a prime location to disseminate the religion of recovery. They are cost effective for companies to produce; they focus on human interest stories, but only one set and only one paid "actor"—the host—is needed, etc. But it is time to pay attention to the message of the religion of recovery. When guests, hosts, audience members, and those of us at home worship at the altar of recovery, what are we getting in return? Recovery religion removes sociological explanations for guests' behavior from public discourse in favor of solely psychological ones. Thus, on these shows, social problems are constructed as either internal psychological weaknesses or interpersonal conflicts between individuals. Individualizing social problems becomes necessary since it is not possible to interview "institutional racism" but it is possible to have a provocative interview with a "skinhead," and so on. Even more importantly, if the causes are individualized, then so must be the solutions. Larger social forces or social facts, as sociology would say, are ignored and instead solutions focus on separate individuals. But what are the social and moral consequences of psychologizing social problems?

Talk shows offer a therapeutic solution to just about every guest: if someone in an inner-city poor neighborhood is stuck in a dead-end job with no hope for a better future, all that is needed is assertiveness training, so seek out help from such a group, and so on. [I] conclude the analysis by asking if a moral code based on recovery religion as preached by talk show hosts is what our nation needs to solve the social problems we face. How can a normative order based on the belief system of "I'm okay, you're okay—so long as you are not in denial" address the structural issues such as the widening gap between the rich and the poor, institutional systems of stratification such as racism and sexism, or even the growing threat of domestic terrorism? We need—and deserve—a moral code more adequate than what Oprah, Phil, Geraldo, Sally, and the rest are offering.

ENDNOTES

[1] Nielsen Media Research. Week of 7/7–7/13/97. www.ultimatetv.com/news/nielsen/syndication.html. This number reflects the ratings for the Oprah Winfrey, Jenny Jones, Sally Jessy Raphael, Ricki Lake, Montel Williams, Maury Povich, and the Jerry Springer Shows.

[2] *The Phil Donahue Show.* 1995. "Their Embryos Were Stolen and Given to Another Family." November 6.

[3] *The Sally Jessy Raphael Show.* 1995. "My Daughter's In Love with a 76-Year-Old." November 17.

[4] *The Phil Donahue Show.* 1996. "Had Sex with My Husband and My Ex-Husband on the Same Day—Result, Twins with Different Dads." February 2.

[5] *The Jerry Springer Show.* July 30, 1997.

[6] Priest, Patricia. 1995. *Public Images: Talk Show Participants and Tell-all TV.* Creskill, NJ: Hampton, p. 35.

[7] Priest, p. 112.

[8] *The Montel Williams Show.* 1995. "Mothers Who Covered Up Their Daughters' Pregnancies." November 16.

[9] *The Phil Donahue Show.* 1996. "High-Powered Women Derailed by Menopause." May 3.

[10] *The Montel Williams Show.* 1996. "Our Father Abused All Four of Us Sisters." February 27.

[11] Heaton, Jeanne Albronda and Nona Leigh Wilson. 1995. *Tuning In Trouble: Talk TV's Destructive Impact on Mental Health.* San Francisco: Jossey-Bass, p. 43.

[12] See Horton, Donald and Anselm Strauss. 1957. "Interaction in Audience-Participation Shows." *The American Journal of Sociology* 62:579–88; and Horton, Donald and R. Richard Wohl. 1956. "Mass Communication and Para-Social Interaction." *Psychiatry* 19:215–29.

[13] Heaton and Wilson, p. 50.

[14] I am indebted to Donileen Loseke for calling my attention to the role of music on talk shows.

[15] See, for example, Bellah, Robert. 1974. "Civil Religion in America." Pp. 21–44 in *American Civil Religion,* edited by Russell R. Richey and Donald G. Jones. New York: Harper & Row; and Wilson, John F. 1979. *Public Religion in American Culture.* Philadelphia: Temple University Press.

[16] Abt, Vicki and Mel Seesholtz. 1994. "The Shameless World of Phil, Sally, and Oprah: Television Talk Shows and the Deconstructing of Society." *Journal of Popular Culture* 28:171–91, p. 177.

[17] Rapping, Elayne. 1996. *The Culture of Recovery: Making Sense of the Self-Help Movement in Women's Lives.* Boston: Beacon. P. 40.

[18] Rapping, p. 34.

[19] This is not, however, to deny the fact that there is a pietistic, passive element in these faiths as well.

[20] Rapping, p. 94.

[21] *The Oprah Winfrey Show.* 1994. "Marianne Williamson: What Is Going On with the World?" January 11, p.10.

[22] *The Oprah Winfrey Show,* "Marianne Williamson," p. 12.

HEALTH AND MEDICINE

44

WHY THE U.S. HEALTH CARE SYSTEM DOES NOT RESPOND TO PEOPLE'S NEEDS

VICENTE NAVARRO

Medical sociology is one of the largest and fastest growing subspecialties within the discipline of sociology. Medical sociologists are concerned with all aspects of the social institution of medicine, including the socialization of doctors, the social construction of health and illness, and the social structure of hospitals and the health care system. The following three readings illustrate different perspectives within the field of medical sociology, beginning with an excerpt from *Dangerous to Your Health: Capitalism and Healthcare* (1993), written by Vicente Navarro, a professor in the School of Public Health at Johns Hopkins University. In this reading, Navarro critically examines the links between health care and social class in the United States. In so doing, he answers the vexing question: Why does one of the wealthiest nations in the world have some of the greatest social inequities in health care?

Health care in the United States is in a state of profound crisis. In 1992 the United States spent $838 billion ($3,010 per person) on health services. No other country in the world spent such a large amount, which came to 14 percent of the Gross National Product, or GNP, almost double the average for capitalist countries with similar levels of economic

From "Dangerous to Your Health: Capitalism and Healthcare," 1993 pp. 151–153. Reprinted with permission of Monthly Review Foundation.

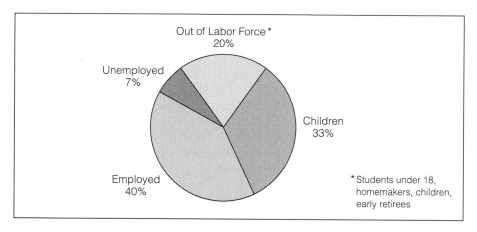

FIGURE 44.1   Who Are the Uninsured?

development. Yet despite this high level of expenditure, 38 million Americans—17 percent of the population—have *no* health benefits, another 50 million have major gaps in their benefits, and the overwhelming majority do not have comprehensive coverage (see Figure 44.1). The average annual cost for long-term care is $27,243, far more than a family earning the median income ($30,000) can afford. Not surprisingly, the inability to pay for health care is the primary cause of personal bankruptcy in this country. People are constantly denied care because they cannot pay their medical bills, or their health benefits are dropped because they cannot pay their health premiums or because they cost their employers or insurers too much. David Himmelstein and Steffie Woolhandler of Harvard University estimate that 100,000 people in the United States die each year from lack of care—three times as many as die from AIDS.

High costs and insufficient coverage are the key characteristics of the U.S. health care non-system, the most inefficient and inhuman of any health care system in any developed capitalist country. The United States and South Africa are the only major countries whose governments do not provide a national health program that guarantees access to health care in time of need. Health care in the United States is not a right; it is a privilege. At a time when the U.S. government declares that it is the great defender of human rights around the world, it continues to ignore this basic right at home. Forty years after the United Nations passed the Declaration of Human Rights, which includes—among other things—the right to access to health care, the U.S. government does not guarantee a right that is guaranteed in most other developed countries. Why?

In order to understand this situation, we must look not only at the practice of medicine but at the society of which this practice is a component. In other words, in order to understand the tree—the health sector—we must study the forest—the society we live in. We therefore have to start our analysis by focusing on the social, economic, and political forces that shape our society and that also shape its health care, including its organization and its funding. This point cannot be overemphasized.

How can we go about understanding this context? This is a good question, and it has a complex answer.

First we need to understand power and how it is distributed. Power is very unevenly distributed. Most of us recognize, for example, that blacks, Hispanics, and other minorities in the United States have less power than whites, and that women have less power than men. Race and gender are categories of power, and much has been written about how racism and sexism continue to operate in the society at large, as well as in its health care system.

But the United States is divided not only by race and gender, but also by *class*. Class is the most important category of power for understanding U.S. society and its system of medicine. Yet class is rarely discussed in either the scientific literature or the mainstream media. It is considered an almost "un-American" category. Yet in other countries, class is considered an extremely important category for understanding how people live, work, dress, vote, enjoy themselves, get sick, and die. In the United States, however, the category of class disappears: the majority of the population is supposed to be in the middle. It is accepted that there are extremes—the rich and the poor—but most Americans are believed to belong to the middle class.

But the United States does have classes. How people live, get sick, and die, as well as the type of health care that they receive, depends not only on their race and gender but primarily on the class to which they belong.

Understanding the class structure of the United States and how it is reproduced over time is of enormous importance if we are to understand U.S. society and its health sector.

The U.S. Class Structure

At the top is a very small group (not more than 1.3 percent of the population) that has enormous power. This is what we can call the corporate class, and it includes individuals whose incomes come primarily from property rather than work. This class is predominantly white and its leaders are predominantly male.

The next group is the middle class. Contrary to popular belief, the middle class does not constitute the majority of Americans, although it is much larger than the corporate class. It includes professionals, small business people, self-employed shopkeepers, artisans, and so on.

The largest group is the working class, which includes almost 75 percent of the population. This is a class whose occupational structure and race and gender composition have changed over the past fifty years. The blue-collar sector of the working class—those working in heavy manufacturing—has declined, while the service sector has grown dramatically. The health sector is the fastest growing sector in the economy, and the health care industry is now the largest employer in the country. The total number of jobs in this sector increased by 639,000 from May 1990 through May 1992, while the total number of jobs *fell* by almost 1.8 million.

At the same time there has been a change from a predominantly white male working class to one in which women and minorities represent more than half of all wage earners. Changes in the labor force in the health care industry reflect the changes in the racial and gender make up of the working class as a whole. Today, most workers in the health sector are women, and 28 percent are minorities.

In the analysis of the U.S. class structure, we can see two striking phenomena that typify our society. One is the enormous concentration of wealth at the top. To cite just one statistic, the top one percent of the population, members of the corporate or capitalist class, owns 40 percent of all the property in this country, including stocks, bonds, and private land.

The other key characteristic of the U.S. class structure is the concentration of income at the top. Nobel Prize winner Paul Samuelson, in his book *Economics*, wrote that "if we made today an income pyramid out of a child's blocks, with each layer portraying $1,000 of income, the peak would be far higher than the Eiffel Tower, but almost all of us would be within a yard of the ground."[1]

The social class structure is different in each of the three major sectors of the economy—the monopolistic sector, the competitive sector, and the state sector.

Of the three sectors, the monopolistic sector is the most influential. It includes the large financial and manufacturing companies and is the world of "corporate America"—the fortune 500 companies and other large employers. This sector employs approximately 25 percent of the labor force. A few companies control each specific area of production or services. A key industry in this sector is the insurance industry, which plays, as we shall see, a very important role in the financing of health services.

The second sector, the market or competitive sector, used to be the largest of the three sectors in terms of both employment and economic activity, but it has declined over the past thirty years. This sector is generally labor intensive and local or regional in scope. The labor force is scattered in small units and seldom unionized. Examples are small businesses, restaurants, drugstores, and, in the medical sector, fee-for-service solo or group practices.

The third major sector is the state (or government) sector, which is in turn divided into two subsectors. In the public service subsector, the government both funds and provides services—an example is the Public Health Service. It does this at all levels of government, federal, state, and local. The other subsector—the contractual subsector—includes those activities that the government funds but that are delivered by the private sector under contract.

For the most part, the government contracts with the monopolistic sector—the defense industry is a prime example. The United States, unlike most developed capitalist countries, does not have a nationalized defense industry that produces armaments; instead, the government contracts with large corporations for their manufacture. Two other examples of this type of contractual arrangement between the government and the private sector are Medicare (the federal program that funds health care for the elderly) and Medicaid (the federal program for the medically indigent). These, along with other federal and state health progams, make up 42 percent of all expenditures in the health sector. The government contracts with private service providers or with health insurance companies for the delivery of health care to the private sector. Most hospitals and physicians are private, and many of the facilities, equipment, drugs, and other commodities used in the health services are also produced and provided by private companies. As Table 44.1 shows, most of the major suppliers to the health sector are also major suppliers to the defense industry.

These corporations are major components of both the military-industrial and medical-industrial complexes. Other components of the medical-industrial complex, besides the medical and hospital equipment industries, are the insurance companies, the drug companies, the hospitals, and the medical professional associations. These are the dominant power holders in the health sector.

The Insurance Industry in the Health Sector

Insurance companies (such as Prudential and John Hancock) write more than 50 percent of the health insurance premiums in this country. They are referred to in the health sector as the *commercial health insurance companies* to distinguish them from the *voluntary health insurance companies,* or the Blues, which until the 1960s controlled most of the premiums. The Blues' share of the private health insurance market dropped from 45 percent in 1965 to 33 percent in 1986, and it continues to decline.

The Blues were established during the Depression of the 1930s by the hospitals (which established Blue Cross) and the American Medical Association (which established Blue Shield) in order to ensure that hospitals and physicians would not run out of patients. For an annual payment—called a premium—these two groups promised to cover many, although not all, of the health care needs of those they insured. Working people could afford to pay a fixed (and at that time, small) amount of money for premiums but could not afford to pay doctors' fees for every service they needed. Later on, after the Depression, the price of premiums increased considerably, but the system of prepayment remained. Blue Cross has continued to be the insurance instrument of the hospital industry and Blue Shield of the medical profession. . . .

TABLE 44.1 Major Manufacturing and Service Companies Operating in the Health Care Industry

Company	Fortune 500 Rank (1984)	Sales (billions $)	Major Areas of Production	Medical Production
IBM	6	45.0	Controls 60 percent U.S. computer, business typewriter, office equipment market	No. 1 in hospital computer market
General Electric	9	27.0	Consumer, industrial, military, technical systems; no. 6 contractor to Pentagon ($4.5 billion in sales); no. 2 producer of nuclear reactors	Diagnostic-imaging equipment; CAT scanners, X-ray, ultrasound, MRI
McDonnell-Douglas	34	9.5	Military and commercial aircraft; F-4 Phantom and F-15 Eagle: DC-9 and DC-10; no. 1 Pentagon defense contractor ($7.7 billion)	Health Services Division, formerly McAuto, fiscal intermediary for NYC Medicaid; acquired Science Dynamics Corp., renamed McDonnell-Douglas Physicians Systems, specializing in medical data bases and electronic claims-processing capabilities
Honeywell	56	6.0	Computer, information, and data systems in aerospace and defense; spacecraft; military and commercial aircraft; 10 percent of business with Pentagon	Controls 5 percent of hospital patient monitoring market; 1981 joint venture with NV Philips, manufacturing medical electronic systems
Siemens AG*	—	14.5	Germany's leading technology firm; world's third largest in telecommunications; supplying Brazil with 4 nuclear reactors	World's largest supplier of X-ray equipment and other diagnostic-imaging machinery
Avon Products	127	3.0	World's largest direct-selling business; cosmetics, toiletries, fragrances	Purchased Malinckrodt in 1982, producer of radiopharmaceuticals, X-ray contrast

*German-based multinational

There is a great deal of competition between the Blues and the commercial insurance companies over control of the premium market. The commercials have been winning the battle, since the insurance companies have far more economic and political influence than the Blues. The large commercial insurance companies are not just health insurers—health is but one piece of their business. Their assets are enormous: Prudential has $116 billion in assets; Metropolitan Life, $94 billion; Aetna, $49 billion; Connecticut General, $31 billion; Travellers, $30 billion; and so on. The boards of directors of the insurance companies are filled with the world's wealthiest people. To take only one example, James Lynn, chief executive officer of Aetna, earned an astounding $23 million in 1990. In 1992, President Clinton's candidate for attorney general Zoë Baird, made $1.5 million as a vice-president of Aetna.

The dominance of the insurance companies in the health care sector has meant that they, rather than the providers of care, are the ones who have a commanding voice in that sector. As a result, it is frequently not physicians and other health professionals who decide what their patients need; it is the insurance companies. What many people do not realize is that any procedures a physician recommends must be approved by the patient's insurance company. A physician can spend up to an hour a day seeking permission to do what he or she considers best for the patient. The insurance companies base their decision on their own criteria of cost-effectiveness, which are not disclosed to either the patient or the physician. This degree of intrusion into the physician-patient relationship by a third party—the insurance company—is unheard of in other countries.

The Power of the Insurance Industry

Table 44.2 shows PAC contributions from the health industry during the 1992 elections. The insurance companies—the commercials and the Blues—as well as the other components of the medical-industrial complex, such as the medical-provider lobbies, the hospital lobbies, the equipment and pharmaceutical lobbies, among others, are the main forces responsible for the fact that the United States is the only major capitalist country without a national health program that guarantees universal and comprehensive health benefits to our population. The overwhelming majority of the population is dissatisfied with health care in this country, and 82 percent wants major and profound changes in the system of funding health care.[2] By a majority or large plurality, Americans since 1952—when the Gallup polls first asked this question—have wanted the federal government to finance health care. But they still do not have it. Back in the 1970s, the labor unions and their allies in Congress—Senator Edward Kennedy and Congresswoman Martha Griffiths—put forward a proposal for a national health program that would cover everyone and would be financed by the federal government, which

TABLE 44.2   Major PAC Contributors

Political action committees that contributed the most money to candidates in the 1992 election	
National Association of Realtors	$2,950,138
National Medical Association	2,936,086
International Brotherhood of Teamsters	2,442,552
Association of Trial Lawyers of America	2,336,135
National Education Association	2,323,122
Political action committees in the health industry that contributed the most money to candidates in the 1992 election	
American Medical Association	$2,936,086
American Dental Association	1,420,958
American Academy of Ophthalmology	801,527
American Chiropractic Association	641,746
American Hospital Association	505,888
American Podiatry Association	401,000
American Optometric Association	398,366
American Health Care Association	382,019
American College of Emergency Physicians	330,725
American Nurses Association	306,519
Association for the Advancement of Psychology	273,743
American Physical Therapy Association	198,941
Eli Lilly & Company	195,530
Pfizer Inc.	188,100
Schering-Plough Corporation	186,050

would then contract directly with the providers of health services (as is done in Canada). The government would be the *single payer for health services,* eliminating the insurance companies. Needless to say, the insurance lobbies and their close friends in Congress mobilized to stop that proposal.

We saw the enormous political influence of the insurance companies during the 1992 election campaign. Even though the majority of Americans would prefer a health system like the Canadian one, not one of the candidates dared to propose it, afraid of antagonizing the insurance industry and the medical-industrial complex. . . . Similarly, the directors of the health components of both the Bush and Clinton campaigns were Washington lobbyists for the insurance companies. The Republicans'chief health advisor was Deborah Steelman, a lobbyist representing the Pharmaceutical Manufacturers Association, Aetna Life and Casualty, and others. The Democrats' chief health advisor was Bruce Fried, also a lobbyist for the major health insurance companies.

The corrupting influence of corporate America over the political process is encouraged by the "revolving door"—the movement of former politicians and the staff of the major health-related congressional committees to jobs in the medical industrial complex. The majority of Washington lobbyists for the medical-industrial complex once worked in the Congress and have retained close contacts there.

Former President Ronald Reagan used to work for the American Medical Association and opposed the establishment of Medicare. In a phonograph record sent by the AMA to doctors' wives, Reagan warned: "If you and I don't stop Medicare, we will spend our sunset years telling our children and children's children what it was like in America when men were free."[3] Both former President Bush and former Vice-President Dan Quayle used to work for the pharmaceutical industry.

The U.S. Constitution starts with that splendid sentence, "We, the People . . ." To be accurate, we should add a footnote that would read "and the medical-industrial complex." The latter has a far greater voice than the people in deciding what can and cannot be done in the health sector.

Class Control of the Health Care Institutions

The corporate class's control over the health care sector does not begin and end with its control of funding; it continues with control over the health care institutions themselves and over the political institutions that influence how these work. Money, the energy that moves the system, passes through institutional channels that are controlled, or heavily influenced, by groups that are similar, although not identical, to those that have dominant influence in the funding of those institutions.

Who controls the health care institutions, such as the medical research foundations, teaching hospitals, voluntary hospitals, and others? The question is difficult to answer. There are many groups that shape these institutions, but one that has enormous power is the board of directors (or trustees, or executive board) of each institution. These boards not only set policy, but generally appoint the executive officers and many members of upper level management in these institutions. Listen to Abraham Flexner, author of the famous *Flexner Report*, which established medical education in the United States as we know it today. Flexner wrote that "the influence of the board of trustees of the university determines in the social and economic realms an atmosphere of timidity, which is not without effect on critical appointments and promotions."[4] Feminists have long been aware of this point and have rightly called for a change in the gender composition of the boards of directors of our health institutions. Blacks, Hispanics, and other minorities have been equally aware of the problems of having all-white boards and have demanded a change in their racial and ethnic composition so that they will better reflect the diversity of the communities they serve.

But the issue of the class composition of these boards is seldom raised. Figure 44.2 compares the class composition of the United States as a whole with the class composition of the boards of trustees of the top ten medical research foundations, the private medical teaching institutions, the state medical teaching institutions, and the voluntary hospitals.

The figure shows vividly the enormous overrepresentation of the corporate and upper middle classes and the dramatic underrepresentation of the majority of the population—members of the lower middle and working classes. Further, the small changes in the gender and racial/ethnic composition of these boards have not had much effect on their class composition. Only in the case of the voluntary not-for-profit hospitals do members of the working class appear on these boards. As R. M. MacIver has written, "The typical board member is associated with large-scale business, a banker, a manufacturer, business executive or prominent lawyer."[5]

You could say—and it has often been said—that there is a justifiable explanation for the class control of these institutions: members of the corporate class are needed to raise funds for the institution. But while that may have been the case in the past, it is not anymore. Most of the funding of the leading private teaching institutions is overwhelmingly public—in other words, the funds come from the majority of the American people, ordinary folks who are not represented on the boards of directors.

This class discrimination is not only the least recognized type of discrimination in the United States, but it is the most persistent and continuous form of discrimination.

There has been an improvement in the representation of women and African Americans in the medical student body. Although these changes are too timid, at least something is being done to correct this discrimination. The strongest, most persistent, and unchangeable discrimination is class discrimination. In 1920, only 12 percent of all medical students came from families at or below the median family income—that is, in the lower economic half of the population. This percentage remained the same in 1992, seventy years later. This is a discrimination that very few people talk about.

Class Power and the State in the Health Sector

Having described the patterns of class dominance over the financing of health care and the administration of health care institutions, let me now touch on a third component of what is going on in the health care sector. This is the class influence on the government, including its executive, legislative, and judicial branches. According to official rhetoric, the U.S. government represents the voice of the people. As one widely used textbook put it, "In our nation, political power reflects the will of all people, not the will of a few at the top."[6]

The reality, however, is otherwise. The overwhelming majority of senators are members of the corporate and upper middle classes. The same applies to the cabinet. Business was the largest single occupational group in cabinet

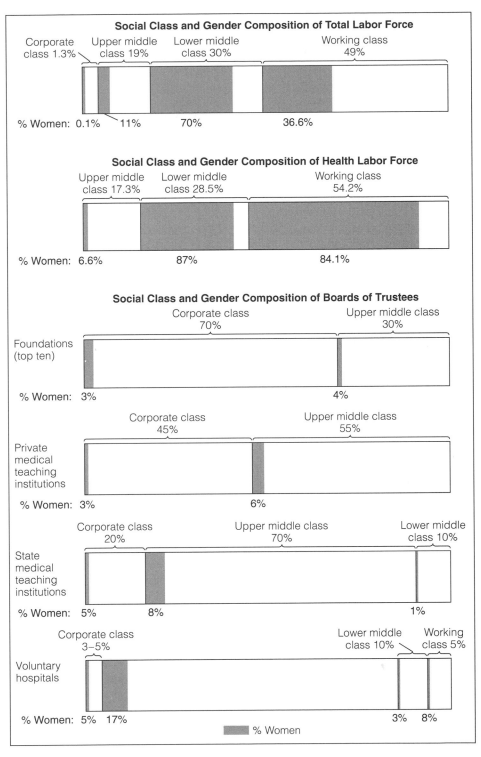

FIGURE 44.2 Social Class and Gender Compositions of U.S. Labor Force, Health Labor Force, and Boards of Trustees in the Health Sector

positions from 1989 to 1990: of all the cabinet members during this period, more than 80 percent had been in business of one sort or another. This situation persists in President Clinton's cabinet. In spite of Clinton's populist message, sustained throughout his presidential campaign, seven of his cabinet members are lawyers with close ties to corporate America. All seven made more than $1 million before being appointed.

The same pattern of class domination holds for the House. A total of 102 congresspeople held stock and well-paying executive positions in banks or other financial institutions, and 81 received regular income from law firms that generally represented big business. Sixty-three percent got income from stock in the top defense contractors; 45 percent from the giant (and federally regulated) oil and gas industries; 22 percent from radio and television companies; 11 percent from commercial airlines; and 9 percent from railroads. Ninety-eight congresspeople were involved in numerous capital gains transactions.

It is important to note that while much has been written about the limited representation of women, and of blacks and other minorities, in top political positions, almost nothing has been written about the very limited class representation in these same bodies.

Some might argue that while there is indeed a pattern of class domination in our major political institutions, they are still representative because these politicians were elected by the majority of citizens, who are, as we saw earlier, mostly working class. The problem with this argument is that the majority of the working class does not vote. People are fully aware of the enormous power that corporate America has over their political institutions: 72 percent, according to a recent *New York Times* poll, believe that the Congress represents powerful economic interests rather than ordinary people.[7] In fact, barely half of the population of voting age goes to the polls in presidential-year Congressional elections (52 percent in 1988 and 54 percent in 1992) and less than half in non-presidential-year Congressional elections (38 percent in 1990). Since the half that votes is predominantly the upper economic half, we can conclude that the lower half, which includes the majority of the working class, does not vote.

Diversity within the Dominant Classes and the Health Policy Debate

There is, however, a diversity of interests within the dominant classes, a diversity that is evident in the proposals for reforming the health care system put forward by different groups. For example, large financial capital (such as the major insurance companies) has different interests than manufacturing companies or medical practitioners (as represented by the AMA). These differences cause conflict. It is these conflicts between different corporate interest groups that are at the center of the debate on health care reform. The large insurance companies support the "managed competition" model, a solution first put forward by Alain Enthoven (former deputy director of defense under Robert McNamara when he was directing the Vietnam War and later health advisor to Prime Minister Margaret Thatcher on her plan to privatize the National Health Service in Great Britain). According to the managed competition proposal, which is suported by the insurance companies, the AMA, the *New York Times,* and the Clinton-Gore administration, employees would have to enroll in insurance-operated health care plans chosen for them by their employers. The employees could expect to see their choice of providers, and their benefits, dramatically reduced.

A few corporate leaders, however, including those in such industries as automobile manufacturing, want the government to play a direct role in controlling the costs because these have become so high. For instance, employee health benefits are a larger component of the cost of a car than the steel it is built from: $700 of the cost of a car now goes to pay for health benefits, compared to only $200 in Canada or Japan. Further, large employers have come to realize that the growing cost of health insurance is cutting into company profits, at least in the short term. In the long term, of course, they can pass these costs on to workers by cutting wages. In fact, the growth in the cost of health benefits is the primary reason wages in the United States have remained constant since 1972. As noted by the Congressional Budget Office, "Since 1973, the increased costs for health care and other benefits have absorbed most of the gains in inflation-adjusted compensation, leaving little room for wages and salaries."[8]

Despite the diversity of proposals for health care reform, there is a bias in the system that explains why some proposals have a far better chance than others, depending on whether or not they conflict with the structure of power that sustains the interests of the various groups. As one perceptive observer has written, the "flaw in the pluralist heaven is that the heavenly chorus sings with a very special accent . . . the system is askew, loaded and unbalanced in favor of a fraction of a minority."[9] The political debate that reflects this pluralism takes place within the framework of a common understanding and acceptance of certain premises and assumptions that consistently benefit some classes rather than others.

Even though a large plurality or a majority of people have, since 1952, wanted a health care system in which the health services are allocated according to need rather than ability to pay, none of the proposals put forward by the White House or by the congressional leadership has even come close to suggesting such a system. This is a clear sign of class dominance.

The Origins of Employment-Based Health Coverage

Understanding class dominance is of paramount importance not only for understanding why the United States does not have a national health plan, but also for understanding why health benefits are provided through the workplace. In 1989, for instance, 56.9 percent of workers received health benefits through their jobs. Why? To answer this question, we must go back to the late 1940s and early 1950s, the period after World War II. The U.S. working class made enormous sacrifices during World War II. It was a war against fascism and nazism, a war for a better future for working people and their children. Not surprisingly, then, at the end of the war people's expectations were high: they believed that their sacrifices had to have served a purpose. Powerful groups were asking for a redistribution of wealth, for the nationalization of banking, and for the establishment of a national health program run by the government. Working people were pushing for these demands, demands that threatened the capitalist and upper middle classes. In response to this threat, these classes developed an aggressive anti-working-class campaign. Congress, where the dominant classes had enormous influence, led the fight. The targets included progressive individuals in all areas of political, social, and academic life. That campaign—called McCarthyism—was brutal.

In 1947, Congress passed the Taft-Hartley Act, which—among other things—outlawed sympathy strikes: for instance, coal miners could not go out on strike in support of steel workers. In other words, class pressure was outlawed. In no other Western developed capitalist country do workers face such restrictions. Indeed, it is not unusual to see a whole city—or even a whole country—in Europe paralyzed by a general strike, in which *all* the workers go on strike in support of demands that would benefit the majority of workers and their families. In the United States, a general strike is forbidden.

The Taft-Hartley Act also mandated that workers and their unions obtain health benefits from their employers through the collective bargaining process rather than, as in Europe, through the state. In other words, the unions had to negotiate the employers' payment of health insurance premiums for the workers and their families. This has meant that workers and their unions have to pressure their employers to get or to extend health benefits. Needless to say, wherever unions are strong, health benefits are extensive; where they are weak—as they are in most sectors of the economy—health benefits are limited.

The United States is therefore the only country in the developed world where workers and their families lose their health benefits when they lose their jobs. Relating health benefits to employment is an enormously effective way to discipline labor. Even changing jobs may mean changing the level of health benefits. According to a *New York Times*/CBS poll conducted in August 1991, 32 percent of working people stayed in jobs they did not like for fear of losing their health benefits.[10] The current shift from high-wage to low-wage, from union to non-union, and from full-time to part-time jobs has also meant a shift from good health benefits (in high-wage, unionized, and full-time jobs) to poor or nonexistent coverage (in low-wage, non-unionized, and part-time jobs). . . .

The same *New York Times*/CBS poll showed that 44.7 percent of those who change jobs or whose employment is for some reason interrupted did not have any form of health benefits for up to twenty-eight months. This percentage was even higher for blacks and Hispanics, who tend to be concentrated in low-wage nonunion jobs. Twenty percent of African Americans and 33 percent of Hispanics are uninsured. Millions of people have loved ones who are sick and are not able to do anything about it because they cannot afford medical care. . . .

All these realities are the result of class power—the power of the dominant class—which is a power unparalleled in any other major capitalist country. Let me give you an example of how unparalleled that power is. We recently saw how Prime Minister Margaret Thatcher had to resign because of her growing unpopularity, which was largely due to the imposition of what the British call a poll tax. According to Thatcher's proposal, local services were to be financed by a flat tax on each household, so that rich households and working-class households would both pay the same amount. The Labour Party loudly denounced the poll tax and mobilized so much opposition that Thatcher was forced out of office.

Yet in this country most of us are forced to pay for health care according to a system that is not unlike the poll tax: every employee in a particular business or industry pays the same amount (we call it a premium rather than a poll tax) for their health benefits, regardless of income. Thus the chairman of Bethlehem Steel, whose annual salary is $1.2 million, pays approximately the same premium for himself and his family as does the unskilled black or white steelworker in one of his mills, in spite of the fact that his income is forty times larger. And it is the Democratic Party that is leading the way in expanding rather than changing this profoundly regressive way of funding health care.

In the United Kingdom, as well as in all the other developed capitalist countries, workers have fought to divorce health benefits from the job and to make the funding of benefits progressive. This is why the overwhelming majority of the labor movements in the Western world made access to health care a universal entitlement, with the government guaranteeing that such a human right is implemented. Part of this human right is the funding of benefits through progressive taxation. In the United States, both the Republican and the Democratic parties have been proponents of the regressive funding of health services.

ENDNOTES

[1] Paul Samuelson, *Economics*, 8th ed. (New York: McGraw-Hill, 1972), p. 110.

[2] Vicente Navarro, *The Politics of the Welfare State.*

[3] Vicki Kemper and Viveca Novak, "What's Blocking Health Care Reform?" *Common Cause Magazine* 18, no. 1 (January/February/March 1992): 8–13, 25.

[4] Abraham Flexner, *Universities: American, English, German,* Rev. ed. (New York: Oxford University Press, 1930), p. 180.

[5] R. M. MacIver, *Academic Freedom in Our Time* (New York: Goodwin Press, 1967), p. 78.

[6] William H. Hartley and William S. Vincent, *American Civics* (Orlando, FL: Harcourt Brace Jovanovich, 1987), p. 434.

[7] *New York Times,* 24 September 1992.

[8] U.S. Congress, Office of the Budget, *Economic Implications of Rising Health Care Costs,* October 1992, p. 37.

[9] E. E. Schattschneider, *The Sovereign People: A Realistic View of Democracy in America* (New York: Holt, Rinehart, & Winston, 1960), p. 31.

[10] *New York Times/*CBS Poll, August 1991.

45

THE RISE OF THE SURGICAL FIX

KATHY DAVIS

One aspect of sociological research on the institution of medicine is the history of changes in medical practices and procedures. When and how did certain forms of treatment become popular? Are these types of treatment driven by medical necessity, or are there other social factors pushing for these changes? In the selection that follows, Kathy Davis, a professor at the University of Utrecht, Netherlands, examines the rise in plastic surgery as a medical practice. Her analysis reveals that not only is plastic surgery one of the most rapidly growing medical specialties, but also that the majority of the "patients" utilizing these procedures are women. Other factors, such as race and social class, also influence who is having plastic surgery done.

Plastic Bodies

The development of cosmetic surgery technology is inextricably connected to a market model of medicine, on the one hand, and to a consumer culture, on the other. With the rise of medicine as a profession, medical cures

From *Reshaping the Female Body* by Kathy Davis, pp. 4–38. Copyright © 1995 Routledge, Inc. Reproduced with permission from Routledge, Inc., part of the Taylor & Francis Group.

and services became something which could be obtained for a fee. In an open market system, the patient is a consumer and, like consumers of other products, free to choose any treatment, provided it can be paid for. The body is no longer simply a dysfunctional object requiring medical intervention, but a commodity not unlike "a car, a refrigerator, a house—which can be continuously upgraded and modified in accordance with new interests and greater resources" (Finkelstein 1991:87). It can be endlessly manipulated— reshaped, restyled, and reconstructed to meet prevailing fashions and cultural values.

Modern cosmetic surgery technology sustains and is a product of the notion of the body as "cultural plastic"—"a construction of life as plastic possibility and weightless choice, undetermined by history, social location, or even individual biography" (Bordo 1990:657). The technologies of cosmetic surgery assume the makeability of the human body, expanding the limits of how the body may be restyled, reshaped and rebuilt. A twin "disdain for material limits" and an "intoxication with change" (ibid., p. 654) make the possibilities for surgical intervention both desirable and endless. Nowhere is this more tellingly manifested than in the use of computer technology whereby potential recipients are given a preview of how they might look after a face lift or breast augmentation. The patient is photographed and the image is duplicated on the screen. The surgeon (God and artist, all in one) uses an electronic pencil on a special board to make the desired changes while the patient watches. Flesh is added or taken away, wrinkles disappear, breasts are inflated, or body shape is transformed. The makeability of the body and the power of medical technology are visually sustained in each demonstration (Balsamo 1993).

Cosmetic surgery is the cultural product of modernity and of a consumer culture which treats the body as a vehicle for self-expression (Bordo 1990; Featherstone 1983, 1990; Finkelstein 1991; Giddens 1991; Turner 1984). By engaging in a wide array of available body maintenance routines, individuals are encouraged to seek their salvation through altering their appearance. ("You are the way you look.") Along with the beauty, fitness, and diet industries, medical technologies can be drawn upon to help turn back the biological clock—to combat the natural deterioration of the body which accompanies age and the rigors of everyday life. The notion of Nature-as-the-ultimate constraint is replaced by Nature-as-something-to-be-improved-upon. Whereas plastic surgery was formerly aimed at repairing bodily deficiencies which made a person noticeably different from the rest of the world, it increasingly came to be seen as a normal intervention for essentially normal bodies. Bodies no longer have to be damaged or impaired to merit surgical alteration. Growing older, gaining or losing weight, or simply failing to meet the transitory cultural norms of beauty are now sufficient cause for surgical improvement. Cosmetic surgery allows us to transcend age, ethnicity, and even sex itself.[1]

From Celebrity Junkie to the Girl Next Door

Cosmetic surgery has increasingly become a mass phenomenon, with the media playing an essential role in making it acceptable for an ever-growing population. Initially, it was associated with the rich and famous (the jet set, celebrities, pop singers). Tales of the surgical exploits of Farah Dibah, Raquel Welch, Sophia Loren, Jane Fonda, Michael Jackson, Joan Collins, and others abounded as the media regaled us with descriptions of lavish clinics where they enjoyed gourmet meals and private suites, along with their face lifts and body sculpting.[2] Models, news commentators, or actresses whose work puts them in the public eye have come to consider cosmetic surgery part of the job. In Beverly Hills, plastic surgeons have their own publicity firms and even accept Visa and MasterCard.[3] The undisputed queen of cosmetic surgery is the pop singer and actress Cher, who has reputedly undergone dozens of operations. She has spent over seventy-five thousand dollars on altering her body ("My body is my capital."), having her stomach corrected to give her navel a "girlish look," her dimples enhanced with silicone, and, most dramatically, two ribs removed to emphasize her waist. By chronicling the operative histories of individuals who are already considered by the public to be beautiful, the media makes its message clear: no one is so beautiful that she cannot become even more so with the help of surgery.

The first articles on cosmetic surgery began to appear between 1965 and 1975, and the end of 1975 marked the beginning of a new era with an increase of nearly two hundred percent in the number published (Dull and West 1987:3). Upscale glossies like *Vogue, Cosmopolitan,* or *Self* as well as most daily newspapers today regularly feature advertisements for clinics specializing in such surgery. Women's magazines frequently provide personal testimonies of the "before and after" variety, which depict women's experiences with various kinds of operations. A typical article describes an ordinary, young, professional woman who "just wants to feel a little better" by having her breasts augmented.[4] She is not portrayed as a celebrity ("My breasts never dominated my life, not like other women.") and her motives seem imminently reasonable—after all, who wouldn't want to feel better? The reader is subsequently taken behind the scenes as she goes through the procedure. Potential unpleasantness and difficulties are downplayed in pictures which show the patient lying barebreasted and smiling on the operating table with circles drawn where the surgeon will cut. ("Here is C., right before the operation. . . . [I]n just over an hour, the silicone implants will be sitting pretty.") Having a breast augmentation becomes a kind of adventure, something to look forward to in pleasant anticipation. The story has a happy ending, the patient emerging with a new body and a boost to her self-confidence as well.

Although magazines occasionally feature a personal testimony about a failed operation ("My life was ruined after having a nose job."), the mishap tends to be attributed to medical malpractice rather than to problems inherent in the operation itself. The patient is simply unfortunate in having run into the one bad apple in the otherwise exemplary bunch of plastic surgeons. In general, surgery is presented as a relatively harmless way to improve appearance—an acceptable path toward happiness and well-being.

There is, of course, the problem of the "plastic surgery junkie"—the individual who indulges in "plastic surgery the way some of us eat chocolate—compulsively."[5] Undeterred by the cost, pain, or terrible bruising, those who are pathologically addicted to having their bodies remade or beautified through surgery cannot be stopped. Although cases of repeated cosmetic surgery receive considerable media attention, the addiction of the recipients tends to be normalized in such public discourse. In her discussion of television's treatment of the cosmetic surgery boom, Dull (1989) shows how "scalpel slaves" may be used to promote the advantages of cosmetic surgery to the general public. For example, in 1986 Oprah Winfrey invited people who had as many as nine cosmetic operations to share their surgical resumes on her show. As the program progressed, the audience's horror and skepticism were gradually transformed. They no longer viewed this involvement as a sign of addiction, but began to see it as simply a matter of being "pro-surgery"—an imminently reasonable choice among all the other choices available to the modern individual.[6]

In short, the media constructs cosmetic surgery as an option which is not only available to everyone, but which bears the promise of an exalted life—one can partake in what was formerly available to the chosen few. Or, as Featherstone (1983) puts it:

> [T]he imagery of consumer culture presents a world of ease and comfort, once the privilege of an elite, now apparently within the reach of all. An ideology of personal consumption presents individuals as free to do their own thing, to construct their own little world in the private sphere. (P. 21)

In such a climate, it is not surprising that cosmetic surgery would seem to be more and more of an option for everyone. Despite its cost, it is available for even those who would normally doubt that they could afford it.

The Cosmetic Surgery Boom

Cosmetic surgery is big business. In the U.S., it takes its place alongside the twenty billion dollar cosmetics industry and the thirty-three billion dollar diet industry as one of the most rapidly expanding fields in the beauty system today (Wolf 1991). Three hundred million dollars are spent every year on cosmetic surgery, and the amount is increasing annually by ten percent. Operations are expensive, ranging from two hundred fifty dollars for a chemical face peel to over five thousand dollars for an abdominoplasty, or tummy tuck.[7] The average plastic surgeon makes a profit of $180,000 a year, earning nearly double the income of a family practitioner, pediatrician, or internist and considerably more than what the average obstetrician or gynecologist would earn.[8]

In 1988, more than two million Americans underwent some form of cosmetic surgery. This figure was up from 590,550 in 1986 and it continues to skyrocket.[9] In the U.S., the number of operations doubled every five years, until it tripled between 1984 and 1986 (Wolf 1991:251). The situation is no different in many European countries. Within the last decade, cosmetic surgery has doubled in Great Britain. As Wolf graphically describes it: "a city the size of San Francisco gets cut open every year in the United States; in Britain, a village the size of Bath." In Germany one hundred eighty million marks are spent annually on cosmetic surgery. More than one hundred thousand Germans have such surgery each year, including ten percent from East Germany (a "new face for a new boss from the West").[10] In the Netherlands it is estimated that between ten and twenty thousand cosmetic surgery operations are performed every year. Since 1982, operations have doubled in frequency and eyelid corrections and tummy tucks are up five hundred and three hundred percent respectively, since 1975 (Starmans 1988).

Nearly ninety percent of the operations are performed on women: all breast corrections, ninety-one percent of face lifts, eighty-six percent of eyelid reconstructions, and sixty-one percent of all nose surgery. In 1987, American women had 94,000 breast reconstructions, 85,000 eyelid corrections, 82,000 nose jobs, 73,230 liposuctions, and 67,000 face lifts—nine times more operations than men had (American Society for Plastic and Reconstructive Surgeons 1987). The only procedures which are performed primarily on men are hair transplants (ninety-five percent) and ear surgery (forty-four percent) (National Center for Health Statistics 1987). Despite reports that men are having faces and necks lifted and sagging eyelids corrected to give them a "competitive advantage" in the business world, women continue to be the primary objects of surgical intervention.[11] Whereas the majority of cosmetic surgery operations have been performed on white women, in 1990 it was estimated that twenty percent of the cosmetic surgery patients in the U.S. were Latinos, African Americans, and Asian Americans. Of these, over sixty percent were women (Kaw 1993).[12]

Cosmetic surgery is the fastest growing specialty in American medicine (Faludi 1991:217). Whereas the total number of physicians has little more than doubled in the last quarter of a century, the number of plastic surgeons has increased fourfold. At the end of World War II, there were only about one hundred plastic surgeons in the U.S. In 1965, there were 1,133 plastic surgeons and in 1990, the number of plastic surgeons had reached 3,850.[13] In Southern California alone, there are 289 practitioners. By 1988, the caseload of registered surgeons had more than doubled, to 750,000 operations annually. Since at least ninety percent of cosmetic surgery is performed in a physician's office or a private clinic,[14] it is not necessary to be a plastic surgeon to be able to perform cosmetic surgery. Face lifts, eyelid corrections, or chemical peeling may be performed by a dermatologist, while otorhinolaryngologists (ENT-specialists) are engaging in nose and ear corrections. There are no standard procedures for preoperative screening and less concern for quality control than would be the case in a hospital setting.[15]

New Technologies

Cosmetic surgery began with the application of reconstructive procedures to recipients who were not disfigured through birth, disease, or accident, but were concerned with improving their appearance. Although this distinction is not always easy to make, plastic surgeons now emphasize the difference between surgery for reconstructive purposes and surgery for aesthetic or cosmetic reasons. In fact, plastic surgeons in the U.S. belong to separate professional organizations from cosmetic surgeons and have different access to medical insurance. Consequently, they have different kinds of patients as well as different status. Although reconstructive surgeons earn less money, their work does not carry the commercial taint attached to surgery for aesthetic purposes. Nor do they face the difficulties of having to justify doing surgery without a clear-cut medical indication.

While much of the growth in plastic surgery has been in cosmetic surgery, it often seems to be a matter of taking earlier reconstructive technologies and putting them to new uses. For example, rhinoplasties, the oldest form of plastic surgery, are now performed in response to the patient's desire to meet a cultural ideal (Millard 1974)—creating "the nose best suited for the individual face."[16] Nose contouring is currently regarded as a solution for "teen angst" and is an increasingly popular graduation gift for adolescents concerned that their noses are too large/too flat/too ethnic to meet the current standards of facial appearance.[17] Ear surgery (otoplasty) has also expanded its horizons (Huffstadt 1981). A relatively simple operation which was frequently performed on the "jug ears" of school-age children is now being perfected to ever more refined interventions. Earlobe reductions have become the "latest nip-and-tuck": overly-long earlobes ("a much overlooked sign of aging") are trimmed down to twenty-five percent of the total ear (a more "ideal" format).[18] Once done to alleviate vision impairment due to sagging eyelids, double eyelid surgery is increasingly employed to westernize the eyes of Asian businessmen, consumer-conscious Korean housewives (Finkelstein 1991) and, more recently Asian American women (Kaw 1993). Braces and the capping of teeth, which used to be the province of orthodontists, has now been transformed into cosmetic dentistry—a rising specialty which can involve a radical reconstruction of the entire face and jaw for aesthetic purposes. In each case, old techniques are refined or applied to different kinds of patients.

In addition, new medical technologies and procedures have been developed since the early sixties which belong exclusively to the domain of cosmetic surgery. For example, face lifts, breast augmentations, and fat removal or body contouring are the most frequently performed procedures. They are done almost exclusively on women for aesthetic or cosmetic reasons.[19] Because these newer procedures mark a shift in both the practice of surgically altering bodily appearance as well as in cultural discourses about the human body, I will discuss them in more detail.

Face Lifts

Although face lifting was first developed in France in 1919, it took another fifty years before it was done to any great extent (Huffstadt 1981). In the U.S., rhytodectomies (the word comes from the Greek word for wrinkle) are now the third most common form of cosmetic surgery. They are performed to smooth out wrinkles or eliminate the sags and puffiness associated with age or the ravages of sunbathing, poor nutrition, smoking, or excessive drinking. The operation involves making an incision from the temples to the front of the ear and then behind the ear to the back of the head. The facial and neck skin are then lifted from the underlying skin and pulled toward the incision. The overlapping skin is cut off and the new edge is sewed to the scalp. It has been compared to "lifting off a wrinkled piece of plastic wrap, smoothing it out and putting it back again."[20]

Face lifts are not the solution for everyone and, as Finkelstein (1991) notes, the ideal candidate often seems to be the one who least needs it. To be ensured of success, the patient should be "of slender build, with soft, smooth skin and minimal subcutaneous fat, with a family story of youthful aging, without serious illness, emotional trauma, or weight fluctuation after operation, and with the desire and skill to augment the surgical improvement by makeup, hairstyling, and enhancing clothes (Goldwyn 1980:693). Surgeons, in fact, recommend that face lifts should only be performed on patients who already have demonstrated concern for their appearance. For those who do not display the "appropriate concern for their appearance," a trip to the local farm is recommended instead (Huffstadt 1981).

Despite these restrictions, more than sixty-seven thousand American women had their faces lifted in 1987—nearly ten times more than the seven thousand male recipients in the same year (American Society of Plastic and Reconstructive Surgeons 1987). The typical face-lift candidate is described as a well-to-do, fashionably-dressed, middle-aged woman between the ages of forty-five and sixty who anticipates having to attract a new mate after a divorce or simply wants to hold her own on the job in the face of younger competition.[21] However, face lifts are increasingly being done on younger women as well. Ever on the lookout for new recipients, one enterprising surgeon found prisons provided a new market for his services. Some female prisoners suffered from "premature aging of the skin due to extensive use of drugs and poor nutrition"; others wanted to have needle marks removed.[22]

Face lifts often go hand in hand with additional surgical procedures. Eyelid corrections take care of telltale sagging or eliminate puffiness associated with fatigue, heavy drinking, or depression. Silicone may be implanted into chin or cheeks to fatten up faces shrunken by age or simply not lush enough to meet current standards of beauty. Dimples can be created surgically in cheeks or a chin enhanced with a ruggedly handsome cleft (Rees and Wood-Smith 1973:510–11). Collagen treatments which involve pumping a protein directly into the skin to plump out the fine lines are becoming increasingly popular.

Face lifts and associated procedures do take off years, but they are not permanent. They have to be redone. For example, surgeons recommend that the patient should have her or his first face lift in the early to mid-forties, the second in the fifties, and the third in the sixties and so on (Rees and Wood-Smith 1973). Moreover, since collagen is quickly absorbed by the body, this kind of treatment is only of temporary benefit and has to be repeated, sometimes more than once a year. It becomes, literally, a form of body maintenance—not unlike getting a permanent or having a facial.[23]

For individuals who cannot afford this kind of maintenance—maintenance which can run up to a total of eight thousand dollars—less drastic procedures for rejuvenating the face are available. Chemical peeling (dissolving the top layers of the skin with acid) or dermabrasion (sanding down the skin with a machine-powered wire brush) can delay face lifts or be used to eliminate fine facial wrinkles caused by exposure to the sun or smoking, acne scars, and other blemishes (Meredith 1988).

Breast Augmentations

Breast corrections (mastopexy, reduction, augmentation) also have a long history. In medieval times, breasts were amputated for tumors and the first case of a breast reduction for aesthetic reasons was reported in 1560.[24] It wasn't until the late nineteenth century, however, that breast reductions were performed to any significant degree. The practice of enlarging breasts did not appear until mid-twentieth century.

Augmentations were first performed in the early 1950s in Japan, but it was not until the early sixties that they became a commercial success. A topless cocktail waitress working in San Francisco became an instant media star in the late fifties when she allowed twenty shots of silicone to be injected directly into her breasts. The press had a field day exploiting Carol Doda's— now forty-four double D—chest. Enthusiasm for this method waned when it was discovered that paraffin or silicone injected directly tended to migrate to other parts of the body, causing cysts and necrosis of the skin. Sponges made of terylene wool, polyvinyl or polyethylene were then introduced to replace the injections. These new materials were an improvement but they often hardened, protruded or caused fluid to accumulate in the breasts, which then had to be drained.

By 1963, inflatable silicone implants were becoming increasingly popular as a way to enlarge small breasts or correct asymmetrical breast development. The implants consisted of bags containing silicone gel or, less commonly, saline solution. Some were coated with a polyurethane foam, although these were later taken off the market by the manufacturers themselves because of their possible carcinogenicity (FDA Medical Bulletin 1991). Silicone implants could be inserted by means of a small incision in the armpit, nipple, or underneath the breast. These implants had the advantage of feeling like real breasts and were less likely to be rejected by the body's immune system, particularly if used in conjunction with steroids. A pocket was created below or behind the chest muscle so that the implant could be inserted.

Although silicone implants also had drawbacks, breast augmentations became one of the most popular forms of cosmetic surgery (Meredith 1988). It is estimated that over one million women in the United States have had their breasts "enhanced," usually by means of silicone implants. Each year one hundred thirty thousand women embark on this operation in the U.S.— the single most commonly performed operation next to liposuctions. The situation is similar in other countries. In Britain, six thousand silicone implant operations are carried out every year. In The Netherlands, there has been a fifty percent increase in the number of augmentations performed since 1982 (van Ham 1990:99)—more breast augmentations per one hundred thousand habitants than in any other country in the world.

Most breast augmentations are performed on women between the ages of twenty and thirty. However, increasingly younger women are having them (two percent of the breast augmentations in the U.S. are performed on women under the age of eighteen) as well as women well into middle age whose breasts have begun to sag after pregnancies and breast feeding. Breast augmentations are increasingly a prerequisite for any job which places a woman in front of the camera.[25]

Fat Removal and Body Contouring

In a culture which suffers under a "tyranny of slenderness" (Chernin 1981) and where the diet industry has reached epidemic proportions, an increasing number of people consider themselves overweight. In the U.S., for example, more than seventy-nine million Americans claim that they weigh too much (Spitzak 1990:9). In this context, it is not surprising that various techniques in cosmetic surgery have been developed for eliminating fat and trimming overweight bodies. Procedures range from tightening abdominal skin that has lost its elasticity due to weight loss, pregnancy, or the normal aging process, to abdominoplasties that involve cutting off an apron of excess skin which has caused discomfort and irritation.

Originally, cosmetic surgery was not considered a substitute for dieting. In recent years, however, a technique has been developed which makes dieting a thing of the past. The lyposuction or suction lipectomy has been developed to remove fatty tissue. Imported from France in 1982, this procedure involves injecting a saline solution, which liquefies the fat, into the area in question. A small incision is then made and fatty deposits are sucked out with a kind of vacuum cleaner. The procedure may be performed in conjunction with abdominoplasties or locally to eliminate saddlebag thighs, trim hips and buttocks and even get rid of "pudding knees." [26] The most extreme form of body contouring or sculpting involves trimming, tucking and remodeling the entire body in a series of nearly simultaneous operations. The advantage to the patient is that she only has to be put under anesthesia once (Pitanguy 1967). For example, fat can be removed from hips and ankles, sagging skin in upper arms and tummy tucked, and a neck lift performed—all in one sitting.

Liposuctions are the fastest growing form of cosmetic surgery in the U.S. In 1986 alone one hundred thousand operations were performed—a number which rose by seventy-eight percent between 1984 and 1986.[27] By 1989 one hundred thirty thousand women alone underwent liposuctions and more than two hundred thousand pounds of body tissue was suctioned out of them (Wolf 1991:261).[28] Although liposuctions are far from safe and have even been known to cause death when too much body tissue is removed, they continue to enjoy an unprecedented popularity.[29]

Problems and Pitfalls

Without a doubt, cosmetic surgery is popular. It is, however, also painful and risky. The most minor intervention causes discomfort, ranging from the dead crust of skin left by a chemical peel to swelling and inflammation of a face lift. Other operations like abdominoplasties, breast corrections, and liposuctions fall under the category of major surgery, requiring hospitalization and sometimes even intensive care. Recovery periods can be long and arduous—painful drains and a slow healing process for breast corrections, wearing a tight girdle after a liposuction to keep the skin from sagging, or having the jaws wired together for two months following cosmetic dentistry are all routine postsurgical experiences. While these discomforts may force the recipient into hiding until her bruised and swollen body returns to some semblance of normalcy and she can show herself to the outside world, there is more involved, in most cosmetic surgery than just discomfort.

Most operations have side effects, many of which are serious and even permanent. Although statistics are not kept, the list of complications accompanying cosmetic operations is long (Goldwyn 1980). For starters, infections, wound disruption, and erosion of overlying skin are a routine byproduct of any operation. Scar tissue can harden or darken. There is no way to prevent this kind of disfigurement, and it is estimated that over twenty percent of all cosmetic surgery involves repairing tissue left over from previous operations.[30] Negative reactions to anesthesia are so common that they are called routine complications, though in some cases they can be fatal.[31]

Each operation has its own specific dangers. Pain, numbness, bruising, discoloration, and depigmentation frequently follow a liposuction, often lingering up to six months after the operation. Face lifts can damage nerves, leaving the person's face permanently numb. More serious disabilities include fat embolisms, blood clots, hypovolemia (fluid depletion), and, in some cases, death. While a breast augmentation is relatively minor surgery, and can even be performed on an outpatient basis, it is, nevertheless, a risky undertaking. Health experts estimate that the chance of side effects is between thirty and fifty percent, some of which are very serious. The least dramatic and most common side effects include decreased sensitivity of the nipples, painful swelling or congestion of the breasts, hardening of the breasts which makes it difficult to lie down comfortably or to raise the arms without the implants shifting position, or asymmetrical breasts (Gurdin 1972). While such side effects are common, they are usually temporary and not health threatening. More serious is the problem of encapsulation, whereby the body reacts to the presence of foreign matter by developing an enclosing capsule of fibrous tissue around the implant. This happens in nearly thirty-five percent of the cases. The implant becomes doorknob-shaped, rock hard, and painful. In some cases, a firm massage on the part of the surgeon (euphemistically called "fluffing them up") will break up the tissue—at great pain to the patient. If this does not work, however, the implants have to be removed—a formidable procedure sometimes requiring that the hardened implants be literally chiseled from the patient's chest wall. More rarely, the implant's outer envelope ruptures or there is gradual leakage of silicone into the body ("gel bleed")—a process which can impair the woman's immune system permanently, leading to arthritis, lupus, connective tissue disease, respiratory problems, or brain damage (Goldblum, Relley, and O'Donnell 1992; Walsh, Solomon, and Espinoza 1989; Weiss 1991). There is still debate about whether the detection of cancerous abnormalities in mammograms is impaired by the presence of an implant or that the implants themselves can cause cancer.

Cosmetic operations often have to be redone. While face lifts fall and have to be repeated every five years, silicone breast implants need to be replaced after fifteen years. Fat which has been removed from thighs or buttocks may return, requiring another liposuction, or the skin may bag and have to be cut and redraped.

Finally, the recipient of cosmetic surgery faces the very real possibility that she may emerge from the operation in worse shape than she was before. Unsuccessful breast augmentations are disfiguring. They leave the recipient with unsightly scars instead of a bigger chest size. An overly tight face lift produces the zombie look—a countenance utterly devoid of expression.[32] Following a liposuction, the skin can develop a corrugated, uneven texture or dents so that the recipient looks worse than she did before the surgery.

Situated Critique

Making sense of both the popularity and the problems of the surgical fix requires situating cosmetic surgery in the cultural and social context from which it emerged. Cosmetic surgery belongs to the cultural landscape of late modernity: consumer capitalism, technological development, liberal individualism, and the belief in the makeability of the human body. It is in this context that cosmetic surgery could emerge as an acceptable means for altering or improving the appearance of the body.

In recent years, however, cosmetic surgery has become increasingly controversial as well. Cosmetic surgery involves a surgical intervention in otherwise healthy bodies. It is a painful and dangerous solution for problems which are rarely life threatening and seldom evoke physical discomfort. And, last but not least, cosmetic surgery is expensive. In an age when cutbacks in health-care expenditure are the order of the day, it is a problematic medical practice.

While cosmetic surgery has become a source of contention in both the U.S. and Europe, these controversies take a different form, depending upon the organization of health care and the political commitment to welfare in each country in question. The organization of health care delivery not only sets limits on who may or may not indulge in the surgical fix, but it shapes the cultural discourses through which the controversial dimensions of cosmetic surgery can be expressed. Like other controversial medical procedures and technologies (in vitro fertilization, fetal monitoring, organ transplants or even female genital excision), cosmetic surgery is justified and criticized for different reasons. . . .

What is missing from debates about cosmetic surgery in both the U.S. and [abroad] is the recipient. Little attention is paid to why patients are willing to take the risk of having cosmetic surgery. Nor have they been consulted in discussions about cosmetic surgery as a matter of welfare. Social policy tends to be made without enlisting the aid of those who are most affected by the outcome. Moreover, the debates have been noticeably silent about the fact that the recipients of cosmetic surgery are primarily women. Why are women so dissatisfied with their appearance that they are prepared to undergo a dangerous operation to have it altered? Why is it taken for granted by the medical profession, the welfare bureaucracy and, for that matter, the general public, that it is the female body which needs surgical alteration?

ENDNOTES

[1] As evidenced by recent strides in sex-change operations—the most radical form of cosmetic surgery.

[2] Pitanguy, a well-known plastic surgeon for the jet set has his private clinic on his own island and is reputed to treat celebrities and society women at the rate of two a day ("I feel I should spend as much time as a painter with a painting would, or a sculptor with a statue."). *The New York Times,* July 8, 1983.

[3] *TV Guide,* October 26, 1991.

[4] Taken from a Belgian women's magazine, *Flair,* May 3, 1991, which is comparable to *Cosmopolitan.*

[5] *Newsweek,* January 11, 1988.

[6] For a discussion of how Oprah's representations of women's experiences with their appearance and the practices of the beauty system can work to empower women, albeit in a somewhat ambivalent mixture of fluff and gravity, sensationalism and social analysis, the reader is referred to Squire (1994).

[7] The prices vary depending upon the extent of the surgery, whether or not the patient is hospitalized, the reputation and expertise of the surgeon, and the geographical region. *Consumers' Digest,* July/August 1986.

[8] Quoted from "Medical Economics" in *The New York Tmes,* February 23, 1992.

[9] It is virtually impossible to obtain accurate statistics on the actual number of cosmetic surgery operations performed each year. In both the U.S. and Europe, statistics are recorded for operations performed in hospitals by registered plastic surgeons. Since the majority of the operations are performed in private settings and many operations are not performed by registered plastic surgeons, such estimates do not begin to cover the actual incidence of operations.

[10] *Der Spiegel* 32 (1992).

[11] In addition to the difference in the number of cosmetic surgery operations performed on men and women, marketing strategies are very different for the sexes. For men, cosmetic surgery is presented as a means to enhance job performance and increase chances to compete, while women are targeted in terms of general attractiveness or changes in identity.

[12] The types of cosmetic surgery are also ethnically specific. White women opt for liposuctions, breast augmentations, or wrinkle removal procedures, whereas Asian women tend to have double-eyelid surgery or nose corrections (Kaw 1993).

[13] *The New York Times,* February 23, 1992.

[14] In the U.S., at least ninety percent of the cosmetic surgery operations are performed in the physician's office or in a private clinic (American Society of Plastic and Reconstructive Surgeons 1988).

[15] *The Los Angeles Times,* December 23, 1991.

[16] *Consumer's Digest,* July/August 1986.

[17] Cosmetic surgery on teenagers is up as much as 300 percent, warns *The New York Times,* December 19, 1989. According to the American Society of Plastic and Reconstructive Surgeons, 73,250 nose jobs were done in 1988—the first year statistics were kept—and sixteen percent of those were performed on patients under eighteen.

[18] *Self,* December 1991.

[19] Breast augmentations are, of course, also done following mastectomies. In 1984, breast reconstructions immediately following a mastectomy accounted for thirty-four percent of the ninety-eight thousand reconstructions. The rest were performed on healthy breasts for the improvement of appearance which makes breast augmentations one of the most common forms of cosmetic surgery. *Consumer's Digest,* July/August 1986. By 1990, the number of reconstructions for cosmetic reasons was up to eighty-five percent. *The Los Angeles Times,* December 10, 1990.

[20] *The New York Times,* February 3, 1982.

[21] Ibid.

[22] This was in response to the governor of California's proposal that in return for state-supported funds to reduce the cost of malpractice insurance, physicians would be required to treat indigent patients or patients for whom there was little medical care available. Grabbing his chance, this plastic surgeon proceeded to offer his services to female prisoners. By 1977, he had operated on more than seventy of them. *The New York Times,* July 25, 1979.

[23] *Consumer's Digest,* July/August 1986.

[24] Gabke and Vaubel (1983) refer to a barber surgeon who amputated the left breast of a maidservant, claiming that it had "assumed such great proportions that she could not support (it), neither standing up nor being seated" (p. 95).

[25] *TV Guide,* October 26, 1991.

[26] *The New York Times,* August 3, 1991 warns about a new "dilemma." "How to wear the new short skirts without being called pudding knees, cottage cheese knees and such?"

[27] *The New York Times,* June 29, 1988.

[28] As one surgeon with a feeling for alliteration explained to me in an informal conversation, the "typical" candidate for a liposuction is "Fat, Forty, and Female."

[29] Early on, eleven deaths were reported as a result of liposuctions. When this number was brought to the attention of a U.S. Senate ad hoc committee, it was pointed out that this is a very low mortality rate for a surgical intervention (.01 percent). However, since the patients getting liposuctions are otherwise healthy, this rate is clearly too high. *The New York Times Magazine,* February 28, 1988.

[30] *Intermediair* (1991):67.

[31] *The Los Angeles Times* reports of a case of a thirty-five-year-old mother of four who was discovered unconscious in the recovery room of the doctor's office after a routine breast augmentation. She was taken by ambulance to a nearby hospital where she died four days later (December 24, 1991). There have been other fatalities, but statistics are not kept on deaths related to medical procedures.

[32] *The New York Times,* February 3, 1982.

REFERENCES

American Society for Plastic and Reconstructive Surgeons. 1987.

American Society for Plastic and Reconstructive Surgeons. 1988. "Estimated Numbers of Cosmetic Procedures Performed by ASPRS Members." Arlington Heights, IL.

Balsamo, Anne. 1993. "On the Cutting Edge: Cosmetic Surgery and the Technological Production of the Gendered Body." *Camera Obscura* 28:207–37.

Bordo, Susan. 1990a. "Feminism, Postmodernism, and Gender-Skepticism." Pp. 133–56 in *Feminism/Postmodernism,* edited by L. J. Nicholson. New York: Routledge.

———. 1990b. "'Material Girl': The Effacements of Postmodern Culture." *Michigan Quarterly Review* 653–77.

548   *Kathy Davis*

———. 1990c. "Reading the Slender Body." Pp. 83–112 in *Body/Politics*, edited by Mary Jacobus, Evelyn Fox Keller, and Sally Shuttleworth. New York: Routledge.
Chernin, Kim. 1981. *The Obsession: Reflections on the Tyranny of Slenderness*. New York: Harper and Row.
Consumer's Digest. July/August 1986.
Der Spiegel. 32 (1992).
Dull, Diana. 1989. "Before and Afters: Television's Treatment of the Boom in Cosmetic Surgery." Presented at the annual meeting of the American Sociological Association, San Francisco, August.
Dull, Diana and Candace West. 1987. "'The Price of Perfection': A Study of the Relations Between Women and Plastic Surgery." Presented at the annual meeting of the American Sociological Association, Chicago, August.
Ehrenreich, Barbara and Deirdre English. 1979. *For Her Own Good*. London: Pluto Press.
Faludi, Susan. 1991. *Backlash: The Undeclared War on American Women*. New York: Crown Publishers, Inc.
FDA Medical Bulletin. July 1991.
Featherstone, Mike. 1983. "The Body in Consumer Culture." *Theory, Culture & Society* 1:18–33.
———. 1990. "Perspectives on Consumer Culture." *Sociology* 24 (1): 5–22.
Finkelstein, Joanne. 1991. *The Fashioned Self*. Cambridge: Polity Press.
Flair. May 3, 1991.
Gabke, Joachim and Ekkehard Vaubel. 1983. *Plastic Surgery Past and Present: Origin and History of Modern Lines of Incision*. Basel: Karger.
Giddens, Anthony. 1991. *Modernity and Self-Identity: Self and Society in the Late Modern Age*. Cambridge: Polity Press.
Goldblum, Randall M., Ronald P. Relley and Alice A. O'Donnell. 1992. "Antibodies to Silicone Elastomers and Reactions to Ventriculoperitoneal Shunts." *Lancet* 340: 510–13.
Goldwyn, Robert M., ed. 1980. *Long-Term Results in Plastic and Reconstructive Surgery*. 2d ed. Boston: Little, Brown.
Gurdin, Michael. 1972. "Augmentation Mammaplasty." In *Long-Term Results in Plastic and Reconstructive Surgery*, edited by Robert M. Goldwyn. Boston: Little, Brown.
Huffstadt, A.J.C., in collaboration with F. G. Bouman, N. H. Groenman, and H. M. A. Marcus-Timmers. 1981. *Kosmetische Chirurgie*. Alphen a.d. Rijn: Stafleu's.
Intermediar. 1991.
Kaw, Eugenia. 1993. "Medicalization of Racial Features: Asian American Women and Cosmetic Surgery." *Medical Anthropology Quarterly* 7 (1): 74–89.
Meredith, B. 1988. *A Change for the Better*. London: Grafton Books.
Millard, D. R., Jr. 1974. "Aesthetic Rhinoplasty." Pp. 371–86 in *Reviews in Plastic Surgery: General Plastic and Reconstructive Surgery*, edited by M. Saad and P. Lichtveldt. New York: American Elsevier.
National Center for Health Statistics. 1987.
Newsweek. January 11, 1988.
Pitanguy, I. 1967. "Abdominal Lipectomy, an Approach to It, Through an Analysis of 300 Consecutive Cases." *Plastic Reconstructive Surgery* 40:384.
Rees, R. D. and D. Wood-Smith. 1973. *Cosmetic Facial Surgery*. Philadelphia: Saunders.
Rheinstein, Peter H. and Grant P. Bagley. 1992. "Update on Breast Implants." *American Family Physician* 45:472–73.
Self, Dec. 1991.
Spitzak, Carole. 1990. *Confessing Excess: Women and the Politics of Body Reduction*. Albany: State University of New York Press.
Squire, Corinne. 1994. "Empowering Women? The Oprah Winfrey Show." *Feminism & Psychology* 4 (1):63–79.

Starmans, P. M. W. 1988. "Wat gebeurt er met de esthetische chirurgie?" *Inzet. Opinieblad van de ziekenfondsen* 1:18–25.

The Los Angeles Times. Dec. 10, 1990.

The New York Times. July 25, 1979.

————. Feb. 3, 1982

————. July 8, 1983.

————. June 29, 1988.

————. July 29, 1988.

————. December 19, 1989.

————. August 3, 1991.

————. February 23, 1992.

The New York Times Magazine. February 28, 1988.

Turner, Bryan S. 1984. *The Body & Society.* Oxford: Basil Blackwell.

TV Guide. October 26, 1991.

van Ham, I. 1990. "Borstvergroting en borstverkleining. Een literatuuronderzoek." *Huisarts en Wetenschap* 33:98–102.

Walsh, Frank W., David A. Solomon, and Luis R. Espinoza. 1989. "Human Adjuvant Disease: A New Cause of Chylous Effusions." *Archives of Internal Medicine* 149: 1194–96.

Weiss, Rick. 1991. "Breast Implant Fears Put Focus on Biomaterials." *Science* 252: 1059–60.

Wolf, Naomi. 1991. *The Beauty Myth: How Images of Beauty Are Used Against Women.* New York: William Morrow.

46

ILLNESS AND IDENTITY

DAVID A. KARP

How should a society treat the mentally ill? For decades, sociologists have researched this question concerning the treatment of the mentally ill, resulting in such classic studies as Erving Goffman's *Asylums* (1961) and David L. Rosenhan's "On Being Sane in Insane Places" (Reading 19). Today, the de-institutionalization movement has meant that fewer mentally ill people are hospitalized; instead, they are more likely to be treated with psychotropic drugs on an outpatient basis. The patient's experience of mental illness is the focus of this reading, taken from David Karp's award-winning book, *Speaking of Sadness: Depression, Disconnection, and the Meanings of Illness* (1996). Here, Karp examines how clinically depressed people experience and interpret their illnesses and their altered senses of self.

From *Speaking of Sadness: Depression, Disconnection, and the Meanings of Illness*, pp. 50–77. Copyright © 1996 by Oxford University Press. Reprinted by permission of Oxford University Press.

You know, I was a mental patient. That was my identity. . . . Depression is very private. Then all of a sudden it becomes public and I was a mental patient. . . . It's no longer just my own pain. I am a mental patient. I am a depressive. I am a depressive (said slowly and with intensity). This is my identity. I can't separate myself from that. When people know me they'll have to know about my psychiatric history, because that's who I am.

—FEMALE GRADUATE STUDENT, AGED 24

At the time we spoke, Karen, whose words open this chapter, had been doing well for more than two years, but described being badly frightened by a recent two-week period during which the all-too-familiar feelings of depression had begun to reappear. Aside from the terror she felt at the prospect of becoming sick, Karen realized that if depression returned, it would mean recasting her identity yet again. After two years with nothing but the "normal" ups and downs of life, she had started to feel that it might be possible to leave behind the mental patient identity she earlier thought she never could shed. By the time of our interview, only her family and a few old friends knew of her several hospitalizations. Her current roommates thought of her simply as Karen, one of about eight students in the large house they shared. She told me, "No one in my life right now knows . . . I'm so eager to talk to you about it [in this interview] because I can't talk about it with people." I said, "It must be hurtful not to be able to talk about so critical a part of your biography," and Karen responded, "Yes, but I don't want to test it with people. . . . [If I told them] they might not say anything, but their perception of me would change."

Karen was willing to be interviewed because I was one of those who knew about her history with depression. Years previously, while taking one of my undergraduate courses, she had confided that she was having a terrible time completing her course work. After much tentative discussion, the word depression finally entered the conversation. She seemed embarrassed by the admission until I opened my desk drawer and showed her a bottle of pills *I* was taking for depression. With this, we began to trade depression experiences and thereby formed the kind of bond felt by those who go through a common difficulty. As her undergraduate years passed, Karen came to my office periodically and during these visits we often spoke about depression. Our shared identity as depressed persons blurred the age and status distinctions that otherwise might have prevented our friendship. . . .

Like nearly everyone whom I talked with, Karen could pinpoint the beginning of her depression career. Although she described a "home filled with feelings of sadness" for as long as she could remember, it was, she said "the beginning of the ninth grade that touched off . . . ten years of depression." She elaborated with the observation, "I was always sad or upset, but I was so busy and social [that the feelings were muted]. You know, things were not doing so well at home, but at school no one knew how much of a hellhole I lived in." She described a home life that was fairly stable until her father became ill when she was a sixth grader. "When he came back from the hospital," she said, "he was very different, unstable [and] extremely violent." Till then Karen had been able to keep the misery of her home life apart from her school world, which served as a refuge. By the ninth grade, however, she "could no longer keep the two worlds separate" and in both places the same intrusive questions, feelings, and ruminations colonized her mind. Now she didn't feel safe anywhere in the world and had these relentless thoughts: "I'm miserable. [There is] such a feeling of emptiness. What the hell am I doing? What is my life all about? What is the point?" "And that," she said, "basically started it."

In the ninth grade Karen had no word for the "it" that had started. When I asked whether she recognized her pain as depression then, she replied, "Did I say this was depression [then]? Did I know [what it was]? It was pain, but I don't think I would have called it depression. I think I would have called it *my* pain." There was another factor that contributed to the anonymity of her misery and kept her pain from having a name—Karen was determined to keep her torment hidden. She said, "I lived with that for . . . a couple of years, from the ninth grade until the eleventh grade. [I lived] with that feeling. . . . But it was all very private. I kept it quiet. It was something inside. I didn't really talk about it. I might have talked about it with some of my friends, but no one understood."

During this time, though, a subtle transformation was taking place in her thinking about "it." Previously, Karen felt that her pain came exclusively from her difficulties at home, but by the eleventh grade she was beginning to suspect that its locus might be elsewhere. She told me, "My family life might have been hell, but it was always, 'Oh [I feel this way] because my father is crazy. It's because of something outside of me.' But it was the first time I'm feeling awful about myself." By the eleventh grade Karen's new consciousness was that there was something really wrong with *her*. Now, her feelings about the pain took a critical turn when she began to say to herself, "I can't live like this. I will not survive. I will not be here. I can't live with the pain. If I have to live with the pain I will eventually kill myself." Despite such a shift in thinking Karen still succeeded in keeping things private until she experienced a very public crisis. It was, moreover, a "crash" that she understood as a major "turning point" in her identity. Here's what she said:

> My whole family life just fell apart. There was no anchor. There was no anchor. . . . [Now] I was able to label it and say it was depression when I crashed in the eleventh grade and was hospitalized. You know, in ninth grade I told you about an experience where I was conscious of feeling pain, or whatever, but no one else knew about it. . . . It is sort of like what my life is like now. I couldn't tell people about it. How can you tell people about it? What do you say? . . .

Then the interview turned to a lengthy discussion about psychiatric hospitals, doctors, and power—all of it negative. She expressed hostility toward doctors who wanted her to "open up" and toward institutional rules that seemed authoritarian and arbitrary. She said, "Psychiatrists and mental health workers have the power to decide when you are going to leave, if you're going to leave, if you can go out on a pass, if you're good, if you're not good." This first hospitalization (eventually there would be four) also started a long history with medications of all sorts. When I asked whether she was treated with medications she replied, "Yup, always medication. That's the big thing. . . . Oh my God, I've had so many. . . . I don't think they really affected me that much. By the time I left I was doing okay. Did I have these problems solved? No, [but] I had an added one. Now I felt crazy." I used Karen's observation about "feeling crazy" as a cue for asking if she had a disease. I said, "Did you now think of yourself as having an illness in the medical sense?" and her answer reflected the ambivalence and confusion I would later routinely hear when I asked this same question of others.

> *I think of it less as an illness and more something that society defines. That's part of it, but then, it is physical. Doesn't that make it an illness? That's a question I ask myself a lot. Depression is a special case because everyone gets depressed. . . . I think that I define it as not an illness. It's a condition. When I hear the term illness I think of sickness. . . . [but] the term mental illness seems to me to be very negative, maybe because I connect it with hospitalization. . . .*

Before it ended, my interview with Karen covered other difficult emotional terrain, including a major suicide attempt, additional periods of hospitalization, stays in halfway houses, a traumatic college experience, failed relationships with therapists, job interviews that required lies about health history, and a personal spiritual transformation. As indicated at the outset, things had gotten better by the time of our interview and Karen believed she was pretty much past her problem with depression. She told me, "A couple of years ago, three years ago, four years ago, I would feel a need to tell people about it because I still felt depressed, because I still felt mentally ill. But now I no longer see myself in that way. I'm other things. I'm Karen the grad student. I'm Karen the one who loves to garden, the one who's interested in a lot of things. I'm not just Karen the mentally ill person." Still, such optimism about being past depression was sometimes distressingly eroded by periods of bad feelings and the ever-present edge of fear that "it" might return in its full-blown, most grotesque form. . . .

A Career View of the Depression Experience

As in many areas of social life, the notion of career seems an extremely useful, sensitizing concept. In his voluminous and influential writings on work, Everett Hughes showed the value of conceptualizing career as "the moving perspective in which the person sees his life as a whole and interprets the meanings of his various attitudes, actions, and the things which happen to him."[1] Hughes' definition directs attention to the subjective aspects of the career process and the ways in which people attach evaluative meanings to the typical sequence of movements constituting their career path. Here I shall be concerned with describing the career features associated with an especially ambiguous illness—depression.

Hughes' definition also suggests that each stage,[2] juncture, or moment in a career requires a redefinition of self. The depression experience is a heuristically valuable instance for studying the intersection of careers and identities. The following data analysis illustrates that much of the depression career is caught up with assessing self, redefining self, reinterpreting past selves, and attempting to construct a future self that will "work" better. Although all careers require periodic reassessments of self, illness careers are especially characterized by critical "turning points" in identity. In his discussion of identity transformations, Anselm Strauss[3] comments on the intersection of career and identity turning points:

> In transformations of identities a person becomes something other than he or she once was. Such shifts necessitate new evaluations of self and others, of events, acts, and objects. . . . Transformation of perception is irreversible; once having changed there is no going back. One can look back, but evaluate only from the new status. . . . Certain critical incidences occur to force a person to recognize that "I am not the same as I was, as I used to be." These critical incidents constitute turning points in the onward movement of persons' careers.

. . . While there is considerable variation in the timing of events, all the respondents in this study described a process remarkably similar to the one implicit in Karen's account. Every person I interviewed moved through these identity turning points in their view of themselves and their problem with depression:

1. A period of *inchoate feelings* during which they lacked the vocabulary to label their experience as depression.
2. A phase during which they conclude that *something is really wrong with me.*
3. A *crisis stage* that thrusts them into a world of therapeutic experts.
4. A stage of *coming to grips with an illness identity* during which they theorize about the cause(s) for their difficulty and evaluate the prospects for getting beyond depression.

Each of these career moments assumes and requires redefinitions of self.

Inchoate Feelings

. . . The ages of respondents in this study range from the early twenties to the middle sixties. All these people described a period of time during which they had no vocabulary for naming their problem. Many traced feelings of emotional discomfort to ages as young as three or four, although they could not associate their feelings with something called "depression" until years later. It was typical for respondents to go for long periods of time feeling different, uncomfortable, marginal, ill-at-ease, scared, and in pain without attaching the notion of depression to their situations. A sampling of comments indicating an inchoate, obscure experience includes these:

> *Well, I knew I was different from other children. I should say that from a very early age it felt like I had this darkness about me. Sort of shadow of myself. And I always had the sense that it wasn't going to go away so easily. And it was like my battle. . . . [female travel agent, aged 41]*

> *An awareness that was more intellectual was apparent to me about my sophomore year in high school, when I'd wake up depressed and drag myself to school. . . . I didn't know that's what it was. I just knew that I had an awful hard time getting out of bed and a hard time making my bed and a hard time, you know, getting myself to school. . . . I kind of just had the feeling that something wasn't right. . . . [It was] just like a constant knot in my stomach. But I didn't think that that was anxiety. I just thought I wasn't feeling good, you know (laughing). [unemployed disabled female, aged 39]*

> *If I think about it, I really can't pinpoint a moment [when I was aware that I was depressed]. . . . [male professor, aged 48]*

Most of those reporting bad feelings from an early age could not conclude that something was "abnormal" because they had no baseline of normalcy for comparison. As might be expected, several respondents in this sample came from what they now describe as severely dysfunctional family circumstances, often characterized by alcoholism and both physical and emotional abuse. These individuals described feeling unsafe at home and often devised strategies to spend as much time as they could elsewhere. . . .

For most respondents the phase of inchoate feelings was the longest in the eventual unfolding of their illness consciousness. Particularly salient in terms of personal identity is the fact that initial definitions of their problem centered on the "structural conditions" of their lives instead of on the structure of their selves. The focus of interpretation was on the situation rather than on the self. Their emerging definition was that escape from the situation would make things right. Over and again individuals recounted fantasies of escape from their families and often from the community in which they grew up. However, initially at least, they felt trapped without a clear notion of how the situation might change.

> *I remember from like five, starting to subtract five from eighteen, to see how many years I have left before I could get out [of the house]. So, I would say the overwhelming feeling was that I felt powerless. I felt a lot of things early. And I felt that I was stuck in this house and these people controlled me, and there wasn't anything I could do about it, and I was stuck there. So I just started*

my little chart at about four and a half or five, counting when I could get out.
[female baker, aged 41]

. . . A decisive juncture in the evolution of a "sickness" self-definition occurs when the circumstances individuals perceive as troubling their lives
change, but mood problems persist. The persistence of problems in the absence of the putative cause requires a redefinition of what is wrong. A huge
cognitive shift occurs when people come to see that the problem may be internal instead of situational; when they conclude that something is likely
wrong with *them* in a manner that transcends their immediate situation.

Something Is Really Wrong with Me

In 1977, Robert Emerson and Sheldon Messinger published a paper entitled
"The Micro-Politics of Trouble"[4] that analyzes the regular processes through
which individuals come to see a personal difficulty as sufficiently troublesome a problem that something ought to be done about it. The materials offered in this [reading] affirm the general process they describe. The process
begins with a state of affairs initially "experienced as difficult, unpleasant, or
unendurable."[5] At first, sufferers try an informal remedy, which sometimes
works. If it doesn't, they seek another remedy. The decision that a consequential problem exists warranting a formal remedy typically follows a "recurring cycle of trouble, remedy, failure, more trouble, and a new remedy,
until the trouble stops or the troubled person forsakes further efforts."[6] Here,
then, is their description of the transformation from vague, inchoate feelings
to a clearer sense that one is sufficiently troubled to seek a remedy.

> Problems originate with the recognition that something is wrong and
> must be remedied. Trouble, in these terms, involves both definitional
> and remedial components. . . . On first apprehension troubles often in-
> volve little more than vague unease. . . . An understanding of the prob-
> lem's dimensions may only begin to emerge as the troubled person thinks
> about them, discusses the matter with others, and begins to implement
> remedial strategies.[7]

Despite the difficulties they have in naming their feelings as a problem,
all of the respondents eventually conclude that something is *really wrong with*
them. To be sure, many used identical phrases in describing their situations.
The phrases "something was really wrong with me" and "I felt that I could
no longer live like this" were repeated over and over. Respondents commented in nearly identical ways on the heightened feeling that "something is
really wrong with me."

When it really became apparent that I was just a mess was in January of 1989. I
made the decision really quickly at the end of 1988 to go to school at [names a
four-year college] and live with my father and my stepmother and commute.
And I packed up all my stuff in my car and went. I was miserable. I cried every

day. Every single day I cried. I think I went to two classes [at the new school] and lasted there only a month. I was absolutely miserable. There was a lot of different factors that were involved with it [but] I just didn't feel right. There was something wrong with me, you know. [unemployed female, aged 23]

I guess it's the fall of '90 when I had done the family therapy. I felt great about that. I was back at Harvard. My work was going okay. I loved myself. I loved my husband. Everything was great. [But] I wanted to die. I had no pleasure in anything What finally got me [was that] I looked at the trees turning and I didn't care. I couldn't believe it. I'd be looking at this big flaming maple and I'd look at it and I'd think, "There it is, it's a maple tree. It's bright orange and red." And nothing in me was touched. At that point I went back to my therapist and said, "There's something really wrong here." [female software quality control manager, aged 31]

. . . These quotes suggest a fundamental transformation in perception and identity at this point in the evolution of a depression consciousness. Respondents now located the source of their problem as somewhere within their bodies and minds, as deep within themselves. Such a belief implies a problematic identity far more basic and immutable than those associated with social statuses. If, for example, someone has a disliked occupational identity, the possibilities for occupational change exist. If the occupational identity becomes onerous enough, it is possible to quit a job. Similarly, without minimizing the difficulties of change, we can choose to become single if married, to change from one religion to another, and, these days, even to change our sex if the motivation is great enough. However, to see oneself as somehow internally flawed poses substantially greater problems for identity change or remediation because one's whole personhood is implicated. Getting rid of a sick self poses far greater problems than dropping certain social statuses. The important point here is that the rejection of situational theories for bad feelings is a critical identity turning point. Full acceptance that one has a damaged self requires acknowledgment that "I am not the same as I was, as I used to be."

Another important dimension of the career process that becomes apparent at this point is the issue of whether to keep the problem private or to make it public, especially to family and friends. The private/public distinction was a dominant theme in respondents' talk throughout the history of their experience with depression. The question of being private or public is, of course, central to one's developing self-identification. As Peter Berger and Hansfried Kellner[8] point out in describing the "social construction of marriage" and Diane Vaughan[9] indicates in analyzing the process of "uncoupling" from a relationship, the moment a new status becomes public is a definitive one in solidifying a person's new identity. In the cases of both creating and disengaging from relationships, people are normally very careful not to make public announcements until they are certain they are ready to adopt new statuses and identities. The significance attached to public announcements of even modest shifts in life style is indicated by the considerable thought people sometimes give to making public such relatively benign decisions as going on diets or quitting cigarettes.

Decisions about "going public" are, of course, greatly magnified when the information to be imparted is negative and, in the case of emotional problems, potentially stigmatizing. As Emerson and Messinger note, the search for a remedy necessarily involves sharing information with others. Still, at this early juncture of dealing with bad feelings, most respondents elected to keep silent about their pain. . . .

Whether or not they made their feelings public, this second phase of their illness career involved the recognition that they possessed a self that was working badly in *every* situation. Although everyone continued to identify the kinds of *social* situations that had caused their bad feelings in the past and precipitated them in the present, the qualitative change at this juncture was in the locus of attention from external to internal causes. At this point respondents were struggling to live their lives in the face of debilitating pain. This stage ended, however, when efforts to control things became impossible.

At some point everyone interviewed experienced a crisis of some sort. For the majority (29) the crisis meant hospitalization. At the point of crisis, whatever their wishes might have been, they could not prevent their situation from becoming public knowledge to family, friends, and co-workers. Whether they were hospitalized or not, everyone reached a point where they felt obliged to rely on psychiatric experts to deal with their difficulty. Receiving an "official" diagnosis of depression and consequent treatment with medications greatly accelerated the need to redefine their past, present, and future in illness terms. The crisis solidified the emerging consciousness that the problem was within themselves. More than that, it was now a problem beyond their own efforts to control.

Crisis

Nearly everyone could pinpoint the precise time, situation, or set of events that moved them from the recognition that something was wrong to the realization that they were desperately sick. They could often remember in vivid detail the moment when things absolutely got out of hand.

> So I went to law school in the fall. I was at Columbia and in the best of times Columbia is a depressing place. I mean, it's a shithole. And you know, I was pretty messed up when I got there. . . . I remember Columbia was a nightmare. . . . So, I was getting to the point where I was paranoid about going to class and so someone talked to the dean and said, "Hey, you've got to do something about this guy, he's off the deep edge." [male administrator, aged 54]

> I think the significant moment was when I got stage fright in high school. There were earlier moments when I felt something was wrong. I can remember feeling

real dizzy when I was on the stage in the 8th grade. But the significant moment was in high school and I was seized by just pure terror. And the fear was so horrible that I couldn't tell it to anybody. I couldn't share it. It was something beyond my ability to communicate. It was so horrible that no one could understand it. [male professor, aged 66]

. . . At the crisis point, people fully enter a therapeutic world of hospitals, mental health experts, and medications. For many, entrance into this world is simultaneous with first receiving the "official" diagnosis of depression.[10] It is difficult to overstate the critical importance of official diagnoses and labeling. The point of diagnosis was a double-edged benchmark in the illness career. On the one hand, knowing that you "have" something that doctors regard as a specific illness imposes definitional boundaries onto an array of behaviors and feelings that previously had no name. Acquiring a clear conception of what one has and having a label to attach to confounding feelings and behaviors was especially significant to those who had gone for years without being able to name their situation. To be diagnosed also suggests the possibility that the condition can be treated and that one's suffering can be diminished. At the same time, being a "depressive" places one in the devalued category of those with mental illness. On the negative side, respondents made comments like these:

I kept going to doctor after doctor, getting like all these new terms put on me. . . . My family was dysfunctional and I was an alcoholic with an eating disorder and bulimia and depression and it was just all these labels. "Oh my God!" [unemployed female, aged 22]

My father went to his allergy doctor who referred us to a guy who turned out to be a reasonable psychiatrist. I'll never forget. He said, "Your daughter is clinically depressed." I remember sitting in his office. He saw us on a Saturday like at six o'clock. He did us a favor. And I remember I just sat there. It was a sort of darkened office. It was the first time I ever cried in front of anybody. [female social worker, aged 38]

And on the liberating side:

They gave me a blood test that measures the level of something in the blood, in the brain. And they pronounced me, they said, "Mr. Smith [a pseudonym], you're depressed." And I said, "Thank God," you know. I wasn't as batty as I thought. It was like the cat was out of the bag. You know? It was a breakthrough. . . . [Before that] depression wasn't in my vocabulary. . . . It was the beginning of being able to sort out a lifetime of feelings, events . . . my entire life. It was the chance for a new beginning. [male salesman, aged 30]

. . . It is impossible to consider the kinds of profound identity changes occasioned by any mental illness without paying special attention to the experience of hospitalization. It is one thing to deal alone with the demons of depression, or to privately see a psychiatrist for the problem, but once a person "shuts down" altogether and seeks asylum or is involuntarily "committed," he or she adds an institutional piece to their biography that is indelible. . . .

A few interviewees described the hospital as truly an asylum that provided relief and allowed them to "crash." Being hospitalized enabled them to give up the struggle of trying to appear and act normally. One person, in fact, described the hospital as a "wonderful place" where "I was taken care of, totally taken care of." Another was relieved "to go somewhere where I won't do anything to myself, where I can get in touch with this." Someone else explained, "I was glad to be there, definitely. It was a break from everything." Sometimes people were glad to be hospitalized since it provided dramatic and definitive evidence that something was really wrong with them when family and friends had been dismissing their complaints. More usual, though, were the responses like that of the person who said that "the experience of hospitalization was devastating to me" and the several who reported that being hospitalized made them feel like "damaged goods."

Of all the tough things associated with depression, nothing would frighten me more than hospitalization. . . .

Many of the 29 people who spoke of their time in hospitals spontaneously acknowledged the extraordinary impact of the experience on the way they thought about themselves. Sometimes they were themselves shocked that they had landed in a hospital. Several mentioned that hospitalization caused them to confront for the first time just how sick they were.

> *I remember being put onto the floor that was probably for the worst people of the sickness, because it was one of those floors where everything was really locked up. So I guess I was in pretty bad shape. [male administrator, aged 54]*

> *So I went to [names hospital] and I remember praying that I would get out. To me it seemed at the time as if the door would close—it was a secure facility— and I would never leave. I know I'm a basket case at this point. . . . The experience of having that severe depression, going to the hospital, and most of all being given shock treatments. . . . It made me feel . . . like damaged goods, impaired in some way that I was just not normal. It did make me feel impaired. [male professor, part-time, aged 48]*

Among the identity-related comments about the hospitalization experience, one set of observations, although made by only a few individuals, caught my attention. Once in the hospital these persons surveyed their environment, both the oppressive physical character of the place and the sad shape of their fellow "inmates," many of whom seemed to them destined for an institutionalized life. However awful their condition, these respondents made a distinction between their trouble and patients who were overtly psychotic. Unlike those unfortunates, they had a choice to make, as they saw it.

Either they would capitulate completely to their depression and possibly, therefore, to a life in the mental health system or they would do whatever necessary to leave the hospital as quickly as possible.

Giving up completely did have some appealing features. Full surrender meant relief from an exhausting battle and absolution from personal responsibility. One woman said,

> I saw these people going back and forth [in and out of the hospital] for their whole lives [and] that I could be one [of them]. If I went in that direction, it somehow absolved me from responsibility. And I teetered on the edge for a long time. It involved a conscious decision . . . [about whether] I'm going to become a [permanent] part of the system because it's safe and where I belong. . . .

. . . It should be noted that one outstanding uniformity in the interviews was the initially strong negative reaction people had to taking drugs. One person was "leery of it" and others variously described the idea of going on medications as "revolting," "certainly not my first choice," and "embarrassing." Others elaborated on the recommendation that they begin drug therapy in ways similar to the nurse who said: "I didn't want to be told that I had something that was going to affect the rest of my life and that could only be solved by taking pills. And there was sort of a rebellion in that: 'No, I'm not like that. I don't need you and your pills.'" . . . [Respondents] held the shared feeling that taking drugs was yet another distressing indication of the severity of a problem they could not control by themselves. The concurrent events of crisis, hospitalization, and beginning a drug regimen worked synergistically to concretize and dramatize respondents' status as patients with an illness that required ongoing treatment by therapeutic experts.

Coming to Grips with an Illness Identity

Whether people are hospitalized or not, involvement with psychiatric experts and medications is the transition point to a number of simultaneous processes, all with implications for the reformulation of identity. They are (1) reconstructing and reinterpreting one's past in terms of current experiences, (2) looking for causes for one's situation, (3) constructing new theories about the nature of depression, and (4) establishing modes of coping behavior. All of these activities require judgments about the appropriate metaphors for describing one's situation. Especially critical to ongoing identity construction is whether respondents approve of illness metaphors for describing their experience. A few individuals were willing clearly to define their condition as a mental illness:

> I know I have a mental illness. I'm beginning to feel that. [But] actually, there is a real relief in that. It's a sense of "Whew! Okay, I don't have to masquerade." I mean, sure I'll masquerade with work, because, listen, I've got to get the bread and butter on the table. But I don't have to masquerade in other ways. . . . It's

sort of like mentally ill people in some ways . . . are my people. There is a fair amount of really chronically mentally ill people at [names hospital where she works]. They're all on heavy-duty meds and I figure like "I know what it's like for you." I mean, I can imagine what it's like. I know some of that pain. I'm sure I don't know all of it, because, you know, I'm not that bad off, but there is sort of a sense like they could understand me and I could understand them in something that's really, really painful. [female physical therapist, aged 42]

. . . Most, however, wanted simultaneously to embrace the definition of their problem as biochemical in nature while rejecting the notion that they suffer from a "mental" illness.

I don't see it as an illness. To me, it seems like part of myself that evolved, part of my personality. And, I mean, it sounds crazy, but it is almost like a dual personality, the happy side of me and the sad side of me. . . . [female nanny, aged 22]

Well, do you have an illness? What do you have?

I tend to think of it as a condition. I don't think of it so much as an illness, although it feels like an illness sometimes. I think it's an unintegrated dimension of myself that's taken [on] kind of a life of its own, that has its own power. . . . [unemployed female, aged 35]

. . . Adopting the view that one is victimized by a biochemically sick self constitutes a comfortable "account" for a history of difficulties and failures and absolves one of reponsibility. On the negative side, however, acceptance of a victim role, while diminishing a sense of personal responsibility, is also enfeebling. To be a victim of biochemical forces beyond one's control gives force to others' definition of oneself as a helpless, passive object of injury. . . .

Respondents generally fall into two broad categories regarding their hopes that they can put depression behind them. First are those who view having depression as a life condition that they will never fully defeat, and second are those who believe either that they are now past the depression forever or that they can attain such a status. As might be expected, the two categories are generally formed by those who have experienced depression as an ongoing chronic thing, on the one hand, in contrast to those who have had periods of depression punctuated by wellness. The role of medications is interesting in establishing for some the idea that depression is something they can leave behind. Among the words that reappeared in comments about drugs was "miracle." Although, as noted, most of those interviewed at first took medication reluctantly, several reported that often for the first time in their lives they felt okay after a drug "kicked in." Generally, subjects were split between those who felt that while there was always the possibility of a recurrence, they essentially could get past depression and those who have surrendered to its inevitability and chronicity in their lives. The following comments summarize the two positions:

I've stopped thinking, "OK, I'm going to get over this depression. I'm going to finally, like, do this primal scream thing, or whatever. . . . [At one point] I did buy into [the idea] of the pursuit of happiness and the pursuit of fulfillment. I hate that word. And the mental health equivalent to finding fulfillment is to fill up the gaps inside of you and everything grows green. And that's what [psychiatry] is really striving for . . . and that's the standard life should be lived on. . . . But then I finally realized that well, maybe I'm in a desert. Maybe your landscape is green, but, you know, I'm in the Sahara and I've stopped trying to get out. . . . I'd rather cure it if I had my choice, but I don't think that is going to happen. My choice is to integrate it into my life. So, no, I don't see it going away. I just see myself becoming, you know, better able to cope with it, more graceful about it. [female mental health worker, aged 27]

I would say that this particular period of my life is a period where I don't have the fear or feeling [that depression will recur]. That's why, for me at least, I'm more inclined now to take the depression as an aberration and to take me in my more expansive, expressive state as the norm. For me, maybe I'm deluding myself, the way I feel now, and it's been three years since the hospitalization and I take no medications of any kind, [is] that I may be out of the woods, so to speak. . . . At the moment I don't have a fear of recurrence, but I do remember having it. [male professor, part-time, aged 48]

Unfortunately, the norm is for people to have repeated bouts with depression. In this regard, the process described here has a feedback-loop quality to it. Individuals move through a crisis with all its attendant identity-altering features, come to grips with the meaning of their experience by constructing theories about causation, and then sometimes reach the point where they feel they have gone beyond the depression experience. A new episode of depression, of course, casts doubt on all the previous interpretive work and requires people to once again move through a process of sense-making and identity construction. In this way, depression is like a virus that keeps mutating since each reliving of an experience, as the philosopher Edmund Husserl tells us, is a new experience. Chronically depressed people are constantly in the throes of an illness that is tragically familiar, but always new. As such, depression often involves a life centered on a nearly continuous process of construction, destruction, and reconstruction of identities in the face of repeated problems. . . .

ENDNOTES

[1] E. Hughes, *Men and Their Work* (New York: Free Press, 1958).

[2] Although the notion of "stage" is difficult to avoid, I want to suggest that in much social science literature the term conveys a determinism that I find unfortunate. Stages imply that, for whatever process being described, everyone must move through them in a predictably timed sequence. Hence, I often use the terms "mo-

ment," "benchmark," or "juncture" in the depression career to suggest a process that is more fluid than the stage idea.

[3] A. Strauss, "Turning Points in Identity." In C. Clark and H. Robboy (eds.), *Social Interaction* (New York: St. Martin's, 1992). The identity transitions described in the pages to follow bear an instructive resemblance to the idea of biographical "epiphanies" developed by Norman Denzin in a number of important books. See N. Denzin, *The Alcoholic Self* (Newbury Park, CA: Sage, 1987); N. Denzin, *Interpretive Interactionism* (Newbury Park, CA: Sage, 1989); N. Denzin, *Interpretive Biography* (Newbury Park, CA: Sage, 1989).

[4] R. Emerson and S. Messinger, "The Micropolitics of Trouble," *Social Problems* 25 (1977):121–33. For another formulation of the trouble idea, see the early work of Charlotte Schwartz. Schwartz's doctoral dissertation studied how 30 people who sought help at a university psychiatric service conceptualized their problem. Her interview data suggested that informants distinguished three mutually exclusive subjective states of trouble. She calls them *exigencies of living* (or momentary difficulties), *normal trouble* (ordinary trouble), and *special trouble* (serious problems). An elaboration of these categories can be found in her work entitled *Clients' Perspectives on Psychiatric Troubles in a College Setting* (unpublished doctoral dissertation, Brandeis University, 1976). See also her article with Merton Kahne entitled "The Social Construction of Trouble and Its Implications for Psychiatrists Working in College Settings," *Journal of the American College Health Asssociation* 25 (February, 1977): 194–97.

[5] R. Emerson and S. Messinger, op. cit., p. 122.

[6] Ibid.

[7] Ibid.

[8] P. Berger and H. Kellner, "Marriage and the Construction of Reality," *Diogenes* 46 (1964):1–25.

[9] D. Vaughan, *Uncoupling: Turning Points in Intimate Relationships* (New York: Oxford, 1986).

[10] Social scientists have been critical of the meaning of psychiatric diagnoses and the processes through which they are established. For examples, see P. Brown, "Diagnostic Conflict and Contradiction in Psychiatry," *Journal of Health and Social Behavior* 28 (1987):37–50 and M. Rosenberg, "A Symbolic Interactionist View of Psychosis," *Journal of Health and Social Behavior* 25 (1984):289–302.

EDUCATION

47

CIVILIZE THEM WITH A STICK

MARY CROW DOG • RICHARD ERDOES

Few students are aware of our nation's policies toward Native Americans, which included the separation of Indian children from their families and cultures so that these children could be "civilized" into the dominant society. Consequently, thousands of Native American children were forced to leave the reservation to attend boarding schools, day schools, or schools in converted Army posts. These total institutions used tactics similar to those used by the military to resocialize the young Native Americans. In the following selection, taken from *Lakota Woman* (1990), Mary Crow Dog and Richard Erdoes reveal how the institution of education can be an agent of social control whose purpose is to assimilate racial-ethnic populations, such as Native Americans, into the dominant culture.

> *. . . Gathered from the cabin, the wickiup, and the tepee,*
> *partly by cajolery and partly by threats;*
> *partly by bribery and partly by force,*
> *they are induced to leave their kindred*
> *to enter these schools and take upon themselves*
> *the outward appearance of civilized life.*
>
> —ANNUAL REPORT OF THE DEPARTMENT OF INTERIOR, 1901

It is almost impossible to explain to a sympathetic white person what a typical old Indian boarding school was like; how it affected the Indian child suddenly dumped into it like a small creature from another world, helpless, defenseless, bewildered, trying desperately and instinctively to survive and sometimes not surviving at all. I think such children were like the victims of Nazi concentration camps trying to tell average, middle-class Americans what their experience had been like. Even now, when these schools are much improved, when the buildings are new, all gleaming steel and glass, the food tolerable, the teachers well trained and well intentioned, even trained in child psychology—unfortunately the psychology of white

---

From *Lakota Woman*, pp. 28–37, 38–39, and 40–41. Copyright © 1990 by Mary Crow Dog and Richard Erdoes. Reprinted with the permission of Grove Weidenfeld.

children, which is different from ours—the shock to the child upon arrival is still tremendous. Some just seem to shrivel up, don't speak for days on end, and have an empty look in their eyes. I know of an 11-year-old on another reservation who hanged herself, and in our school, while I was there, a girl jumped out of the window, trying to kill herself to escape an unbearable situation. That first shock is always there.

Although the old tiyospaye has been destroyed, in the traditional Sioux families, especially in those where there is no drinking, the child is never left alone. It is always surrounded by relatives, carried around, enveloped in warmth. It is treated with the respect due to any human being, even a small one. It is seldom forced to do anything against its will, seldom screamed at, and never beaten. That much, at least, is left of the old family group among full-bloods. And then suddenly a bus or car arrives, full of strangers, usually white strangers, who yank the child out of the arms of those who love it, taking it screaming to the boarding school. The only word I can think of for what is done to these children is kidnapping.

Even now, in a good school, there is impersonality instead of close human contact; a sterile, cold atmosphere, an unfamiliar routine, language problems, and above all the maza-skan-skan, that damn clock—white man's time as opposed to Indian time, which is natural time. Like eating when you are hungry and sleeping when you are tired, not when that damn clock says you must. But I was not taken to one of the better, modern schools. I was taken to the old-fashioned mission school at St. Francis, run by the nuns and Catholic fathers, built sometime around the turn of the century and not improved a bit when I arrived, not improved as far as the buildings, the food, the teachers, or their methods were concerned.

In the old days, nature was our people's only school and they needed no other. Girls had their toy tipis and dolls, boys their toy bows and arrows. Both rode and swam and played the rough Indian games together. Kids watched their peers and elders and naturally grew from children into adults. Life in the tipi circle was harmonious—until the whiskey peddlers arrived with their wagons and barrels of "Injun whiskey." I often wished I could have grown up in the old, before-whiskey days.

Oddly enough, we owed our unspeakable boarding schools to the do-gooders, the white Indian-lovers. The schools were intended as an alternative to the outright extermination seriously advocated by generals Sherman and Sheridan, as well as by most settlers and prospectors overrunning our land. "You don't have to kill those poor benighted heathen," the do-gooders said, "in order to solve the Indian Problem. Just give us a chance to turn them into useful farmhands, laborers, and chambermaids who will break their backs for you at low wages." In that way the boarding schools were born. The kids were taken away from their villages and pueblos, in their blankets and moccasins, kept completely isolated from their families—sometimes for as long as ten years—suddenly coming back, their short hair slick with pomade, their necks raw from stiff, high collars, their thick jackets always short in the sleeves and pinching under the arms, their tight patent leather shoes giving them corns, the girls in starched white blouses and clumsy, high-buttoned boots—caricatures of white people. When they found out—and they found out quickly—that they were neither wanted by whites nor by Indians, they got good and drunk, many of them staying drunk for the rest of their lives. I still have a poster I found among my grandfather's stuff, given to him by the missionaries to tack up on his wall. It reads:

1. Let Jesus save you.
2. Come out of your blanket, cut your hair, and dress like a white man.
3. Have a Christian family with one wife for life only.
4. Live in a house like your white brother. Work hard and wash often.
5. Learn the value of a hard-earned dollar. Do not waste your money on giveaways. Be punctual.
6. Believe that property and wealth are signs of divine approval.
7. Keep away from saloons and strong spirits.
8. Speak the language of your white brother. Send your children to school to do likewise.
9. Go to church often and regularly.
10. Do not go to Indian dances or to the medicine men.

The people who were stuck upon "solving the Indian Problem" by making us into whites retreated from this position only step by step in the wake of Indian protests.

The mission school at St. Francis was a curse for our family for generations. My grandmother went there, then my mother, then my sisters and I. At one time or other, every one of us tried to run away. Grandma told me once about the bad times she had experienced at St. Francis. In those days they let students go home only for one week every year. Two days were used up for transportation, which meant spending just five days out of 365 with her family. And that was an improvement. Before grandma's time, on many reservations they did not let the students go home at all until they had finished school. Anybody who disobeyed the nuns was severely punished. The building in which my grandmother stayed had three floors, for girls only. Way up in the attic were little cells, about five by five by ten feet. One time she was in church and instead of praying she was playing jacks. As punishment they took her to one of those little cubicles where she stayed in darkness because the windows had been boarded up. They left her there for a whole week with only bread and water for nourishment. After she came out she promptly ran away, together with three other girls. They were found and brought back. The nuns stripped them naked and whipped them. They used a horse buggy whip on my grandmother. Then she was put back into the attic—for two weeks.

My mother had much the same experiences but never wanted to talk about them, and then there I was, in the same place. The school is now run by the BIA—the Bureau of Indian Affairs—but only since about 15 years ago. When

I was there, during the 1960s, it was still run by the Church. The Jesuit fathers ran the boys' wing and the Sisters of the Sacred Heart ran us—with the help of the strap. Nothing had changed since my grandmother's days. I have been told recently that even in the '70s they were still beating children at that school. All I got out of school was being taught how to pray. I learned quickly that I would be beaten if I failed in my devotions or, God forbid, prayed the wrong way, especially prayed in Indian to Wakan Tanka, the Indian Creator.

The girls' wing was built like an F and was run like a penal institution. Every morning at five o'clock the sisters would come into our large dormitory to wake us up, and immediately we had to kneel down at the sides of our beds and recite the prayers. At six o'clock we were herded into the church for more of the same. I did not take kindly to the discipline and to marching by the clock, left-right, left-right. I was never one to like being forced to do something. I do something because I feel like doing it. I felt this way always, as far as I can remember, and my sister Barbara felt the same way. An old medicine man once told me: "Us Lakotas are not like dogs who can be trained, who can be beaten and keep on wagging their tails, licking the hand that whipped them. We are like cats, little cats, big cats, wildcats, bobcats, mountain lions. It doesn't matter what kind, but cats who can't be tamed, who scratch if you step on their tails." But I was only a kitten and my claws were still small.

Barbara was still in the school when I arrived and during my first year or two she could still protect me a little bit. When Barb was a seventh grader she ran away together with five other girls, early in the morning before sunrise. They brought them back in the evening. The girls had to wait for two hours in front of the mother superior's office. They were hungry and cold, frozen through. It was wintertime and they had been running the whole day without food, trying to make good their escape. The mother superior asked each girl, "Would you do this again?" She told them that as punishment they would not be allowed to visit home for a month and that she'd keep them busy on work details until the skin on their knees and elbows had worn off. At the end of her speech she told each girl, "Get up from this chair and lean over it." She then lifted the girls' skirts and pulled down their underpants. Not little girls either, but teenagers. She had a leather strap about a foot long and four inches wide fastened to a stick, and beat the girls, one after another, until they cried. Barb did not give her that satisfaction but just clenched her teeth. There was one girl, Barb told me, the nun kept on beating and beating until her arm got tired.

I did not escape my share of the strap. Once, when I was 13 years old, I refused to go to Mass. I did not want to go to church because I did not feel well. A nun grabbed me by the hair, dragged me upstairs, made me stoop over, pulled my dress up (we were not allowed at the time to wear jeans), pulled my panties down, and gave me what they called "swats"—25 swats with a board around which Scotch tape had been wound. She hurt me badly.

My classroom was right next to the principal's office and almost every day I could hear him swatting the boys. Beating was the common punishment for not doing one's homework, or for being late to school. It had such a bad effect upon me that I hated and mistrusted every white person on sight, because I met only one kind. It was not until much later that I met sincere white people I could relate to and be friends with. Racism breeds racism in reverse.

The routine at St. Francis was dreary. Six A.M., kneeling in church for an hour or so; seven o'clock, breakfast; eight o'clock, scrub the floor, peel spuds, make classes. We had to mop the dining room twice every day and scrub the tables. If you were caught taking a rest, doodling on the bench with a fingernail or knife, or just rapping, the nun would come up with a dish towel and just slap it across your face, saying, "You're not supposed to be talking, you're supposed to be working!" Monday mornings we had cornmeal mush, Tuesday oatmeal, Wednesday rice and raisins, Thursday cornflakes, and Friday all the leftovers mixed together or sometimes fish. Frequently the food had bugs or rocks in it. We were eating hot dogs that were weeks old, while the nuns were dining on ham, whipped potatoes, sweet peas, and cranberry sauce. In winter our dorm was icy cold while the nuns' rooms were always warm.

I have seen little girls arrive at the school, first graders, just fresh from home and totally unprepared for what awaited them, little girls with pretty braids, and the first thing the nuns did was chop their hair off and tie up what was left behind their ears. Next they would dump the children into tubs of alcohol, a sort of rubbing alcohol, "to get the germs off." Many of the nuns were German immigrants, some from Bavaria, so that we sometimes speculated whether Bavaria was some sort of Dracula country inhabited by monsters. For the sake of objectivity I ought to mention that two of the German fathers were great linguists and that the only Lakota-English dictionaries and grammars which are worth anything were put together by them.

At night some of the girls would huddle in bed together for comfort and reassurance. Then the nun in charge of the dorm would come in and say, "What are the two of you doing in bed together? I smell evil in this room. You girls are evil incarnate. You are sinning. You are going to hell and burn forever. You can act that way in the devil's frying pan." She would get them out of bed in the middle of the night, making them kneel and pray until morning. We had not the slightest idea what it was all about. At home we slept two and three in a bed for animal warmth and a feeling of security.

The nuns and the girls in the two top grades were constantly battling it out physically with fists, nails, and hair-pulling. I myself was growing from a kitten into an undersized cat. My claws were getting bigger and were itching for action. About 1969 or 1970 a strange young white girl appeared on the reservation. She looked about 18 or 20 years old. She was pretty and had long, blond hair down to her waist, patched jeans, boots, and a backpack. She was different from any other white person we had met before. I think her name was Wise. I do not know how she managed to overcome our reluctance and distrust, getting us into a corner, making us listen to her, asking us how we were treated. She told us that she was from New York. She was the first real hippie or Yippie we had come across. She told us of people called the Black Panthers, Young Lords, and Weathermen. She said, "Black people are getting it on. Indians are getting it on in St. Paul and California. How about you?" She also said, "Why don't you put out an underground paper, mimeograph it. It's easy. Tell it like it is. Let it all hang out." She spoke a strange lingo but we caught on fast.

Charlene Left Hand Bull and Gina One Star were two full-blood girls I used to hang out with. We did everything together. They were willing to join me in a Sioux uprising. We put together a newspaper which we called the *Red Panther*. In it we wrote how bad the school was, what kind of slop we had to eat—slimy, rotten, blackened potatoes for two weeks—the way we were beaten. I think I was the one who wrote the worst article about our principal of the moment, Father Keeler. I put all my anger and venom into it. I called him a goddam wasičun son of a bitch. I wrote that he knew nothing about Indians and should go back to where he came from, teaching white children whom he could relate to. I wrote that we knew which priests slept with which nuns and that all they ever could think about was filling their bellies and buying a new car. It was the kind of writing which foamed at the mouth, but which also lifted a great deal of weight from one's soul.

On Saint Patrick's Day, when everybody was at the big powwow, we distributed our newspapers. We put them on windshields and bulletin boards, in desks and pews, in dorms and toilets. But someone saw us and snitched on us. The shit hit the fan. The three of us were taken before a board meeting. Our parents, in my case my mother, had to come. They were told that ours was a most serious matter, the worst thing that had ever happened in the school's long history. One of the nuns told my mother, "Your daughter really needs to be talked to." "What's wrong with my daughter?" my mother asked. She was given one of our *Red Panther* newspapers. The nun pointed out its name to her and then my piece, waiting for mom's reaction. After a while she asked, "Well, what have you got to say to this? What do you think?"

My mother said, "Well, when I went to school here, some years back, I was treated a lot worse than these kids are. I really can't see how they can have any complaints, because we was treated a lot stricter. We could not even wear skirts halfway up our knees. These girls have it made. But you should forgive them because they are young. And it's supposed to be a free country, free speech and all that. I don't believe what they done is wrong." So all I got out of it was scrubbing six flights of stairs on my hands and knees, every day. And no boy-side privileges.

The boys and girls were still pretty much separated. The only time one could meet a member of the opposite sex was during free time, between 4 and 5:30, in the study hall or on benches or the volleyball court outside, and that was strictly supervised. One day Charlene and I went over to the boys' side. We were on the ball team and they had to let us practice. We played three extra minutes, only three minutes more than we were supposed to. Here was the nuns' opportunity for revenge. We got 25 swats. I told Charlene, "We are getting too old to have our bare asses whipped that way. We are old enough to have babies. Enough of this shit. Next time we fight back." Charlene only said, "Hoka-hay!". . .

In a school like this there is always a lot of favoritism. At St. Francis it was strongly tinged with racism. Girls who were near-white, who came from what the nuns called "nice families," got preferential treatment. They waited on the faculty and got to eat ham or eggs and bacon in the morning. They got the easy jobs while the skins, who did not have the right kind of background—myself among them—always wound up in the laundry room sorting out 10-bushel baskets of dirty boys' socks every day. Or we wound up scrubbing the floors and doing all the dishes. The school therefore fostered fights and antagonism between whites and breeds, and between breeds and skins. At one time Charlene and I had to iron all the robes and vestments the priests wore when saying Mass. We had to fold them up and put them into a chest in the back of the church. In a corner, looking over our shoulders, was a statue of the crucified Savior, all bloody and beaten up. Charlene looked up and said, "Look at that poor Indian. The pigs sure worked him over." That was the closest I ever came to seeing Jesus.

I was held up as a bad example and didn't mind. I was old enough to have a boyfriend and promptly got one. At the school we had an hour and a half for ourselves. Between the boys' and the girls' wings were some benches where one could sit. My boyfriend and I used to go there just to hold hands and talk. The nuns were very uptight about any boy-girl stuff. They had an exaggerated fear of anything having even the faintest connection with sex. One day in religion class, an all-girl class, Sister Bernard singled me out for some remarks, pointing me out as a bad example, an example that should be shown. She said that I was too free with my body. That I was holding hands which meant that I was not a good example to follow. She also said that I wore unchaste dresses, skirts which were too short, too suggestive, shorter than regulations permitted, and for that I would be punished. She dressed me down before the whole class, carrying on and on about my unchastity. . . .

We got a new priest in English. During one of his first classes he asked one of the boys a certain question. The boy was shy. He spoke poor English, but he had the right answer. The priest told him, "You did not say it right. Correct yourself. Say it over again." The boy got flustered and stammered. He could hardly get out a word. But the priest kept after him: "Didn't you hear? I told you to do the whole thing over. Get it right this time." He kept on and on.

I stood up and said, "Father, don't be doing that. If you go into an Indian's home and try to talk Indian, they might laugh at you and say, 'Do it over correctly. Get it right this time!'"

He shouted at me, "Mary, you stay after class. Sit down right now!"

I stayed after class, until after the bell. He told me, "Get over here!" He grabbed me by the arm, pushing me against the blackboard, shouting, "Why are you always mocking us? You have no reason to do this."

I said, "Sure I do. You were making fun of him. You embarrassed him. He needs strengthening, not weakening. You hurt him. I did not hurt you."

He twisted my arm and pushed real hard. I turned around and hit him in the face, giving him a bloody nose. After that I ran out of the room, slamming the door behind me. He and I went to Sister Bernard's office. I told her, "Today I quit school. I'm not taking any more of this, none of this shit anymore. None of this treatment. Better give me my diploma. I can't waste any more time on you people."

Sister Bernard looked at me for a long, long time. She said, "All right, Mary Ellen, go home today. Come back in a few days and get your diploma." And that was that. Oddly enough, that priest turned out okay. He taught a class in grammar, orthography, composition, things like that. I think he wanted more respect in class. He was still young and unsure of himself. But I was in there too long. I didn't feel like hearing it. Later he became a good friend of the Indians, a personal friend of myself and my husband. He stood up for us during Wounded Knee and after. He stood up to his superiors, stuck his neck way out, became a real people's priest. He even learned our language. He died prematurely of cancer. It is not only the good Indians who die young, but the good whites, too. It is the timid ones who know how to take care of themselves who grow old. I am still grateful to that priest for what he did for us later and for the quarrel he picked with me—or did I pick it with him?—because it ended a situation which had become unendurable for me. The day of my fight with him was my last day in school.

48

PREPARING FOR POWER
Cultural Capital and Curricula
in America's Elite Boarding Schools

PETER W. COOKSON, JR.
CAROLINE HODGES PERSELL

In addition to teaching individuals life skills, such as reading, writing, and critical thinking, another important function of education is to help select the future employment of students. Thus, education tracks and trains people for certain jobs. Many jobs in society are based on *credentialing,* or the requirement of certain educational degrees in order to be hired and promoted. Schools also provide the valued *cultural capital* of the middle and upper classes. This knowledge of cultural background, norms, and skills of the upper classes enables students to obtain higher socioeconomic statuses. This reading by Peter W. Cookson, Jr. and Caroline Hodges Persell is taken from their 1985 book of the same title, and it examines the cultural capital students gain in elite boarding schools.

Borrowing from the British, early American headmasters and teachers advocated a boarding school curriculum that was classical, conservative, and disciplined. It wasn't until the latter part of the nineteenth century that such "soft" subjects as English, history, and mathematics were given a place beside Latin, Greek, rhetoric, and logic in the syllabus. It was the early schoolmasters' belief that young minds, especially boys' minds, if left to their own devices, were undisciplined, even anarchic. The only reliable antidote to mental flabbiness was a rigorous, regular regime of mental calisthenics. A boy who could not flawlessly recite long Latin passages was required to increase his mental workouts. Classical languages were to the mind what cold showers were to the body: tonics against waywardness.

Girls, with some exceptions, were not thought of as needing much mental preparation for their future roles as wives and mothers. Their heads were best left uncluttered by thought; too much book learning could give a girl ideas about independence. Besides, the great majority of them were not going on to college, where even more classical languages were required.

From *Preparing for Power: America's Elite Boarding Schools,* pp. 73–84. Copyright © 1985 by Peter W. Cookson, Jr. and Caroline Hodges Persell. Reprinted with the permission of BasicBooks, a member of Perseus Books, L.L.C.

As an intellectual status symbol, the classical curriculum helped distinguish gentlemen from virtually everyone else and thus defined the difference between an "educated" man and an untutored one, as well as the difference between high culture and popular culture. Such a division is critical to exclude nonmembers from groups seeking status. For a long time a classical curriculum was the only path to admission to a university, as Harvard and many others required candidates to demonstrate proficiency in Latin and Greek (Levine 1980). Thus, the curriculum of boarding schools has long served both social and practical functions.

Culture, much like real estate or stocks, can be considered a form of capital. As the French scholars Pierre Bourdieu and Jean-Claude Passeron (1977) have indicated, the accumulation of cultural capital can be used to reinforce class differences. Cultural capital is socially created: What constitutes the "best in Western civilization" is not arrived at by happenstance, nor was it decided upon by public election. The more deeply embedded the values, the more likely they will be perceived as value free and universal.

Thus curriculum is the nursery of culture and the classical curriculum is the cradle of high culture. The definition of what is a classical course of study has evolved, of course, since the nineteenth century. Greek and Latin are no longer required subjects in most schools—electives abound. But the disciplined and trained mind is still the major objective of the boarding school curriculum.

> The Groton curriculum is predicated on the belief that certain qualities of mind are of major importance: precise and articulate communication; the ability to compute accurately and to reason quantitatively; a grasp of scientific approaches to problem-solving; an understanding of the cultural, social, scientific, and political background of Western civilization; and the ability to reason carefully and logically and to think imaginatively and sensitively. Consequently the School puts considerable emphasis on language, mathematics, science, history, and the arts. (*Groton School* 1981–82:15)

The contrast between the relatively lean curricula of many public schools and the abundant courses offered by boarding schools is apparent. In catalogues of the boarding school's academic requirements, courses are usually grouped by subject matter, and at the larger schools course listings and descriptions can go on for several dozen pages. Far from sounding dreary, the courses described in most catalogues are designed to whet the intellectual appetite. Elective subjects in particular have intriguing titles such as "Hemingway: The Man and His Work," "Varieties of the Poetic Experience," "Effecting Political Change," "Rendezvous with Armageddon," and for those with a scientific bent, "Vertebrate Zoology" and "Mammalian Anatomy and Physiology."

Boarding school students are urged to read deeply and widely. A term course on modern American literature may include works from as many as

10 authors, ranging from William Faulkner to Jack Kerouac. Almost all schools offer a course in Shakespeare in which six or seven plays will be read.

In history, original works are far more likely to be assigned than excerpts from a textbook. A course on the presidency at one school included the following required readings: Rossiter, *The American Presidency;* Hofstadter, *The American Political Tradition;* Hargrove, *Presidential Leadership;* Schlesinger, *A Thousand Days;* Kearns, *Lyndon Johnson and the American Dream;* and White, *Breach of Faith.* Courses often use a college-level text, such as Garraty's *The American Nation* or Palmer's *A History of the Modern World.* Economic history is taught as well—in one school we observed a discussion of the interplay between politics and the Depression of 1837—and the idea that there are multiple viewpoints in history is stressed. It is little wonder that many prep school graduates find their first year of college relatively easy.

An advanced-placement English class uses a collection of *The Canterbury Tales* by Geoffrey Chaucer that includes the original middle English on the left page and a modern English translation on the right. An advanced third-year French course includes three or four novels as well as two books of grammar and readings. Even social science courses require a great deal of reading. In a course called "An Introduction to Human Behavior," students are assigned 11 texts including works from B. F. Skinner, Sigmund Freud, Erich Fromm, Jean Piaget, and Rollo May.

Diploma requirements usually include four years of English, three years of math, three years in one foreign language, two years of history or social science, two years of laboratory science, and one year of art. Many schools require a year of philosophy or religion and also may have such noncredit diploma requirements as four years of physical education, a library skills course, introduction to computers, and a seminar on human sexuality. On average, American public high school seniors take one year less English and math, and more than a year less foreign language than boarding school students (Coleman, Hoffer, and Kilgore 1982:90). Moreover, in the past two decades there has been a historical decline in the number of academic subjects taken by students in the public schools (Adleman 1983).

Because success on the Scholastic Aptitude Test is so critical for admission to a selective college, it is not uncommon for schools to offer English review classes that are specifically designed to help students prepare for the tests. Most schools also offer tutorials and remedial opportunities for students who are weak in a particular subject. For foreign students there is often a course in English as a second language.

As the arts will be part of the future roles of boarding school students, the music, art, and theater programs at many schools are enriching, with special courses such as "The Sound and Sense of Music," "Advanced Drawing," and "The Creative Eye in Film." Student art work is usually on display, and almost every school will produce several full-length plays each year, for example, *Arsenic and Old Lace, A Thurber Carnival, Dracula,* and *The Mousetrap.*

Music is a cherished tradition in many boarding schools, in keeping with their British ancestry. The long-standing "Songs" at Harrow, made famous because Winston Churchill liked to return to them for solace during World War II, are a remarkable display of school solidarity. All 750 boys participate, wearing identical morning coats with tails. Every seat is filled in the circular, sharply tiered replica of Shakespeare's Globe Theater as the boys rise in unison, their voices resonating in the rotunda.

The belief that a well-rounded education includes some "hands-on" experience and travel runs deep in the prep view of learning. Virtually every boarding school provides opportunities for its students to study and work off campus. As volunteers, Taft students, for instance, can "tutor on a one-to-one basis in inner-city schools in Waterbury, act as teachers' helpers in Waterbury Public Schools and work with retarded children at Southbury Training School." They can also work in convalescent homes, hospitals, and day-care centers, and act as "apprentices to veterinarians and help with Girl Scout troops" (*Taft* 1981–82:21). At the Ethel Walker School in Connecticut, girls can go on whale watches, trips to the theater, or work in the office of a local politician. The Madeira School in Virginia has a co-curriculum program requiring students to spend every Wednesday participating in volunteer or internship situations.

Generally speaking, the schools that take the position that manual labor and firsthand experience are good for the soul as well as the mind and body, are more progressive in orientation than other schools. At the Putney School every student has to take a tour of duty at the cow barn, starting at 5:30 A.M. In their own words, "Putney's work program is ambitious. We grow much of our own food, mill our own lumber, pick up our own trash, and have a large part in building our buildings. . . . Stoves won't heat until wood is cut and split" (*The Putney School* 1982:3).

Various styles of student-built structures dot the campus of the Colorado Rocky Mountain School, and at the tiny Midland School in California, there is no service staff, except for one cook. When the water pump breaks, faculty and students fix it, and when buildings are to be built, faculty and students pitch in. "We choose to live simply, to distinguish between our needs and our wants, to do without many of the comforts which often obscure the significant things in life" (*Midland School* 1983:1). The creed of self-reliance is reenacted every day at Midland. When a trustee offered to buy the school a swimming pool, he was turned down. Lounging around a pool is not part of the Midland philosophy.

Travel is very much part of the prep way of life and is continued right through the school year. Not only are semesters or a year abroad (usually in France or Spain) offered, but at some of the smaller schools, everyone goes on an extensive field trip. Every March at the Verde Valley School in Arizona the students travel to "Hopi, Navajo and Zuni reservations, to small villages in northern Mexico, to isolated Spanish-American communities in northern

New Mexico and to ethnic neighborhoods of Southwestern cities. They live with native families, attend and teach in schools, work on ranches, and participate in the lives of the host families and their communities" (*Verde Valley School* 1982–83:9). Not all boarding schools, of course, place such a high value on rubbing shoulders with the outside world. At most of the academies, entrepreneurial, and girls' schools the emphasis is on service rather than sharing.

While boarding schools may vary in their general philosophy, the actual curricula do not widely differ. The pressures exerted on prep schools to get their students into good colleges means that virtually all students must study the same core subjects. Although not quick to embrace educational innovation, many boarding schools have added computers to their curricula. This has no doubt been encouraged by announcements by a number of Ivy League and other elite colleges that they want their future applicants to be "computer literate." While people at most boarding schools, or anywhere else for that matter, are not quite sure what is meant by computer literate, they are trying to provide well-equipped computer rooms and teachers who can move their students toward computer proficiency.

For students who have particular interests that cannot be met by the formal curriculum, almost all schools offer independent study, which gives students and teachers at boarding schools a great deal of intellectual flexibility. At Groton, for example, independent study can cover a diverse set of topics including listening to the works of Wagner, conducting a scientific experiment, or studying a special aspect of history.

The boarding school curriculum offers students an abundant buffet of regular course work, electives, volunteer opportunities, travel, and independent study, from which to choose a course of study. By encouraging students to treat academic work as an exciting challenge rather than just a job to be done, the prep schools not only pass on culture but increase their students' competitive edge in the scramble for admission to selective colleges.

The Importance of Sports

Even the most diligent student cannot sit in classrooms all day, and because the prep philosophy emphasizes the whole person, boarding schools offer an impressive array of extracurricular activities, the most important of which is athletics. At progressive schools, the competitive nature of sport is deemphasized. The "afternoon out-of-door program" at Putney, for example, allows for a wide variety of outdoor activities that are noncompetitive; in fact, "skiing is the ideal sport for Putney as one may ski chiefly to enjoy himself, the air, the snow" (*The Putney School* 1982:15).

Putney's sense that sport should be part of a communion with nature is not shared by most other schools, however. At most prep schools sport is about competition and, even more important, about winning. An athletically powerful prep school will field varsity, junior varsity, and third-string teams in most major sports. A typical coed or boys' school will offer football, soccer, cross-country, water polo, ice hockey, swimming, squash, basketball, wrestling, winter track, gymnastics, tennis, golf, baseball, track, and lacrosse. For the faint-hearted there are alternative activities such as modern dance, cycling, tai chi, yoga, ballet, and for the hopelessly unathletic, a "fitness" class. A truly traditional prep school will also have crew like their English forebears at Eton and Harrow. Certain schools have retained such British games as "Fives," but most stop short of the mayhem masquerading as a game called rugby.

Prep teams compete with college freshmen teams, other prep teams, and occasionally with public schools, although public school competitors are picked with care. Not only is there the possible problem of humiliation on the field, there is the even more explosive problem of fraternization in the stands when prep meets townie. Some schools, known as "jock" schools, act essentially as farm teams for Ivy League colleges, consistently providing them with athletes who have been polished by the prep experience. Many prep schools take public high school graduates for a postgraduate year, as a way of adding some size and weight to their football teams.

Prep girls also love sports; they participate as much as the boys, often in the same sports, and with as much vigor. A girls' field hockey game between Exeter and Andover is as intense as when the varsity football teams clash. Horseback riding at girls' schools is still popular; a number of the girls go on to ride in the show or hunt circuit. Unlike many of the girls in public schools, the boarding-school girl is discouraged from being a spectator. Loafing is considered to be almost as bad for girls as it is for boys.

During the school year the halls of nearly all prep schools are decorated with either bulletins of sporting outcomes or posters urging victory in some upcoming game. Pep rallies are common, as are assemblies when awards are given and competitive spirit is eulogized. Often the whole school will be bussed to an opponent's campus if the game is considered to be crucial or if the rivalry is long-standing.

Alumni return to see games, and there are frequent contests between alumni and varsity teams. Because preps retain the love of fitness and sports, it is not uncommon for the old warriors to give the young warriors a thrashing. Similarly, the prep life also invariably includes ritual competitions between, say, the girls' field hockey team and a pick-up faculty team.

Nowhere is the spirit of victory more pronounced than on the ice of the hockey rink. Few public schools can afford a hockey rink so prep schools can attract the best players without much competition. Some prep schools import a few Canadians each year to fill out the roster. Speed, strength, endurance, and fearlessness are the qualities that produce winning hockey and more than one freshman team from an Ivy League college has found itself outskated by a prep team. Whatever else may be, in Holden Caulfield's term, "phony" about prep schools, sports are for real. This emphasis on sport is not without its critics. At the Harrow School in London, the new headmaster, who was an all-England rugby player, has begun a program to reward artistic and musical prowess as well as athletic and academic skills.

The athletic facilities at prep schools are impressive and, at the larger schools, lavish. Acres and acres of playing fields, scores of tennis courts, one or more gyms, a hockey rink, a golf course, swimming pools, squash courts, workout rooms—all can be found on many prep school campuses. Generally, the facilities are extremely well maintained. The equipment most preps use is the best, as are the uniforms. One boy described how "when your gym clothes get dirty, you simply turn them in at the locker room for a fresh set." The cost of all this, of course, is extraordinary, but considered necessary, because excellence in sport is part of the definition of a gentleman or gentlewoman.

The pressure for athletic success is intense on many campuses, and a student's, as well as a school's, social standing can ride on the narrow margin between victory and defeat. Perhaps because of this, schools generally take great pains to play schools of their own size and social eliteness. A study of who plays whom among prep schools reveals that schools will travel great distances, at considerable expense, to play other prep schools whose students and traditions are similar to their own.

Extracurriculars and Preparation for Life

Not all prep school extracurricular activities require sweating, however. Like public school students, preps can work on the school newspaper or yearbook, help to organize a dance, or be part of a blood donor drive, and are much more likely than their public school counterparts to be involved in such activities. For example, one in three boarding school students is involved in student government compared to one in five public school students, and two in five are involved in the school newspaper or yearbook compared to one in five. This evidence is consistent with other research. Coleman, Hoffer, and Kilgore (1982) found that private school students participate more in extracurricular activities than do public school students. The fact that more boarding school students than public school students are involved in activities provides additional opportunities for them to practice their verbal, interpersonal, and leadership skills.

The catalogue of clubs at prep schools is nearly endless. The opportunity for students to develop special nonacademic interests is one of the qualities of life at prep schools that distinguishes them from many public schools. Special interest clubs for chess, sailing, bowling, or gun clubs are popular at boys' schools. One elite boys' school has a "war games" club. As the boys at this school are feverishly calculating their country's next strategic arms move, the girls in a Connecticut school are attending a meeting of Amnesty International. Girls, in general, tend to spend their off hours studying the gentler arts such as gourmet cooking and art history. One girls' school has a club with a permanent service mission to the governor's office.

At some schools students can learn printing, metalwork, or woodworking. The shop for the latter at Groton is amply equipped and much of the work turned out by the students is of professional quality. The less traditional schools offer clubs for vegetarian cooking, weaving, quilting, folk music, and—in subtle juxtaposition to the Connecticut girls' school—international cooking. At western schools the horse still reigns supreme, and many students spend endless hours riding, training, cleaning, and loving their own horse or a horse they have leased from the school.

With the prep emphasis on music, choirs, glee clubs, madrigals, chamber music groups, as well as informal ensembles are all given places to practice. Most schools also have individual practice rooms, and like athletic teams, many prep musicians travel to other schools for concerts and performances.

Some schools offer a five-week "Winterim," during which students and faculty propose and organize a variety of off- and on-campus activities and studies. Such a program breaks the monotony of the usual class routine in the middle of winter, a season teachers repeatedly told us was the worst time at boarding school. It also enables students and faculty to explore new areas or interests in a safe way, that is, without grades.

In prep schools there is a perceived need for students to exercise authority as apprentice leaders early in their educational careers. The tradition of delegating real authority to students has British roots, where head boys and prefects have real power within the public schools. Head boys can discipline other boys by setting punishments and are treated by headmaster and housemasters alike as a part of the administration. In the United States, student power is generally more limited, although at the progressive schools students can be quite involved in the administrative decision-making process.

Virtually all prep schools have a student government. The formal structure of government usually includes a student body president, vice president, treasurer, secretary, class presidents, and dorm prefects, representatives, or "whips," as they are called at one school. Clubs also have presidents and there are always committees to be headed. Some schools have student-faculty senates and in schools like Wooster, in Connecticut, students are expected to play a major part in the disciplinary system. An ambitious student can obtain a great deal of experience in committee work, developing transferable skills for later leadership positions in finance, law, management, or politics.

The office of student body president or head prefect is used by the administration primarily as an extension of the official school culture, and most of the students who fill these offices are quite good at advancing the school's best public relations face. A successful student body president, like a good head, is artful in developing an easy leadership style, which is useful because he or she is in a structural political dilemma. Elected by the students but responsible to the school administration, the student politician is a classic go-between, always running the danger of being seen as "selling out" by students and as "uncooperative" by the administration. Occasionally students rebel against too much pandering to the administration and elect a rebel leader, who makes it his or her business to be a thorn in the side of the administration. A number of heads and deans of students watch elections closely, because if elections go "badly" it could mean a difficult year for them.

The actual content of real power varies by school. At some, authority is more apparent than real; at others, student power can affect important school decisions. At Putney, the "Big Committee" is composed of the school director, student leaders, and teachers. The powers of the Big Committee are laid out in the school's constitution, and students at Putney have real input into the decision-making process. At the Thacher School in California, the Student Leadership Council, which is composed of the school chairman, presidents of the three lower classes, and head prefects, is not only responsible for student activities and events, but also grants funds to groups who petition for special allocations. The power of the purse is learned early in the life of a prep school student. At the Westtown School in Pennsylvania, the student council arrives at decisions not by voting yea or nay, "but by following the Quaker custom of arriving at a 'sense of the meeting'" (*Westtown School* 1982–83:25).

Not all students, of course, participate in school politics; it may well be that many of the students most admired by their peers never run, or never would run, for a political position. The guerrilla leaders who emerge and flourish in the student underlife—or counterculture—may have far greater real power than the "superschoolies" that tend to get elected to public office.

In most coeducational schools, boys tend to monopolize positions of power. The highest offices are generally held by boys; girls are found in the vice presidential and secretarial positions. Politics can be important to prep families, and we suspect that a number of prep boys arrive at boarding school with a good supply of political ambition. One of the reasons advanced in support of all-girls' schools is that girls can gain important leadership experience there.

Some schools try to capture what they see as the best aspects of single-sex and coed schools. They do this by having boys and girls elect distinct school leaders, by having certain customs, places, and events that they share only with members of their own sex, and by having classes, certain other activities, and social events be coeducational. These schools, often called coordinate schools, see themselves as offering the chance to form strong single-sex bonds, to build self-confidence in adolescents, and to provide experience in working and relating to members of both sexes. Girls at coed schools more generally are likely to say they think in 10 years they will find the social skills they learned to be the most valuable part of their boarding-school experience.

Learning by Example

Part of the social learning students obtain is exposure to significant public personalities. Virtually all the schools have guest speaker programs in which well-known people can be seen and heard. Some of the speakers that have appeared at Miss Porter's School in the last several years include Alex Haley, author; Russell Baker, humorist; Arthur Miller, playwright; and Dick Gregory, comedian. At the boys' schools there is a tendency to invite men who are successful in politics and journalism. Recent speakers at the Hill School include James A. Baker III, Secretary of the Treasury (Hill class of 1948); James Reston, columnist; Frank Borman, astronaut and president of Eastern Airlines; and William Proxmire, United States senator (Hill class of 1934).

Inviting successful alumni to return for talks is one of the ways boarding schools can pass on a sense of the school's efficacy. Throughout the year panels, assemblies, and forums are organized for these occasions. Often the alumni speakers will also have informal sessions with students, visit classrooms, and stay for lunch, tea, or supper.

In keeping with cultural environments of prep schools, especially the select 16 schools, professional musicians, actors, and dancers are regularly invited to perform. Art and sculpture exhibits are common and some schools, such as Andover and Exeter, have permanent art galleries. The art at prep schools is generally either original works by artists such as Toulouse-Lautrec, Matisse, or Daumier, or the work of established contemporary artists such as Frank Stella, who graduated from Andover. At a large school there may be so much cultural activity that it is unnecessary to leave campus for any kind of high cultural event.

Those who come to elite boarding schools to talk or perform are the makers of culture. For adolescents seeking to be the best, these successful individuals give them a sense of importance and empowerment. All around them are the symbols of their special importance—in Groton's main hallway hangs a personal letter from Ronald Reagan to the headmaster, reminding the students that Groton "boasts a former President of the United States and some of America's finest statesmen." Five or six books a year will be published by a school's alumni; Exeter in particular has many alumni authors, including James Agee, Nathaniel G. Benchley, John Knowles, Dwight Macdonald, Jr., Arthur M. Schlesinger Jr., Sloan Wilson, and Gore Vidal. Roger L. Stevens, Alan Jay Lerner, and Edward Albee are all Choate-Rosemary Hall alumni, adding luster to a theater program that trains many professional actresses and actors. A student at an elite school is part of a world where success is expected, and celebrity and power are part of the unfolding of life. Not every school is as culturally rich as the elite eastern prep schools, but in the main, most schools work hard to develop an appreciation for high culture. At the Orme School in Arizona, a week is set aside each year in which the whole school participates in looking at art, watching art being made, and making art.

Nowhere is the drive for athletic, cultural, and academic excellence more apparent than in the awards, honors, and prizes that are given to outstanding teams or students at the end of each year. Sporting trophies are often large silver cups with the names of annual champions engraved on several sides. At some schools the triumphs have come with enough regularity to warrant building several hundred yards of glass casing to hold the dozens of medals, trophies, and other mementos that are the victors' spoils. Pictures of past winning teams, looking directly into the camera, seem frozen in time.

Academic prizes tend to be slightly less flashy but no less important. Much like British schoolmasters, American schoolmasters believe in rewarding excellence, so most schools give a number of cultural, service, and academic prizes at the end of each year. There is usually at least one prize in each academic discipline, as well as prizes for overall achievement and effort. There are service prizes for dedicated volunteers, as well as debating and creative writing prizes. Almost all schools have cum laude and other honor societies.

Sitting through a graduation ceremony at a boarding school can be an endurance test—some schools give so many prizes that one could fly from New York to Boston and back in the time it takes to go from the classics prize to the prize for the best woodworking or weaving project. But of course, the greatest prize of all is graduation, and more than a few schools chisel, paint, etch, or carve the names of the graduates into wood, stone, or metal to immortalize their passage from the total institution into the world.

REFERENCES

Adleman, Clifford. 1983. "Devaluation, Diffusion and the College Connection: A Study of High School Transcripts, 1964–1981." Washington, DC: National Commission on Excellence in Education.

Bourdieu, Pierre and Jean-Claude Passeron. 1977. *Reproduction: In Education, Society, and Culture.* Beverly Hills, CA: Sage.

Coleman, James S., Thomas Hoffer, and Sally Kilgore. 1982. *High School Achievement.* New York: Basic Books, p. 90.

Levine, Steven B. 1980. "The Rise of American Boarding Schools and the Development of a National Upper Class." *Social Problems* 28:63–94.

49

FAILING AT FAIRNESS
Hidden Lessons

MYRA SADKER • DAVID SADKER

Few social institutions mold the social environment as faithfully as schools do. The institution of education reinforces social inequality by teaching the dominant culture's values and biases. The following reading by Myra Sadker and David Sadker, professors of education at The American University, examines how the social institution of education has replicated social hierarchies that perpetuate gender inequality. In this excerpt, taken from their 1994 book, *Failing at Fairness: How Our Schools Cheat Girls,* they illustrate the gender biases that permeate the institution of education.

Sitting in the same classroom, reading the same textbook, listening to the same teacher, boys and girls receive very different educations. From grade school through graduate school, female students are more likely to be invisible members of classrooms. Teachers interact with males more frequently, ask them better questions, and give them more precise and helpful feedback. Over the course of years the uneven distribution of teacher time, energy, attention, and talent, with boys getting the lion's share, takes its toll on girls. Since gender bias is not a noisy problem, most people are unaware of the secret sexist lessons and the quiet losses they engender.

Girls are the majority of our nation's schoolchildren, yet they are second-class educational citizens. The problems they face—loss of self-esteem, decline in achievement, and elimination of career options—are at the heart of the educational process. Until educational sexism is eradicated, more than half our children will be shortchanged and their gifts lost to society.

Award-winning author Susan Faludi discovered that backlash "is most powerful when it goes private, when it lodges inside a woman's mind and turns her vision inward, until she imagines the pressure is all in her head, until she begins to enforce the backlash too—on herself." [1] Psychological backlash internalized by adult women is a frightening concept, but what is even more terrifying is a curriculum of sexist school lessons becoming secret mind games played against female children, our daughters, tomorrow's women.

Reprinted with the permission of Scribner, a Division of Simon & Schuster, from *Failing at Fairness: How America's Schools Cheat Girls* by Myra Sadker and David Sadker. Copyright © 1994 by Myra Sadker and David Sadker.

After almost two decades of research grants and thousands of hours of classroom observation, we remain amazed at the stubborn persistence of these hidden sexist lessons. When we began our investigation of gender bias, we looked first in the classrooms of one of Washington, D.C.'s elite and expensive private schools. Uncertain of exactly what to look for, we wrote nothing down; we just observed. The classroom was a whirlwind of activity, so fast paced we could easily miss the quick but vital phrase or gesture, the insidious incident, the tiny inequity that held a world of meaning. As we watched, we had to push ourselves beyond the blind spots of socialization and gradually focus on the nature of the interaction between teacher and student. On the second day we saw our first example of sexism, a quick, jarring flash within the hectic pace of the school day:

Two second-graders are kneeling beside a large box. They whisper excitedly to each other as they pull out wooden blocks, colored balls, counting sticks. So absorbed are these two small children in examining and sorting the materials, they are visibly startled by the teacher's impatient voice as she hovers over them. "Ann! Julia! Get your cotton-pickin' hands out of the math box. Move over so the boys can get in there and do their work."

Isolated here on the page of a book, this incident is not difficult to interpret. It becomes even more disturbing if you think of it with the teacher making a racial distinction. Picture Ann and Julia as African American children moved away so white children can gain access to the math materials. If Ann and Julia's parents had observed this exchange, they might justifiably wonder whether their tuition dollars were well spent. But few parents actually watch teachers in action, and fewer still have learned to interpret the meaning behind fast-paced classroom events.

The incident unsettles, but it must be considered within the context of numerous interactions this harried teacher had that day. While she talked to the two girls, she was also keeping a wary eye on fourteen other active children. Unless you actually shadowed the teacher, stood right next to her as we did, you might not have seen or heard the event. After all, it lasted only a few seconds.

It took us almost a year to develop an observation system that would register the hundreds of daily classroom interactions, teasing out the gender bias embedded in them. Trained raters coded classrooms in math, reading, English, and social studies. They observed students from different racial and ethnic backgrounds. They saw lessons taught by women and by men, by teachers of different races. In short, they analyzed America's classrooms. By the end of the year we had thousands of observation sheets, and after another year of statistical analysis, we discovered a syntax of sexism so elusive that most teachers and students were completely unaware of its influence.[2]

Recently a producer of NBC's "Dateline" contacted us to learn more about our discovery that girls don't receive their fair share of education. Jane Paulcy, the show's anchorwoman, wanted to visit classrooms, capture these covert sexist lessons on videotape, and expose them before a television audience. The task was to extricate sound bites of sexism from a fifth-grade classroom where the teacher, chosen to be the subject of the exposé, was aware she was being scrutinized for sex bias.

"Dateline" had been taping in her class for two days when we received a concerned phone call. "This is a fair teacher," the producer said. "How can we show sexism on our show when there's no gender bias in this teacher's class?" We drove to the NBC studio in Washington, D.C., and found two "Dateline" staffers, intelligent women concerned about fair treatment in school, sitting on the floor in a darkened room staring at the videotape of a fifth-grade class. "We've been playing this over and over. The teacher is terrific. There's no bias in her teaching. Come watch."

After about twenty minutes of viewing, we realized it was a case of déjà vu: The episodal sexist themes and recurring incidents were all too familiar. The teacher was terrific, but she was more effective for half of the students than she was for the other. She was, in fact, a classic example of the hundreds of skillful well-intentioned professionals we have seen who inadvertently teach boys better than girls.

We had forgotten how difficult it was to recognize subtle sexism before you learn how to look. It was as if the "Dateline" staff members were wearing blinders. We halted the tape, pointed out the sexist behaviors, related them to incidents in our research, and played the tape again. There is a classic "aha!" effect in education when people finally "get it." Once the hidden lessons of unconscious bias are understood, classrooms never look the same again to the trained observer.

Much of the unintentional gender bias in that fifth-grade class could not be shown in the short time allowed by television, but the sound bites of sexism were also there. "Dateline" chose to show a segregated math group: boys sitting on the teacher's right side and girls on her left. After giving the math book to a girl to hold open at the page of examples, the teacher turned her back to the girls and focused on the boys, teaching them actively and directly. Occasionally she turned to the girls' side, but only to read the examples in the book. This teacher, although aware that she was being observed for sexism, had unwittingly transformed the girls into passive spectators, an audience for the boys. All but one, that is: The girl holding the math book had become a prop.

"Dateline" also showed a lively discussion in the school library. With both girls' hands and boys' hands waving for attention, the librarian chose boy after boy to speak. In one interaction she peered through the forest of girls' hands waving directly in front of her to acknowledge the raised hand of a boy in the back of the room. Startled by the teacher's attention, the boy muttered, "I was just stretching."

The next day we discussed the show with future teachers, our students at The American University. They were bewildered. "Those teachers really were sexist. They didn't mean to be, but they were. How could that happen—with the cameras and everyone watching?" When we took those students into classrooms to discover the hidden lessons for themselves, they began to understand. It is difficult to detect sexism unless you know precisely how to observe. And if a lifetime of socialization makes it difficult to spot gender bias even when you're looking for it, how much harder it is to avoid the traps when you are the one doing the teaching.

Among Schoolchildren

Subtle sexism is visible to only the most astute readers of *Among Schoolchildren,* Tracy Kidder's chronicle of real-life educator Chris Zajac. A thirty-four-year-old teacher in Mt. Holyoke, Massachusetts, Mrs. Zajac is a no-nonsense veteran of the classroom. She does not allow her fifth-grade students to misbehave, forget to do their homework, or give up without trying their hardest. Underlying her strict exterior is a woman who cares about schoolchildren. Our students admired her dedication and respected her as a good human being, and it took several readings and discussions before they discovered her inadvertent gender bias. Then came the questions: Does Mrs. Zajac work harder teaching boys than girls? Does she know there is sex bias in her classroom?

These questions probably do not occur to most readers of *Among Schoolchildren* and might jolt both Chris Zajac and the author who so meticulously described the classroom. Here's how Tracy Kidder begins the story of a year in the life of this New England teacher:

> Mrs. Zajac wasn't born yesterday. She knows you didn't do your best work on this paper, Clarence. Don't you remember Mrs. Zajac saying that if you didn't do your best, she'd make you do it over? As for you, Claude, God forbid that you should ever need brain surgery. But Mrs. Zajac hopes that if you do, the doctor won't open up your head and walk off saying he's almost done, as you said when Mrs. Zajac asked you for your penmanship, which, by the way, looks like you did it and ran. Felipe, the reason you have hiccups is, your mouth is always open and the wind rushes in. You're in fifth grade now. So, Felipe, put a lock on it. Zip it up. Then go get a drink of water. Mrs. Zajac means business, Robert. The sooner you realize she never said everybody in the room has to do the work except for Robert, the sooner you'll get along with her. And . . . Clarence. Mrs. Zajac knows you didn't try. You don't just hand in junk to Mrs. Zajac. She's been teaching an awful lot of years. She didn't fall off the turnip cart yesterday. She told you she was an old-lady teacher."[3]

Swiftly, adroitly, Kidder introduces the main characters in the classroom— Clarence, Claude, Felipe, Robert, and back to Clarence, the boy in whom Mrs. Zajac invests most. But where are the girls?

As our students analyzed the book and actually examined who Mrs. Zajac was speaking to, they saw that page after page she spent time with the boys—disciplining them, struggling to help them understand, teaching them with all the energy and talent she could muster. In contrast, the pages that showed Mrs. Zajac working with girls were few and far between.

When we ask teachers at our workshops why they spend more time helping boys, they say, "Because boys need it more" or "Boys have trouble reading, writing, doing math. They can't even sit still. They need me more." In *Among Schoolchildren,* Chris Zajac feels that way, too. Kidder describes how she allows boys to take her over because she thinks they need her.

So teachers of good intention, such as Chris Zajac, respond to boys and teach them more actively, but their time and attention are not limitless. While the teachers are spending time with boys, the girls are being ignored and shortchanged. The only girl clearly realized in *Among Schoolchildren* is Judith, a child who is so alert that she has a vast English vocabulary even though her parents speak only Spanish. But while Judith is a girl of brilliant potential, she rarely reaps the benefit of Mrs. Zajac's active teaching attention. In fact, rather than trouble her teacher and claim time and attention for herself, Judith helps Mrs. Zajac, freeing her to work with the more demanding boys. Mrs. Zajac knows she isn't giving this talented girl what she needs and deserves: "If only I had more time," she thinks as she looks at Judith.

On a field trip to old Sturbridge Village, the children have segregated themselves by sex on the bus, with the boys claiming the back. In a moment of quiet reflection, Chris realizes that in her classroom "the boys rarely give her a chance to spend much time with her girls." She changes her seat, joins the girls, and sings jump rope songs with them for the remainder of the trip.[4]

But her time spent with the girls is short-lived—the length of the day-long field trip—and her recognition of the gender gap in time and attention is brief: a paragraph-long flash of understanding in a book of more than three hundred pages. On the whole, Chris Zajac does not invest her talent in girls. But nurturing children is not unlike tending a garden: Neglect, even when benign, is withering; time and attention bear fruit. Mrs. Zajac and other caring teachers across the country are unaware of the full impact of uneven treatment. They do not realize the high academic and emotional price many girls pay for being too good. Drawn from years of research, the episodes that follow demonstrate the sexist lessons taught daily in America's classrooms.[5] Pulled out of the numerous incidents in a school day, these inequities become enlarged, as if observed through a magnifying glass, so we can see clearly how they extinguish learning and shatter self-esteem. Imagine yourself in a sixth-grade science class like the one we observed in Maryland.

The teacher is writing a list of inventors and their discoveries on the board:

Elias Howe	sewing machine
Robert Fulton	steamboat
Thomas A. Edison	light bulb
James Otis	elevator

Alexander Graham Bell	telephone
Cyrus McCormick	reaper
Eli Whitney	cotton gin
Orville and Wilbur Wright	airplane

A girl raises her hand and asks, "It looks like all the inventors were men. Didn't women invent anything?" The teacher does not add any female inventors to the list, nor does he discuss new scholarship recognizing the involvement of women in inventions such as the cotton gin. He does not explain how hard it was in times past for women to obtain patents in their own names, and therefore we may never know how many female inventors are excluded from the pages of our history books. Instead he grins, winks, and says, "Sweetheart, don't worry about it. It's the same with famous writers and painters. It's the man's job to create things and the woman's job to look beautiful so she can inspire him." Several boys laugh. A few clown around by flexing their muscles as they exclaim, "Yes!" One girl rolls her eyes toward the ceiling and shakes her head in disgust. The incident lasts less than a minute, and the discussion of male inventors continues.

We sometimes ask our students at The American University to list twenty famous women from American history. There are only a few restrictions. They cannot include figures from sports or entertainment. Presidents' wives are not allowed unless they are clearly famous in their own right. Most students cannot do it. The seeds of their ignorance were sown in their earliest years of schooling.

In the 1970s, analyses of best-selling history books showed a biological oddity, a nation with only founding fathers.[6] More space was given to the six-shooter than to the women's suffrage movement. In fact, the typical history text gave only two sentences to enfranchising half the population. Science texts continued the picture of a one-gender world, with the exception of Marie Curie who was permitted to stand behind her husband and peer over his shoulder as he looked into a microscope. Today's history and science texts are better—but not much.[7]

At our workshops we ask teachers and parents to tell or write about any sexism they have seen in their schools. We have been collecting their stories for years.[8] A Utah teacher told us: "Last year I had my U.S. history class write biographies about famous Americans. When I collected all one hundred and fifty, I was dismayed to find only five on women. When I asked my kids why, they said they didn't know any famous women. When I examined their textbook more closely, I saw there were few females in it. And there were even fewer books on famous American women in our school library."

Teachers add to textbook bias when they produce sexist materials of their own. One parent described her efforts to stop a teacher-made worksheet that perpetuated stereotypes of yesteryear:

A few years ago my daughter came home upset over her grade. When I looked at her paper, I got more angry than she was. At the top of the worksheet were the faces of a man and a woman. At the bottom were different objects—nails, a saw, a sewing needle, thread, a hammer, a screwdriver, a broom. The directions said to draw a line from the woman to the objects that go with her. In our house my husband does the cooking and I do the repair work, so you can imagine what the lines on my daughter's paper looked like. There was a huge red F in the middle of her worksheet. I called the teacher right away. She was very understanding and assured me the F wouldn't count. A small victory, I thought, and forgot about it.

This year my son is in her class. Guess what he brought home last week. Same worksheet—same F. Nothing had changed at all.

When girls do not see themselves in the pages of textbooks, when teachers do not point out or confront the omissions, our daughters learn that to be female is to be an absent partner in the development of our nation. And when teachers add their stereotypes to the curriculum bias in books, the message becomes even more damaging.

In a 1992 survey in *Glamour*, 74 percent of those responding said that they had "a teacher who was biased against females or paid more attention to the boys." Math class was selected as the place where inequities were most likely to occur. Fifty-eight percent picked it as their most sexist subject. Physical education was second, and science came in third, selected by 47 percent of the respondents.[9] Women at our workshops recall remarks made by math and science teachers that years later still leave them upset and angry:

In my A.P. physics class in high school in 1984 there were only three girls and twenty-seven boys. The three girls, myself included, consistently scored at the top end of the scale. On one test I earned a 98. The next closest boy earned an 88. The teacher handed the tests back saying, "Boys, you are failing. These three pretty cookies are outscoring you guys on every test." He told the boys it was embarrassing for them to be beaten by a girl. He always referred to us (the girls) as "Cookie" or made our names sound very cutesy!

Sometimes the humiliating lessons come not from school policies, teachers, or books but from boys, the very individuals that adolescent girls most want to impress:

The New England high school was having an assembly during the last period on Friday, and the auditorium was packed with more than a thousand students, who were restless as they listened to announcements. A heavy, awkward tenth-grader made her way across the stage to reach the microphone located in the center. As she walked, several male students made loud barking noises to signify she was a dog. Others oinked like pigs. Later a slender long-haired senior walked to the mike; she was greeted by catcalls and whistles. Nobody attempted to stop the demeaning and hurtful public evaluation of the appearance of these teenage girls.

Tolerated under the assumption that "boys will be boys" and hormone levels are high in high school, sexual harassment is a way of life in America's schools. While teachers and administrators look the other way, sexually denigrating comments, pinching, touching, and propositioning happen daily. Sensitive and insecure about their appearance, some girls are so intimidated they suffer in silence. Others fight back only to find this heightens the harassment. Many girls don't even realize they have a right to protest. And when they do come forward, bringing school sexual harassment into the open, it is often dealt with quickly and nervously; it is swept under the rug, turned aside, or even turned against the girl who had the courage to complain. A teacher at a workshop in Indiana told us: "In our school a girl was pinched on the derriere by two boys and verbally harassed. When she reported the incident to the principal, she was told that her dress was inappropriate and that she had asked for it."

Intimidating comments and offensive sexual jokes are even more common in college and sometimes are even made public as part of a classroom lecture and discussion. A female faculty member, teaching at a university that was historically all male, told us about one of the most popular teachers on campus, an economics professor:

> *He would show slides illustrating an economic theory and insert women in bikinis in the middle "to keep students interested." He illustrated different phases of the economic cycle by showing a slide of a woman's breast and pointed out how far away from the nipple each phase was. When a number of female students complained, the local newspaper supported the professor and criticized the "ultrasensitive coeds." That semester the university gave the professor the Teacher of the Year award.*

Although sexually harassing remarks, stories, and jokes occur only occasionally in classrooms, female silence is the norm. During our two-year study of colleges, our raters found that girls grow quieter as they grow older. In coeducational classes, college women are even less likely to participate in discussions than elementary and secondary school girls. In the typical college classroom, 45 percent of students do not speak; the majority of these voiceless students are women.[10]

Breaking the Sound Barrier

Women who have spent years learning the silence in elementary, secondary, and college classrooms have trouble regaining their voices. In our workshops we often set up a role play to demonstrate classroom sex bias. Four volunteers, two women and two men, are asked to pretend to be students in a middle school social studies lesson. They have no script; their only direction is to take a piece of paper with them as David, playing the part of the social studies teacher, ushers them to four chairs in front of the room. He tells the audience that he will condense all the research on sexism in the classroom into a ten-minute lesson, so the bias will look blatant, even overwhelming. The job of the parents and teachers in the audience is to detect the different forms of egregious sexism. He begins the lesson.

"Today we're going to discuss the chapter in your book, 'The Gathering Clouds of War,' about the American Revolution. But first I'd like you to take out your homework so I can check it." David walks over to Sarah, the first student in the line of four. (In real life she is an English teacher at the local high school.)

"Let's see your paper, Sarah." He pauses to look it over. "Questions three and seven are not correct." Sarah looks concerned.

David moves to Peggy (who is a communications professor at a state college). "Oh, Peggy, Peggy, Peggy!" She looks up as everyone stares. David holds up Peggy's paper. "Would you all look at this. It is sooo neat. You print just like a typewriter. This is the kind of paper I like to put on the bulletin board for open school night." Peggy looks down, smiles, blushes, looks up wide-eyed, and bats her eyelashes. She is not faking or exaggerating these behaviors. Before our eyes she has returned to childhood as the stereotypical good girl with pretty penmanship. The lessons have been well learned.

Next, David stops by Tony (who is a vocational education teacher) and looks at the blank paper he is holding. "Tony, you've missed questions three, seven, and eleven. I think you would do better on your assignments if you used the bold headings to guide your reading. I know you can get this if you try harder." Tony nods earnestly as David moves to Roy. Sarah, who missed questions three and seven, looks perplexed.

David scans Roy's paper and hands it back. "Roy, where's your homework?"

Roy (a college physics teacher) stammers, "Here it is," and again offers the blank paper that served as homework for the others in the role play.

"Roy, that's not your history homework. That's science." Roy still looks puzzled. "Trust me, Roy," David says. "No matter what you come up with, it won't be history homework. Now, where is it?"

"The dog ate it," Roy mutters, getting the picture and falling into the bad boy role.

Next, David discusses revolutionary battles, military tactics, and male leaders—George Washington, John and Samuel Adams, Paul Revere, Benjamin Franklin, Thomas Jefferson, and more. He calls on Roy and Tony more than twenty times each. When they don't know the answer, he probes, jokes, challenges, offers hints. He calls on Sarah only twice. She misses both her questions because David gives her less than half a second to speak. After effusively praising Peggy's pretty paper, David never calls on her again. As the lesson progresses, Sarah's face takes on a sad, almost vacant expression. Peggy keeps on smiling.

When the scene of blatant sexism is over, many in the audience want to know how the two women felt.

"That was me all through school," Peggy blurts out. "I did very well. My work was neat. I was always prepared. I would have had the right answer if someone had called on me. But they never did."

"Why did you watch the two males get all the attention?" we ask. "If you weren't called on, why didn't you call out?"

"I tried. I just couldn't do it."

"Why? You weren't wearing a muzzle. The men were calling out."

"I know. I felt terrible. It reminded me of all those years in school when I wanted to say something but couldn't."

"What about you, Sarah?" we ask. "Why didn't you just shout out an answer?"

"It never occurred to me to do it," Sarah says, then pauses. "No, that's not true. I thought about it, but I didn't want to be out there where I might get laughed at or ridiculed."

David has taught this role play class hundreds and hundreds of times in workshops in big cities and small towns all across the United States. Each time he demonstrates sex bias by blatantly and offensively ignoring female students, and almost always the adult women, put back into the role of twelve-year-olds, sit and say nothing; once again they become the nice girls watching the boys in action. Inside they may feel sad or furious or relieved, but like Sarah and Peggy, they remain silent.

When women try to get into classroom interaction, they rarely act directly. Instead they doodle, write letters, pass notes, and wait for the teacher to notice them. In a California workshop, one parent who was playing the part of a student developed an elaborate pantomime. She reached into her large purse, pulled out a file, and began to do her nails. When that failed to attract David's attention, she brought out a brush, makeup, and a mirror. But David continued to ignore her, talking only with the two males.

"I was so mad I wanted to hit you," the woman fumed at the end of the role play when she was invited to express her feelings.

"What did you do to show your anger?" David asked.

"I didn't do anything." Then she paused, realizing the passive-aggressive but ultimately powerless strategy she had pursued. "No, I did do something—my nails," she said sadly.

After hundreds of these role plays, we are still astonished at how quickly the veneer of adulthood melts away. Grown women and men replay behavior they learned as children at school. The role plays are always revealing—funny, sad, and sometimes they even have a troubling twist.

At a workshop for college students at a large university in the Midwest, one of the young women ignored in the role play did not exhibit the usual behavior of silence or passive hostility. Instead, in the middle of the workshop in front of her classmates, she began to sob. She explained later in private that as one of only a few girls in the university's agricultural program, she had been either ignored or harassed. That week in an overenrolled course an instructor had announced, "There are too many students in this class. Every-one with ovaries—out!"

"What did you do?"

"What could I do? I left. Later I told my adviser about it. He was sympathetic but said if there was no room, I should consider another major."

Silent Losses

Each time a girl opens a book and reads a womanless history, she learns she is worth less. Each time the teacher passes over a girl to elicit the ideas and opinions of boys, that girl is conditioned to be silent and to defer. As teachers use their expertise to question, praise, probe, clarify, and correct boys, they help these male students sharpen ideas, refine their thinking, gain their voice, and achieve more. When female students are offered the left-overs of teacher time and attention, morsels of amorphous feedback, they achieve less.

Then girls and women learn to speak softly or not at all; to submerge honest feelings, withhold opinions, and defer to boys; to avoid math and science as male domains; to value neatness and quiet more than assertiveness and creativity; to emphasize appearance and hide intelligence. Through this curriculum in sexism they are turned into educational spectators instead of players; but education is not a spectator sport.

When blatantly sexual or sexist remarks become an accepted part of classroom conversation, female students are degraded. Sexual harassment in business and the military now causes shock waves and legal suits. Sexual harassment in schools is dismissed as normal and unavoidable "boys will be boys" behavior; but by being targeted, girls are being intimidated and caused to feel like members of an inferior class.

Like a thief in school, sexist lessons subvert education, twisting it into a system of socialization that robs potential. Consider this record of silent, devastating losses.[11]

- ▼ In the early grades, girls are ahead of or equal to boys on almost every standardized measure of achievement and psychological well-being. By the time they graduate from high school or college, they have fallen back. Girls enter school ahead but leave behind.[12]
- ▼ In high school, girls score lower on the SAT and ACT tests, which are critical for college admission. The greatest gender gap is in the crucial areas of science and math.
- ▼ Girls score far lower on College Board Achievement tests, which are required by most of the highly selective colleges.
- ▼ Boys are much more likely to be awarded state and national college scholarships.

▼ The gap does not narrow in college. Women score lower on all sections of the Graduate Record Exam, which is necessary to enter many graduate programs.

▼ Women also trail on most tests needed to enter professional schools: the GMAT for business school, the LSAT for law school, and the MCAT for medical school.

▼ From elementary school through higher education, female students receive less active instruction, both in the quantity and in the quality of teacher time and attention.[13]

In addition to the loss of academic achievement, girls suffer other difficulties:

▼ Eating disorders among girls in middle and secondary schools and in college are rampant and increasing.[14]

▼ Incidents of school-based sexual harassment are now reported with alarming frequency.[15]

▼ One in ten teenage girls becomes pregnant each year. Unlike boys, when girls drop out, they usually stay out.[16]

▼ As girls go through school, their self-esteem plummets, and the danger of depression increases.[17]

▼ Economic penalties follow women after graduation. Careers that have a high percentage of female workers, such as teaching and nursing, are poorly paid. And even when women work in the same jobs as men, they earn less money. Most of America's poor live in households that are headed by women.

If the cure for cancer is forming in the mind of one of our daughters, it is less likely to become a reality than if it is forming in the mind of one of our sons. Until this changes, everybody loses.

ENDNOTES

[1] Susan Faludi, *Backlash: The Undeclared War against American Women* (New York: Crown, 1991), p. xxii.

[2] Our first study, which analyzed gender bias in elementary and secondary classrooms, lasted more than three years and was funded by the National Institute of Education. The report submitted to the government was Myra Sadker and David Sadker, *Year 3: Final Report: Promoting Effectiveness in Classroom Instruction* (Washington, DC: National Institute of Education, 1984); Myra Sadker and David Sadker, "Sexism in the Schoolroom of the Eighties," *Psychology Today*, March 1985, pp. 54–57; Myra Sadker and David Sadker, "Sexism in the Classroom: From Grade School to Graduate School," *Phi Delta Kappan* 67, no. 7 (March 1986):512–15. We also reported this study as one of the contributing authors to Wellesley College Center for Research on Women, *How Schools Shortchange Girls: The AAUW Report* (Washington, DC: American Association of University Women Educational Foundation), 1992.

[3] Tracy Kidder, *Among Schoolchildren* (Boston: Houghton Mifflin, 1989), p. 3.

[4] Kidder, *Among Schoolchildren*, p. 262.

[5] These episodes are drawn primarily from our three-year study of sex bias in elementary and secondary classrooms. They are also taken from classroom observations conducted as we supervised student teachers at The American University and as we consulted with schools around the country and assessed their classrooms for gender bias.

[6] Janice Law Trecker, "Women in U.S. History High School Textbooks," *Social Education* 35 (1971):249–60.

[7] Lenore Weitzman and Diane Rizzo, *Biased Textbooks: Images of Males and Females in Elementary School Textbooks* (Washington, DC: Resource Center on Sex Roles in Education, 1976); Terry Saario, Carol Jacklin, and Carol Tittle, "Sex Role Stereotyping in the Public Schools," *Harvard Educational Review* 43:386–416; Women on Words and Images, *Dick and Jane As Victims: Sex Stereotyping in Children's Readers* (Princeton, NJ: Carolingian Press, 1972).

[8] For more than a decade we have offered workshops on gender bias for educators and parents around the country. At these workshops we have collected anecdotes and stories from students, teachers, and parents about sex bias that they faced at school.

[9] "This Is What You Thought: Were Any of Your Teachers Biased against Females?" *Glamour*, August 1992, p. 157.

[10] Following our three-year study of elementary and secondary classrooms, we conducted a two-year study of college classrooms and were sponsored by the Fund for the Improvement of Postsecondary Education. The project report submitted to the government was Myra Sadker and David Sadker, *Final Report: Project Effect (Effectiveness and Equity in College Teaching)*, Washington, DC: Fund for the Improvement of Postsecondary Education, 1986; Myra Sadker and David Sadker, "Confronting Sexism in the College Classroom," in Susan Gabriel and Isaiah Smithson (eds.), *Gender in the Classroom: Power and Pedagogy* (Urbana: University of Illinois Press, 1990), pp. 176–87.

[11] Myra Sadker, David Sadker, and Susan Klein, "The Issue of Gender in Elementary and Secondary Education," in Gerald Grant (ed.), *Review of Research in Education*, vol. 17. (Washington, DC: American Educational Research Association, 1991); Wellesley College Center for Research on Women, *How Schools Shortchange Girls: The AAUW Report*.

[12] Data documenting the loss of academic achievement were obtained from reports, tables, news releases, and studies issued by test publishers. The Educational Testing Service in Princeton, New Jersey, provided several reports and statistics related to the Preliminary Scholastic Aptitude Test, the Scholastic Aptitude Test, the Achievement tests, the Graduate Record Exam, and the Graduate Management Admissions Test. While the Graduate Record Exam data were from 1987–1988 (the most recently published), all other data reflected 1991 and 1992 test administrations. The American College Testing Program data were derived from a variety of profile and normative reports for 1990 and 1991 issued by American College Testing in Iowa City, Iowa.

Professional organizations and schools often contract with testing services to develop and administer their admissions tests. For example, the Medical College Admission Test (MCAT) is developed by ACT in Iowa City. For each of these admission tests the professional association responsible was contacted first, and it provided the requisite information. These organizations included the Association of American Medical Colleges, the Graduate Management Admissions Council, and the Law School Data Assembly Service.

[13] Sadker and Sadker, *Year 3: Final Report;* Sadker and Sadker, *Final Report: Project Effect.*

[14] K. L. Nagel and Karen H. Jones, "Sociological Factors in the Development of Eating Disorders," *Adolescence* 27 (Spring 1992):107–13; Claire Wiseman, James Gray,

James Mosimann, and Anthony Ahrens, "Cultural Expectations of Thinness in Women: An Update," *International Journal of Eating Disorders* 11, no. 1 (1992):85–89; Eric Button, "Self-Esteem in Girls Aged 11–12. Baseline Findings from a Planned Prospective Study of Vulnerability to Eating Disorders," *Journal of Adolescence* 13 (December 7, 1990):407–13.

[15] Jean O'Gorman Hughes and Bernice Sandler, *Peer Harassment: Hassles for Women on Campus* (Washington, DC: Project on the Status and Education of Women, Association of American Colleges, 1988); Nan Stein, "Sexual Harassment in Schools," *The School Administrator,* January 1993, pp. 14–21.

[16] Janice Earle, *Counselor/Advocates: Keeping Pregnant and Parenting Teens in School* (Alexandria, VA: National Association of State Boards of Education, 1990).

[17] A vast body of research documents girls' declining self-esteem at adolescence: Betty Allgood-Merten, Peter Lewinsohn, and Hyman Hops, "Sex Differences and Adolescent Depression," *Journal of Abnormal Psychology* 99, no. 1 (February 1990): 55–63; Herman Brutsaert, "Changing Sources of Self-Esteem among Girls and Boys in Secondary Schools," *Urban Education* 24, no. 4 (January 1990):432–39; Kevin Kelly and LaVerne Jordan. "Effects of Academic Achievement and Gender on Academic and Social Self-Concept: A Replication Study," *Journal of Counseling and Development* 69 (November–December 1990):173–77; Keith Widaman, et al. "Differences in Adolescents' Self-Concept As a Function of Academic Level, Ethnicity, and Gender," *American Journal of Mental Retardation* 96, no. 4 (1992):387–404; Sheila Williams and Rob McGee, "Adolescents' Self-Perceptions of Their Strengths," *Journal of Youth and Adolescence* 20, no. 3 (June 1991):325–37.

THE FAMILY

50

GAY AND LESBIAN FAMILIES ARE HERE

JUDITH STACEY

Some scholars argue that to understand completely the current debate about family, we need to examine the changing definitions of family. For example, many people define *family* only in terms of heterosexual marriage and blood ties. If we delineate family based on only these two criteria, think of all the people this definition leaves out, including adopted and foster children, cohabiting couples, gay and lesbian couples, and friends who are often closer

From *In the Name of the Family* by Judith Stacey in *All Our Families,* edited by Mary Ann Mason, pp. 105–128, 164–167. Copyright © 1996 Oxford University Press. Reprinted with permission from Oxford University Press.

than blood relatives. In the following selection, taken from *In the Name of the Family: Rethinking Family Values in the Post Modern Age* (1996), Judith Stacey challenges us to examine our heterosexist and narrow definitions of family. Stacey, a professor of sociology at the University of Southern California, argues that gay and lesbian families already exist in large numbers; they are not deviant; and many of these families are fighting for the same rights as heterosexual families, including the right to adopt children and the right to have the economic and legal benefits of marriage.

In 1992 in Houston, I talked about the cultural war going on for the soul of America. And that war is still going on! We cannot worship the false god of gay rights. To put that sort of relationship on the same level as marriage is a moral lie.

—Pat Buchanan, February 10, 1996

Homosexuality is a peculiar and rare human trait that affects only a small percentage of the population and is of little interest to the rest.

—Jonathan Rauch 1994

I came to Beijing to the Fourth World Conference of Women to speak on behalf of lesbian families. We are part of families. We are daughters, we are sisters, we are aunts, nieces, cousins. In addition, many of us are mothers and grandmothers. We share concerns for our families that are the same concerns of women around the world.

—Bonnie Tinker, *Love Makes a Family,* September 1995

Until but a short time ago, gay and lesbian families seemed quite a queer concept, even preposterous, if not oxymoronic, not only to scholars and the general public, but even to most lesbians and gay men. The grass roots movement for gay liberation that exploded into public visibility in 1969, when gays resisted a police raid at the Stonewall bar in New York City, struggled along with the militant feminist movement of that period to liberate gays and women *from* perceived evils and injustices represented by the family, rather than *for* access to its blessings and privileges. During the early 1970s, marches for gay pride and women's liberation flaunted provocative, countercultural banners, like "Smash The Family" and "Smash Monogamy." Their legacy is a lasting public association of gay liberation and feminism with family subversion. Yet how "queer" such antifamily rhetoric sounds today, when gays and lesbians are in the thick of a vigorous profamily movement of their own.

Gay and lesbian families are indisputably here. In June of 1993, police chief Tom Potter joined his lesbian, police officer daughter in a Portland, Oregon, gay pride march for "family values." By the late 1980s an astonishing "gay-by boom" had swelled the ranks of children living with gay and lesbian parents to between six to fourteen million.[1] *Family Values* is the title of a popular 1993 book by and about a lesbian's successful struggle to become a legal second mother to one of these "turkey-baster" babies, the son she and his biological mother have co-parented since his birth.[2] In 1989 Denmark became the first nation in the world to legalize a form of gay marriage, termed "registered partnerships," and its Nordic neighbors, Norway and Sweden, soon followed suit. In 1993, thousands of gay and lesbian couples participated in a mass wedding ceremony on the Washington Mall during the largest demonstration for gay rights in U.S. history. Three years later, on March 25, 1996, Mayor of San Francisco Willie Brown proudly presided over a civic ceremony to celebrate the domestic partnerships of nearly 200 same-sex couples. "We're leading the way here in San Francisco," the mayor declared, "for the rest of the nation to fully embrace the diversity of people in love, regardless of their gender or sexual orientation."[3] By then thousands of gay and lesbian couples across the nation were eagerly awaiting the outcome of *Baehr v. Lewin,* cautiously optimistic that Hawaii's Supreme Court will soon order the state to become the first in the United States, and in the modern world, to grant full legal marriage rights to same-sex couples. As this work went to press in May 1996, the Republican party had just made gay marriage opposition a wedge issue in their presidential campaign.

Gay and lesbian families are undeniably here, yet they are not queer, if one uses the term in the sense of "odd" to signify a marginal or deviant population.[4] It is nearly impossible to define this category of families in a manner that could successfully distinguish all of its members, needs, relationships, or even their values, from those of all other families. In fact, it is almost impossible to define this category in a satisfactory, substantive way at all. What should count as a gay or lesbian family? Even if we bracket the thorny matter of how to define an individual as gay or lesbian and rely on self-identification, we still face a jesuitical challenge. Should we count only families in which every single member is gay? Clearly there are not very many, if even any, of these. Or does the presence of just one gay member color a family gay? Just as clearly, there are very many of these, including those of Ronald Reagan, Colin Powell, Phyllis Schlafly and Newt Gingrich.[5] More to the point, why would we want to designate a family type according to the sexual identity of one or more of its members? No research, as we will see, has ever shown a uniform, distinctive pattern of relationships, structure, or even of "family values," among families that include self-identified gays. Of course, most nongays restrict the term gay family to units that contain one or two gay parents and their children. However, even such families that most commonsensically qualify as gay or lesbian are as diverse as are those which do not.

Gay and lesbian families come in different sizes, shapes, ethnicities, races, religions, resources, creeds, and quirks, and even engage in diverse sexual practices. The more one attempts to arrive at a coherent, defensible sorting principle, the more evident it becomes that the category "gay and lesbian family" signals nothing so much as the consequential social fact of widespread, institutionalized homophobia.[6] The gay and lesbian family label marks the cognitive dissonance, and even emotional threat, that much of the nongay public experiences upon recognizing that gays can participate in family life at all. What unifies such families is their need to contend with the particular array of psychic, social, legal, practical, and even physical challenges to their very existence that institutionalized hostility to homosexuality produces. Paradoxically, the label "gay and lesbian family" would become irrelevant if the nongay population could only "get used to it."

In this [article] I hope to facilitate such a process of normalization, ironically, perhaps, to allow the marker "gay and lesbian" as a family category once again to seem queer—as queer, that is, as it now seems to identify a *family*, rather than an individual or a desire, as heterosexual. . . . Gay and lesbian families represent such a new, embattled, visible and necessarily self-conscious, genre of postmodern kinship, that they more readily expose the widening gap between the complex reality of postmodern family forms and the simplistic modern family ideology that still undergirds most public rhetoric, policy and law concerning families. In short, I hope to demonstrate that, contrary to Jonathan Rauch's well-meaning claim in the second epigraph above, the experience of "homosexuals"[7] should be of immense interest to everyone else. Nongay families, family scholars and policymakers alike can learn a great deal from examining the experience, struggles, conflicts, needs, and achievements of contemporary gay and lesbian families. . . .

A More, or Less, Perfect Union?

Much nearer at hand . . . than most ever dared to imagine has come the momentous prospect of legal gay marriage. The idea of same-sex marriage used to draw nearly as many jeers from gays and lesbians as from nongays. As one lesbian couple recalls, "In 1981, we were a very, very small handful of lesbians who got married. We took a lot of flak from other lesbians, as well as heterosexuals. In 1981, we didn't know any other lesbians, not a single one, who had had a ceremony in Santa Cruz, and a lot of lesbians live in that city. Everybody was on our case about it. They said, What are you doing?, How heterosexual. We really had to sell it."[8]

Less than a decade later, gay and lesbian couples could proudly announce their weddings and anniversaries, not only in the gay press, which now includes specialized magazines for gay and lesbian couples, like *Partners Magazine*, but even in such mainstream, Midwestern newspapers as the Minneapolis *Star Tribune*.[9] Jewish rabbis, Protestant ministers, Quaker meetings, and even some Catholic priests regularly perform gay and lesbian wedding or commitment ceremonies. This phenomenon is memorialized in cultural productions within the gay community, like "Chicks In White Satin," a documentary about a Jewish lesbian wedding which won prizes at recent gay film festivals, but it has also become a fashionable pop culture motif. In December 1995, the long-running TV sitcom program "Roseanne" featured a gay male wedding in a much-hyped episode called "December Bride." Even more provocative, however, was a prime-time lesbian wedding that aired one month later on "Friends," the highest rated sitcom of the 1995–1996 television season. Making a cameo appearance on the January 18, 1996 episode, Candice Gingrich, the lesbian half-sister of right-wing Speaker of the House Newt Gingrich, conducted a wedding ceremony which joined the characters who play a lesbian couple on the series "in holy matrimony" and pronounced them "wife and wife."

When the very first social science research collection about gay parents was published in 1987, not even one decade ago, its editor concluded that however desirable such unions might be, "it is highly unlikely that marriages between same-sex individuals will be legalized in any state in the foreseeable future." [10] Yet, almost immediately thereafter, precisely this specter began to exercise imaginations across the political spectrum. A national poll reported by the *San Francisco Examiner* in 1989 found that 86 percent of lesbians and gay men supported legalizing same-sex marriage.[11] However, it is the pending *Baehr v. Lewin* court decision concerning same-sex marriage rights in Hawaii that has thrust this issue into escalating levels of front-page and prime-time prominence. Amidst rampant rumors that thousands of mainland gay and lesbian couples were stocking their hope chests with Hawaiian excursion fares, poised to fly to tropical altars the instant the first gay matrimonial bans falter, right-wing Christian groups began actively mobilizing resistance. Militant antiabortion leader Randall Terry of Operation Rescue flew to Hawaii in February 1996 to fight "queer marriage," and right-wing Christian women's leader and radio broadcast personality Beverly LaHaye urged her "Godly" listeners to fight gay marriage in Hawaii.[12]

Meanwhile, fearing that Hawaii will become a gay marriage mecca, state legislators have rushed to introduce bills that exclude same-sex marriages performed in other states from being recognized in their own, because the "full faith and credit" clause of the U.S. Constitution obligates interstate recognition of legal marriages. While fourteen states had rejected such bills by May 1995, eight others had passed them, and contests were underway in numerous others, including California.[13] On May 8, 1996, gay marriage galloped onto the nation's center political stage when Republicans introduced the Defense of Marriage Act (DOMA) which defines marriage in exclusively heterosexual terms, as "a legal union between one man and one woman as husband and wife." [14] The last legislation that Republican presidential candidate Bob Dole co-sponsored before he resigned from the Senate to pursue his White House bid full throttle, DOMA exploits homophobia to defeat President Clinton and the Democrats in November 1996. With Clinton severely bruised by the political debacle incited by his support for gay rights in the military when he first took office, but still dependent upon the support of his gay constituency, the President indeed found himself "wedged" between a rock and a very hard place. Unsurprisingly, he tried to waffle. Naming this a "time when we need to do things to strengthen the American family," Clinton publicly opposed same-sex marriage at the same time that he tried to reaffirm support for gay rights and to expose the divisive Republican strategy.[15]

Polemics favoring and opposing gay marriage rights now proliferate in editorial pages and legislatures across the nation, and mainstream religious bodies find themselves compelled to confront the issue. In March 1996 the Vatican felt called upon not merely to condemn same-sex marriage as a "moral disorder," but also to warn Catholics that they would themselves risk "moral censure" if they were to support "the election of the candidate who has formally promised to translate into law the homosexual demand."[16] Just one day after the Vatican published this admonition, the Central Conference of American Rabbis, which represents the large, generally liberal wing of Judaism, took a momentous action in direct opposition. The Conference resoundingly endorsed a resolution to "support the right of gay and lesbian couples to share fully and equally in the rights of civil marriage." Unsurprisingly, Orthodox rabbis immediately condemned the action as prohibited in the Bible and "another breakdown in the family unit."[17] One week later, in another historic development, a lead editorial in the *New York Times* strongly endorsed gay marriage.[18]

As with child custody, the campaign for gay marriage clings to legal footholds carved by racial justice pioneers. It is startling to recall how recent it was that the Supreme Court finally struck down antimiscegenation laws. Not until 1967, that is only two years before Stonewall, did the high court, in *Loving v. Virginia,* find state restrictions on interracial marriages to be unconstitutional. (Twenty states still had such restrictions on the books in 1967, only one state fewer than the twenty-one which currently prohibit sodomy.) A handful of gay couples quickly sought to marry in the 1970s through appeals to this precedent, but until three lesbian and gay male couples sued Hawaii in *Baehr v. Lewin* for equal rights to choose marriage partners without restrictions on gender, all U.S. courts had dismissed the analogy. In a historic ruling in 1993, the Hawaiian state Supreme Court remanded this suit to the state, requiring it to demonstrate a "compelling state interest" in prohibiting same-sex marriage, a strict scrutiny standard that few believe the state will be able to meet. Significantly, the case was neither argued nor adjudicated as a gay rights issue. Rather, just as ERA opponents once had warned and advocates had denied, passage of an equal rights amendment to Hawaii's state constitution in 1972 paved the legal foundation for *Baehr.*[19]

Most gay activists and legal scholars anticipate a victory for gay marriage when *Baehr* is finally decided early in 1997, but they do not all look forward to this prospect with great delight. Although most of their constituents desire the right to marry, gay activists and theorists continue to vigorously debate the politics and effects of this campaign. Refining earlier feminist and socialist critiques of the gender and class inequities of marriage, an articulate, vocal minority seeks not to extend the right to marry, but to dismantle an institution they regard as inherently, and irredeemably, hierarchical, unequal, conservative, and repressive. Nancy Polikoff, one of the most articulate lesbian legal activist-scholars opposed to the marriage campaign, argues that

> Advocating lesbian and gay marriage will detract from, and even contradict, efforts to unhook economic benefits from marriage and make basic health care and other necessities available to all. It will also require a rhetorical strategy that emphasizes similarities between our relationships and heterosexual marriages, values long-term monogamous coupling above all other relationships, and denies the potential of lesbian and gay marriage to transform the gendered nature of marriage for all people. I fear that the very process of employing that rhetorical strategy for the years it will take to achieve its objective will lead our movement's public representatives, and the countless lesbians and gay men who hear us, to believe exactly what we say.[20]

A second perspective supports legal marriage as one long-term goal of the gay rights movement, but voices serious strategic objections to making this a priority before there is sufficient public support to sustain a favorable ruling in Hawaii or the nation. Such critics fear that a premature victory will prove pyrrhic, because efforts to defend it against the vehement backlash it has already begun to incite are apt to fail, after sapping resources and time better devoted to other urgent struggles for gay rights. Rather than risk a major setback for the gay movement, they advise an incremental approach to establishing legal family status for gay and lesbian kin ties through a multifaceted struggle for family diversity.[21]

However, the largest, and most diverse, contingent of gay activist voices now supports the marriage rights campaign, perhaps because gay marriage can be read to harmonize with virtually every hue on the gay ideological spectrum. Pro-gay marriage arguments range from profoundly conservative to liberal humanist to radical and deconstructive. Conservatives, like those radicals who still oppose marriage, view it as an institution that promotes monogamy, commitment and social stability, along with interests in private property, social conformity and mainstream values. They likewise agree that legalizing gay marriage would further marginalize sexual radicals by segregating counter-cultural gays and lesbians from the "whitebread" gay couples who could then choose to marry their way into Middle America. Radicals and conservatives, in other words, envision the same prospect, but regard it with inverse sentiments.[22]

Liberal gays support legal marriage, of course, not only to affirm the legitimacy of their relationships and help sustain them in a hostile world, but as a straightforward matter of equal civil rights. As one long-coupled gay man expresses it: "I resent the fact that married people get lower taxes. But as long as there is this institution of marriage and heterosexuals have that privilege, then gay people should be able to do it too."[23] Liberals also recognize that marriage rights provide access to the social advantages of divorce law. "I used to say, 'Why do we want to get married? It doesn't work for straight people,'" one gay lawyer comments. "But now I say we should care: They have the privilege of divorce and we don't. We're left out there to twirl around in pain."[24]

Less obvious or familiar, however, are cogent arguments in favor of gay marriage that some feminist and other critical gay legal theorists have developed in response to opposition within the gay community. Nan Hunter, for example, rejects feminist legal colleague Nancy Polikoff's belief that marriage is an unalterably sexist and heterosexist institution. Building upon critical theories that reject the notion that social institutions or categories have inherent, fixed meanings apart from their social contexts, Hunter argues that legalized same-sex marriage would have "enormous potential to destabilize the gendered definition of marriage for everyone."[25]

Evan Wolfson, director of the Marriage Project of the gay legal rights organization Lambda Legal Defense, who has submitted a brief in support of *Baehr,* pursues the logic of "anti-essentialism" even more consistently. The institution of marriage is neither inherently equal nor unequal, he argues, but depends upon an everchanging cultural and political context.[26] (Anyone who doubts this need only consider such examples as polygamy, arranged marriages, or the same-sex unions in early Western history documented by the late Princeton historian, John Boswell.) Hoping to use marriage precisely to change its context, gay philosopher Richard Mohr argues that access to legal marriage would provide an opportunity to reconstruct its meaning by serving "as a nurturing ground for social marriage, and not (as now) as that which legally defines and creates marriage and so precludes legal examination of it." For Mohr, social marriage represents "the fused intersection of love's sanctity and necessity's demands," and does not necessarily depend upon sexual monogamy.[27]

Support for gay marriage, not long ago anathema to radicals and conservatives, gays and nongays, alike, now issues forth from ethical and political perspectives as diverse, and even incompatible, as these. The cultural and political context has changed so dramatically since Stonewall that it now seems easier to understand why marriage has come to enjoy overwhelming support in the gay community than to grasp the depth of resistance to the institution that characterized the early movement. Still, I take seriously many of the strategic concerns about the costly political risks posed by a premature campaign. Although surveys and electoral struggles suggest a gradual growth in public support for gay rights, that support is tepid, uneven and fickle, as the debacle over Clinton's attempt to combat legal exclusion of gays from the military made distressingly clear. Thus, while 52 percent of those surveyed in a 1994 *Time* magazine/CNN poll claimed to consider gay lifestyle acceptable, 64 percent did not want to legalize gay marriages or to permit gay couples to adopt children.[28]

Gay marriage, despite its apparent compatibility with mainstream family values sentiment, raises far more threatening questions than does military service about gender relations, sexuality and family life. Few contemporary politicians, irrespective of their personal convictions, display the courage to confront this contradiction, even when urged to do so by gay conservatives. In *Virtually Normal: An Argument about Homosexuality*, *New Republic* editor Andrew Sullivan develops the "conservative case for gay marriage," that he earlier published as an op-ed, which stresses the contribution gay marriage could make to a conservative agenda for family and political life. A review of Sullivan's book in the *New Yorker* points out that, "here is where the advocates of gay rights can steal the conservatives' clothes."[29] The epigraph to this [article] by Jonathan Rauch about the insignificance of the homosexual minority comes from a *Wall Street Journal* op-ed he wrote to persuade Republicans that they should support legal gay marriage, not only because it is consistent with conservative values, but to guard against the possibility that gay rights advocates will exploit the party's inconsistency on this issue to political advantage.[30]

The logic behind the conservative case for gay marriage strikes me as compelling. Most importantly, gay marriage would strengthen the ranks of those endangered two-parent, "intact," married-couples families whose praises conservative, "profamily" enthusiasts never seem to tire of singing. Unsurprisingly, however, the case has won few nongay conservative converts to the cause. After all, homophobia is a matter of passion and politics, not logic. The religious right regards homosexuality as an abomination, and it has effectively consolidated its influence over the Republican Party. For example, in 1994, Republicans in the Montana state senate went so far as to pass a bill that would require anyone convicted of homosexual acts to register for life as a violent offender. They reversed their vote in response to an outpouring of public outrage.[31] It was not long afterward, however, that Republican presidential contender Robert Dole returned the thousand-dollar campaign contribution from the gay Log Cabin Republicans in the name, of course, of family values. Nor have figures prominent in the centrist, secular neo-family-values campaign or the communitarian movement, whose professed values affirm both communal support for marital commitment and for tolerance, displayed much concern for such consistency.[32] And even when, in the 1995 fall preelection season, President Clinton sought to "shore up" his standing among gays and lesbians by announcing his administration's support of a bill to outlaw employment discrimination against gays, he specifically withheld his support from gay marriage.[33] First Lady Hillary Rodham Clinton's [1996] book, *It Takes a Village*, ostensibly written to challenge "false nostalgia for family values," fails even to mention gay marriage or gay families, let alone to advocate village rights and resources for children whose parents are gay.[34]

Despite my personal political baptism in the heady, anti-family crucible of early second wave feminism, I, for one, have converted to the long-term cause. A "postmodern" ideological stew of discordant convictions enticed me to this table. Like Wolfson, Mohr, and Hunter, I have come to believe that legitimizing gay and lesbian marriages would promote a democratic, pluralistic expansion of the meaning, practice, and politics of family life in the United States. This could help to supplant the destructive sanctity of the *family* with respect for diverse and vibrant *families.*

To begin with, the liberal implications of legal gay marriage are far from trivial, as the current rush by the states and Congress to nullify them should confirm. The Supreme Court is certain to have its docket flooded far into the next century with constitutional conflicts that a favorable decision in Hawaii, or elsewhere, will unleash. Under the "full faith and credit" provision of the Constitution, which requires the 50 states to recognize each other's laws, legal gay marriage in one state could begin to threaten anti-sodomy laws in all the others. Policing marital sex would be difficult to legitimate, and differential prosecution of conjugal sex among same-sex couples could violate equal protection legislation. Likewise, if gay marriages were legalized, the myriad state barriers to child custody, adoption, fertility services, inheritance, and other family rights that lesbians and gay men currently suffer could also become subject to legal challenge. Moreover, it seems hard to overestimate the profound cultural implications for the struggle against the pernicious effects of legally condoned homophobia that would ensue were lesbian and gay relationships to be admitted into the ranks of legitimate kinship. In a society that forbids most public school teachers and counselors even the merest expression of tolerance for homosexuality, while lesbian and gay youth attempt suicide at rates three to five times greater than other youth,[35] granting full recognition to even just whitebread lesbian and gay relationships could have dramatic, and salutary, consequences.

Of course, considerations truer to some of my earlier, more visionary feminist convictions also invite me to join the gay wedding procession. For while I share some of Polikoff's disbelief that same-sex marriage can in itself dismantle the patterned gender and sexual injustices of the institution, I do believe it could make a potent contribution to those projects. . . . Moreover, as Mohr suggests, admitting gays to the wedding banquet invites gays and nongays alike to consider the kinds of place settings that could best accommodate the diverse needs of all contemporary families.

Subjecting the conjugal institution to this sort of heightened democratic scrutiny could help it to assume varied creative forms. If we begin to value the meaning and quality of intimate bonds over their customary forms, there are few limits to the kinds of marriage and kinship patterns people might wish to devise. The "companionate marriage," a much celebrated, but less often realized, ideal of modern sociological lore, could take on new life. Two friends might decide to marry without basing their bond on erotic or romantic attachment, as Dorthe, a prominent Danish lesbian activist who had initially opposed the campaign for gay marriage, fantasized after her nation's parliament approved gay registered partnerships: "If I am going to marry it will be with one of my oldest friends in order to share pensions and things like that. But I'd never marry a lover. That is the advantage of being married to a close friend. Then, you never have to marry a lover!" [36] Or, more radical still, perhaps some might dare to question the dyadic limitations of Western marriage and seek some of the benefits of extended family life through small-group marriages arranged to share resources, nurturance and labor. After all, if it is true that "The Two-Parent Family Is Better" [37] than a single-parent family, as family-values crusaders like David Popenoe tirelessly proclaim, might not three-, four-, or more-parent families be better yet, as many utopian communards have long believed?

While conservative advocates of gay marriage surely would balk at such radical visions, they correctly realize that putative champions of committed relationships and of two-parent families who oppose gay marriage can be charged with gross hypocrisy on this score. For access to legal marriage not only would promote long-term, committed intimacy among gay couples, but also would afford invaluable protection to the children of gay parents, as well as indirect protection to closeted gay youth who reside with nongay parents. Clearly, only through a process of massive denial of the fact that millions of children living in gay and lesbian families are here, and here to stay, can anyone genuinely concerned with the best interests of children deny their parents the right to marry.

In the face of arguments for legalizing gay marriage as compelling and incongruent as these, it is hard to dispute Evan Wolfson's enthusiastic claim that "the brilliance of our movement's taking on marriage is that marriage is, at once and truly, both conservative and transformative, easily understood in basic human terms of equality and respect, and liberating in its individual and social potential." [38]

ENDNOTES

Epigraph Sources: Buchanan quoted in Susan Yoachum and David Tuller, "Right Makes Might in Iowa," *San Francisco Chronicle,* February 12, 1996: A1, 11; Rauch (see bibliographic entry); Bonnie Tinker, "Love Makes a Family," Presentation to 1995 United Nations International Women's Conference, Beijing, September 14.

[1] The estimate that at least six million children were living with a gay parent by 1985 appeared in Schulenberg, *Gay Parenting,* and has been accepted or revised upward by most scholars since then. See, for example, Bozett, *Gay and Lesbian Parents,* 39; Patterson, "Children of Lesbian and Gay Parents"; Allen and Demo, "The Families of Lesbians and Gay Men: A New Frontier in Family Research."

[2] Burke, *Family Values: A Lesbian Mother's Fight for Her Son.*

[3] Goldberg, "Virtual Marriages for Same-Sex Couples."

[4] Many gay activist groups and scholars, however, have begun to reclaim the term "queer" as a badge of pride, in much the same way that the Black power movement of the 1960s reclaimed the formerly derogatory term of blacks.

[5] Reagan and Schlafly both have gay sons, Powell has a lesbian daughter, and Gingrich has a lesbian half-sister.

[6] For a sensitive discussion of the definitional difficulties involved in research on gay and lesbian families, see Allen and Demo, "Families of Lesbians and Gay Men," 112–13.

[7] Most gay and lesbian scholars and activists reject the term "homosexual" because it originated within a medical model that classified homosexuality as a sexual perversion or disease and because the term emphasizes sexuality as at the core of the individual's identity. In this [article], I follow the generally preferred contemporary practice of using the terms "lesbians" and "gay men," but I also occasionally employ the term "gay" generically to include both women and men. I also play with the multiple, and currently shifting, meanings of the term "queer," by specifying whether I am using the term in its older pejorative sense, in its newer sense of proudly challenging fixed notions of gender and sexuality, or in its more colloquial sense of simply "odd."

[8] Quoted in Sherman, ed., *Lesbian and Gay Marriage*, 191.

[9] Ibid., 173.

[10] Bozett, epilogue to *Gay and Lesbian Parents*, 232.

[11] Cited in Sherman, *Lesbian and Gay Marriage*, 9, fn 6. A more recent poll conducted by *The Advocate* suggests that the trend of support for gay marriage is increasing. See Wolfson, "Crossing the Threshold," 583.

[12] Terry announced his plans January 24, 1996, on "Randall Terry Live," and LaHaye made her pitch the next day, January 25, 1996, on "Beverly LaHaye Live."

[13] Dunlap, "Some States Trying to Stop Gay Marriages Before They Start," A18; Dunlap, "Fearing a Toehold for Gay Marriage, Conservative Rush to Bar the Door," A7. Lockhead, "GOP Bill Targets Same-Sex Marriages," *San Francisco Chronicle*, May 9, 1996, A1, 15.

[14] Ibid., A1.

[15] Press Briefing by Mike McCurry, White House, May 14, 1996, Office of the Press Secretary.

[16] "Vatican Denounces Gay-Marriage Idea," *New York Times*, March 29, 1996, A8.

[17] Dunlap, "Reform Rabbis Vote to Back Gay Marriage," A8.

[18] "The Freedom to Marry," *New York Times*, April 7, 1996, Editorials/Letters, p. 10.

[19] The decision stated that the sexual orientation of the parties was irrelevant, because same-sex spouses could be of any sexual orientation. It was the gender discrimination involved in limiting one's choice of spouse that violated the state constitution. See Wolfson, "Crossing the Threshold," 573.

[20] Polikoff, "We Will Get What We Ask For: Why Legalizing Gay and Lesbian Marriage Will Not 'Dismantle the Legal Structure of Gender in Every Marriage.'"

[21] Law Professor Thomas Coleman, who is executive director of the "Family Diversity Project" in California, expresses these views in Sherman, 128–29.

[22] Sullivan, "The Conservative Case for Gay Marriage"; Rauch, "A Pro-Gay, Pro-Family Policy."

[23] Tede Matthews in Sherman, 57.

[24] Kirk Johnson quoted in Wolfson, 567.

[25] Hunter, "Marriage, Law and Gender," 12.

[26] Wolfson, "Crossing the Threshold."

[27] Mohr, *A More Perfect Union,* 48, 41, 50.

[28] "Some Progress Found in Poll on Gay Rights," *San Francisco Chronicle,* June 20, 1994.

[29] Ryan, "No Easy Way Out," 90. Sullivan, "Here Comes the Groom."

[30] Rauch, "Pro-Gay, Pro-Family Policy."

[31] Herscher, "After Reconsidering, Montana Junks Gay Sex Bill," A2.

[32] See chap. 3, pp. 69–71 above.

[33] Clinton, according to his senior adviser George Stephanopoulos, "thinks the proper role for the government is to work on the fight against discrimination, but he does not believe we should support (gay) marriage." Quoted in Sandalow and Tuller, "White House Tells Gays It Backs Them," A2.

[34] Clinton, *It Takes a Village,* book jacket copy.

[35] Remafedi, *Death by Denial.*

[36] Quoted in Miller, *Out in the World,* 350.

[37] This is the title and central argument of Popenoe's *New York Times* op-ed discussed above .

[38] Wolfson, "Crossing the Threshold," 599.

REFERENCES

Allen, Katherine R. and David H. Demo. 1995. "The Families of Lesbians and Gay Men: A New Frontier in Family Research." *Journal of Marriage and the Family* 57 (February):111–27.

Bozett, Frederick W., ed. 1987. *Gay and Lesbian Parents.* New York: Praeger.

Burke, Phyllis. 1993. *Family Values: A Lesbian Mother's Fight for Her Son.* New York: Random House.

Clinton, Hillary Rodham. 1996. *It Takes a Village: And Other Lessons Children Teach Us.* New York: Simon & Schuster.

Dunlap, David W. 1995. "Some States Trying to Stop Gay Marriages Before They Start," *New York Times,* March 15, p. A18.

Goldberg, Carey. 1996. "Virtual Marriages for Same-Sex Couples." *New York Times,* March 26, p. A8.

Herscher, Elaine. 1995. "After Reconsidering, Montana Junks Gay Sex Bill," *San Francisco Chronicle,* March 24.

Hunter, Nan D. 1991. "Marriage, Law, and Gender: A Feminist Inquiry." *Law & Sexuality* 1(1):9–30.

Miller, Neil. 1992. *Out in the World: Gay and Lesbian Life from Buenos Aires to Bangkok.* New York: Random House.

Mohr, Richard. 1994. *A More Perfect Union: Why Straight America Must Stand Up for Gay Rights.* Boston: Beacon.

Patterson, Charlotte J. 1992. "Children of Lesbian and Gay Parents." *Child Development* 63:1025–42.

Polikoff, Nancy. 1993. "We Will Get What We Ask For: Why Legalizing Gay and Lesbian Marriage Will Not 'Dismantle the Legal Structure of Gender in Every Marriage,'" *Virginia Law Review* 79:1549–50.

Popenoe, David. 1992. "The Controversial Truth: The Two-Parent Family Is Better." *New York Times,* December 26, p. 13.

Rauch, Jonathan. 1994. "A Pro-Gay, Pro-Family Policy." *Wall Street Journal,* November 29, p. A22.

Remafedi, Gary. 1994. *Death by Denial.* Boston: Alyson Publications.

Ryan, Alan, ed. 1995. "No Easy Way Out." *New Yorker,* September 11, 90.

Sandalow, Marc and David Tuller. 1995. "White House Tells Gays It Backs Them." *San Francisco Chronicle,* October 21, p. A2.

Sherman, Suzanne, ed. 1992. *Lesbian and Gay Marriage: Private Commitments, Public Ceremonies.* Philadelphia: Temple University Press.

Sullivan, Andrew. 1989. "Here Comes the Groom: A (Conservative) Case for Gay Marriage." *New Republic* 201(9):20–21.

Wolfson, Evan. 1994–95. "Crossing the Threshold: Equal Marriage Rights for Lesbians and Gay Men and the Intra-Community Critique." *Review of Law & Social Change* 21:3.

51

THE MEANING OF MOTHERHOOD IN BLACK CULTURE

PATRICIA HILL COLLINS

In this selection, taken from *Black Feminist Thought* (1990), Patricia Hill Collins observes how motherhood is socially constructed within the black community. Collins, a professor in the Department of African American Studies at the University of Cincinnati, states that black children often are raised by "othermothers," grandmothers and extended kin relations. These racial-ethnic differences in family formation patterns and parenting challenge the dominant culture's stereotype of the nuclear family. Moreover, Collins' research illustrates that the family, regardless of its membership or structure, is an institution that primarily socializes children and stabilizes adults.

Bloodmothers, Othermothers, and Women-Centered Networks

In African American communities, the boundaries distinguishing biological mothers of children from other women who care for children are often fluid and changing. Biological mothers or bloodmothers are expected to care for

From *Black Feminist Thought: Knowledge, Consciousness, and the Politics of Empowerment,* pp. 119–32. Copyright © 1990 by Unwin Hyman, Inc. Reprinted with the permission of Routledge, Inc.

their children. But African and African American communities have also recognized that vesting one person with full responsibility for mothering a child
may not be wise or possible. As a result, "othermothers," women who assist
bloodmothers by sharing mothering responsibilities, traditionally have been
central to the institution of Black motherhood.[1]

The centrality of women in African American extended families is well
known.[2] Organized, resilient, women-centered networks of bloodmothers
and othermothers are key in understanding this centrality: Grandmothers,
sisters, aunts, or cousins acted as othermothers by taking on child care responsibilities for each other's children. When needed, temporary child-care
arrangements turned into long-term care or informal adoption.[3]

In African American communities, these women-centered networks of
community-based child care often extend beyond the boundaries of biologically related extended families to support "fictive kin."[4] Civil rights activist
Ella Baker describes how informal adoption by othermothers functioned in
the Southern, rural community of her childhood:

> *My aunt who had thirteen children of her own raised three more. She had become
> a midwife, and a child was born who was covered with sores. Nobody was partic-
> ularly wanting the child, so she took the child and raised him . . . and another
> mother decided she didn't want to be bothered with two children. So my aunt
> took one and raised him. . . . They were part of the family.*[5]

Even when relationships were not between kin or fictive kin, African
American community norms were such that neighbors cared for each other's
children. In the following passage, Sara Brooks, a Southern domestic worker,
describes the importance of the community-based child care that a neighbor
offered her daughter. In doing so, she also shows how the African American
cultural value placed on cooperative child care found institutional support in
the adverse conditions under which so many Black women mothered.

> *She kept Vivian and she didn't charge me nothin either. You see, people used to
> look after each other, but now it's not that way. I reckon it's because we all was
> poor, and I guess they put theirself in the place of the person that they was helpin.*[6]

Othermothers were key not only in supporting children but also in supporting bloodmothers who, for whatever reason, were ill-prepared or had little
desire to care for their children. Given the pressures from the larger political
economy, the emphasis placed on community-based child care and the respect given to othermothers who assume the responsibilities of child care
have served a critical function in African American communities. Children
orphaned by sale or death of their parents under slavery; children conceived
through rape; children of young mothers; children born into extreme poverty;
or children, who for other reasons have been rejected by their bloodmothers,
have all been supported by othermothers who, like Ella Baker's aunt, took in
additional children, even when they had enough of their own.

Providing As Part of Mothering

The work done by African American women in providing the economic resources essential to Black family well-being affects motherhood in a contradictory fashion. On the one hand, African American women have long integrated their activities as economic providers into their mothering relationships. In contrast to the cult of true womanhood where work is defined as being in opposition to and incompatible with motherhood, work for Black women has been an important and valued dimension of Afro-centric definitions of Black motherhood. On the other hand, African American women's experiences as mothers under oppression were such that the type and purpose of work Black women were forced to do greatly impacted on the type of mothering relationships bloodmothers and othermothers had with Black children.

While slavery both disrupted West African family patterns and exposed enslaved Africans to the gender ideologies and practices of slaveowners, it simultaneously made it impossible, had they wanted to do so, for enslaved Africans to implement slaveowners' ideologies. Thus, the separate spheres of providing as a male domain and affective nurturing as a female domain did not develop within African American families.[7] Providing for Black children's physical survival and attending to their affective, emotional needs continued as interdependent dimensions of an Afrocentric ideology of motherhood. However, by changing the conditions under which Black women worked and the purpose of the work itself, slavery introduced the problem of how best to continue traditional Afrocentric values under oppressive conditions. Institutions of community-based child care, informal adoption, greater reliance on othermothers, all emerge as adaptations to the exigencies of combining exploitative work with nurturing children.

In spite of the change in political status brought on by emancipation, the majority of African American women remained exploited agricultural workers. However, their placement in southern political economies allowed them to combine child care with field labor. Sara Brooks describes how strong the links between providing and caring for others were for her:

> *When I was about nine I was nursin my sister Sally—I'm about seven or eight years older than Sally. And when I would put her to sleep, instead of me goin somewhere and sit down and play, I'd get my little old hoe and get out there and work right in the field around the house.*[8]

Black women's shift from southern agriculture to domestic work in southern and northern towns and cities represented a change in the type of work done, but not in the meaning of work to women and their families. Whether they wanted to or not, the majority of African American women had to work and could not afford the luxury of motherhood as a noneconomically productive, female "occupation."

Community Othermothers and Social Activism

Black women's experiences as othermothers have provided a foundation for Black women's social activism. Black women's feelings of responsibility for nurturing the children in their own extended family network have stimulated a more generalized ethic of care where Black women feel accountable to all the Black community's children.

This notion of Black women as community othermothers for all Black children traditionally allowed Black women to treat biologically unrelated children as if they were members of their own families. For example, sociologist Karen Fields describes how her grandmother, Mamie Garvin Fields, draws on her power as a community othermother when dealing with unfamiliar children.

> *She will say to a child on the street who looks up to no good, picking out a name at random, "Aren't you Miz Pinckney's boy?" in that same reproving tone. If the reply is, "No, ma'am, my mother is Miz Gadsden," whatever threat there was dissipates.*[9]

The use of family language in referring to members of the Black community also illustrates this dimension of Black motherhood. For example, Mamie Garvin Fields describes how she became active in surveying the poor housing conditions of Black people in Charleston.

> *I was one of the volunteers they got to make a survey of the places where we were paying extortious rents for indescribable property. I said "we," although it wasn't Bob and me. We had our own home, and so did many of the Federated Women. Yet we still felt like it really was "we" living in those terrible places, and it was up to us to do something about them.*[10]

To take another example, while describing her increasingly successful efforts to teach a boy who had given other teachers problems, my daughter's kindergarten teacher stated, "You know how it can be—the majority of the children in the learning disabled classes are *our children*. I know he didn't belong there, so I volunteered to take him." In these statements, both women invoke the language of family to describe the ties that bind them as Black women to their responsibilities to other members of the Black community as family.

Sociologist Cheryl Gilkes suggests that community othermother relationships are sometimes behind Black women's decisions to become community activists.[11] Gilkes notes that many of the Black women community activists in her study became involved in community organizing in response to the needs of their own children and of those in their communities. The following comment is typical of how many of the Black women in Gilkes' study relate to Black children: "There were a lot of summer programs springing up for kids, but they were exclusive . . . and I found that most of *our kids* (emphasis mine) were excluded."[12] For many women, what began as the daily expression of their obligations as community othermothers, as was the case for the kindergarten teacher, developed into full-fledged roles as community leaders.

ENDNOTES

[1] The terms used in this section appear in Rosalie Riegle Troester, "Turbulence and Tenderness: Mothers, Daughters, and Othermothers" in Paula Marshall's *Brown Girl, Brownstones,* and in *SAGE: A Scholarly Journal on Black Women* 1 (Fall 1984): 13–16.

[2] See Tanner's discussion of matrifocality, 1974; see also Carrie Allen McCray, "The Black Woman and Family Roles," in *The Black Woman,* ed. LaFrances Rogers-Rose (Beverly Hills, CA: Sage, 1980), pp. 67–78; Elmer Martin and Joanne Mitchell Martin, *The Black Extended Family* (Chicago: University of Chicago, 1978); Joyce Aschenbrenner, *Lifelines, Black Families in Chicago* (Prospect Heights, IL: Waveland, 1975); and Carol B. Stack, *All Our Kin* (New York: Harper & Row, 1974).

[3] Martin and Martin, *The Black Extended Family;* Stack, *All Our Kin;* and Virginia Young, "Family and Childhood in a Southern Negro Community," *American Anthropologist* 72 (1970):269–88.

[4] Stack, *All Our Kin.*

[5] Ellen Cantarow, *Moving the Mountain: Women Working for Social Change* (Old Westbury, NY: Feminist Press, 1980), p. 59.

[6] Thordis Simonsen, ed., *You May Plow Here: The Narrative of Sara Brooks* (New York: Touchstone, 1986), p. 81.

[7] Deborah White, *Arn't I a Woman? Female Slaves in the Plantation South* (New York: Norton, 1984); Bonnie Thornton Dill, "Our Mothers' Grief: Racial Ethnic Women and the Maintenance of Families," Research Paper 4, Center for Research on Women (Memphis, TN: Memphis State University, 1986); Leith Mullings, "Uneven Development: Class, Race and Gender in the United States before 1900," in *Women's Work, Development and the Division of Labor by Gender,* eds. Eleanor Leacock and Helen Safa (South Hadley, MA: Bergin & Garvey, 1986), pp. 41–57.

[8] Simonsen, *You May Plow Here,* p. 86.

[9] Mamie Garvin Fields and Karen Fields, *Lemon Swamp and Other Places: A Carolina Memoir* (New York: Free Press, 1983), p. xvii.

[10] Ibid, p. 195.

[11] Cheryl Gilkes, "'Holding Back the Ocean with a Broom,' Black Women and Community Work," in Rogers-Rose, *The Black Woman,* pp. 217–31; "Going Up for the Oppressed: The Career Mobility of Black Women Community Workers," *Journal of Social Issues* 39 (1983):115–39.

[12] Gilkes, "'Holding Back,'" p. 219.

52

THE TIME BIND
When Work Becomes
Home and Home Becomes Work

ARLIE RUSSELL HOCHSCHILD

What are the relationships between work life and family life? How do individuals negotiate the role demands of both social institutions? Arlie Russell Hochschild, a professor of sociology at the University of California at Berkeley, investigates these questions in her three-year study of a large corporation, which she calls "Amerco." Hochschild interviewed 130 employees, including middle and upper management, clerks and factory workers, most of whom were working parents. Hochschild also talked with human resource specialists, psychologists, child-care workers, and homemakers who were married to Amerco employees. In this selection, adapted from her book *The Time Bind: When Work Becomes Home and Home Becomes Work* (1997), Hochschild discusses her findings about the changing relationship between work life and home life for many working parents.

It's 7:40 A.M. when Cassie Bell, 4, arrives at the Spotted Deer Child-Care Center, her hair half-combed, a blanket in one hand, a fudge bar in the other. "I'm late," her mother, Gwen, a sturdy young woman whose short-cropped hair frames a pleasant face, explains to the child-care worker in charge. "Cassie wanted the fudge bar so bad, I gave it to her," she adds apologetically.

"*Pleeese*, can't you take me with you?" Cassie pleads.

"You know I can't take you to work," Gwen replies in a tone that suggests that she has been expecting this request. Cassie's shoulders droop. But she has struck a hard bargain—the morning fudge bar—aware of her mother's anxiety about the long day that lies ahead at the center. As Gwen explains later, she continually feels that she owes Cassie more time than she gives her—she has a "time debt."

Arriving at her office just before 8, Gwen finds on her desk a cup of coffee in her personal mug, milk no sugar (exactly as she likes it), prepared by a co-worker who managed to get in ahead of her. As the assistant to the head

From *The Time Bind: When Work Becomes Home and Home Becomes Work* by Arlie Russell Hochschild. Copyright © 1997 by Arlie Russell Hochschild. Reprinted by permission of Henry Holt and Company, L.L.C.

of public relations at a company I will call Amerco, Gwen has to handle responses to any reports that may appear about the company in the press—a challenging job, but one that gives her satisfaction. As she prepares for her first meeting of the day, she misses her daughter, but she also feels relief; there's a lot to get done at Amerco.

Gwen used to work a straight eight-hour day. But over the last three years, her workday has gradually stretched to eight and a half or nine hours, not counting the e-mail messages and faxes she answers from home. She complains about her hours to her co-workers and listens to their complaints—but she loves her job. Gwen picks up Cassie at 5:45 and gives her a long, affectionate hug.

At home, Gwen's husband, John, a computer programmer, plays with their daughter while Gwen prepares dinner. To protect the dinner "hour"—8:00–8:30—Gwen checks that the phone machine is on, hears the phone ring during dinner but resists the urge to answer. After Cassie's bath, Gwen and Cassie have "quality time," or "Q.T.," as John affectionately calls it. Half an hour later, at 9:30, Gwen tucks Cassie into bed.

There are, in a sense, two Bell households: the rushed family they actually are and the relaxed family they imagine they might be if only they had time. Gwen and John complain that they are in a time bind. What they say they want seems so modest—time to throw a ball, to read to Cassie, to witness the small dramas of her development, not to speak of having a little fun and romance themselves. Yet even these modest wishes seem strangely out of reach. Before going to bed, Gwen has to e-mail messages to her colleagues in preparation for the next day's meeting; John goes to bed early, exhausted—he's out the door by 7 every morning.

Nationwide, many working parents are in the same boat. More mothers of small children than ever now work outside the home. In 1993, 56 percent of women with children between 6 and 17 worked outside the home full time year round; 43 percent of women with children 6 and under did the same. Meanwhile, fathers of small children are not cutting back hours of work to help out at home. If anything, they have increased their hours at work. According to a 1993 national survey conducted by the Families and Work Institute in New York, American men average 48.8 hours of work a week, and women 41.7 hours, including overtime and commuting. All in all, more women are on the economic train, and for many—men and women alike—that train is going faster.

But Amerco has "family-friendly" policies. If your division head and supervisor agree, you can work part time, share a job with another worker, work some hours at home, take parental leave or use "flex time." But hardly anyone uses these policies. In seven years, only two Amerco fathers have taken formal parental leave. Fewer than 1 percent have taken advantage of the opportunity to work part time. Of all such policies, only flex time—which rearranges but does not shorten work time—has had a significant number of takers (perhaps a third of working parents at Amerco).

Forgoing family-friendly policies is not exclusive to Amerco workers. A 1991 study of 188 companies conducted by the Families and Work Institute found that while a majority offered part-time shifts, fewer than 5 percent of employees made use of them. Thirty-five percent offered "flex place"—work from home—and fewer than 3 percent of their employees took advantage of it. And an earlier Bureau of Labor Statistics survey asked workers whether they preferred a shorter workweek, a longer one or their present schedule. About 62 percent preferred their present schedule; 28 percent would have preferred longer hours. Fewer than 10 percent said they wanted a cut in hours.

Still, I found it hard to believe that people didn't protest their long hours at work. So I contacted Bright Horizons, a company that runs 136 company-based child-care centers associated with corporations, hospitals and Federal agencies in 25 states. Bright Horizons allowed me to add questions to a questionnaire they sent out to 3,000 parents whose children attended the centers. The respondents, mainly middle-class parents in their early 30s, largely confirmed the picture I'd found at Amerco. A third of fathers and a fifth of mothers described themselves as "workaholic," and 1 out of 3 said their partners were.

To be sure, some parents have tried to shorten their hours. Twenty-one percent of the nation's women voluntarily work part time, as do 7 percent of men. A number of others make under-the-table arrangements that don't show up on surveys. But while working parents say they need more time at home, the main story of their lives does not center on a struggle to get it. Why? Given the hours parents are working these days, why aren't they taking advantage of an opportunity to reduce their time at work?

The most widely held explanation is that working parents cannot afford to work shorter hours. Certainly this is true for many. But if money is the whole explanation, why would it be that at places like Amerco, the best-paid employees—upper-level managers and professionals—were the least interested in part-time work or job sharing, while clerical workers who earned less were more interested?

Similarly, if money were the answer, we would expect poorer new mothers to return to work more quickly after giving birth than rich mothers. But among working women nationwide, well-to-do new mothers are not much more likely to stay home after 13 weeks with a new baby than low-income new mothers. When asked what they look for in a job, only a third of respondents in a recent study said salary came first. Money is important, but by itself, money does not explain why many people don't want to cut back hours at work.

A second explanation goes that workers don't dare ask for time off because they are afraid it would make them vulnerable to layoffs. With recent downsizings at many large corporations, and with well-paying, secure jobs being replaced by lower-paying, insecure ones, it occurred to me that perhaps employees are "working scared." But when I asked Amerco employees whether they worked long hours for fear of getting on a layoff list, virtually everyone said no. Even among a particularly vulnerable group—factory workers who were laid off in the downturn of the early 1980s and were later rehired—most did not cite fear for their jobs as the only, or main, reason they worked overtime. For unionized workers, layoffs are assigned by seniority, and for nonunionized workers, layoffs are usually related to the profitability of the division a person works in, not to an individual work schedule.

Were workers uninformed about the company's family-friendly policies? No. Some even mentioned that they were proud to work for a company that offered such enlightened policies. Were rigid middle managers standing in the way of workers using these policies? Sometimes. But when I compared Amerco employees who worked for flexible managers with those who worked for rigid managers, I found that the flexible managers reported only a few more applicants than the rigid ones. The evidence, however counter-intuitive, pointed to a paradox: workers at the company I studied weren't protesting the time bind. They were accommodating to it.

Why? I did not anticipate the conclusion I found myself coming to: namely, that work has become a form of "home" and home has become "work." The worlds of home and work have not begun to blur, as the con-ventional wisdom goes, but to reverse places. We are used to thinking that home is where most people feel the most appreciated, the most truly "them-selves," the most secure, the most relaxed. We are used to thinking that work is where most people feel like "just a number" or "a cog in a machine." It is where they have to be "on," have to "act," where they are least secure and most harried.

But new management techniques so pervasive in corporate life have helped transform the workplace into a more appreciative, personal sort of so-cial world. Meanwhile, at home the divorce rate has risen, and the emotional demands have become more baffling and complex. In addition to teething, tantrums and the normal developments of growing children, the needs of el-derly parents are creating more tasks for the modern family—as are the blending, unblending, reblending of new stepparents, stepchildren, exes and former in-laws.

This idea began to dawn on me during one of my first interviews with an Amerco worker. Linda Avery, a friendly, 38-year-old mother, is a shift super-visor at an Amerco plant. When I meet her in the factory's coffee-break room over a couple of Cokes, she is wearing blue jeans and a pink jersey, her hair pulled back in a long, blond ponytail. Linda's husband, Bill, is a technician in the same plant. By working different shifts, they manage to share the care of their 2-year-old son and Linda's 16-year-old daughter from a previous mar-riage. "Bill works the 7 A.M. to 3 P.M. shift while I watch the baby," she ex-plains. "Then I work the 3 P.M. to 11 P.M. shift and he watches the baby. My daughter works at Walgreen's after school."

Linda is working overtime, and so I begin by asking whether Amerco required the overtime or whether she volunteered for it. "Oh, I put in for it," she replies. I ask her whether, if finances and company policy permitted, she'd be interested in cutting back on the overtime. She takes off her safety glasses, rubs her face and, without answering my question, explains: "I get home, and the minute I turn the key, my daughter is right there. Granted, she needs somebody to talk to about her day. . . . The baby is still up. He should have been in bed two hours ago, and that upsets me. The dishes are piled in the sink. My daughter comes right up to the door and complains about anything her stepfather said or did, and she wants to talk about her job. My husband is in the other room hollering to my daughter, 'Tracy, I don't ever get any time to talk to your mother, because you're always monopolizing her time before I even get a chance!' They all come at me at once."

Linda's description of the urgency of demands and the unarbitrated quarrels that await her homecoming contrast with her account of arriving at her job as a shift supervisor: "I usually come to work early, just to get away from the house. When I arrive, people are there waiting. We sit, we talk, we joke. I let them know what's going on, who has to be where, what changes I've made for the shift that day. We sit and chitchat for 5 or 10 minutes. There's laughing, joking, fun."

For Linda, home has come to feel like work and work has come to feel a bit like home. Indeed, she feels she can get relief from the "work" of being at home only by going to the "home" of work. Why has her life at home come to seem like this? Linda explains it this way: "My husband's a great help watching our baby. But as far as doing housework or even taking the baby when I'm at home, no. He figures he works five days a week; he's not going to come home and clean. But he doesn't stop to think that I work seven days a week. Why should I have to come home and do the housework without help from anybody else? My husband and I have been through this over and over again. Even if he would just pick up from the kitchen table and stack the dishes for me, that would make a big difference. He does nothing. On his weekends off, he goes fishing. If I want any time off, I have to get a sitter. He'll help out if I'm not here, but the minute I am, all the work at home is mine."

With a light laugh, she continues: "So I take a lot of overtime. The more I get out of the house, the better I am. It's a terrible thing to say, but that's the way I feel."

When Bill feels the need for time off, to relax, to have fun, to feel free, he climbs in his truck and takes his free time without his family. Largely in response, Linda grabs what she also calls "free time"—at work. Neither Linda nor Bill Avery wants more time together at home, not as things are arranged now.

How do Linda and Bill Avery fit into the broader picture of American family and work life? Current research suggests that however hectic their lives, women who do paid work feel less depressed, think better of themselves and are more satisfied than women who stay at home. One study reported that women who work outside the home feel more valued at home than housewives do. Meanwhile, work is where many women feel like "good mothers." As Linda reflects: "I'm a good mom at home, but I'm a better mom at work. At home, I get into fights with Tracy. I want her to apply to a junior college, but she's not interested. At work, I think I'm better at seeing the other person's point of view."

Many workers feel more confident they could "get the job done" at work than at home. One study found that only 59 percent of workers feel their "performance" in the family is "good or unusually good," while 86 percent rank their performance on the job this way.

Forces at work and at home are simultaneously reinforcing this "reversal." This lure of work has been enhanced in recent years by the rise of company cultural engineering—in particular, the shift from Frederick Taylor's principles of scientific management to the Total Quality principles originally set out by W. Edwards Deming. Under the influence of a Taylorist world view, the manager's job was to coerce the worker's mind and body, not to appeal to the worker's heart. The Taylorized worker was de-skilled, replaceable and cheap, and as a consequence felt bored, demeaned and unappreciated.

Using modern participative management techniques, many companies now train workers to make their own work decisions, and then set before their newly "empowered" employees moral as well as financial incentives. At Amerco, the Total Quality worker is invited to feel recognized for job accomplishments. Amerco regularly strengthens the familylike ties of co-workers by holding "recognition ceremonies" honoring particular workers or self-managed production teams. Amerco employees speak of "belonging to the Amerco family," and proudly wear their "Total Quality" pins or "High Performance Team" T-shirts, symbols of their loyalty to the company and of its loyalty to them.

The company occasionally decorates a section of the factory and serves refreshments. The production teams, too, have regular get-togethers. In a New Age recasting of an old business slogan—"The Customer Is Always Right"—Amerco proposes that its workers "Value the Internal Customer." This means: Be as polite and considerate to co-workers inside the company as you would be to customers outside it. How many recognition ceremonies for competent performance are being offered at home? Who is valuing the internal customer there?

Amerco also tries to take on the role of a helpful relative with regard to employee problems at work and at home. The education-and-training division offers employees free courses (on company time) in "Dealing With Anger," "How to Give and Accept Criticism," "How to Cope With Difficult People."

At home, of course, people seldom receive anything like this much help on issues basic to family life. There, no courses are being offered on "Dealing With Your Child's Disappointment in You" or "How to Treat Your Spouse Like an Internal Customer."

If Total Quality calls for "re-skilling" the worker in an "enriched" job environment, technological developments have long been de-skilling parents at home. Over the centuries, store-bought goods have replaced homespun cloth, homemade soap and home-baked foods. Day care for children, retirement homes for the elderly, even psychotherapy are, in a way, commercial substitutes for jobs that a mother once did at home. Even family-generated entertainment has, to some extent, been replaced by television, video games and the VCR. I sometimes watched Amerco families sitting together after their dinners, mute but cozy, watching sitcoms in which television mothers, fathers and children related in an animated way to one another while the viewing family engaged in relational loafing.

The one "skill" still required of family members is the hardest one of all—the emotional work of forging, deepening or repairing family relationships. It takes time to develop this skill, and even then things can go awry. Family ties are complicated. People get hurt. Yet as broken homes become more common—and as the sense of belonging to a geographical community grows less and less secure in an age of mobility—the corporate world has created a sense of "neighborhood," of "feminine culture," of family at work. Life at work can be insecure; the company can fire workers. But workers aren't so secure at home, either. Many employees have been working for Amerco for 20 years but are on their second or third marriages or relationships. The shifting balance between these two "divorce rates" may be the most powerful reason why tired parents flee a world of unresolved quarrels and unwashed laundry for the orderliness, harmony and managed cheer of work. People are getting their "pink slips" at home.

Amerco workers have not only turned their offices into "home" and their homes into workplaces; many have also begun to "Taylorize" time at home, where families are succumbing to a cult of efficiency previously associated mainly with the office and factory. Meanwhile, work time, with its ever longer hours, has become more hospitable to sociability—periods of talking with friends on e-mail, patching up quarrels, gossiping. Within the long workday of many Amerco employees are great hidden pockets of inefficiency while, in the far smaller number of waking weekday hours at home, they are, despite themselves, forced to act increasingly time-conscious and efficient.

The Averys respond to their time bind at home by trying to value and protect "quality time." A concept unknown to their parents and grandparents, "quality time" has become a powerful symbol of the struggle against the growing pressures at home. It reflects the extent to which modern parents feel the flow of time to be running against them. The premise behind "quality time" is that the time we devote to relationships can somehow be separated from ordinary time. Relationships go on during quantity time, of course, but then we are only passively, not actively, wholeheartedly, specializing in our emotional ties. We aren't "on." Quality time at home becomes like an office appointment. You don't want to be caught "goofing off around the water cooler" when you are "at work."

Quality time holds out the hope that scheduling intense periods of togetherness can compensate for an overall loss of time in such a way that a relationship will suffer no loss of quality. But this is just another way of transferring the cult of efficiency from office to home. We must now get our relationships in good repair in less time. Instead of nine hours a day with a child, we declare ourselves capable of getting "the same result" with one intensely focused hour.

Parents now more commonly speak of time as if it is a threatened form of personal capital they have no choice but to manage and invest. What's new here is the spread into the home of a financial manager's attitude toward time. Working parents at Amerco owe what they think of as time debts at home. This is because they are, in a sense, inadvertently "Taylorizing" the house—speeding up the pace of home life as Taylor once tried to "scientifically" speed up the pace of factory life.

Advertisers of products aimed at women have recognized that this new reality provides an opportunity to sell products, and have turned the very pressure that threatens to explode the home into a positive attribute. Take, for example, an ad promoting Instant Quaker Oatmeal: it shows a smiling mother ready for the office in her square-shouldered suit, hugging her happy son. A caption reads: "Nicky is a very picky eater. With Instant Quaker Oatmeal, I can give him a terrific hot breakfast in just 90 seconds. And I don't have to spend any time coaxing him to eat it!" Here, the modern mother seems to have absorbed the lessons of Frederick Taylor as she presses for efficiency at home because she is in a hurry to get to work.

Part of modern parenthood seems to include coping with the resistance of real children who are not so eager to get their cereal so fast. Some parents try desperately not to appease their children with special gifts or smooth-talking promises about the future. But when time is scarce, even the best parents find themselves passing a system-wide familial speed-up along to the most vulnerable workers on the line. Parents are then obliged to try to control the damage done by a reversal of worlds. They monitor mealtime, homework time, bedtime, trying to cut out "wasted" time.

In response, children often protest the pace, the deadlines, the grand irrationality of "efficient" family life. Children dawdle. They refuse to leave places when it's time to leave. They insist on leaving places when it's not time to leave. Surely, this is part of the usual stop-and-go of childhood itself, but perhaps, too, it is the plea of children for more family time and more control over what time there is. This only adds to the feeling that life at home has become hard work.

Instead of trying to arrange shorter or more flexible work schedules, Amerco parents often avoid confronting the reality of the time bind. Some minimize their ideas about how much care a child, a partner or they themselves "really need." They make do with less time, less attention, less understanding and less support at home than they once imagined possible. They *emotionally downsize* life. In essence, they deny the needs of family members, and they themselves become emotional ascetics. If they once "needed" time with each other, they are now increasingly "fine" without it.

Another way that working parents try to evade the time bind is to buy themselves out of it—an approach that puts women in particular at the heart of a contradiction. Like men, women absorb the work-family speed-up far more than they resist it; but unlike men, they still shoulder most of the work-load at home. And women still represent in people's minds the heart and soul of family life. They're the ones—especially women of the urban middle and upper-middle classes—who feel most acutely the need to save time, who are the most tempted by the new "time saving" goods and services—and who wind up feeling the most guilty about it. For example, Playgroup Connections, a Washington-area business started by a former executive recruiter, matches playmates to one another. One mother hired the service to find her child a French-speaking playmate.

In several cities, children home alone can call a number for "Grandma, Please!" and reach an adult who has the time to talk with them, sing to them or help them with their homework. An ad for Kindercare Learning Centers, a for-profit child-care chain, pitches its appeal this way: "You want your child to be active, tolerant, smart, loved, emotionally stable, self-aware, artistic and get a two-hour nap. Anything else?" It goes on to note that Kindercare accepts children 6 weeks to 12 years old and provides a number to call for the Kindercare nearest you. Another typical service organizes children's birth-day parties, making out invitations ("sure hope you can come") and providing party favors, entertainment, a decorated cake and balloons. Creative Memories is a service that puts ancestral photos into family albums for you.

An overwhelming majority of the working mothers I spoke with recoiled from the idea of buying themselves out of parental duties. A bought birthday party was "too impersonal," a 90-second breakfast "too fast." Yet a surprising amount of lunchtime conversation between female friends at Amerco was devoted to expressing complex, conflicting feelings about the lure of trading time for one service or another. The temptation to order flash-frozen dinners or to call a local number for a homework helper did not come up because such services had not yet appeared at Spotted Deer Child-Care Center. But many women dwelled on the question of how to decide where a mother's job began and ended, especially with regard to baby sitters and television. One mother said to another in the breakroom of an Amerco plant: "Damon doesn't settle down until 10 at night, so he hates me to wake him up in the morning and I hate to do it. He's cranky. He pulls the covers up. I put on car-toons. That way, I can dress him and he doesn't object. I don't like to use TV that way. It's like a drug. But I do it."

The other mother countered: "Well, Todd is up before we are, so that's not a problem. It's after dinner, when I feel like watching a little television, that I feel guilty, because he gets too much TV at the sitter's."

As task after task falls into the realm of time-saving goods and services, questions arise about the moral meanings attached to doing or not doing such tasks. Is it being a good mother to bake a child's birthday cake (alone or together with one's partner)? Or can we gratefully save time by ordering it, and be good mothers by planning the party? Can we save more time by hiring a planning service, and be good mothers simply by watching our children have a good time? "Wouldn't that be nice!" one Amerco mother exclaimed. As the idea of the "good mother" retreats before the pressures of work and the expansion of motherly services, mothers are in fact continually reinventing themselves.

The final way working parents tried to evade the time bind was to develop what I call "potential selves." The potential selves that I discovered in my Amerco interviews were fantasy creations of time-poor parents who dreamed of living as time millionaires.

One man, a gifted 55-year-old engineer in research and development at Amerco, told how he had dreamed of taking his daughters on a camping trip in the Sierra Mountains: "I bought all the gear three years ago when they were 5 and 7, the tent, the sleeping bags, the air mattresses, the backpacks, the ponchos. I got a map of the area. I even got the freeze-dried food. Since then the kids and I have talked about it a lot, and gone over what we're going to do. They've been on me to do it for a long time. I feel bad about it. I keep putting it off, but we'll do it, I just don't know when."

Banished to garages and attics of many Amerco workers were expensive electric saws, cameras, skis and musical instruments, all bought with wages it took time to earn. These items were to their owners what Cassie's fudge bar was to her—a substitute for time, a talisman, a reminder of the potential self.

Obviously, not everyone, not even a majority of Americans, is making a home out of work and a workplace out of home. But in the working world, it is a growing reality, and one we need to face. Increasing numbers of women are discovering a great male secret—that work can be an escape from the pressures of home, pressures that the changing nature of work itself are only intensifying. Neither men nor women are going to take up "family-friendly" policies, whether corporate or governmental, as long as the current realities of work and home remain as they are. For a substantial number of time-bound parents, the stripped-down home and the neighborhood devoid of community are simply losing out to the pull of the workplace.

There are several broader, historical causes of this reversal of realms. The last 30 years have witnessed the rapid rise of women in the workplace. At the same time, job mobility has taken families farther from relatives who might lend a hand, and made it harder to make close friends of neighbors who could help out. Moreover, as women have acquired more education and have joined men at work, they have absorbed the views of an older, male-oriented work world, its views of a "real career," far more than men have taken up their share of the work at home. One reason women have changed more than men is that the world of "male" work seems more honorable and valuable than the "female" world of home and children.

So where do we go from here? There is surely no going back to the mythical 1950s family that confined women to the home. Most women don't wish to return to a full-time role at home—and couldn't afford it even if they did.

But equally troubling is a workaholic culture that strands both men and women outside the home.

For a while now, scholars on work-family issues have pointed to Sweden, Norway and Denmark as better models of work-family balance. Today, for example, almost all Swedish fathers take two paid weeks off from work at the birth of their children, and about half of fathers and most mothers take additional "parental leave" during the child's first or second year. Research shows that men who take family leave when their children are very young are more likely to be involved with their children as they grow older. When I mentioned this Swedish record of paternity leave to a focus group of American male managers, one of them replied, "Right, we've already heard about Sweden." To this executive, paternity leave was a good idea not for the U.S. today, but for some "potential society" in another place and time.

Meanwhile, children are paying the price. In her book *When the Bough Breaks: The Cost of Neglecting Our Children,* the economist Sylvia Hewlett claims that "compared with the previous generation, young people today are more likely to underperform at school; commit suicide; need psychiatric help; suffer a severe eating disorder; bear a child out of wedlock; take drugs; be the victim of a violent crime." But we needn't dwell on sledgehammer problems like heroin or suicide to realize that children like those at Spotted Deer need more of our time. If other advanced nations with two-job families can give children the time they need, why can't we?

Author's Note: Over three years, I interviewed 130 respondents for a book. They spoke freely and allowed me to follow them through "typical" days, on the understanding that I would protect their anonymity. I have changed the names of the company and of those I interviewed, and altered certain identifying details. Their words appear here as they were spoken.—A.R.H.

53

THE McDONALDIZATION OF SOCIETY

GEORGE RITZER

In this reading, the first of four to focus on social change, George Ritzer focuses on the larger consequences of having an organization, such as McDonald's, in society. Ritzer, a professor of sociology at the University of Maryland, argues that societies are being transformed by a process he labels "McDonaldization," in which the principles of the fast-food restaurant have come to influence other aspects of the social structure, such as the family, politics, education, travel, and leisure. Ritzer also summarizes the societal costs and benefits of this widespread social change.

A wide-ranging process of *rationalization* is occurring across American society and is having an increasingly powerful impact in many other parts of the world. It encompasses such disparate phenomena as fast-food restaurants, TV dinners, packaged tours, industrial robots, plea bargaining, and open-heart surgery on an assembly-line basis. As widespread and as important as these developments are, it is clear that we have barely begun a process that promises even more extraordinary changes (e.g., genetic engineering) in the years to come. We can think of rationalization as a historical process and rationality as the end result of that development. As a historical process, rationalization has distinctive roots in the Western world. Writing in the late nineteenth and early twentieth centuries, the great German sociologist Max Weber saw his society as the center of the ongoing process of rationalization and the bureaucracy as its paradigm case. The model of rationalization, at least in contemporary America, is no longer the bureaucracy, but might be better thought of as the fast-food restaurant. As a result, our concern here is with what might be termed the "McDonaldization of Society." While the fast-food restaurant is not the ultimate expression of rationality, it is the current exemplar for future developments in rationalization.

From *Journal of American Culture* 6, no. 1 (1983):100–107. Reprinted with the permission of the publisher.

A society characterized by rationality is one which emphasizes *efficiency, predictability, calculability, substitution of nonhuman for human technology,* and *control over uncertainty.* In discussing the various dimensions of rationalization, we will be little concerned with the gains already made, and yet to be realized, by greater rationalization. These advantages are widely discussed in schools and in the mass media. In fact, we are in danger of being seduced by the innumerable advantages already offered, and promised in the future, by rationalization. The glitter of these accomplishments and promises has served to distract most people from the grave dangers posed by progressive rationalization. In other words, we are ultimately concerned here with the irrational consequences that often flow from rational systems. Thus, the second major theme of this essay might be termed "the irrationality of rationality." . . .

Efficiency

The process of rationalization leads to a society in which a great deal of emphasis is placed on finding the best or optimum means to any given end. Whatever a group of people define as an end, and everything they so define, is to be pursued by attempting to find the best means to achieve the end. Thus, in the Germany of Weber's day, the bureaucracy was seen as the most efficient means of handling a wide array of administrative tasks. Somewhat later, the Nazis came to develop the concentration camp, its ovens, and other devices as the optimum method of collecting and murdering millions of Jews and other people. The efficiency that Weber described in turn-of-the-century Germany, and which later came to characterize many Nazi activities, has become a basic principle of life in virtually every sector of a rational society.

The modern American family, often with two wage earners, has little time to prepare elaborate meals. For the relatively few who still cook such meals, there is likely to be great reliance on cookbooks that make cooking from scratch much more efficient. However, such cooking is relatively rare today. Most families take as their objective quickly and easily prepared meals. To this end, much use is made of prepackaged meals and frozen TV dinners.

For many modern families, the TV dinner is no longer efficient enough. To many people, eating out, particularly in a fast-food restaurant, is a far more efficient way of obtaining their meals. Fast-food restaurants capitalize on this by being organized so that diners are fed as efficiently as possible. They offer a limited, simple menu that can be cooked and served in an assembly-line fashion. The latest development in fast-food restaurants, the addition of drive-through windows, constitutes an effort to increase still further the efficiency of the dining experience. The family now can simply drive through, pick up its order, and eat it while driving to the next, undoubtedly efficiently organized, activity. The success of the fast-food restaurant has come full circle with frozen-food manufacturers now touting products for the home modeled after those served in fast-food restaurants.

Increasingly, efficiently organized food production and distribution systems lie at the base of the ability of people to eat their food efficiently at home, in the fast-food restaurant, or in their cars. Farms, groves, ranches, slaughterhouses, warehouses, transportation systems, and retailers are all oriented toward increasing efficiency. A notable example is chicken production where they are mass-bred, force-fed (often with many chemicals), slaughtered on an assembly line, iced or fast frozen, and shipped to all parts of the country. Some may argue that such chickens do not taste as good as the fresh-killed, local variety, but their complaints are likely to be drowned in a flood of mass-produced chickens. Then there is bacon which is more efficiently shipped, stored, and sold when it is preserved by sodium nitrate, a chemical which is unfortunately thought by many to be carcinogenic. Whatever one may say about the quality or the danger of the products, the fact remains that they are all shaped by the drive for efficiency. . . .

One of the most interesting and important aspects of efficiency is that it often comes to be not a means but an end in itself. This "displacement of goals" is a major problem in a rationalizing society. We have, for example, the bureaucrats who slavishly follow the rules even though their inflexibility negatively affects the organization's ability to achieve its goals. Then there are the bureaucrats who are so concerned with efficiency that they lose sight of the ultimate goals the means are designed to achieve. A good example was the Nazi concentration camp officers who, in devoting so much attention to maximizing the efficiency of the camps' operation, lost sight of the fact that the ultimate purpose of the camps was the murder of millions of people.

Predictability

A second component of rationalization involves the effort to ensure predictability from one place to another. In a rational society, people want to know what to expect when they enter a given setting or acquire some sort of commodity. They neither want nor expect surprises. They want to know that if they journey to another locale, the setting they enter or the commodity they buy will be essentially the same as the setting they entered or product they purchased earlier. Furthermore, people want to be sure that what they encounter is much like what they encountered at earlier times. In order to ensure predictability over time and place, a rational society must emphasize such things as discipline, order, systemization, formalization, routine, consistency, and methodical operation.

One of the attractions of TV dinners for modern families is that they are highly predictable. The TV dinner composed of fried chicken, mashed potatoes, green peas, and peach cobbler is exactly the same from one time to another and one city to another. Home cooking from scratch is, conversely, a notoriously unpredictable enterprise with little assurance that dishes will taste the same time after time. However, the cookbook cannot eliminate all unpredictability. There are often simply too many ingredients and other variables involved. Thus the cookbook dish is far less predictable than the TV dinner or a wide array of other prepared dishes.

Fast-food restaurants rank very high on the dimension of predictability. In order to help ensure consistency, the fast-food restaurant offers only a limited menu. Predictable end products are made possible by the use of similar raw materials, technologies, and preparation and serving techniques. Not only the food is predictable; the physical structures, the logo, the "ambience," and even the personnel are as well.

The food that is shipped to our homes and our fast-food restaurants is itself affected by the process of increasing predictability. Thus our favorite white bread is indistinguishable from one place to another. In fact, food producers have made great efforts to ensure such predictability.

On packaged tours, travelers can be fairly sure that the people they travel with will be much like themselves. The planes, buses, hotel accommodations, restaurants, and at least the way in which the sites are visited are very similar from one location to another. Many people go on packaged tours *because* they are far more predictable than travel undertaken on an individual basis.

Amusement parks used to be highly unpredictable affairs. People could never be sure, from one park to another, precisely what sorts of rides, events, foods, visitors, and employees they would encounter. All of that has changed in the era of the theme parks inspired by Disneyland. Such parks seek to ensure predictability in various ways. For example, a specific type of young person is hired in these parks, and they are all trained in much the same way, so that they have a robot-like predictability.

Other leisure-time activities have grown similarly predictable. Camping in the wild is loaded with uncertainties—bugs, bears, rain, cold, and the like. To make camping more predictable, organized grounds have sprung up around the country. Gone are many of the elements of unpredictability replaced by RVs, paved-over parking lots, sanitized campsites, fences and enclosed camp centers that provide laundry and food services, recreational activities, television, and video games. Sporting events, too, have in a variety of ways been made more predictable. The use of artificial turf in baseball makes for a more predictable bounce of a ball. . . .

Calculability or Quantity Rather than Quality

It could easily be argued that the emphasis on quantifiable measures, on things that can be counted, is *the* most defining characteristic of a rational society. Quality is notoriously difficult to evaluate. How do we assess the quality of a hamburger, or a physician, or a student? Instead of even trying, in an increasing number of cases, a rational society seeks to develop a series of quantifiable measures that it takes as surrogates for quality. This urge to quantify has given great impetus to the development of the computer and has, in turn, been spurred by the widespread use and increasing sophistication of the computer.

The fact is that many aspects of modern rational society, especially as far as calculable issues are concerned, are made possible and more widespread by the computer. We need not belabor the ability of the computer to handle large numbers of virtually anything, but somewhat less obvious is the use of the computer to give the illusion of personal attention in a world made increasingly impersonal in large part because of the computer's capacity to turn virtually everything into quantifiable dimensions. We have all now had many experiences where we open a letter personally addressed to us only to find a computer letter. We are aware that the names and addresses of millions of people have been stored on tape and that with the aid of a number of word processors a form letter has been sent to every name on the list. Although the computer is able to give a sense of personal attention, most people are nothing more than an item on a huge mailing list.

Our main concern here, though, is not with the computer, but with the emphasis on quantity rather than quality that it has helped foster. One of the most obvious examples in the university is the emphasis given to grades and cumulative grade point averages. With less and less contact between professor and student, there is little real effort to assess the quality of what students know, let alone the quality of their overall abilities. Instead, the sole measure of the quality of most college students is their grade in a given course and their grade point averages. Another blatant example is the emphasis on a variety of uniform exams such as SATs and GREs in which the essence of an applicant is reduced to a few simple scores and percentiles.

Within the educational institution, the importance of grades is well known, but somewhat less known is the way quantifiable factors have become an essential part of the process of evaluating college professors. For example, teaching ability is very hard to evaluate. Administrators have difficulty assessing teaching quality and thus substitute quantitative scores. Of course each score involves qualitative judgments, but this is conveniently ignored. Student opinion polls are taken and the scores are summed, averaged, and compared. Those who score well are deemed good teachers while those who don't are seen as poor teachers. There are many problems involved in relying on these scores such as the fact that easy teachers in "gut" courses may well obtain high ratings while rigorous teachers of difficult courses are likely to score poorly. . . .

In the work world we find many examples of the effort to substitute quantity for quality. Scientific management was heavily oriented to turning everything work-related into quantifiable dimensions. Instead of relying on the "rule of thumb" of the operator, scientific management sought to develop precise measures of how much work was to be done by each and every motion of the worker. Everything that could be was reduced to numbers, and all these numbers were then analyzable using a variety of mathematical formulae. The assembly line is similarly oriented to a variety of quantifiable dimensions such as optimizing the speed of the line, minimizing time for each task, lowering the price of the finished product, increasing sales and ultimately increasing profits. The divisional system pioneered by General Motors and thought to be one of the major reasons for its past success was oriented to the reduction of the performance of each division to a few, bottom-line numbers. By monitoring and comparing these numbers, General Motors was able to exercise control over the results without getting involved in the day-to-day activities of each division. . . .

Thus, the third dimension of rationalization, calculability or the emphasis on quantity rather than quality, has wide applicability to the social world. It is truly central, if not the central, component of a rationalizing society. To return to our favorite example, it is the case that McDonald's expends far more effort telling us how many billions of hamburgers it has sold than it does in telling us about the quality of those burgers. Relatedly, it touts the size of its product (the "Big Mac") more than the quality of the product (it is not the "Good Mac"). The bottom line in many settings is the number of customers processed, the speed with which they are processed, and the profits produced. Quality is secondary, if indeed there is any concern at all for it.

Substitution of Nonhuman Technology

In spite of Herculean efforts, there are important limits to the ability to rationalize what human beings think and do. Seemingly no matter what one does, people still retain at least the ultimate capacity to think and act in a variety of unanticipated ways. Thus, in spite of great efforts to make human behavior more efficient, more predictable, more calculable, people continue to act in unforeseen ways. People continue to make home-cooked meals from scratch, to camp in tents in the wild, to eat in old-fashioned diners, and to sabotage the assembly lines. Because of these realities, there is great interest among those who foster increasing rationality in using rational technologies to limit individual independence and ultimately to replace human beings with machines and other technologies that lack the ability to think and act in unpredictable ways.

McDonald's does not yet have robots to serve us food, but it does have teenagers whose ability to act autonomously is almost completely eliminated by techniques, procedures, routines, and machines. There are numerous examples of this including rules which prescribe all the things a counterperson should do in dealing with a customer as well as a large variety of technologies which determine the actions of workers such as drink dispensers which shut themselves off when the cup is full; buzzers, lights, and bells which indicate when food (e.g., french fries) is done; and cash registers which have the prices of each item programmed in. One of the latest attempts to constrain individual action is Denny's use of pre-measured packages of dehydrated food that are "cooked" simply by putting them under the hot water tap. Because of such tools and machines, as well as the elaborate rules dictating worker behavior, people often feel like they are dealing with human robots when they relate to the personnel of a fast-food restaurant. When human robots are found, mechanical robots cannot be far behind. Once people are reduced to a few robot-like actions, it is a relatively easy step to replace them with mechanical robots. Thus, Burgerworld is reportedly opening a prototypical restaurant in which mechanical robots serve the food.

Much of the recent history of work, especially manual work, is a history of efforts to replace human technology with nonhuman technology. Scientific management was oriented to the development of an elaborate and rigid set of rules about how jobs were to be done. The workers were to blindly and obediently follow those rules and not to do the work the way they saw fit. The various skills needed to perform a task were carefully delineated and broken down into a series of routine steps that could be taught to all workers. The skills, in other words, were built into the routines rather than belonging to skilled craftspersons. Similar points can be made about the assembly line, which is basically a set of nonhuman technologies that have the needed steps and skills built into them. The human worker is reduced to performing a limited number of simple, repetitive operations. However, the control of this technology over the individual worker is so great and omnipresent that individual workers have reacted negatively manifesting such things as tardiness, absenteeism, turnover, and even sabotage. We are now witnessing a new stage in this technological development with automated processes now totally replacing many workers with robots. With the coming of robots we have reached the ultimate stage in the replacement of humans with nonhuman technology.

Even religion and religious crusades have not been unaffected by the spread of nonhuman technologies. The growth of large religious organizations, the use of Madison Avenue techniques, and even drive-in churches all reflect the incursion of modern technology. But it is in the electronic church, religion through the TV screens, that replacement of human by nonhuman technology in religion is most visible and has its most important manifestation. . . .

Control

This leads us to the fifth major dimension of rationalization—control. Rational systems are oriented toward, and structured to expedite, control in a variety of senses. At the most general level, we can say that rational systems are set up to allow for greater control over the uncertainties of life—birth, death, food production and distribution, housing, religious salvation, and many, many others. More specifically, rational systems are oriented to gaining greater control over the major source of uncertainty in social life—other people. Among other things, this means control over subordinates by superiors and control of clients and customers by workers.

There are many examples of rationalization oriented toward gaining greater control over the uncertainties of life. The burgeoning of the genetic engineering movement can be seen as being aimed at gaining better control over the production of life itself. Similarly, amniocentesis can be seen as a technique which will allow the parents to determine the kind of child they will have. The efforts to rationalize food production and distribution can be seen as being aimed at gaining greater control over the problems of hunger and starvation. A steady and regular supply of food can make life itself more certain for large numbers of people who today live under the threat of death from starvation.

At a more specific level, the rationalization of food preparation and serving at McDonald's gives it great control over its employees. The automobile assembly line has a similar impact. In fact, the vast majority of the structures of a rational society exert extraordinary control over the people who labor in them. But because of the limits that still exist on the degree of control that rational structures can exercise over individuals, many rationalizing employers are driven to seek to more fully rationalize their operations and totally eliminate the worker. The result is an automated, robot-like technology over which, barring some *2001* rebellion, there is almost total control.

In addition to control over employees, rational systems are also interested in controlling the customer/clients they serve. For example, the fast-food restaurant with its counter, the absence of waiters and waitresses, the limited seating, and the drive-through windows all tend to lead customers to do certain things and not to do others.

Irrationality of Rationality

Although not an inherent part of rationalization, the *irrationality of rationality* is a seemingly inevitable byproduct of the process. We can think of the irrationality of rationality in several ways. At the most general level it can simply be seen as an overarching label for all the negative effects of rationalization. More specifically, it can be seen as the opposite of rationality, at least in some of its senses. For example, there are the inefficiencies and unpredictabilities that are often produced by seemingly rational systems. Thus, although bureaucracies are constructed to bring about greater efficiency in organizational work, the fact is that there are notorious inefficiencies such as the "red tape" associated with the operation of most bureaucracies. Or take the example of the arms race in which a focus on quantifiable aspects of nuclear weapons may well have made the occurrence of nuclear war more, rather than less, unpredictable.

Of greatest importance, however, is the variety of negative effects that rational systems have on the individuals who live, work, and are served by them. We might say that *rational systems are not reasonable systems.* As we've already discussed, rationality brings with it great dehumanization as people are reduced to acting like robots. Among the dehumanizing aspects of a rational society are large lecture classes, computer letters, pray TV, work on the automobile assembly line, and dining at a fast-food restaurant. Rationalization also tends to bring with it disenchantment leaving much of our lives without any mystery or excitement. Production by a hand craftsman is far more mysterious than an assembly-line technology where each worker does a single, very limited operation. Camping in an RV tends to suffer in comparison to the joys to be derived from camping in the wild. Overall a fully rational society would be a very bleak and uninteresting place.

Conclusions

Rationalization, with McDonald's as the paradigm case, is occurring throughout America and, increasingly, other societies. In virtually every sector of society, more and more emphasis is placed on efficiency, predictability, calculability, replacement of human by nonhuman technology, and control over uncertainty. Although progressive rationalization has brought with it innumerable advantages, it has also created a number of problems, the various irrationalities of rationality, which threaten to accelerate in the years to come. These problems, and their acceleration, should not be taken as a case for the return to a less rational form of society. Such a return is not only impossible but also undesirable. What is needed is not a less rational society, but greater control over the process of rationalization involving, among other things, efforts to ameliorate its irrational consequences.

54

HOW WILL THE INTERNET CHANGE SOCIETY?

Conrad L. Kanagy • Donald B. Kraybill

This selection is a study of social change written by two sociologists, Conrad L. Kanagy, at Elizabethtown College, and Donald B. Kraybill, at Messiah College. In their research, Kanagy and Kraybill examine how the Internet has changed society. In particular, they investigate how the Internet is changing culture, social structure, and rituals in American society and beyond. Will the Internet create a global community of similar norms and values that transcends national boundaries? What are the limitations of new technologies, such as the Internet, in creating and changing social structure? These and other questions are addressed by Kanagy and Kraybill in this excerpt from their 1999 book, *The Riddles of Human Society.*

On March 14, 1994, police handcuffed Matt Mihaly, a 21-year-old student at Cornell University, and drove him to the Tompkins County Hospital. During the intake process, hospital personnel pressed him: "Do you want to kill yourself? Do you ever hear voices? Are you a danger to yourself?" Matt insisted he was fine. But against his strong protests, an ambulance transported him to the mental health ward of another hospital, where he spent two days in mandatory group therapy sessions. Then he was released.

How did Mihaly get himself into this predicament? Depressed over a broken romance, drunk and reeling in self-pity, he posted the following note to an Internet news group:

> *I am planning on killing myself. . . . I want some information on drugs that induce a relatively painless death. . . . If I can't get the information, I'll probably just try taking a few packs of sleeping pills. . . . Please don't post back stuff about how I shouldn't do it, OK?*

Mihaly insists that he wasn't serious when he sent the message, just angry and depressed. His case initiated serious debate about privacy and free speech on the Internet.[1]

From *The Riddles of Human Society: An Introduction to Society* by Conrad L. Kanagy and Donald B. Kraybill, pp. 260–268, 337–338. Copyright © 1999 Pine Forge Press. Reprinted by permission of Sage Publications, Inc.

The norms of Internet culture remain fuzzy. Technological advances are speeding ahead of social regulation. Are people free to write whatever they want and to anybody they want? How much privacy should we have on the Internet? Should Matt have been hospitalized for his statement? Such gaps between social norms and policy on one hand and technological expertise on the other are typical during rapid social change.

The Social Construction of the Internet

The first Internet exchanges occurred in November 1969 under the authority of the U.S. Department of Defense.[2] The internet was born as ARPANET, a worldwide network of computers linking a few university scientists, military personnel, and computer experts. ARPANET's purpose was to enhance U.S. military prowess in the Cold War against communism. Initial communication was formal and official, some users worried that personal e-mail messages might violate U.S. postal laws. But by the mid-1980s, ARPANET was linked to other networks. The change created near chaos, a "full-scale Mardi Gras parade." By 1990 ARPANET had been shut down, and private companies were overseeing activity in cyberspace.[3]

To many college students today, the Internet is a taken-for-granted part of the objective social world, just like cable TV and Nintendo. They've grown up in a digital world. They've internalized expectations for high-speed communication on the Internet. They watch less television than their parents did, finding its old-fashioned pace too slow. They want technology they can interact with and control. The world has shrunk for these students; it lies at their fingertips.

Clearly, use of the Internet is changing our world. In fact, its effects might parallel the transformations brought about by the invention of the printing press. Both technologies expand exponentially the access of ordinary persons to information once held by experts and elites. Sociologists are beginning to develop a sociology of the Internet to study these social changes, and this subfield is likely to grow rapidly in the next several years.[4]

Culture and the Internet

We already know a few things about the beliefs, norms, and values of Internet culture. For instance, social scientists have been debating for some time the reality of Internet communities, or **virtual communities**.[5] Some have argued that such communities are little more than social networks, because they lack

---

Virtual communities are networks of relationships in which people identify with one another and share feelings for one another but don't share their physical selves or physical space. They share cyberselves and cyberspace.

the typical characteristics of communities—things like residential proximity and economic dependence. However, digital technology has been pressing us to renovate some standard definitions, and the concept of community may be one of them. What do you think? What elements of community are represented in your online relationships? Are chat rooms communities?

In the age of television, many bemoaned the loss of written text as a form of communication. Interestingly, text-based communication has returned on the Internet. The need for writing, reading, and critical expression are as great as, or greater than, ever. But electronic text is extemporaneous, transitory, and soon trashed, unlike the enduring works of Shakespeare and other classic writers.

A problem with text-based communication is the difficulty of expressing emotions and feelings. To counter this difficulty, many Internet users resort to "smileys," combinations of characters that symbolize emotional responses. Besides smileys, people communicating on the Internet are using some new forms of abbreviation and spelling, such as *jc* for "just curious," *bmf* for "biting my fingernails," *brb* for "be right back," *imho* for "in my humble opinion," and *lol* for "laughing out loud."

Internet norms, sometimes referred to as netiquette, are in the process of being defined.[6] Because of the rapid growth and fluidity of the Internet, ambiguity abounds about how people should behave in cyberspace. However, threats of censorship have hastened the development of some norms. Internet users are particularly concerned that outrageous behavior by some will prompt government agencies to censor the Internet. Certain legal norms probably will be defined eventually. In addition, subcultural groups will undoubtedly develop their own particular norms, just as subcultures do in the real world.

What are the values of Internet users that will shape these norms? Don Tapscott, in *Growing Up Digital,* identifies several themes that are important to this subculture. For example, independence, free expression, and inclusion, which are core American values as well. These values are undoubtedly reinforced for Internet users by the freedom and diversity of Internet communication. Other cyberculture values, however, have been socially constructed and reinforced through electronic interaction.

- ▾ Openness characterizes Internet communication.
- ▾ Innovation created the Internet and continues to shape it.
- ▾ An investigative spirit is encouraged by the vast scope of the Internet wilderness.
- ▾ Immediacy is driven by the speed of Internet processing.
- ▾ Internet users, particularly the younger ones, are skeptical of corporate interests and the greed driving some efforts to shape Internet technology.

▼ Authenticity and trust are expected in the open environment of the Internet, where the cooperation of the parts (individuals) is needed to preserve the whole.[7]

Although several of these cyberculture values intersect with more traditional American values, others are relatively new and are likely to influence the cultural values of the larger society in years to come.

Social Structure and the Internet

The changes brought about by the Internet will accelerate as the number of youth who have been socialized into cyberculture grows. Some refer to this generation as the "net generation." These are the children of the baby boomers, the cohort born between 1945 and 1964, who now represent 29% of the U.S. population. The net generation, or "N-geners," born since 1977, comprise 30% of the U.S. population. The baby boomers represent the television generation, their children the digital generation. In their youth, many baby boomers sat staring at programs like *MASH, The Brady Bunch,* and *The Jeffersons.* But N-geners controlled a host of interactive devices, such as Nintendo games and computers. For people who grew up with these technologies, their operation is second nature. The Internet will develop and become more influential as the people who grew up with it become a larger part of the population.[8]

The two cohorts—baby boomers and N-geners—have unique intergenerational problems. In place of a generation gap, where the growing-up experiences of children and parents are simply different, we may have a "generation lap," as children outpace their parents in the race for technological knowledge. Young children often know much more than their parents about the computer. In one study by researchers at Carnegie Mellon University, children were the heaviest computer users in a large majority of families. Two-thirds of children in another survey said they are more proficient on the computer than their parents. In Finland, 5,000 N-geners teach computing to the country's teachers.[9] The "generation lap" turns typical patterns of socialization upside down: The parents, who typically teach their children, are now learning from them. As a result, children and youth have become the gatekeepers of technology and information for their families, teachers, and supervisors. This generational shift means that some entry-level employees will have greater skills and knowledge in some areas than their supervisors, managers, and administrators.

The new generation gap has four themes:

▼ Older people are anxious about the new technology being embraced by youth.

▼ Older people are uneasy about the new media, such as the Internet, which are part of everyday life among youth.

▼ Older media (newspapers, radio, television) are apprehensive about the newer media.

▼ The digital revolution, unlike previous revolutions, is not completely controlled by adults.[10]

Reconciliation between baby boomers and N-geners may lie in the willingness of N-geners to share their knowledge and the humility of baby boomers to receive it.

The digital revolution may create other structural fault lines as well. Some fear that computer technology will exacerbate the existing divide between rich and poor. In fact, only 7% of low-income households have a computer, while among those making more than $50,000 a year, 53% have a computer. Thus economic poverty leads to information poverty, which leads to even greater economic poverty. In addition, racial discrimination in society leads to racial discrimination in media and technology access.[11] Blacks are two-thirds less likely to have a computer than whites, and two-thirds of white students have used the Web as opposed to fewer than half of black students.[12] On the brighter side, the Internet has the potential to equalize without regard to race, sex, or economics. Students in poor, inner-city schools could have access equal to those in wealthy, suburban schools. The challenge for the government and for educators is to ensure such equality. Whether in the final analysis the Internet will increase or diminish social inequality remains to be seen.

Structural differences in technology use also occur in the global arena: . . . developed and developing countries differ substantially in their resources. Information technology will probably heighten those differences. In 1996, 66% of households connected to the Internet were in North America. Even developed countries in Western Europe fall behind the United States in Internet access and use. At the same time, the Internet has the potential to democratize political systems around the world, by giving everyone equal access to information, regardless of cultural or political boundaries. The Internet makes possible the development of a truly global culture, where children in Hong Kong can learn the same information as children in Papua New Guinea. They can also learn about each other.

Ritual and the Internet

Although some social divisions are sharpened by digital technology, the Internet levels the playing field for individuals communicating through e-mail, chat rooms, bulletin boards, and discussion lists. The only symbols of communication are written words; facial expressions, voice intonations, hand gestures, and physical appearance are gone. The context of each individual's social world—family life, occupation, income, residence—is minimized. Such **decontextualization** is quite different from the high context of face-to-face interaction, where we can see the person. The decontextualized nature of Internet culture is the opposite of, say, Amish life, which is a high-context culture that values face-to-face interaction and knowledge of everyone in the community. In a high context culture, social actors know many background details of each other—home, habits, lifestyle, friends, and work. Conversation is embedded in this rich social context.

On the Internet, everyone is alike. The decontextualized space of the Internet brings a new openness in communication and weakens the features that often lead to discrimination and prejudice. People with disabilities, who usually face discrimination, can interact without the scorn of prejudice. Age, beauty, size, body odor, color of hair and eyes, and facial hair lose their power. Labels, stereotypes, and stigmas disappear.

In Goffman's terms, on the Internet the frontstage is the same for everyone, without the typical props, signals, sounds, and appearances of social life. Individuals can create any frontstage that they wish. It may not be real, but who will ever know? Said one 14-year-old: "I'd have to say I'm very shy unless I know a person very well. This doesn't happen though in cyberspace. On the Net, I am one of the most outgoing people I know. Probably why I spend so much time there." [13]

In general, we all have greater control over disclosure and our presentation of self on the Internet than in other social contexts. If we dislike someone, we can break off the communication without serious consequences, especially if we have kept our identity disguised. We'll likely never see the other person, and if we do, we won't recognize each other.

Relationships on the Internet are often disposable, fragile, and superficial. At the same time, however, they can be deeply intimate and personal, because so much contextual baggage is left behind. Some of the values of N-geners arise from these characteristics of ritual interaction on the Internet.[14]

Decontextualized interaction on the Internet poses some interesting dilemmas, which some voice as concerns:

▼ Individuals can enter chat rooms or post messages to bulletin boards using multiple identities. Some deliberately create artificial identities to deceive unsuspecting individuals. On-line romances have occasionally resulted in fraud or homicide. Children can be manipulated and harmed by menacing adults.[15]

▼ Another danger is Internet addiction, sometimes called "netomania" or "on-lineaholism." Some view this condition as a symptom of a

Decontextualization is the loss of identifiable social landmarks in human interaction. In a decontextualized social world like the Internet, we don't have the contextual knowledge—the other person's facial expressions and gestures, a physical setting such as a home or office, and the other person's friends or family—that we usually use to interpret our interaction.

psychiatric disorder; others see it as a disorder in its own right.[16] One analyst, Kimberly Young, has written a self-help guide called *Caught in the Net* to aid those who abandon family, friends, and work to be on-line. She believes up to 5 million Internet users may be addicted.[17] Examples of those with symptoms of Internet addiction include a 31-year-old man who spent more than 100 hours a week on-line, ignoring others and stopping only for sleep. In another case, a 21-year-old college student disappeared, only to be found in the computer lab hooked on seven consecutive days of on-line chat. Some individuals with Internet addiction have reported an average of five psychiatric disorders, including manic-depressive disorder, social phobia, bulimia or binge eating, impulse-control problems, and substance abuse.[18]

▾ Some experts fear that N-geners are losing their social skills. Others are concerned about the short attention span that N-geners may develop through overexposure to interactive communication. Some fear the Internet is stressing children and spreading them too thin. Others worry about the cruelty that children may experience on the Internet. Some argue that the opportunity to create one's homepage leads to vanity— an artificially heightened self-esteem.[19]

All these issues raise a host of ethical questions for an Internet society. How much freedom should Internet users have? How much control should the government and other social institutions exert? Is it ethical to change one's identity on-line? When is on-line deception potentially harmful to individuals and society? Is Internet addiction harmful? Should we have Internet police to regulate activity in chat rooms and discussion groups? Should individuals be held accountable for everything they write on the Internet? How much further will the Internet renovate social relations?[20]

Summary: Internet

Because the development of the Internet is relatively new, we can't really consider its renovation yet. But the recent development of the Internet provides a fascinating opportunity to watch a culture being constructed from scratch.

The construction of the Internet reflects to some extent the cultural norms and structural divisions of the larger society. The Internet has the potential, however, to make the same information available to everyone, regardless of race, class, education, occupation, or residence.

The rituals of interaction on the Internet are still being shaped. It is a decontextualized environment where we can minimize everyday prejudices by carefully controlling the presentation of self. We can remain relatively anonymous while still being intimate. We can create relationships with few obligations but with high levels of authenticity.

It remains to be seen whether the Internet will remain a communication medium of the middle and upper classes or whether, like television, it will override class lines and serve the masses.

ENDNOTES

[1] Kim Neely, "Caught in the Net," *Rolling Stone,* 1 December 1994.

[2] For on-line resources about the history of the Internet, see <http://info.isoc.org/guest/zakon/Internet/History/Timeline_of_Network_History>; <http://info.isoc.org/guest/zakon/Internet/History/How_the_Internet_came_to_Be>; <http://info.isoc.org/guest/zakon/Internet/History/Brief_History_of_the_Internet>.

[3] Edwin Diamond and Stephen Bates, "The Ancient History of the Internet," *American Heritage* 46 (1995):34–41.

[4] For related resources, see <http://www.itcs.com/elawley/bourdieu.html> and <http://jefferson.village.virginia.edu/>.

[5] Howard Reingold, *Virtual Communities: Homesteading on the Electronic Frontier* (New York: Harper Perennial, 1993), p. 5.

[6] For an on-line description of netiquette, see <http://rs6000.adm.fau.edu/rinaldi/netiquette.html>. Another valuable resource, titled "A Primer on How to Work with the Usenet Community," is available through the news group news.announce.newusers, with the archive name usernet/primer/part1.

[7] A substantial part of our discussion of the Internet is based on Don Tapscott, *Growing Up Digital* (New York: McGraw-Hill, 1998).

[8] For more on the age profile of Internet users, see Thomas E. Miller, "Segmenting the Internet," *American Demographics* 18 (1996):48–50.

[9] Don Tapscott, *Growing Up Digital* (New York: McGraw-Hill, 1998).

[10] Ibid., pp. 48–50.

[11] Don Tapscott, *Growing Up Digital* (New York: McGraw-Hill, 1998).

[12] *Time,* "World White Web," 27 April 1998.

[13] Ibid., p. 93.

[14] Don Tapscott, *Growing Up Digital* (New York: McGraw-Hill, 1998).

[15] Ibid.

[16] Ibid.

[17] Vincent Kiernan, "Some Scholars Question Research Methods of Expert on Internet Addiction," *The Chronicle of Higher Education,* 29 May 1998.

[18] Malcolm Ritter, *Associated Press,* 2 June 1998.

[19] Don Tapscott, *Growing Up Digital* (New York: McGraw-Hill, 1998).

[20] Given its recent development, we do not offer any suggestions as to how the Internet will be renovated in the future.

55

―――――

ONE WORLD, READY OR NOT
The Manic Logic of Global Capitalism

WILLIAM GREIDER

This reading by journalist William Greider is an excerpt from his 1997 book, *One World, Ready or Not: The Manic Logic of Global Capitalism.* Greider explores how the global economic revolution is reshaping international politics and the daily realities of millions of lives. The growth of multinational corporations and the inability of nation-states to regulate them have numerous consequences for capitalists and workers. In the following selection, Greider discusses the rise of global capitalism and the legacy of social problems it is creating for both developed and developing countries.

Imagine a wondrous new machine, strong and supple, a machine that reaps as it destroys. It is huge and mobile, something like the machines of modern agriculture but vastly more complicated and powerful. Think of this awesome machine running over open terrain and ignoring familiar boundaries. It plows across fields and fencerows with a fierce momentum that is exhilarating to behold and also frightening. As it goes, the machine throws off enormous mows of wealth and bounty while it leaves behind great furrows of wreckage.

Now imagine that there are skillful hands on board, but no one is at the wheel. In fact, this machine has no wheel nor any internal governor to control the speed and direction. It is sustained by its own forward motion, guided mainly by its own appetites. And it is accelerating.

The machine is modern capitalism driven by the imperatives of global industrial revolution. The metaphor is imperfect, but it offers a simplified way to visualize what is dauntingly complex and abstract and impossibly diffuse—the drama of a free-running economic system that is reordering the world.

The logic of commerce and capital has overpowered the inertia of politics and launched an epoch of great social transformations. Settled facts of material life are being revised for rich and poor nations alike. Social under-

―――――

Adapted with permission of Simon & Schuster from *One World, Ready or Not: The Manic Logic of Global Capitalism* by William Greider. Copyright © 1997 by William Greider.

standings that were formed by the hard political struggles of the twentieth century are put in doubt. Old verities about the rank ordering of nations are revised, and a new map of the world is gradually being drawn. These great changes sweep over the affairs of mere governments and destabilize the established political orders in both advanced and primitive societies. Everything seems new and strange. Nothing seems certain.

Economic revolution, similar to the impulse of political revolution, liberates masses of people and at the same time projects new aspects of tyranny. Old worlds are destroyed and new ones emerge. The past is upended and new social values are created alongside the fabulous new wealth. Marvelous inventions are made plentiful. Great fortunes are accumulated. Millions of peasants find ways to escape from muddy poverty.

Yet masses of people are also tangibly deprived of their claims to self-sufficiency, the independent means of sustaining hearth and home. People and communities, even nations, find themselves losing control over their own destinies, ensnared by the revolutionary demands of commerce.

The great paradox of this economic revolution is that its new technologies enable people and nations to take sudden leaps into modernity, while at the same time they promote the renewal of once-forbidden barbarisms. Amid the newness of things, exploitation of the weak by the strong also flourishes again.

The present economic revolution, like revolutions of the past, is fueled by invention and human ingenuity and a universal aspiration to build and accumulate. But it is also driven by a palpable sense of insecurity. No one can be said to control the energies of unfettered capital, not important governments or financiers, not dictators or democrats.

And, in the race to the future, no one dares to fall a step behind, not nations or major corporations. Even the most effective leaders of business and finance share in the uncertainty, knowing as they do that the uncompromising dynamics can someday turn on the revolutionaries themselves.

As history confirms, every revolution gradually accumulates its own tensions and instabilities, the unresolved contradictions that deepen and eventually lead it to falter or break down. Likewise, this revolution is steadily creating the predicate for its own collapse. The imperatives driving enterprise and finance and leading to great social transformations reveal, in turn, the inherent contradictions that are also propelling the world toward some new version of breakdown, the prospect of an economic or political cataclysm of unknowable dimensions.

Our wondrous machine, with all its great power and creativity, appears to be running out of control toward some sort of abyss. Amid revolutionary fervor, such warnings may sound far-fetched and, as history tells us, usually go unheeded until one day, sometimes quite suddenly, they are confirmed by reality. . . .

Before the machine can be understood, one must first be able to see it. The daunting shape and scope of the global system are usually described by

opaque statistics from business and economics, but only the most sophisticated can grasp the explosive dynamics in those numbers. To visualize this
great drama in its full dimensions, one must also see the people.

When I visited Bangkok, in Thailand, the newspapers were preoccu-
pied with the melancholy saga of Honey, a work elephant who was severely
injured when a truck sideswiped her on the highway. As doctors tried to
mend the elephant's smashed hip, contributions poured in from heartsick
citizens, including the king. Elephants have been the emblem of Thai culture
for at least seven centuries, but are now gradually dying out. Honey's death
prompted editorial reflections on the price of prosperity.

The new national symbol of Thailand, one could say, is the traffic jam.
Bangkok's are the worst in Asia, citizens remark with an air of disgusted
pride. Their daily commuting routines are the longest in developing Asia,
and Thais manipulate schedules endlessly to try to avoid the hours of steaming in tropical congestions of cars. The problem is that Thais are buying cars
much faster than the government is building a modern transportation system. Thailand may emerge as Toyota's biggest overseas market aside from
the United States.[1]

In Poland, the newly chartered Warsaw Stock Exchange was under way
in a stately old pre-Communist building on Aleje Jeroszolimskie. Trading
was quite thin since only two dozen companies had their shares listed and
Poles were already experiencing the turbulence of Adam Smith's *niewidzialna
ręka rynku,* "the invisible hand of the market." Stock prices rose fabulously in
1993, and many of the pioneer investors became instantly wealthy, zloty millionaires, at least on paper. The stock market crashed the following spring.
As shares fell 40 to 70 percent in ten days, the Polish traders adopted the style
of gallows humor familiar to mature financial markets around the world.
Watching stocks plunge 27 percent in a single day, a broker observed: "The
Warsaw Stock Exchange still awaits its first suicide."[2]

The lobby of Warsaw's Victoria Intercontinental Hotel, a favorite of foreign business travelers, was filled with hopeful plungers. Each morning
Polish entrepreneurs would spread their business prospectuses across the
broad coffee tables and sit back, a bit fidgety, while visiting investors from
Frankfurt or New York or Milan inspected the numbers.

On the city's industrial outskirts, meanwhile, workers at the Huta Luchini
steelworks were on strike. They closed down the mill to demand a share
of the ownership. These steelworkers had once been revolutionaries themselves, among the militant members of Solidarity, the free trade union that
arose to confront the Polish Communist regime in the early 1980s and had
campaigned for the autonomy of workers and enterprises organized on principles of self-management. The Warsaw steelworks is now owned by an Italian conglomerate.

In China, as the November days turned crisp and cold, the citizens of
Beijing shopped at sidewalk markets for the traditional supplies of winter
cabbage. High, squared-off mounds of cabbages attended by merchants in

blue smocks with white kerchiefs on their heads were stacked at street corners along Chang An—Avenue of Eternal Peace—the mainstream boulevard. Farmers hauled cabbages into the city every day, stacked on trucks, bicycle-powered wagons and overloaded handcarts. The ritual reflects a national memory of poverty and famine. Every autumn a family acquires its store of winter cabbages as insurance against the ancient threat of scarcity. One can see the cabbages hanging atop communal walls or outside apartment windows, their outer leaves blackened by Beijing's sooty air.

Meanwhile, traffic on the boulevard was abruptly interrupted to make way for a caravan of important personages—a fleet of limousines and police escorts racing down the center lanes, with blue lights flashing. It was Jean Chrètien, the Canadian prime minister, and a trade delegation from Ottawa and the provinces. Kohl, Mitterand, Major, Balladur, Bentsen, Brown, Christopher—visiting political leaders from the most advanced economies, statesmen seeking contracts for home companies and access to China's explosive market, have become a commonplace.

As usual, McDonald's was already there, selling burgers to consumers. From Kuala Lumpur to Moscow, the company acts like an advanced scout for the global revolution, somehow able to detect the emergence of disposable incomes before other firms see it. Chinese buy their winter cabbages and also fast food. McDonald's measures its market potential with numbers like these: In the United States, there is a McDonald's restaurant for every 29,000 Americans. In China, despite rapid expansion, there is one McDonald's for every 40 million Chinese.

In Tokyo, the Sony Corporation, an authentic symbol of Japan's manufacturing excellence, is on the verge of becoming an un-Japanese company. The human resources manager, Yasunori Kirihara, lamented the prospect but explained it as an inevitable consequence of global economic integration. At present, he said, Sony's employees are split roughly fifty-fifty between Japanese and foreigners. As Sony continues to relocate its factories elsewhere, from Southeast Asia to Mexico, the substantial majority of its workforce, about 60 percent, will soon be outside Japan.

A new Japanese word, *kudoka,* has been popularized in business and political circles to describe this phenomenon. *Kudoka,* I was told, did not exist in the language before the 1980s. Its meaning should be familiar to American industrial workers who have seen their manufacturing jobs disappear. In English, it means "hollowing out."

In Everett, Washington, just north of Seattle, workers on the assembly line for Boeing's new 777, the company's latest addition to its line of large-body aircraft, gossiped that they might be shut down by the earthquake in Kobe, Japan. The main body section of the "Triple Seven," as Boeing people call their new plane, is manufactured by Mitsubishi Heavy Industries, though its plant, as it turned out, was not damaged by the quake. The 777 is a brilliant expression of America's productive prowess in advanced technologies, but their aircraft is manufactured, piece by piece, in twelve different countries.

As these scattered glimpses suggest, the symptoms of upheaval can be found most anywhere, since people in distant places are now connected by powerful strands of the same marketplace. The convergence has no fixed center, no reliable boundaries or settled outcomes. As enterprise opens up new territories, the maps keep changing—changing so rapidly that it has already become commonplace to speak of "one world" markets for everything from cars to capital. The earth's diverse societies are being rearranged and united in complicated ways by global capitalism. The idea evokes benumbed resignation among many. The complexity of it overwhelms. The enormity makes people feel small and helpless.

The essence of this industrial revolution, like others before it, is that commerce and finance have leapt inventively beyond the existing order and existing consciousness of peoples and societies. The global system of trade and production is fast constructing a new functional reality for most everyone's life, a new order based upon its own dynamics and not confined by the traditional social understandings. People may wish to turn away from that fact, but there is essentially no place to hide, not if one lives in any of the industrialized nations.

The only option people really have is to catch up with the reality. The only way to escape a sense of helplessness is to confront this new world on its own terms and try to understand its larger implications. The actual system, as we shall see, does not conform to the economic theory it presumes to follow. Nor are people and nations actually powerless to influence its behavior, as conventional wisdom asserts. But people and nations may restore a sense of control over their own destinies only if they are willing to face the complexity, only by grasping the operating imperatives that drive the global system and the full scope of human consequences that it yields.

Grasping the meaning of this new order requires one to set aside reflexive national loyalties in order to see the system whole. I have tried at least to do that. Above all, I avoid the standard nationalist complaints (most often aimed at Japan) that preoccupy so many books about the global economy, especially books written by Americans. (While I have tried to stand outside national identity and see things in a spirit of universality, I do not imagine for a moment that I have succeeded fully. Like most people, I am bound by culture and personal experience, by limitations of language and native biases, to one nation.)

The usual question—is America winning or losing?—can be disposed of quickly. The answer is yes. America is winning, and yes, it is losing. Some sectors of Americans are triumphant and other sectors are devastated, but not in equal measures. The same rough answer applies in differing degrees throughout most of the world, especially among the wealthiest nations— Germany, France or Britain, even Japan.

Books that nominate one country or another as "the winner" of global competition have a very short shelf life since these things change so rapidly.

In 1992, a best-selling author heralded Europe, led by Germany, as the likely champion for its superior economic system; eighteen months later Europe and Germany were mired in gloomy forecasts from their own business leaders, complaining about their failure to keep up with American flexibility. Likewise, the United States has been written off and revived a number of times. Even Japan, so wealthy that many thought it had already won the race, is now experiencing its own tangible crisis of self-doubt.[3]

The obsession with nations in competition misses the point of what is happening: The global economy divides every society into new camps of conflicting economic interests. It undermines every nation's ability to maintain social cohesion. It mocks the assumption of shared political values that supposedly unite people in the nation-state.

That is the fundamental reason politics has become so muddled in the leading capitalist democracies. In recent years, voters have turned on established parties and leaders, sometimes quite brutally, in the United States, Canada, Italy, France, Sweden and Japan, to name the most spectacular cases. Nor is there any ideological consistency to these voter rebellions. Socialists were tossed out in socialist Sweden, then restored to power a few years later. In a single election, the Conservative Party of Canada was reduced from governing majority to a remnant of two parliamentary seats. The business party that ruled Japan without interruption for four decades, the Liberal Democrats, was ousted by dissident reformers, then regained power in an unstable coalition of its own, this time led by a socialist.

Deeper political instability lies ahead for these societies because the global economy has put a different political question on the table: What exactly is the national interest in these new circumstances? No elected government in the richest countries, neither right nor left, has produced a definition that convinces its own electorate. Indeed, some important governments, clinging to the inherited postwar orthodoxy, are pursuing economic strategies that arguably do injury to majorities of their own citizens. This reflects not only the heavy hand of defunct theory, but also that insecure politicians do not know what else to do.

Political confusion in the dominant economies is set against a fundamental countervailing reality: For most people living in most parts of the world, the global economy began in 1492. In their history, the centuries of conquest and economic colonization were integral to the rise of industrial capitalism in Europe and North America, but the returns were never really shared with them. Books by Americans proclaiming "one world" may seem quite precious and self-centered to those people. For them, the global economy long ago consigned most regions of the world to lowly status as commodity producers—the hewers and haulers, the rubber tappers, tin miners and cane cutters. What William Faulkner said of the American South applies as well to those colonialized nations that used to be known as the Third World: the past is never dead, it is not even past. (The global economy has a language problem: The old labels for categories of nations are confused or obsolete. "Third World," a condescending term coined for the Cold War, is not meaningless. Even the "West" is useless if it is meant to designate the advanced economies, since Japan is among them and booming Asia lies west of the United States, not east. We are reduced to cruder terms like rich and poor nations, advanced and primitive economies.)

From the perspective of most of these countries, the present industrial revolution is a rare opening in history, a chance to get out from under. Some of them are succeeding, climbing rapidly in wealth and establishing at least a fragile basis for national self-sufficiency. Dozens of others are trying to do the same. All of them approach the present with deep historical skepticism, the memory of how many times their aspirations were thwarted by the leading economic powers, how many previous openings turned out to be illusory.

When all the larger economic and political questions are exhausted, the heaviest legacy of this new "one world" may be the psychological blow to national arrogance. Americans reflexively think of themselves as without any real peers. Number One. In their own racialist ways so do the Japanese and the Germans. Tribal assumptions of inherited superiority are embedded in the cultures of the French and Chinese and Muslims, among many others. These folk illusions are now under vigorous assault, contradicted by the emerging economic reality.

During my travels I experienced certain small epiphanies: The amazement of watching a great modern industrial factory at work. The anguish of encountering exploited young people, peasant children turned into low-wage industrial workers, struggling to understand their own condition. The simple delight any tourist feels at glimpsing the weird variety of human life and also the underlying sameness.

The most powerful moments, however, were the recurring experience of witnessing poor people who dwell in marginal backwaters doing industrial work of the most advanced order. People of color, people who are black, yellow, red, brown, who exist in surroundings of primitive scarcity, are making complex things of world-class quality, mastering modern technologies that used to be confined to a select few. The tools of advanced civilization are being shared with other tribes. Multinational corporations, awesomely powerful and imperiously aloof, are the ironic vehicle for accomplishing this generous act of history.

The confident presumption that certain high-caliber work can be done only by certain people (mainly, it is assumed, by well-educated white people in a few chosen countries) is mistaken. Observing these scenes of industrial activity, I thought first of the explosive implications for the future of work and prosperity in the advanced economies, including America. The portents are stark and threatening. Yet the meaning also has to be understood in the broader sweep of human history. Watching former peasants making high-tech goods for the global market, I eventually reached a simpler, more nourishing understanding. Of course, I thought. People are capable, everywhere in the world.

Is it conceivable that commerce, pursuing narrow self-interested ends, might accomplish what idealistic politics has never been able to achieve—defeating stubborn ideas of racial superiority? I returned from my travels imagining it might someday be possible. Certainly, enormous conflicts lie ahead for the peoples of the world, political and economic collisions, possibly including the violence of wars between rival economies. Nevertheless, the process of globalization is visibly dismantling enduring stereotypes of race and culture, ancient assumptions of supremacy. This transformation will someday be understood as the most radical dimension of the revolution. . . .

The raw energies of the global system, its power of excitement, can be glimpsed in the daily headlines about important business deals. Anheuser-Busch buys a stake in Kirin, Japan's biggest brewery, also a 5 percent share of China's Tsingtao, then acquires 10 percent of Antarctica, the leading beer of Brazil. Siemens of Germany forms a partnership with Skoda Plzen to manufacture steam turbines in the Czech Republic. Volvo opens an assembly line near Xian, China, with Chinese machinists making Swedish tour buses. Switzerland's Roche bids $5.3 billion for the U.S. pharmaceutical Syntex, while Smith-Kline Beecham buys another American company for $2.3 billion. NEC, the Japanese electronics giant, agrees to collaborate with Samsung, the Korean multinational, to make DRAM memory chips, probably at a plant in Portugal, to supply the $5 billion European market.

The problem, of course, is that the stories are too diverse and plentiful to make the motivating principles very clear. As the announcements of new ventures accumulate in breathtaking number, the effect is like the blur of a major blizzard. IBM announces quarterly losses of $8 billion and plans to cut 35,000 jobs. Bausch & Lomb begins making contact lenses and Ray-Ban sunglasses in India. Colgate-Palmolive opens a toothbrush factory in Colombia. AT&T forms an alliance with the national telephone companies of Sweden, Switzerland and the Netherlands; its American rival MCI pairs off with British Telecommunications.

Coca-Cola returns to Vietnam, this time without the U.S. military forces. Toyota picks Kentucky to make automobiles, BMW picks South Carolina, Mercedes picks Alabama. Ford and General Motors hope the Chinese government will pick them to make cars in China.[4]

John F. Welch Jr., CEO of General Electric and widely admired for hard-headed corporate strategies, has warned fellow executives not to be lulled by self-congratulations or press clippings about how American companies have regained an edge over foreign competitors. "These things are going to get tougher," he predicted in mid-1994. "The shakeouts will be more brutal. The pace of change is more rapid." What lies ahead, Welch said, is "a hurricane."[5]

The accumulating evidence supports this warning. After two decades of dramatic changes, the revolutionary pressures are not abating or leveling off into familiar patterns. The dynamics appear to be accelerating. What is the nature of the storm upon us? A new structure of power is gradually emerging in the world, forcing great changes everywhere it asserts itself. The broad dimensions are defined by a baseline of unsettling facts:

1. During the last generation the world's 500 largest multinational corporations have grown sevenfold in sales. Yet the worldwide employment of these global firms has remained virtually flat since the early 1970s, hovering around 26 million people. The major multinationals grew in sales from $721 billion in 1971 to $5.2 trillion in 1991, claiming a steadily growing share of commerce (one third of all manufacturing exports, three fourths of commodity trade, four fifths of the trade in technology and management services). Yet the human labor required for each unit of their output is diminished dramatically.

While this galaxy of major global firms grew in size, its center of gravity also shifted. America's flagship companies, from du Pont and IBM to GE and General Motors, were the modern progenitors of globalized manufacturing after World War II, but the United States has lost its dominance. In 1971, 280 of the largest 500 multinationals were American-based. By 1991, the United States had only 157 on the list.

Europe's largest companies surpassed America's in number and sales volume during the last half of the 1980s. By 1991, Europe had 168 of the largest 500. Japan, meanwhile, had risen in twenty years from 53 to 119. A few important multinational corporations have even emerged in countries that were once very poor—Korea, Taiwan, even Thailand. The corporate girth of nations is gradually dispersing, leveling out.[6]

2. The basic mechanism of globalization—companies investing capital in foreign countries, buying existing assets or building new factories—has accelerated explosively during the last fifteen years. The volume of direct foreign investment nearly quadrupled during the 1980s, reaching $2 trillion in the 1990s. The largest portion of that capital flow, about 25 percent, actually went into the United States during the 1980s, reversing the historic pattern. The United States became a debtor nation and sold off domestic assets to foreign investors; Japanese auto companies, among others, prudently located assembly plants in the States.[7]

Direct investing across borders cooled off for several years amid the major recessions of the early 1990s, but as it resumed the heaviest flows of capital were aimed in a different direction—building new production in the so-called emerging markets of Asia and selected nations in Latin America and Eastern Europe. Indeed, another historic relationship seemed broken: the utter dependence of poor nations on the prosperous. This time around, while the advanced economies remained stagnant or mired in recession, a league of poorer economies was enjoying a spectacular investment boom.

The growth of transnational corporate investments, the steady dispersal of production elements across many nations, has nearly obliterated the traditional understanding of trade. Though many of them know better, economists and politicians continue to portray the global trading system in terms that the public can understand—that is, as a collection of nations buying and selling things to each other. However, as the volume of world trade has grown, the traditional role of national markets is increasingly eclipsed by an alternative system: trade generated within the multinational companies themselves as they export and import among their own foreign-based subsidiaries.

According to one scholarly estimate, more than 40 percent of U.S. exports and nearly 50 percent of its imports are actually goods that travel not in the open marketplace, but through these intrafirm channels. A U.S. computer company ships design components to its assembly plant in Malaysia, then distributes the finished hardware back to the United States and to other buyers in Asia and Europe. A typical Japanese plant located in America "imports" most of its components from its parent corporation and allied suppliers, then "exports" products back to the parent in Japan or sister affiliates in other countries.[8]

All of this intrafirm traffic is counted in the national trade statistics, but national identities are increasingly irrelevant to the buyers and sellers. Nation-to-nation trade flows are driven more and more by the proprietary strategies of the multinational corporations organizing their own diversified production, less and less by traditional concepts of comparative advantage among nations or the economic policies of home governments.

The shifting content of trade has led many leading governments, including the one in Washington, to embrace a strategy that might confound some citizens (if it were explained to them clearly) because it seems to offend nationalist intuition. The governments are actively promoting the dispersal of capital investment and production to foreign locations on the assumption that this will lead to increased exports for home-based production (and more jobs for domestic workers). As the flagship multinationals make more things overseas, they will presumably ship more homemade goods to their overseas affiliates. That, anyway, is the logic governments embrace.

3. Finance capital—the trading of stocks, bonds, currencies, and more exotic forms of financial paper—has accelerated its movements around the world at an astonishing pace. International bank loans more than quadrupled from 1980 to 1991, reaching $3.6 trillion. Global bond financing expanded likewise. Cross-border stockholdings in the so-called Triad—Europe, Japan and the United States—nearly doubled in a few years in the late 1980s.

The global exchange markets in national currencies—swapping dollars for yen or deutschemarks for francs or scores of other such trades—are moving faster still. Foreign-exchange trading totaled more than $1.2 trillion a day by the early 1990s, compared to only $640 billion a day as recently as 1989. Since financial traders usually move in and out of different currencies in order to buy or sell a nation's stocks or bonds, this furious pace of currency exchange reflects the magnifying presence of borderless finance.

The entire global volume of publicly traded financial assets (about $24 trillion) turns over every twenty-four days. The International Monetary Fund, which attempts to monitor such matters, claims that this quickening pace is unexceptional since, it points out, the trading in U.S. government bonds is even faster. The entire traded volume of U.S. treasury debt ($2.6 trillion) turns over every eight days.[9]

Despite the staggering volume the financial trading across borders is mostly transacted by a very small community: the world's largest thirty to fifty banks and a handful of major brokerages that do the actual trades in behalf of investor clients—wealthy individuals and the various pools of private capital, smaller banks and brokerages, pension funds, mutual funds and so on—as well as the banks' own portfolios.

As the volume has swelled, the global financial markets have become much more powerful—and much more erratic. Sentiment and prices can shift suddenly and sharply, cascading losses across innocent bystanders like the multinational corporations that depend on predictable currency values for their cross-border trade or national governments that watch helplessly as global finance raises their domestic interest rates or devalues their currencies. "Crisis" has become an overworked word. Market economists speak more politely of "disturbances." These are the decisive breaks in prices that occur when global investors suddenly lose confidence in one investment sector or an entire country and abruptly shift huge amounts of capital elsewhere quick as the electronic impulses of modern banking.

To make sense out of these bewildering facts, it helps to think of the global system in cruder terms, as a galaxy of four broad, competing power blocs—each losing or gaining influence over events. The biggest, most obvious loser in these terms is labor, both the organized union workers and wage earners in general. Wages are both rising and falling around the world, but workers at both ends of the global economy have lost substantial control over their labor markets and the terms of employment. "Now capital has wings," as New York financier Robert A. Johnson explained succinctly. "Capital can deal with twenty labor markets at once and pick and choose among them. Labor is fixed in one place. So power has shifted."

National governments, likewise, have lost ground on the whole, partly because many have retreated from trying to exercise their power over commerce and finance, implicitly ceding to the revolutionary spirit. In the advanced economies, most governments have become mere salesmen, promoting the fortunes of their own multinationals in the hope that this will provide a core prosperity that keeps everyone afloat. The clearest evidence that this strategy is not working is the condition of labor markets in the wealthiest nations: either mass unemployment or declining real wages (nominal pay adjusted for inflation), and, in some cases, both of these deleterious effects.

The more subtle evidence of the dilemma of leading governments is their deteriorating fiscal condition: most are threatened by rising, seemingly permanent budget deficits and accumulating debt. The swollen fiscal deficits of the United States are the largest in size, but far from the worst in relative terms. The general fiscal crisis of rich nations is driven by the same fundamental—disappointing economic growth that, year after year, fails to generate the tax revenues needed to keep up with the public obligations established in more prosperous times. The modern welfare state, the social protections that rich nations enacted to ameliorate the harsh inequalities of industrial capitalism, is now in peril. Some would say it is already obsolete.

Ironically, the governments of developing countries, at least the most successful ones, are less enthralled by the global system's theory and rhetoric and more willing to impose their own terms on capital and trade. Given their own historical memory, poor countries attempt, if they can, to bargain with the system—making nationalistic trade-offs with global firms and investors. Some succeed; many are overwhelmed.

The multinational corporations are, collectively, the muscle and brains of this new system, the engineers who are designing the brilliant networks of new relationships. It is their success at globalization that has inevitably weakened labor and degraded the control of governments. Some smart organizations are even reconfiguring themselves into what business futurists have dubbed "the virtual corporation," a quick-witted company so dispersed that it resembles the ganglia of a nervous system, a brain attached to many distant nodes but without much bodily substance at the center.[10]

Despite their supple strengths the great multinationals are, one by one, insecure themselves. Even the most muscular industrial giants are quite vulnerable if they fail to adapt to the imperatives of reducing costs and improving rates of return. Critics who focus on the awesome size and sprawl of the global corporations find this point difficult to accept, but the executives of Volkswagen, GM, Volvo, IBM, Eastman Kodak and Pan American Airlines can attest to it. Those well-known firms, among many others, have experienced the harsh consequences of straying from the path of revolution. Their stocks were hammered, their managements ousted, tens of thousands of employees discarded. Behind corporate facades, the anxiety is genuine.

The Robespierre of this revolution is finance capital. Its principles are transparent and pure: maximizing the return on capital without regard to national identity or political and social consequences. Global finance collectively acts as the disinterested enforcer of these imperatives, like a Committee of Public Safety presiding over the Terror (though historians would note that Robespierre's revolutionaries pursued the opposite objective of reducing the great inequalities of wealth).

Financial investors monitor and punish corporations or whole industrial sectors if their returns weaken. Finance disciplines governments or even entire regions of the globe if those places appear to be creating impediments to profitable enterprise or unpleasant surprises for capital. If this sounds dictatorial, the global financiers also adhere to their own rough version of egalitarian values: they will turn on anyone, even their own home country's industry and government, if the defense of free capital seems to require it.

As the Jacobins learned during the French Revolution, it is the most zealous, principled advocates of new values who are ultimately most at risk in a revolutionary environment. Master financiers seem to appreciate this, too. George Soros, the Hungarian American billionaire who became fabulously wealthy by grasping the new principles of global investing before others, often emphasizes his own fallibility. In early 1994, when Soros got things wrong, he lost $600 million during two days of brisk disturbance in global bond markets. When Robespierre got things wrong, he was guillotined before a cheering mob in the Place de la Révolution.

Even the most powerful players—titans of finance or the multinationals regularly demonized in popular lore—are themselves dwarfed by the system and subject to its harsh, overwhelming consequences. To describe the power structure of the global system does not imply that anyone is in charge of the revolution. The revolution runs itself. This point is critical to understanding its anarchic energies and oblivious disregard for parochial victims or, for that matter, the seeming impotence of enterprises themselves to control things. This revolution is following historical patterns of behavior that industrial capitalism has reiterated across the centuries—an explosive cycle of renewal, migration and destruction that is typically ignited by human invention.

ENDNOTES

Author's Note: As these notes reflect, I have relied on many diverse sources, but none was more valuable than the *Financial Times* of London. The *Financial Times* provides an authoritative snapshot of action in the global economy every day, with superb reporting and analysis, much more comprehensive than anything published in the United States.

[1] The elephant population of Thailand has declined to 1,975 in the wild and 2,938 domesticated animals, according to Rodney Tasker, *Far Eastern Economic Review,* April 29, 1993. Daily commuting time in Thailand is the longest in Asia, according to a survey of affluent consumers: *Far Eastern Economic Review,* August 27, 1992. Thai auto sales and traffic jams: Victor Mallet, *Financial Times,* November 27, 1993.

[2] The Warsaw stock market crash: *Warsaw Voice,* April 24, 1994.

[3] Economist Lester Thurow wrote as recently as 1992: "History and human nature tells us that it will be far easier for the Americans and the Japanese to avoid doing what they must do if they are to win. Future historians will record that the twenty-first century belonged to the House of Europe!" *Head to Head: Coming Economic Battles among Japan, Europe, and America* (New York: Morrow, 1992).

[4] Anheuser-Busch: *Financial Times,* June 29 and July 30, 1993, and February 23, 1995; Siemens: *Financial Times,* July 21, 1993; Taiwan Aerospace: *Financial Times,* July 24, 1993; drug company mergers: *Financial Times,* May 4, 1994; NEC-Samsung: *Financial Times,* February 7, 1995; IBM losses: *Wall Street Journal,* July 28, 1993; Bausch & Lomb, Colgate-Palmolive: *Wall Street Journal,* August 4, 1993; AT&T: *Financial Times,* June 24, 1994; Coca-Cola: *Financial Times,* July 22, 1993.

[5] John F. Welch Jr., *Wall Street Journal,* June 21, 1994.

[6] The 500 largest global firms are described in *Multinationals and the National Interest: Playing by Different Rules,* Office of Technology Assessment, U.S. Congress, Septem-

ber 1993. American firms still dominate among the largest, accounting for 7 of the 20 biggest multinationals, as ranked by foreign assets.

The top 20 are, in order: Royal Dutch Shell (UK/Netherlands), Ford, GM, Exxon, IBM (U.S.), British Petroleum (UK), Asea Brown Boveri (Switzerland/ Sweden), Nestlé (Switzerland), Philips Electronics (Netherlands), Mobil (U.S.), Unilever (UK, Netherlands), Matsushita Electric (Japan), Fiat (Italy), Siemens (Germany), Sony (Japan), Volkswagen (Germany), Elf Aquitaine (France), Mitsubishi (Japan), GE and du Pont (U.S.). Cited in "World Investment Report 1993: Transnational Corporations and Integrated International Production," United Nations, from *Financial Times,* July 21, 1993.

[7] *Multinationals and National Interest,* OTA. The biggest owners of the $2 trillion in foreign productive assets continue to be U.S. firms, with a total of $474 billion, followed by Britain, $259 billion, and Japan, $251 billion: *Financial Times,* July 21, 1993.

[8] The intrafirm trade patterns vary from country to country. For Japanese manufacturing, 51 percent of all exports from affiliates were to the parent companies or other sister affiliates in 1989, according to John H. Dunning, *Multinational Enterprises and the Global Economy* (Reading, MA: Addison-Wesley, 1993).

[9] Bank lending growth is from the annual reports of the Bank for International Settlements. Other financial data is from "International Capital Markets, Part I," International Monetary Fund, 1993.

[10] William H. Davidow and Michael S. Malone, *The Virtual Corporation: Structuring and Revitalizing the Corporation for the 21st Century* (New York: HarperCollins, 1992).

56

WHAT CAN WE DO?
Becoming Part of the Solution

ALLAN G. JOHNSON

This last reading is by Allan G. Johnson, a sociologist at the Hartford College for Women of the University of Hartford. Johnson studies the dynamics of privilege, power, and oppression. He is especially interested in understanding how and why systems of privilege are created and maintained in society. In this selection, adapted from *Privilege, Power, and Difference* (2001), Johnson outlines how every individual can be involved in creating solutions to social problems caused by social inequality. He suggests we learn new strategies to effectively become aware of how each of us is privileged and contributes to

Excerpted and adapted from the chapter titled "Unraveling the Gender Knot," included in *The Gender Knot: Unraveling Our Patriarchal Legacy,* by permission of Temple University Press. Copyright © 1997 by Allan G. Johnson. All rights reserved.

the oppression of others based on that privilege. With that awareness comes the ability to better affect social change.

The challenge we face is to change patterns of exclusion, rejection, privilege, harassment, discrimination, and violence that are everywhere in this society and have existed for hundreds (or, in the case of gender, thousands) of years. We have to begin by thinking about the trouble and the challenge in new and more productive ways. . . . Here is a summary of the tools we have to start with.

Large numbers of people have sat on the sidelines and seen themselves as neither part of the problem nor the solution. Beyond this shared trait, however, they are far from homogeneous. Everyone is aware of the whites, heterosexuals, and men who intentionally act out in oppressive ways. But there is less attention to the millions of people who know inequities exist and want to be part of the solution. Their silence and invisibility allow the trouble to continue. Removing what silences them and stands in their way can tap an enormous potential of energy for change.

The problem of privilege and oppression is deep and wide, and to work with it we have to be able to see it clearly so that we can talk about it in useful ways. To do that, we have to reclaim some difficult language that names what's going on, language that has been so misused and maligned that it generates more heat than light. We can't just stop using words like *racism, sexism,* and *privilege,* however, because these are tools that focus our awareness on the problem and all the forms it takes. Once we can see and talk about what's going on, we can analyze how it works as a system. We can identify points of leverage where change can begin.

Reclaiming the language takes us directly to the core reality that the problem is privilege and the power that maintains it. Privilege exists when one group has something that is systematically denied to others not because of who they are or what they've done or not done, but because of the social category they belong to.

Privilege is a feature of social systems, not individuals. People have or don't have privilege depending on the system they're in and the social categories other people put them in. To say, then, that I have race privilege says less about me personally than it does about the society we all live in and how it is organized to assign privilege on the basis of a socially defined set of racial categories that change historically and often overlap. The challenge facing me as an individual has more to do with how I participate in society as a recipient of race privilege and how those choices oppose or support the system itself.

In dealing with the problem of privilege, we have to get used to being surrounded by paradox. Very often those who have privilege don't know it, for example, which is a key aspect of privilege. Also paradoxical is the fact that privilege doesn't necessarily lead to a "good life," which can prompt people in privileged groups to deny resentfully that they even have it. But privilege doesn't equate with being happy. It involves having what others don't have and the struggle to hang on to it at their expense, neither of which is a recipe for joy, personal fulfillment, or spiritual contentment. . . .

To be an effective part of the solution, we have to realize that privilege and oppression are not a thing of the past. It's happening right now. It isn't just a collection of wounds inflicted long ago that now need to be healed. The wounding goes on as I write these words and as you read them, and unless people work to change the system that promotes it, personal healing by itself cannot be the answer. Healing wounds is no more a solution to the oppression that causes the wounding than military hospitals are a solution to war. Healing is a necessary process, but it isn't enough. . . .

Since privilege is rooted primarily in systems—such as families, schools, and workplaces—change isn't simply a matter of changing people. People, of course, will have to change in order for systems to change, but the most important point is that changing people isn't enough. The solution also has to include entire systems, such as capitalism, whose paths of least resistance shape how we feel, think, and behave as individuals, how we see ourselves and one another.

As they work for change, it's easy for members of privileged groups to lose sight of the reality of privilege and its consequences and the truth that the trouble around privilege is their trouble as much as anyone else's. This happens in large part because systems of privilege provide endless ways of seeing and thinking about the world that make privilege invisible. These include denying and minimizing the trouble; blaming the victim; calling the trouble something else; assuming everyone prefers things the way they are; mistaking intentions with consequences; attributing the trouble to others and not their own participation in social systems that produce it; and balancing the trouble with troubles of their own. The more aware people can be of how these behaviors limit their effectiveness, the more they can contribute to change both in themselves and the systems where they work and live.

With these tools in hand, we can begin to think about how to make ourselves part of the solution to the problem of privilege and oppression. . . .

STUBBORN OUNCES
(To One Who Doubts the Worth of Doing Anything
if You Can't Do Everything)

> You say the little efforts that I make
> will do no good; they will never prevail
> to tip the hovering scale
> where Justice hangs in balance.
>   I don't think
> I ever thought they would.
> But I am prejudiced beyond debate
> In favor of my right to choose which side
> shall feel the stubborn ounces of my weight.[1]

Stubborn Ounces: What Can We Do?

There are no easy answers to the question of what can we do about the problem of privilege. There is no twelve-step program, no neat set of instructions. Most important, there is no way around or over it: the only way out is through it. We won't end oppression by pretending it isn't there or that we don't have to deal with it.

Some people complain that those who work for social change are being "divisive" when they draw attention to gender or race or social class and the oppressive systems organized around them. But when members of dominant groups mark differences by excluding or discriminating against subordinate groups and treating them as "other," they aren't accused of being divisive. Usually it's only when someone calls attention to how differences are used for oppressive purposes that the charge of divisiveness comes up.

In a sense, it *is* divisive to say that oppression and privilege exist, but only insofar as it points to divisions that already exist and to the perception that the status quo is normal and unremarkable. Oppression promotes the worst kind of divisiveness because it cuts us off from one another and, by silencing us about the truth, cuts us off from ourselves as well. Not only must we participate in oppression by living in an oppressive society, we also must act as though oppression didn't exist, denying the reality of our own experience and its consequences for people's lives, including our own.

What does it mean to go out by going through? What can we do that will make a difference? I don't have the answers, but I do have some suggestions.

Acknowledge That the Trouble Exists

A key to the continued existence of every oppressive system is unawareness, because oppression contradicts so many basic human values that it invariably arouses opposition when people know about it. The Soviet Union and its East European satellites, for example, were riddled with contradictions so widely known among their people that the oppressive regimes fell apart with an ease and speed that astonished the world. An awareness of oppression compels people to speak out, to break the silence that continued oppression depends on.

This is why most oppressive cultures mask the reality of oppression by denying its existence, trivializing it, calling it something else, blaming it on those most victimized by it, or diverting attention from it. Instead of treating oppression as a serious problem, we go to war or get embroiled in controversial "issues" such as capital gains tax cuts or "family values" or immigrant workers. There would be far more active opposition to racism, for example, if white people lived with an ongoing awareness of how it actually affects the everyday lives of those it oppresses as "not white." As we have seen, however, the vast majority of white people *don't* do this.

It's one thing to become aware and quite another to stay that way. The greatest challenge when we first become aware of a critical perspective on the world is simply to hang on to it. Every system's paths of least resistance invariably lead away from critical awareness of how the system works. In some ways, it's harder and more important to pay attention to systems of privilege than it is to people's behavior and the paths of least resistance that shape it. . . .

Pay Attention

Understanding how privilege and oppression operate and how you participate in them is where the work for change begins. It's easy to have opinions, but it takes work to know what you're talking about. The simplest way to begin is by reading, and making reading about privilege part of your life. Unless you have the luxury of a personal teacher, you can't understand this issue without reading, just as you'd need to read about a foreign country before you traveled there for the first time, or about a car before you tried to work under the hood. Many people assume they already know what they need to know because it's part of everyday life. But they're usually wrong. Just as the last thing a fish would discover is water, the last thing people discover is society itself and something as pervasive as the dynamics of privilege.

We also have to be open to the idea that what we think we know is, if not wrong, so deeply shaped by systems of privilege that it misses most of the truth. This is why activists talk with one another and spend time reading one another's writing: seeing things clearly is tricky. This is also why people who are critical of the status quo are so often self-critical as well: they know how complex and elusive the truth really is and what a challenge it is to work toward it. People working for change are often accused of being orthodox and rigid, but in practice they are typically among the most self-critical people around. . . .

Little Risks: Do Something

The more you pay attention to privilege and oppression, the more you'll see opportunities to do something about them. You don't have to mount an expedition to find those opportunities; they're all over the place, beginning in yourself. As I became aware of how male privilege encourages me to control conversations, for example, I also realized how easily men dominate group meetings by controlling the agenda and interrupting, without women's objecting to it. This pattern is especially striking in groups that are mostly female but in which most of the talking nonetheless comes from a few men. I would find myself sitting in meetings and suddenly the preponderance of male voices would jump out at me, an unmistakable sign of male privilege, in full bloom.

As I've seen what's going on, I've had to decide what to do about this little path of least resistance and my relation to it that leads me to follow it so readily. With some effort, I've tried out new ways of listening more and talking less. At times my methods have felt contrived and artificial, such as telling myself to shut up for a while or even counting slowly to ten (or more) to give others a chance to step into the space afforded by silence. With time and practice, new paths have become easier to follow and I spend less time monitoring myself. But awareness is never automatic or permanent, for paths of least resistance will be there to choose or not as long as male privilege exists.

As you become more aware, questions will arise about what goes on at work, in the media, in families, in communities, in religious institutions, in government, on the street, and at school—in short, just about everywhere. The questions don't come all at once (for which we can be grateful), although they sometimes come in a rush that can feel overwhelming. If you remind yourself that it isn't up to you to do it all, however, you can see plenty of situations in which you can make a difference, sometimes in surprisingly simple ways. Consider the following possibilities:

Make noise, be seen. Stand up, volunteer, speak out, write letters, sign petitions, show up. Every oppressive system feeds on silence. Don't collude in silence. Breaking the silence is especially important for dominant groups, because it undermines the assumption of solidarity that dominance depends on. If this feels too risky, you can practice being aware of how silence reflects your investment in solidarity with other dominant-group members. This can be a place to begin working on how you participate in making privilege and oppression happen: "Today I said nothing, colluded in silence, and this is how I benefited from it. Maybe tomorrow I can try something different."

Find little ways to withdraw support from paths of least resistance and people's choices to follow them, starting with yourself. It can be as simple as not laughing at a racist or heterosexist joke or saying you don't think it's funny, or writing a letter to your senator or representative or the editor of your newspaper, objecting to an instance of sexism in the media. When my local newspaper ran an article whose headline referred to sexual harassment as "earthy behavior," for example, I wrote a letter pointing out that harassment isn't "earthy."

The key to withdrawing support is to interrupt the flow of business as usual. We can subvert the assumption that we're all going along with the status quo by simply not going along. When we do this, we stop the flow, if only for a moment, but in that moment other people can notice and start to think and question. It's a perfect time to suggest the possibility of alternatives, such as humor that isn't at someone else's expense, or of ways to think about discrimination, harassment, and violence that do justice to the reality of what's going on and how it affects people. . . .

Dare to make people feel uncomfortable, beginning with yourself. At the next local school board meeting, for example, you can ask why principals and other administrators are almost always white and male (unless your system is an exception that proves the rule), while the teachers they supervise are mostly women and people of color. Or look at the names and mascots used by local sports teams and see if they exploit the heritage and identity of Native Americans; if that's the case, ask principals and coaches and owners about it.[2] Consider asking similar kinds of questions about privilege and difference in your place of worship, workplace, and local government. . . .

Some will say it isn't "nice" to make people uncomfortable, but oppressive systems do a lot more than make people feel uncomfortable, and there isn't anything "nice" about allowing that to continue unchallenged. Besides, discomfort is an unavoidable part of any meaningful process of education. We can't grow without being willing to challenge our assumptions and take ourselves to the edge of our competencies, where we're bound to feel uncomfortable. If we can't tolerate ambiguity, uncertainty, and discomfort, then we'll never get beneath superficial appearances or learn or change anything of much value, including ourselves.

And if history is any guide, discomfort—to put it mildly—is also an unavoidable part of changing systems of privilege. As sociologist William Gamson noted in his study of social movements, "the meek don't make it."[3] To succeed, movements must be willing to disrupt business as usual and make those in power as uncomfortable as possible. Women didn't win the right to vote, for example, by reasoning with men and showing them the merits of their position. To even get men's attention, they had to take to the streets in large numbers at considerable risk to themselves. At the very least they had to be willing to suffer ridicule and ostracism, but it often got worse than that. In England, for example, suffragettes were jailed and, when they went on hunger strikes, were force fed through tubes run down their throats. The modern women's movement has had to depend no less on the willingness of women to put themselves on the line in order to make men so uncomfortable that they've had to pay attention and, eventually, to act.

It has been no different with the civil rights movement. Under the leadership of men like Martin Luther King, the movement was dedicated to the principle of nonviolence. As with the movement for women's suffrage, however, they could get white people's attention only through mass demonstrations and marches. Whites typically responded with violence and intimidation.[4] As Douglas McAdam showed in his study of that period, the Federal government intervened and enacted civil rights legislation only when white violence against civil rights demonstrators became so extreme that the government was compelled to act.[5] . . .

Openly choose and model alternative paths. As we identify paths of least resistance, we can identify alternatives and then follow them openly so that other people can see what we're doing. Paths of least resistance become more visible when people choose alternatives, just as rules become more visible when someone breaks them. Modeling new paths creates tension in a system, which moves toward resolution. We don't have to convince anyone of anything. As Gandhi put it, the work begins with us as we try to be the change we want to see happen in the world. If you think this has no effect, watch how people react to the slightest departures from established paths and how much effort they expend trying to ignore or explain away or challenge those who choose alternative paths.

Actively promote change in how systems are organized around privilege. The possibilities here are almost endless, because social life is complicated and privilege is everywhere. You can, for example,

Speak out for equality in the workplace.

Promote diversity awareness and training.

Support equal pay and promotion.

Oppose the devaluing of women and people of color and the work they do, from dead-end jobs to glass ceilings.

Support the well-being of mothers and children and defend women's right to control their bodies and their lives.

Object to the punitive dismantling of welfare and attempts to limit women's access to reproductive health services.

Speak out against violence and harassment wherever they occur, whether at home, at work, or on the street.

Support government and private services for women who are victimized by male violence. Volunteer at the local rape crisis center or battered-women's shelter. Join and support groups that intervene with and counsel violent men.

Call for and support clear and effective anti-harassment policies in workplaces, unions, schools, professional associations, religious institutions, and political parties, as well as public spaces such as parks, sidewalks, and malls.

Object to theaters and video stores that carry violent pornography. This doesn't require a debate about censorship—just the exercise of freedom of speech to articulate pornography's role in the oppression of women and to express how its opponents feel about it.

Ask questions about how work, education, religion, and family are shaped by core values and principles that support race privilege, gender privilege, and other forms of privilege. You might accept women's entry into combat branches of the military or the upper reaches of corporate power as "progress," for example. But you could also raise questions about what happens to people and societies when political and economic institutions are organized around control, domination, "power over," and, by extension, competition and the use of violence. Is it progress to allow selected women to share control with men over oppressive systems?

Support the right of women and men to love whomever they choose. Raise awareness of homophobia and heterosexism. For example, ask school officials and teachers about what's happening to gay and lesbian students in local schools. If they don't know, ask them to find out, since it's a safe bet these students are being harassed, suppressed, and oppressed by others at one of the most vulnerable stages of life. When sexual orientation is discussed, whether in the media or among friends, raise questions about its relation to patriarchy. Remember that it isn't necessary to have answers to questions in order to ask them.

Pay attention to how different forms of oppression interact with one another. There has been a great deal of struggle within women's movements, for example, about the relationship between gender oppression and other forms of oppression, especially those based on race and social class. White middle- and upper-middle-class feminists have been criticized for pursuing their own agenda to the detriment of women who aren't privileged by class or race. Raising concerns about glass ceilings that keep women out of top corporate and professional positions, for example, does little to help working- or lower-class women. There has also been debate over whether some forms of oppression are more important to attack first or produce more oppressive consequences than other forms.

One way out of this conflict is to realize that patriarchy isn't problematic just because it emphasizes *male* dominance, but because it promotes dominance and control as ends in themselves. In that sense, all forms of oppression draw support from common roots, and whatever we do that calls attention to those roots undermines *all* forms of oppression. If working against patriarchy is seen simply as enabling some women to get a bigger piece of the pie, then some women probably will "succeed" at the expense of others who are disadvantaged by race, class, ethnicity, and other characteristics. One could make the same argument about movements for racial justice: If it just means enabling well-placed blacks to get ahead, then it won't end racial oppression for the vast majority. But if we identify the core problem as *any* society organized around principles of domination and privilege, then changing *that* requires us to pay attention to all the forms of oppression those principles promote. Whether we begin with race or gender or ethnicity or class or the capitalist system, if we name the problem correctly we'll wind up going in the same general direction.

Work with other people. This is one of the most important principles of participating in social change. From expanding consciousness to taking risks, being in the company of people who support what you're trying to do makes all the difference in the world. For starters, you can read and talk about books and issues and just plain hang out with other people who want to understand and do something about privilege and oppression. The roots of the modern women's movement were in consciousness-raising groups where women did little more than talk about themselves and try to figure out how they were shaped by a patriarchal society. It may not have looked like much at the time, but it laid the foundation for huge social change. . . .

It is especially important to form alliances across difference—for men to ally with women, whites with people of color, heterosexuals with lesbians and gay men. What does this mean? As Paul Kivel [author of *Uprooting Racism* (1996)] argues, one of the keys to being a good ally is a willingness to listen—for whites to listen to people of color, for example—and to give credence to what people say about their own experience.[6] This isn't easy to do, of course, since whites, heterosexuals, and men may not like what they hear about their privilege from those who are most damaged by it. It is difficult to hear anger about privilege and oppression and not take it personally, but that is what allies have to be willing to do. It's also difficult for members of privileged groups to realize how mistrusted they are by subordinate groups and to not take that personally as well. . . .

Don't keep it to yourself. A corollary of looking for company is not to restrict your focus to the tight little circle of your own life. It isn't enough to work out private solutions to social problems like oppression and keep them to yourself. It isn't enough to clean up your own act and then walk away, to find ways to avoid the worst consequences of oppression and privilege at home and inside yourself and think that's taking responsibility. Privilege and oppression aren't a personal problem that can be solved through personal solutions. At some point, taking responsibility means acting in a larger context, even if that means letting just one other person know what you're doing. It makes sense to start with yourself, but it's equally important not to end with yourself.

A good way to convert personal change into something larger is to join an organization dedicated to changing the systems that produce privilege and oppression. Most college and university campuses, for example, have student organizations that focus on issues of gender, race, and sexual orientation. There are also national organizations working for change, often through local and statewide branches. Consider, for example, the National Organization for Women (NOW), the National Association for the Advancement of Colored People (NAACP), the National Conference for Community and Justice (formerly the National Conference of Christians and Jews), the National Gay and Lesbian Task Force, the Southern Poverty Law Center, the National Organization of Men Against Sexism, the Feminist Majority, the National Abortion Rights Action League, the Southern Christian Leadership Conference, and the National Urban League. . . .

Don't let other people set the standard for you. Start where you are and work from there. Make lists of all the things you could actually imagine *doing*—from reading another book about inequality to suggesting policy changes at work to protesting against capitalism to raising questions about who cleans the bathroom at home—and rank them from the most risky to the least. Start with the least risky and set reasonable goals ("What small risk for change will

I take *today*?"). As you get more experienced at taking risks, you can move up your list. You can commit yourself to whatever the next steps are for you, the tolerable risks, the contributions that offer some way—however small it might seem—to help balance the scales. As long as you do something, it counts.

In the end, taking responsibility doesn't have to involve guilt and blame, letting someone off the hook, or being on the hook yourself. It simply means acknowledging an obligation to make a contribution to finding a way out of the trouble we're all in, and to find constructive ways to act on that obligation. You don't have to do anything dramatic or earth-shaking to help change happen. As powerful as oppressive systems are, they cannot stand the strain of lots of people doing something about it, beginning with the simplest act of naming the system out loud.

What's in It for Me?

It's risky to promote change. You risk being seen as odd, being excluded or punished for asking questions and setting examples that make people uncomfortable or threaten privilege. We've all adapted in one way or another to life in a society organized around competition, privilege, and difference. Paths of least resistance may perpetuate oppression, but they also have the advantage of being familiar and predictable and therefore can seem preferable to untried alternatives and the unknown. There are inner risks—of feeling lost, confused, and scared—along with outer risks of being rejected or worse. Obviously, then, working for change isn't a path of least resistance, which raises the question of why anyone should follow Gandhi's advice and do it anyway.

It's an easier question to answer for subordinate groups than it is for dominants, which helps explain why the former have done most of the work for change. Those on the losing end have much to gain by striving to undo the system that oppresses them, not only for themselves in the short run, but for the sake of future generations. The answer comes less easily for those in dominant groups, but they don't have to look very far to see that they have much to gain—especially in the long run—that more than balances what they stand to lose.[7]

When whites, heterosexuals, and men join the movement against privilege and oppression, they can begin to undo the costs of participating in an oppressive system as the dominant group. Few men, for example, realize how much they deaden themselves in order to support (if only by their silence) a system that privileges them at women's expense, that values maleness by devaluing femaleness, that makes women invisible in order to make men appear larger than life. Most men don't realize the impoverishment to their emotional and spiritual lives, the price they pay in personal authenticity and integrity, how they compromise their humanity, how they limit the connections they can have with other people, how they distort their sexuality to live up to core patriarchal values of control. They don't realize how much they have to live a lie in order to interact on a daily basis with their mothers, wives, sisters, daughters, women friends and co-workers—all members of the group male privilege oppresses. So the first thing men can do is claim a sense of aliveness and realness that doesn't depend on superiority and control, and a connection to themselves and the world—which they may not even realize was missing until they begin to feel its return.

In similar ways, most whites don't realize how much energy it takes to defend against their continuing vulnerability to guilt and blame and to avoid seeing how much trouble the world is in and the central role they play in it. When whites do nothing about racial privilege and oppression, they put themselves on the defensive, in the no-safe-place-to-hide position of every dominator class. But when white people make a commitment to participate in change, to be more than part of the problem, they free themselves to live in the world without feeling open to guilt simply for being white.

In perhaps more subtle ways, homophobia and heterosexism take a toll on heterosexuals. The persecution of lesbians, for example, is a powerful weapon of sexism that encourages women to silence themselves, to disavow feminism, and tolerate male privilege for fear that if they speak out, they'll be labeled as lesbians and ostracized.[8] In similar ways, the fear of being called gay is enough to make men conform to masculine stereotypes that don't reflect who they really are and to go along with an oppressive gender system they may not believe in. And because homosexuals all come from families, parents and siblings may also pay a huge emotional price for the effects of prejudice, discrimination, and persecution directed at their loved ones.

With greater authenticity and aliveness comes the opportunity to go beyond the state of arrested development, the perpetual adolescence that privilege promotes in dominant groups, to move away from unhealthy dependencies on the subordination and undervalued labor of others and toward healthy interdependencies free of oppressive cultural baggage.

When people join together to end any form of oppression, they act with courage to take responsibility to do the right thing, and this empowers them in ways that can extend to every corner of their lives. Whenever we act with courage, a halo effect makes that same courage available to us in other times and places. When we step into our legacies and take responsibility for them, we can see how easily fear keeps us from acting for change in ourselves and in the systems we participate in. As we do the work, we build a growing store of experience to draw on in figuring out how to act with courage again and again. As our inner and outer lives become less bound by the strictures of fear and compromise, we can claim a deeper meaning for our lives than we've known before.

The human capacity to choose how to participate in the world empowers all of us to pass along something different from what's been passed to us. With each strand of the knot of privilege that we help to work loose and unravel, we don't act simply for ourselves, we join a process of creative resistance to oppression that's been unfolding for thousands of years. We become part of the long tradition of people who have dared to make a difference—to look at things as they are, to imagine something better, and to plant seeds of change in themselves, in others, and in the world.

ENDNOTES

[1] Bonaro W. Overstreet, *Hands Laid Upon the Wind* (New York: Norton, 1955), p. 15.

[2] For more on this, see Ward Churchill, "Crimes Against Humanity," *Z Magazine* 6 (March 1993):43–47. Reprinted in Margaret L. Andersen and Patricia Hill Collins (eds.), *Race, Class, and Gender*, 3d ed. (Belmont, CA: Wadsworth, 1998), pp. 413–20.

[3] William A. Gamson, "Violence and Political Power: The Meek Don't Make It," *Psychology Today* 8 (July 1974):35–41.

[4] For more on this, see the excellent PBS documentary of the civil rights movement, *Eyes on the Prize*.

[5] Doug McAdam, *Political Process and the Development of Black Insurgency 1930–1970* (Chicago: University of Chicago Press, 1982).

[6] See Kivel, *Uprooting Racism: How White People Can Work for Racial Justice* (Philadelphia: New Society Publishers, 1996), part 3, "Being Allies."

[7] A lot of what follows came out of a brainstorming session with my friend and colleague Jane Tuohy as we worked out the design for a gender workshop.

[8] See Suzanne Pharr, *Homophobia: A Weapon of Sexism* (Inverness, CA: Chardon Press, 1988).